The Complete Air Fryer Cookbook

1500 Quick & Easy Recipes That Anyone Can Cook at Home

By Jemma Madison

Table of Contents

3

4

Breakfast

Crispy Southwestern Ham Egg Cups

Prep time: 5 minutes **Cooking time:** 12 minutes
Servings: 2

Ingredients

4 (1-ounce) slices deli ham
4 large eggs
2 tablespoons diced white onion
2 tablespoons diced red bell pepper
2 tablespoons full-fat sour cream
1/4 cup diced green bell pepper
1/2 cup shredded medium Cheddar cheese

Directions

Set one slice of ham on the bottom of four baking cups. In a large bowl, whisk eggs with sour cream. Stir in green pepper, red pepper, and onion.

Pour the egg mixture into ham-lined baking cups. Top with Cheddar. Place cups into the fryer basket. Adjust the temperature to 320F and set the timer for 12 minutes or until the tops are browned. Serve warm.

Buffalo Egg Cups

Prep time: 10 minutes **Cooking time:** 15 minutes
Servings: 2

Ingredients

4 large eggs
2 tbs buffalo sauce
2 ounces full-fat cream cheese
1/2 cup shredded sharp Cheddar cheese

Directions

Crack eggs into two (4") ramekins. In a small microwave-safe bowl, mix cream cheese, buffalo sauce, and Cheddar. Microwave for 20 seconds and then stir. Place a spoonful into each ramekin on top of the eggs.

Place ramekins into the air fryer basket. Adjust the temperature to 320F and set the timer for 15 minutes Serve warm.

Quick and Easy Bacon Strips

Prep time: 5 minutes **Cooking time:** 12 minutes
Servings: 2

Ingredients

8 slices sugar free bacon

Directions

Place bacon strips into the air fryer basket. Adjust the temperature to 400F and set the timer for 12 minutes. After 6 minutes, flip bacon and continue cooking time. Serve warm.

"Banana" Nut Cake

Prep time: 15 minutes **Cooking time:** 25 minutes
Servings: 6

Ingredients

1 cup blanched finely ground almond flour
1/2 cup powdered Erythritol
1/2 teaspoon ground cinnamon
1/4 cup unsalted butter, melted
1/4 cup chopped walnuts
2 tablespoons ground golden flaxseed
2 teaspoons baking powder
1/4 cup full-fat sour cream
2 large eggs
2 1/2 teaspoons banana extract
1 teaspoon vanilla extract

Directions

In a large bowl, merge almond flour, Erythritol, flaxseed, baking powder, and cinnamon.

Stir in butter, banana extract, vanilla extract, and sour cream. Add eggs to the mixture and gently stir until fully combined. Stir in the walnuts.

Pour into 6" nonstick cake pan and place into the air fryer basket. Adjust the temperature to 300F and set the timer for 25 minutes.

Cake will be golden and a toothpick inserted in center will come out clean when fully cooked. Allow to fully cool to avoid crumbling.

Veggie Frittata

Prep time: 15 minutes **Cooking time:** 12 minutes
Servings: 4

Ingredients

6 large eggs
1/2 cup chopped broccoli
1/4 cup chopped yellow onion
1/4 cup heavy whipping cream
1/4 cup chopped green bell pepper

Directions

In a large bowl, merge eggs and heavy whipping cream. Mix in broccoli, onion, and bell pepper. Pour into a 6" round oven-safe baking dish. Set baking dish into the air fryer basket.

Adjust the temperature to 350F and set the timer for 12 minutes. Eggs should be firm and cooked fully when the frittata is done. Serve warm.

Pumpkin Spice Muffins

Prep time: 10 minutes **Cooking time:** 15 minutes
Servings: 2

Ingredients

1 cup blanched finely ground almond flour
1/4 cup unsalted butter, softened
1/4 cup pure pumpkin purée
1 teaspoon vanilla extract
1/2 cup granular Erythritol
1/2 teaspoon baking powder
1/2 teaspoon ground cinnamon
1/4 teaspoon ground nutmeg
2 large eggs

Directions

In a large bowl, merge almond flour, Erythritol, baking powder, butter, pumpkin purée, cinnamon, nutmeg, and vanilla. Gently stir in eggs.

Evenly pour the batter into six silicone muffin cups. Place muffin cups into the air fryer basket, working in batches if necessary.

Adjust the temperature to 300F and set the timer for 15 minutes. When completely cooked, a toothpick inserted in center will come out mostly clean. Serve warm.

Lemon Poppy Seed Cake

Prep time: 10 minutes **Cooking time:** 14 minutes
Servings: 6

Ingredients

1 cup blanched finely ground almond flour
1/2 cup powdered Erythritol
1/4 cup unsweetened almond milk
2 large eggs
1 teaspoon poppy seeds
1/2 teaspoon baking powder
1/4 cup unsalted butter, melted
1 teaspoon vanilla extract
1 medium lemon

Directions

In a large bowl, merge almond flour, Erythritol, baking powder, butter, almond milk, eggs, and vanilla. Divide the lemon in half and press the juice into a small bowl, then add to the batter.

Using a fine grater, zest the lemon and add 1 tablespoon zest to the batter and stir. Add poppy seeds to batter.
Pour batter into nonstick 6" round cake pan. Place pan into the air fryer basket.

Adjust the temperature to 300F and set the timer for 14 minutes. When fully cooked, a toothpick inserted in center will come out mostly clean. The cake will finish cooking and firm up as it cools. Serve at room temperature.

Pancake Cake

Prep time: 10 minutes **Cooking time:** 7 minutes
Servings: 4

Ingredients

1/2 cup finely ground almond flour
2 tablespoons unsalted butter, softened
1 large egg
1/2 teaspoon ground cinnamon
1/2 teaspoon baking powder
1/2 teaspoon unflavored gelatin
1/2 tbs vanilla extract
1/4 cup powdered Erythritol

Directions

In a large bowl, merge almond flour, Erythritol, and baking powder. Add butter, egg, gelatin, vanilla, and cinnamon. Pour into 6" round baking pan.

Place pan into the air fryer basket. Adjust the temperature to 300F and set the timer for 7 minutes. When the cake is completely cooked, a toothpick will come out clean. Cut cake into four and serve.

Bacon, Egg, and Cheese Roll Ups

Prep time: 15 minutes **Cooking time:** 15 minutes
Servings: 4

Ingredients

2 tablespoons butter	1/2 medium green
1/4 cup onion	pepper, seeded and sliced
12 slices bacon	1 cup Cheddar cheese
1/2 cup mild salsa	6 large eggs

Directions

In a medium skillet over medium heat, dissolve butter. Attach onion and pepper to the skillet and sauté until fragrant and onions are translucent, about 3 minutes. Pour eggs in a bowl and set into a pan.

On work surface, set three slices of bacon side by side, overlapping about 1/4". Set 1/4 cup scrambled eggs in a heap on the side closest to you and whisk cheese over the eggs. Tightly set the bacon around the eggs. Set each roll into the air fryer basket. Adjust the temperature to 350F. Set the rolls halfway through the cooking time. Serve immediately with salsa for dipping.

Breakfast Stuffed Poblanos

Prep time: 15 minutes **Cooking time:** 15 minutes
Servings: 4

Ingredients

1/2 pound spicy ground pork breakfast sausage	4 ounces full-fat cream cheese, softened
1/4 cup canned tomatoes and green chilies, drained	8 tablespoons shredded pepper jack cheese
4 large poblano peppers	4 large eggs
1/2 cup full-fat sour cream	

Directions

In a skillet, crumble and brown the ground sausage until no pink remains. Detach sausage and drain the fat from the pan. Crack eggs into the pan, scramble, and cook until no longer runny.

Place cooked sausage in a large bowl and fold in cream cheese. Mix in diced tomatoes and chilies. Gently fold in eggs.

Cut a 4"–5" slit in the top of each poblano, removing the seeds and white membrane with a small knife. Separate the filling into four **Servings:** and spoon carefully into each pepper. Top each with 2 tablespoons pepper jack cheese.
Place each pepper into the air fryer basket.
Adjust the temperature to 350F and set the timer for 15 minutes.

Peppers will be soft and cheese will be browned when ready. Serve immediately with sour cream on top.

Air Fryer "Hard-Boiled" Eggs

Prep time: 12 minutes **Cooking time:** 18 minutes
Servings: 4

Ingredients

4 large eggs	1 cup water

Directions

Place eggs into a 4-cup round baking-safe dish and pour water over eggs. Place dish into the air fryer basket.
Adjust the temperature to 300F and set the timer for 18 minutes. Store cooked eggs in the refrigerator until ready to use or peel and eat warm.

Cheesy Cauliflower Hash Browns

Prep time: 20 minutes **Cooking time:** 12 minutes
Servings: 4

Ingredients

11/2(12-ounce) steamer bag cauliflower	1 cup shredded sharp Cheddar cheese
1 large egg	

Directions

Place bag in microwave and cook according to package instructions. Allow to cool completely and put cauliflower into a cheesecloth or kitchen towel and squeeze to remove excess moisture.

Pulse cauliflower with a fork and add egg and cheese. Divide a piece of parchment to fit your air fryer basket. Set 1/4 of the mixture and form it into a hash brown patty shape. Place it onto the parchment and into the air fryer basket, working in batches if necessary.
Adjust the temperature to 400F and set the timer for 12 minutes.

Flip the hash browns halfway through the cooking time. When completely cooked, they will be golden brown. Serve immediately.

Scrambled Eggs

Prep time: 5 minutes **Cooking time:** 15 minutes
Servings: 2

Ingredients

4 large eggs
1/2 cup shredded sharp
Cheddar cheese

2 tablespoons unsalted
butter, melted

Directions

Crack eggs into 2-cup round baking dish and whisk.
Place dish into the air fryer basket.

Adjust the temperature to 400F and set the timer for
10 minutes. After 5 minutes, stir the eggs and add the
butter and cheese. Let cook 3 more minutes and stir
again.

Allow eggs to finish cooking an additional 2 minutes
or remove if they are to your desired liking. Use a fork
to fluff. Serve warm.

Loaded Cauliflower Breakfast Bake

Prep time: 15 minutes **Cooking time:** 20 minutes
Servings: 4
Ingredients

6 large eggs
11/2 cups chopped
cauliflower

1cup shredded medium
Cheddar cheese
1 medium avocado, peeled
and pitted
12 slices sugar-free bacon,
cooked and crumbled

1/4 cup heavy whipping
cream
2scallions, sliced on the
bias
8 tablespoons full-fat sour
cream

Directions

In a medium bowl, merge eggs and cream together.
Pour into a 4-cup round baking dish. Add cauliflower
and mix, and then top with Cheddar. Place dish into
the air fryer basket.

Adjust the temperature to 320F and set the timer for
20
minutes. When completely cooked, eggs will be firm
and cheese will be browned. Slice into four pieces.

Slice avocado and divide evenly among pieces. Set
each piece with 2 tablespoons sour cream, sliced
scallions, and crumbled bacon.

Cinnamon Roll Sticks

Prep time: 10 minutes **Cooking time:** 7 minutes
Servings: 4

Ingredients

cup shredded mozzarella
cheese
1 ounce full-fat cream
cheese
1 teaspoon vanilla extract

1 large egg

2 teaspoons unsweetened
vanilla almond milk

1/3 cup blanched finely
ground almond flour
1/2 teaspoon baking
soda
1/2 cup granular
Erythritol
1 tbsp unsalted butter,
melted
1/2 teaspoon ground
cinnamon tablespoons
powdered Erythritol

Directions

Set mozzarella in a large microwave-safe bowl and
break cream cheese into small pieces and place into
bowl. Microwave for 45 seconds. Stir in almond flour,
baking soda, 1/4 cup granular Erythritol, and vanilla.
Soft dough should form. Microwave the mix for
additional 15 seconds if it becomes too stiff.

Mix egg into the dough, using your hands if necessary.
Divide a piece of parchment to fit your air fryer
basket. Press the dough into an 8" × 5" rectangle on
the parchment and cut into eight (1") sticks.

In a small bowl, merge butter, cinnamon, and
remaining granular Erythritol. Garnish half the
mixture over the top of the sticks and place them into
the air fryer basket.
Adjust the temperature to 400F and set the timer for 7
minutes.

Halfway through the cooking time, flip the sticks and
brush with remaining butter mixture. When done,
sticks should be crispy.

To make glaze, whisk powdered Erythritol and
almond milk in a small bowl. Drizzle over cinnamon
sticks. Serve warm.

Swiss chard Frittata

Prep time: 5 minutes **Cooking time:** 20 minutes
Servings: 4

Ingredients

6 eggs, beaten	4 oz. Swiss chard chopped
1/2 teaspoon ground turmeric	1/2 teaspoon salt
	1/4 cup coconut cream
	tbsp coconut oil, melted

Directions

In the mixing bowl mix all Ingredients except coconut oil and make the small fritters. Preheat the air fryer to 385F.

Brush it with coconut oil and put the fritters inside. Cook them for 10 minutes per side.

Cauliflower Avocado Toast

Prep time: 15 minutes **Cooking time:** 8 minutes
Servings: 2

Ingredients

1(12-ounce) steamer bag cauliflower	1/2 cup shredded mozzarella cheese
1 large egg	1 ripe medium avocado
1/2 teaspoon garlic powder	1/4 teaspoon ground black pepper

Directions

Cook cauliflower according to package instructions. Remove from bag and place into cheesecloth or clean towel to remove excess moisture. Place cauliflower into a large bowl and mix in egg and mozzarella.

Divide a piece of parchment to fit your air fryer basket. Separate the cauliflower mixture into two, and place it on the parchment in two mounds. Press out the cauliflower mounds into a 1/4"-thick rectangle. Place the parchment into the air fryer basket.

Adjust the temperature to 400F and set the timer for 8 minutes. Turn over the cauliflower halfway through the cooking time. When the timer beeps, remove the parchment and allow the cauliflower to cool 5 minutes.

Divide open the avocado and remove the pit. Scoop out the inside, place it in a medium bowl, and mash it with garlic powder and pepper. Spread onto the cauliflower. Serve immediately.

Spaghetti Squash Fritters

Prep time: 15 minutes **Cooking time:** 8 minutes
Servings: 4

Ingredients

2 cups cooked spaghetti squash	2 tablespoons unsalted butter, softened
1/4 cup finely ground almond flour	1/2 teaspoon garlic powder
	1large egg
1 teaspoon dried parsley	2 stalks green onion, sliced

Directions

Detach excess moisture from the squash using a cheesecloth or kitchen towel.

Mix all Ingredients in a large bowl. Form into four patties.
Divide a piece of parchment to fit your air fryer basket. Place each patty on the parchment and place into the air fryer basket.

Adjust the temperature to 400F and set the timer for 8 minutes. Turn over the patties halfway through the cooking time. Serve warm.

Sausage and Cheese Balls

Prep time: 12 minutes **Cooking time:** 12 minutes
Servings: 16

Ingredients

1pound (454 g) pork breakfast sausage	1 ounce (28 g) full-fat cream cheese, softened
1/2 cup shredded Cheddar cheese	1 large egg

Directions

Mix all Ingredients in a large bowl. Form into sixteen (1-inch) balls. Place the balls into the air fryer basket. Adjust the temperature to 400F (204C) and air fry for 12 minutes.

Shake the basket two or three times during cooking. Sausage balls will be browned on the outside and have an internal temperature of at least 145°F (63°C) when completely cooked. Serve warm.

Cheesy Bell Pepper Eggs

Prep time: 10 minutes **Cooking time:** 15 minutes
Servings: 4

Ingredients

4 medium green bell peppers ounces (85 g) cooked ham, chopped 1cup mild Cheddar cheese	1/4 medium onion, peeled and chopped 8 large eggs

Directions

Cut the tops off each bell pepper. Remove the seeds and the white membranes with a small knife. Place ham and onion into each pepper.

Crack 2 eggs into each pepper. Top with 1/4 cup cheese per pepper. Place into the air fryer basket.

Adjust the temperature to 390F (199C) and air fry for 15 minutes. When fully cooked, peppers will be tender and eggs will be firm. Serve immediately.

Bacon-and-Eggs Avocado

Prep time: 5 minutes **Cooking time:** 17 minutes
Servings: 1

Ingredients

1large egg Fresh parsley, for serving (optional)	1 avocado, halved, peeled, and pitted slices bacon Sea salt flakes, for garnish (optional)

Directions

Set the air fryer basket with avocado oil. Preheat the air fryer to 320F (160C). Fill a small bowl with cool water.
Soft-boil the egg Place the egg in the air fryer basket. Air fry for 6 minutes for a soft yolk or 7 minutes for a cooked yolk. Bring the egg to the bowl of cool water and let sit for 2 minutes. Peel and set aside.

Use a spoon to carve out extra space in the center of the avocado halves until the cavities are big enough to fit the soft-boiled egg. Place the soft-boiled egg in the center of one half of the avocado and replace the other half of the avocado on top, so the avocado appears whole on the outside.

Starting at one end of the avocado, wrap the bacon around the avocado to completely cover it.

Place the bacon-wrapped avocado in the air fryer basket and air fry for 5 minutes. Flip the avocado over and air fry for another 5 minutes or until the bacon is cooked to your liking. Serve on a bed of fresh parsley, if desired, and sprinkle with salt flakes, if desired. Best served fresh.

Double-Dipped Mini Cinnamon Biscuits

Prep time: 15 minutes **Cooking time:** 13 minutes
Servings: 8

Ingredients

2 cups blanched almond flour 1/4 cup unsweetened, unflavored almond milk 1teaspoon baking powder 1/2 teaspoon fine sea salt 1 large egg Glaze	1/2 cup Swerve confectioners'-style sweetener or equivalent amount of liquid or powdered sweetener 1/4 cup plus 2 tbsp(3/4 stick) very cold unsalted butter 1 teaspoon vanilla extract teaspoons ground cinnamon
1/2 cup Swerve confectioners'-style sweetener or equivalent amount of powdered sweetener	1/4 cup heavy cream or unsweetened, unflavored almond milk

Directions

Preheat the air fryer to 350F (177C). Line a pie pan that fits into your air fryer with parchment paper.

In a medium-sized bowl, mix together the almond flour, sweetener (if powdered; do not add liquid sweetener), baking powder, and salt. Cut the butter into 1/2-inch squares, and then use a hand mixer to work the butter into the dry Ingredients.

In a small bowl, pour together the almond milk, egg, and vanilla extract (if using liquid sweetener, add it as well) until blended. With a fork, merge the wet Ingredients into the dry Ingredients until large clumps form. Attach the cinnamon and use your hands to swirl it into the dough.
Form the dough into sixteen 1-inch balls and place them on the prepared pan, spacing them about 1/2 inches apart. (If you're using a smaller air fryer, work in batches if necessary.) Bake in the air fryer until golden, 10 to 13 minutes. Detach from the air fryer and let cool on the pan for at least 5 minutes.

While the biscuits bake, make the glaze Place the powdered sweetener in a small bowl and slowly stir in the heavy cream with a fork.

When the biscuits have cooled somewhat, dip the tops into the glaze, allow it to dry a bit, and then dip again for a thick glaze. Serve warm or at room temperature. Store unglazed biscuits in an

airtight container in the refrigerator. Reheat in a preheated 350F (177C) air fryer for 5 minutes, or until warmed through, and dip in the glaze as instructed above.

Mexican Shakshuka

Prep time: 5 minutes **Cooking time:** 6 minutes
Servings: 1

Ingredients

1/2 cup salsa
1/2 teaspoon fine sea salt
1/4 teaspoon smoked paprika
For Garnish

2 large eggs, room temperature
1/8 teaspoon ground cumin
2 tablespoons cilantro leaves

Directions

Preheat the air fryer to 400F (204C). Place the salsa in a pie pan or a casserole dish that will fit into your air fryer. Crack the eggs into the salsa and sprinkle them with the salt, paprika, and cumin.

Set the pan in the air fryer and bake for 6 minutes Detach from the air fryer and garnish with the cilantro before serving. Best served fresh.

Heritage Eggs

Prep time: 5 minutes **Cooking time:** 8 minutes
Servings: 2

Ingredients

2 teaspoons unsalted butter (or coconut oil for dairy-free), for greasing the ramekins
large eggs
3 tablespoons finely grated Parmesan cheese (or Kite Hill brand chive cream cheese style spread, softened, for dairy-free)

1/2 teaspoon fine sea salt
2 teaspoons chopped fresh thyme
2 tablespoons heavy cream (or unsweetened, unflavored almond milk for dairy-free)
Fresh thyme leaves, for garnish (optional)

Directions

Preheat the air fryer to 400F (204C). Grease two (4-ounce / 113-g) ramekins with the butter. Crack 2 eggs into each ramekin and divide the thyme, salt, and pepper between the ramekins. Pour 1 tablespoon of the heavy cream into each ramekin. Sprinkle each ramekin with 11/2 tablespoons of the Parmesan cheese.

Set the ramekins in the air fryer and bake for 8 minutes for soft-cooked yolks (longer if you desire a harder yolk).

Brush with a sprinkle of ground black pepper and thyme leaves, if desired. Best served fresh.

Cayenne Pepper Eggs

Prep time: 10 minutes **Cooking time:** 12 minutes
Servings: 4

Ingredients

1 teaspoon cayenne pepper

1 tablespoon butter melted
8 eggs

Directions

Preheat the air fryer to 395F. Then brush the air fryer basket with butter and crack the eggs inside. Sprinkle the eggs with cayenne pepper and cook them for 12 minutes.

Breakfast Pizza

Prep time: 5 minutes **Cooking time:** 8 minutes
Servings: 1

Ingredients

2 large eggs
1/4 cup diced onions
) 6 pepperoni slices (omit for vegetarian)
1/4 teaspoon fine sea salt
1/4 cup Parmesan cheese (omit for dairy-free
1/4 cup pizza sauce, warmed, for serving

1/4 cup unsweetened, unflavored almond milk (or unflavored hemp milk for nut-free)
1/8 tbsp ground black pepper
1/4 teaspoon dried oregano leaves

Directions

Preheat the air fryer to 350F (177C). Grease a cake pan.
In a bowl, use a fork to merge together the eggs, almond milk, salt, and pepper. Add the onions and stir to mix. Pour the mixture into the greased pan. Top with the cheese (if using), pepperoni slices (if using), and oregano.
Set the pan in the air fryer and bake for 8 minutes, or until the eggs are cooked to your liking.

Set the eggs from the sides of the pan with a spatula and place them on a serving plate. Drizzle the pizza sauce on top. Best served fresh.

Breakfast Sammy's

Prep time: 15 minutes **Cooking time:** 20 minutes
Servings: 4

Ingredients

Biscuits
2 cups almond flour, plus more if necessary
1/4 cup unsalted butter (or lard for dairy-free)
5 large eggs
1/4 teaspoon ground black pepper

6 large egg whites
1/2 teaspoon fine sea salt
1 1/2 tbsp baking powder
Eggs
10 thin slices ham
1/2 teaspoon fine sea salt
5 (1-ounce / 28-g) slices Cheddar cheese (omit for dairy-free)

Directions

Set the air fryer basket with avocado oil. Preheat the air fryer to 350F (177C). Grease two pie pans or two baking pans that will fit inside your air fryer.

Make the biscuits In a medium-sized bowl, whip the egg whites with a hand mixer until very stiff. Set aside. In a separate bowl, merge together the almond flour, baking powder, and salt until well combined. Cut in the butter.

Using a large spoon, divide the dough into 5 equal portions and drop them about 1 inch apart on one of the greased pie pans. (If you're using a smaller air fryer, work in batches if necessary.) Set the pan in the device and bake for 11 to 14 minutes, until the biscuits are golden brown. Detach from the air fryer and set aside to cool.
Make the eggs Set the air fryer to 375F (191C). Crack the eggs into the remaining greased pie pan and sprinkle with the salt and pepper. Place the eggs in the air fryer to bake for 5 minutes, or until they are cooked to your liking.
Open the air fryer and top each egg yolk with a slice of cheese (if using). Bake for another minute.

Once the biscuits are cool, slice them in half lengthwise. Place 1 cooked egg topped with cheese and 2 slices of ham in each biscuit.

Store leftover biscuits, eggs, and ham in separate airtight containers in the fridge for up to 3 days. Reheat the biscuits and eggs on a baking sheet in a preheated 350F (177C) air fryer for 5 minutes, or until warmed through.

Denver Omelet

Prep time: 5 minutes **Cooking time:** 8 minutes
Servings: 1

Ingredients

2 large eggs
1/4 teaspoon fine sea salt
1/8 teaspoon ground black pepper
2 tablespoons diced green onions, plus more for garnish
1/4 cup red bell peppers
Quartered cherry tomatoes, for serving (optional)

1/4 cup unsweetened, unflavored almond milk
1/4 cup diced ham (omit for vegetarian)
1/4 cup shredded Cheddar cheese (about 1 ounce / 28 g) (omit for dairy-free)

Directions

Preheat the air fryer to 350F (177C). Grease a cake pan and set aside.

In a bowl, use a fork to merge together the eggs, almond milk, salt, and pepper. Add the ham, bell peppers, and green onions. Pour the mixture into the greased pan. Add the cheese on top (if using).

Set the pan in the basket of the air fryer. Bake for 8 minutes, or until the eggs are cooked to your liking.

Detach the omelet from the sides of the pan with a spatula and place it on a serving plate. Garnish with green onions and serve with cherry tomatoes, if desired. Best served fresh.

Green Eggs and Ham

Prep time: 5 minutes **Cooking time:** 10 minutes
Servings: 12

Ingredients

1large Hass avocado, halved and pitted
2 tablespoons green onions, plus more for garnish
1/4 cup Cheddar cheese (omit for dairy-free)

2 large eggs
2 thin slices ham
1/4 teaspoon ground black pepper
1/2 teaspoon fine sea salt

Directions

Preheat the air fryer to 400F (204C). Place a slice of ham into the cavity of each avocado half. Crack an egg on top of the ham, then sprinkle on the green onions, salt, and pepper.

Set the avocado halves in the air fryer cut side up and air fry for 10 minutes. Top with the cheese (if using) and air fry for 30 seconds more or until the cheese is melted. Garnish with chopped green onions. Best served fresh.

Gyro Breakfast Patties with Tzatziki

Prep time: 10 minutes **Cooking time:** 20 minutes
Servings: 16

Ingredients

Patties
1/2 cup diced red onions
1/4 cup sliced black olives
2 tablespoons tomato sauce
1 teaspoon fine sea salt
1 cup full-fat sour cream

1/2 teaspoon garlic, or
1 clove garlic, minced
1 teaspoon Greek seasoning 1cloves garlic, minced
For Garnish
Serving
Diced red onions Sliced black olives

2 pounds (907 g) ground lamb or beef
1teaspoon dried oregano leaves

Tzatziki
1 small cucumber, chopped
1/4 teaspoon dried dill weed, or 1 teaspoon finely chopped fresh dill
1/2 teaspoon fine sea salt

1/2 cup crumbled feta cheese
Sliced cucumbers

Directions

Preheat the air fryer to 350F (177C). Place the ground lamb, onions, olives, tomato sauce, oregano, Greek seasoning, garlic, and salt in a large bowl. Mix well to combine the ingredients. Using your hands, form the mixture into sixteen 3-inch patties. Place about 5 of the patties in the air fryer and air fry for 20 minutes, flipping halfway through. Detach the patties and place them on a serving platter. Repeat with the remaining patties.

While the patties cook, make the Tzatziki Place all the ingredients in a small bowl and stir well. Close and set in the fridge until ready to serve. Garnish with ground black pepper before serving. Serve the patties with a dollop of Tzatziki, a sprinkle of crumbled feta cheese, diced red onions, sliced black olives, and sliced cucumbers.

Keto Quiche

Prep time: 10 minutes **Cooking time:** 1 hour
Servings: 1
Ingredients

Crust
1large egg, beaten

1/4 teaspoon fine sea salt
1 cup shredded Swiss cheese 1/2 cup chicken
1/3 cup minced leeks or sliced green onions
1 tablespoon unsalted butter, melted

11/4 cups almond flour
11/4 cups grated Parmesan
Filling
4 ounces 113g cream cheese 4 large eggs, beaten
3/4 teaspoon fine sea salt
1/8 tbsp cayenne pepper
Chopped green onions, for garnish

Directions

Preheat the air fryer to 325F (163C). Grease a pie pan. Set two large pieces of parchment paper with avocado oil and set them on the countertop.
Set the crust In a medium-sized bowl, combine the flour, cheese, and salt and mix well. Attach the egg and mix until the dough is well combined and stiff.

Place the dough in the center of one of the greased pieces of parchment. Top with the other piece of parchment. Roll out the dough.
Press the pie crust into the prepared pie pan. Place it in the air fryer and bake for 12 minutes, or until it starts to lightly brown.

While the crust bakes, make the filling In a large bowl, combine the broth, Swiss cheese, cream cheese, and butter. Stir in the eggs, leeks, salt, and cayenne pepper. When the crust is processed, pour the mixture into the crust.

Place the quiche in the air fryer and bake for 15 minutes. Turn the heat down to 300F (149C) and bake for an additional 30 minutes

Allow the quiche to cool for 10 minutes before garnishing it with chopped green onions and cutting it into wedges.

BLT Breakfast Wrap

Prep time: 5 minutes **Cooking time:** 10 minutes
Servings: 4

Ingredients

8 ounces (227 g) reduced-sodium bacon
8 large romaine lettuce leaves 4 Roma tomatoes, sliced

8 tablespoons mayonnaise
Salt and ground black pepper, to taste

Directions

Set the bacon in a single layer in the air fryer basket. (It's OK if the bacon sits a bit on the sides.) Set the air fryer to 350F (177C) and air fry for 10 minutes. Check for crispiness and air fry for 2 to 3 minutes longer if needed. Cook in batches, if necessary, and drain the grease in between batches.

Scatter 1 tablespoon of mayonnaise on each of the lettuce leaves and top with the tomatoes and cooked bacon. Flavor to taste with salt and freshly ground black pepper. Roll the lettuce leaves as you would a burrito, securing with a toothpick if desired

Biscuits Casserole

Prep time: 10 minutes **Cooking time:** 15 minutes
Servings: 8

Ingredients

12 ounces biscuits, quartered
A pinch of salt and black pepper
2 and 1/2 cups milk

1/2 pound sausage, chopped
Cooking spray
3 tablespoons flour

Directions

Set your air fryer with cooking spray and heat it over 350 degrees F. Add biscuits on the bottom and mix with sausage.

Add flour, milk, salt and pepper, toss a bit and cook for 15 minutes. Divide among plates and serve for breakfast. Enjoy!

Everything Bagels

Prep time: 15 minutes **Cooking time:** 16 minutes
Servings: 6

Ingredients

13/4 cups shredded Mozzarella cheese or goat cheese Mozzarella
1 tablespoon apple cider vinegar

11/2 teaspoons everything bagel seasoning

1large egg, beaten
2 tablespoons unsalted butter or coconut oil
1 tablespoon baking powder 1/8 teaspoon fine sea salt
1 cup blanched almond flour

Directions

Make the dough Put the Mozzarella and butter in a large microwave-safe bowl and microwave. Stir well. Add the egg and vinegar. Using a hand mixer on medium, combine well. Add the almond flour, baking powder, and salt and, using the mixer, combine well. Set a piece of parchment on the countertop and place the dough on it. Knead it for about 3 minutes. Preheat the air fryer to 350F (177C). Spray a baking sheet or pie pan that will fit into your air fryer with avocado oil.

Divide the dough into 6 equal portions. Roll 1 portion into a log that is 6 inches long and about 1/2 inch thick. Form the log into a circle and seal the edges together, making a bagel shape. Set the bagels on the greased baking sheet. Spray the bagels with avocado oil and top with everything bagel seasoning, pressing the seasoning into the dough with your hands. Set the bagels in the air fryer and bake for 14 minutes, or until cooked through and golden brown, flipping after 6 minutes. Remove the bagels from the air fryer and allow them to cool slightly before slicing them in half and serving.

Tasty Hash

Prep time: 10 minutes **Cooking time:** 15 minutes
Servings: 6

Ingredients

16 ounces hash browns
1/4 cup olive oil
1/2 teaspoon garlic powder
2 tablespoon chives, chopped

1/2 teaspoon paprika
1 egg, whisked
Salt and black pepper to the taste
1 cup cheddar, shredded

Directions

Add oil to your air fryer, heat it up at 350 degrees F and add hash browns. Also add paprika, garlic powder, salt, pepper and egg, toss and cook for 15 minutes.

Add cheddar and chives, toss, divide among plates and serve. Enjoy!

Breakfast Cobbler

Prep time: 20 minutes **Cooking time:** 30 minutes
Servings: 4

Ingredients

Filling
2 cloves garlic, minced
1/4 cup minced onions
1/2 teaspoon ground
black pepper
1 teaspoon baking
powder
3/4 cup beef
3large egg whites
1/4 teaspoon fine sea salt
Fresh thyme leaves, for
garnish

10 ounces (283 g) bulk
pork sausage, crumbled
1/2 teaspoon fine sea salt
1(8-ounce / 227-g)
package cream cheese (or
Kite Hill brand cream
cheese style softened
Biscuits
3/4 cup blanched almond
flour
2 1/2 tablespoons very
cold unsalted butter, cut
into
1/4-inch pieces

Directions

Preheat the air fryer to 400F (204C). Place the sausage,
onions, and garlic in a pie pan. Using your hands, break up
the sausage into small pieces and spread it evenly
throughout the pie pan. Season with the salt and pepper.
Set the pan in the device and bake for 5 minutes.

While the sausage cooks, place the cream cheese and broth
in a food processor or blender and purée until smooth.
Detach the pork from the air fryer and use a fork or metal
spatula to crumble it more. Pour the cream cheese mixture
into the sausage and stir to combine. Set aside. Make the
biscuits Place the egg whites in a medium-sized mixing
bowl or the bowl of a stand mixer and whip with a hand
mixer or stand mixer until stiff peaks form.

In a separate medium-sized bowl, merge together the
almond flour, baking powder, and salt, and then cut in the
butter.
When processed, the mixture should still have chunks of
butter. Flip the flour mixture into the egg whites with a
rubber spatula. Spoon the dough into 4 equal-sized
biscuits, making sure the butter is evenly distributed. Place
the biscuits on top of the sausage and cook in the air fryer
for 5 minutes.

Tofu Scramble

Prep time: 5 minutes **Cooking time:** 30 minutes
Servings: 4

Ingredients

2 tablespoons soy sauce
1tofu block, cubed
2cups broccoli florets
1/2 teaspoon onion
powder 1/2 teaspoon
garlic powder
Salt and black pepper

1 teaspoon turmeric,
ground 1tablespoons extra
virgin olive oil
2 and 1/2 cup red
potatoes, cubed
1/2 cup yellow onion

Directions

Merge tofu with 1 tablespoon oil, salt, pepper, soy
sauce, garlic powder, onion powder, turmeric and
onion in a bowl, stir and leave aside.

In a separate bowl, merge potatoes with the rest of the
oil, a pinch of salt and pepper and toss to coat.
Set potatoes in your air fryer at 350 degrees F and
bake for 15 minutes, shaking once.

Add tofu and its marinade to your air fryer and bake for 15
minutes. Attach broccoli to the fryer and cook everything
for 5 minutes more. Serve right away

Sausage, Eggs and Cheese Mix

Prep time: 10 minutes **Cooking time:** 20 minutes
Servings: 4

Ingredients

10 ounces sausages,
cooked and crumbled
1cup cheddar cheese,
shredded
1 cup milk

1 cup mozzarella cheese,
shredded
8 eggs, whisked
Cooking spray
Salt,black pepper to the
taste

Directions

In a bowl, mix sausages with cheese, mozzarella, eggs,
milk, salt and pepper and whisk well. Heat up your air
fryer at 380 degrees F, spray cooking oil, add eggs and
sausage mix and cook for 20 minutes. Divide among
plates and serve. Enjoy!

Nutty Granola

Prep time: 5 minutes **Cooking time:** 1 hour **Servings:** 4

Ingredients

1/2 cup pecans, coarsely chopped
1/4 cup unsweetened flaked coconut
1/4 cup flaxseed or chia seeds 2 tablespoons sunflower seeds
2 tablespoons melted butter 1/4 cup Swerve

1/2 cup walnuts or almonds, chopped
1/4 cup almond flour
2 tablespoons water
1/2 teaspoon ground cinnamon
1/2 teaspoon vanilla extract 1/4 teaspoon ground nutmeg 1/4 teaspoon salt

Directions

Preheat the air fryer to 250F (121C). Divide a piece of parchment paper to fit inside the air fryer basket. In a large bowl, toss the nuts, coconut, almond flour, ground flaxseed or chia seeds, sunflower seeds, butter, Swerve, cinnamon, vanilla, nutmeg, salt, and water until thoroughly combined.

Spread the granola on the parchment paper and flatten to an even thickness. Air fry for about an hour, or until golden throughout. Detach from the air fryer and allow to fully cool. Break the granola into bite-size pieces and store in a covered container for up to a week.

Portobello Eggs Benedict

Prep time: 10 minutes **Cooking time:** 14 minutes **Servings:** 2

Ingredients

1tablespoon olive oil
1cloves garlic, minced
1/4 teaspoon dried thyme
Salt and ground black pepper, to taste
2 large eggs
1 teaspoon truffle oil (optional)

2Portobello mushrooms, stems removed and gills scraped out
2 tablespoons grated Pecorino Romano cheese
1 tablespoon chopped fresh parsley, for garnish
2 Roma tomatoes, halved lengthwise

Directions

Preheat the air fryer to 400F (204C). In a small bowl, merge the olive oil, garlic, and thyme. Brush the mixture over the mushrooms and tomatoes until thoroughly coated. Flavor to taste with salt and freshly ground black pepper. Arrange the vegetables, cut side up, in the air fryer basket.

Set an egg into the center of each mushroom and sprinkle with cheese. Air fry for 10 to 14 minutes until the vegetables are tender and the whites are firm. When cool enough to handle, slice the tomatoes and set on top of the eggs. Scatter parsley on top and drizzle with truffle oil, if desired, just before serving.

Broccoli-Mushroom Frittata

Prep time: 10 minutes **Cooking time:** 20 minutes **Servings:** 2

Ingredients

1tablespoon olive oil
6 eggs
1/4 cup finely chopped onion
1/4 cup Parmesan cheese
1/2 teaspoon salt

11/2 cups broccoli florets, finely chopped
1/4 teaspoon freshly ground black pepper
1/2 cup sliced brown mushrooms

Directions

In a nonstick cake pan, combine the olive oil, broccoli, mushrooms, onion, salt, and pepper. Stir until the vegetables are thoroughly coated with oil. Place the cake pan in the air fryer basket and set the air fryer to 400F (204C).

Air fry for 5 minutes until the vegetables soften. Meanwhile, in a medium bowl, whisk the eggs and Parmesan until thoroughly combined. Merge the egg mixture into the pan and shake gently to distribute the vegetables. Air fry for another 15 minutes until the eggs are set. Detach from the air fryer and let sit for 5 minutes to cool slightly. Use a silicone spatula to lift the frittata onto a plate before serving gently.

Lemon-Blueberry Muffins

Prep time: 5 minutes **Cooking time:** 25 minutes **Servings:** 6

Ingredients

1 1/4 cups almond flour
3 tablespoons Swerve
3tablespoons melted butter 1tablespoon almond milk

1teaspoon baking powder
2large eggs
1 tablespoon fresh lemon juice
1/2 cup fresh blueberries

Directions

Preheat the air fryer to 350F (177C). Lightly coat 6 silicone muffin cups with vegetable oil. Set aside. In a bowl, merge the almond flour, Swerve, and baking soda. Set aside.

In a separate bowl, merge together the eggs, butter, milk, and lemon juice. Attach the egg mixture to the flour mixture and stir until just combined. Roll in the blueberries and let the batter sit for 5 minutes. Set the muffin batter into the muffin cups, about two-thirds full. Air fry for 20 to 25 minutes, or until a toothpick inserted into the center of a muffin comes out clean. Detach the basket from the device and let the muffins cool for about 5.

Turkey Sausage Breakfast Pizza

Prep time: 10 minutes **Cooking time:** 24 minutes
Servings: 2

Ingredients

4 large eggs, divided
1 tablespoon water
2 tablespoons coconut
flour

3 tablespoons grated
Parmesan cheese
1/2 cup shredded
provolone cheese

2 scallions, thinly sliced

1/2 teaspoon garlic
powder
1/2 teaspoon onion
powder
1/2 teaspoon dried
oregano
1 link cooked turkey
sausage, chopped (about 2
ounces / 57 g)
2 sun-dried tomatoes,
finely
chopped

Directions

Preheat the air fryer to 400F (204C). Set a cake pan
with parchment paper and lightly coat the paper with
olive oil. In a large bowl, whisk 2 of the eggs with the
water, garlic powder, onion powder, and dried oregano.
Add the coconut flour, breaking up any lumps with your
hands as you add it to the bowl. Toss the coconut flour
into the egg mixture, mixing until smooth. Stir in the
Parmesan cheese. Set the mixture to rest for a few minutes
until thick and dough- like.

Transfer the mixture to the prepared pan. Use a spatula
to scatter it evenly and slightly up the sides of the pan.
Air fry until the crust is set but still light in color, about
10 minutes. Top with the cheeses, sausage, and sun-dried
tomatoes.

Break the remaining eggs into a bowl, and then slide
them onto the pizza. Return the pizza to the air fryer.
Air fry 10 to 14 minutes until the egg whites are set
and the yolks are the desired doneness. Top with the
scallions and allow to rest for 5 minutes before
serving.

Air Fried Tomato Breakfast Quiche

Prep time: 10 minutes **Cooking time:** 30 minutes
Servings: 1

Ingredients

2 tablespoons yellow
onion, chopped
1/2 cup gouda cheese,
shredded
1/4 cup tomatoes,
chopped

1/4 cup milk
2 eggs
Salt and black pepper to
the taste
Cooking spray

Directions

Set a ramekin with cooking spray. Crack eggs, add
onion, milk, cheese, tomatoes, salt and pepper and stir.
Attach this in your air fryer's pan and cook at 340
degrees F for 30 minutes. Serve hot. Enjoy!

Cheese Air Fried Bake

Prep time: 10 minutes **Cooking time:** 20 minutes
Servings: 4

Ingredients

4 bacon slices, cooked
and crumbled
1 pound breakfast sausage,
casings removed and
chopped 2 eggs
Cooking spray

Salt and black pepper to
the taste

2 and 1/2 cups cheddar
cheese
1/2 teaspoon onion
powder
2 cups milk
1/2 tablespoons parsley,
chopped

Directions

In a bowl, mix eggs with milk, cheese, onion powder,
salt, pepper and parsley and whisk well. Grease your
air fryer with cooking spray, heat it up at 320 degrees
F and add bacon and sausage. Add eggs mix, spread
and cook for 20 minutes. Divide among plates and
serve. Enjoy!

Turkey Burrito

Prep time: 10 minutes **Cooking time:** 10 minutes
Servings: 2

Ingredients

4 slices turkey breast
already cooked
1 small avocado, peeled,
pitted and sliced
2 tablespoons salsa

2 eggs
1/2 red bell pepper, sliced
Salt and black pepper
1/8 cup mozzarella
cheese, grated Tortillas for
serving

Directions

In a bowl, merge eggs with salt and pepper to the
taste, set them in a pan and set it in the air fryer's
basket.
Cook at 400 degrees F, take pan out of the device and
transfer eggs to a plate.

Set tortillas on a working surface, divide eggs on them,
also divide turkey meat, bell pepper, cheese, salsa and
avocado. Roll your burritos and Set them in your
device after you've lined it with some tin foil. Set up
the burritos at 300 degrees F, divide them on plates
and serve. Enjoy!

Oatmeal Casserole

Prep time: 10 minutes **Cooking time:** 20 minutes
Servings: 8

Ingredients

2 cups rolled oats
1 teaspoon baking powder
2/3 cup blueberries
1/3 cup brown sugar
1 eggs
1tablespoons butter
Cooking spray

1 teaspoon cinnamon powder 1/2 cup chocolate chips
1 banana, peeled and mashed 2cups milk
1 teaspoon vanilla extract

Directions

In a bowl, mix sugar with baking powder, cinnamon, chocolate chips, blueberries and banana and stir.
In a separate bowl, merge eggs with vanilla extract and butter and stir.

Heat up your air fryer at 320 degrees F, grease with cooking spray and add oats on the bottom.
Add cinnamon mix and eggs mix, toss and cook for 20 minutes.

Stir one more time, divide into bowls and serve for breakfast. Enjoy!

Ham Breakfast

Prep time: 10 minutes **Cooking time:** 15 minutes
Servings: 6

Ingredients

6 cups French bread, cubed
10 ounces ham, cubed
4 ounces cheddar cheese, shredded
1 tablespoon mustard
Cooking spray

4 ounces green chilies, chopped

5 eggs
2 cups milk
Salt and black pepper to the taste

Directions

Warmth up your air fryer at 350 degrees F and grease it with cooking spray. In a bowl, mix eggs with milk, cheese, mustard, salt and pepper and stir.

Attach bread cubes in your air fryer and mix with chilies and ham. Add eggs mix, spread and cook for 15 minutes.
Divide among plates and serve. Enjoy!

Tomato and Bacon Breakfast

Prep time: 10 minutes **Cooking time:** 30 minutes
Servings: 6

Ingredients

1 pound white bread, cubed
1/4 cup olive oil
28 ounces canned tomatoes, chopped
1/2 teaspoon red pepper, crushed
1/2 pound Monterey jack, shredded
2 tablespoons stock

1 pound smoked bacon, cooked and chopped

1/2 pound cheddar, shredded 2 tablespoons chives, chopped
1 yellow onion, chopped
Salt and black pepper to the taste
8 eggs, whisked

Directions

Add the oil to your air fryer and heat it up at 350 degrees F. Add bread, bacon, onion, tomatoes, red pepper and stock and stir.

Add eggs, cheddar and Monterey jack and cook everything for 20 minutes. Divide among plates, sprinkle chives and serve. Enjoy!

Creamy Hash Browns

Prep time: 10 minutes **Cooking time:** 20 minutes
Servings: 6

Ingredients

2 pounds hash browns
1 cup whole milk
1 yellow onion, chopped
6 green onions, chopped
Salt and black pepper to the taste
6 eggs

8 bacon slices, chopped
9 ounces cream cheese
1 cup cheddar cheese, shredded
Cooking spray

Directions

Warmth up your air fryer at 350 degrees F and grease it with cooking spray.

In a bowl, mix eggs with milk, cream cheese, cheddar cheese, bacon, onion, salt and pepper and whisk well. Add hash browns to your air fryer add eggs mix over them and cook for 20 minutes. Divide among plates and serve. Enjoy!

Blackberry French toast

Prep time: 10 minutes **Cooking time:** 20 minutes
Servings: 6

Ingredients

1 cup blackberry jam, warm 12 ounces bread loaf, cubed
1 teaspoon cinnamon powder
1 teaspoon vanilla extract
4 eggs

8 ounces cream cheese, cubed
1/2 cup brown sugar
Cooking spray
2 cups half and half

Directions

Set your air fryer with cooking spray and heat it up at 300 degrees F. Add blueberry jam on the bottom, layer half of the bread cubes, then add cream cheese and Set with the rest of the bread.

In a bowl, mix eggs with half and half, cinnamon, sugar and vanilla, whisk well and add over bread mix. Cook for 20 minutes and serve for breakfast. Enjoy!

Smoked Sausage Breakfast Mix

Prep time: 10 minutes **Cooking time:** 30 minutes
Servings: 4

Ingredients

1 and 1/2 pounds smoked sausage, chopped and browned
1 cup milk
16 ounces cheddar cheese, shredded

1 and 1/2 teaspoons thyme, chopped

1 and 1/2 cups grits 4 and 1/2 cups water
A pinch of salt and black pepper
1/4 teaspoon garlic powder
Cooking spray
4 eggs, whisked

Directions

Put the water in a pot, bring to a boil over medium heat, and add grits, stir, and cover.

Add cheese, stir until it melts and mix with milk, thyme, salt, pepper, garlic powder and eggs and whisk really well.
Heat up your air fryer at 300 degrees F, grease with cooking spray and add browned sausage.

Add grits mix, spread and cook for 25 minutes.
Divide among plates and serve for breakfast. Enjoy!

Delicious Potato Frittata

Prep time: 10 minutes **Cooking time:** 20 minutes
Servings: 6

Ingredients

6 ounces jarred roasted red bell peppers, chopped
12 eggs, whisked
2 tablespoons parsley, chopped
2 tablespoons chives, chopped

1/2 cup parmesan, grated
3 garlic cloves, minced
16 potato wedges
6 tablespoons ricotta cheese
Salt and black pepper to the taste
Cooking spray

Directions

In a bowl, mix eggs with red peppers, garlic, parsley, salt, pepper and ricotta and whisk well. Heat up your air fryer at 300 degrees F and grease it with cooking spray.
Add half of the potato wedges on the bottom and sprinkle half of the parmesan all over.

Add half of the egg mix; add the rest of the potatoes and the rest of the parmesan. Add the rest of the eggs mix, sprinkle chives and cook for 20 minutes. Divide among plates and serve for breakfast. Enjoy!

Asparagus Frittata

Prep time: 10 minutes **Cooking time:** 5 minutes
Servings: 2

Ingredients

4 eggs, whisked
10 asparagus tips, steamed
Salt and black pepper to the taste

2 tablespoons parmesan, grated
Cooking spray
4 tablespoons milk

Directions

In a bowl, mix eggs with parmesan, milk, salt and pepper and whisk well. Heat up your air fryer at 400 degrees F and grease with cooking spray.

Add asparagus, add eggs mix, toss a bit and cook for 5 minutes. Divide frittata on plates and serve for breakfast. Enjoy!

Special Corn Flakes Breakfast Casserole

Prep time: 10 minutes **Cooking time:** 8 minutes
Servings: 5

Ingredients

1/3 cup milk
2 eggs, whisked
4 tablespoons cream cheese, whipped
1 and 1/2 cups corn flakes, crumbled
3 teaspoons sugar
1/4 tbs nutmeg, ground
5 bread slices
1/4 cup blueberries

Directions

In a bowl, merge eggs with sugar, nutmeg and milk and whisk well. In another bowl, merge cream cheese with blueberries and whisk well.

Put corn flakes in a third bowl. Spread blueberry mix on each bread slice, then dip in eggs mix and dredge in corn flakes at the end.

Place bread in your air fryer's basket, heat up at 400 degrees F and bake for 8 minutes. Divide among plates and serve for breakfast. Enjoy!

Ham Breakfast Pie

Prep time: 10 minutes **Cooking time:** 25 minutes
Servings: 6

Ingredients

16 ounces crescent rolls dough
2 eggs, whisked
2 cups ham, cooked and chopped
Salt and black pepper to the taste
2 cups cheddar cheese, grated 1 tablespoon parmesan, grated
Cooking spray

Directions

Set your air fryer's pan with cooking spray and press half of the crescent rolls dough on the bottom. In a bowl, mix eggs with cheddar cheese, parmesan, salt and pepper, pour well and add over dough.

Scatter ham, divide the rest of the crescent rolls dough in strips, set them over ham and cook at 300 degrees F.
Divide pie and serve for breakfast. Enjoy!

Breakfast Veggie Mix

Prep time: 10 minutes **Cooking time:** 25 minutes
Servings: 6

Ingredients

1 yellow onion
1 red bell pepper
12 ounces sourdough bread
4 ounces parmesan
2 tablespoons mustard
Salt and black pepper to the taste
2 tablespoons olive oil
8 ounces brie
8 eggs
1 gold potato
3 cups milk

Directions

Set up your air fryer at 350 degrees F, add oil, onion, potato and bell pepper and cook for 5 minutes.
In a bowl, merge eggs with milk, salt, pepper and mustard and whisk well.

Attach bread and brie to your air fryer, add half of the eggs mix and add half of the parmesan as well.
Add the rest of the bread and parmesan, toss just a little bit and cook for 20 minutes. Divide among plates and serve for breakfast. Enjoy!

Fast Eggs and Tomatoes

Prep time: 5 minutes **Cooking time:** 10 minutes
Servings: 4

Ingredients

4 eggs
2 tablespoons parmesan,
Salt and black pepper
Cooking spray
2 ounces milk
8 cherry tomatoes

Directions

Set your air fryer with cooking spray and heat it up at 200 degrees F. In a bowl, merge eggs with cheese, milk, salt and pepper and whisk.

Attach this mix to your air fryer and cook for 6 minutes.
Attach tomatoes, cook your scrambled eggs for 3 minutes, divide among plates and serve. Enjoy!

Breakfast Mushroom Quiche

Prep time: 10 minutes **Cooking time:** 10 minutes
Servings: 4

Ingredients

1 tablespoon flour	1 tablespoon butter, soft
2 button mushrooms, chopped	3 eggs
1 small yellow onion, chopped	9 inch pie dough
	A pinch of nutmeg, ground
	2 tbsp ham, chopped
Salt and black pepper to the taste	1/4 cup Swiss cheese, grated
1/2 teaspoon thyme, dried	1/3 cup heavy cream

Directions

Dust a working surface with the flour and roll the pie dough. Press in on the bottom of the pie pan your air fryer has. In a bowl, mix butter with mushrooms, ham, onion, eggs, heavy cream, salt, pepper, thyme and nutmeg and whisk well.

Add this over pie crust, spread, sprinkle Swiss cheese all over and place pie pan in your air fryer. Cook your quiche at 400 degrees F for 10 minutes. Slice and serve for breakfast. Enjoy!

Duo-Cheese Roll

Prep time: 10 minutes **Cooking time:** 20 minutes
Servings: 12

Ingredients

2 1/2 cups shredded Mozzarella cheese	1 cup blanched finely ground almond flour
2 ounces (57 g) cream cheese, softened	1/2 teaspoon vanilla extract
1/2 cup Erythritol	1 tbsp ground cinnamon

Directions

In a large microwave-safe bowl, combine Mozzarella cheese, cream cheese, and flour. Microwave the mixture on high 90 seconds until cheese is melted. Add vanilla extract and Erythritol, and mix until a dough forms.

When the dough is processed to work with your hands, about 2 minutes, spread it out into a 12-inch × 4-inch rectangle on ungreased parchment paper. Evenly sprinkle dough with cinnamon.

Begin at the long side of the dough; roll lengthwise to form a log. Slice the log into twelve even pieces. Divide rolls between two ungreased 6-inch round nonstick baking dishes. Place one dish into air fryer basket. Adjust the temperature to 375F (190C) and set the timer for 10 minutes. Cinnamon rolls will be done when golden around the edges and mostly firm. Repeat with second dish. Allow rolls to cool in dishes 10 minutes before serving.

Sausage with Peppers

Prep time: 15 minutes **Cooking time:** 15 minutes
Servings: 4

Ingredients

1/2 pound (227 g) spicy ground pork breakfast sausage	4 ounces (113 g) full-fat cream cheese, softened
	4 large eggs
1/4 cup canned diced tomatoes and green chiles, drained	8 tablespoons shredded pepper jack cheese
	4 large poblano peppers
1/2 cup full-fat sour cream	

Directions

In a skillet medium heat, crumble and brown the ground sausage until no pink remains. Detach sausage and drain the fat from the pan. Crack eggs into the pan, scramble, and cook until no longer runny.

Place cooked sausage in a large bowl and fold in cream cheese. Mix in diced tomatoes and chilies. Gently fold in eggs.
Cut a 4-inch–5-inch slit in the top of each poblano, removing the seeds and white membrane with a small knife. Separate the filling into four **Servings:** and spoon carefully into each pepper. Top each with 2 tablespoons pepper jack cheese.

Place each pepper into the air fryer basket.
Adjust the temperature to 350F (180C) and set the timer for 15 minutes.

Peppers will be soft and cheese will be browned when ready. Serve immediately with sour cream on top.

Chocolate Chip Muffin

Prep time: 5 minutes **Cooking time:** 15 minutes
Servings: 6

Ingredients

1 1/2 cups finely ground almond flour	4 tablespoons salted butter, melted
1/3 cup granular brown Erythritol	2 large eggs, whisked
	1 tbsp baking powder
	1/2 cup low-carb chocolate chips

Directions

In a large bowl, combine all Ingredients. Evenly pour batter into six silicone muffin cups greased with cooking spray.

Place muffin cups into air fryer basket. Adjust the temperature to 320°F (160°C) and set the timer for 15 minutes. Muffins will be golden brown when done.

Let muffins cool in cups 15 minutes to avoid crumbling. Serve warm.

Simple Ham and Pepper Omelet

Prep time: 5 minutes **Cooking time:** 8 minutes
Servings: 1

Ingredients

2 large eggs
1/4 teaspoon fine sea salt
1/8 teaspoon ground black pepper
2 tablespoons diced green onions, plus more for garnish
1/4 cup diced red bell peppers
Quartered cherry tomatoes, for serving (optional)

1/4 cup unsweetened, unflavored almond milk
1/4 cup diced ham (omit for vegetarian)
1/4 cup shredded Cheddar cheese (about 1 ounce / 28g) (omit for dairy-free)

Directions

Preheat the air fryer to 350F (180C). Grease a 6 by 3-inch cake pan and set aside.
In a bowl, use a fork to whisk together the eggs, almond milk, salt, and
pepper. Add the ham, bell peppers, and green onions. Pour the mixture into the greased pan. Add the cheese on top (if using).
Set the pan in the basket of the air fryer. Cook for 8 minutes, or until
the eggs are cooked to your liking.
Detach the omelet from the sides of the pan with a spatula and place it on a serving plate. Garnish with green onions and serve with cherry tomatoes, if desired. Best served fresh.

Ham with Avocado

Prep time: 5 minutes **Cooking time:** 10 minutes
Servings: 2

Ingredients

1 large Hass avocado, halved and pitted
2 tablespoons green onions, plus more for garnish
1/4 cup Cheddar cheese (omit for dairy-free)

2 large eggs
2 thin slices ham
1/4 teaspoon ground black pepper

1/2 teaspoon fine sea salt

Directions

Preheat the air fryer to 400F (205C). Place a slice of ham into the cavity of each avocado half. Crack an egg on top of the ham, then sprinkle on the green onions, salt, and pepper.

Set the avocado halves in the air fryer cut side up and cook for 10 minutes. Top with the cheese (if using) and cook for 30 seconds more, or until the cheese is melted. Garnish with chopped green onions. Best served fresh.

Sausage Eggs with Smoky Mustard Sauce

Prep time: 20 minutes **Cooking time:** 12 minutes
Servings: 8

Ingredients

1 pound (454 g) pork sausage
1 large egg
2 tablespoons milk
1/4 cup mayonnaise
1 tablespoon Dijon mustard
1 teaspoon chipotle hot sauce

8 soft-boiled or hard-boiled eggs, peeled

1 cup crushed pork rinds
2 tablespoons sour cream
Smoky Mustard Sauce

Directions

Preheat the air fryer to 390F (199C) Divide the sausage into 8 portions. Take each portion of sausage, pat it down into a patty, and place 1 egg in the middle, gently wrapping the sausage around the egg until the egg is completely covered. (Wet your hands slightly if you find the sausage to be too sticky.) Repeat with the remaining eggs and sausage.

In a small bowl, merge the egg and milk until frothy. In another shallow bowl, place the crushed pork rinds. Working one at a time, dip a sausage-wrapped egg into the beaten egg and then into the pork rinds, gently rolling to coat evenly. Repeat with the remaining sausage- wrapped eggs.

Set the eggs in the device, and lightly spray with olive oil. Air fry for 10 to 12 minutes, pausing halfway through the baking time to turn the eggs, until the eggs are hot and the sausage is cooked. To make the sauce In a bowl, merge the mayonnaise, sour cream, Dijon, and hot sauce. Whisk until thoroughly combined. Serve with the Scotch eggs.

Pecan and Almond Granola

Prep time: 10 minutes **Cooking time:** 5 minutes
Servings: 6

Ingredients

2 cups pecans, chopped
1 cup almond slivers
1/3 cup sunflower seeds
1/4 cup golden flaxseed
2 tablespoons unsalted butter
1/4 cup granular Erythritol

1 cup unsweetened coconut flakes
1/4 cup low-carb, sugar-free chocolate chips
1 teaspoon ground cinnamon

Directions

In a large bowl, mix all Ingredients. Place the mixture into a 4-cup round baking dish. Place dish into the air fryer basket. Adjust the temperature to 320F (160C) and set the timer for 5 minutes. Allow to cool completely before serving.

Gold Muffin

Prep time: 5 minutes **Cooking time:** 15 minutes
Servings: 6

Ingredients

1 cup blanched finely ground almond flour	2 tablespoons salted butter, melted
1/4 cup granular Erythritol	1 large egg, whisked
2 teaspoons baking powder	1 teaspoon ground allspice

Directions

In a large bowl, combine all Ingredients. Evenly pour batter into six silicone muffin cups greased with cooking spray.

Place muffin cups into air fryer basket. Adjust the temperature to 320°F (160°C) and set the timer for 15 minutes. Cooked muffins should be golden brown.

Let muffins cool in cups 15 minutes to avoid crumbling. Serve warm

Lemony Cake

Prep time: 10 minutes **Cooking time:** 14 minutes
Servings: 6

Ingredients

1 cup blanched finely ground almond flour	1/2 teaspoon baking powder
1/2 cup powdered Erythritol	1/4 cup unsalted butter, melted
1/4 cup unsweetened almond milk	1 teaspoon vanilla extract
1 teaspoon poppy seeds	1 medium lemon
	2 large eggs

Directions

In a large bowl, merge almond flour, Erythritol, baking powder, butter, almond milk, eggs, and vanilla. Divide the lemon in half and press the juice into a small bowl, then add to the batter.

Using a fine grater, zest the lemon and add 1 tablespoon zest to the batter and stir. Add poppy seeds to batter.
Pour batter into nonstick 6-inch round cake pan. Place pan into the air fryer basket.

Adjust the temperature to 300°F (150°C) and set the timer for 14 minutes. When fully cooked, a toothpick inserted in center will come out mostly clean. The cake will finish cooking and firm up as it cools. Serve at room temperature.

Bacon Lettuce Wraps

Prep time: 20 minutes **Cooking time:** 30 minutes
Servings: 4

Ingredients

8 ounces (227 g) (about 12 slices) reduced-sodium bacon	8 tablespoons mayonnaise
8 large romaine lettuce leaves 4 Roma tomatoes, sliced	Salt and freshly ground black pepper

Directions

Set the bacon in a single layer in the air fryer basket. (It's OK if the bacon sits a bit on the sides.) Set the air fryer to 350F (180C) and cook for 10 minutes. Check for crispiness and cook for 2 to 3 minutes longer if needed. Cook in batches, if necessary, and drain the grease in between batches.

Scatter 1 tablespoon of mayonnaise on each of the lettuce leaves and top with the tomatoes and cooked bacon. Flavor to taste with salt and freshly ground black pepper. Roll the lettuce leaves as you would a burrito, securing with a toothpick if desired.

Broccoli and Mushroom Frittata

Prep time: 15 minutes **Cooking time:** 20 minutes
Servings: 2

Ingredients

1 tablespoon olive oil	11/2 cups broccoli florets, finely chopped
1/2 cup sliced brown mushrooms	6 eggs
1/4 cup finely chopped onion	1/2 teaspoon salt
1/4 teaspoon freshly ground black pepper	1/4 cup Parmesan cheese

Directions

In an 8-inch nonstick cake pan, combine the olive oil, broccoli, mushrooms, onion, salt, and pepper. Stir until the vegetables are thoroughly coated with oil. Place the cake pan in the air fryer basket and set the air fryer to 400F (205C). Air fry for 5 minutes until the vegetables soften.

Meanwhile, in a medium bowl, whisk the eggs and Parmesan until thoroughly combined. Merge the egg mixture into the pan and shake gently to distribute the vegetables. Air fry for another 15 minutes until the eggs are set.

Detach from the air fryer and let sit for 5 minutes to cool slightly. Use a silicone spatula to lift the frittata onto a plate before serving gently.

Mozzarella Almond Bagels

Prep time: 15 minutes **Cooking time:** 14 minutes
Servings: 6

Ingredients

13/4 cups shredded
Mozzarella cheese
1 large egg, beaten
1 cup almond flour
1 tablespoon baking
powder
1/8 teaspoon fine sea salt

2 tablespoons unsalted
butter or coconut oil
1 tablespoon apple cider
vinegar
11/2 teaspoons everything
bagel seasoning

Directions

Make the dough Put the Mozzarella and butter in a
large microwave- safe bowl and microwave for 1 to 2
minutes. Stir well. Add the egg and vinegar. Using a
hand mixer on medium, combine well. Add the
almond flour, baking powder, and salt and, using the
mixer, combine well.
Set a parchment paper on the countertop and place
the dough on it. Knead it for about 3 minutes.

Preheat the air fryer to 350F (180C). Spray a baking
sheet or pie pan that will fit into your air fryer with
avocado oil.
Divide the dough into 6 equal portions. Roll 1 portion
into a log that is 6 -inches long and about 1/2 -inch
thick. Form the log into a circle and seal the edges
together, making a bagel shape.

Set the bagels on the greased baking sheet. Spray the
bagels with avocado oil and top with everything bagel
seasoning, pressing the seasoning into the dough with
your hands.

Set the bagels in the air fryer and cook for 14 minutes, or
until cooked through and golden brown, flipping after 6
minutes. Remove the bagels from the air fryer and allow
them to cool slightly before slicing them in half and
serving.

Bell Pepper and Ham Omelet

Prep time: 5 minutes **Cooking time:** 15 minutes
Servings: 2

Ingredients

3 large eggs
1/4 cup seeded green bell
pepper

2 tablespoons peeled and
chopped yellow onion
1/4 cup chopped cooked
no-sugar-added ham

1 tablespoon salted butter,
melted
1/4 tbsp ground black
pepper
1/4 teaspoon salt

Directions

Crack eggs into an ungreased 6-inch round nonstick
baking dish. Mix in butter, bell pepper, onion, ham,
salt, and black pepper.

Place dish into air fryer basket. Adjust the temperature
to 320°F (160°C) and set the timer for 15 minutes.
The eggs will be fully cooked and firm in the middle
when done.
Slice in half and serve warm on two medium plates.

Turkey Sausage and Avocado Burger

Prep time: 5 minutes **Cooking time:** 15 minutes
Servings: 4

Ingredients

1 pound (454 g) ground
turkey breakfast sausage
1/2 teaspoon salt
2 tablespoons mayonnaise

1/4 teaspoon ground
black pepper
1/4 cup green bell pepper
1 medium avocado,
peeled, pitted, and sliced

Directions

In a large bowl, mix sausage with salt, black pepper,
bell pepper, and mayonnaise. Form meat into four
patties.
Place patties into ungreased air fryer basket. Adjust the
temperature to 370F and set the timer for 15 minutes,
turning patties halfway through cooking. Burgers will
be done when dark brown and they have an internal
temperature of at least 165F (74C).

Serve burgers topped with avocado slices on four
medium plates.

Chicken Bake

Prep time: 5 minutes **Cooking time:** 25 minutes
Servings: 4

Ingredients

1 cup ground chicken
1 egg, beaten
1 teaspoon coconut oil
1/4 cup Mozzarella, shredded
1 teaspoon Italian seasonings

Directions

In the mixing bowl, mix all Ingredients until you get a homogenous mixture. Then put it in the air fryer basket and bake at 370F for 25 minutes.

Avocado Spread

Prep time: 10 minutes **Cooking time:** 10 minutes
Servings: 4

Ingredients

1 teaspoon garlic powder
1 tablespoon pork rinds, chopped
1 tablespoon cream cheese
1 avocado, pitted, peeled, chopped
1 egg

Directions

Preheat the air fryer to 375F. Mix beaten egg with pork rinds and pour the mixture in the air fryer. Cook it at 385F for 10 minutes. Stir the cooked egg mixture well.

Then mix it with garlic powder, avocado, and cream cheese. Blend the mixture well.

Duo-Cheese Sausage Meatball

Prep time: 10 minutes **Cooking time:** 15 minutes
Servings: 18

Ingredients

1 pound (454 g) ground pork breakfast sausage
1/2 cup shredded sharp Cheddar cheese 1 ounce (28 g) cream cheese, softened
1/4 teaspoon ground black pepper
1/2 teaspoon salt
1 large egg, whisked

Directions

Combine all Ingredients in a large bowl. Form mixture into eighteen 1-inch meatballs. Place meatballs into ungreased air fryer basket. Set the heat to 400F and set the timer for 15 minutes, shaking basket three times during cooking. Meatballs will be browned on the outside and have an internal temperature of at least 145F (63C) when completely cooked. Serve warm.

Pork Sausage and Cream Cheese Biscuit

Prep time: 20 minutes **Cooking time:** 30 minutes
Servings: 4

Ingredients

Filling
1/4 cup minced onions
2 cloves garlic, minced
1/2 teaspoon fine sea salt
1 (8-ounce / 227-g) package cream cheese (or Kite Hill brand cream cheese style spread for dairy-free), softened
Biscuits
3/4 cup blanched almond flour
2 1/2 tablespoons very cold unsalted butter, cut into 1/4-inch pieces
10 ounces (283 g) bulk pork sausage, crumbled
1/2 teaspoon ground black pepper
3/4 cup beef or chicken broth
1 teaspoon baking powder
Fresh thyme leaves, for garnish
3 large egg whites
1/4 teaspoon fine sea salt

Directions

Preheat the air fryer to 400F (205C). Place the sausage, onions, and garlic in a 7-inch pie pan. Using your hands, break up the sausage into small pieces and spread it evenly throughout the pie pan. Season with the salt and pepper. Set the pan in the device and cook for 5 minutes.

While the sausage cooks, place the cream cheese and broth in a food processor or blender and purée until smooth.

Detach the pork from the air fryer and use a fork or metal spatula to crumble it more. Pour the cream cheese mixture into the sausage and stir to combine. Set aside.

Make the biscuits Place the egg whites in a medium-sized mixing bowl or the bowl of a stand mixer and whip with a hand mixer or stand mixer until stiff peaks form.
In a separate medium-sized bowl, merge together the almond flour, baking powder, and salt, and then cut in the butter.

Scoop the dough into 4 equal-sized biscuits, making sure the butter is evenly distributed. Place the biscuits on top of the sausage and cook in the air fryer for 5 minutes

Kale Mix

Prep time: 5 minutes **Cooking time:** 20 minutes
Servings: 4

Ingredients

4 kalamata olives, chopped	2 oz. Provolone cheese, grated
1/2 teaspoon smoked paprika	4 eggs, beaten
	1 cup kale, chopped

Directions

Mix all Ingredients in the mixing bowl. Then pour it in the air fryer basket. Flatten the mixture and cook it at 360F for 20 minutes

Sausage Egg Cup

Prep time: 10 minutes **Cooking time:** 15 minutes
Servings: 6

Ingredients

12 ounces (340 g) ground pork breakfast sausage	1/2 teaspoon salt
1/4 tbs ground black pepper	6 large eggs
	1/2 tbs red pepper flakes

Directions

Place sausage in six 4-inch ramekins (about 2 ounces (57 g) per ramekin) greased with cooking oil. Press sausage down to cover bottom and about 1/2-inch up the sides of ramekins. Beat one egg into each ramekin and sprinkle evenly with salt, black pepper, and red pepper flakes.
Place ramekins into air fryer basket. Adjust the temperature to 350F (180C) and set the timer for 15 minutes. Egg cups will be done when sausage is fully cooked to at least 145F (63C) and the egg is firm. Serve warm.

Spinach and Tomato Egg

Prep time: 10 minutes **Cooking time:** 15 minutes
Servings: 4

Ingredients

2 cups 100% liquid egg whites	3 tablespoons salted butter, melted
1/4 tbsp onion powder	1/2 medium Roma tomato, cored and diced
1/2 cup chopped fresh spinach leaves	1/4 teaspoon salt

Directions

In a large bowl, merge egg whites with butter, salt, and onion powder. Stir in tomato and spinach, and then pour evenly into four 4-inch ramekins greased with cooking spray. Place ramekins into air fryer basket. Adjust the temperature to 300F (150C) and set the timer for 15 minutes. Eggs will be fully cooked and firm in the center when done. Serve warm.

Turkey Sausage with Tabasco Sauce

Prep time: 15 minutes **Cooking time:** 20 minutes
Servings: 8

Ingredients

11/2 pounds (680g) 85% lean ground turkey	1/4 onion, grated
1 teaspoon Tabasco sauce	3 cloves garlic, chopped
	1 teaspoon Creole seasoning
1/2 teaspoon paprika	1/2 teaspoon cayenne
1 teaspoon dried thyme	

Directions

Preheat the air fryer to 370F (188C). In a large bowl, merge the turkey, garlic, onion, Tabasco, Creole seasoning, thyme, paprika, and cayenne. Mix with clean hands until thoroughly combined. Shape into 16 patties, about 1/2 -inch thick. (Wet your hands slightly if you find the sausage too sticky to handle.)

Working in batches if necessary, arrange the patties in a single layer in the air fryer basket. Pausing halfway through the **Cooking time:**to flip the patties, air fry until a thermometer inserted into the thickest portion registers 165F (74C).

Mozzarella Balls

Prep time: 15 minutes **Cooking time:** 12 minutes
Servings: 6

Ingredients

4 tablespoons coconut flour	1/2 cup Mozzarella cheese, shredded
1 teaspoon Erythritol	
2 tablespoons coconut oil, softened	1 egg, beaten
	1/4 teaspoon baking powder

Directions

In the mixing bowl, mix coconut flour with Mozzarella cheese, Erythritol, coconut oil, baking powder, and egg. Knead the dough. Make the balls and put them in the air fryer. Cook the balls at 365F for 12 minutes.

Keto Wrap

Prep time: 10 minutes **Cooking time:** 15 minutes
Servings: 2

Ingredients

1/2 cup ground
pork
1 teaspoon plain yogurt
1/2 teaspoon dried
oregano

1 jalapeno pepper,
chopped
4 lettuce leaves
1 teaspoon coconut oil

Directions

Mix the ground pork with jalapeno pepper and ground
oregano. Then preheat the air fryer to 365F.

Add coconut oil and ground pork mixture. Cook the
mixture for 15 minutes. Stir it from time to time.
Then fill lettuce leaves with ground pork mixture. Add
plain yogurt and wrap the lettuce leaves.

Avocado Bake

Prep time: 10 minutes **Cooking time:** 20 minutes
Servings: 2

Ingredients

1 avocado, pitted, halved
2 eggs

1 oz. Parmesan, grated
1/2 teaspoon ground
nutmeg

Directions

Crack the eggs in the avocado hole and top them with
Parmesan and ground nutmeg. Then put the eggplants
in the air fryer basket and cook at 375F for 20
minutes.

Swiss Chard Bake

Prep time: 10 minutes **Cooking time:** 15 minutes
Servings: 4

Ingredients

4 eggs, beaten
2 oz. Swiss chard,
chopped
1 oz. Provolone cheese,
grated

1 tablespoon coconut
cream
1/2 teaspoon coconut oil

Directions

Set the air fryer basket with coconut oil. Then pour eggs
inside. Add coconut cream, Provolone cheese, and Swiss
Chard. Cook the meal at 375F for 16 minutes or until the
eggs are firm.

Tender Muffins

Prep time: 15 minutes **Cooking time:** 12 minutes
Servings: 4

Ingredients

4 slices of ham, chopped
4 eggs, beaten
1 teaspoon coconut oil,
softened

1/4 cup coconut cream
1 teaspoon dried dill
1/2 teaspoon chives,
chopped

Directions

In the mixing bowl, mix ham with eggs, coconut
cream, dried dill, coconut oil, and chives. Put the
mixture in the muffin molds and bale at 365F for 12
minutes.

Fish Eggs

Prep time: 5 minutes **Cooking time:** 20 minutes
Servings: 4

Ingredients

1 teaspoon chives,
chopped
4 eggs, beaten
1/2 teaspoon ground
coriander

5 oz. cod fillet, chopped,
boiled

1/2 teaspoon salt
1/2 tbsp coconut oil,
melted

Directions

Shred the cod fillet and mix it with chives, eggs,
ground coriander, and salt. Brush the air fryer basket
with coconut oil and pour the egg mixture inside. Bake
the fish eggs at 360F for 20 minutes.

Chilies Casserole

Prep time: 10 minutes **Cooking time:** 15 minutes
Servings: 2

Ingredients

1 chili pepper, chopped
1/4 cup Mozzarella,
shredded
1/2 tbsp ground
cinnamon

1 cup ground chicken
1/4 cup cauliflower,
chopped
1/2 teaspoon coconut oil

Directions

Mix chili pepper with ground chicken, Mozzarella,
ground cinnamon, and cauliflower. Brush the air fryer
basket with coconut oil and put the mixture inside.
Bake the casserole at 375F for 15 minutes.

Brussels Sprouts with Bacon

Prep time: 5 minutes **Cooking time:** 12 minutes
Servings: 4

Ingredients

2 cups trimmed Brussels sprouts
1/4 teaspoon ground black pepper
2 tablespoons balsamic vinegar
1/4 teaspoon salt
2 tablespoons olive oil
2 slices cooked sugar-free bacon, crumbled

Directions

In a large bowl, merge Brussels sprouts in olive oil, and then sprinkle with salt and pepper. Place into ungreased air fryer basket. Adjust the temperature to 375F (190C) and set the timer for 12 minutes, shaking the basket halfway through cooking. Brussels sprouts will be tender and browned when done.

Place sprouts in a large serving dish and drizzle with balsamic vinegar. Sprinkle bacon over top. Serve warm.

Air Fried Radishes

Prep time: 10 minutes **Cooking time:** 10 minutes
Servings: 4

Ingredients

1 pound (454 g) radishes
1/2 tbs garlic powder
1/2 teaspoon dried parsley 1/4 teaspoon dried oregano
2 tablespoons unsalted butter, melted
1/4 teaspoon ground black pepper

Directions

Detach roots from radishes and cut into quarters. In a small bowl, attach butter and seasonings. Merge the radishes in the herb butter and place into the air fryer basket. Adjust the temperature to 350F (180C) and set the timer for 10 minutes. Halfway through the cooking time, merge the radishes in the air fryer basket. Serve warm.

Bacon-Wrapped Asparagus

Prep time: 5 minutes **Cooking time:** 10 minutes
Servings: 4

Ingredients

8 slices reduced-sodium bacon, cut in half
16 thick (about 1 pound 454 g) asparagus spears, trimmed of woody ends

Directions

Preheat the air fryer to 350F (180C). Set a half piece of bacon around the center of each stalk of asparagus.

Working in batches, if necessary, arranges seam-side down in a single layer in the air fryer basket. Cook for 10 minutes until the bacon is crisp and the stalks are tender.

Air Fried Asparagus

Prep time: 5 minutes **Cooking time:** 12 minutes
Servings: 4

Ingredients

1 tablespoon olive oil
1/4 teaspoon salt
1/4 teaspoon ground black pepper
1 pound (454 g) asparagus spears, ends trimmed
1 tablespoon salted butter, melted

Directions

In a bowl, whisk olive oil over asparagus spears and sprinkle with salt and pepper.

Place spears into ungreased air fryer basket. Set the temperature to 375F (190C) and set the timer for 12 minutes, shaking the basket halfway through cooking. Asparagus will be lightly browned and tender when done.
Transfer to a large dish and drizzle with butter. Serve warm.

Cheesy Asparagus

Prep time: 10 minutes **Cooking time:** 18 minutes
Servings: 4

Ingredients

1/2 cup heavy whipping cream
1/2 cup Parmesan cheese
1 pound (454 g) asparagus, ends trimmed, chopped into 1-inch pieces
2 ounces (57 g) cream cheese, softened
1/4 teaspoon salt
1/4 teaspoon ground black pepper

Directions

In a medium bowl, merge together heavy cream, Parmesan, and cream cheese until combined. Place asparagus into an ungreased 6-inch round nonstick baking dish. Pour cheese mixture over top and sprinkle with salt and pepper. Place dish into air fryer basket. Adjust the temperature to 350F (180C) and set the timer for 18 minutes. Asparagus will be tender when done. Serve warm.

Cheesy Bean Mushroom Casserole

Prep time: 10 minutes **Cooking time:** 12 minutes
Servings: 4

Ingredients

1 pound fresh green beans
1/2 onion, sliced
1/2 cup chicken stock
1 clove garlic, minced
1 tablespoon olive oil
1/2 teaspoon salt
1/2 cup grated Cheddar cheese
1 (8-ounce / 227-g) package sliced brown mushrooms
1/4 teaspoon freshly ground black pepper
4 ounces 113 g cream cheese
1/4 tbs ground nutmeg

Directions

Preheat the air fryer to 400F (205C). Coat a 6-cup casserole dish with olive oil and set aside. In a large bowl, combine the green beans, mushrooms, onion, garlic, olive oil, salt, and pepper. merge until the vegetables are thoroughly coated with the oil and seasonings.

Transfer the mixture to the air fryer basket. Pausing halfway through the **Cooking time:**to shake the basket, air fry for 10 minutes until tender.

While the vegetables are cooking, in a 2-cup glass measuring cup, warm the cream cheese and chicken stock in the microwave on high for 1 to 2 minutes until the cream cheese is melted. Add the nutmeg and whisk until smooth.

Transfer the vegetables to the prepared casserole dish and pour the cream cheese mixture over the top. Top with the Cheddar cheese. Air fry for another 10 minutes until the cheese is melted and beginning to brown.

Crispy Green Beans

Prep time: 5 minutes **Cooking time:** 8 minutes
Servings: 4

Ingredients

2 teaspoons olive oil
1/4 teaspoon salt
1/4 teaspoon ground black pepper
1/2 pound (227g) fresh green beans, ends trimmed

Directions

In a large bowl, whisk olive oil over green beans and sprinkle with salt and pepper.

Place green beans into ungreased air fryer basket. Adjust the temperature to 350°F (180°C) and set the timer for 8 minutes, shaking the basket two times during cooking. Green beans will be dark golden and crispy at the edges when done. Serve warm.

Air Fried Zucchini Salad

Prep time: 5 minutes **Cooking time:** 7 minutes
Servings: 4

Ingredients

2 medium zucchini, thinly sliced
2 tablespoons chopped fresh mint
Zest and juice of 1/2 lemon
1/4 cup crumbled feta cheese Freshly ground black pepper
1/4 cup chopped fresh parsley
1 clove garlic, minced
5 tbsp olive oil, divided

Directions

Preheat the air fryer to 400F (205C). In a bowl, merge the zucchini slices with 1 tablespoon of the olive oil.

Working in batches if necessary, arrange the zucchini slices in an even layer in the air fryer basket. Pausing halfway through the **Cooking time:**to shake the basket, air fry for 5 to 7 minutes until soft and lightly browned on each side.

Meanwhile, in a bowl, merge the remaining 4 tablespoons olive oil, parsley, mint, lemon zest, lemon juice, and garlic.
Set the zucchini on a plate and drizzle with the dressing. Sprinkle the feta and black pepper on top. Serve warm or at room temperature.

Zucchini Fritters

Prep time: 15 minutes **Cooking time:** 10 minutes
Servings: 4

Ingredients

2 zucchini, grated (about 1 pound / 454 g)	1 teaspoon salt
1/4 cup almond flour	1 large egg
1 tablespoon olive oil	1/4 cup grated Parmesan cheese
1/4 teaspoon dried thyme	1/4 tbsp ground turmeric
1/4 teaspoon freshly ground black pepper	1/2 lemon, sliced into wedges

Directions

Preheat the air fryer to 400F (205C). Divide a piece of parchment paper to fit slightly smaller than the bottom of the air fryer.

Place the zucchini in a large colander and sprinkle with the salt. Let sit for 5 to 10 minutes. Press as much liquid as you can from the zucchini and place in a large mixing bowl. Add the almond flour, Parmesan, egg, thyme, turmeric, and black pepper. Stir gently until thoroughly combined.

Shape the mixture into 8 patties and arrange on the parchment paper. Brush lightly with the olive oil. Serve warm with the lemon wedges.

Zucchini and Tomato Boats

Prep time: 5 minutes **Cooking time:** 10 minutes
Servings: 4

Ingredients

1 large zucchini ends removed, halved lengthwise	1/4 teaspoon salt
	1/4 cup feta cheese
1 tablespoon balsamic vinegar	1 tablespoon olive oil
	6 grape tomatoes, quartered

Directions

Use a spoon to scoop out 2 tablespoons from center of each zucchini half, making just enough space to fill with tomatoes and feta.

Place tomatoes evenly in centers of zucchini halves and sprinkle with salt. Place into ungreased air fryer basket. Adjust the temperature to 350°F (180°C) and set the timer for 10 minutes. When done, zucchini will be tender.

Transfer boats to a serving tray and sprinkle with feta, and then drizzle with vinegar and olive oil. Serve warm.

Air Fried Cauliflower

Prep time: 15 minutes **Cooking time:** 20 minutes
Servings: 4

Ingredients

1/4 cup olive oil	2 teaspoons curry powder
1/4 teaspoon freshly ground black pepper	1 head cauliflower, cut into bite-size florets
1/2 teaspoon salt	1/2 red onion, sliced
2 tablespoons freshly chopped parsley, for garnish (optional)	

Directions

Preheat the air fryer to 400F (205C). In a large bowl, merge the olive oil, curry powder, salt, and pepper. Add the cauliflower and onion. Toss gently until the vegetables are completely coated with the oil mixture. Transfer the vegetables to the basket of the air fryer.

Pausing about halfway through the **Cooking time:** to shake the basket, air fry for 20 minutes. Top with the parsley, if desired, before serving.

Cheese Cauliflower Mash

Prep time: 10 minutes **Cooking time:** 15 minutes
Servings: 6

Ingredients

1 (12-ounce / 340-g) steamer bag cauliflower florets, cooked according to package instructions	2 tablespoons salted butter, softened
2 ounces (57 g) cream cheese, softened	1/2 cup shredded sharp Cheddar cheese
1/4 teaspoon ground black pepper	1/2 teaspoon salt
	1/4 cup pickled jalapeños

Directions

Set cooked cauliflower into a food processor with remaining
Ingredients. Pulse twenty times until cauliflower is smooth and all Ingredients are combined.

Spoon mash into an ungreased 6-inch round nonstick baking dish. Place dish into air fryer basket. Adjust the temperature to 380F (193C) and set the timer for 15 minutes. The top will be golden brown when done. Serve warm.

Cheesy Cauliflower Tots

Prep time: 15 minutes **Cooking time:** 12 minutes
Servings: 16

Ingredients

1 large head cauliflower	1 cup shredded Mozzarella cheese
1/2 cup grated Parmesan cheese	1/4 teaspoon dried parsley
1 large egg	1/4 teaspoon garlic powder 1/8 teaspoon onion powder

Directions

On the stovetop, set a large pot with 2 cups water and place a steamer in the pan. Bring water to a boil. Divide the cauliflower into florets and set on steamer basket. Cover pot with lid.

Allow cauliflower to steam 7 minutes until fork tender. Remove from steamer basket and place into cheesecloth or clean kitchen towel and let cool. Squeeze over sink to remove as much excess moisture as possible. The mixture will be too soft to form into tots if not all the moisture is removed. Beat with a fork to a smooth consistency.

Put the cauliflower into a large mixing bowl and add Mozzarella, Parmesan, egg, garlic powder, parsley, and onion powder. Stir until fully combined. The mixture should be wet but easy to mold.

Take 2 tablespoons of the mixture and roll into tot shape. Repeat with remaining mixture. Place into the air fryer basket.

Adjust the temperature to 320F (160C) and set the timer for 12 minutes. Turn tots halfway through the cooking time. Cauliflower tots should be golden when fully cooked. Serve warm.

Cauliflower with Lime Juice

Prep time: 10 minutes **Cooking time:** 7 minutes
Servings: 4

Ingredients

2 cups chopped cauliflower florets	1/2 teaspoon garlic powder
2 tbsp coconut oil, melted	1 medium lime
2 tbsp chopped cilantro	2 teaspoons chili powder

Directions

In a bowl, merge cauliflower with coconut oil. Sprinkle with chili powder and garlic powder. Set seasoned cauliflower into the air fryer basket.

Set the temperature to 350F (180C). Cauliflower will be juicy and begin to turn golden at the edges. Set into serving bowl. Divide the lime into quarters and squeeze juice over cauliflower. Garnish with cilantro.

Cheesy Cauliflower Rice Balls

Prep time: 10 minutes **Cooking time:** 8 minutes
Servings: 4

Ingredients

1 (10-ounce / 283-g) steamer bag cauliflower rice, cooked according to package instructions	1/2 cup shredded Mozzarella cheese
	1 large egg
2 ounces (57 g) plain pork rinds, finely crushed	1/2 teaspoon Italian seasoning
1/4 teaspoon salt	

Directions

Place cauliflower into a large bowl and mix with Mozzarella. Whisk egg in a separate medium bowl. Place pork rinds into another large bowl with salt and Italian seasoning.

Separate cauliflower mixture into four equal sections and form each into a ball. Carefully dip a ball into whisked egg, and then roll in pork rinds. Repeat with remaining balls.

Place cauliflower balls into ungreased air fryer basket. Adjust the temperature to 400F (205C) and set the timer for 8 minutes. Rice balls will be golden when done.
Use a spatula to move cauliflower balls to a large dish for serving carefully. Serve warm.

Broccoli with Sesame Dressing

Prep time: 5 minutes **Cooking time:** 10 minutes
Servings: 4

Ingredients

6 cups broccoli florets	2 tablespoons sesame seeds
1 tablespoon olive oil	2 tablespoons rice vinegar
2 tablespoons coconut aminos	1/2 teaspoon Swerve
	1/4 teaspoon salt
1/4 tbsp red pepper flakes	2 tablespoons sesame oil

Directions

Preheat the air fryer to 400F (205C). In a bowl, merge the broccoli with the olive oil and salt until thoroughly coated.
Transfer the broccoli to the air fryer basket. Pausing halfway through the cooking time to shake the basket, air fry for 10 minutes.

Meanwhile, in the same large bowl, whisk together the sesame seeds, vinegar, coconut aminos, sesame oil, Serve, and red pepper flakes (if using). Transfer the broccoli to the bowl and toss until thoroughly coated with the seasonings. Serve warm or at room temperature.

Breakfast Calzone

Prep time: 15 minutes
Cooking time: 15 minutes **Servings:** 4

Ingredients

11/2 cups shredded mozzarella cheese	1 large whole egg
1ounce full-fat cream cheese	8 tablespoons shredded mild Cheddar cheese
4 large eggs, scrambled	1/2 pound cooked breakfast sausage, crumbled
1/2 cup finely ground almond flour	

Directions

In a large microwave-safe bowl, add mozzarella, almond flour, and cream cheese. Microwave for 1 minute. Stir until the mixture is smooth and forms a ball. Add the egg and stir until dough forms.

Set dough between two sheets of parchment and roll out to 1/4" thickness. Cut the dough into four rectangles. Mix scrambled eggs and cooked sausage together in a large bowl. Divide the mixture evenly among each piece of dough, placing it on the lower half of the rectangle. Sprinkle each with 2 tablespoons Cheddar.

Fold over the rectangle to cover the egg and meat mixture. Pinch, roll, or use a wet fork to close the edges completely. Divide a piece of parchment to fit your air fryer basket and place the calzones onto the parchment. Place parchment into the air fryer basket.

Adjust the temperature to 380F and set the timer for 15 minutes. Flip the calzones halfway through the cooking time. When done, calzones should be golden in color. Serve immediately.

Cheesy Broccoli with Bacon

Prep time: 10 minutes **Cooking time:** 10 minutes
Servings: 2

Ingredients

3 cups fresh broccoli florets	1/2 cup shredded sharp Cheddar cheese
4 slices sugar-free bacon, cooked and crumbled	1 scallion, sliced on the bias
1 tablespoon coconut oil	1/4 cup full-fat sour cream

Directions

Set broccoli into the air fryer basket and drizzle it with coconut oil. Adjust the temperature to 350F (180C) and set the timer for 10 minutes.

Toss the basket two or three times during cooking to avoid burned spots. When broccoli begins to crisp at ends, remove from fryer. Top with shredded cheese, sour cream, and crumbled bacon and garnish with scallion slices.

Golden Broccoli Salad

Prep time: 5 minutes **Cooking time:** 7 minutes
Servings: 4

Ingredients

2 cups fresh broccoli florets, chopped	1/4 teaspoon salt
1/8 teaspoon ground black pepper	1 tablespoon olive oil
1/4 cup sliced roasted almonds	1/4 cup shredded Parmesan cheese
	1/4 cup lemon juice, divided

Directions

In a large bowl, toss broccoli and olive oil together. Sprinkle with salt and pepper, then drizzle with 2 tablespoons lemon juice.

Place broccoli into ungreased air fryer basket. Adjust the temperature to 350F (180C) and set the timer for 7 minutes, shaking the basket halfway through cooking. Broccoli will be golden on the edges when done. Place broccoli into a large serving bowl and drizzle with remaining lemon juice. Sprinkle with Parmesan and almonds. Serve warm.

Sausage-Stuffed Mushroom Caps

Prep time: 10 minutes **Cooking time:** 8 minutes
Servings: 3

Ingredients

6 large Portobello mushroom caps	2 tablespoons blanched finely ground almond flour
1/2 pound (227g) Italian sausage	1/4 cup grated Parmesan cheese
1 tbsp minced fresh garlic	1/4 cup chopped onion

Directions

Use a spoon to hollow out each mushroom cap, reserving scrapings. In a medium skillet over medium heat, brown the sausage about 10 minutes or until fully cooked and no pink remains. Drain and then add reserved mushroom scrapings, onion, almond flour, Parmesan, and garlic. Gently fold Ingredients together and continue cooking an additional minute, then remove from heat.

Evenly spoon the mixture into mushroom caps and place the caps into a 6-inch round pan. Place pan into the air fryer basket. Adjust the temperature to 375F (190C) and set the timer for 8 minutes. When finished cooking, the tops will be browned and bubbling. Serve warm.

Tomato Salad with Arugula

Prep time: 10 minutes **Cooking time:** 10 minutes
Servings: 4

Ingredients

4 green tomatoes
1 large egg, lightly beaten
1/2 cup peanut flour
1 cup mayonnaise
1/2 cup sour cream
2 tablespoons finely chopped fresh parsley
1/2 teaspoon garlic powder
1 (5-ounce / 142-g) bag arugula Buttermilk Dressing

1/2 teaspoon salt
1 tablespoon Creole seasoning
2 teaspoons fresh lemon juice
1 teaspoon dried chives
1/2 teaspoon salt
1/2 teaspoon onion powder
1 teaspoon dried dill

Directions

Preheat the air fryer to 400F (205C). Divide the tomatoes into 1/2-inch slices and sprinkle with the salt. Let sit for 5 to 10 minutes. Set the egg in a small shallow bowl. In another small shallow bowl, combine the peanut flour and Creole seasoning. Soak each tomato slice into the egg wash, and then dip into the peanut flour mixture, turning to coat evenly.

Working in batches if necessary, arranges the tomato slices in a single layer in the air fryer basket and spray both sides lightly with olive oil. Air fry until browned and crisp, 8 to 10 minutes.

To make the buttermilk dressing In a small bowl, whisk together the mayonnaise, sour cream, lemon juice, parsley, dill, chives, salt, garlic powder, and onion powder.
Serve the tomato slices on top of a bed of the arugula with the dressing on the side.

Herb Tomato Egg Cups

Prep time: 10 minutes **Cooking time:** 12 minutes
Serve 6

Ingredients

5 eggs
½ cup tomatoes, chopped
Salt

1 medium onion, chopped
2 tbsp fresh parsley, chopped
2 tbsp fresh basil, chopped Pepper

Directions

Preheat the air fryer to 300 F. In a mixing bowl, whisk eggs with pepper and salt. Add onion, basil, parsley, and tomatoes and stir well. Pour egg mixture into the silicone muffin molds. Place muffin molds into the air fryer basket and cook for 10-12 minutes. Serve and enjoy.

Tasty Egg Bites

Prep time: 10 minutes **Cooking time:** 12 minutes
Serve 6

Ingredients

6 eggs
2 green onions, sliced
2 bacon slices, cooked & chopped
Pepper Salt

¼ tsp mustard powder
1 tbsp milk
¼ cup cheddar cheese, shredded
1 tbsp heavy cream

Directions

Preheat the air fryer to 350 F. In a bowl, whisk eggs with mustard powder, cream, pepper, and salt until fluffy.

Add green onions, cheese, and bacon and stir well. Pour egg mixture into the silicone muffin molds. Place muffin molds into the air fryer basket and cook for 10-12 minutes or until eggs are set. Serve and enjoy.

Cheese Sandwich

Prep time: 10 minutes **Cooking time:** 5 minutes
Serve 2

Ingredients

4 bread slices
4 oz cheddar cheese slices
2 tbsp butter

¼ tsp garlic powder
1 tomato, cut into slices

Directions

Preheat the air fryer to 350 F. Spread butter on one side of each bread slice. Take two bread slices and top with cheddar cheese slices and tomato slices.

Cover with remaining bread slices. Make sure buttered side up. Sprinkle garlic powder on top of sandwiches. Place sandwiches into the air fryer basket and cook for 4-5 minutes. Serve and enjoy.

Easy French Toast

Prep time: 10 minutes **Cooking time:** 10 minutes
Serve 2

Ingredients

2 eggs
¼ tsp cinnamon
½ cup milk

4 bread slices
1 tbsp sugar
1 tsp vanilla

Directions

Preheat the air fryer to 380 F. In a shallow bowl, whisk eggs with milk, sugar, vanilla, and cinnamon. Dip bread slices in egg mixture from both sides.

Place bread slices into the air fryer basket and cook for 4 minutes. Turn bread slices and cook for 6 minutes more. **Serve:** and enjoy.

Flavorful Banana Muffins

Prep time: 10 minutes **Cooking time:** 15 minutes
Serve: 10

Ingredients

1 egg	¾ cup self-rising flour
1 tsp vanilla	½ cup brown sugar
1 tsp cinnamon	1/3 cup olive oil
2 ripe bananas	

Directions

Preheat the air fryer to 320 F. mIn a mixing bowl, add ripe bananas and mash using a fork. Add oil, brown sugar, vanilla, and egg and stir until well combined.

Add cinnamon and flour and mix until just combined. Spoon batter into the silicone muffin molds. Place muffin molds into the air fryer basket and cook for 15 minutes. **Serve:** and enjoy.

Quick & Easy Granola

Prep time: 10 minutes **Cooking time:** 10 minutes
Serve: 4

Ingredients

1 cup rolled oats	2 tbsp butter, melted 3
1 tsp vanilla	tbsp honey
1 tsp cinnamon	½ cup almonds, sliced
	Pinch of salt

Directions

In a mixing bowl, mix together oats, vanilla, butter, honey, cinnamon, almonds, and salt. Add granola mixture into the parchment-lined air fryer basket and cook for 10 minutes. Stir after every 2-3 minutes. **Serve:** and enjoy.

Breakfast Hush Puppies

Prep time: 10 minutes **Cooking time:** 10 minutes
Serve: 4

Ingredients

1 egg	¼ cup onion, chopped
¾ cup milk	½ tsp garlic powder
½ tsp onion powder	¼ tsp sugar
1 ½ tsp baking powder	¾ cup all-purpose flour
½ tsp salt	1 cup yellow cornmeal

Directions

In a mixing bowl, mix together cornmeal, flour, baking powder, sugar, onion, garlic powder, onion powder, and salt Add milk and egg and mix until well combined.

Make small balls from the cornmeal mixture and place into the parchment-lined air fryer basket and cook for 10 minutes. Turn halfway through. **Serve:** and enjoy.

Tasty Breakfast Potatoes

Prep time: 10 minutes **Cooking time:** 25 minutes
Serve: 4

Ingredients

1 ½ lbs. potatoes, diced	¼ tsp fennel seed
¼ tsp garlic powder	¼ cup onion, diced
Salt	Pepper
	2 bell peppers, sliced

Directions

Preheat the air fryer to 360 F. In a mixing bowl, toss potatoes with remaining Ingredients.

Add potato mixture into the air fryer basket and cook for 20-25 minutes. Stir after every 5 minutes. **Serve:** and enjoy.

Blueberry Oatmeal

Prep time: 10 minutes **Cooking time:** 15 minutes
Serve: 2

Ingredients

1 egg	¼ cup blueberries
2 tbsp maple syrup	¼ tsp baking powder
2 tbsp butter, melted	1/3 cup milk
½ tsp vanilla	½ tsp cinnamon
¾ cup rolled oats	¼ tsp salt

Directions

In a mixing bowl, mix together oats, egg, cinnamon, vanilla, baking powder, maple syrup, milk, and salt. Add blueberries and fold well.

Pour oat mixture into the two greased ramekins. Place ramekins into the air fryer basket and cook at 300 F for 12-15 minutes. **Serve:** and enjoy.

Banana Bread

Prep time: 10 minutes **Cooking time:** 15 minutes
Serve: 6

Ingredients

1 egg	¼ cup butter, melted
1/3 cup walnuts, chopped	3 bananas, overripe &
1 cup sugar	mashed
1 ½ cups all-purpose flour	½ tsp salt
1 tsp baking soda	

Directions

In a mixing bowl, mix together flour, baking soda, sugar, walnuts, and salt. Add melted butter, egg, and mashed bananas and mix until well combined.

Pour batter into the greased loaf pan. Place loaf pan into the air fryer basket and cook at 350 F for 12-15 minutes. Slice and **Serve:**.

Air Fryer Brussels Sprouts

Prep time: 15 minutes **Cooking time:** 25 minutes
Serve: 1

Ingredients

1 teaspoon avocado oil	½ teaspoon salt
½ teaspoon ground black pepper	1 teaspoon balsamic vinegar
	10 ounces Brussels sprouts
2 teaspoons crumbled cooked bacon	

Directions

Preheat an air fryer carefully to 350°F (175 degrees C). In a mixing dish, combine the oil, salt, and pepper. Turn the Brussels sprouts to coat. Cook for 5 minutes in the air fryer, then shake the sprouts and cook for another 5 minutes.

Place the sprouts in a serving dish, drizzle with balsamic vinegar; toss to coat. Garnish with bacon.

Air-Fryer Roasted Veggies

Prep time: 15 minutes **Cooking time:** 25 minutes
Serve: 1

Ingredients

½ cup diced zucchini	½ cup diced sweet red pepper
¼ teaspoon salt	¼ teaspoon ground black pepper
2 teaspoons vegetable oil	
½ cup diced summer squash	½ cup diced mushrooms
½ cup diced cauliflower	½ cup diced asparagus
	1/4 teaspoon seasoning

Directions

Preheat the air fryer carefully to 360°F (180 degrees C).
Combine the veggies, oil, salt, pepper, and preferred spice in a mixing dish. Toss to coat and place in a frying basket.
Cook for 10 minutes, stirring every 5 minutes.

Air Fryer Apple Pies

Prep time: 15 minutes **Cooking time:** 20 minutes
Serve: 1

Ingredients

4 tablespoons butter	6 tablespoons brown sugar
1 teaspoon ground cinnamon	2 medium Granny Smith apples, diced
2 teaspoons cold water	14 ounces pastry for a 9-inch double-crust pie
¼ cup powdered sugar	cooking spray
½ tablespoon grapeseed oil	1 teaspoon cornstarch
1 teaspoon milk, or more as needed	

Directions

Combine the brown sugar, apples, butter, and cinnamon in a nonstick pan. Cook for 5 minutes over medium heat or until the apples are softened.

Coldwater should be used to dissolve cornstarch. Cook, constantly stirring, until the sauce thickens, approximately 2 minutes. Remove the apple pie filling from the heat and leave it aside to cool while preparing the crust.

On a lightly floured board, roll out the pie crust carefully to smooth the surface of the dough. Next, cut the dough into rectangles small enough to fit in your air fryer simultaneously. Repeat with the remaining crust,
re-rolling any scraps of dough as needed until you have 8 equal rectangles.

Wet the edges of four rectangles and place some apple filling in the center, about 1/2-inch from the edges. Roll out the remaining four rectangles, making them somewhat larger than the filled ones. Place these rectangles on the filling and use a fork to seal the edges. Make four little slits on the tops of the pies.

Cooking spray should be sprayed on the air fryer basket. Brush the tops of two pies with grapeseed oil and arrange them, spatula-style, in the air fryer basket.

Set the temperature to 385°F after inserting the basket (195 degrees C). 8 minutes in the oven or until golden brown. Remove the pies from the basket and repeat with the other two pies.

In a small mixing dish, combine powdered sugar and milk. Allow the glaze to dry on the heated pies. Pies can be **Serve:**d warm or at room temperature

Air Fryer Roasted Asparagus

Prep time: 20 minutes **Cooking time:** 20 minutes
Serve: 1

Ingredients

1 bunch fresh asparagus,
trimmed avocado oil
cooking spray
½ teaspoon Himalayan
pink salt
¼ teaspoon red pepper
flakes

½ teaspoon garlic powder
¼ cup freshly grated
Parmesan cheese
¼ teaspoon ground multi-
colored peppercorns

Directions

Preheat the air fryer carefully to 375°F (190 degrees
C). Using parchment paper, line the basket. Mist the
asparagus stalks with avocado oil and place them in
the air
fryer basket.

Garlic powder, pink Himalayan salt, pepper, and red
pepper flakes are optional. Garnish with Parmesan
cheese. 7 to 9 minutes in the air fryer until asparagus
spears brown.

Air Fryer Corn Nuts

Prep time: 20 minutes **Cooking time:** 25 minutes
Serve: 1

Ingredients

14 ounces giant white corn
3 tablespoons vegetable oil

1 ½ teaspoons salt

Directions

Place the corn in a big bowl, cover with water, and set
aside to rehydrate for 8 hours overnight.

Drain the corn and put it out on a wide baking sheet
in an equal layer. Using paper towels, pat dry. Allow
for a 20-minute air-drying period.

Preheat the air fryer carefully to 400°F (200 degrees
C).
Put the corn in a large mixing dish. Mix in the oil and
salt. Stir until everything is uniformly covered.
Place the corn in a uniform layer in the air fryer basket
in batches.

The **Cooking time:**is 10 minutes. Cook for another
10 minutes after shaking the basket. Shake the basket
and cook for 5 minutes more before transferring to a
paper towel-lined dish. Rep with the leftover corn.
Allow corn nuts to cool for about 20 minutes or until
crisp.

Air Fryer Breakfast Frittata

Prep time: 15 minutes **Cooking time:** 18 minutes
Serve: 1

Ingredients

¼ pound breakfast
sausage fully cooked and
crumbled
4 eggs, lightly beaten
1 green onion, chopped

½ cup shredded Cheddar-
Monterey Jack cheese
blend 2 tbsp red bell
pepper, diced
1 pinch cayenne pepper
(Optional) cooking spray

Directions

Combine sausage, eggs, and Cheddar-Monterey
cheese. Combine the Jack cheese, bell pepper, onion,
and cayenne in a mixing dish.

Preheat the air fryer carefully to 360°F (180 degrees
C). Coat a 6x2 inch nonstick cake pan with cooking
spray.
Fill the prepared cake pan halfway with the egg
mixture.
Cook in the air fryer for 18 to 20 minutes, or until the
frittata is set.

Air Fryer Wiener Schnitzel

Prep time: 15 minutes **Cooking time:** 22 minutes
Serve: 1

Ingredients

1 pound veal, scallopini
cut
2 tablespoons lemon juice
¼ cup all-purpose flour,
1 egg
nonstick cooking spray
1 cup panko breadcrumbs

salt and ground black
pepper to taste

1 tablespoon chopped
fresh parsley
1 lemon, cut into wedges

Directions

Preheat an air fryer carefully to 400°F (200 degrees C).
Sprinkle lemon juice, salt, and pepper over the veal in
a clean work area.

Fill a flat plate halfway with flour. In a separate dish,
combine the egg and parsley. In a third dish, place the
breadcrumbs. Dredge each veal cutlet in flour, then in
the egg-parsley mixture, and last in breadcrumbs,
pressing down to ensure that the breadcrumbs adhere.

Spray the air fryer basket properly with nonstick
cooking spray. Place the breaded veal cutlets in the
basket, being careful not to overcrowd it. Nonstick
cooking spray should be sprayed on the tops. 5
minutes in the oven Cook for 5 minutes more after
flipping, spraying any chalky parts with nonstick
cooking spray. Rep with the leftover veal. With lemon
slices, **Serve:**.

Air Fryer Plantain Chips

Prep time: 10 minutes **Cooking time:** 18 minutes
Serve: 1

Ingredients

1 green plantain avocado
oil spray

1 pinch salt

Directions

Preheat an air fryer carefully to 350°F (175 degrees C).
Plantain should be cut on both ends and scored along
the side only through the skin. Remove the peel from
the plantain and chop it in half. Then, using a
vegetable peeler, cut the peel into strips.

Avocado oil should be sprayed on the air fryer basket.
Fill the basket with plantain strips, ensuring sure they
don't touch. Oil the tops of the plantain slices.

Cook for 7 to 9 minutes in a preheated air fryer. Turn
each strip over with tongs and continue frying until
crispy, 3 to 5 minutes more. Sprinkle with salt right
away.

Air Fryer Potato Chips

Prep time: 18 minutes **Cooking time:** 20 minutes
Serve: 1

Ingredients

1 large russet potato,
peeled cooking spray

1 teaspoon smoked
Cheddar salt (such as
Batterman)

Directions

Set a man doline to the thinnest setting and cut the
potato into thin slices. Soak sliced potatoes in a dish
of water for 15 minutes. Then, pour off the water,
cover the potatoes with new water and soak for 15
minutes.

Meanwhile, prepare the air fryer to 400°F (200°C) for
10 minutes. Cooking spray should be sprayed on the
air fryer basket.

Remove the potatoes from the water and carefully dry
them. Sprinkle with smoked Cheddar salt and place it
in the air fryer basket, avoiding overcrowding.
Cooking spray should be sprayed on the potatoes. 8
minutes in the air fryer. Shake the potatoes in the air
fryer. Cook for another 7 minutes, or until the
potatoes are golden brown. Check to see if they're not
becoming too hot and starting to burn.

Air Fryer Ranch-Stuffed Olives

Prep time: 20 minutes **Cooking time:** 20 minutes
Serve: 1

Ingredients

3 ounces cream cheese,
softened
1 (5.75 ounces) can jumbo
pitted black olives, drained
1 cup panko breadcrumbs

2 teaspoons dry ranch
dressing mix
½ cup all-purpose flour
1 large egg, beaten
nonstick cooking spray

Directions

Preheat an air fryer carefully to 400°F (200 degrees C).
In a mixing bowl, blend cream cheese and ranch
powder until well incorporated. Fill a resealable plastic
bag halfway with the mixture. Snip a tiny piece of the
cheese mixture with scissors and pipe it into the olives.

In a mixing dish, combine the flour and baking
powder. Place the egg in a second bowl and the
breadcrumbs in a third. Coat the olives in flour first,
then in egg, then in flour again, then in egg again, and
finally in breadcrumbs. Spray the tops of the olives
with cooking spray before placing them in the air fryer
basket.

Cook for 8 minutes in a hot air fryer, shaking halfway
through.

Air Fryer Spicy Bay Scallops

Prep time: 15 minutes **Cooking time:** 25 minutes
Serve: 1

Ingredients

1 pound bay scallops,
rinsed and patted dry
1 teaspoon garlic powder
2 teaspoons smoked
paprika
⅛ teaspoon cayenne red
pepper

2 teaspoons chili powder
2 teaspoons olive oil
¼ teaspoon ground black
pepper

Directions

Preheat an air fryer carefully to 400°F (200 degrees C).
Add bay scallops, smoked paprika, chili powder, olive
oil, garlic powder, pepper, and cayenne pepper in a
mixing bowl. Place in the air fryer basket.

Cook until the scallops are cooked through, about 8
minutes, shaking the basket halfway through.

"Everything" Seasoning Air Fryer Asparagus

Prep time: 15 minutes **Cooking time:** 20 minutes
Serve: 1

Ingredients

1-pound thin asparagus
1 tablespoon olive oil
4 wedge (blank)s lemon wedges

1 tablespoon everything bagel seasoning
1 pinch salt to taste

Directions

Rinse and trim the asparagus, removing any woody ends. Drizzle olive oil over asparagus on a platter. Toss with the bagel seasoning until well

blended. Arrange the asparagus in a single layer in the air fryer basket. If necessary, work in bunches.

Preheat the air fryer carefully carefully to 390°F (200 degrees C). 5–6 minutes, flipping with tongs halfway through, until slightly soft. If necessary, season with salt. With lemon slices, **Serve:**.

Air Fryer Fingerling Potatoes with Dip

Prep time: 20 minutes **Cooking time:** 25 minutes
Serve: 1

Ingredients

12 ounces fingerling potatoes, halved lengthwise
1 tablespoon olive oil
1/3 cup reduced-fat sour cream,
2 tablespoons mayonnaise
2 tablespoons finely grated Parmesan cheese
1 tablespoon chopped fresh parsley

1 teaspoon garlic powder,
1/4 teaspoon paprika salt and ground black pepper to taste
1 1/2 tablespoons ranch dressing mix (such as Hidden Valley Ranch®)
1 tablespoon white vinegar

Directions

Preheat an air fryer carefully for 5 minutes at 390 degrees F (200 degrees C).

Combine the potatoes, olive oil, garlic powder, paprika, salt, and pepper in a mixing bowl. Transfer the potatoes to the air fryer basket after tossing until coated.
Cook, shaking the basket halfway through until the potatoes are cooked through and crispy, 15 to 17 minutes in a preheated air fryer.

In a separate bowl, combine sour cream, mayonnaise, Parmesan cheese, ranch dressing mix, and vinegar while the potatoes are boiling.

Transfer the cooked potatoes to a platter and sprinkle with parsley. **Serve:** right away with dipping sauce.

Keto Air Fryer Jalapeno Poppers

Prep time: 15 minutes **Cooking time:** 20 minutes
Serve: 1

Ingredients

6 jalapeno peppers, halved and seeded
6 bacon strips, halved lengthwise

7 1/2 ounces garden vegetable cream cheese (such as Philadelphia®)

Directions

Preheat the air fryer carefully to 390°F (200 degrees C).
Fill each half of jalapeño with cream cheese and wrap a split bacon strip. To secure, tuck in the bacon ends or use toothpicks.

Place the jalapeno poppers in the air fryer basket, working in batches as necessary to minimize congestion.

Cook in a preheated air fryer for 10 to 12 minutes, or until the bacon is done to your preference.

Air Fryer Shortbread Cookie Fries

Prep time: 15 minutes **Cooking time:** 18 minutes
Serve: 1

Ingredients

1 1/4 cups all-purpose flour
1/3 cup strawberry jam
3 tablespoons white sugar
1/3 cup lemon curd

1/2 cup butter
1/8 teaspoon ground dried chipotle pepper (Optional)

Directions

In a medium mixing bowl, combine the flour and sugar. Using a pastry blender, cut in the butter until the mixture resembles fine crumbs and begins to cling. Make a ball out of the
Ingredients and knead it until smooth.

Preheat an air fryer carefully to 350°F (190 degrees C). On a lightly floured surface, roll out the dough to 1/4-inch thickness. Cut into 3- to 4-inch-long 1/2-inch-wide "fries." Sprinkle with more sugar if desired.

Arrange the fries in the air fryer basket in a single layer. Cook for 3 to 4 minutes, or until gently browned. Allow cooling in the basket until hard enough to transfer to a wire rack to finish cooling. Rep with the remaining dough.

To make strawberry "ketchup," use the back of a spoon to push jam through a fine-mesh sieve. Next, stir in the chipotle powder. Next, whip the lemon curd until it is dippable for the "mustard." Serve the strawberry ketchup and lemon curd mustard with the sugar cookie fries.

Air Fryer Keto Thumbprint Cookies

Prep time: 15 minutes **Cooking time:** 22 minutes
Serve: 1

Ingredients

1 cup almond flour	2 ounces cream cheese,
1 egg	softened
3 tablespoons low-calorie	1 teaspoon baking powder
natural sweetener (such as	3 ½ tablespoons reduced-
Swerve®)	sugar raspberry pre**Serve:**s

Directions

In a mixing bowl, combine the flour, cream cheese, sweetener, egg, and baking powder until a moist dough forms.

Place the bowl in the freezer for 20 minutes or until the dough is cold enough to shape into balls.

According to the manufacturer's instructions, preheat an air fryer carefully to 400°F (200°C). Then, using parchment paper, line the basket.

Roll the dough into ten balls and set them in the prepared basket. In the center of each cookie, make a thumbprint. Fill each indentation with 1 spoonful of pre**Serve:**s. Cook for 7 minutes in a warm air fryer until the edges are golden brown.

Cool the cookies entirely before removing them from the parchment paper, about 15 minutes, or they will crumble.

Air Fryer Spicy Roasted Peanuts

Prep time: 10 minutes **Cooking time:** 18 minutes
Serve: 1

Ingredients

2 tablespoons olive oil	3 teaspoons seafood
salt to taste	seasoning
½ teaspoon cayenne	8 ounces raw Spanish
pepper	peanuts

Directions

Preheat an air fryer carefully to 320°F (160 degrees C). Combine olive oil, seafood seasoning, and cayenne pepper in a large mixing bowl. Stir in the peanuts until they are equally coated.

Place the peanuts in the air fryer basket. Cook the peanuts for 10 minutes in the air fryer. Cook for a further 10 minutes, tossing occasionally.

Remove the air fryer basket and season the peanuts to taste. Cook for 5 minutes more after tossing the peanuts one last time. Allow the peanuts to cool on a dish lined with paper towels

Air Fryer Roasted Salsa Verde

Prep time: 18 minutes **Cooking time:** 20 minutes
Serve: 1

Ingredients

1-pound tomatillos	1 serrano pepper, halved
1 jalapeno pepper, halved	and seeded
and seeded	1 serving cooking spray
½ large white onion, cut	4 cloves garlic, peeled
½ cup chopped cilantro	½ lime, juiced, or more to
1 pinch salt to taste	taste

Directions

Preheat the air fryer carefully to 390°F (200 degrees C).
Remove the husks from the tomatillos and rinse them; cut the tomatillos in half. Place the tomatillos and peppers in the air fryer basket, skin side down. Add the onion. To aid in the roasting process, lightly coat veggies with cooking spray. 5 minutes in the air fryer.

Open the basket and place the garlic cloves inside. Spray lightly with cooking spray and continue to air fry for 5 minutes.

Allow 10 minutes for the veggies to cool. Transfer to a food processor bowl. Combine the cilantro, lime juice, and salt in a mixing bowl. Pulse several times until the veggies are finely chopped, reaching the ideal consistency. Refrigerate or **Serve:** at room temperature to let flavors mingle

Air Fryer Spinach and Feta Casserole

Prep time: 15 minutes **Cooking time:** 20 minutes
Serve: 1

Ingredients

cooking spray	1 (13.5 ounces) can of
1 cup cottage cheese	spinach
2 eggs, beaten	2 tablespoons butter,
	melted
¼ cup crumbled feta	2 tablespoons all-purpose
cheese	flour
⅛ teaspoon ground	
nutmeg	
1 clove garlic, minced, or	1 ½ teaspoons onion
more to taste	powder

Directions

Preheat an air fryer carefully to 375°F (190 degrees C). Set aside an 8- inch pie tin sprayed with cooking spray.

In a mixing bowl, combine spinach, feta cheese, flour, butter, cottage cheese, eggs, garlic, onion powder, and nutmeg. Stir until all of the Ingredients are properly combined. Pour into the pie pan that has been prepared.
Air fry until the center is set, 15 to 20 minutes.

Air Fryer Peri Peri Fries

Prep time: 15 minutes **Cooking time:** 25 minutes
Serve: 1

Ingredients

2 pounds russet potatoes
¼ teaspoon chili powder
⅛ tbs ground white pepper
2 tbs grapeseed oil

¼ tbsp smoked paprika
¼ teaspoon garlic granules
½ teaspoon salt

Directions

Peel the potatoes and cut them into 3/8-inch slices. Place for 15 minutes in a water basin to remove most of the starch. Remove to a clean kitchen towel to dry. Preheat the air fryer carefully for 5 minutes at 350 degrees F (180 degrees C).

Combine paprika, chili powder, garlic, white pepper, and salt in a small bowl. Mix the potatoes with the grapeseed oil in a medium basin. Fill the air fryer basket halfway with the mixture.

Cook for 10 minutes in an air fryer, shaking periodically. Raise the temperature to 400°F (200°C) and continue to air fry for 12 to 15 minutes, or until golden brown. Pour the fries into a bowl, sprinkle with the seasoning mix, and shake to coat evenly. If necessary, taste and adjust the salt. **Serve:** right away.

Air Fryer Chile Verde Burritos

Prep time: 20 minutes **Cooking time:** 20 minutes
Serve: 1

Ingredients

2 cups finely chopped leftover pulled pork
cooking spray

2 tablespoons cotija cheese
10 (6 inches) flour tortillas
1 cup salsa Verde

Directions

According to the manufacturer's instructions, preheat an air fryer carefully to 400°F (200°C).

Combine the pulled pork, salsa Verde, and cotija cheese in a mixing bowl. Stir until everything is well blended. Fill the bottom half of a tortilla with a heaping scoop of filling. Make two folds on either side of the big fold to form an envelope. Roll it up, tucking the filling in with the tips of your fingers as you go. Rep with the remaining tortillas.

Spray the air fryer basket with nonstick cooking spray. Place several burritos in the basket, seam side down, being careful not to overcrowd them. Coat the burritos' tops with cooking spray.

6 minutes in the air fryer Rep with the leftover burritos. If preferred, **Serve:** with more salsa Verde for dipping.

Air Fryer Boursin-Stuffed Wontons

Prep time: 15 minutes **Cooking time:** 25 minutes
Serve: 1

Ingredients

18 wonton wrappers
cooking spray

6 tbsp garlic and herb cheese spread (such as Boursin®) water, as needed

Directions

Preheat the air fryer carefully to 325°F (160 degrees C).
Place the wonton wrappers on a clean work area and separate them. 1 teaspoon garlic and herb cheese should be placed in the center of each wonton. Wet the sides of each wonton with a pastry brush or your finger and fold in half, pressing carefully to make a perfect seal. Wet the wrapper tips and push them together. Spray generously with cooking spray and place on a clean platter.

Coat the inside basket with cooking spray and arrange half of the packed wontons inside. 4 minutes in the air fryer until lightly browned. Rep with the remaining wontons. Allow cooling for a few minutes before serving.

Air Fryer Sugared Pecans

Prep time: 20 minutes **Cooking time:** 25 minutes
Serve: 1

Ingredients

2 tablespoons salted butter, melted
¼ teaspoon ground cinnamon

¼ cup white sugar
1 egg white
1 cup pecan halves

Directions

Preheat an air fryer carefully to 300°F (150 degrees C). Aluminum foil should be used to line the air fryer basket.
Melt the butter and pour it into the prepared basket.

Combine the egg white, sugar, and cinnamon in a mixing dish. Toss in the pecans until evenly coated. Spread the contents of the lined basket out.

5 minutes in the air fryer. Shake the basket and continue to air fry for 5 minutes. Shake the basket again and continue to air fry for 2 to 4 minutes.

Air Fryer Pizza Dogs

Prep time: 15 minutes **Cooking time:** 20 minutes
Serve: 1

Ingredients
2 hot dogs
½ cup pizza sauce
2 hot dog buns
2 teaspoons sliced olives
4 slices pepperoni, halved
¼ cup shredded
mozzarella cheese

Directions

Preheat an air fryer carefully to 390°F (200 degrees C). Make four slits down the center of each hot dog. Cook the hot dogs in the air fryer basket for 3 minutes. Using tongs, transfer to a chopping board.

Insert a pepperoni half into each hot dog slit. Fill the buns with the pizza sauce, hot dogs, mozzarella cheese, and olives.

Return the hot dogs to the air fryer basket and cook for 2 minutes, or until the buns are crisp and the cheese has melted.

Air Fryer Zucchini Chips

Prep time: 15 minutes **Cooking time:** 18 minutes
Serve: 1

Ingredients
1 cup panko
breadcrumbs
1 medium zucchini, thinly
sliced
1 large egg, beaten
¾ cup grated Parmesan
cheese
cooking spray

Directions

Before prepping the zucchini, Preheat an air fryer carefully to 350 degrees F (175 degrees C).

On a plate, combine panko and Parmesan cheese. Dip 1 zucchini slice into the beaten egg, then into the panko mixture, pressing down to coat. Repeat with the remaining zucchini slices on a wire baking rack. Coat the zucchini slices lightly with cooking spray.

Place as many zucchini slices as you can in the air fryer basket without overlapping them.

The **Cooking time:** is 10 minutes. Toss with tongs. Cook for another 2 minutes. Remove from the air fryer and continue with the remaining zucchini slices.

Air Fryer Sausage Patties

Prep time: 15 minutes **Cooking time:** 22 minutes
Serve: 1

Ingredients
1 (12 ounces) package
sausage patties
1 serving nonstick cooking
spray

Directions

Preheat an air fryer carefully to 400°F (200 degrees C). Place the sausage patties in a single layer in the basket, working in batches if required.

Cook for 5 minutes in a hot air fryer. Remove the basket, flip the sausage, and cook for another 3 minutes, or until an instant-read thermometer placed into the middle of a patty registers 160 degrees F (70 degrees C).

Air Fryer Steak and Mushrooms

Prep time: 18 minutes **Cooking time:** 20 minutes
Serve: 1

Ingredients
¼ cup Worcestershire
sauce
1 tablespoon olive oil
1 teaspoon parsley flakes
1 teaspoon paprika
8 ounces button
mushrooms, sliced
1 pound beef sirloin steak,
cut into 1-inch cubes

1 teaspoon crushed chili
flakes

Directions

Combine the steak, mushrooms, Worcestershire sauce, olive oil, parsley, paprika, and chili flakes in a mixing bowl. Refrigerate for at least 4 hours or overnight. 30 minutes before cooking, remove from refrigerator. Preheat an air fryer carefully to 400°F (200 degrees C). Remove the steak mixture from the marinade and set it aside. Place the steak and mushrooms in the air fryer basket.

Cook for 5 minutes in a hot air fryer. Cook for 5 minutes more after tossing. Transfer the steak and mushrooms to a serving platter and set aside for 5 minutes to rest.

Air Fryer Sweet Potato Hash

Prep time: 15 minutes **Cooking time:** 25 minutes
Serve: 1

Ingredients

2 large, sweet potatoes
2 tablespoons olive oil
1 tablespoon smoked
paprika 1 teaspoon sea salt
1 teaspoon dried dill weed

2 slices bacon, cut into
small pieces
1 teaspoon ground black
pepper

Directions

Preheat an air fryer carefully to 400°F (200 degrees C).
Combine sweet potato, bacon, olive oil, paprika, salt,
pepper, and dill in a large mixing bowl.

Place the mixture in the air fryer that has been
warmed. Cook for 12 to 16 minutes, depending on the
size of your pan. After 10 minutes, check and stir,
then every 3 minutes until crispy and golden.

Air Fryer Apple Crumble

Prep time: 15 minutes **Cooking time:** 20 minutes
Serve: 1

Ingredients

1 cup all-purpose flour
¼ cup cold salted butter,
cubed
½ teaspoon baking
powder
2 ½ cups peeled, cored,
and diced apples

½ cup white sugar
½ teaspoon ground
cinnamon
¼ teaspoon ground
nutmeg
cooking spray

Directions

Preheat an air fryer carefully to 350°F (175 degrees C).
Combine the flour, sugar, and butter in a medium
mixing bowl. Mix with your hands until the mixture is
crumbly. Next, combine the cinnamon, baking
powder, and nutmeg in a mixing bowl.

Nonstick cooking spray should be sprayed into two 4
1/2-inch ramekins. Fill ramekins halfway with crumble
and top with apples. Repeat twice more, finishing with
a mounded crumble on top.

Wrap the ramekins with big strips of foil, tucking the
ends beneath to keep them from flying away. Cook
until the apples are soft, about 16 to 20 minutes in the
air fryer. Remove the foil and continue to air fry until
the crumble is golden brown, 2 to 4 minutes more.

Basic Air Fryer Hot Dogs

Prep time: 10 minutes **Cooking time:** 18 minutes
Serve: 1

Ingredients

4 hot dog buns

4 hot dogs

Directions

Preheat the air fryer carefully to 390°F (200 degrees
C). Place the buns in the air fryer basket and cook for
2 minutes. Then, place the buns on a platter.

Cook the hot dogs in the air fryer basket for 3
minutes. Place hot dogs in buns.

Air Fryer Tofu

Prep time: 20 minutes **Cooking time:** 20 minutes
Serve: 1

Ingredients

8 ounces firm tofu
1 tablespoon low-sodium
soy sauce
½ teaspoon sesame oil

1 large clove garlic, finely
chopped
1 tablespoon olive oil

Directions

Place the tofu on a dish lined with paper towels. Cover
with additional paper towels and a second plate. Set a
4- to 5-pound weight on top and press the tofu for 30
minutes; drain and discard any excess liquid before
cutting the tofu into 1/2-inch cubes.

Whisk together the soy sauce, olive oil, garlic, and
sesame oil in a small bowl. Marinate the tofu cubes for
15 to 20 minutes.

Preheat an air fryer carefully to 350°F (180 degrees C).
Place the tofu in the air fryer basket in a single layer.
Without shaking the fryer, air-fried for 5 minutes.
Continue air frying, tossing periodically, for about 10
minutes more, or until browned.

Air Fryer Roasted Bananas

Prep time: 15 minutes **Cooking time:** 25 minutes
Serve: 1

Ingredients
1 banana, sliced into 1/8-
inch-thick diagonals
avocado oil cooking spray

Directions

The parchment paper should be used to line the air fryer basket.

Preheat an air fryer carefully to 375°F (190 degrees C). Place the banana slices in the basket, ensuring they don't touch; cook in batches if required. Avocado oil should be sprayed on banana slices.

Cook for 5 minutes in the air fryer. Remove the basket and carefully turn the banana slices (soft). Cook for another 2 to 3 minutes, or until the banana slices are browning and caramelized. Remove from the basket with caution.

Air Fryer Crab Rangoon

Prep time: 20 minutes **Cooking time:** 25 minutes
Serve: 1

Ingredients
1 (8 ounces) package cream cheese	4 ounces lump crab meat
1 teaspoon soy sauce	1 serving nonstick cooking spray
2 tbs chopped scallions	1 teaspoon Worcestershire sauce
2 tbs Asian sweet chili sauce	24 each wonton wrappers

Directions

In a mixing bowl, add cream cheese, crab meat, scallions, soy sauce, and Worcestershire sauce, whisk until well blended. Preheat an air fryer carefully to 350°F (175 degrees C). Coat the air fryer basket with cooking spray. Warm water should be placed in a small dish.

On a clean work area, arrange 12 wonton wrappers. 1 teaspoon cream cheese mixture should be placed in the center of each wonton wrapper. Wet the sides of each wonton wrapper with your index finger after dipping it into the warm water. Crimp the wrapper corners upwards until they meet in the middle to make dumplings.

Spray the tops of the dumplings with cooking spray and place them in the prepared basket. Cook dumplings for 8 to 10 minutes, or until desired crispness is achieved. Transfer to a plate lined with paper towels. While the first dumplings are cooking, construct the remaining dumplings using the leftover wrappers and filling.
Serve: with sweet chili sauce as a dipping sauce.

Air Fryer Fish Sticks

Prep time: 15 minutes **Cooking time:** 20 minutes
Serve: 1

Ingredients
1 pound cod fillets	¼ cup all-purpose flour
½ cup panko breadcrumbs	¼ cup grated Parmesan cheese
1 egg	½ teaspoon black pepper
1 tablespoon parsley flakes,	cooking spray
1 teaspoon paprika	

Directions

Preheat an air fryer carefully to 400°F (200 degrees C). Pat the fish dry using paper towels before slicing it into 1x3-inch pieces.

In a small bowl, combine the flour and salt. In a separate shallow dish, beat the egg. In a third shallow dish, combine panko, Parmesan cheese, parsley, paprika, and pepper.
Each fish stick should be coated in flour, then dipped in beaten egg, and then coated in seasoned panko mixture.
Spray the air fryer basket with nonstick cooking spray. Arrange half of the sticks in the basket, ensuring none of them is a contact. Cooking spray should be sprayed on the top of each stick. Cook for 5 minutes in a hot air fryer. Cook for a further 5 minutes after flipping the fish sticks. Rep with the rest of the fish sticks.

Air-Fryer Asparagus Fries

Prep time: 15 minutes **Cooking time:** 22 minutes
Serve: 1

Ingredients
1 large egg	1 teaspoon honey
1 cup panko breadcrumbs	½ cup grated Parmesan cheese
12 asparagus spears,	¼ cup Greek yogurt
¼ cup stone-ground mustard	
1 pinch cayenne pepper (Optional)	

Directions

Preheat an air fryer carefully to 400°F (200 degrees C). In a long, thin bowl, whisk together the egg and honey. In a separate dish, combine panko and Parmesan cheese. Coat each asparagus stalk in the egg mixture before rolling in the panko mixture to coat.

Cook 6 spears in the air fryer for 4 to 6 minutes, or until desired brownness is achieved. Rep with the remaining spears.

Combine the mustard, yogurt, and cayenne pepper in a small bowl. Serve with asparagus spears and dipping sauce.

Air Fryer Hasselback Potatoes

Prep time: 15 minutes **Cooking time:** 18 minutes
Serve: 1

Ingredients

4 medium Yukon Gold potatoes	1 tablespoon olive oil
3 cloves garlic, crushed	3 tbsp melted butter
salt and ground black pepper to taste	½ tbsp ground paprika
	1 tablespoon chopped fresh parsley

Directions

Preheat an air fryer carefully to 350°F (175 degrees C). Make 1/4-inch or 1/2-inch slices across the full length of each potato, making sure the knife only cuts through to the bottom 1/2-inch, leaving the bottom of the potato intact.
Combine the butter, olive oil, garlic, and paprika in a small mixing bowl. Brush some of the mixtures into the slits of each potato. Season with salt and pepper to taste.

Cook the potatoes in the air fryer basket for 15 minutes. Brushing the potatoes with the butter mixture again, being careful to get it all the way down into the fanned-out slices to prevent them from drying out. Cook for another 15 minutes, or until the potatoes are tender.

Remove the potatoes from the basket and brush with any leftover butter mixture. **Serve:** immediately garnished with chopped parsley.

Air Fryer Ranch Pork Chops

Prep time: 10 minutes **Cooking time:** 18 minutes
Serve: 1

Ingredients

4 boneless	cooking spray
2 teaspoons dry ranch salad dressing mix	
aluminum foil	

Directions

Place the pork chops on a dish and coat both sides lightly with cooking spray. Allow both sides to remain at room temperature for 10 minutes after sprinkling with ranch seasoning mix.

Preheat an air fryer carefully to 390 degrees F and coat the
basket with cooking spray (200 degrees C). Place the chops in the preheated air fryer, working in batches if required to avoid overcrowding.

5 minutes in the oven Cook for another 5 minutes on the other side. Allow it to rest for 5 minutes on a foil-covered dish before serving

Air Fryer Meatloaf

Prep time: 18 minutes **Cooking time:** 20 minutes
Serve: 1

Ingredients

1-pound lean ground beef	3 tablespoons dry breadcrumbs
1 egg, lightly beaten	
1 tablespoon chopped fresh thyme	ground black pepper to taste 2 mushrooms, thickly sliced
1 teaspoon salt	
1 tablespoon olive oil, or as needed	1 small onion, chopped

Directions

Preheat an air fryer carefully at 392°F (200 degrees C). Combine ground beef, egg, breadcrumbs, onion, thyme, salt, and pepper in a mixing bowl. Knead and completely combine.

Smooth the top of the beef mixture in a baking pan. Coat the mushrooms in olive oil and press them into the top. Insert the pan into the air fryer basket and place it in it. Set the air fryer to 25 minutes and roast the meatloaf until it is well browned.

Allow the meatloaf to rest for at least 10 minutes before slicing it into wedges and serving it.

Air Fryer Portobello Pizzas for Two

Prep time: 15 minutes **Cooking time:** 20 minutes
Serve: 1

Ingredients

2 tablespoons olive oil	1 tbsp Italian seasoning
2 portobello mushroom caps, gills removed	6 tablespoons pizza sauce
	2 tbsp sliced black olives
5 tablespoons shredded mozzarella cheese, divided	8 pepperoni slices

Directions

Preheat an air fryer carefully to 350°F (175 degrees C). 1 tablespoon olive oil, rubbed on each mushroom. Fill each with 1/2 teaspoon Italian spice.
Place the mushrooms, cap sides up, in the air fryer basket. 3 minutes in the air fryer Turn the mushrooms over in the basket so that the cap is facing down.

Divide the pizza sauce evenly between the two mushrooms. 2 tablespoons shredded mozzarella and 1 tablespoon chopped olives on top 3 minutes in the air fryer Cover each pizza with 4 pepperoni pieces and the remaining mozzarella cheese. The pepperoni must be weighed down with cheese, or the fan will blow them off the pie. Air fried for 2 minutes, or until the cheese is melted and the pepperoni is browned.

Air-Fryer Tempura Veggies

Prep time: 15 minutes **Cooking time:** 25 minutes
Serve: 1

Ingredients

- ½ cup all-purpose flour
- 2 eggs
- ½ teaspoon ground black pepper
- 1 cup panko breadcrumbs
- ½ cup whole asparagus spears
- ½ cup sweet pepper rings
- ½ cup zucchini slices
- ½ teaspoon salt, divided, or more to taste
- 2 tablespoons water
- 2 teaspoons vegetable oil
- ½ cup whole green beans
- ½ cup red onion rings
- ½ cup avocado wedges

Directions

Combine the flour, 1/4 teaspoon salt, and pepper in a small bowl. In a separate shallow bowl, properly whisk together the eggs and water. In a third shallow dish, combine panko and oil. Season the panko and flour mixture as desired.

Sprinkle the remaining 1/4 teaspoon salt over the veggies. To coat, dip in the flour mixture, then the egg mixture, and finally the panko mixture. Preheat the air fryer carefully to 400 degrees Fahrenheit (200 degrees Celsius) and the oven to 200 degrees Fahrenheit (95 degrees C).

Place half of the veggies in the air fryer basket in a single layer. Cook for about 10 minutes, or until golden brown. If desired, season with more salt. Place the veggies in the oven to remain warm. Rep with the remaining veggies.

Air Fryer Pasta Chips

Prep time: 20 minutes **Cooking time:** 25 minutes
Serve: 1

Ingredients

- 2 cups farfalle pasta
- 1 tablespoon olive oil
- 1 teaspoon Italian seasoning
- ½ cup Parmesan cheese
- 1 teaspoon garlic powder
- ½ teaspoon salt

Directions

A big saucepan of lightly salted water should be brought to a boil. Cook farfalle pasta at a boil, tossing periodically, for 8 minutes, or until soft yet firm to the biting. Rinse, but do not drain. Allow for a 2-minute rest.

Preheat an air fryer carefully to 400°F (200 degrees C). Drizzle olive oil over the spaghetti in a large mixing basin. Combine the Parmesan cheese, garlic powder, Italian seasoning, and salt in a mixing bowl. Gently combine all of the Ingredients in a mixing bowl.

Cook the pasta in batches in the air fryer basket for 5 minutes. Cook for 2 to 3 minutes more after flipping with a spatula. Transfer to a plate lined with paper towels. Separate any spaghetti chips that have been glued together. Rep with the remaining spaghetti. Allow cooling completely before crisping the last time.

Air Fryer Avocado Fries

Prep time: 15 minutes **Cooking time:** 22 minutes
Serve: 1

Ingredients

- ¼ cup all-purpose flour
- 1 egg
- ¼ teaspoon salt
- 1 ripe avocado, halved, seeded, peeled, and cut into 8 slices
- ½ teaspoon ground black pepper
- 1 teaspoon water
- ½ cup panko breadcrumbs
- cooking spray

Directions

Preheat the air fryer carefully to 400°F (200 degrees C).
In a small bowl, combine the flour, pepper, and salt. In a second shallow dish, whisk together the egg and water. Finally, in a third shallow dish, place the panko.

Dredge an avocado slice in flour, brushing off any excess. Allow the extra egg to drip out before dipping. Finally, coat both sides of the slice with panko. Repeat with the remaining slices on a dish.

Spray avocado slices liberally with cooking spray and place sprayed side down in the air fryer bowl. Also, spray the tops of the avocado slices. Cook for 4 minutes in a hot air fryer. Cook until the avocado slices are browned, about 3 minutes more

Air Fryer Celery Root Fries

Prep time: 20 minutes **Cooking time:** 20 minutes
Serve: 1

Ingredients

½ celeriac (celery root), peeled and cut into 1/2-inch sticks

1 tablespoon brown mustard

1 tablespoon olive oil

⅓ cup vegan mayonnaise

1 tablespoon lime juice

3 cups water,

1 teaspoon powdered horseradish

1 pinch salt and ground black pepper

Directions

Place the celery root in a basin. Pour in the lime juice and water. Allow resting for 20 minutes after mixing. Preheat the air fryer carefully to 400°F (200 degrees C). Make the mayonnaise sauce. Combine vegan mayonnaise, mustard, and horseradish powder in a mixing bowl. Store in the refrigerator, covered, until required.

Drain and dry the celery root sticks before reserving them in a basin. Season the fries with salt and pepper after drizzling them with oil. To coat evenly, toss everything together. Place the celery root in the air fryer basket. Cook for about 10 minutes, testing for doneness halfway through. Shake the basket and cook for another 8 minutes, or until the fries are crisp and golden. **Serve:** the fries right away, with vegan mayo on the side.

Air Fryer Fried Okra

Prep time: 15 minutes **Cooking time:** 25 minutes
Serve: 1

Ingredients

1 large egg

1 cup cornmeal

¼ cup all-purpose flour
cooking spray

½ pound okra pods, cut into 1/2-inch slices

salt to taste

Directions

In a shallow bowl, beat the egg; carefully fold in the cut okra. In a gallon-size resealable plastic bag, combine cornmeal and flour. Place 5 okra slices in the cornmeal mixture, seal the bag, and shake. Transfer the breaded okra to a dish. Repeat with the rest of the okra slices.

Preheat the air fryer carefully to 400°F (200 degrees C). Spray half of the breaded okra pieces with cooking spray in the air fryer basket. Cook for 4 minutes. Shake the basket and respray the okra with frying spray.

Cook for another 4 minutes. Cook for 2 minutes after shaking the basket one more. Remove the okra from the basket and season with salt and pepper to taste. Repeat with the rest of the okra slices.

Lumpia in the Air Fryer

Prep time: 15 minutes **Cooking time:** 20 minutes
Serve: 1

Ingredients

1-pound Italian hot sausage links

¼ cup diced onions

½ cup finely chopped water chestnuts

2 cloves garlic, minced

¼ teaspoon ground ginger

½ cup finely sliced green onions

½ cup chopped carrots

2 tablespoons soy sauce

½ teaspoon salt

16 spring roll wrappers

avocado oil cooking spray

Directions

Remove the casing from the sausage and cook it in a pan over medium heat for 4 to 5 minutes, or until slightly browned. Combine the green onions, onions, carrots, and water chestnuts in a mixing bowl. Cook and stir for 5 to 7 minutes, or until the onions are tender and transparent. Cook for 1 to 2 minutes after adding the garlic. Soy sauce, salt, and ginger to taste. Remove from heat after stirring until the filling is fully mixed.

Place a spring roll wrapper at an angle on a plate. Fill the wrapper with a scant 1/4 cup of the filling. Fold the bottom corner over the filling and tuck in the edges to construct a roll. Wet your finger and softly wet the edges. Rep with the rest of the wrappers and filling. Each roll should be sprayed with avocado oil spray.

Preheat an air fryer carefully to 390°F (198 degrees C). Place the lumpia rolls in the basket, making sure they don't touch; cook in batches as needed. Fry for 4 minutes, then turn and cook for another 4 minutes, or until the crispy skins.

Easy Air Fryer Apple Pies

Prep time: 15 minutes **Cooking time:** 18 minutes
Serve: 1

Ingredients

1 (14.1 ounces) package refrigerated pie crusts (2 pie crusts)

2 tablespoons cinnamon sugar, or to taste

1 (21 ounces) can apple pie filling

1 egg, beaten

1 serving cooking spray

Directions

Roll out 1 pie crust using a rolling pin on a lightly floured board. Cut the pie dough into 10 circles with a 2-1/4-inch round biscuit or cookie cutter. Repeat with the remaining pie dough to make 20 pie crust circles.

Fill approximately half of each circle with apple pie filling. Make a tiny pie by adding a second pie crust circle on top. Don't overfill the container. Crimp the edges of the tiny pies with a fork to seal them.Enjoy.

VEGAN

Air Grilled Tofu

(**Ready in about** 15 minutes | **Servings:** 3)

Ingredients

8 ounces firm tofu, pressed and cut into bite-sized cubes 1 tablespoon tamari sauce
1/2 teaspoon onion powder

1 teaspoon peanut oil
1/2 teaspoon garlic powder

Directions

Toss the tofu cubes in a bowl with the tamari sauce, peanut oil, garlic powder, and onion powder.

Cook your tofu for about 13 minutes in a preheated Air Fryer at 380 degrees F, shaking the basket once or twice to ensure even browning. Good appetite!

Golden Beet Salad with Tahini Sauce

(**Ready in about** 40 minutes | **Servings:** 2)

Ingredients

2 golden beets
Sea salt and ground black pepper, to taste
2 tablespoons soy sauce
1/2 jalapeno pepper, chopped
1 clove garlic, pressed

1 tablespoon sesame oil
2 tablespoons tahini
2 cups baby spinach
1 tablespoon white vinegar
1/4 teaspoon ground cumin

Directions

Toss the golden beets with sesame oil. Cook the golden beets in the preheated Air Fryer at 400 degrees F for 40 minutes, turning them over once or twice to ensure even cooking.

Let your beets cool completely and then, slice them with a sharp knife. Place

the beets in a salad bowl and add in salt, pepper and baby spinach.

In a small mixing dish, whisk the remaining Ingredients until well combined.

Spoon the sauce over your beets, toss to combine and **Serve:** immediately. Bon appétit!

Easy Roasted Fennel

(**Ready in about** 25 minutes | **Servings:** 3)

Ingredients

1 pound fennel bulbs, sliced
1/2 teaspoon dried marjoram
1 tablespoon olive oil

1/2 teaspoon dried basil
1/4 cup vegan mayonnaise
Sea salt and ground black pepper, to taste

Directions

Toss the fennel slices with the olive oil and spices and transfer them to the Air Fryer cooking basket.

Roast the fennel at 370 degrees F for about 20 minutes, shaking the basket once or twice to promote even cooking. **Serve:** the fennel slice with mayonnaise and enjoy!

Asian-Style Brussels Sprouts

(**Ready in about** 20 minutes | **Servings:** 3)

Ingredients

1 pound Brussels sprouts, trimmed and halved
1 tablespoon agave syrup
1 teaspoon rice vinegar
1 clove garlic, minced
1 tbs sesame seeds, toasted

2 tablespoons Shoyu sauce
1 teaspoon coconut oil
1/2 teaspoon Gochujang paste
2 scallion stalks, chopped

Directions

Toss the Brussels sprouts with coconut oil, Shoyu sauce, agave syrup, rice vinegar, Gochujang paste and garlic. Cook the Brussels sprouts in the preheated Air Fryer at 380 degrees F for 15 minutes, shaking the basket halfway through the cooking time.

Place the roasted Brussels sprouts on a serving platter and garnish with scallions and sesame seeds. **Serve:** immediately!

Authentic Platanos Maduros

(**Ready in about** 15 minutes | **Servings:** 2)

Ingredients

1 very ripe, sweet plantain	1 teaspoon Caribbean
1 tbsp coconut oil, melted	Sorrel Rum Spice Mix

Directions

Cut your plantain into slices. Toss your plantain with Caribbean Sorrel Rum Spice Mix and coconut oil. Cook your plantain in the preheated Air Fryer at 400 degrees F for 10 minutes, shaking the cooking basket halfway through the cooking time. **Serve:** immediately and enjoy!

Cauliflower Oatmeal Fritters

(**Ready in about** 20 minutes | **Servings:** 3)

Ingredients

1/2 pound cauliflower florets	1 tablespoons flaxseed meal
2 tablespoons sunflower seeds	4 tablespoons pumpkin seeds butter
1 glove garlic, chopped	1/2 tbsp smoked paprika
Kosher salt and freshly ground black pepper, to taste	2 tablespoons hemp hearts
	1 cup rolled oats
1 tablespoon canola oil	
1 small yellow onion	

Directions

In a food processor or blender, combine all of the Ingredients and blend until well combined. After that, form the mixture into small patties and place them in the Air Fryer cooking basket.

Cook the cauliflower patties for 16 minutes in a preheated Air Fryer at 375°F, shaking the basket halfway through to ensure even browning. Good appetite!

Famous Everything Bagel Kale Chips

(**Ready in about** 12 minutes | **Servings:** 1)

Ingredients

2 cups loosely packed kale leaves, stems removed	1 tablespoon nutritional yeast flakes
Coarse salt and ground black pepper, to taste	1/2 teaspoon poppy seeds, lightly toasted
1 teaspoon sesame seeds, lightly toasted	1 teaspoon olive oil
	1/4 teaspoon garlic powder

Directions

Toss the kale leaves with olive oil, nutritional yeast, salt and black pepper.

Cook your kale at 250 degrees F for 12 minutes, shaking the basket every 4 minutes to promote even cooking.

Place the kale leaves on a platter and sprinkle evenly with sesame seeds, poppy seeds and garlic powder while still hot. Enjoy.

Korean-Style Broccoli

(**Ready in about** 12 minutes | **Servings:** 2)

Ingredients

1/2 pound broccoli florets	1 tablespoon soy sauce
1/4 teaspoon coriander seeds	1/2 teaspoon gochukaru (Korean red chili powder)
1/2 teaspoon garlic powder	Sea salt and ground black pepper, to taste
1 tablespoon brown sugar	
1 tablespoon sesame oil	

Directions

Toss the broccoli florets with the other Ingredients until well coated. Air fry your broccoli at 390 degrees F for about 10 minutes, shaking the basket halfway through the cooking time. **Serve:** with your favorite vegan dip. Enjoy!

Louisiana-Style Eggplant Cutlets

(**Ready in about** 45 minutes | **Servings:** 3)

Ingredients

1 pound eggplant, cut lengthwise into 1/2-inch thick slices
1 cup fresh bread crumbs
Sea salt and ground black pepper, to taste
1 cup tomato sauce
1/4 cup almond milk
1/4 cup plain flour
1 teaspoon Cajun seasoning mix
1 teaspoon brown mustard 1/2 teaspoon chili powder

Directions

Toss your eggplant with 1 teaspoon of salt and leave it for 30 minutes; drain and rinse the eggplant and set it aside.

In a shallow bowl, mix the flour with almond milk until well combined. In a separate bowl, mix the breadcrumbs with Cajun seasoning mix, salt and black pepper.

Dip your eggplant in the flour mixture, then, coat each slice with the breadcrumb mixture, pressing to adhere.

Cook the breaded eggplant at 400 degrees F for 10 minutes, flipping them halfway through the **Cooking time:**to ensure even browning.

In the meantime, mix the remaining Ingredients for the sauce. Divide the tomato mixture between eggplant cutlets and continue to cook for another 5 minutes or until thoroughly cooked.

Transfer the warm eggplant cutlets to a wire rack to stay crispy. Bon appétit

Fried Green Beans

(**Ready in about** 10 minutes | **Servings:** 2)

Ingredients

1/2 pound green beans, cleaned and trimmed
1 tspn extra-virgin olive oil
1/2 tbsp shallot powder
1/4 tbsp cumin powder
1/2 teaspoon cayenne pepper
1 tablespoon soy sauce
1/2 teaspoon onion powder
1/2 tbsp garlic powder
1/4 cup pecans,chopped
Himalayan salt and freshly ground black pepper, to taste
1 tablespoon lime juice

Directions

Toss the green beans with olive oil, spices and lime juice.

Cook the green beans in your Air Fryer at 400 degrees F for 5 minutes, shaking the basket halfway through the Cooking time to promote even cooking.

Toss the green beans with soy sauce and Serve garnished with chopped pecans. Bon appétit!

Portobello Mushroom Schnitzel

(**Ready in about** 10 minutes | **Servings:** 2)

Ingredients

7 ounces Portobello mushrooms
1/3 cup beer
1/2 teaspoon porcini powder
1/2 teaspoon dried basil
1/4 cup chickpea flour ground black pepper, to taste
Kosher salt
1/4 cup plain flour
1/2 tbsp garlic powder
1 cup breadcrumbs
1/4 teaspoon dried oregano 1/4 teaspoon ground cumin 1/4 teaspoon ground bay leaf
1/2 teaspoon shallot powder

Directions

Set aside the Portobello mushrooms after patting them dry.

Then, in a rimmed plate, combine the flour and beer thoroughly. In a separate bowl, combine the breadcrumbs and spices.

Dip the mushrooms in the flour mixture, then in the breadcrumb mixture.

Cook the breaded mushrooms for 6 to 7 minutes in a preheated Air Fryer at 380 degrees F, flipping halfway through the cooking time. Consume while warm.

Quinoa-Stuffed Winter Squash

(**Ready in about** 30 minutes | **Servings:** 2)

Ingredients

1/2 cup quinoa
1 teaspoon sesame oil

1 clove garlic, pressed
1 tablespoon fresh parsley, roughly chopped
1 cup loosely mixed greens, torn into small pieces
1 small winter squash, halved lengthwise
Sea salt and ground black pepper, to taste

Directions

Rinse your quinoa, drain it and transfer to a pot with 1 cup of lightly salted water; bring to a boil.

Turn the heat to a simmer and continue to cook, covered, for about 10 minutes; add in the mixed greens and continue to cook for 5 minutes longer.

Stir in the sesame oil and garlic and stir to combine. Divide the quinoa mixture between the winter squash halves and sprinkle it with the salt and pepper.

Cook your squash in the preheated Air Fryer at 400 degrees F for about 12 minutes.

Place the stuffed squash on individual plates, garnish with fresh parsley and **Serve:**. Bon appétit!

Baby Potatoes with Garlic-Rosemary Sauce

(**Ready in about** 50 minutes | **Servings:** 3)

Ingredients

1 pound baby potatoes, scrubbed	1/2 garlic bulb, slice the top 1/4-inch off the garlic head
1 tablespoon fresh rosemary leaves, chopped	1/2 cup white wine
Salt and freshly ground black pepper	1 tablespoon olive oil
	1 teaspoon sherry vinegar

Directions

Brush the baby potatoes with olive oil and transfer them to the air Fryer cooking basket. Cook the baby potatoes at 400 degrees F for 12 minutes, shaking the basket halfway through the cooking time.

Place the garlic bulb into the center of a piece of aluminum foil. Drizzle the garlic bulb with a nonstick cooking spray and wrap tightly in foil.

Cook the garlic at 390 degrees F for about 25 minutes or until the cloves are tender. Let it cool for about 10 minutes; remove the cloves by squeezing them out of the skins; mash the garlic and add it to a saucepan.

Stir the remaining Ingredients into the saucepan and let it simmer for 10 to 15 minutes until the sauce has reduced by half. Spoon the sauce over the baby potatoes and **Serve:** warm. Bon appétit!

Italian-Style Tomato Cutlets

(**Ready in about** 10 minutes | **Servings:** 2)

Ingredients

1 beefsteak tomato – sliced into halves	1/2 cup almond milk
1/2 cup breadcrumbs	1/2 cup all-purpose flour
	1 tbsp Italian seasoning mix

Directions

Pat the beefsteak tomato dry and set it aside.

In a shallow bowl, mix the all-purpose flour with almond milk. In another bowl, mix breadcrumbs with Italian seasoning mix.

Dip the beefsteak tomatoes in the flour mixture; then, coat the beefsteak tomatoes with the breadcrumb mixture, pressing to adhere to both sides.

Cook your tomatoes at 360 degrees F for about 5 minutes; turn them over and cook on the other side for 5 minutes longer. **Serve:** at room temperature and enjoy!

Old-Fashioned Potato Wedges

(**Ready in about** 15 minutes | **Servings:** 2)

Ingredients

2 medium potatoes, scrubbed and cut wedges	1 teaspoon garlic powder
1 teaspoon shallot powder	1 teaspoon olive oil
1/4 tbsp cayenne pepper	Kosher salt and ground black pepper, to season

Directions

Toss the potato wedges with olive oil and spices and transfer them to the Air Fryer cooking basket.

Cook the potato wedges at 400 degrees F for 6 minutes; shake the basket and cook for another 6 to 8 minutes.

Serve: with your favorite vegan dip. Bon appétit!

Paprika Squash Fries

(**Ready in about** 15 minutes | **Servings:** 3)

Ingredients

1/4 cup rice milk	1/4 cup almond flour
2 tbsp nutritional yeast	Sea salt and ground black pepper, to taste
1/4 tbsp shallot powder	
1/2 teaspoon paprika	1/2 teaspoon garlic powder
1 pound butternut squash	1 cup tortilla chips, crushed

Directions

Combine the milk flour, nutritional yeast, and spices in a mixing bowl. Place the crushed tortilla chips in a separate shallow bowl. Dip the butternut squash sticks into the batter, then roll them in the crushed tortilla chips until thoroughly coated.

Place the squash pieces in the cooking basket of the Air Fryer. Cook the squash fries for about 12 minutes at 400 degrees F, shaking the basket once or twice. Good appetite!

Green Potato Croquettes

(**Ready in about** 45 minutes | **Servings:** 2)

Ingredients

1/2 pound cup russet potatoes

1 cups loosely packed mixed greens, torn into pieces

1/4 teaspoon red pepper flakes, crushed

1/2 teaspoon garlic, pressed

1 teaspoon olive oil

Sea salt and ground black pepper, to taste

2 tablespoons oat milk

Directions

Cook your potatoes for about 30 minutes until they are fork-tender; peel the potatoes and add them to a mixing bowl. Mash your potatoes and stir in the remaining Ingredients.

Shape the mixture into bite-sized balls and place them in the cooking basket; sprits the balls with a nonstick cooking oil. Cook the croquettes at 390 degrees F for about 13 minutes, shaking the cooking basket halfway through the cooking time.

Serve: with tomato ketchup if desired. Bon appétit!

Easy Homemade Falafel

(**Ready in about** 15 minutes | **Servings:** 3)

Ingredients

1 cup dry chickpeas, soaked overnight

2 tablespoons fresh parsley

Sea salt and ground black pepper, to taste

2 tablespoons fresh cilantro

1 small onion, sliced

1/2 teaspoon cayenne pepper

2 cloves garlic

1/2 teaspoon ground cumin

Directions

Drain and rinse your chickpeas and place them in a bowl of a food processor.

Add in the remaining Ingredients and blitz until the Ingredients form a coarse meal. Roll the mixture into small balls with oiled hands.

Cook your falafel in the preheated Air Fryer at 395 degrees F for 5 minutes; turn them over and cook for another 5 to 6 minutes. Bon appétit!

Italian-Style Pasta Chips

(**Ready in about** 15 minutes | **Servings:** 2)

Ingredients

1 cup dry rice pasta

1/2 teaspoon dried oregano 1/2 teaspoon dried basil

Kosher salt and ground black pepper, to taste

1 tbsp nutritional yeast

1 teaspoon dried parsley flakes

1 teaspoon olive oil

Directions

Cook the pasta according to the manufacturer's instructions. Drain your pasta and toss it with the remaining Ingredients.

Cook the pasta chips at 390 degrees F for about 10 minutes, shaking the cooking basket halfway through the cooking time.

The pasta chips will crisp up as it cools.

Serve: with tomato ketchup if desired. Bon appétit!

Shawarma Roasted Chickpeas

(**Ready in about** 20 minutes | **Servings:** 2)

Ingredients

8 ounces canned chickpeas

1/4 teaspoon turmeric powder

1/2 teaspoon ground coriander

1/4 teaspoon ground ginger

1/4 teaspoon allspice

1/4 teaspoon cinnamon

1/4 teaspoon smoked paprika

Coarse sea salt and freshly ground black pepper, to taste

Directions

Rinse the chickpeas under cold running water and pat them dry with kitchen towels.

Place the spices in a plastic bag with the chickpeas and shake until the chickpeas are evenly coated with the spices.

Transfer the spiced chickpeas to the Air Fryer cooking basket after sprinkling them with nonstick cooking oil.

Cook your chickpeas for 13 minutes in a 395°F preheated Air Fryer. Cook for an additional 6 minutes at 350 degrees F in your Air Fryer.

Bell Pepper Fries

(**Ready in about** 15 minutes | **Servings:** 2)

Ingredients

1 cup flour
1/2 teaspoon dried marjoram 1/2 teaspoon turmeric powder

2 large bell peppers

1 cup oat milk
Sea salt and ground black pepper, to taste
1 cup seasoned breadcrumbs

Directions

In a shallow bowl, thoroughly combine the flour, milk, marjoram, turmeric, salt and black pepper. In another bowl, place seasoned breadcrumbs.

Dip the pepper rings in the flour mixture; then, coat the rings with the seasoned breadcrumbs, pressing to adhere.

Transfer the pepper rings to the Air Fryer cooking basket and spritz them with a nonstick spray.

Cook the pepper rings at 380 degrees F for about 10 minutes, shaking the basket halfway through the **Cooking time:**to promote even cooking. Bon appétit!

Polish Placki Ziemniaczan

(**Ready in about** 10 minutes | **Servings:** 2)

Ingredients

1/2 pound potatoes, peeled and finely grated

1/2 teaspoon turmeric powder
2 tablespoons granulated sugar
2 ounces sour cream

1/4 cup all-purpose flour
2 tablespoons breadcrumbs
Kosher salt and ground black pepper, to taste
2 tablespoons breadcrumbs

Directions

Place the grated potatoes in a triple layer of cheesecloth; now, twist and squeeze the potatoes until no more liquid comes out of them.

Place the potatoes in a mixing bowl; stir in the onion, flour, turmeric powder, breadcrumbs, salt and black pepper.

Cook them at 380 degrees for about 10 minutes, turning over after 5 minutes. **Serve:** with granulated sugar and sour cream. Enjoy!

Favorite Lentil Burgers

(**Ready in about** 15 minutes | **Servings:** 3)

Ingredients

1/2 cup wild rice, cooked
1 cup red lentils, cooked
1/2 small onion, quartered
1/4 cup walnuts

Sea salt and ground black pepper, to taste
1/2 teaspoon cayenne pepper

1/2 small beet, peeled and quartered
1 garlic clove

2 tablespoons breadcrumbs
1 tablespoon vegan barbecue sauce

Directions

Pulse all of the Ingredients in a food processor until a moldable dough forms.

Form the mixture into equal patties and place them in the Air Fryer cooking basket that has been lightly oiled.

Cook your burgers for about 15 minutes at 380 degrees F, flipping halfway through.

Enjoy! **Serve:** on burger buns.

Traditional Indian Pakora

(**Ready in about** 35 minutes | **Servings:** 2)

Ingredients

1 large zucchini, grated
2 scallion stalks, chopped
1/2 teaspoon paprika

14 teaspoon ginger-garlic paste

1/2 tbsp baking powder
1/4 teaspoon curry powder
1/2 cup besan flour
Sea salt and ground black pepper, to taste
1 teaspoon olive oil

Directions

Sprinkle the salt over the grated zucchini and leave it for 20 minutes. Then, squeeze the zucchini and drain off the excess liquid.

Mix the grated zucchini with the flour, baking powder, scallions, paprika, curry powder and ginger-garlic paste. Salt and pepper to taste.

Shape the mixture into patties and transfer them to the Air Fryer cooking basket. Brush the zucchini patties with 1 teaspoon of olive oil.

Cook the pakora at 380 degrees F for about 12 minutes, flipping them halfway through the cooking time.

Serve on dinner rolls and enjoy!

The Best Crispy Tofu

(**Ready in about** 55 minutes | **Servings:** 4)

Ingredients

16 ounces firm tofu, pressed and cubed
1 teaspoon cider vinegar
5 tablespoons cornstarch
1/2 teaspoon shallot powder
1/2 teaspoon porcini powder
1 teaspoon garlic powder
1 tablespoon tamari sauce
1 tablespoon vegan oyster
1 teaspoon pure maple syrup
1 tablespoon sesame oil
1 teaspoon sriracha

Directions

Toss the tofu with the oyster sauce, tamari sauce, vinegar, maple syrup, sriracha, shallot powder, porcini powder, garlic powder, and sesame oil. Let it marinate for 30 minutes.

Toss the marinated tofu with the cornstarch.

Cook at 360 degrees F for 10 minutes; turn them over and cook for 12 minutes more. Bon appétit!

Crunchy Eggplant Rounds

(**Ready in about** 45 minutes | **Servings:** 4)

Ingredients

1 (1-pound) eggplant, sliced 1/2 cup flax meal
Coarse sea salt and ground black pepper, to taste
1 cup cornbread crumbs, crushed
1/2 cup rice flour
1/2 cup vegan parmesan
1 cup water
1 teaspoon paprika

Directions

Toss the eggplant with 1 tablespoon of salt and let it stand for 30 minutes. Drain and rinse well.

Mix the flax meal, rice flour, salt, black pepper, and paprika in a bowl. Then, pour in the water and whisk to combine well.

In another shallow bowl, mix the cornbread crumbs and vegan parmesan.

Dip the eggplant slices in the flour mixture, then in the crumb mixture; press to coat on all sides. Transfer to the lightly greased Air Fryer basket.

Cook at 370 degrees F for 6 minutes. Turn each slice over and cook an additional 5 minutes.

Serve: garnished with spicy ketchup if desired. Bon appétit!

Classic Vegan Chili

(**Ready in about** 40 minutes | **Servings:** 3)

Ingredients

1 tablespoon olive oil
2 red bell peppers, seeded and chopped
1 red chili pepper, seeded and minced
1 teaspoon ground cumin
1/2 teaspoon mustard seeds 1/2 teaspoon celery seeds
1 cup vegetable broth
1 bay leaf
1 teaspoon cider vinegar
1/2 yellow onion, chopped
Sea salt and ground black pepper, to taste
2 garlic cloves, minced
1 teaspoon cayenne pepper
1 ybsp Mexican oregano
1 can (28-ounces) diced tomatoes with juice
1 (15-ounce) can black beans, rinsed and drained
1 avocado, sliced

Directions

Begin by preheating your Air Fryer to 365°F.

In a baking pan, heat the olive oil until it begins to sizzle. Then, in the baking pan, sauté the onion, garlic, and peppers. 4 to 6 minutes in a preheated oven

Now, combine the salt, black pepper, cumin, cayenne pepper, oregano, mustard seeds, celery seeds, tomatoes, and broth in a mixing bowl. Cook, stirring every 4 minutes, for 20 minutes.

Stir in the canned beans, bay leaf, and cider vinegar; cook for another 8 minutes, stirring halfway through. Serve in individual bowls with avocado slices on top. Enjoy!

Indian Plantain Chips (Kerala Neenthram)

(**Ready in about** 30 minutes | **Servings:** 2)

Ingredients

1 pound plantain, thinly sliced
2 tablespoons coconut oil
1 tablespoon turmeric

Directions

Fill a large enough cup with water and add the turmeric to the water.

Soak the plantain slices in the turmeric water for 15 minutes. Brush with coconut oil and transfer to the Air Fryer basket.

Cook in the preheated Air Fryer at 400 degrees F for 10 minutes, shaking the cooking basket halfway through the cooking time. **Serve:** at room temperature. Enjoy!

Cinnamon Pear Chips

(**Ready in about** 25 minutes | **Servings:** 1)

Ingredients

1 medium pear, cored and thinly sliced

2 tablespoons cinnamon & sugar mixture

Directions

Toss the pear slices with the cinnamon & sugar mixture. Transfer them to the lightly greased Air Fryer basket.

Bake in the preheated Air Fryer at 380 degrees F for 8 minutes, turning them over halfway through the cooking time. Transfer to wire rack to cool. Bon appétit!

Dad's Roasted Pepper Salad

(**Ready in about** 25 minutes + chilling time | **Servings:** 4)

Ingredients

2 yellow bell peppers
1 Serrano pepper
2 tablespoons cider vinegar
Sea salt, to taste
1 tbsp cayenne pepper
1/4 cup loosely packed fresh Italian parsley leaves, roughly chopped

2 green bell peppers
4 tablespoons olive oil
2 garlic cloves, peeled and pressed
1/2 teaspoon mixed peppercorns, crushed
1/2 cup pine nuts
2 red bell peppers

Directions

Start by preheating your Air Fryer to 400 degrees F. Brush the Air Fryer basket lightly with cooking oil.

Then, roast the peppers for 5 minutes. Give the peppers a half turn; place them back in the cooking basket and roast for another 5 minutes.

Turn them one more time and roast until the skin is charred and soft or 5 more minutes. Peel the peppers and let them cool to room temperature. In a small mixing dish, whisk the olive oil, vinegar, garlic, cayenne pepper, salt, and crushed peppercorns. Dress the salad and set aside.

Add the pine nuts to the cooking basket. Roast at 360 degrees F for 4 minutes; give the nuts a good toss. Put the cooking basket back again and roast for a further 3 to 4 minutes. Scatter the toasted nuts over the peppers and garnish with parsley. Bon appétit!

Swiss Chard and Potato Fritters

(**Ready in about** 35 minutes | **Servings:** 4)

Ingredients

8 baby potatoes
1 garlic clove, pressed
1 cup Swiss chard, torn into small pieces
1 tablespoon flax seed, soaked in
1 cup vegan cheese, shredded

2 tablespoons olive oil
1/2 cup leeks, chopped
Sea salt and ground black pepper, to your liking
1/4 cup chickpea flour
3 tablespoon water (vegan egg)

Directions

Begin by preheating your Air Fryer to 400°F.

Drizzle the potatoes with olive oil. Cook the potatoes in the Air Fryer basket for about 15 minutes, shaking the basket occasionally.

Crush the potatoes lightly to split them; mash the potatoes with the remaining Ingredients.

Make patties out of the potato mixture.

Bake for 14 minutes in a preheated Air Fryer at 380 degrees F, flipping halfway through the cooking time. Good appetite!

Easy Granola with Raisins and Nuts

(**Ready in about** 40 minutes | **Servings:** 8)

Ingredients

1 cups rolled oats
1/3 cup almonds chopped
1/4 cup whole wheat pastry flour
1/2 teaspoon cinnamon
1/3 cup coconut oil, melted
1/2 tbs coconut extract

1/2 cup walnuts, chopped
1/4 cup raisins
1/4 teaspoon nutmeg, preferably freshly grated
1/2 teaspoon salt
1/3 cup agave nectar
1/2 teaspoon vanilla extract

Directions

Thoroughly combine all Ingredients. Then, spread the mixture onto the Air Fryer trays. Spritz with cooking spray.

Bake at 230 degrees F for 25 minutes; rotate the trays and bake 10 to 15 minutes more. This granola can be stored in an airtight container for up to 2 weeks. Enjoy!

Aromatic Baked Potatoes with Chives

(**Ready in about** 45 minutes | **Servings:** 2)

Ingredients

4 medium baking potatoes, peeled
1/4 teaspoon smoked paprika
2 tablespoons chives, chopped

1/4 teaspoon red pepper flakes
2 garlic cloves, minced
2 tablespoons olive oil
1 tablespoon sea salt

Directions

Toss the potatoes with the olive oil, seasoning, and garlic.

Place them in the Air Fryer basket. Cook in the preheated Air Fryer at 400 degrees F for 40 minutes or until fork tender.

Garnish with fresh chopped chives. Bon appétit!

Classic Baked Banana

(**Ready in about** 20 minutes | **Servings:** 2)

Ingredients

2 just-ripe bananas
1/4 teaspoon grated nutmeg 1/2 teaspoon ground cinnamon

2 teaspoons lime juice
2 tablespoons honey
A pinch of salt

Directions

Toss the banana with all Ingredients until well coated. Transfer your bananas to the parchment-lined cooking basket.

Bake in the preheated Air Fryer at 370 degrees F for 12 minutes, turning them over halfway through the cooking time. Enjoy!

Garlic-Roasted Brussels Sprouts with Mustard

(**Ready in about** 20 minutes | **Servings:** 3)

Ingredients

1 pound Brussels sprouts, halved
2 garlic cloves, minced
2 tablespoons olive oil

Sea salt and freshly ground black pepper, to taste
1 tablespoon Dijon mustard

Directions

Combine the Brussels sprouts, olive oil, salt, black pepper, and garlic in a mixing bowl.

Cook for 15 minutes at 380°F in a preheated Air Fryer, shaking the basket occasionally.

Enjoy with a dollop of Dijon mustard!

Baked Oatmeal with Berries

(**Ready in about** 30 minutes | **Servings:** 4)

Ingredients

1 cup fresh strawberries
1/2 cup dried cranberries
A pinch of grated nutmeg
1 ½ cups rolled oats
4 tablespoons agave syrup
1/2 teaspoon vanilla extract

1/2 teaspoon baking powder A pinch of sea salt
1/2 teaspoon ground cinnamon
1 ½ cups coconut milk

Directions

Spritz a baking pan with cooking spray.

Place 1/2 cup of strawberries on the bottom of the pan; place the cranberries over that.

In a mixing bowl, thoroughly combine the rolled oats, baking powder, salt, nutmeg, cinnamon, vanilla, agave syrup, and milk. Pour the oatmeal mixtures over the fruits; allow it to soak for 15 minutes. Top with the remaining fruits.

Bake at 330 degrees F for 12 minutes. **Serve:** warm or at room temperature. Enjoy.

Green Beans with Oyster Mushrooms

(**Ready in about** 20 minutes | **Servings:** 3)

Ingredients

1 tablespoon extra-virgin olive oil
2 cups oyster mushrooms, sliced
Sea salt and ground black pepper, to taste

1/2 cup scallions, chopped
12 ounces fresh green beans, trimmed
1 tablespoon soy sauce
2 garlic cloves, minced

Directions

Start by preheating your Air Fryer to 390 degrees F. Heat the oil and sauté the garlic and scallions until tender and fragrant, about 5 minutes.

Add the remaining ingredients and stir to combine well.

Increase the temperature to 400 degrees F and cook for a further 5 minutes. **Serve:** warm.

Hoisin-Glazed Bok Choy

(**Ready in about** 10 minutes | **Servings:** 4)

Ingredients

1 pound baby Bok choy, bottoms removed, leaves separated
½ teaspoon sage
1 tbsp all-purpose flour
1 teaspoon onion powder
2 garlic cloves, minced
2 tablespoons sesame oil
2 tablespoons hoisin sauce

Directions

Place the Bok choy, garlic, onion powder, and sage in the lightly greased Air Fryer basket.

Cook in the preheated Air Fryer at 350 degrees F for 3 minutes. In a small mixing dish, whisk the hoisin sauce, sesame oil, and flour. Drizzle the sauce over the Bok choy. Cook for a further 3 minutes. Bon appétit!

Herb Roasted Potatoes and Peppers

(**Ready in about** 30 minutes | **Servings:** 4)

Ingredients

1 pound russet potatoes, cut into 1-inch chunks
1 teaspoon dried rosemary
1 teaspoon dried basil
1 teaspoon dried parsley flakes
1/2 teaspoon smoked paprika
2 bell peppers, seeded and cut into 1-inch chunks
1 teaspoon dried oregano
2 tablespoons olive oil
Sea salt and ground black pepper, to taste

Directions

Toss everything into the Air Fryer basket. Roast for 15 minutes at 400°F, tossing the basket halfway through. Working in batches is recommended. **Serve:** immediately and enjoy.

Spicy Roasted Cashew Nuts

(**Ready in about** 20 minutes | **Servings:** 4)

Ingredients

1 cup whole cashews
Salt and ground black pepper, to taste
1 teaspoon olive oil
1/2 teaspoon smoked paprika
1/2 teaspoon ancho chili powder

Directions

In a mixing bowl, combine all of the Ingredients.

Line the Air Fryer basket with parchment paper. In the basket, arrange the spiced cashews in a single layer.

Roast for 6 to 8 minutes at 350°F, shaking the basket once or twice. Working in batches is recommended. Enjoy!

Corn on the Cob with Spicy Avocado Spread

(**Ready in about** 15 minutes | **Servings:** 4)

Ingredients

4 corn cobs
1 clove garlic, pressed
1 tablespoon fresh lime juice
1/2 teaspoon cayenne pepper
1 teaspoon hot sauce
1 tablespoon soy sauce
1/2 teaspoon dried dill
1 avocado, pitted, peeled and mashed
4 teaspoons nutritional yeast
Sea salt and ground black pepper, to taste
2 heaping tablespoons fresh cilantro leaves, roughly chopped

Directions

Spritz the corn with cooking spray. Cook at 390 degrees F for 6 minutes, turning them over halfway through the cooking time.

In the meantime, mix the avocado, lime juice, soy sauce, nutritional yeast, cayenne pepper, dill, salt, black pepper, and hot sauce.

Spread the avocado mixture all over the corn on the cob. Garnish with fresh cilantro leaves. Bon appétit!

Winter Squash and Tomato Bake

(**Ready in about** 30 minutes | **Servings:** 4)

Ingredients

Cashew Cream
1/4 cup lime juice
1 tablespoon tahini
Sea salt, to taste

1/2 cup water Squash
2 ripe tomatoes, crushed
2 tablespoons olive oil
1 cup vegetable broth
2 tablespoons olive oil
1/2 teaspoon dried basil
2 garlic cloves, minced
1/2 cup sunflower seeds, soaked overnight, rinsed and drained
2 teaspoons nutritional yeast
1 pound winter squash, peeled and sliced
Sea salt and ground black pepper, to taste Sauce
6 ounces spinach, torn into small pieces
1/2 teaspoon dried rosemary

Directions

Mix the Ingredients for the cashew cream in your food processor until creamy and uniform. Re**Serve:**.

Place the squash slices in the lightly greased casserole dish. Add the olive oil, salt, and black pepper.

Mix all the Ingredients for the sauce. Pour the sauce over the vegetables. Bake in the preheated Air Fryer at 390 degrees F for 15 minutes.

Top with the cashew cream and bake an additional 5 minutes or until everything is thoroughly heated.

Transfer to a wire rack to cool slightly before sling and serving.

Mashed Potatoes with Roasted Peppers

(**Ready in about** 1 hour | **Servings:** 4)

Ingredients

4 potatoes
1 pound bell peppers, seeded and quartered lengthwise
2 Fresno peppers, seeded and halved lengthwise
2 tablespoons cider vinegar
1/2 teaspoon dried dill

1 tbs vegan margarine
4 tablespoons olive oil
1 teaspoon garlic powder
4 garlic cloves, pressed
Kosher salt, to taste

1/2 teaspoon freshly ground black pepper

Directions

Place the potatoes in the Air Fryer basket and cook at 400 degrees F for 40 minutes. Discard the skin and mash the potatoes with the vegan margarine and garlic powder.

Then, roast the peppers at 400 degrees F for 5 minutes. Give the peppers a

half turn; place them back in the cooking basket and roast for another 5 minutes.

Turn them one more time and roast until the skin is charred and soft or 5 more minutes. Peel the peppers and let them cool to room temperature.

Toss your peppers with the remaining Ingredients and **Serve:** with the mashed potatoes. Bon appétit!

Hungarian Mushroom Pilaf

(**Ready in about** 50 minutes | **Servings:** 4)

Ingredients

1 ½ cups white rice
1 pound fresh porcini mushrooms, sliced
2 tablespoons olive oil
1 onion, chopped
1/2 teaspoon dried tarragon

3 cups vegetable broth
2 garlic cloves
2 tablespoons olive oil
1 teaspoon dried thyme
1/4 cup dry vermouth
1 teaspoon sweet Hungarian paprika

Directions

Place the rice and broth in a large saucepan, add water; and bring to a boil. Cover, turn the heat down to low, and continue cooking for 16 to 18 minutes more. Set aside for 5 to 10 minutes.

Now, stir the hot cooked rice with the remaining Ingredients in a lightly greased baking dish.

Cook in the preheated Air Fryer at 370 degrees for 20 minutes, checking periodically to ensure even cooking.

Serve: in individual bowls. Bon appétit!

Rosemary Au Gratin Potatoes

(**Ready in about** 45 minutes | **Servings:** 4)

Ingredients

2 pounds potatoes
1/2 cup almonds, soaked overnight
1 cup unsweetened almond milk
2 tablespoons nutritional yeast
Kosher salt and ground black pepper, to taste

1/4 cup sunflower kernels, soaked overnight
1 teaspoon shallot powder
2 fresh garlic cloves, minced 1/2 cup water
1 tablespoon fresh rosemary
1 teaspoon cayenne pepper

Directions

Bring a large pan of water to a boil. Cook the whole potatoes for about 20 minutes. Drain the potatoes and let sit until cool enough to handle.

Peel your potatoes and slice into 1/8-inch rounds.

Add the sunflower kernels, almonds, almond milk, nutritional yeast, shallot powder, and garlic to your food processor; blend until uniform, smooth, and creamy. Add the water and blend for 30 seconds more.

Place 1/2 of the potatoes overlapping in a single layer in the lightly greased casserole dish. Spoon 1/2 of the sauce on top of the potatoes. Repeat the layers, ending with the sauce.

Top with salt, black pepper, cayenne pepper, and fresh rosemary. Bake in the preheated Air Fryer at 325 degrees F for 20 minutes. Serve warm.

Cinnamon Sugar Tortilla Chips

(**Ready in about** 20 minutes | **Servings:** 4

Ingredients

4 (10-inch) flour tortillas
1 ½ tablespoons ground cinnamon

1/4 cup vegan margarine, melted
1/4 cup caster sugar

Directions

Slice each tortilla into eight slices. Brush the tortilla pieces with the melted margarine.

In a mixing bowl, thoroughly combine the cinnamon and sugar. Toss the cinnamon mixture with the tortillas.

Transfer to the cooking basket and cook at 360 degrees F for 8 minutes or until lightly golden. Work in batches.

They will crisp up as they cool. **Serve:** and enjoy!

Kid-Friendly Vegetable Fritters

(**Ready in about** 20 minutes | **Servings:** 4)

Ingredients

1 pound broccoli florets	1 tablespoon ground
1 yellow onion, finely	flaxseeds
chopped	1/2 cup cornmeal
1 sweet pepper, seeded	2 garlic cloves, pressed
and chopped	1 carrot, grated
1 teaspoon turmeric	Salt and ground black
powder 1/2 teaspoon	pepper, to taste
ground cumin 1/2 cup all-	2 tablespoons olive oil
purpose flour	

Directions

Blanch the broccoli in salted boiling water for 3 to 4 minutes, or until al dente. Drain well and place in a mixing bowl with the remaining Ingredients; mash the broccoli florets. Form the mixture into patties and place them in the Air Fryer basket that has been lightly greased.

Cook for 6 minutes at 400 degrees F, turning them over halfway through; work in batches.

Warm with your favourite Vegenaise sauce. Enjoy

Onion Rings with Spicy Ketchup

(**Ready in about** 30 minutes | **Servings:** 2)

Ingredients

1 onion, sliced into rings	1 teaspoon curry powder
1/2 cup oat milk	1/3 cup all-purpose flour
1 teaspoon cayenne pepper	Salt and ground black
1/2 cup cornmeal	pepper, to your liking
4 tablespoons vegan	1/4 cup spicy ketchup
parmesan	

Directions

Place the onion rings in the bowl with cold water; let them soak approximately 20 minutes; drain the onion rings and pat dry using a kitchen towel.In a shallow bowl, mix the flour, milk, curry powder, cayenne pepper, salt, and black pepper. Mix to combine well.

Mix the cornmeal and vegan parmesan in another shallow bowl. Dip the onion rings in the flour/milk mixture; then, dredge in the cornmeal mixture.

Spritz the Air Fryer basket with cooking spray; arrange the breaded onion rings in the Air Fryer basket.

Cook in the preheated Air Fryer at 400 degrees F for 4 to 5 minutes, turning them over halfway through the cooking time. **Serve:** with spicy ketchup. Bon appétit!

Barbecue Tofu with Green Beans

(**Ready in about** 1 hour | **Servings:** 3)

Ingredients

12 ounces super firm tofu,	1 tablespoon white vinegar
pressed and cubed	1/4 cup ketchup
1 tablespoon coconut	1/4 teaspoon ground
sugar	black pepper
1 tablespoon mustard	
1/2 teaspoon sea salt	1/4 tbsp smoked paprika
1/2 tbs freshly grated	2 tablespoons olive oil
ginger	1 pound green beans
2 cloves garlic, minced	

Directions

Toss the tofu with the ketchup, white vinegar, coconut sugar, mustard, black pepper, sea salt, paprika, ginger, garlic, and olive oil. Let it marinate for 30 minutes.

Cook at 360 degrees F for 10 minutes; turn them over and cook for 12 minutes more. Re**Serve:**.

Place the green beans in the lightly greased Air Fryer basket. Roast at 400 degrees F for 5 minutes. Bon appétit!

Vegetable Skewers

Prep time: 10 minutes **Cooking time:** 10 minutes **Serve:** 4

Ingredients

1 eggplant, cut into 1-inch	1/2 onion, cut into 1-inch
pieces	pieces
2 bell peppers, cut into 1-	1 tbsp olive oil
inch pieces	1 tsp garlic powder
1 zucchini, cut 1-inch	¼ tsp paprika Pepper, Salt
pieces	

Directions

Preheat the air fryer to 390 F. In a mixing bowl, toss veggies with oil, garlic powder, paprika, pepper, and salt until well coated.

Thread vegetables onto the soaked wooden skewers. Place vegetable skewers into the air fryer basket and cook for 10 minutes. Turn halfway through. **Serve:** and enjoy.

Healthy Jicama & Green Beans

Prep time: 10 minutes **Cooking time:** 45 minutes
Serve: 6

Ingredients
12 oz green beans, sliced in half	1 tsp dried thyme
3 garlic cloves, minced	3 tbsp canola oil
1 tsp dried rosemary	1/2 tsp salt
	1 medium jicama, cubed

Directions

Preheat the air fryer to 400 F. Add green beans, jicama, and remaining ingredients into the mixing bowl and toss well.

Spread green beans and jicama mixture into the air fryer basket and cook for 45 minutes. Stir halfway through. **Serve:** and enjoy.

Crispy Brussels Sprouts

Prep time: 10 minutes **Cooking time:** 15 minutes
Serve: 4

Ingredients
2 cups Brussels sprouts	1/4 cup almonds, crushed
2 tbsp everything bagel seasoning Pepper	Salt
	2 tbsp canola oil

Directions

Preheat the air fryer to 375 F. Add Brussels sprouts into the saucepan with 2 cups of water. Cover and cook for 10 minutes. Drain well and let it cool completely.

Cut each Brussels sprouts in half. Add Brussels sprouts and remaining ingredients into the bowl and toss to coat. Add Brussels sprouts into the air fryer basket and cook for 15 minutes. Stir halfway through. **Serve:** and enjoy.

Flavorful Green Beans

Prep time: 5 minutes **Cooking time:** 10 minutes
Serve: 2

Ingredients
2 cups green beans	1/8 tsp cayenne pepper
1/2 tsp dried oregano	1/8 tsp ground allspice
1/4 tsp ground coriander	1/2 tsp salt
1/4 tsp ground cumin	2 tbsp canola oil
1/4 tsp ground cinnamon	

Directions

Preheat the air fryer to 370 F. Add green beans and remaining ingredients into the mixing bowl and toss well.
Add green beans into the air fryer basket and cook for 8-10 minutes. Stir halfway through. **Serve:** and enjoy.

Easy Ratatouille

Prep time: 10 minutes **Cooking time:** 15 minutes
Serve: 6

Ingredients
1 eggplant, diced	2 bell peppers, diced
2 tbsp herb de Provence	1 onion, diced
1 tbsp vinegar	1 1/2 tbsp olive oil
3 tomatoes, diced	2 garlic cloves, chopped
Pepper	Salt

Directions

Preheat the air fryer to 400 F. Add all ingredients into the bowl and toss well and transfer into the air fryer baking dish. Place baking dish into the air fryer basket and cook for 15 minutes. **Serve:** and enjoy.

Tasty Zucchini Chips

Prep time: 10 minutes **Cooking time:** 12 minutes
Serve: 3

Ingredients
1 large zucchini, cut into slices	3 tbsp roasted pecans, crushed
1 tbsp olive oil	1 tbsp Bagel seasoning
3 tbsp almond flour	

Directions

Preheat the air fryer to 350 F. Add zucchini slices, crushed pecans, almond flour, oil, and bagel seasoning into the mixing bowl and toss until well coated.

Arrange zucchini slices into the air fryer basket and cook for 12 minutes. Turn halfway through. **Serve:** and enjoy.

Crispy Cauliflower Tots

Prep time: 10 minutes **Cooking time:** 12 minutes
Serve: 4

Ingredients
1 large cauliflower head, cut into florets	2 tbsp arrowroot
1/4 cup extra-virgin olive oil	3 tbsp hot sauce
	1 tbsp olive oil Pepper
	Salt

Directions

Preheat the air fryer to 380 F. Toss cauliflower florets with oil and coat with arrowroot. Add cauliflower florets into the air fryer basket and cook for 6 minutes. Meanwhile, in a mixing bowl, mix together hot sauce and extra-virgin olive oil.

Once cauliflower florets are cooked then transfer them into the sauce and toss well. Return cauliflower florets into the air fryer basket and cook for 6 minutes more. Serve and enjoy.

Crispy Tofu Cubes

Prep time: 10 minutes **Cooking time:** 15 minutes
Serve: 4

Ingredients
15 oz extra-firm tofu, pressed and cut into cubes
2 tbsp soy sauce
1 tsp sesame oil
1 tbsp rice vinegar

Directions

Preheat the air fryer to 400 F. In a mixing bowl, mix together tofu, vinegar, sesame oil, and soy sauce. Allow to sit for 20 minutes.

Add tofu into the air fryer basket and cook for 12-15 minutes. Stir halfway through. **Serve:** and enjoy.

Herb Olives

Prep time: 10 minutes **Cooking time:** 5 minutes
Serve: 4

Ingredients
2 cups olives
2 tbsp canola oil
1/2 tsp dried fennel seeds
2 tsp garlic, minced
Salt
1/2 tsp red pepper flakes, crushed
1/2 tsp dried oregano
Pepper

Directions

Preheat the air fryer to 300 F. Add olives and remaining ingredients into the bowl and toss to coat well.

Add olives into the air fryer basket and cook for 5 minutes. **Serve:** and enjoy.

Tasty Carrots Chips

Prep time: 10 minutes **Cooking time:** 12 minutes
Serve: 4

Ingredients
12 oz carrot chips
1/4 tsp pepper
1/4 tsp paprika
1 tbsp canola oil
¼ tsp chili powder
1/2 tsp garlic powder
1/2 tsp salt

Directions

Preheat the air fryer to 375 F. Add carrot chips and remaining ingredients into the bowl and toss well.

Add carrot chips into the air fryer basket and cook for 12 minutes. Stir halfway through.
Serve: and enjoy.

Air Fryer Vegan Buffalo Tofu Bites

Prep time: 20 minutes **Cooking time:** 20 minutes
Serve: 1

Ingredients
1 (8 ounces) container extra-firm tofu
4 tablespoons cornstarch
⅛ teaspoon garlic powder
⅛ teaspoon onion powder
⅔ cup vegan Buffalo wing sauce (such as Frank's®)
4 tbsp unsweetened rice milk
¾ cup panko breadcrumbs
⅛ teaspoon paprika
⅛ tbsp ground black pepper

Directions

Take the tofu block out of the packaging and discard the liquid. Wrap tofu in cheesecloth, set on a platter, and cover with a heavy saucepan for 10 minutes to press out any residual liquid. Remove the cheesecloth from the tofu and chop it into 20 1-inch bite-sized pieces. Place in a freezer-safe container and place in the freezer for 8 hours overnight.

Remove the frozen tofu from the freezer and defrost it on paper towels or a dry cheesecloth. Allow airing to dry.
Fill a resealable plastic bag halfway with cornstarch while the tofu is thawing. Fill a small bowl halfway with rice milk.
Preheat an air fryer carefully to 375°F (190 degrees C). Place the tofu in the bag with the cornstarch, close, and shake to cover the tofu pieces fully. Remove the tofu and coat each piece with rice milk.

In a resealable plastic bag, combine the breadcrumbs, garlic powder, paprika, onion powder, and pepper with the cornstarch residue; shake until thoroughly combined. Return each piece of tofu to the bag with the breadcrumbs, one at a time. Shake the bag until the tofu is thoroughly covered, then gently shake off the excess and lay the tofu on a wire rack while you repeat with the other tofu pieces.

Cook for 10 minutes in the air fryer basket with covered tofu. To loosen the fragments, shake the basket. Cook for 3 minutes more, or until browned. Toss fried tofu bits in a basin with 1/3 cup buffalo sauce to coat. Drizzle the remaining buffalo sauce over the tofu and toss to cover.
Serve: right away.

Air Fryer Baked Potatoes

Prep time: 18 minutes **Cooking time:** 20 minutes
Serve: 1

Ingredients

2 large russet potatoes, scrubbed

½ teaspoon coarse sea salt
1 tablespoon peanut oil

Directions

Preheat the air fryer carefully to 400°F (200 degrees C).
Potatoes should be brushed with peanut oil and seasoned with salt. Place them in the air fryer basket, then in the air fryer.

Cook until potatoes are tender, about 1 hour. Prick them with a fork to see whether they're done.

Air Fryer Vegan Buffalo Cauliflower

Prep time: 15 minutes **Cooking time:** 25 minutes
Serve: 1

Ingredients

1 ½ pound cauliflower florets
¾ cup all-purpose flour
1 teaspoon paprika
¼ teaspoon ground black pepper nonstick cooking spray

4 tbsp Egg substitute, liquid
½ teaspoon salt
1 teaspoon garlic powder
½ cup vegan Buffalo wing sauce (such as Frank's®)

Directions

Preheat the air fryer carefully to 400°F (200 degrees C).
In a large mixing basin, combine cauliflower florets. Stir the egg replacement into the florets to coat.

Combine the flour, garlic powder, paprika, salt, and pepper in a large plastic resealable bag. Shake and zip until evenly blended. 1/2 of the florets should be dipped in seasoned flour. Zip it up and shake it to coat. Fill the air fryer basket with florets. Nonstick cooking spray should be sprayed on the tops.

5 minutes in the air fryer. Cook for 5 minutes more after flipping the cauliflower and spraying any powdery places. Repeat with the rest of the cauliflower florets.

Meanwhile, prepare the buffalo wing sauce in a skillet over medium heat. Place the cauliflower in a large mixing basin. Toss the top with the wing sauce until uniformly covered. Serve right away.

Air Fryer Vegan Sweet Potato Fritters

Prep time: 15 minutes **Cooking time:** 20 minutes
Serve: 1

Ingredients

1 ½ cups shredded sweet potato
¼ cup finely diced onions
½ teaspoon salt
¼ teaspoon ground turmeric avocado oil

½ cup almond flour cooking spray
½ tablespoon olive oil
½ tbsp ground black pepper

Directions

Preheat an air fryer carefully to 350°F (175 degrees C). Combine the shredded sweet potato, almond flour, onions, olive oil, salt, pepper, and turmeric in a mixing bowl. Using a large cookie scoop, divide the mixture into 9 balls and shape it into patties. Place the patties in the air fryer basket, ensuring they don't touch. Coat the tops with cooking spray.

Cook in a preheated air fryer for 10 to 12 minutes, or until the cakes begin to brown on the edges. Flip the patties over, coat with cooking spray, and continue to air fry for 6 to 8 minutes. Allow for a 1-minute rest before removing from the air fryer basket.

Air Fryer Apple Dumplings

Prep time: 10 minutes **Cooking time:** 18 minutes
Serve: 1

Ingredients

2 tablespoons sultana raisins
2 small apples, peeled and cored
2 tablespoons butter, melted

2 sheets puff pastry
1 tablespoon brown sugar

Directions

Preheat an air fryer carefully to 320°F (180 degrees C). Aluminum foil should be used to line the air fryer basket.
In a mixing dish, combine sultanas and brown sugar.

Place a sheet of puff pastry on a clean work surface. Fill the core of an apple with the sultana mixture and place it on the crust. Fold the dough around the apple to cover it completely. Repeat with the rest of the pastry, apple, and filling.

Brush the dumplings with melted butter and place them in the prepared basket. Cook the dumplings for 25 minutes, or until golden brown and the apples are tender.

Vegan Air Fryer Taquitos

Prep time: 20 minutes **Cooking time:** 25 minutes
Serve: 1

Ingredients

1 large russet potato, peeled
2 tablespoons diced onions
1 clove garlic, minced
2 tablespoons unsweetened, plain almond milk
salt and ground black pepper to taste

1 teaspoon plant-based butter
¼ cup plant-based butter (such as Country Crock®)
6 corn tortillas
avocado oil cooking spray

Directions

Fill a saucepan halfway with salted water and bring to a boil. Reduce the heat to medium-low and cook until the vegetables are soft, about 20 minutes.
While the potato is boiling, heat 1 teaspoon plant-based butter in a pan and sauté onions for 3 to 5 minutes, or until tender and translucent. Cook until the garlic is aromatic, approximately 1 minute.

Set aside some time Drain the potato and place it in a bowl. Mash in 1/4 cup plant-based butter and almond milk, season with salt and pepper. Combine the onion and garlic in a mixing bowl.

Heat tortillas in a pan or directly on the gas stove grates till warm and flexible. Place 3 teaspoons of the potato mixture down the middle of each tortilla, fold it over, and roll it up.

Preheat an air fryer carefully to 400°F (200 degrees C). Place the taquitos in the air fryer basket without touching and spritz with avocado oil. If necessary, cook in batches.
6 to 9 minutes in the air fryer until the taquitos are golden brown and crispy. Turn the taquitos over, spray with avocado oil, and continue to air fry for 3 to 5 minutes.

Air Fryer Potato Wedges

Prep time: 18 minutes **Cooking time:** 20 minutes
Serve: 1

Ingredients

2 medium Russet potatoes, cut into wedges

½ teaspoon paprika
½ teaspoon chili powder

1 ½ tablespoon olive oil
⅛ tbsp ground black pepper
½ teaspoon parsley flakes
½ teaspoon sea salt

Directions

Preheat the air fryer carefully to 400°F (200 degrees C).
In a large mixing basin, combine the potato wedges. Next, mix olive oil, paprika, parsley, chili, salt, and pepper until completely combined.

Cook for 10 minutes with 8 wedges in the air fryer basket.
Cook for an additional 5 minutes after flipping the wedges with tongs. Rep with the remaining 8 wedges.

Vegan Jalapeno Cornbread in the Air Fryer

Prep time: 15 minutes **Cooking time:** 18 minutes
Serve: 1

Ingredients

1 tablespoon flaxseed meal cooking spray
1 cup stone-ground yellow cornmeal
2 tablespoons white sugar
1 teaspoon kosher salt

⅓ cup vegetable oil

⅔ cup all-purpose flour
3 tablespoons water
¼ cup nutritional yeast
2 ¼ tbsp baking powder
1 cup unsweeten almond milk
½ tbsp ground black pepper
1 large jalapeno pepper, seeded and minced

Directions

In a small dish, combine water and flaxseed meal and let aside for 10 minutes. Meanwhile, prepare an air fryer to 350°F (175°C) according to the manufacturer's recommendations. Coat a 6-inch heat-resistant inner pot with cooking spray.

Combine cornmeal, sugar, baking powder, flour, nutritional yeast, salt, and pepper in a medium mixing bowl. Stir in the flaxseed and water combination, almond milk, and oil until it barely comes together and there are no lumps. Pour into the prepared pot and set in the air fryer; stir in the jalapeno.

Cook for 15 minutes in a preheated air fryer. Remove the inner pot with tongs, turn the cornbread, and continue to air fry for another 5 minutes, or until a toothpick inserted into the middle comes out clean.
Serve: hot.

Air Fryer Root Vegetables with Vegan Aioli

Prep time: 15 minutes **Cooking time:** 22 minutes
Serve: 1

Ingredients

1 clove garlic, minced
½ teaspoon fresh lemon juice
1 tablespoon minced fresh rosemary
3 cloves garlic, finely minced
1-pound parsnips, peeled and cut vertically into pieces
1 pound baby red potatoes, cut lengthwise into 4 or 6 pieces

½ tbs grated lemon zest

½ cup vegan mayonnaise
salt and ground black pepper to taste
½ teaspoon ground black pepper
4 tbsp extra virgin olive oil
½ pound baby carrots split lengthwise
½ red onion cut lengthwise into 1/2-inch slices
1 teaspoon kosher salt

Directions

In a small bowl, combine mayonnaise, garlic, lemon juice, salt, and pepper to make the garlic aioli; refrigerate until ready to **Serve:**. If your air fryer manufacturer suggests preheating, preheat it to 400 degrees F (200 degrees C).

In a small bowl, combine the olive oil, rosemary, garlic, salt, and pepper; leave aside to blend the flavors. Next, combine the parsnips, potatoes, carrots, and onion in a large mixing dish. Stir in the olive oil-rosemary mixture until the veggies are well covered. Place a part of the veggies in the air fryer basket in a single layer, then properly add a rack and another layer of vegetables.

Cook for 15 minutes in an air fryer. When the timer goes off, **Serve:** the vegetables, and keep warm, or continue cooking in 5-minute intervals until the vegetables are done and browning to your liking.

Place the remaining veggies in the air fryer basket and cook for 15 minutes, monitoring doneness as required. Use the rack again if you have more veggies than fit in a single layer. When all veggies are cooked, **Serve:** with garlic aioli and lemon zest on top.

Air Fryer Fingerling Potatoes

Prep time: 10 minutes **Cooking time:** 18 minutes
Serve: 1

Ingredients

1 pound fingerling potatoes, halved lengthwise
½ teaspoon parsley flakes
salt, black pepper to taste

½ teaspoon ground paprika
1 tablespoon olive oil
½ teaspoon garlic powder

Directions

Preheat an air fryer carefully to 400°F (200 degrees C). In a large mixing dish, combine potato halves. Stir in olive oil, paprika, parsley, garlic powder, salt, and pepper until evenly covered. Cook the potatoes in the prepared air fryer basket for 10 minutes. Cook, often stirring until the desired crispness is obtained, about 5 minutes more.

Air Fryer Pakoras

Prep time: 15 minutes **Cooking time:** 25 minutes
Serve: 1

Ingredients

2 cups chopped cauliflower
1 cup diced yellow potatoes
¾ cup water
1 clove garlic, minced
1 tablespoon salt
½ teaspoon ground cayenne pepper
1 serving cooking spray

1 ¼ cups chickpea flour (bean)

½ red onion, chopped
1 teaspoon curry powder
1 teaspoon coriander
½ teaspoon cumin

Directions

In a large mixing bowl, combine cauliflower, potatoes, chickpea flour, water, red onion, salt, garlic, curry powder, coriander, cayenne pepper, and cumin. Set aside for 10 minutes to relax.

Preheat the air fryer carefully to 350°F (175 degrees C).
Coat the air fryer basket with cooking spray. 2 tablespoons cauliflower mixture, flattened in the basket Repeat as many times as the space in your basket permits without the pakoras touching. Spray the tops of each pakora with nonstick cooking spray.

8 minutes in the oven Cook for an additional 8 minutes on the otherside. Transfer to a plate lined with paper towels. Rep with the remaining batter.

Hasselback Air Fryer Potatoes

Prep time: 15 minutes **Cooking time:** 25 minutes
Serve: 1

Ingredients

4 (6 ounces) russet potatoes, scrubbed and dried
2 chopsticks
½ teaspoon chopped fresh chives (Optional)

4 tablespoons olive oil, or as needed
salt and ground black pepper to taste

Directions

Preheat the air fryer carefully to 350°F (180 degrees C).
1 potato, cut a very thin slice lengthwise from the flattest side. Place the potato cut side down on a chopping board to lay uniformly without rolling. Place chopsticks along the top and bottom sides of the potato lengthwise. Slice the potato evenly across the length to form 1/4-inch slices, ensuring sure the knife comes to rest on the chopsticks each time to keep the bottom of the potato intact. Rep with the remaining potatoes. Brush oil on the outsides and between the slices. Season with salt and pepper to taste.

Place the potatoes in the air fryer dish and cook for 15 minutes. Brush with oil and cook for another 15 minutes until the edges are crispy and the centers are soft. **Serve:** garnished with chives.

Air Fryer Corn on The Cob

Prep time: 15 minutes **Cooking time:** 18 minutes
Serve: 1

Ingredients

¼ cup mayonnaise
1 teaspoon lime juice
¼ teaspoon chili powder
4 sprigs of fresh cilantro

2 teaspoons crumbled cotija cheese
2 ears corn, shucked and halved

Directions

Preheat an air fryer carefully to 400°F (200 degrees C).
In a shallow bowl, combine mayonnaise, cotija cheese, lime juice, and chili powder.

Roll each piece of corn in the mayonnaise mixture until it is evenly coated on both sides. Cook for 8 minutes with all four pieces of corn in the air fryer basket. Garnish with cilantro if desired.

Air Fryer Turkey Fajitas

Prep time: 10 minutes **Cooking time:** 18 minutes
Serve: 1

Ingredients

½ teaspoon onion powder
1 large red onion, halved and sliced into strips
1-pound skinless, boneless turkey breast
1 teaspoon freshly ground black pepper
2 limes, divided

½ tablespoon paprika
1 medium yellow bell pepper
1 jalapeno pepper

1 tablespoon chili powder
½ tablespoon dried Mexican oregano
1 ½ tablespoon vegetable oil, divided
1 large red bell pepper, sliced into strips
1 tablespoon ground cumin
1 teaspoon garlic powder
¼ cup chopped fresh cilantro

Directions

Combine chili powder, cumin, paprika, oregano, pepper, garlic powder, and onion powder in a small bowl. 1 lime juice squeezed over the turkey breast Season the meat with the spice combination. 1 tablespoon of oil Set aside after tossing to coat.

Cover the bell peppers and onion with the remaining oil
in a bowl. To coat, toss everything together.
The manufacturer's instructions preheat an air fryer carefully to 375°F (190°C).

In a preheated air fryer, cook the bell peppers and onion for 8 minutes. Cook for another 5 minutes after shaking. Add the jalapenos. 5 minutes in the oven Shake the basket and arrange the turkey strips in a single layer on top of the veggies. Cook for 7 to 8 minutes with the basket closed. Open the basket, shake it to disperse the mixture, and cook for another 5 minutes, or until the turkey strips are crispy and no longer pink in the middle and the peppers are soft.

Remove the fajitas from the basket and set them in a dish or on a tray. Garnish with cilantro and squeeze the remaining lime juice over the top.

Air Fryer Mushrooms

Prep time: 20 minutes **Cooking time:** 20 minutes
Serve: 1

Ingredients

1 (8 ounces) package cremini mushrooms, halved or quartered
½ teaspoon garlic granules

1 teaspoon low-sodium soy sauce
2 tablespoons avocado oil
salt and ground black pepper to taste

Directions

Preheat the air fryer carefully to 375°F (190 degrees C).

In a mixing bowl, combine the mushrooms, avocado oil, soy sauce, garlic granules, salt, and pepper; toss to coat. Place in the air fryer bowl. Cook the mushrooms for 10 minutes in the air fryer, shaking periodically.

Air Fryer Broiled Grapefruit

Prep time: 15 minutes **Cooking time:** 25 minutes
Serve: 1

Ingredients

1 red grapefruit, refrigerated
1 tablespoon softened butter
½ teaspoon ground cinnamon

2 teaspoons brown sugar
aluminum foil

1 tablespoon brown sugar

Directions

Preheat the air fryer carefully to 400°F (200 degrees C).

If the grapefruit isn't lying flat, cut it in half crosswise and slice a tiny sliver from the bottom of each side. Next, cut along the outside edge of the grapefruit and between each segment with a sharp paring knife to make the fruit easier to consume once cooked.

Combine melted butter and 1 tablespoon brown sugar in a small mixing dish. Distribute the mixture evenly over each grapefruit half. Finish with the remaining brown sugar.

Place each grapefruit half on one 5-inch square of aluminum foil and

fold up the edges to capture any juices. Then, place the air fryer basket in the air fryer.

Broil in the air fryer for 6 to 7 minutes, or until the sugar mixture is bubbling. Before serving, sprinkle the fruit with cinnamon.

Air Fryer Turkey Fajitas

Prep time: 20 minutes **Cooking time:** 20 minutes
Serve: 1

Ingredients

½ tablespoon dried Mexican oregano
1 medium yellow bell pepper, sliced into strips
1 large red onion, halved and sliced into strips
2 limes, divided

1-pound skinless, boneless turkey breast
1 large red bell pepper, sliced into strips

½ tablespoon paprika
1 tablespoon chili powder
1 teaspoon garlic powder
1 teaspoon freshly ground black pepper
½ teaspoon onion powder
1 tablespoon ground cumin
1 ½ tablespoon vegetable oil, divided
1 jalapeno pepper, seeded and chopped

Directions

Combine chili powder, cumin, paprika, oregano, pepper, garlic powder, and onion powder in a small bowl. 1 lime juice squeezed over the turkey breast Season the meat with the spice combination. 1 tablespoon of oil Set aside after tossing to coat.

Cover the bell peppers and onion with the remaining oil in a bowl. To coat, toss everything together. The manufacturer's instructions preheat an air fryer carefully to 375°F (190°C).

In a preheated air fryer, cook the bell peppers and onion for 8 minutes. Cook for another 5 minutes after shaking. Add the jalapenos. 5 minutes in the oven Shake the basket and arrange the turkey strips in a single layer on top of the veggies. Cook for 7 to 8 minutes with the basket closed. Open the basket, shake it to disperse the mixture, and cook for another 5 minutes, or until the turkey strips are crispy and no longer pink in the middle and the peppers are soft.

Remove the fajitas from the basket and set them in a dish or on a tray. Garnish with cilantro and squeeze the remaining lime juice over the top.

Air Fryer Roasted Garlic

Prep time: 15 minutes **Cooking time:** 20 minutes
Serve: 1

Ingredients

1 head garlic aluminum foil	1 tbsp extra-virgin olive oil
¼ teaspoon salt	¼ tbs ground black pepper

Directions

Preheat the air fryer carefully to 380°F (190 degrees C).
Remove the top of the garlic head and set it on a square piece of aluminum foil. Wrap the foil around the garlic. Season with salt and pepper and drizzle with olive oil. Fold the ends of the foil over the garlic to form a pouch.
16 to 20 minutes in the air fryer until the garlic is tender. Open the foil package with extreme caution, as hot steam will escape.

Air Fryer Latkes

Prep time: 15 minutes **Cooking time:** 25 minutes
Serve: 1

Ingredients

1 (16 ounces) package frozen shredded hash brown potatoes	1 egg
	2 tablespoons matzo meal
½ cup shredded onion	cooking spray
avocado oil	kosher salt and ground black pepper to taste

Directions

The manufacturer's instructions preheat an air fryer carefully to 375°F (190°C). Next, prepare a piece of parchment or waxed paper.

Place the thawed potatoes and shredded onion between layers of paper towels. Cover with extra paper towels and wring out as much liquid as possible.

Combine the egg, salt, and pepper in a large mixing bowl. With a fork, mix in the potatoes and onion. Stir in the matzo meal until the ingredients are uniformly distributed. Form the mixture into ten 3- to 4- inch broad patties with your hands. Place the patties on a sheet of parchment or waxed paper.

Cooking spray should be sprayed on the air fryer basket. Place half of the patties properly in the basket and coat with cooking spray generously.

Air-fry for 10 to 12 minutes, or until the exterior is crispy and dark golden brown. (If you like a softer latke, check for doneness at 8 minutes.) Transfer the latkes to a plate. In the same manner, cook the remaining patties and coat them with cooking spray before cooking.

Air Fryer Stuffed Mushrooms

Prep time: 15 minutes **Cooking time:** 20 minutes
Serve: 1

Ingredients

1 (16 ounces) package whole white button mushrooms	4 ounces cream cheese, softened
¼ cup finely shredded sharp Cheddar cheese	¼ teaspoon ground paprika
	1 pinch salt
cooking spray	2 scallions

Directions

Gently clean the mushrooms with a moist towel. Remove and discard the stems. Separate the white and green sections of the scallions. Preheat an air fryer carefully to 360°F (182 degrees C).

In a small mixing dish, combine cream cheese, Cheddar cheese, the white sections of the scallions, paprika, and salt. Stuff the filling into the mushrooms, pushing it in with the back of a small spoon to fill the cavity. Cooking sprays the air fryer basket and place the mushrooms inside. You may need to perform two batches depending on the size of your air fryer. Cook for 8 minutes or until the filling is gently browned. Rep with the remaining mushrooms.

Air Fryer Turkey Breast

Prep time: 15 minutes **Cooking time:** 25 minutes
Serve: 1

Ingredients

1 tablespoon finely chopped fresh rosemary	1 teaspoon finely minced fresh garlic
½ teaspoon salt	¼ teaspoon ground black pepper
1 teaspoon finely chopped fresh chives	2 tbsp cold unsalted butter
2 ¾ pounds skin-on, bone-in split turkey breast	

Directions

Preheat the air fryer carefully to 350°F (175 degrees C).
Combine the rosemary, chives, garlic, salt, and pepper on a chopping board. Place thin slices of butter on the herbs and spices and mash until thoroughly combined.

Pat the turkey breast dry and massage it on both sides and beneath the skin with herbed butter.
Place the turkey in the air fryer basket, skin side down, and cook for 20 minutes.

Turn the turkey skin-side up and fry for another 18 minutes, or until an instant-read thermometer placed near the bone registers 165 degrees F (74 degrees C). Transfer to a dish and tent with aluminum foil for 10 minutes to rest. **Serve:** heated, sliced.

Air Fryer French Fries

Prep time: 15 minutes **Cooking time:** 20 minutes
Serve: 1

Ingredients

1 pound russet potatoes, peeled	1 pinch cayenne pepper
½ teaspoon kosher salt	2 teaspoons vegetable oil

Directions

Each potato should be cut lengthwise into 3/8-inch-thick slices. Sections should be cut into 3/8-inch-wide sticks as well.
Cover potatoes with water and soak for 5 minutes to allow extra starches to be released. Drain and cover with a few inches of boiling water (or place in a bowl of boiling water). Allow for a 10-minute resting period.

Drain the potatoes and pat them dry with paper towels. Blot out any excess water and set it aside for at least 10 minutes to cool fully. Drizzle with oil, season with cayenne pepper, and toss to coat in a mixing bowl.

Preheat the air fryer carefully to 375°F (190 degrees C). In the fryer basket, stack potatoes in a double layer. The **Cooking time:**is 15 minutes. Slide the basket out, toss the fries, cook until golden brown, approximately 10 minutes longer. In a mixing dish, toss the fries with salt. **Serve:** right away.

Air-Fryer Fries

Prep time: 20 minutes **Cooking time:** 20 minutes
Serve: 1

Ingredients

1-pound potatoes	¼ teaspoon salt
1 teaspoon vegetable oil	1/4 teaspoon seasoning

Directions

Allow potatoes to soak in water for 30 minutes. Using paper towels, drain and wipe dry. Drizzle oil over the vegetables and toss to coat.

Preheat the air fryer carefully to 400°F (200 degrees C).
Arrange the potatoes in the fryer basket in a double layer. Cook, tossing every 5 minutes, for 15 to 20 minutes, or until golden brown. Season with salt and pepper to taste.

Air Fryer Baba Ghanoush

Prep time: 20 minutes **Cooking time:** 25 minutes
Serve: 1

Ingredients

5 ½ tablespoons olive oil, divided	1 medium eggplant, halved lengthwise
½ teaspoon kosher salt	1 tablespoon chopped fresh parsley
1 bulb garlic	¼ teaspoon ground cumin
¼ cup tahini	2 tablespoons lemon juice, or more to taste
⅛ teaspoon smoked paprika	
2 tbsp crumbled feta cheese	
½ teaspoon lemon zest	

Directions

Season the cut sides of the eggplant with salt. Allow for a 20- to 30- minute resting period. Then, using paper towels, blot dry.

Preheat an air fryer carefully to 400°F (200 degrees C). 1 tablespoon olive oil on the sliced sides of the eggplant. Remove the top 1/4 inch of the garlic bulb to expose the cloves. Wrap the bulb in aluminum foil after brushing it with 1/2 tablespoon olive oil. In the air fryer basket, combine the eggplant and garlic.

Cook in a preheated air fryer for 15 to 20 minutes, or until the eggplant and garlic are soft, and the eggplant is a deep golden-brown color. Allow cooling for about 10 minutes after removing from the oven.

Scoop out the flesh of the eggplant and place it in the bowl of a food processor. Pulse in tahini, lemon juice, 4 cloves, roasted garlic, remaining 4 tablespoons of olive oil, cumin, and paprika until smooth. **Serve:** with feta cheese, parsley, and lemon zest on top.

Air Fryer Roasted Pineapple

Prep time: 15 minutes **Cooking time:** 22 minutes
Serve: 1

Ingredients
1 fresh pineapple

Directions

Preheat the air fryer carefully to 375°F (190 degrees C). Then, using parchment paper, line the air fryer basket.
Using a pineapple core or slicer, core the pineapple and
cut it into rings.

Fill the prepared basket with pineapple rings.
8 to 10 minutes in the air fryer until the slices roast.
Flip the slices over and continue to air fry for 3 to 5 minutes.

Air Fryer Blueberry Chimichangas

Prep time: 15 minutes **Cooking time:** 25 minutes
Serve: 1

Ingredients

½ (8 ounces) package Neufchatel cheese, softened
1 teaspoon vanilla extract
½ tbsp ground cinnamon
5 (7 inches) flour tortillas
avocado oil cooking spray
1 ½ tablespoon white sugar
2 tablespoons sour cream
1 (6 ounces) container blueberries
2 ½ tablespoons white sugar

Directions

Combine Neufchatel cheese, sour cream, sugar, and vanilla extract in a mixing bowl and whisk with an electric hand mixer. Fold in the blueberries with care.

Heat tortillas until soft and malleable in a big pan or directly on the grates of a gas burner. 1/4 cup blueberry mixture should be placed down the center of each tortilla. Fold the top and bottom of the tortillas over the filling, then wrap each tortilla into a burrito form. Mist with avocado oil and set in an air fryer basket.

Cook the chimichangas in the air fryer at 400 degrees F (200 degrees C) for 4 to 6 minutes, or until golden brown. 1 to 2 minutes more, flip each chimichanga over, spritz with cooking spray, and air fry until golden brown. Allow cooling slightly.

In a small dish, combine the sugar and cinnamon. Each chimichangashould be sprayed with avocado oil and rolled with cinnamon sugar.

Air Fryer Polenta Fries

Prep time: 18 minutes **Cooking time:** 20 minutes
Serve: 1

Ingredients

1 (16 ounces) package prepared polenta nonstick olive oil cooking spray
salt and ground black pepper to taste

Directions

Preheat an air fryer carefully to 350°F (175 degrees C). Cut the polenta into long, thin slices that resemble French fries.

Cooking spray should be sprayed on the bottom of the basket. Place half of the polenta fries in the basket and spritz the tops gently with cooking spray. Season with salt and pepper to taste.

Cook for 10 minutes in a preheated air fryer. Flip the fries with a spatula and cook for another 5 minutes, or until crispy. Place the fries on a dish lined with paper towels. Repeat with the other half of the fries.

Air Fryer Falafel

Prep time: 20 minutes **Cooking time:** 25 minutes
Serve: 1

Ingredients

1 cup dry garbanzo beans
¾ cup fresh flat-leafed parsley stems removed
¼ teaspoon baking soda
2 tbsp chickpea flour
1 tbsp ground cumin
salt and ground black pepper to taste
1 ½ cups fresh cilantro, stems removed
1 clove garlic
1 small red onion, quartered
1 tbsp sriracha sauce
1 tbsp ground coriander
½ tbsp baking powder
cooking spray

Directions

Soak chickpeas for 24 hours in a large amount of cold water. Rub your fingers through the wet chickpeas to help loosen and remove the skins. Rinse and drain well. To dry, spread chickpeas on a wide clean dish towel. In a food processor, combine chickpeas, cilantro, parsley, onion, and garlic until rough paste forms. Transfer the mixture to a large mixing basin. Chickpea flour, coriander, cumin, sriracha, salt, and pepper. Allow the mixture to rest for 1 hour, covered.

Preheat an air fryer carefully to 375°F (190 degrees C). To the chickpea mixture, add the baking powder and baking soda. Using your hands, mix until just blended. Create 15 equal-sized balls and softly press them to form patties. Cooking spray should be sprayed on the falafel patties.
Cook for 10 minutes in a preheated air fryer with 7 falafel patties. Cook for 10 to 12 minutes, transfer cooked falafel to a platter and repeat with the remaining 8 falafel.

Air Fryer Roasted Okra

Prep time: 15 minutes **Cooking time:** 20 minutes
Serve: 1

Ingredients

½ pound okra ends trimmed, and pods sliced
⅛ tbsp black pepper
¼ teaspoon salt
1 teaspoon olive oil

Directions

Preheat an air fryer carefully to 350°F (175 degrees C). Combine the okra, olive oil, salt, and pepper in a mixing dish. Place in the air fryer basket in a single layer. Cook for 5 minutes in the air fryer. Cook for 5 minutes more after tossing. Cook for 2 minutes more after tossing. **Serve:** right away In a shallow dish, combine panko breadcrumbs, salt, Italian seasoning, and pepper. Then, in a separate dish, softly beat the remaining egg. Each rice ball should be dipped in egg first, then the panko mixture. Next, spray the air fryer basket with cooking spray and place the rice balls in it.

BEEF, PORK AND LAMB

Paprika Porterhouse Steak with Cauliflower

(**Ready in about** 20 minutes | **Servings:** 4)

Ingredients

1 pound Porterhouse steak, sliced
Coarse sea salt and ground black pepper, to taste
1/2 teaspoon shallot powder

1 teaspoon butter, room temperature
1/2 teaspoon porcini powder 1 teaspoon granulated garlic
1 teaspoon smoked paprika

1 pound cauliflower, torn into florets

Directions

Brush all sides of the steak with butter and season with all spices. Season the cauliflower to taste with salt and pepper.

Place the steak in the cooking basket and roast for 12 minutes at 400 degrees F, turning halfway through.

Remove the cauliflower from the basket and cook your steak for another 2 to 3 minutes, if necessary. Garnish the steak with the cauliflower. Consume while warm.

Chuck Roast with Sweet 'n' Sticky Sauce

(**Ready in about** 35 minutes | **Servings:** 3)

Ingredients

1 pound chuck roast
2 tablespoons butter softened
1 tablespoon coriander, chopped
1 tablespoon fish sauce
2 tablespoons honey

Sea salt and ground black pepper, to taste

1 tablespoon fresh scallions, chopped
1 teaspoon soy sauce

Directions

Season the chuck roast with salt and pepper; spritz a nonstick cooking oil all over the beef.

Air fry at 400 degrees F for 30 to 35 minutes, flipping the chuck roast halfway through the cooking time.

While the roast is cooking, heat the other

Ingredients in a sauté pan over medium-high heat. Bring to a boil and reduce the heat; let it simmer, partially covered, until the sauce has thickened and reduced.

Slice the chuck roast into thick cuts and **Serve:** garnished with sweet 'n' sticky sauce. Bon appétit!

Italian Sausage Peperonata Pomodoro

(**Ready in about** 15 minutes | **Servings:** 2)

Ingredients

2 bell peppers, sliced
1 chili pepper
2 smoked beef sausages
1 teaspoon Italian spice mix
1 garlic clove, minced

1 yellow onion, sliced
1 teaspoon olive oil
2 medium-sized tomatoes, peeled and crushed

Directions

Spritz the sides and bottom of the cooking basket with a nonstick cooking oil. Add the peppers, onion and sausage to the cooking basket.

Cook at 390 degrees F for 10 minutes, shaking the basket periodically. Re**Serve:**.

Heat the olive oil in a medium-sized saucepan over medium-high flame until sizzling; add in the tomatoes and garlic; let it cook for 2 to 3 minutes.

Stir in the peppers, onion and Italian spice mix. Continue to cook for 1 minute longer or until heated through. Fold in the sausages and **Serve:** warm. Bon appétit!

Flank Steak with Dijon Honey Butter

(**Ready in about** 15 minutes | **Servings:** 3)

Ingredients

1 pound flank steak
1/2 teaspoon olive oil
3 tablespoons butter

Sea salt and red pepper flakes, to taste
1 teaspoon Dijon mustard
1 teaspoon honey

Directions

Brush the flank steak with olive oil and season with salt and pepper.

Cook at 400 degrees F for 6 minutes. Then, turn the steak halfway through the **Cooking time:** and continue to cook for a further 6 minutes.

In the meantime, prepare the Dijon honey butter by whisking the remaining Ingredients.

Serve: the warm flank steak dolloped with the Dijon honey butter. Bon appétit!

Easy Homemade Hamburgers

(**Ready in about** 15 minutes | **Servings:** 2)

Ingredients

3/4 pound lean ground chuck
1 teaspoon garlic, minced
1 teaspoon soy sauce
3 tablespoons onion, minced
1/4 teaspoon ground cumin
2 burger buns

Kosher salt and ground black pepper, to taste
1/2 teaspoon smoked paprika
1/2 teaspoon mustard seeds
1/2 teaspoon cayenne pepper

Directions

Thoroughly combine the ground chuck, salt, black pepper, onion, garlic and soy sauce in a mixing dish.

Season with smoked paprika, ground cumin, cayenne pepper and mustard seeds. Mix to combine well.

Shape the mixture into 2 equal patties.

Spritz your patties with a nonstick cooking spray. Air fry your burgers at 380

degrees F for about 11 minutes or to your desired degree of doneness.

Place your burgers on burger buns and **Serve:** with favorite toppings. Devour!

Greek-Style Roast Beef

(**Ready in about** 55 minutes | **Servings:** 3)

Ingredients

1 clove garlic, halved
1 zucchini, sliced lengthwise
2 teaspoons olive oil
1/2 cup Greek-style yogurt

1 ½ pounds beef eye round
roast
1 teaspoon Greek spice mix Sea salt, to season

Directions

Rub the beef eye round roast with garlic halves.

Brush the beef eye round roast and zucchini with olive oil. Sprinkle with spices and place the beef in the cooking basket.

Roast in your Air Fryer at 400 degrees F for 40 minutes. Turn the beef over.

Add the zucchini to the cooking basket and continue to cook for 12 minutes more or until cooked through. **Serve:** warm, garnished with Greek-style yogurt. Enjoy!

Chuck Roast with Rustic Potatoes

(**Ready in about** 50 minutes | **Servings:** 3)

Ingredients

1 tablespoon brown mustard
2 tablespoons BBQ sauce
1 tablespoon Worcester sauce 1 ½ pounds chuck roast
Coarse sea salt and ground black pepper, to taste
1 teaspoon granulated garlic
1 teaspoon dried marjoram

2 tablespoons tomato paste, preferably homemade
1 pound medium-sized russet potatoes, quartered
1 teaspoon shallot powder
1/2 tbsp cayenne pepper

Directions

In a small bowl, combine the mustard, tomato paste, BBQ sauce, and Worcester sauce. This mixture should be rubbed all over the chuck roast.

Place the chuck roast in the Air Fryer cooking basket that has been lightly greased with melted butter and season with salt and pepper.

Air fry for 30 minutes at 400°F; turn over and scatter potato chunks around the beef. Cook for an additional 15 minutes. Check to ensure that the beef is thoroughly cooked.

Seasonings should be tasted and adjusted. Place the meat on a cutting board and set aside. **Serve:** the beef warm, sliced against the grain.

Marinated London Broil

(**Ready in about** 25 minutes+ marinating time | **Servings:** 2)

Ingredients

2 tablespoons soy sauce
1 teaspoon mustard
2 tablespoons wine vinegar
1 tablespoon honey
Salt and black pepper, to taste

1 tablespoon olive oil
2 garlic cloves, minced
1 pound London broil
1/2 teaspoon paprika

Directions

In a ceramic dish, mix the soy sauce, garlic, mustard, oil, wine vinegar and honey. Add in the London broil and let it marinate for 2 hours in your refrigerator.

Season the London broil with paprika, salt and pepper.

Cook in the preheated Air Fryer at 400 degrees F for 10 minutes; turn over and continue to cook for a further 10 minutes.

Slice the London broil against the grain and eat warm. Enjoy!

Mayo Roasted Sirloin Steak

(**Ready in about** 20 minutes | **Servings:** 3)

Ingredients

1 pound sirloin steak, cubed
1 teaspoon garlic, minced
1/2 teaspoon dried basil
Kosher salt

1 tbsp red wine vinegar
1/2 cup mayonnaise
1/2 tbs cayenne pepper
ground black pepper, to season

Directions

Pat dry the sirloin steak with paper towels.

In a small mixing dish, thoroughly combine the remaining Ingredients until everything is well incorporated.

Toss the cubed steak with the mayonnaise mixture and transfer to the Air Fryer cooking basket.

Cook in the preheated Air Fryer at 400 degrees F for 7 minutes. Shake the basket and continue to cook for a further 7 minutes. Bon appétit!

Easy Beef Burritos

(**Ready in about** 25 minutes | **Servings:** 3)

Ingredients

1 pound rump steak
1/2 tbsp shallot powder
1/2 tbsp porcini powder

1 teaspoon piri piri powder
1 teaspoon lard, melted
1/2 teaspoon celery seeds

Sea salt and crushed red pepper, to taste
½ tb dried Mexican oregano
3 (approx 7-8" dia) whole-wheat tortillas

Directions

Toss the rump steak with the spices and melted lard. Cook in your Air Fryer at 390 degrees F for 20 minutes, turning it halfway through the cooking time. Place on a cutting board to cool slightly. Slice against the grain into thin strips.

Spoon the beef strips onto wheat tortillas; top with your favorite fixings, roll them up and **Serve:**. Enjoy!

Beef Sausage-Stuffed Zucchini

(**Ready in about** 30 minutes | **Servings:** 2)

Ingredients

1/2 pound beef sausage, crumbled

1/4 cup tomato paste
1/2 cup sharp cheddar cheese, grated

1/2 teaspoon garlic, pressed
1/2 cup tortilla chips
2 small-sized zucchini, halved lengthwise and seeds removed

Directions

In a mixing bowl, thoroughly combine the beef sausage, tortilla chips, garlic and tomato paste. Divide the sausage mixture between the zucchini halves. Bake in the preheated Air Fryer at 400 degrees F for 20 minutes.

London Broil with Herb Butter

(**Ready in about** 30 minutes | **Servings:** 3)

Ingredients

1 pound London broil
Herb butter
1 teaspoon basil, chopped
1 tablespoon chives
Coarse sea salt and crushed black peppercorns, to taste

2 tablespoons butter, at room temperature
1 tablespoon cilantro, chopped
1 tablespoon lemon juice

Directions

Pat the London broil dry with paper towels. Mix all Ingredients for the herb butter.

Cook in the preheated Air Fryer at 400 degrees F for 14 minutes; turn over, brush with the herb butter and continue to cook for a further 12 minutes.

Slice the London broil against the grain and **Serve:** warm.

BBQ Glazed Beef Riblets

(**Ready in about** 15 minutes + marinating time | **Servings:** 3)

Ingredients

1 pound beef riblets	Sea salt and red pepper, to
1/4 cup tomato paste	taste
1/4 cup Worcestershire	1 tablespoon oyster sauce
sauce	1 tablespoon stone-
2 tablespoons hot sauce	ground mustard
2 tablespoons rice vinegar	

Directions

Combine all Ingredients in a glass dish, cover, and refrigerate for at least 2 hours.

Remove the riblets from the marinade and place them in the Air Fryer cooking basket.

Cook for 12 minutes in a preheated Air Fryer at 360°F, shaking the basket halfway through to ensure even cooking.

In a small skillet over medium heat, heat the reServe:d marinade; spoon the glaze over the riblets and **Serve:** immediately.

American-Style Roast Beef

(**Ready in about** 30 minutes | **Servings:** 3)

Ingredients

1 pound beef eye of round	1 tbsp red pepper flakes
roast	1 teaspoon sesame oil
1/4 teaspoon dried bay	Sea salt and black pepper,
laurel 1/2 teaspoon cumin	to taste
powder	
1 sprig thyme, crushed	

Directions

Simply toss the beef with the remaining Ingredients; toss until well coated on all sides.

Cook in the preheated Air Fryer at 390 degrees F for 15 to 20 minutes, flipping the meat halfway through to cook on the other side.

Remove from the cooking basket, cover loosely with foil and let rest for 15 minutes before carving and serving. Bon appétit!

Porterhouse Steak with Tangy Sauce

(**Ready in about** 20 minutes | **Servings:** 2)

Ingredients

1/2 pound Porterhouse	1 teaspoon sesame oil
steak, cut into four pcs	Salt and pepper, to season
1 teaspoon garlic paste	1 habanero pepper,
1 teaspoon ginger juice	minced
1 tablespoon soy sauce	2 tablespoons brown sugar
	1 tablespoon fish sauce

Directions

Pat the steak dry and generously season it with salt and black pepper.

Cook in the preheated Air Fryer at 400 degrees F for 7 minutes; turn on the other side and cook an additional 7 to 8 minutes.

To make the sauce, heat the remaining Ingredients in a small saucepan over medium-high heat; let it simmer for a few minutes until heated through.

Spoon the sauce over the steak and **Serve:** over hot cooked rice or egg noodles. Bon appétit!

Chicago-Style Beef Sandwich

(**Ready in about** 25 minutes | **Servings:** 2)

Ingredients

1/2 pound chuck,	1 tablespoon soy
boneless	sauce
1/4 teaspoon ground bay	1/2 teaspoon cayenne
laurel	pepper
1/2 teaspoon shallot	1 tablespoon olive oil
powder	1/4 tbsp porcini powder
Kosher salt and ground	2 ciabatta rolls, sliced in
black pepper, to taste	half
1 cup pickled vegetables,	1/2 teaspoon garlic
chopped	powder

Directions

Toss the chuck roast with the olive oil, soy sauce, and spices until thoroughly coated.

Cook for 20 minutes in a preheated Air Fryer at 400 degrees F, turning halfway through the cooking time.

Adjust the seasonings and shred the meat with two forks.

Place a generous portion of the meat and pickled vegetables on the bottom halves of the ciabatta rolls. Place the ciabatta roll tops on top of the sandwiches. **Serve:** right away and enjoy!

Classic Beef Jerky

(**Ready in about** 4 hours 30 minutes | **Servings:** 4)

Ingredients

6 ounces top round steak, cut into 1/8-inch thick strips
2 tablespoons Worcestershire sauce
1 teaspoon hot sauce
1 teaspoon onion powder
1/2 teaspoon fresh garlic, crushed
1 teaspoon liquid smoke
1/2 tablespoon honey

Directions

Transfer the strips of steak to a large Ziplock bag; add in the other Ingredients, seal the bag and shake to combine well. Refrigerate for at least 30 minutes.

Cook in the preheated Air Fryer at 160 degrees F for about 4 hours, until it is dry and firm.

Refrigerate in an airtight container for up to 1 month. Bon appétit!

Mediterranean Burgers with Onion Jam

(**Ready in about** 20 minutes | **Servings:** 2)

Ingredients

1/2 pound ground chuck
1/2 teaspoon garlic, minced
1 teaspoon brown mustard
2 burger buns
2 ounces Haloumi cheese
1 medium tomato, sliced
2 Romaine lettuce leaves
Onion jam
Sea salt and ground black pepper, to taste
2 tablespoons scallions, chopped

Kosher salt and ground black pepper, to taste

2 tablespoons butter, at room temperature
2 red onions, sliced
1 cup red wine
2 tablespoons honey
1 tablespoon fresh lemon juice

Directions

Mix the ground chuck, scallions, garlic, mustard, salt and black pepper until well combined; shape the mixture into two equal patties.

Spritz a cooking basket with a nonstick cooking spray. Air fry your burgers at 370 degrees F for about 11 minutes or to your desired degree of doneness.

Meanwhile, make the onion jam. In a small saucepan, melt the butter; once hot, cook the onions for about 4 minutes. Turn the heat to simmer, add salt, black pepper and wine and cook until liquid evaporates.

Stir in the honey and continue to simmer until the onions are a jam-like consistency; afterwards, drizzle with freshly squeezed lemon juice. Top the bottom halves of the burger buns with the warm beef patty. Top with haloumi cheese, tomato, lettuce and onion jam. Set the bun tops in place and **Serve:** right now. Enjoy!

New York Strip with Mustard Butter

(**Ready in about** 20 minutes | **Servings:** 4)

Ingredients

1 tablespoon peanut oil
Sea salt and freshly cracked black pepper, to taste
1/2 stick butter, softened
1/2 teaspoon honey
2 pounds New York Strip
1 teaspoon whole-grain mustard
1 teaspoon cayenne pepper

Directions

Season the steak with cayenne pepper, salt, and black pepper after rubbing it with peanut oil.

Cook for 7 minutes in a preheated Air Fryer at 400 degrees F, then flip and cook for another 7 minutes.

Meanwhile, whisk together the butter, whole-grain mustard, and honey to make the mustard butter.

Serve: the roasted New York Strip with the mustard butter on the side. Good appetite!

Dad's Meatloaf with a Twist

(**Ready in about** 35 minutes | **Servings:** 2)

Ingredients

1 tablespoon olive oil
1 Italian pepper, deveined and chopped
1/2 pound ground beef
1/2 teaspoon liquid smoke
1 tablespoon Dijon mustard 1/2 cup crushed corn flakes
4 tablespoons tomato paste
1/2 tbsp garlic, minced
1 tablespoon soy sauce
1 onion, chopped
1 Serrano pepper, deveined and chopped
1 teaspoon Italian seasoning mix

Directions

Start by preheating your Air Fryer to 350 degrees F.

In a mixing bowl, thoroughly combine the onion, garlic, peppers, ground beef, soy sauce, mustard and crushed corn flakes. Salt to taste.

Mix until everything is well incorporated and press into a lightly greased meatloaf pan.

Air fry for about 25 minutes. Whisk the tomato paste with the Italian seasoning mix and liquid smoke; spread the mixture over the top of your meatloaf.

Continue to cook for 3 minutes more. Let it rest for 6 minutes before slicing and serving. Bon appétit!

Tex-Mex Taco Pizza

(**Ready in about** 20 minutes | **Servings:** 1)

Ingredients

1 teaspoon lard, melted	4 ounces ground beef sirloin
2 tablespoons jarred salsa	1/4 teaspoon Mexican oregano
4 ounces pizza dough	
1/2 teaspoon granulated garlic	1/2 teaspoon basil
2 ounces cheddar cheese grated	1 plum tomato, sliced

Directions

Melt the lard in a skillet over medium-high heat; once hot, cook the beef until no longer pink, about 5 minutes.

Roll the dough out and transfer it to the Air Fryer cooking basket. Spread the jarred salsa over the dough.

Sprinkle Mexican oregano, basil, garlic and cheese over the salsa. Top with the sautéed beef, then with the sliced tomato.

Bake in your Air Fryer at 375 degrees F for about 11 minutes until the bottom

of crust is lightly browned. Bon appétit!

Dijon Top Chuck with Herbs

(**Ready in about** 1 hour | **Servings:** 3)

Ingredients

1 ½ pounds top chuck	1 tablespoon Dijon mustard
Sea salt and ground black pepper, to taste	1 teaspoon dried thyme
1/2 teaspoon fennel seeds	2 teaspoons olive oil
	1 teaspoon dried marjoram

Directions

Begin by preheating your Air Fryer to 380°F.

In a Ziploc bag, combine all of the Ingredients and shake well to combine. Spray the bottom of the Air Fryer basket with cooking spray next.

Cook for 50 minutes, turning every 10 to 15 minutes, with the beef in the cooking basket. Allow for a 5- to 7-minute rest before slicing and serving. Enjoy!

Mediterranean-Style Beef Steak and Zucchini

(**Ready in about** 20 minutes | **Servings:** 4)

Ingredients

1 ½ pounds beef steak	1 teaspoon dried rosemary
1 teaspoon dried basil	1 teaspoon dried oregano
2 tablespoons extra-virgin olive oil	1 pound zucchini
	2 tbs fresh chives, chopped

Directions

Start by preheating your Air Fryer to 400 degrees F.

Toss the steak and zucchini with the spices and olive oil. Transfer to the cooking basket and cook for 6 minutes.

Now, shale the basket and cook another 6 minutes. **Serve:** immediately garnished with fresh chives. Enjoy!

Tender Marinated Flank Steak

(**Ready in about** 20 minutes + marinating time | **Servings:** 4)

Ingredients

1 ½ pounds flank steak	1/2 cup apple cider vinegar
2 tbs soy sauce Salt, to taste	1/2 teaspoon ground black pepper
1/2 teaspoon dried basil	
1/2 teaspoon red pepper flakes, crushed	1 teaspoon thyme
	1/2 cup red wine

Directions

Add all Ingredients to a large ceramic bowl. Cover and let it marinate for 3 hours in your refrigerator.

Transfer the flank steak to the Air Fryer basket that is previously greased with nonstick cooking oil.

Cook in the preheated Air Fryer at 400 degrees F for 12 minutes, flipping over halfway through the cooking time. Bon appétit!

Peperonata with Beef Sausage

(**Ready in about** 35 minutes | **Servings:** 4)

Ingredients

2 teaspoons canola oil
1 serrano pepper, sliced
1 shallot, sliced

1/2 dried thyme
1 teaspoon fennel seeds

2 pounds thin beef
parboiled sausage

1 green bell pepper, sliced
Sea salt and pepper, to
taste
2 bell peppers, sliced
1 teaspoon dried rosemary
1/2 teaspoon mustard
seeds

Directions

Brush the sides and bottom of the cooking basket with
1 teaspoon of canola oil. Add the peppers and shallot
to the cooking basket.

Toss them with the spices and cook at 390 degrees F
for 15 minutes, shaking the basket occasionally.
Re**Serve:**.

Turn the temperature to 380 degrees F

Then, add the remaining 1 teaspoon of oil. Once hot,
add the sausage and cook in the preheated Air Frye for
15 minutes, flipping them halfway through the cooking
time.

Serve: with re**Serve:**d pepper mixture. Bon appétit!

Scotch Fillet with Sweet 'n' Sticky Sauce

(**Ready in about** 40 minutes | **Servings:** 4)

Ingredients

2 pounds scotch fillet,
sliced into strips
2 tablespoons honey
Sauce
2 garlic cloves, minced
1/2 cup beef broth
1/2 teaspoon dried dill

2 green onions, chopped
4 tablespoons tortilla
chips, crushed
1 tablespoon butter
1/2 tbs dried rosemary
1 tablespoons fish sauce

Directions

Start by preheating your Air Fryer to 390 degrees F.

Coat the beef strips with the crushed tortilla chips on
all sides. Spritz with cooking spray on all sides and
transfer them to the cooking basket.

Cook for 30 minutes, shaking the basket every 10
minutes.

Meanwhile, heat the sauce ingredient in a saucepan
over medium-high heat. Bring to a boil and reduce the
heat; cook until the sauce has thickened slightly.

Add the steak to the sauce; let it sit approximately 8
minutes. **Serve:** over the hot egg noodles if desired.

Kid-Friendly Mini Meatloaves

(**Ready in about** 30 minutes | **Servings:** 4)

Ingredients

2 tablespoons bacon,
chopped
1 small-sized onion,
chopped
1/2 teaspoon dried
mustard seeds
1/2 teaspoon dried
marjoram
1/2 cup panko crumbs

1 garlic clove, minced
1 pound ground beef
1/2 teaspoon dried
basil
4 tablespoons tomato
puree
1 bell pepper, chopped
Salt and black pepper, to
taste

Directions

Cook the bacon for 1 to 2 minutes in a nonstick skillet
over medium-high heat; add the onion, bell pepper, and
garlic and cook for another 3 minutes, or until fragrant.

Turn off the heat. Combine the ground beef, spices,
and panko crumbs in a mixing bowl. Stir until
everything is well combined. Make four mini
meatloaves out of the mixture.

Preheat your Air Fryer to 350 degrees Fahrenheit.
Spray the cooking basket with nonstick cooking spray.

Cook the mini meatloaves in the cooking basket for 10
minutes, then turn them over, top with the tomato
puree, and cook for another 10 minutes. Good
appetite!

Mayonnaise and Rosemary Grilled Steak

(**Ready in about** 20 minutes | **Servings:** 4)

Ingredients

1 cup mayonnaise
1 teaspoon smoked
paprika
1 ½ pounds short loin
steak
1 teaspoon garlic, minced
Sea salt, to taste

1 tablespoon fresh
rosemary, finely chopped
2 tablespoons
Worcestershire sauce

1/2 teaspoon ground black
pepper

Directions

Combine the mayonnaise, rosemary, Worcestershire
sauce, salt, pepper, paprika, and garlic; mix to combine
well.

Now, brush the mayonnaise mixture over both sides of
the steak. Lower the steak onto the grill pan.

Grill in the preheated Air Fryer at 390 degrees F for 8
minutes. Turn the steaks over and grill an additional 7
minutes. Check for doneness with a meat thermometer.
Serve: warm and enjoy!

Quick Sausage and Veggie Sandwiches

(**Ready in about** 35 minutes | **Servings:** 4)

Ingredients

4 bell peppers
4 medium-sized tomatoes, halved
4 spring onions
1 tablespoon mustard

2 tablespoons canola oil
4 beef sausages
4 hot dog buns

Directions

Start by preheating your Air Fryer to 400 degrees F.

Add the bell peppers to the cooking basket. Drizzle 1 tablespoon of canola oil all over the bell peppers.

Cook for 5 minutes. Turn the temperature down to 350 degrees F. Add the tomatoes and spring onions to the cooking basket and cook an additional 10 minutes.

Re**Serve:** your vegetables.

Then, add the sausages to the cooking basket. Drizzle with the remaining tablespoon of canola oil.

Cook in the preheated Air Fryer at 380 degrees F for 15 minutes, flipping them halfway through the cooking time.

Add the sausage to a hot dog bun; top with the air-fried vegetables and mustard; **Serve:**.

Cheesy Beef Burrito

(**Ready in about** 20 minutes | **Servings:** 4)

Ingredients

1 pound rump steak
1/2 teaspoon cayenne pepper
1 teaspoon piri piri powder
Salt and ground black pepper, to taste

1 cup iceberg lettuce, shredded

1 teaspoon garlic powder
1/2 teaspoon onion powder
1 teaspoon Mexican oregano
4 large whole wheat tortillas
1 cup Mexican cheese blend

Directions

Toss the rump steak with the garlic powder, onion powder, cayenne pepper, piri piri powder, Mexican oregano, salt, and black pepper.

Cook in the preheated Air Fryer at 390 degrees F for 10 minutes. Slice against the grain into thin strips. Add the cheese blend and cook for 2 minutes more.

Spoon the beef mixture onto the wheat tortillas; top with lettuce; roll up burrito-style and **Serve:**.

Homemade Beef Empanadas

(**Ready in about** 35 minutes | **Servings:** 5)

Ingredients

1 teaspoon olive oil
1/2 pound ground beef chuck

1/2 cup tomato paste 1/2 cup vegetable broth
10 Goya discs pastry dough
2 egg whites, beaten

1 garlic clove, minced
1/2 teaspoon dried oregano
1/2 onion, chopped
Salt and ground pepper, to taste
1 tablespoon raisins

Directions

Heat the oil in a saucepan over medium-high heat. Once hot, sauté the onion and garlic until tender, about 3 minutes.

Then, add the beef and continue to sauté an additional 4 minutes, crumbling with a fork.

Add the raisins, oregano, tomato paste, vegetable broth, salt, and black pepper. Reduce the heat to low and cook an additional 15 minutes.

Preheat the Air Fryer to 330 degrees F. Brush the Air Fryer basket with cooking oil. Divide the sauce between discs. Fold each of the discs in half and seal the edges. Brush the tops with the beaten eggs.

Bake for 7 to 8 minutes, working with batches. **Serve:** with salsa sauce if desired. Enjoy!

Indonesian Beef with Peanut Sauce

(**Ready in about** 25 minutes + marinating time | **Servings:** 4)

Ingredients

2 pounds filet mignon, sliced into bite-sized strips
2 tablespoons tamari sauce
1 tablespoon mustard
1 tablespoon honey
2 tablespoons lime juice
1/4 cup peanut butter

2 tablespoons sesame oil
1 tablespoon oyster sauce
1 tablespoon ginger-garlic paste
1 teaspoon chili powder
1 teaspoon red pepper flakes 2 tablespoons water

Directions

In a large ceramic dish, combine the beef strips, oyster sauce, sesame oil, tamari sauce, ginger-garlic paste, mustard, honey, and chilli powder.

Allow it to marinate in the refrigerator for 2 hours, covered.

Cook for 18 minutes in a preheated Air Fryer at 400 degrees F, shaking halfway through. basket on occasion

Combine the peanut butter, lime juice, red pepper flakes, and water in a mixing bowl. **Serve:** the sauce over the air-fried beef strips while they're still warm.

Beef Skewers with Pearl Onions and Eggplant

(**Ready in about** 1 hour 30 minutes | **Servings:** 4)

Ingredients

1 ½ pounds beef stew meat cubes
1 tablespoon yellow mustard
1 cup pearl onions
1 medium-sized eggplant,
1/4 cup sour cream
1/4 cup mayonnaise
1 tablespoon Worcestershire sauce
1 ½-inch cubes Sea salt and ground black pepper, to taste

Directions

In a mixing bowl, toss all Ingredients until everything is well coated. Place in your refrigerator, cover, and let it marinate for 1 hour.

Soak wooden skewers in water for 15 minutes

Thread the beef cubes, pearl onions and eggplant onto skewers. Cook in preheated Air Fryer at 395 degrees F for 12 minutes, flipping halfway through the cooking time. **Serve:** warm.

Sunday Tender Skirt Steak

(**Ready in about** 20 minutes + marinating time | **Servings:** 4)

Ingredients

1/3 cup soy sauce
2 tablespoons champagne vinegar
1 teaspoon celery seeds
1 teaspoon paprika
Sea salt and ground black pepper, to taste
4 tablespoon molasses
1 tbsp porcini powder
2 garlic cloves, minced
1 ½ pounds skirt steak, cut into slices
1 teaspoon shallot powder

Directions

Place the soy sauce, molasses, garlic, vinegar, shallot powder, porcini powder, celery seeds, paprika, and beef in a large resealable plastic bag. Shake well and let it marinate overnight.

Discard the marinade and place the beef in the Air Fryer basket. Season with salt and black pepper to taste.

Cook in the preheated Air Fryer at 400 degrees F for 12 minutes, flipping and basting with the re**Serve:**d marinade halfway through the cooking time. Bon appétit!

Beef with Creamed Mushroom Sauce

(**Ready in about** 20 minutes | **Servings:** 5)

Ingredients

2 tablespoons butter
Salt and cracked black pepper, to taste

1/2 tbs dried rosemary
1 pound Cremini mushrooms, sliced
1 cup sour cream
1/2 teaspoon curry powder
2 pounds sirloin, cut into four pieces
1 teaspoon cayenne pepper
1/4 teaspoon dried thyme
1 teaspoon mustard
1/2 teaspoon dried dill

Directions

Start by preheating your Air Fryer to 396 degrees F. Grease a baking pan with butter.

Add the sirloin, salt, black pepper, cayenne pepper, rosemary, dill, and thyme to the baking pan. Cook for 9 minutes.

Next, stir in the mushrooms, sour cream, mustard, and curry powder. Continue to cook another 5 minutes or until everything is heated through.

Spoon onto individual serving plates. Bon appétit!

Juicy Strip Steak

(**Ready in about** 30 minutes | **Servings:** 4)

Ingredients

1 ½ pounds strip steak, sliced
2 tablespoons honey
2 tablespoons champagne vinegar
1/2 teaspoon coriander seeds
1/3 cup Shoyu sauce
1 tbsp ginger-garlic paste
1 teaspoon mustard seeds
1 tablespoon cornstarch
1/4 cup chickpea flour

Directions

Start by preheating your Air Fryer to 395 degrees F. Spritz the Air Fryer basket with cooking oil.

Toss the strip steak with chickpea flour. Cook the strip steak for 12 minutes; flip them over and cook an additional 10 minutes.

In the meantime, heat the saucepan over medium-high heat. Add the Shoyu sauce, honey, mustard seeds, champagne vinegar, ginger-garlic paste, and coriander seeds.

Reduce the heat and simmer until the sauce is heated through. Make the slurry by whisking the cornstarch with 1 tablespoon of water.

Now, whisk in the cornstarch slurry and continue to simmer until the sauce has thickened. Spoon the sauce over the steak and **Serve:**.

Birthday Party Cheeseburger Pizza

(**Ready in about** 20 minutes | **Servings:** 4)

Ingredients

Nonstick cooking oil
1 pound ground beef
1/2 teaspoon basil
1/2 teaspoon oregano
2 spring onions, chopped
4 burger buns
1/4 cup marinara sauce

Kosher salt and ground
black pepper, to taste
1/4 teaspoon red pepper
flakes
1 cup mozzarella cheese,
shredded

Directions

Start by preheating your Air Fryer to 370 degrees F. Spritz the Air Fryer basket with cooking oil.

Add the ground beef and cook for 10 minutes, crumbling with a spatula. Season with salt, black pepper, oregano, basil, and red peppers.

Spread the marinara pasta on each half of burger bun. Place the spring onions and ground meat mixture on the buns equally.

Set the temperature to 350 degrees F. Place the burger pizza in the Air Fryer basket. Top with mozzarella cheese.

Bake approximately 4 minutes or until cheese is bubbling. Top with another half of burger bun and **Serve:**. Bon appétit!

Filipino Tortang Giniling

(**Ready in about** 20 minutes | **Servings:** 3)

Ingredients

1 teaspoon lard
1/2 teaspoon ground bay
leaf 1/2 teaspoon ground
pepper Sea salt, to taste
1 tomato, sliced
6 eggs
1/2 cup Colby cheese,
shredded

2/3 pound ground beef
1 green bell pepper,
seeded and chopped
1 red bell pepper, seeded
and chopped
1/3 cup double cream
1/4 teaspoon chili powder

Directions

Melt the lard in a cast-iron skillet over medium-high heat. Add the ground beef and cook for 4 minutes until no longer pink, crumbling with a spatula.

Add the ground beef mixture, along with the spices to the baking pan. Now, add the bell peppers.

In a mixing bowl, whisk the eggs with double cream. Spoon the mixture over the meat and peppers in the pan.

Cook in the preheated Air Fryer at 355 degrees F for 10 minutes.

Top with the cheese and tomato slices. Continue to cook for 5 minutes more or until the eggs are golden and the cheese has melted.

Pastrami and Cheddar Quiche

(**Ready in about** 20 minutes | **Servings:** 2)

Ingredients

4 eggs
2 spring onions, chopped

1/2 cup Cheddar cheese,
grated Sea salt, to taste
1 cup pastrami, sliced

1 bell pepper, chopped
1/4 cup Greek-style
yogurt
1/4 teaspoon ground
black pepper

Directions

Begin by preheating your Air Fryer to 330 degrees F. Spritz the baking pan with cooking oil.

Then, thoroughly combine all of the Ingredients and pour the mixture into the prepared baking pan.

Cook for 7 to 9 minutes, or until the eggs are set. Place on a cooling rack for 10 minutes before slicing and serving.

Roasted Blade Steak with Green Beans

(**Ready in about** 25 minutes | **Servings:** 4)

Ingredients

2 garlic cloves, smashed
1 tablespoon Cajun
seasoning
1/2 teaspoon Tabasco
pepper sauce
1 ½ pounds blade steak

1/2 tbsp cayenne pepper
2 cups green beans
2 teaspoons sunflower oil
Sea salt and ground black
pepper, to taste

Directions

Start by preheating your Air Fryer to 330 degrees F.

Mix the garlic, oil, cayenne pepper, and Cajun seasoning to make a paste. Rub it over both sides of the blade steak.

Cook for 13 minutes in the preheated Air Fryer. Now, flip the steak and cook an additional 8 minutes.

Heat the green beans in a saucepan. Add a few tablespoons of water, Tabasco, salt, and black pepper; heat until it wilts or about 10 minutes.

Serve: the roasted blade steak with green beans on the side. Bon appétit!

Indian Beef Samosas

(**Ready in about** 35 minutes | **Servings:** 8)

Ingredients

1 tablespoon sesame oil
2 cloves garlic, minced
2 tablespoons green chili peppers, chopped
Salt and ground black pepper, to taste
1 teaspoon coriander
1 (16-ounce) package phyllo dough

4 tablespoons shallots, minced
4 ounces bacon, chopped
1/2 pound ground chuck
1 teaspoon turmeric
1 teaspoon cumin powder
1 cup frozen peas, thawed
1 egg, beaten with 2 tablespoons of water (egg wash)

Directions

Heat the oil in a saucepan over medium-high heat. Once hot, sauté the shallots, garlic, and chili peppers until tender, about 3 minutes.

Then, add the beef and bacon; continue to sauté an additional 4 minutes, crumbling with a fork. Season with the salt, pepper, cumin powder, turmeric, and coriander. Stir in peas.

Then, preheat your Air Fryer to 330 degrees F. Brush the Air Fryer basket with cooking oil.

Place 1 to 2 tablespoons of the mixture onto each phyllo sheet. Fold the sheets into triangles, pressing the edges. Brush the tops with egg wash.

Bake for 7 to 8 minutes, working with batches. **Serve:** with Indian tomato sauce if desired. Enjoy!

Grilled Vienna Sausage with Broccoli

(**Ready in about** 25 minutes | **Servings:** 4)

Ingredients

1 pound beef Vienna sausage
1 tablespoon fresh lemon juice
1 pound broccoli

1 teaspoon yellow mustard
1/4 teaspoon black pepper
1/2 cup mayonnaise
1 teaspoon garlic powder

Directions

Start by preheating your Air Fryer to 380 degrees F. Spritz the grill pan with cooking oil.

Cut the sausages into serving sized pieces. Cook the sausages for 15 minutes, shaking the basket occasionally to get all sides browned. Set aside.

In the meantime, whisk the mayonnaise with mustard, lemon juice, garlic powder, and black pepper. Toss the broccoli with the mayo mixture.

Turn up temperature to 400 degrees F. Cook broccoli for 6 minutes, turning halfway through the cooking time.

Serve: the sausage with the grilled broccoli on the side. Bon appétit!

Aromatic T-Bone Steak with Garlic

(**Ready in about** 20 minutes | **Servings:** 3)

Ingredients

1 pound T-bone steak
2 tablespoons olive oil
1/4 cup tamari sauce
4 tablespoons tomato paste
1 teaspoon dried rosemary
1/2 teaspoon dried basil
1 teaspoon Sriracha sauce

1/4 cup all-purpose flour
2 teaspoons brown sugar
4 garlic cloves, halved
2 tablespoons white vinegar
2 heaping tablespoons cilantro, chopped

Directions

Rub the garlic halves all over the T-bone steak. Toss the steak with the flour.

Drizzle the oil all over the steak and transfer it to the grill pan; grill the steak in the preheated Air Fryer at 400 degrees F for 10 minutes.

Meanwhile, whisk the tamari sauce, sugar, tomato paste, Sriracha, vinegar, rosemary, and basil. Cook an additional 5 minutes

Serve: garnished with fresh cilantro. Bon appétit!

Sausage Scallion Balls

(**Ready in about** 20 minutes | **Servings:** 4)

Ingredients

1 ½ pounds beef sausage meat
1 cup rolled oats
1 teaspoon Worcestershire sauce

1/2 teaspoon granulated garlic

4 teaspoons mustard

4 tablespoons scallions, chopped
1 teaspoon paprika
Flaky sea salt freshly ground black pepper, to taste
1/2 teaspoon dried oregano
1 teaspoon dried basil
4 pickled cucumbers

Directions

Start by preheating your Air Fryer to 380 degrees F. Spritz the Air Fryer basket with cooking oil.

In a mixing bowl, thoroughly combine the sausage meat, oats, scallions, Worcestershire sauce, salt, black pepper, paprika, garlic, basil, and oregano.

Then, form the mixture into equal sized meatballs using a tablespoon.

Place the meatballs in the Air Fryer basket and cook for 15 minutes, turning halfway through the cooking time.

Serve: with mustard and cucumbers. Bon appétit!

Cube Steak with Cowboy Sauce

(**Ready in about** 20 minutes | **Servings:** 4)

Ingredients

1 ½ pounds cube steak
Salt, to taste
4 ounces butter
2 tablespoon fresh parsley, finely chopped
1 tablespoon fresh horseradish, grated

1/4 tbsp ground black pepper, or more to taste
2 garlic cloves, chopped
1 teaspoon cayenne pepper
2 scallions, finely chopped

Directions

Season the cube steak with salt and black pepper after patting it dry. Cooking oil should be sprayed into the Air Fryer basket. Place the meat in the basket.

Cook for 14 minutes in a preheated Air Fryer at 400 degrees F.

In the meantime, melt the butter in a skillet over medium heat. Stir in the remaining Ingredients and continue to cook until the sauce thickens and reduces slightly.

Serve: the warm cube steaks with Cowboy sauce right away.

Spicy Short Ribs with Red Wine Sauce

(**Ready in about** 20 minutes + marinating time | **Servings:** 4)

Ingredients

1 ½ pounds short ribs
1 lemon, juiced
1 cup red wine
1 teaspoon black pepper
1 teaspoon paprika
1 cup ketchup
1 teaspoon salt

1/2 cup tamari sauce
1 teaspoon fresh ginger, grated
1 teaspoon chipotle chili powder
1 teaspoon garlic powder
1 teaspoon cumin

Directions

In a ceramic bowl, place the beef ribs, wine, tamari sauce, lemon juice, ginger, salt, black pepper, paprika, and chipotle chili powder. Cover and let it marinate for 3 hours in the refrigerator.

Discard the marinade and add the short ribs to the Air Fryer basket. Cook in the preheated Air fry at 380 degrees F for 10 minutes, turning them over halfway through the cooking time. In the meantime, heat the saucepan over medium heat; add the re**Serve:**d marinade and stir in the ketchup, garlic powder, and cumin. Cook until the sauce has thickened slightly. Pour the sauce over the warm ribs and **Serve:** immediately. Bon appétit!

Beef Schnitzel with Buttermilk Spaetzle

(**Ready in about** 20 minutes | **Servings:** 2)

Ingredients

1 egg, beaten
1 teaspoon paprika
1/2 tbs coarse sea salt
2 thin-cut minute steaks
Buttermilk Spaetzle
1/2 cup buttermilk
1/2 teaspoon salt

1/2 teaspoon ground black pepper
1/2 cup tortilla chips
2 eggs
1 tablespoon ghee, melted
1/2 cup all-purpose flour

Directions

Start by preheating your Air Fryer to 360 degrees F.

In a shallow bowl, whisk the egg with black pepper, paprika, and salt. Thoroughly combine the ghee with the crushed tortilla chips and coarse sea salt in another shallow bowl.

Using a meat mallet, pound the schnitzel to 1/4-inch thick.

Dip the schnitzel into the egg mixture; then, roll the schnitzel over the crumb mixture until coated on all sides.

Cook for 13 minutes in the preheated Air Fryer.

To make the spaetzle, whisk the eggs, buttermilk, flour, and salt in a bowl. Bring a large saucepan of salted water to a boil. Push the spaetzle mixture through the holes of a potato ricer into the boiling water; slice them off using a table knife. Work in batches. When the spaetzle float, take them out with a slotted spoon. Repeat with the rest of the spaetzle mixture.

Serve: with warm schnitzel. Enjoy!

Cilantro-Mint Pork BBQ Thai Style

Prep time: 10 minutes **Cooking time:** 15 minutes
Servings: 3

Ingredients

1 minced hot Chile
1 minced shallot
3 tablespoons basil

3 tablespoons cilantro

1-pound ground pork
2 tablespoons fish sauce
3 tablespoons chopped mint

2 tablespoons lime juice

Directions

In a shallow dish, mix well all ingredients with hands. Form into 1-inch ovals.

Thread ovals in skewers. Place on a skewer rack in the air fryer. For 15 minutes, cook on 360F. Halfway through cooking time, turnover skewers. If needed, cook in batches. **Serve:** and enjoy.

Beef Sausage Goulash

(**Ready in about** 40 minutes | **Servings:** 2)

Ingredients

1 tablespoon lard, melted
2 red chilies, finely chopped
1 teaspoon ginger-garlic paste
4 beef good quality sausages, thinly sliced
2 teaspoons smoked paprika

1 bell pepper, chopped
1/4 teaspoon ground black pepper
1 shallot, chopped
Sea salt, to taste
1 cup beef bone broth
1/2 cup tomato puree
2 handfuls spring greens, shredded

Directions

Melt the lard in a Dutch oven over medium-high flame; sauté the shallots and peppers about 4 minutes or until fragrant. Add the ginger-garlic paste and cook an additional minute. Season with salt and black pepper and transfer to a lightly greased baking pan.

Then, brown the sausages, stirring occasionally, working in batches. Add to the baking pan. Add the smoked paprika, broth, and tomato puree. Lower the pan onto the Air Fryer basket. Bake at 325 degrees F for 30 minutes.

Stir in the spring greens and cook for 5 minutes more or until they wilt. **Serve:** over the hot rice if desired. Bon appétit!

Mom's Toad in the Hole

(**Ready in about** 45 minutes | **Servings:** 4)

Ingredients

6 beef sausages

A pinch of salt
2 eggs

1 tablespoon butter, melted
1 cup semi-skimmed milk
1 cup plain flour

Directions

Cook the sausages in the preheated Air Fryer at 380 degrees F for 15 minutes, shaking halfway through the cooking time.

Meanwhile, make up the batter mix.

Tip the flour into a bowl with salt; make a well in the middle and crack the eggs into it. Mix with an electric whisk; now, slowly and gradually pour in the milk, whisking all the time.

Place the sausages in a lightly greased baking pan. Pour the prepared batter over the sausages.

Cook in the preheated Air Fryer at 370 degrees F approximately 25 minutes, until golden and risen. **Serve:** with gravy if desired. Bon appétit!

Beef Nuggets with Cheesy Mushrooms

(**Ready in about** 25 minutes | **Servings:** 4)

Ingredients

2 eggs, beaten
1 cup tortilla chips, crushed
salt and ground black pepper, to taste
1 pound button mushrooms
1 pound cube steak, cut into bite-size pieces

4 tablespoons yogurt
1 teaspoon dry mesquite flavored seasoning mix
Coarse
1/2 teaspoon onion powder

1 cup Swiss cheese, shredded

Directions

In a shallow bowl, whisk together the eggs and yoghurt. Combine the tortilla chips, mesquite seasoning, salt, pepper, and onion powder in a resealable bag.

Dip the steaks in the egg mixture, then place them in the bag and shake to coat on all sides.

Cook for 14 minutes at 400 degrees F, flipping halfway through.time.

Place the mushrooms in the cooking basket that has been lightly oiled. Shredded Swiss cheese on top.

5 minutes in a preheated Air Fryer at 400 degrees F. **Serve:** alongside the beef nuggets. Good appetite!

Crispy Fried Pork Chops the Southern Way

Prep time: 15 minutes **Cooking time:** 25 minutes
Servings: 4

Ingredients

1/2 cup all-purpose flour
1/2 cup low-fat buttermilk
4 bone-in pork chops
1 teaspoon paprika

11/2 teaspoon Tabasco sauce
1/2 teaspoon black pepper

Directions

Place the buttermilk and hot sauce in a Ziploc bag and add the pork chops. Allow to marinate for at least an hour in the fridge.

In a bowl, combine the flour, paprika, and black pepper.

Remove pork from the Ziploc bag and dredge in the flour mixture. Preheat the air fryer to 390F. Spray the pork chops with oil. Set in the device and cook for 25 minutes.

Crispy Roast Garlic-Salt Pork

Prep time: 10 minutes **Cooking time:** 45 minutes
Servings: 4

Ingredients
1 teaspoon Chinese five-spice powder	2 pounds of pork belly
2 teaspoons garlic salt	1 teaspoon white pepper

Directions

Preheat the air fryer to 390F. Mix all the spices in a bowl to create the dry rub. Score the skin of the pork belly with a knife and season the entire pork with the spice rub. Set in the air fryer basket and cook for 40 to 45 minutes until the skin is crispy. Chop before serving.

Curry Pork Roast in Coconut Sauce

Prep time: 25 minutes **Cooking time:** 60 minutes
Servings: 6

Ingredients
1/2 teaspoon curry powder	1/2 teaspoon ground turmeric powder
1 can unsweetened coconut milk	3pounds of pork shoulder
1 tablespoon sugar	Salt and pepper to taste
2tablespoons fish sauce	2tablespoons soy sauce

Directions

Place all ingredients in a bowl and allow the meat to marinate in the fridge for at least 2 hours.

Preheat the air fryer to 390F. Place the grill pan accessory in the air fryer. Grill the meat for 20 minutes making sure to flip the pork every 10 minutes for even grilling and cook in batches. Meanwhile, merge the marinade into a saucepan and allow to simmer for 10 minutes until the sauce thickens. Baste the pork with the sauce before serving.

Pork Taquitos

Prep time: 10 minutes **Cooking time:** 16 minutes
Servings: 8

Ingredients
1juiced lime	10 whole-wheat tortillas
2 1/2 C. shredded mozzarella cheese	30 ounces of cooked and shredded pork tenderloin

Directions

Preparing the Ingredients. Ensure your air fryer is preheated to 380 degrees. Drizzle pork with lime juice and gently mix.
Heat tortillas in the microwave with a dampened paper towel to soften. Add about 3 ounces of pork and 1/4 cup of shredded cheese to each tortilla. Tightly roll them up.

Lamb Burgers

Prep time: 15 minutes **Cooking time:** 8 minutes
Servings: 6

Ingredients
2 pounds ground lamb	Salt and ground black pepper, as required
1tablespoon onion powder	

Directions

In a bowl, attach all the ingredients and mix well. Make 6 equal-sized patties from the mixture. Arrange the patties onto a cooking tray.

Arrange the drip pan in the bottom of the Instant Vortex Plus Air Fryer Oven cooking chamber. Select "Air Fry" and then adjust the temperature to 360 degrees F. Set the timer for 8 minutes and press the "Start". When the display shows "Add Food" inserts the cooking rack in the center position. When the display shows "Turn Food" turns the burgers.When **Cooking time:**is complete, remove the tray from Vortex and **Serve:** hot.

Cajun Bacon Pork Loin Fillet

Prep time: 10 minutes **Cooking time:** 20 minutes
Servings: 6

Ingredients
11/2 pounds pork loin fillet or pork tenderloin	2 tablespoons Cajun Spice Mix Salt
6 slices bacon	Olive oil spray
3 tablespoons olive oil	

Directions

Preparing the Ingredients. Divide the pork in half so that it will fit in the air fryer basket.

Place both pieces of meat in a resalable plastic bag. Add the oil, Cajun seasoning, and salt to taste, if using. Seal the bag and massage to coat all of the meat with the oil and seasonings. Marinate in the refrigerator.

Air Frying. Remove the pork from the bag and wrap 3 bacon slices around each piece. Spray the Pro Breeze air fryer basket with olive oil spray. Place the meat in the air fryer. Set the Pro Breeze air fryer to 350°F for 15 minutes. Increase the temperature to 400°F for 5 minutes.

Let the meat rest for 10 minutes. Slice into 6 medallions and Serve

Pork Tenders with Bell Peppers

Prep time: 5 minutes **Cooking time:** 15 minutes
Servings: 4

Ingredients
11 Oz Pork Tenderloin	1 tbsp. Olive Oil
1Bell Pepper, in thin strips	1 Red Onion, sliced
Pepper to taste	1Tsps. Provencal Herbs
1/2 tbsp. Mustard	Black

Directions

Preparing the Ingredients. Preheat the Pro Breeze air fryer to 390 degrees. In the oven dish, mix the bell pepper strips with the onion, herbs, and some salt and pepper to taste.

Attach half a tablespoon of olive oil Divide the pork tenderloin into four pieces and rub it with salt, pepper, and mustard.
Thinly coat the pieces with remaining olive oil and place them upright in the oven dish on top of the pepper mixture

Air Frying. Place the bowl into the Air fryer. Set the timer to 20 minutes and roast the meat and the vegetables
Turn the meat and mix the peppers halfway through
Serve: with a fresh salad

Wonton Meatballs

Prep time: 15 minutes **Cooking time:** 10 minutes
Servings: 4

Ingredients
1-pound ground pork	1/4 cup chopped green
2 large eggs	onions
fresh ginger cloves garlic,	1/4 cup chopped fresh
minced	cilantro tablespoon
1teaspoons soy sauce	minced
	1teaspoon oyster sauce
1/2 teaspoon kosher salt	1 teaspoon black pepper

Directions

Preparing the Ingredients, merge the pork, eggs, green onions, cilantro, ginger, garlic, soy sauce, oyster sauce, salt, and pepper.

Merge on low speed until all of the ingredients are incorporated, 2 to 3 minutes. Form the mixture into 12 meatballs and arrange in a single layer in the air fryer basket.

Air Frying. Set the Pro Breeze air fryer to 350F for 10 minutes. Use a meat thermometer to ensure the meatballs have reached an internal temperature of 145F. Set the meatballs to a bowl and **Serve**

Easy Air Fryer Marinated Pork Tenderloin

Prep time: 1 hour and 10 minutes **Cooking time:** 30 minutes
Servings: 4 to 6

Ingredients
1/4 cup olive oil	1/4 cup of soy sauce
1/4 cup freshly squeezed	1 tablespoon Dijon
lemon juice	mustard
	1 teaspoon salt
1/2 teaspoon freshly	1pounds pork tenderloin
ground black pepper	1garlic clove, minced

Directions

Preparing the Ingredients. In a mixing bowl, make the marinade. Mix the olive oil, soy sauce, lemon juice, minced garlic, Dijon mustard, salt, and pepper. Re**Serve:** 1/4 cup of the marinade.

Place the tenderloin in a large bowl and pour the remaining marinade over the meat. Cover and marinate in the refrigerator for about 1 hour. Place the marinated pork tenderloin into the air fryer basket.

Air Frying. Set the temperature of your Pro Breeze AF to 400F. Set the timer and roast for 10 minutes. Using tongs flip the pork and baste it with half of the re**Serve:**d marinade. Reset the timer and roast for 10 minutes more.
Using tongs, flip the pork, and then baste with the remaining marinade.

Reset the timer and roast for another 10 minutes, for a total Cooking time of 30 minutes.

Barbecue Flavored Pork Ribs

Prep time: 5 minutes **Cooking time:** 15 minutes
Servings: 6

Ingredients
1/4 cup honey, divided	2 tablespoons tomato
3/4 cup BBQ sauce	ketchup
1 tablespoon soy sauce	1tablespoon
13/4 pound pork ribs	Worcestershire sauce
1/2 teaspoon garlic	Freshly ground white
powder	pepper, to taste

Directions

Preparing the Ingredients. In a large bowl, merge 3 tablespoons of honey and the remaining ingredients except for the pork ribs. Refrigerate to marinate for about 20 minutes.

Preheat the Pro Breeze air fryer to 355 degrees F. Place the ribs in an Air fryer basket.

Air Frying. Cook for about 13 minutes. Detach the ribs from the Air fryer and coat with remaining honey.
Serve: hot.

Perfect Air Fried Pork Chops

Prep time: 5 minutes **Cooking time:** 17 minutes
Servings: 4

Ingredients

3 cups bread crumbs
2 tablespoons vegetable oil
2 teaspoons salt
1/4 teaspoon garlic powder
6 (1/2-inch-thick) bone-in pork chops
1/2 cup grated Parmesan cheese
2 teaspoons sweet paprika
1/2 teaspoon onion powder

Directions

Preparing the Ingredients. Spray the Pro Breeze air fryer basket with olive oil. In a large resalable bag, combine the bread crumbs, Parmesan cheese, oil, salt, paprika, onion powder, and garlic powder. Secure the bag and shake it a few times for the spices to blend. Place the pork chops, one by one, in the bag and shake to coat.

Air Frying. Place the pork chops in the greased Pro Breeze air fryer basket in a single layer. Be careful not to overcrowd the basket. Spray the chops generously with olive oil to avoid powdery, uncooked breading.

Set the temperature of your Pro Breeze AF to 360°F. Set the timer and roast for 10 minutes.

Using tongs, flip the chops. Spray them generously with olive oil. Reset the timer and roast for 7 minutes more.

Balsamic-Glazed Pork Chops

Prep time: 5 minutes **Cooking time:** 50
Servings: 4

Ingredients

3/4 cup balsamic vinegar
11/2 tablespoons sugar
4pork rib chops
1 tablespoon butter
1/2tablespoons olive oil
1/4tablespoons salt

Directions

Preparing the Ingredients. Place all ingredients in a bowl and allow the meat to marinate in the fridge for at least 2 hours. Preheat the Pro Breeze air fryer to 390°F. Place the grill pan accessory in the air fryer.

Air Frying. Grill the pork chops for 20 minutes making sure to flip the meat every 10 minutes for even grilling. Meanwhile, pour the balsamic vinegar into a saucepan and allow simmering for at least 10 minutes until the sauce thickens. Brush the meat with the glaze before serving.

Rustic Pork Ribs

Prep time: 5 minutes **Cooking time:** 15 minutes
Servings: 4

Ingredients

1rack of pork ribs
1/2 teaspoon dried thyme
1/2 teaspoon onion powder 1/2 teaspoon garlic powder
1 tablespoon cornstarch
1 tablespoon soy sauce
3tablespoons dry red wine
1/2 teaspoon ground black pepper
1 teaspoon smoked salt
1/2 teaspoon olive oil

Directions

Preparing the Ingredients. Warmth your Air fryer to 390 degrees F. Place all ingredients in a mixing bowl and let them marinate for at least 1 hour.

Air Frying. Cook the marinated ribs for approximately 25 minutes at 390 degrees F. **Serve:** hot.

Air Fryer Baby Back Ribs

Prep time: 5 minutes **Cooking time:** 25 minutes
Servings: 4

Ingredients

1rack baby back ribs

1 teaspoon freshly ground black pepper
2tablespoons salt
1 tablespoon garlic powder
1 cup barbecue sauce (any type)

Directions

Preparing the Ingredients. Dry the ribs with a paper towel.
Season the ribs with garlic powder, pepper, and salt. Place the seasoned ribs into the air fryer.

Air Frying. Set the temperature of your Pro Breeze AF to 400°F. Set the timer and grill for 10 minutes. Using tongs, flip the ribs.

Parmesan Crusted Pork Chops

Prep time: 10 minutes **Cooking time:** 15 minutes
Servings: 8

Ingredients

3 tbsp. grated parmesan cheese
1/4 tsp. chili powder
1/4 tsp. pepper
4-6 thick boneless pork chops

2beaten eggs
1C. pork rind crumbs
1/2 tsp. salt
1/2 tsp. onion powder
1 tsp. smoked paprika

Directions

Ensure your air fryer is preheated to 400 degrees. With pepper and salt, season both sides of pork chops.
In a food processor, pulse pork rinds into crumbs. Mix crumbs with other seasonings.Beat eggs and add to another bowl.

Dip pork chops into eggs then into pork rind crumb mixture. Spray down the air fryer with olive oil and add pork chops to the basket. Set temperature to 400F, and set time to 15 minutes.

Crispy Pork Dumplings

Prep time: 10 minutes **Cooking time:** 10 minutes
Servings: 8

Ingredients

5 lb. Ground pork 1tbsp. Olive oil
Half of 1 pkg. Dumpling wrappers

5 tsp. each Black pepper and salt

Directions

Set the Air Fryer temperature setting at 390 Fahrenheit.
Mix the fixings. Prepare each dumpling using two teaspoons of the pork mixture. Seal the edges with a portion of water to make the triangle form. Lightly spritz the Air Fryer basket using a cooking oil spray as needed. Add the dumplings to air-fry for eight minutes. **Serve:** when they're ready.

Pork Joint

Prep time: 10 minutes **Cooking time:** 20 minutes
Servings: 10

Ingredients

3 cups Cooked shredded pork tenderloin or chicken
Lime juice

10 small flour tortillas
2.5cups Fat-free shredded Mozzarella

Directions

Set the Air Fryer at 380 Fahrenheit. Sprinkle the juice over the pork. Microwave five of the tortillas at a time (putting a damp paper towel over them for 10 seconds). Add three ounces of pork and 1/4 of a cup of cheese to each tortilla. Tightly roll the tortillas. Line the tortillas onto a greased foil-lined pan. Spray an even coat of cooking oil spray over the tortillas.

Chorizo and Beef Burger

Prep time: 10 minutes **Cooking time:** 15 minutes
Servings: 4

Ingredients

3/4 pound 80/20 ground beef
5 slices pickled jalapeños, chopped
2 teaspoons chili powder

1/4 pound Mexican-style ground chorizo
1 teaspoon minced garlic
1/4 teaspoon cumin
1/4 cup chopped onion

Directions

In a large bowl, mix all ingredients. Divide the mixture into four sections and form them into burger patties. Place burger patties into the air fryer basket, working in batches if necessary.

Adjust the temperature to 375F and set the timer for 15 minutes. Turn over the patties halfway through the cooking time. **Serve:** warm.

Crispy Brats

Prep time: 5 minutes **Cooking time:** 15 minutes
Servings: 4

Ingredients

4 (3-ounce) beef bratwursts

Directions

Place brats into the air fryer basket. Adjust the temperature to 375F and set the timer for 15 minutes. **Serve:** warm.

Almond Flour 'n Egg Crusted Beef

Prep time: 10 Minutes **Cooking time:** 15 minutes
Servings: 1

Ingredients

1/2 cup almond flour	1/2-pound beef schnitzel
1egg beaten	2tablespoons vegetable oil
1 slice of lemon to **Serve:**	

Directions

Preheat the air fryer for 5 minutes. Mix the oil and almond flour together. Dip the schnitzel into the egg and dredge in the almond flour mixture.

Press the almond flour so that it sticks on to the beef. Set in the air fryer and cook for 15 minutes at 3500F. **Serve:** with a slice of lemon.

Easy Teriyaki BBQ Recipe

Prep time: 10 Minutes **Cooking time:** 15 minutes
Servings: 2

Ingredients

1tablespoon honey	1 tablespoon soy sauce
1 tablespoon mirin	1 thumb-sized piece of
14 oz. lean diced steak,	fresh
with fat trimmed	ginger, grated

Directions

Merge all Ingredients in a bowl and marinate for at least an hour. Turning over halfway through marinating time.
Thread mead into skewers. Place on skewer rack.
Cook for 5 minutes at 390oF or to desired doneness.
Serve: and enjoy.

Apricot Glazed Pork Tenderloins

Prep time: 10 Minutes **Cooking time:** 30 minutes
Servings: 3
Ingredients

1/2teaspoon salt	1/2 teaspoon pepper
2tablespoons minced fresh	2tablespoons olive oil,
rosemary or 1 tablespoon	divided
dried rosemary, crushed	4garlic cloves, minced
3 tablespoons lemon juice	Apricot Glaze Ingredients
1 cup apricot	2 garlic cloves, minced
	1-lb pork tenderloin

Directions

Mix well pepper, salt, garlic, oil, and rosemary. Brush all over pork. If needed cut pork crosswise in half to fit in air fryer. Lightly grease baking pan of air fryer with cooking spray. Add pork. For 3 minutes per side, brown pork in a preheated 390F air fryer. Meanwhile, mix well all glaze Ingredients in a small bowl. Baste pork every 5 minutes. Cook for 20 minutes at 330F. **Serve:** and enjoy.

Baby Back Rib Recipe from Kansas City

Prep time: 10 Minutes **Cooking time:** 50 minutes
Servings: 2

Ingredients

1/4 cup apple cider vinegar 1/4 cup molasses	1/4 teaspoon cayenne pepper
1 tablespoon brown sugar	1 tablespoon liquid smoke
1 tbsp Worcestershire sauce	seasoning, hickory
1 teaspoon dry mustard	Salt and pepper to taste
1-pound pork ribs, small	1cup ketchup
2cloves of garlic	

Directions

Bring all ingredients in a Ziploc bag and allow marinating in the fridge for at least 2 hours. Preheat the air fryer to 390F. Place the grill pan accessory in the air fryer.

Grill meat for 25 minutes per batch. Flip the meat halfway through the cooking time.

Bacon, Spinach and Feta Quiche

Prep time: 10 Minutes **Cooking time:** 30 minutes
Servings: 3

Ingredients

6 EGGS	salt and freshly ground
1/2-pound fresh spinach	pepper to taste
3 slices bacon, chopped	1/2 pinch cayenne pepper
11/2 teaspoons butter	1/2 pinch salt
1-1 /2 ounces crumbled	1/4 onion, diced
feta cheese	

Directions

Lightly grease baking pan of air fryer with butter. Add spinach and for 2 minutes, cook on 360F.
Drain well the spinach and squeeze dry. Chop and set aside.

Add bacon in air fryer pan and cook for 6 minutes or until crisped. Discard excess fat.
Stir in onion and season with salt. Cook for another 5 minutes. Stir in chopped spinach and cook for another 5 minutes to heat through.

Meanwhile, in a bowl whisk well eggs, cayenne pepper, black pepper, and salt. Remove basket, evenly spread mixture in pan, and pour in eggs. Sprinkle feta cheese on top.

Cook for another 15 minutes, until eggs are cooked to desired doneness. **Serve:** and enjoy.

Bacon Cheeseburger Casserole

Prep time: 10 Minutes **Cooking time:** 35 minutes
Servings: 6

Ingredients

1small onion, chopped
1 tablespoon Worcestershire sauce
1/2 can (15 ounces) tomato sauce
1/4 cup sliced dill pickles
6 bacon strips, cooked and crumbled
8-ounces frozen Tater Tots
1 tbsp ground mustard
1-pound ground beef
1/2 cup grape tomatoes, chopped
1/2 cup shredded cheddar cheese
4-ounces process cheese (Velveeta)

Directions

Lightly grease baking pan of air fryer with cooking spray. Add beef and half of onions. For 10 minutes, cook on 390F. Halfway through cooking time, stir and crumble beef.

Stir in Worcestershire, mustard, Velveeta, and tomato sauce. Mix well. Cook for 4 minutes until melted. Mix well and evenly spread in pan. Top with cheddar cheese and then bacon strips.

Evenly top with tater tots. Cover pan with foil. Cook for 15 minutes at 390F. Uncover and bake for 10 minutes more until tops are lightly browned. **Serve:** and enjoy topped with pickles and tomatoes and remaining onion.

Baked Cheese 'n Pepperoni Calzone

Prep time: 10 Minutes **Cooking time:** 25 minutes
Servings: 4

Ingredients

1cup chopped pepperoni
1 to 2 tablespoons 2% milk
1 tablespoon grated Parmesan cheese
1/4 cup shredded part-skim mozzarella cheese
1 loaf frozen bread dough, thawed
1/2 teaspoon Italian seasoning, optional
1/2 cup pasta sauce with meat

Directions

In a bowl mix well mozzarella cheese, pizza sauce, and pepperoni. On a lightly floured surface, divide dough into four portions. Set each into a 6-in. circle; top each with a scant 1/3 cup pepperoni mixture. Fold dough over filling; pinch edges to seal.

Lightly grease baking pan of air fryer with cooking spray. Place dough in a single layer and if needed, cook in batches. For 25 minutes, cook on 330F preheated air fryer or until dough is lightly browned. **Serve:** and enjoy.

Beef Recipe Texas-Rodeo Style

Prep time: 10 Minutes **Cooking time:** 1 hour **Servings:** 6

Ingredients

1/2 cup honey
1/2 teaspoon dry mustard
1clove of garlic, minced
Salt and pepper to taste
1/2 cup ketchup
3pounds beef steak sliced
1 tablespoon chili powder
2onion, chopped

Directions

Stick all Ingredients in a Ziploc bag and allow marinating in the fridge for at least 2 hours. Preheat the air fryer to 390F. Place the grill pan accessory in the air fryer.

Grill the beef for 15 minutes per batch making sure that you flip it every 8 minutes for even grilling. Meanwhile, pour the marinade on a saucepan and allow simmering over medium heat until the sauce thickens. Baste the beef with the sauce before serving.

Beef Roast in Worcestershire-Rosemary

Prep time: 10 Minutes **Cooking time:** 2 hours **Servings:** 6

Ingredients

1onion, chopped
1 tbs Worcestershire sauce
3 stalks of celery, sliced
1-pound beef chuck roast
2cloves of garlic, minced
1 tablespoon butter
1 teaspoon thyme
1 teaspoon rosemary
2cups water
3tablespoons olive oil

Directions

Preheat the air fryer for 5 minutes. Set all Ingredients in a deep baking dish that will fit in the air fryer. Bake for 2 hours at 350F. Braise the meat with its sauce every 30 minutes until cooked.

Beefy Bell Pepper 'n Egg Scramble

Prep time: 10 Minutes **Cooking time:** 30 minutes
Servings: 4

Ingredients

1green bell pepper, seeded and chopped
3tablespoons olive oil
6 cups eggs, beaten
1-pound ground beef
2cloves of garlic, minced
Salt and pepper to taste
1 onion, chopped

Directions

Preheat the air fryer for 5 minutes with baking pan insert.
In a baking dish mix the ground beef, onion, garlic, olive oil, and bell pepper. Season with salt and pepper to taste.
Pour in the beaten eggs and give a good stir. Place the dish with the beef and egg mixture in the air fryer. Bake for 30 minutes at 330F.

Beefy 'n Cheesy Spanish Rice Casserole

Prep time: 10 Minutes **Cooking time:** 50 minutes
Servings: 3

Ingredients

2 tablespoons chopped green bell pepper	1/2-pound lean ground beef 1/2 cup water
1/2 teaspoon salt	1/2 teaspoon brown sugar
1/2 pinch ground black pepper	1/4 teaspoon ground cumin
1/3 cup uncooked long grain rice	2 tablespoon chopped fresh cilantro
1/4 cup Chile sauce	1/4 cup finely chopped onion
1/4 teaspoon Worcestershire sauce	1/4 cup shredded Cheddar cheese

Directions

Lightly grease baking pan of air fryer with cooking spray. Add ground beef. For 10 minutes, cook on 360F. Halfway through cooking time, stir and crumble beef. Discard excess fat, Stir in pepper, Worcestershire sauce, cumin, brown sugar, salt, Chile sauce, rice, water, tomatoes, green bell pepper, and onion. Mix well. Cover pan with foil and cook for 25 minutes. Stirring occasionally.

Give it one last good stir, press down firmly and sprinkle cheese on top. Cook uncovered for 15 minutes at 390oF until tops are lightly browned. **Serve:** and enjoy with chopped cilantro.

Beefy Steak Topped with Chimichurri Sauce

Prep time: 10 Minutes **Cooking time:** 60 minutes
Servings: 6

Ingredients

1 cup commercial chimichurri	Salt and pepper to taste
	3 pounds steak

Directions

Stick all Ingredients in a Ziploc bag and marinate in the fridge for 2 hours. Preheat the air fryer to 390F. Place the grill pan accessory in the air fryer. Grill the skirt steak for 20 minutes per batch. Flip the steak every 10 minutes for even grilling.

Bourbon-BBQ Sauce Marinated Beef BBQ

Prep time: 10 Minutes **Cooking time:** 60 minutes
Servings: 4

Ingredients

1/4 cup bourbon	1/4 cup barbecue sauce
Salt and pepper to taste	tablespoon Worcestershire sauce pounds beef steak, pounded

Directions

Stick all Ingredients in a Ziploc bag and allow marinating in the fridge for at least 2 hours. Preheat the air fryer to 390F. Place the grill pan accessory in the air fryer. Set on the grill pan and cook for 20 minutes per batch.

Halfway through the cooking time, give a stir to cook evenly. Meanwhile, pour the marinade on a saucepan and allow to simmer until the sauce thickens. **Serve:** beef with the bourbon sauce.

Buttered Garlic-Thyme Roast Beef

Prep time: 10 Minutes **Cooking time:** 2 hours
Servings: 12

Ingredients

11/2 tablespoon garlic	1 teaspoon black pepper
1 cup beef stock	1 teaspoon salt
1 teaspoon thyme leaves, chopped	1 tablespoons butter
	3-pound eye of round roast
6 tablespoons olive oil	

Directions

Place in a Ziploc bag all the Ingredients and allow to marinate in the fridge for 2 hours. Preheat the air fryer for 5 minutes. Transfer all Ingredients in a baking dish that will fit in the air fryer. Set in the air fryer and cook for 2 hours for 400F. Baste the beef with the sauce every 30 minutes.

Cajun 'n Coriander Seasoned Ribs

Prep time: 10 Minutes **Cooking time:** 1 hour
Servings: 4

Ingredients

1/4 cup brown sugar	1 teaspoon coriander seed
1/2 teaspoon lemon	powder
1 tablespoon paprika	2 slabs spareribs
2 tbsp onion powder	2 teaspoon Cajun
1 tablespoon salt	seasoning

Directions

Preheat the air fryer to 390F. Place the grill pan accessory in the air fryer. In a small bowl, combine the spaces. Rub the spice mixture on to the spareribs. Place the spareribs on the grill pan and cook for 20 minutes per batch. **Serve:** with your favorite barbecue sauce.

Cajun Sweet-Sour Grilled Pork

Prep time: 10 Minutes **Cooking time:** 12 minutes
Servings: 3

Ingredients

1/4 cup brown sugar	1-lb pork loin, sliced into
1/4 cup cider vinegar	1-inch cubes
3 tablespoons brown sugar	2 tbsp Cajun seasoning

Directions

In a shallow dish, mix well pork loin, 3 tablespoons brown sugar, and Cajun seasoning. Toss well to coat. Marinate in the ref for 3 hours. In a medium bowl mix well, brown sugar and vinegar for basting.

Thread pork pieces in skewers. Baste with sauce and place on skewer rack in air fryer. For 12 minutes, cook on 360F. Halfway through cooking time, turnover skewers and baste with sauce. If needed, cook in batches. **Serve:** and enjoy.

Pork Stew

Prep time: 10 minutes **Cooking time:** 35 minutes
Serve:s 4- 6

Ingredients

1lb. of pork chops	4oz. of chopped asparagus
4cups of beef broth	1 tsp. of paprika
1 tsp. of salt	3yellow onions
1 tsp. of chili powder	A cup of chopped bok choy
1 tbsp. of ground celery	1/2 tsp. of Erythritol

Directions

Peel the onions and slice them. Chop the pork chops into bite-sized pieces. Combine the pork with salt, paprika, and chili powder and stir well. Set pressure cooker to Sauté mode and pour in the constituents.

Close pressure cooker lid and Cook for about 35 minutes. When the **Cooking time:**elapses, remove the stew from the pressure cooker and **Serve:**.

Capers 'n Olives Topped Flank Steak

Prep time: 10 Minutes **Cooking time:** 45 minutes
Servings: 4

Ingredients

1anchovy fillet, minced	1 tablespoon capers,
1 clove of garlic, minced	minced 1/3 cup olive oil
2pounds flank steak, pounded	2 tablespoons garlic powder 2 tablespoons
2tablespoons fresh oregano	onion powder
2 tbs smoked paprika	1 cup pitted olives
	Salt and pepper to taste

Directions

Preheat the air fryer to 390F. Place the grill pan accessory in the air fryer. Season the steak with salt and pepper. Rub the oregano, paprika, onion powder, and garlic powder all over the steak.

Set on the grill pan and cook for 45 minutes. Make sure to flip the meat every 10 minutes for even cooking. Meanwhile, mix together the olive oil, olives, capers, garlic, and anchovy fillets. **Serve:** the steak with the tapenade.

Caraway, Sichuan 'n Cumin Lamb Kebabs

Prep time: 10 Minutes **Cooking time:** 1 hour
Servings: 3

Ingredients

11/2 pounds lamb shoulder, bones removed and cut pcs	1 teaspoon sugar
	1 tbs Sichuan peppercorns
2 tbs cumin seeds, toasted	2 tbs caraway seeds, toasted
2 tbs red pepper flakes	Salt and pepper to taste

Directions

Place all Ingredients in bowl and allow the meat to marinate in the fridge for at least 2 hours. Preheat the air fryer to 390F. Place the grill pan accessory in the air fryer. Grill the meat for 15 minutes per batch. Flip the meat every 8 minutes for even grilling.

Pulled Beef

Prep time: 15 minutes **Cooking time:** 8 hours 10 minutes
Servings: 4 - 6

Ingredients

1lb. of beef chuck	1 cup of tomato paste
1 tsp. of black pepper(ground)	1 tbsp. of mustard
	1 tsp. of paprika
1 tbsp. of onion powder	1 tbsp. of apple cider vinegar treatment
1 tbsp. of salt	
1 tbsp. of sour cream	4 cups of beef broth

Directions

Chop the beef chuck into medium-sized pieces, sprinkle it with salt and ground black pepper, and stir well.
Set the pressure cooker to Slow Cook mode. Pour the chopped beef to the pressure cooker and add the beef broth. Close the lid and cook for about 8 hours. Combine the tomato paste, sour cream, mustard, onion powder, paprika, apple cider vinegar treatment, and honey together in a mixing bowl.

Whisk the amalgamation until it is smooth. When the **Cooking time:**ends, remove the cooked beef from the pressure cooker and shred it.

Return the shredded beef to the pressure cooker and sprinkle it with the honey mixture. Stir it carefully and close the lid. Cook the dish on Pressure mode for about 10 minutes. When the dish is cooked, allow it to rest briefly before serving.

Beef Steak

Prep time: 25 minutes **Cooking time:** 25 minutes
Servings: 2 - 4

Ingredients

1lb. of beef steak	1 tbsp. of freshly squeezed lemon juice
1 tsp. of salt	
3tbsp. of fresh rosemary	3tbsp. of balsamic vinegar
1 tsp. of paprika	1 tbsp. of olive oil
1 tsp. of ground black pepper	1 tbsp. of minced garlic
	1 cup of red wine
1 onion	

Directions

Mix salt, paprika, fresh rosemary, ground black pepper and minced garlic in a mixing bowl. Peel the onion and chop it and place the chopped onion and spice mixture in a blender.

Add freshly squeezed lemon juice, balsamic vinegar, organic extra virgin olive oil, and burgundy or merlot wine. Blend the amalgamation until it smoothens. Mix beef steak with all the spice mixture and then leave it in a refrigerator for a quarter-hour to marinate.

Switch to Sauté mode and transfer the marinated steak into pressure cooker and sauté the meat for ten minutes while stirring frequently.

Beef Ragout

Prep time: 15 minutes **Cooking time:** 35 minutes
Servings: 5-7

Ingredients

2 lb. of beef brisket	4 white onions tsp. of sugar
1 tbsp. of butter	
3 Servings of water	1/2 cup of fresh parsley
1cup of cherry tomatoes	1 cup of cream
1 tbsp. of fresh thyme	2 carrots
1 cup of tomato juice	11 tsp. of fresh rosemary
5 oz. of fennel	1/4 cup of fresh dill

Directions

Wash the thyme, dill and parsley and chop them. Chop the beef brisket roughly. Wash cherry tomatoes and cut them into halves. Chop the fennel. Peel the onions and carrots and chop them roughly.
Place all of the Ingredients into a pressure cooker and set the pressure cooker on Sauté mode. Add water, sugar, cream, tomato juice, fresh rosemary, and butter into the pressure cooker and stir well.

Garlic Roasted Beef

Prep time: 15 minutes **Cooking time:** 40 minutes
Servings: 2-4

Ingredients

2 tbsp. of minced garlic	7 oz. of mushrooms
1tsp. of garlic powder	1 tsp. of salt
1 tsp. of black pepper (ground)	1 tbsp. of extra-virgin olive oil
1cups of chicken stock	1 cup of chopped celery stalk
2yellow onions	
1 lb. of beef brisket	

Directions

Merge garlic powder, salt and ground black pepper together in a mixing bowl and stir. Rub the beef brisket with all the spice mixture. Set the pressure cooker to Sauté mode and place the beef brisket in the pressure cooker.

Sauté the meat for about 5 minutes on them, until golden brown. Add celery stalk. Peel the onions, chop vegetables, and slice mushrooms. Detach the beef brisket from the pressure cooker. Put the vegetables into pressure the cooker. Sprinkle the constituents with the organic olive oil and sauté for 10 minutes, stirring frequently. Add the chicken stock, garlic and beef brisket.

Close the pressure cooker lid and cook the dish on Keep Warm mode roughly for about 25 minutes. When the Cooking time ends, release pressure on the cooker and open the lid. Stir the amalgamation and Serve.

Pork Satay

Prep time: 10 minutes **Cooking time:** 25 minutes
Servings: 3-5

Ingredients

12 oz. of pork loin	3 tbsp. of apple cider vinegar treatment
1tbsp. of essential olive oil	
1 tbsp. of sesame oil	1/2 tsp. of red pepper cayenne
1 tsp. of turmeric	
1 tsp. of basil	1 tsp. of Erythritol
1 tsp. of cilantro	1 tsp. of soy sauce
11 tbsp. of fish sauce	

Directions

Chop the pork loin into medium-sized pieces. Place the pork loin in the mixing bowl.

Sprinkle the meat with apple cider vinegar, organic olive oil, sesame oil, turmeric, cayenne, cilantro, basil, Erythritol, soy sauce, and fish sauce, stir well. Thread the meat on the skewers. Set the strain cooker to Sauté mode. Place the skewers in the pressure cooker and Cook the pork satay for about 25 minutes. When cooked, transfer the satays to a wide bowl and allow them to rest before serving.

Beef with Horseradish

Prep time: 10 minutes **Cooking time:** 30 minutes
Servings: 4-6

Ingredients

5 oz. of horseradish	1 lb. of beef brisket
1cup of cream	1 tbsp. of thyme
1 tsp. of coriander	1/2 cup of chicken stock
1 tsp. of oregano	1 tbsp. of fresh dill
1 tsp. of salt	1garlic cloves
1 tbsp. of olive oil	

Directions

Chop the beef rump and sprinkle it with salt. Peel the onions and slice them. Mix the sliced onions with the extra virgin olive oil and stir well.

Mix the burgundy or merlot wine, bay leaves, black-eyed peas, groundginger thyme, red pepper cayenne, freshly squeezed lemon juice, cilantro, oregano, and minced garlic together in a mixing bowl. Set pressure cooker to Sauté mode and add the sliced onion mixture to pressure cooker and sauté for about 10 minutes, stirring frequently.

Add the chopped beef rump and allow it marinate for a handful of minutes. Stir well and close the strain cooker lid. Cook the dish on Sauté mode for about 40 minutes. When the Cooking time ends, open pressure cooker lid and stir again. Transfer the dish to serving bowls. **Serve:** immediately and Enjoy!

Turmeric Meatballs

Prep time: 10 minutes **Cooking time:** 10 minutes
Servings: 5-7

Ingredients

1tbsp. of turmeric	1 tsp. of ground ginger
1/2 tsp. of oregano	1 tsp. of minced garlic
1 tsp. of salt	1 zucchini
10 oz. of ground pork	1 tbsp. of organic olive oil
1 egg yolk	1 tsp. of cilantro

Directions

Mix the turmeric, ground ginger, salt, oregano, and cilantro in a mixing bowl and stir well. Add ground pork into the contents and stir again. Add the egg yolk and minced garlic. Chop the zucchini and transfer it to the blender. Blend the vegetable mixture until smooth. Add zucchini into the meat mixture and stir well. Make medium-sized meatballs from your meat mixture.

Set pressure to succeed cooker to Pressure mode. Pour the organic olive oil into the pressure cooker contents. Place the meatballs in the pressure cooker and close the lid. Cook for about 10 minutes. When the dish is cooked, release pressure and open the load cooker lid. Remove the meatballs and **Serve:**.

Meatballs Soup

Prep time: 10 minutes **Cooking time:** 15 minutes
Servings: 6- 8

Ingredients

7 oz. of ground pork
2carrot
A tbsp. of minced garlic
1 tsp. of ground black
pepper
1/2 cup of dill
An egg

1 tsp. of oregano
1 onion
6 cups of chicken stock
1 tsp. of paprika
1 tbsp. of flour

Directions

Skin the carrot and onion and chop them. Combine the vegetables together and transfer them into the pressure cooker. Set the load cooker to Pressure mode. Add chicken stock and paprika. Combine the soil pork, oregano, flour, and ground pork in a mixing bowl.

Beat the egg and pour them into the pork mixture. Stir the Ingredients carefully. Make small meatballs using the ground pork mixture place them in the pressure cooker.

Close the cooker lid and cook for about 14 minutes. Wash the dill and chop it. When the dish is cooked, ladle it into serving bowls. Sprinkle the soup with the dill and **Serve:**.

Pork Belly with Peanuts

Prep time: 10 minutes **Cooking time:** 25 minutes
Servings: 4- 6

Ingredients

5 oz. of peanut
1lb. of pork belly
1 tsp. of ground black
pepper
1 tbsp. of cilantro
1garlic cloves

1 cup of chicken stock
1 tbsp. of salt
1 tsp. of onion powder
1 tsp. of paprika
3tbsp. of fresh rosemary

Directions

Rub the pork belly with salt, ground black pepper, onion powder, paprika, and cilantro. Set pressure cooker to Pressure mode. Put the pork belly into the cooker followed by rosemary and chicken stock.

Close pressure cooker lid and cook for about 25 minutes. Crush the peanuts. When the **Cooking time:**ends, open pressure cooker lid and remove the pork belly. Dry the pork belly with a paper towel. After that, slice it and sprinkle crushed peanuts before serving.

Pork with Every One of the Almonds and Sage

Prep time: 15 minutes **Cooking time:** 40 minutes
Servings: 5-7

Ingredients

3 lb. of pork loin
3 tbsp. of sage
3 garlic cloves
1 tsp. of lemon zest
1 tbsp. of almond flakes
A cup of almond milk

3 carrots
5 tbsp. of chicken stock
5tbsp. of extra-virgin olive
oil
1 tbsp. of salt

Directions

Pat the pork loin with the sage and leave them to chill for about 10 minutes. Peel the garlic cloves and carrots. Cut the carrots into halves. Place the garlic cloves, halved carrots, and lemon zest into the pressure cooker.

Add the fundamental organic olive oil, almond milk, salt, and almond flakes. Set pressure cooker to Sauté mode.
Put the pork into pressure cooker and close its lid. Cook the dish on meat mode for about 40 minutes.

When the **Cooking time:**elapses, open the cooker and remove the pork. Allow the pork-meal to cool a bit. Slice it and **Serve:** while warm.

Rack of Lamb

Prep time: 15 minutes **Cooking time:** 25 minutes
Servings: 4-6

Ingredients

13 oz. of lamb rack
1tbsp. of Erythritol
A tsp. of ground black
pepper
3tbsp. of butter
1 tsp. of curry
1 tsp. of fresh rosemary

A cup of burgundy or
merlot wine
1 cup of chicken stock
1 onion
1 tbsp. of extra virgin
organic olive oil
1 tsp. of cilantro

Directions

Combine Erythritol, ground black pepper, cilantro, chicken stock, curry, and rosemary in a mixing bowl and stir.

Peel the onion and chop it. Add the chopped onion in the mixture and stir. Place the lamb rack chicken stock mixture and allow it to marinate for about 10 minutes Set pressure cooker to Pressure mode. Add the butter into pressure cooker and melt it. Add the marinated lamb rack and sprinkle it with curry.

Secure the lid and cook for about 25 minutes. When the **Cooking time:**elapses, remove your rack of lamb meal from the cooker. Allow it to cool before serving.

Glazed Sausage

Prep time: 10 minutes **Cooking time:** 15 minutes
Servings: 4-6

Ingredients

1 tbsp. of Erythritol
1 tbsp. of butter
1 lb. of ground pork
1 tbsp. of liquid stevia
1 tsp. of oregano
1 tsp. of water

1 tbsp. of coconut flour
6 oz. of ground chicken
1 tbsp. of salt
1 tsp. of cilantro
1 onion
1 tbsp. of ground black pepper

Directions

Peel the onion and grate it. Pour the grated onion, ground pork, ground chicken, salt, oregano, cilantro, and ground black pepper in a mixing bowl. Add the coconut flour and mix well. Combine liquid stevia, Erythritol, and water in another bowl.

Stir the mixture well to dissolve Erythritol, make medium-sized sausages patties from the meat mixture. Set the pressure cooker to Sauté mode. Add the butter into the cooker and allow it melt. Pour the sausage patties into the pressure cooker and sauté the patties for about 4 minutes.

Sprinkle the sausage patties with liquid stevia mixture and close the lid. Cook the dish for another 10 minutes on Sauté mode. When the **Cooking time:**ends, remove the cooked sausage patties from pressure cooker and **Serve:**.

Roast Lamb Shoulder

Prep time: 10 minutes **Cooking time:** 60 minutes
Serving 2

Ingredients

1 lb. boneless lamb shoulder roast
4 cloves garlic, minced
3 tablespoon olive oil, divided Salt
2 lb. baby potatoes halved

1 tablespoon rosemary, chopped
2 teaspoon thyme leaves
Black pepper

Directions

Toss potatoes with all the herbs, seasonings, and oil in a baking tray. Choose "Power Button" of Air Fry Oven and turn the dial to select the "Air Roast" mode.

Choose the Time button and again turn the dial to set the Cooking time to 60 minutes.

Now rest the Temp button and rotate the dial to set the temperature at 370 degrees F. Once preheated, set the lamb baking tray in the oven and close its lid. Slice and **Serve:** warm.

Ginger Pork Chops

Prep time: 10 minutes **Cooking time:** 35 minutes
Servings: 3-5

Ingredients

2 tbsp. of ground ginger
1 lb. of pork chop
1 tsp. of ground black pepper
1 tsp. of garlic powder

1 cup of soy sauce
1 tsp. of parsley
1 tbsp. of freshly-squeezed lemon juice
1 cup of water

Directions

Combine the soy sauce and water in a mixing bowl. Add fresh lemon juice and mix.

Sprinkle the mixture with ground ginger, parsley, ground black pepper, and garlic powder. Add freshly squeezed lemon juice and stir well.

Cut the pork chop roughly using a sharp object. Put the pork on the soy sauce mixture and allow it to sit for about 15 minutes.

Set pressure cooker to Sauté mode. Place the amalgamation into the cooker and close its lid. Cook the dish for about 35 minutes. When cooked, open pressure cooker lid and **Serve:** the ginger pork chops while hot.

Salisbury Steak

Prep time: 10 minutes **Cooking time:** 15 minutes
Servings: 3-5

Ingredients

1/2 cup of onion soup mix
A cup of water
1 lb. of ground beef
A tsp. of ground white pepper

2 eggs
1 tsp. of tomato paste
A tbsp. of mustard
1 tsp. of salt
1 tbsp. of extra virgin organic olive oil

Directions

Whisk the eggs in the mixing bowl and whisk them. Add the mustard, salt, and ground white pepper, stir well until smooth. Dip the beef in the egg mixture and ensure it mixes well. Make mid-sized balls from the meat mixture and flatten them.

Set the pressure cooker to Sauté mode and pour the olive oil into pressure and preheat it in sauté mode. Add the steaks and sauté the dish for 2 minutes on both sides. Combine the tomato paste and onion soup together and stir well.

Pour the soup mixture to the pressure cooker and close the lid. Cook the dish on Pressure mode for about 5 minutes. When the **Cooking time:**elapses, remove Salisbury steak from the pressure cooker and **Serve:** with gravy.

Pork Chili

Prep time: 15 minutes **Cooking time:** 45 minutes
Servings: 6-8

Ingredients

1cup of black soybeans
10 oz. of ground pork
Λ tsp. of cilantro
1 tsp. of oregano
1 tsp. of tomato paste
3carrots

1 cup of chicken stock
1 tbsp. of butter
1 cup of chopped bok
choy 1/4 cup of green
beans 3**Servings:** of water
2red onions
Λ tbsp. of salt

Directions

Combine the ground pork with tomato paste, butter, cilantro, and oregano, and salt, stirs well.
Set pressure cooker to Sauté mode and add the ground pork mixture.

Sauté the mixture for about 2 minutes while stirring frequently. Add the green beans and water; peel the carrots and red onions. Chop the vegetables and add them in to the pressure cooker.

Sprinkle the stew mixture with bok choy, and stir. Close pressure cooker lid and cook the dish on Pressure mode for about 40 minutes.

When the **Cooking time:**elapses, open the pressure cooker lid and mix the chili well. Transfer the pork chili to serving bowls.

Marinated Pork Steak

Prep time: 20 minutes **Cooking time:** 25 minutes
Servings: 4-6

Ingredients

1/4 cup of beer
1tsp. of cayenne pepper
1 tsp. of cilantro
1 tsp. of oregano
1 tbsp. of salt

¼ cup of virgin olive oil
1 onion
1 tsp. of ground black
pepper
1 lb. of pork tenderloin

Directions

Combine the red pepper cayenne, extra virgin organic olive oil, cilantro, oregano, salt, and ground black pepper together in a mixing bowl.

Peel the onion and grind it. Add the onion to the spice contents and mix it until smooth, add beer and stir well. Dip the pork tenderloin in the beer mixture and allow it to marinate for at least 10 minutes. Set pressure cooker to Pressure mode.

Transfer the marinated meat to the pressure cooker and cook for about 25 minutes. When the Cooking time ends, release the cooker's pressure and open its lid. Remove the cooked meat from the cooker and **Serve:**.

Lamb Estrada's

Prep time: 15 minutes **Cooking time:** 25 minutes
Servings: 3-5

Ingredients

2 onions
1 tbsp. of extra virgin
essential olive oil
1 tsp. of oregano
1lb. of lamb
1/4 cup of burgundy or
merlot wine
1 tsp. of apple cider
vinegar

1 tbsp. of paprika
1 tbsp. of cilantro
1/2 tsp. of bay leaf
1 tbsp. of sea salt
1/4 chili
1 tsp. of black-eyed peas

Directions

Chop the lamb roughly and combine the chopped lamb with oregano, cilantro, sea salt, chili, red, apple cider vinegar treatment, and black- eyed peas in a mixing bowl and stir well. Let the mixture sit. Peel the onions and blend well using a blender.

Take the chopped meat and hang with wooden skewers. Spread the meat with the blended onion. Preheat pressure cooker on Sauté mode for about 3 minutes. Place the lamb skewers in the pressure cooker and sprinkle the meat with olive oil.

Secure the lid and cook for about 25 minutes. When your lamp espetadas is cooked, remove it from the pressure cooker and allow it to cool before serving.

Onion Lamb Kebabs

Prep time: 10 minutes **Cooking time:** 20 minutes
Serving 4

Ingredients

18 oz. lamb kebab
1teaspoon chili powder
2oz. onion, chopped

1 teaspoon cumin powder
1 egg
2teaspoon sesame oil

Directions

Whisk onion with egg, chili powder, oil, cumin powder, and salt in a bowl. Add lamb to coat well then thread it on the skewers. Place these lamb skewers in the Air fryer basket.

Choose "Power Button" of Air Fry Oven and turn the dial to select the "Air Fry" mode. Choose the Time button and again turn the dial to set the **Cooking time:**to 20 minutes.

Now press the Temp button and rotate the dial to set the temperature at 395 degrees F. Once preheated, place the Air fryer basket in the oven and close its lid. Slice and **Serve:** warm.

Lamb Cutlets

Prep time: 10 minutes **Cooking time:** 12 minutes
Servings: 3-5

Ingredients

14 oz. of ground lamb
2 white onions
1 tbsp. of salt
1/2 tsp. of ground rosemary
1 cup of fresh basil
1/4 tsp. of sage
1 egg

1tsp. of ground black pepper
1 tsp. of cilantro
1 tsp. of organic essential olive oil
1 tsp. of minced garlic
1 tsp. of paprika

Directions

Combine the ground lamb, ground black pepper, egg, salt, cilantro, ground rosemary, minced garlic, and paprika in a mixing bowl and stir well.

Peel the onions and dice them. Add the diced onion on the ground lamb mixture and stir well. Chop the basil and pour sage over it. Set pressure cooker to Sauté mode. Pour the virgin organic olive oil in to the pressure cooker and add basil mixture.

Sauté the amalgamation for about 2 minutes while stirring frequently. Remove the basil mixture from the cooker. Make medium-sized cutlets from the lamb mixture and hang them in the pressure cooker. Cook the cutlets for about 10 minutes or until golden brown on both sides. Remove the lamb cutlets from the cooker and allow it to cool before serving.

Lamb with Thyme

Prep time: 10 minutes **Cooking time:** 45 minutes
Servings: 6-8

Ingredients

1cup of fresh thyme
1 tbsp. of turmeric
1 tsp. of oregano
1lb. of lamb
1/4 cup of rice wine
1 tsp. of Erythritol
1/4 cup of chicken stock

1 tbsp. of essential olive oil
1 tbsp. of ground black pepper
4tbsp. of butter
1 tsp. of paprika

Directions

Chop the fresh thyme and mix it with oregano, ground black pepper, paprika, rice wine, Erythritol, chicken stock, and turmeric.

Sprinkle the lamb with the spice mixture and stir it carefully. Transfer the lamb mixture to a pressure cooker and add olive oil.

Close the pressure cooker lid and cook the dish on meat mode for about 45 minutes. When the lamb meal is cooked remove it from the pressure cooker. Allow it to rest and slice it. Enjoy!

Lamb Chops with Rosemary Sauce

Prep time: 10 minutes **Cooking time:** 52 minutes
Serving 8

Ingredients

8 lamb loin chops
Salt & black pepper to taste
For the sauce
1 tablespoon rosemary leaves
1 oz. plain flour
6 fl. oz. vegetable stock
2tablespoons cream, whipping

1small onion, peeled and chopped
1 onion, peeled and chopped
1 oz. butter
6 fl. oz. milk
Salt and black pepper, to taste

Directions

Place the lamb loin chops, and onion in a baking tray, then drizzle salt and black pepper on top. Choose "Power Button" of Air Fry Oven and turn the dial to select the "Bake" mode. Choose the Time button and again turn the dial to set the **Cooking time:**to 45 minutes.

Now press the Temp button and rotate the dial to set the temperature at 350 degrees F. Once preheated, set the lamb baking tray in the oven and close its lid.

Set the white sauce by melting butter in a saucepan the sti in onions Sauté for 5 minutes, then stir flour and stir cook for 2 minutes. Stir in the rest of the ingredients and mix well. Pour the sauce over baked chops and **Serve:**.

Garlicky Lamb Chops

Prep time: 10 minutes **Cooking time:** 45 minutes
Serving 8

Ingredients

8 medium lamb chops
2 garlic cloves, crushed
1teaspoon dried oregano
1 teaspoon salt

3 thin lemon slices
1/2 teaspoon black pepper
1/4 cup olive oil

Directions

Set the medium lamb chops in a baking tray and rub them with olive oil. Attach lemon slices, garlic, oregano, salt, and black pepper on top of the lamb chops.

Choose "Power Button" of Air Fry Oven and turn the dial to select the "Air Roast" mode. Choose the Time button and again turn the dial to set the **Cooking time:**to 45 minutes.

Now press the Temp button and rotate the dial to set the temperature at 400 degrees F. Once preheated, set the lamb baking tray in the oven and close its lid. Slice and **Serve:** warm.

New England Lamb

Prep time: 10 minutes **Cooking time:** 60 minutes
Serving 6

Ingredients

2 tablespoon canola oil	2 lbs. boneless leg of lamb,
1 onion, chopped	diced
2 leeks white portion only,	2 tablespoons minced
sliced	fresh parsley, divided
2 carrots, sliced	1/2 teaspoon dried
3 potatoes, peeled and	rosemary, crushed
sliced	
1/2 teaspoon salt	1/4 teaspoon black pepper
3 tablespoons butter,	1/4 teaspoon dried thyme,
melted	crushed

Directions

Toss the lamb cubes with all the veggies, oil, and seasonings in a baking tray. Choose "Power Button" of Air Fry Oven and turn the dial to select the "Air Roast" mode.

Choose the Time button and again turn the dial to set the **Cooking time:** to 60 minutes. Now press the Temp button and rotate the dial to set the temperature at 350 degrees F. Once preheated, set the lamb baking tray in the oven and close its lid. Slice and **Serve:** warm.

Zucchini Lamb Meatballs

Prep time: 10 minutes **Cooking time:** 15 minutes
Serving 4

Ingredients

1 lb. ground lamb avocado	1/2 tablespoon garlic ghee
oil spray	1 red bell pepper diced
1/3 cup red onion diced	1/3 cup cilantro diced
1/3 cup zucchini diced	1 tablespoon gyro
	seasoning
1/2 teaspoon cumin	1/2 teaspoon coriander
2 garlic cloves minced	Salt and black pepper to
1/2 teaspoon turmeric	taste

Directions

Mix the lamb minced with all the meatball Ingredients in a bowl. Do small meatballs out of this mixture and place them in the Air fryer basket. Choose "Power Button" of Air Fry Oven and turn the dial to select the "Air Fry" mode.

Choose the Time button and again turn the dial to set the **Cooking time:** to 15 minutes. Now press the Temp button and rotate the dial to set the temperature at 370 degrees F.
Once preheated, place the Air fryer basket in the oven and close its lid. Slice and **Serve:** warm.

Mint Lamb with Roasted Hazelnuts

Prep time: 10 minutes **Cooking time:** 25 minutes
Serving 2

Ingredients

1/4 cup hazelnuts, toasted	2/3 lb. shoulder of lamb
1 tablespoon hazelnut oil	cut into strips
2 tablespoon fresh mint	1/4 cup of water
leaves chopped	1/2 cup white wine
Salt and black pepper to	1/2 cup frozen peas
taste	

Directions

Toss lamb with hazelnuts, spices, and all the Ingredients in a baking pan. Choose "Power Button" of Air Fry Oven and turn the dial to select the "Bake" mode.

Choose the Time button and again turn the dial to set the **Cooking time:** to 25 minutes. Now press the Temp button and rotate the dial to set the temperature at 370 degrees F.

Once preheated, place the baking pan in the oven and close its lid. Slice and **Serve:** warm.

Lamb Rack with Lemon Crust

Prep time: 10 minutes **Cooking time:** 25 minutes Serving 5

Ingredients

1.7 lbs. frenched rack of	1/2 teaspoon salt
lamb	Salt and black pepper, to
0.13-lb. dry breadcrumbs	taste
1 teaspoon cumin seeds	1/2 teaspoon Grated
1 teaspoon ground cumin	lemon rind
1 teaspoon oil	1 egg, beaten
1 teaspoon grated garlic	

Directions

Place the lamb rack in a baking tray and pour the whisked egg on top. Whisk rest of the crusting Ingredients in a bowl and spread over the lamb.

Choose "Power Button" of Air Fry Oven and turn the dial to select the "Air Fry" mode.
Choose the Time button and again turn the dial to set the **Cooking time:** to 25 minutes.

Now press the Temp button and rotate the dial to set the temperature at 350 degrees F. Once preheated, set the lamb baking tray in the oven and close its lid. Slice and **Serve:** warm.

Braised Lamb Shanks

Prep time: 10 minutes **Cooking time:** 20 minutes
Serving 4

Ingredients

4 lamb shanks	1/2 teaspoon black
11/2 teaspoons salt	pepper 4 garlic cloves, crushed
2 tablespoons olive oil	4 to 6 sprigs fresh rosemary
2 tablespoons balsamic vinegar	3 cups beef broth, divided

Directions

Place the sham shanks in a baking pan. Whisk rest of the Ingredients in a bowl and pour over the shanks. Place these shanks in the Air fryer basket.

Choose "Power Button" of Air Fry Oven and turn the dial to select the "Air Fry" mode. Choose the Time button and again turn the dial to set the **Cooking time:**to 20 minutes.

Now press the Temp button and rotate the dial to set the temperature at 360 degrees F.Once preheated, place the Air fryer basket in the oven and close its lid. Slice and **Serve:** warm.

Za'atar Lamb Chops

Prep time: 10 minutes **Cooking time:** 10 minutes
Serving 8

Ingredients

8 lamb loin chops, bone-in	1/2 fresh lemon
3 garlic cloves, crushed	1teaspoon olive oil
1 1/4 teaspoon salt	Black pepper, to taste
1 tablespoon Za'atar	

Directions

Rub the lamb chops with oil, zaatar, salt, lemon juice, garlic, and black pepper. Place these chops in the Air fryer basket.

Choose "Power Button" of Air Fry Oven and turn the dial to select the "Air Fry" mode. Choose the Time button and again turn the dial to set the **Cooking time:**to 10 minutes.

Now press the Temp button and rotate the dial to set the temperature at 400 degrees F. Once preheated, place the air fryer basket in the oven and close its lid. Flip the chops when cooked halfway through then resume cooking. **Serve:** warm.

Lamb Sirloin Steak

Prep time: 10 minutes **Cooking time:** 15 minutes
Serving 2

Ingredients

1/2 onion	4 slices ginger
5 cloves garlic	1 teaspoon fennel, ground
1 teaspoon cinnamon ground	1 teaspoon salt
1 teaspoon cayenne	1teaspoon garam masala
1-lb. boneless lamb sirloin steaks	1/2 teaspoon cardamom ground

Directions

In a blender, jug adds all the Ingredients except the chops.
Rub the chops with this blended mixture and marinate for 30 minutes. Transfer the chops to the Air fryer basket.

Choose "Power Button" of Air Fry Oven and turn the dial to select the "Air Fry" mode. Choose the Time button and again turn the dial to set the **Cooking time:**to 15 minutes.

Now press the Temp button and rotate the dial to set the temperature at 330 degrees F. Once preheated, place the Air fryer basket in the oven and close its lid. Flip the chops when cooked halfway through then resume cooking. **Serve:** warm.

Lemony Lamb Chops

Prep time: 10 minutes **Cooking time:** 25 minutes
Serving 2

Ingredients

2 medium lamb chops	1/4 cup lemon juice

Directions

Liberally rub the lamb chops with lemon juice. Place the lemony chops in the Air fryer basket.

Choose "Power Button" of Air Fry Oven and turn the dial to select the "Air Fry" mode. Choose the Time button and again turn the dial to set the **Cooking time:**to 25 minutes.

Now press the Temp button and rotate the dial to set the temperature at 350 degrees F. Once preheated, place the Air fryer basket in the oven and close its lid.

Flip the chops when cooked halfway through then resume cooking. **Serve:** warm.

Garlicky Rosemary Lamb Chops

Prep time: 10 minutes **Cooking time:** 12 minutes
Serving 4

Ingredients

4 lamb chops	2 teaspoon olive oil
1teaspoon fresh rosemary	2teaspoon garlic puree Salt
2garlic cloves, minced	and black pepper

Directions

Place lamb chops in the Air fryer basket. Rub them with olive oil, rosemary, garlic, garlic puree, salt, and black pepper

Choose "Power Button" of Air Fry Oven and turn the dial to select the "Air Fry" mode. Choose the Time button and again turn the dial to set the **Cooking time:**to 12 minutes.

Now press the Temp button and rotate the dial to set the temperature at 350 degrees F.

Once preheated, place the Air fryer basket in the oven and close its lid. Flip the chops when cooked halfway through then resume cooking. **Serve:** warm.

Lamb Tomato Bake

Prep time: 10 minutes **Cooking time:** 35 minutes
Serving 6

Ingredients

25 oz. potatoes, boiled	Sauce
14 oz. lean lamb mince	1teaspoon cinnamon
12 oz. white sauce	1 tablespoon olive oil
23 oz. jar tomato pasta	

Directions

Mash the potatoes in a bowl and stir in white sauce and cinnamon. Sauté lamb mince with olive oil in a frying pan until brown.

Layer a casserole dish with tomato pasta sauce. Top the sauce with lamb mince. Spread the potato mash over the lamb in an even layer.

Choose "Power Button" of Air Fry Oven and turn the dial to select the "Bake" mode. Choose the Time button and again turn the dial to set the **Cooking time:**to 35 minutes.

Now press the Temp button and rotate the dial to set the temperature at 350 degrees F. Once preheated, place casserole dish in the oven and close its lid. **Serve:** warm.

Lamb Potato Chips Baked

Prep time: 10 minutes **Cooking time:** 25 minutes
Serving 4

Ingredients

1/2 lb. minced lamb	1 pinch salt and black
1tbs. parsley chopped	pepper
2teaspoon curry powder	1 lb. potato cooked, mashed
1 ½ oz.potato chips crushed	1 oz. cheese grated

Directions

Mix lamb, curry powder, seasoning and parsley. Spread this lamb mixture in a casserole dish.

Top the lamb mixture with potato mash, cheese, and potato chips. Choose "Power Button" of Air Fry Oven and turn the dial to select the "Bake" mode.

Choose the Time button and again turn the dial to set the **Cooking time:**to 20 minutes.

Now press the Temp button and rotate the dial to set the temperature at 350 degrees F. Once preheated, place casserole dish in the oven and close its lid. **Serve:** warm.

Reuben Egg Rolls

Prep time: 10 minutes **Cooking time:** 5 minutes
Serving 4-6

Ingredients

Swiss cheese Can of sauerkraut	Sliced deli corned beef
Egg roll wrappers	

Directions

Cut corned beef and Swiss cheese into thin slices. Drain sauerkraut and dry well. Take egg roll wrapper and moisten edges with water. Stack center with corned beef and cheese till you reach desired thickness. Top off with sauerkraut.

Fold corner closest to you over the edge of filling. Bring up sides and glue with water. Add to air fryer basket and spritz with olive oil. Cook 4 minutes at 400 degrees, then flip and cook another 4 minutes.

Greek Macaroni Bake

Prep time: 10 minutes **Cooking time:** 46 minutes
Serving 6

Ingredients

1 tablespoon olive oil
1 garlic cloves, minced
1 lb. lean lamb mince
1 beef or lamb stock cube
1 tablespoon dried
oregano 14 oz. macaroni,
boiled
2 tablespoons parmesan,
grated

1 large onion, chopped
finely
1 teaspoon ground
cinnamon
9 Oz. tub ricotta
2 cups tomatoes chopped

bread, to **Serve:** optional
2 tablespoons milk

Directions

Sauté onion with oil in a frying pan for 10 minutes.
Stir in garlic and cook for 1 minute, then remove it
from the heat.

Toss lamb mince then sauté until brown.
Stir in cinnamon, tomatoes, oregano, and stock cubes.
Cook this mixture on a simmer for 15 minutes.

Meanwhile, blend ricotta with parmesan, milk and
garlic in a blender. Spread the lamb tomatoes mixture
in a casserole dish and top it with ricotta mixture.

Choose "Power Button" of Air Fry Oven and turn the
dial to select the "Bake" mode. Choose the Time
button and again turn the dial to set the **Cooking
time:** to 30 minutes. Now press the Temp button and
rotate the dial to set the temperature at 350 degrees F.

Once preheated, place casserole dish in the oven and
close its lid. **Serve:** warm.

Air Fryer Burgers

Prep time: 10 minutes **Cooking time:** 10 minutes
Serving 4

Ingredients

1 pound lean ground beef
1 tsp. dried parsley
1/2 tsp. salt
Few drops of liquid
smoke

1/2 tsp. dried oregano
1/2 tsp. pepper
1/2 tsp. onion powder
1 tsp. Worcestershire sauce

Directions

Ensure your air fryer is preheated to 350 degrees. Mix
all seasonings together till combined.

Place beef in a bowl and add seasonings. Mix well, but
do not over mix. Make 4 patties from the mixture and
using your thumb, making an indent in the center of
each patty.
Add patties to air fryer basket and cook 10 minutes.
No need to turn!

Greek lamb Farfalle

Prep time: 10 minutes **Cooking time:** 20 minutes
Serving 4

Ingredients

1 tablespoon olive oil
2 garlic cloves, finely
chopped
1 lb. pack lamb
mince
1/2 cup frozen spinach,
defrosted
1 ball half-fat
mozzarella, torn

1 onion, finely chopped
2 teaspoon dried oregano
1/4 cup pitted black olives
3/4 lb. tin chopped
tomatoes
2 tablespoons dill, stems
removed and chopped
9 Oz. farfalle, boiled

Directions

Sauté onion and garlic with oil in a pan over moderate
heat for 5 minutes. Stir in tomatoes, spinach, dill,
lamb, and olives, then stir cook for 5 minutes.

Spread the lamb in a casserole dish and toss in the
pasta.
Top the pasta lamb mix with mozzarella cheese.
Choose "Power Button" of Air Fry Oven and turn the
dial to select the "Bake" mode.

Choose the Time button and again turn the dial to set
the **Cooking time:** to 10 minutes. Now press the
Temp button and rotate the dial to set the temperature
at 350 degrees F.
Once preheated, place casserole dish in the oven and
close its lid. **Serve:** warm.

Beef Empanadas

Prep time: 10 minutes **Cooking time:** 15 minutes
Serving 8

Ingredients

1 tsp. water
1 egg white

1 C. picadillo
8 Goya empanada discs
(thawed)

Directions

Ensure your air fryer is preheated to 325. Spray basket
with olive oil. Place 2 tablespoons of picadillo into the
center of each disc. Set disc in half and use a fork to
seal edges. Repeat with all Ingredients.

Whisk egg white with water and brush tops of
empanadas with egg wash. Add 2-3 empanadas to air
fryer, cooking 8 minutes until golden. Repeat till you
cook all filled empanadas.

Lamb Orzo Bake

Prep time: 10 minutes **Cooking time:** 2hr. 15 minutes
Serving 6

Ingredients

Lamb	1tablespoon olive oil
1 2/3 lbs. lamb shoulder, diced	2teaspoon dried oregano and thyme
2onions, chopped	1 teaspoon dried mint
2bay leaves	1/2 tbsp ground cumin
14 oz. tin cherry tomatoes	1 tbs smoked paprika
1cups vegetable stock, hot	Pasta
2 1/2 oz. peppered peppers halved	2 1/2 0z. pitted kalamata olives halved
2oz. orzo pasta	2 oz. sun-blushed tomatoes, chopped
1/4 cup feta, crumbled	
Finely grated zest 1 lemon	

Directions

Rub the lamb shoulder with all its seasonings and oil. Place the lamb should in a baking tray. Choose "Power Button" of Air Fry Oven and turn the dial to select the "Bake" mode. Choose the Time button and again turn the dial to set the Cooking time to 1 hr. 45 minutes.

Now press the Temp button and rotate the dial to set the temperature at 350 degrees F. Once preheated, set the lamb baking tray in the oven and close its lid. Meanwhile, cook orzo, with hot stock, peppers, tomatoes, olives, salt and black pepper in a cooking pot for 30 minutes. **Serve:** the lamb with orzo.

Herbed Roast Beef

Prep time: 10 minutes **Cooking time:** 15 minutes
Serving 10-12

Ingredients

1/2 tsp. fresh rosemary	1/4 tsp. pepper
4-pound top round roast beef	1tsp. dried thyme
2tsp. olive oil	1 tsp. salt

Directions

Ensure your air fryer is preheated to 360 degrees. Rub olive oil all over beef. Mix rosemary, thyme, pepper, and salt together and proceed to rub all sides of beef with spice mixture.

Place seasoned beef into air fryer and cook 20 minutes.
Allow roast to rest 10 minutes before slicing to **Serve:**.

Minced Lamb Casserole

Prep time: 10 minutes **Cooking time:** 30 minutes
Serving 4

Ingredients

2 tablespoons olive oil	4 fresh mushrooms, sliced
1medium onion, chopped	2cups bottled marinara sauce
1/2 lb. ground lamb	1 egg, beaten
1 teaspoon butter	1 cup small pasta shells, cooked
4teaspoons flour	
1 cup milk	
1 cup cheddar cheese, grated	

Directions

Put a wok on moderate heat and add oil to heat. Toss in onion and sauté until soft. Stir in mushrooms and lamb, and then cook until meat is brown. Add marinara sauce and cook it to a simmer.

Stir in pasta then spread this mixture in a casserole dish.
Set the sauce by melting butter in a saucepan over moderate heat. Stir in flour and whisk well, pour in the milk. Mix well and whisk 1/4 cup sauce with egg then return it to the saucepan.

Stir cook for 1 minute then pour this sauce over the lamb.
Drizzle cheese over the lamb casserole. Choose "Power Button" of Air Fry Oven and turn the dial to select the "Bake" mode. Choose the Time button and again turn the dial to set the **Cooking time:**to 30 minutes.

Now press the Temp button and rotate the dial to set the temperature at 350 degrees F. Once preheated, place casserole dish in the oven and close its lid. **Serve:** warm.

Beef Taco Fried Egg Rolls

Prep time: 10 minutes **Cooking time:** 15 minutes
Serving 8

Ingredients

1tsp. cilantro	1chopped garlic cloves
1 C. shredded Mexican cheese	1/2 can cilantro lime rote
	1/2 chopped onion
1/2 packet taco seasoning	1 tbsp. olive oil
16 egg roll wrappers	1 pound lean ground beef

Directions

Ensure that your air fryer is preheated to 400 degrees. Add onions and garlic to a skillet, cooking till fragrant. Then add taco seasoning, pepper, salt, and beef, cooking till beef is broke up into tiny pieces and cooked thoroughly. Add rotel and stir well.

Lay out egg wrappers and brush with water to soften a bit.
Load wrappers with beef filling and add cheese to each.
Fold diagonally to close and use water to secure edges.
Brush filled egg wrappers with olive oil and add to the air fryer. Cook 8 minutes, flip, and cook another 4 minutes.
Serve:d sprinkled with cilantro.

Lamb Baked with Tomato Topping

Prep time: 10 minutes **Cooking time:** 1hr 40 minutes
Serving 8

Ingredients

8 lamb shoulder chops, trimmed	1tablespoon olive oil
	1/4 cup plain flour
1 large brown onion, chopped	2medium carrots, peeled and diced
2garlic cloves, crushed	2 tablespoons tomato paste
2 1/2 cups beef stock	1 cup frozen peas
2cups potato gems	2 dried bay leaves

Directions

Dust the lamb chops with flour and sear it in a pan layered with olive oil. Sear the lamb chops for 4 minutes per side. Transfer the chops to a baking tray.

Add onion, garlic, and carrot to the same pan. Sauté for 5 minutes, then stir in tomato paste, stock and all other Ingredients. Stir cook for 4 minutes then pour this sauce over the chops.

Choose "Power Button" of Air Fry Oven and turn the dial to select the "Bake" mode. Choose the Time button and again turn the dial to set the **Cooking time:**to 1 hr. 30 minutes. Now press the Temp button and rotate the dial to set the temperature at 350 degrees F. Once preheated, place the baking pan in the oven and close its lid. **Serve:** warm.

Pub Style Corned Beef Egg Rolls

Prep time: 10 minutes **Cooking time:** 5 minutes
Serving 10

Ingredients

Olive oil	1/2 C. orange marmalade
4 C. corned beef and cabbage	10 egg roll wrappers
	Brandy Mustard Sauce
1egg	1/16th tsp. pepper
1tbsp. whole grain mustard 1 tsp. dry mustard powder	1/2 C. chicken stock
	1/4 C. brandy
1 C. heavy cream	5 slices of Swiss cheese
1/4 tsp. curry powder	1 minced shallot
1/2 tbsp. cilantro	3/4 C. dry white wine
2tbsp. ghee	

Directions

To make mustard sauce, add shallots and ghee to skillet, cooking until softened. Then add brandy and wine, heating to a low boil. Cook 5 minutes for liquids to reduce. Add stock and seasonings. Simmer 5 minutes.
Turn down heat and add heavy cream. Cook on low till sauce reduces and it covers the back of a spoon. Place sauce in the fridge to chill.

Crack the egg in a bowl and set to the side. Lay out an egg wrapper with the corner towards you. Brush the edges with egg wash. Place 1/3 cup of corned beef mixture into the center along with 2 tablespoons of marmalade and 1/2 a slice of Swiss cheese.

Fold the bottom corner over filling. As you are folding the sides, make sure they are stick well to the first flap you made. Place filled rolls into prepared air fryer basket. Spritz rolls with olive oil. Cook 10 minutes at 390 degrees, shaking halfway through cooking. **Serve:** rolls with Brandy Mustard sauce and devour!

Roasted Stuffed Peppers

Prep time: 10 minutes **Cooking time:** 5 minutes
Serving 4

Ingredients

4 ounces shredded cheddar cheese	1/2 tsp. salt
	1/2 tsp. pepper
1tsp. Worcestershire sauce	1/2 C. tomato sauce
8 ounces lean ground beef	1 tsp. olive oil
1 minced garlic clove	1/2 chopped onion
2green peppers	

Directions

Ensure your air fryer is preheated to 390 degrees. Spray with olive oil. Cut stems off bell peppers and remove seeds. Cook in boiling salted water for 3 minutes.
Sauté garlic and onion together in a skillet until golden in color. Take skillet off the heat. Mix pepper, salt,

Air Fryer Beef Steak

Prep time: 10 minutes **Cooking time:** 17 minutes
Serving 4

Ingredients

1tbsp. olive oil Pepper and   1pounds of rib eye steak
salt

Directions

Flavor meat on both sides with pepper and salt.
Massage all sides of meat with olive oil.
Preheat air fryer to 356 degrees and spritz with olive oil.
Cook steak 7 minutes. Flip and cook an additional 6
minutes. Let meat sit 2-5 minutes to rest. Slice and **Serve:**
with salad.

Beef and Broccoli

Prep time: 10 minutes **Cooking time:** 10 minutes
Serving 4

Ingredients

1minced garlic clove	1 tsp. almond flour
1 tbsp. olive oil	1 sliced ginger root
1 tsp. sweetener of choice	1 tsp. low-sodium soy sauce
2tsp. sesame oil	1 pounds of broccoli
1/3 C. oyster sauce	1/3 C. sherry
3/4 pound round steak	

Directions

Remove stems from broccoli and slice into florets.
Slice steak into thin strips.

Combine sweetener, soy sauce, sherry, almond flour,
sesame oil, and oyster sauce together, stirring till
sweetener dissolves.

Put strips of steak into the mixture and allow to
marinate 45 minutes to 2 hours. Add broccoli and
marinated steak to air fryer. Place garlic, ginger, and
olive oil on top. Cook 12 minutes at 400 degrees.
Serve: with cauliflower rice!

Air Fryer Beef Fajitas

Prep time: 10 minutes **Cooking time:** 5 minutes
Serving 4-6

Ingredients

Beef	1/8 C. carne aside
Fajita veggies	1tsp. chili powder
2 pounds beef flap meat	1-2 tsp. pepper
Diet 7-Up	1 onion
1-2 tsp. salt	2 bell peppers

Directions

Slice flap meat into manageable pieces and place into a
bowl. Season meat with carne seasoning and pour diet
soda over meat. Cover and chill overnight. Ensure
your air fryer is preheated to 380 degrees.

Place a parchment liner into air fryer basket and spray
with olive oil. Place beef in layers into the basket.
Cook 8-10 minutes. Remove and set to the side.

Juicy Tender Pork Chops

Prep time: 10 minutes **Cooking time:** 12 minutes
Serve: 4

Ingredients

4 pork chops, boneless	½ tsp garlic powder
1 tsp chili powder	2 tbsp brown sugar
Salt	Pepper

Directions

Preheat the air fryer to 400 F. In a small bowl, mix
together brown sugar, chili powder, garlic powder,
pepper, and salt and rub all over pork chops.

Place pork chops into the air fryer basket and cook for
12 minutes. Turn halfway through. **Serve:** and enjoy.

Meatballs

Prep time: 10 minutes **Cooking time:** 12 minutes
Serve: 6

Ingredients

1 egg	½ lb. ground pork
½ tsp onion powder	½ tsp Italian seasoning
1 tbsp parmesan cheese, grated	2 tbsp milk
	1 lb. ground beef
2 tbsp fresh mint, chopped	2 tbsp parsley, chopped
1/3 cup breadcrumbs	Salt
Pepper	

Directions

Preheat the air fryer to 380 F. Add ground meat and
remaining Ingredients into the mixing bowl and mix
until well combined. Make small balls from the meat
mixture and place into the air fryer basket and cook
for 10-12 minutes. **Serve:** and enjoy.

Moist & Tender Ham

Prep time: 10 minutes **Cooking time:** 35 minutes
Serve: 4

Ingredients

3 lbs. cooked ham For glaze	1 tsp dry mustard
1 tbsp pineapple juice	1 tbsp honey
	2 tbsp brown sugar

Directions

Preheat the air fryer to 320 F. Wrap ham in aluminum foil and place into the air fryer basket and cook for 25 minutes. In a small bowl, mix together pineapple juice, brown sugar, honey, and mustard.

After 25 minutes brush ham with glaze and cook for 10-15 minutes more. Slice and **Serve:**.

Juicy Pork Tenderloin

Prep time: 10 minutes **Cooking time:** 18 minutes
Serve: 4

Ingredients

1 ½ lbs. pork tenderloin	½ tsp Italian seasoning
1 tbsp balsamic vinegar	Salt
1 tsp Dijon mustard	1 tsp olive oil
Pepper	

Directions

Preheat the air fryer to 400 F. In a small bowl, mix together mustard, vinegar, Italian seasoning, pepper, and salt.

Brush pork tenderloin with oil and rub with mustard mixture. Place pork tenderloin into the air fryer basket and cook for 16-18 minutes. Slice and **Serve:**.

Steak Kebab

Prep time: 10 minutes **Cooking time:** 10 minutes
Serve: 4

Ingredients

1 lb. sirloin steak, cut into 1-inch pieces	1 bell pepper, cut into 1-inch pieces
For marinade	2 tbsp vinegar
1 tsp ginger garlic paste	1/4 cup soy sauce
2 tbsp olive oil	1 onion, cut 1-inch pieces
1 tsp pepper	

Directions

Preheat the air fryer to 350 F. Add meat pieces and remaining Ingredients into the zip-lock bag. Seal bag and place in the refrigerator overnight. Thread marinated meat pieces, onion, and bell pepper onto the skewers.

Place skewers into the air fryer basket and cook for 10 minutes. Turn halfway through. **Serve:** and enjoy.

Onion Garlic Pork Chops

Prep time: 10 minutes **Cooking time:** 12 minutes
Serve: 4

Ingredients

4 pork chops, boneless	1/2 tsp celery seeds, crushed
1/2 tsp granulated onion	
2 tsp canola oil	1/2 tsp salt
1/2 tsp parsley	1/2 tsp granulated garlic

Directions

Preheat the air fryer to 350 F. In a small bowl, mix together garlic, celery seeds, onion, parsley, and salt. Brush pork chops with oil and rub with spice mixture. Place pork chops into the air fryer basket and cook for 12 minutes. Turn halfway through. **Serve:** and enjoy.

Easy Beef Roast

Prep time: 10 minutes **Cooking time:** 45 minutes
Serve: 8

Ingredients

2 1/2 lbs. beef roast	1 tsp rosemary
1/2 tsp onion powder	1 tsp dill
2 tbsp canola oil	1/2 tsp garlic powder
1/2 tsp pepper Salt	

Directions

Preheat the air fryer to 360 F. In a small bowl, mix together rosemary, pepper, garlic powder, onion powder, dill, and oil and rub all over the beef roast.

Place beef roast into the air fryer basket and cook for 45 minutes. **Serve:** and enjoy.

Flavorful Pork Patties

Prep time: 10 minutes **Cooking time:** 35 minutes
Serve: 6

Ingredients

1 egg, lightly beaten	1 tsp garlic powder
1 tsp smoked paprika	1 carrot, minced
1 onion, minced	2 lbs. ground pork
1/2 cup almond flour	Salt
Pepper	

Directions

Preheat the air fryer to 375 F. Add meat and remaining Ingredients into the large bowl and mix until well combined.

Make patties from the meat mixture and place into the air fryer basket and cook for 35 minutes. Turn patties after 20 minutes. **Serve:** and enjoy.

Lemon Herb Lamb Chops

Prep time: 10 minutes **Cooking time:** 8 minutes **Serve:** 4

Ingredients

1 lb. lamb chops	2 tbsp fresh lemon juice
1 tsp rosemary	2 tbsp canola oil
1 tsp oregano	1 tsp thyme
1 tsp coriander	1 tsp salt

Directions

Preheat the air fryer to 390 F. Add lamb chops and remaining Ingredients into the zip-lock bag. Seal bag and place in the refrigerator for 1 hour.

Place marinated lamb chops into the air fryer basket and cook for 8 minutes. Turn lamb chops halfway through. Serve and enjoy.

Dutch Oven Beef Stew

Prep time: 15 minutes **Cooking time:** 25 minutes
Serve: 1

Ingredients

½ cup all-purpose flour	1 tbsp ground paprika
salt and ground black pepper to taste	1 ½ tablespoon Worcestershire sauce
2 pounds cubed beef stew meat	2 tablespoons extra-virgin olive oil
2 large potatoes, cubed	1 (8 ounces) package mushrooms
4 cups beef broth	
1 stalk celery, chopped	3 medium carrots, sliced
1 medium onion, chopped	2 cloves garlic, minced
2 bay leaves	

Directions

Combine the flour, paprika, salt, and pepper in a medium mixing bowl. Toss the steak in the flour mixture until evenly covered.

Heat the oil over medium-high heat in a cast-iron Dutch oven or big saucepan. Sear the meat for 2 to 3 minutes per side, or until nicely browned. Cover and stir in the broth, potatoes, mushrooms, carrots, onion, celery, Worcestershire sauce, garlic, and bay leaves.

Reduce heat to medium and simmer, stirring periodically, for 2 ½ hours, or until soft meat and veggies.

Beef Stroganoff Sauce with Meatballs

Prep time: 20 minutes **Cooking time:** 20 minutes
Serve: 1

Ingredients

½ teaspoon vegetable oil,	3 tablespoons Worcestershire sauce
1 teaspoon ground mustard	
1 egg	⅓ cup dry breadcrumbs
½ small onion, chopped	salt and ground black pepper to taste
1 pound ground sirloin	
¼ cup butter, divided	1 (16 ounces) package mushrooms, sliced
2 tbs. all-purpose flour	
10.5 ounces can beef broth	⅓ cup sour cream

Directions

Preheat the oven carefully to 350 degrees Fahrenheit (175 degrees C). Coat a baking sheet with cooking spray.

Combine the ground sirloin, Worcestershire sauce, egg, breadcrumbs, onion, salt, and pepper in a mixing bowl. Combine thoroughly. Make meatballs the size of golf balls. Place on the baking sheet that has been prepared. Bake for 15 minutes, or until the meatballs are no longer pink in the center.

In a large pan over medium heat, melt 2 tablespoons of butter. Cook and stir until the mushrooms are tender about 10 minutes. Push the mushrooms to the pan's side.

Melt the remaining 2 tablespoons of butter in the skillet and mix in the flour. Bring the broth and mustard to a boil.

Dried Beef Ball

Prep time: 15 minutes **Cooking time:** 25 minutes
Serve: 1

Ingredients

5 ounces dried beef, chopped	2 (8 ounces) packages cream cheese, softened
1 tablespoon Worcestershire sauce	½ teaspoon seasoned salt
	6 green onions, chopped

Directions

Set aside approximately a half cup of the chopped dry beef. Combine the remaining meat, cream cheese, green onions, Worcestershire sauce, and seasoned salt in a separate medium bowl. Roll into a ball after thoroughly mixing. Roll the ball in the re**Serve:**d beef, covering it all the way around.

Simple Beef Stew

Prep time: 15 minutes **Cooking time:** 20 minutes
Serve: 1

Ingredients

3 tablespoons vegetable oil	2 pounds room temperature beef stew meat, cut into 1 1/2-inch cube
1 teaspoon minced garlic	
3 stalks celery, chopped	
½ cup all-purpose flour	1 yellow onion, roughly chopped
3 yellow potatoes, or more to taste, cubed	1 teaspoon dried basil
1 (32 ounces) carton low-sodium beef broth	1 (15 ounces) can have crushed tomatoes
1 cup baby carrots	1 teaspoon Creole seasoning

Directions

In a big saucepan, heat the oil over medium-high heat. Cook and stir for 10 to 15 minutes, or until the meat, flour, onion, and garlic are browned.

Stir in the broth, tomatoes, potatoes, celery, and carrots, followed by mthe Creole spice and basil. Bring to a boil. Reduce heat to maintain a simmer and cook, uncovered, for 1 hour, or until potatoes are soft, meat is cooked, and gravy is thick.

Confetti Beef Tacos

Prep time: 20 minutes **Cooking time:** 25 minutes
Serve: 1

Ingredients

1 pound ground beef	2 teaspoons chili powder
½ teaspoon salt	11 ounces can corn, drained
1 cup prepared chunky salsa	12 taco shells, warmed

Directions

Warm-up a big nonstick skillet over medium heat. Cook for 8 to 10 minutes, breaking up the ground beef into small crumbles and stirring regularly. Drain drippings and season with chili powder and salt. Heat through the corn and salsa. **Serve:** in taco shells with your choice of toppings.

Beef Taco Noodle Bake

Prep time: 15 minutes **Cooking time:** 20 minutes
Serve: 1

Ingredients

PAM® Original No-Stick Cooking Spray	6 ounces dry extra-wide egg noodles, uncooked
2 cups frozen Southwest mixed vegetables (corn, black beans, red peppers)	1 (10 ounces) can Ro*Tel® Original Diced Tomatoes & Green Chilies, undrained
1 (10 ounces) can red enchilada sauce	1 ¼ cups water
1 ¼ cups shredded Mexican blend cheese	1 teaspoon Sour cream
1 pound ground chuck beef (80% lean)	¼ cup thinly sliced green onions

Directions

Preheat the oven carefully to 400°F. Coat a 13x9 inch glass baking dish with nonstick cooking spray. In a baking dish, place uncooked noodles.

Melt butter in a large pan over medium-high heat. Cook it for 5 to 7 minutes, or until the beef is crumbled and no longer pink. Drain. Stir in the veggies, undrained tomatoes, enchilada sauce, and water. Bring the water to a boil. Pour the mixture over the noodles.

Cover securely with foil and bake for 15 minutes. Cover with foil after stirring and sprinkling with cheese. Bake for another 10 minutes or until the noodles are soft. Garnish with green onions. If desired, top with sour cream.

Filipino Corned Beef and Cabbage

Prep time: 15 minutes **Cooking time:** 18 minutes
Serve: 1

Ingredients

⅓ cup butter	1 teaspoon olive oil
½ onion, chopped	⅓ small head cabbage, cored and cut into strips
3 cloves garlic, minced	¼ cup chicken stock
4 Roma tomatoes, cubed	
1 (12 ounces) can corned beef	

Directions

In a large saucepan over medium heat, melt the butter and oil. Cook until the onion and garlic are tender and transparent, about 5 minutes. Heat through the tomatoes, approximately 3 minutes.

Cook until the cabbage is tender, about 5 minutes. Heat through with a splash of chicken stock, about 3 minutes. Cook until the corned beef is cooked through, and the flavors have blended for about 10 minutes.

Slow Cooker Barbecue Beef

Prep time: 15 minutes **Cooking time:** 22 minutes
Serve: 1

Ingredients

3 tablespoons all-purpose flour	15 ounces tomato sauce
½ cup chopped onion	3 pounds chuck roast
1 ½ teaspoon chili powder	⅓ cup brown sugar
1 clove garlic, minced	1 teaspoon mustard powder
	2 cubes beef bouillon

Directions

The flour should be rubbed into the roast. Place the roast in the bottom of the slow cooker. Combine the tomato sauce, onion, brown sugar, bouillon, chili powder, garlic powder, and mustard powder in a mixing bowl. Combine thoroughly. Cover the slow cooker and cook on high for 8 hours or low for 14 to 16 hours.

Blue Cheese Beef Tenderloin

Prep time: 10 minutes **Cooking time:** 18 minutes
Serve: 1

Ingredients

3 pounds beef tenderloin	½ cup teriyaki sauce
½ cup red wine	2 cloves garlic, chopped
4 ounces blue cheese crumbled	⅓ cup mayonnaise
⅔ cup sour cream	1 ½ teaspoon Worcestershire sauce

Directions

In a shallow dish, place the meat. Pour teriyaki sauce, red wine, and garlic over the steak. Allow beef to marinate for 30 minutes in the refrigerator. Preheat the oven carefully to 450°F (230 degrees C). Place the tenderloin on a broiler pan and cook for 15 minutes in a preheated oven. Reduce the heat to 375 degrees F (190 degrees C) and continue to cook for 30 to 40 minutes, or until done to preference. Allow for a 10-minute rest before slicing, Combine blue cheese, mayonnaise, sour cream, and Worcestershire sauce in a skillet over low heat. Stir until smooth and **Serve:** over tenderloin slices.

Slow Cooker Roast Beef

Prep time: 15 minutes **Cooking time:** 20 minutes
Serve: 1

Ingredients

⅓ cup soy sauce	1 pack dry onion soup mix
3 pounds beef chuck roast	2 tbs freshly black pepper

Directions

Mix the soy sauce and dry onion soup in the slow cooker. Insert the chuck roast into the slow cooker. Pour in enough water to cover the top 1/2 inch of the roast. Season with ground pepper to taste. Cook on low for 22 hours, covered.

Mushroom Beef Burgers

Prep time: 18 minutes **Cooking time:** 20 minutes
Serve: 1

Ingredients

2 pounds ground beef	1 (8 ounces) package mushrooms, chopped,
1 teaspoon salt	
3 cloves garlic, minced	1 teaspoon Italian seasoning
½ teaspoon ground black pepper	cooking spray

Directions

Remove the ground beef from the refrigerator and set it aside for 20 minutes to come to room temperature. Combine mushrooms, onion, garlic, Italian seasoning, salt, and pepper in a large mixing bowl. Add in the meat. Make 1/2-inch-thick patties out of the meat mixture.
Cooking spray should be sprayed on an indoor grill pan. Cook patties in batches for approximately 10 minutes on each side or browned and no longer pink in the center.

Corned Beef Hash

Prep time: 15 minutes **Cooking time:** 25 minutes
Serve: 1

Ingredients

6 large potatoes, peeled and diced	1 (12 ounces) can corned beef, cut into chunks
1 cup beef broth	1 medium onion, chopped

Directions

Combine the potatoes, corned beef, onion, and beef stock in a large deep pan over medium heat. Cover and cook until the potatoes are mashed, and the liquid has almost evaporated. **Serve:** with a well-mixed sauce.

Hot Beef Dip

Prep time: 15 minutes **Cooking time:** 20 minutes
Serve: 1

Ingredients

2 (8 ounces) jars dried chipped beef

2 (8 ounces) packages cream cheese, softened

1 onion, finely chopped

1 green bell pepper chopped

1 (8 ounces) package shredded Cheddar cheese

Directions

Preheat the oven carefully to 350°F (175 degrees C). In a small baking dish, combine the dry chipped beef, green bell pepper, onion, cream cheese, and Cheddar cheese.

Bake for 45 minutes, uncovered, in a preheated oven, or until the center is bubbling and the sides are gently browned.

Smothered Beef Short Ribs

Prep time: 20 minutes **Cooking time:** 20 minutes
Serve: 1

Ingredients

½ cup olive oil

4 pounds beef short ribs

1 cup all-purpose flour

salt and pepper to taste

2 cups chopped onions

1 cup chopped celery

1 cup chopped carrots

2 tbsp minced garlic

1 tablespoon dried thyme

8 cups beef stock

1 cup red wine

3 bay leaves

¼ cup chopped fresh parsley

Directions

In a big saucepan, heat the oil over medium-high heat. Season the ribs with salt and pepper to taste, then coat them in flour. Fry the ribs in small batches in the oil, adding oil as required to sear the meat. This should take between 2 and 3 minutes for each batch. Set aside the ribs.
Sauté the onions in the same saucepan for 2 minutes.

Cook for 1 minute more after adding the celery and carrots. Season to taste with salt and pepper, then toss in the garlic, bay leaves, and thyme and cook for 1 minute longer.

Deglaze the saucepan with the red wine, scraping away any particles accumulated on the bottom. Bring the stock to a boil, then lower to low heat and simmer. Continue to boil for 2 hours, or until the sauce thickens. **Serve:** with the parsley stirred in.

Corned Beef and Swiss Dip

Prep time: 15 minutes **Cooking time:** 25 minutes **Serve:** 1

Ingredients

1 tablespoon vegetable oil

¾ onion, chopped

3 (2.5 ounces) packages deli-sliced corned beef diced

2 (8 ounces) packages cream cheese, softened

1 ½ cups mayonnaise

1 pound loaf Italian bread

1 cup shredded Swiss cheese

1 (8 ounces) carton sour cream

1 teaspoon garlic powder

Directions

Preheat the oven carefully to 350°F (175 degrees C). In a pan over medium heat, heat the vegetable oil. Cook and stir onion for 5 to 7 minutes, or until tender. Place the onion in a large mixing basin.

Combine corned beef, cream cheese, mayonnaise, sour cream, Swiss cheese, and garlic powder in a mixing bowl. Mix until everything is well blended.

Slice a slice of bread off the top of the loaf and hollow out the center of the loaf to make a long bread bowl. At least 1/2 inch of bread should be left on the sides. If desired, save bread chunks from the center of the loaf for dipping.
Fill the bread dish halfway with the corned beef mixture.

Patsy's Best Barbeque Beef

Prep time: 15 minutes **Cooking time:** 22 minutes
Serve: 1

Ingredients

⅛ teaspoon hot pepper sauce

3 large onions, chopped

3 tablespoons cider vinegar

1 bunch celery, chopped

1 teaspoon pepper

6 pounds boneless beef chuck roast

2 teaspoons chili powder

2 tbs salt

1 medium green bell pepper, chopped

1 ¼ cups ketchup

½ cup water

3 tbs barbeque sauce

Directions

In a large mixing basin, combine the celery, onions, green pepper, ketchup, water, barbeque sauce, vinegar, and hot pepper sauce. Chili powder, salt, and pepper to taste.

Chef John's Beef Goulash

Prep time: 20 minutes **Cooking time:** 25 minutes
Serve: 1

Ingredients

2 ½ pounds boneless beef chuck roast	2 tablespoons vegetable oil
2 teaspoons olive oil	2 onions, chopped
2 tablespoons Hungarian paprika	½ teaspoon salt
1 teaspoon freshly ground black pepper	2 teaspoons caraway seeds, crushed
1 tbsp dried marjoram	½ teaspoon ground thyme
½ teaspoon cayenne pepper	salt and ground black pepper to taste
¼ cup tomato paste	4 cups chicken broth, divided
2 tablespoons balsamic vinegar	3 cloves garlic, crushed
1 bay leaf	½ teaspoon salt, or to taste
	1 teaspoon white sugar

Directions

Season the meat with salt and pepper. Heat the vegetable oil in a large pan over high heat; cook and stir the beef in batches until browned on both sides, about 5 minutes per batch. Transfer to a large stockpot, leaving the drippings in the skillet. Return skillet to medium heat; toss onions into saved drippings, sprinkle olive oil over onions, season with 1/2 teaspoon salt, and cook for 5 minutes, or until onion has softened. Add to the stockpot with the meat.

In a pan, toast the paprika, caraway seeds, black pepper, marjoram, thyme, and cayenne pepper until aromatic, approximately 3 minutes. Stir in 1 cup chicken stock before adding to the meat and onion combination. 3 cups of the chicken broth should be added to the beef mixture. Bring tomato paste, garlic, vinegar, sugar, 1/2 teaspoon salt, and bay leaf to a boil in a stockpot over high heat. Reduce the heat to low and simmer for 1 1/2 to 2 hours, or until a fork easily inserts into the meat.

DSF's Shredded Beef

Prep time: 15 minutes **Cooking time:** 25 minutes
Serve: 1

Ingredients

1 ½ pounds rump roast	1 ¼ cups water
garlic powder, or to taste	salt and ground black pepper to taste

Directions

Season the rump roast well with garlic powder, salt, and pepper before placing it in the crock of a slow cooker. Fill the crock with water.

Cook for 5 hours on high. Transfer the roast to a chopping board and shred it with two forks.

Beef Kebabs with Pomegranate Couscous

Prep time: 15 minutes **Cooking time:** 18 minutes
Serve: 1

Ingredients

2 ounces feta cheese, crumbled	¼ cup whole-milk plain Greek yogurt
½ teaspoon lemon zest	1 tablespoon water, or more as needed
1 teaspoon lemon juice	1 cup cherry tomatoes
12 ounces beef top sirloin, cut into 1-inch cubes	1 tablespoon Baharat (Middle Eastern spice mix)
1 red bell pepper	2 portobello mushrooms, stem and ribs removed, cut into 1-inch pieces
1 small red onion, cut into 1/2-inch wedges	1 tbsp chopped fresh mint
2 cups reduced-sodium chicken broth	⅓ cup pomegranate seeds
1 ½ cups Israeli (large pearl) couscous	¼ cup chopped pistachios
1 teaspoon Baharat (Middle Eastern spice mix)	

Directions

In a small mixing bowl, combine the feta, yogurt, lemon juice, and zest to make the feta sauce. Thin with water to achieve the required consistency.

In a medium saucepan, bring broth to a boil to prepare the couscous. Mix in the couscous. Reduce heat to low and cover for 8 to 10 minutes, or until couscous is cooked and liquid is absorbed. Using a fork, fluff the rice. Pomegranate seeds, pistachios, mint, and Baharat are optional. To mix, toss everything together.

Preheat an outside grill to medium (325 to 375 degrees Fahrenheit (160 to 190 degrees Celsius)). Toss the meat cubes in the Baharat to coat. Thread eight 10-inch metal skewers with steak, bell pepper, tomatoes, onion, and mushrooms.
Grill the kebabs, turning once or twice until the veggies are soft and the meat is slightly pink in the center, 8 to 12 minutes. Kebabs should be **Serve:**d with couscous and feta sauce on the side.

Easy Ginger Beef

Prep time: 10 minutes **Cooking time:** 18 minutes
Serve: 1

Ingredients

1 pound round steak, thinly sliced	1 teaspoon butter
1 (1 inch) piece fresh ginger root	1 red bell pepper
¼ cup sweet and sour sauce 4 cups cooked rice	12 mushrooms
	1 tablespoon soy sauce
	1 onion

Directions

Combine the steak, ginger, and soy sauce, flip to coat. Marinate in the refrigerator for at least 30 minutes and up to overnight. Heat a wok over high heat and add the meat mixture. Cook, covered, for 5 minutes, or until meat is browned. Remove the meat from the wok.

Melt the butter over high heat; add the bell pepper, onion, mushrooms, and sweet and sour sauce. Cook, covered, for 3 minutes, or until the veggies soften. Cook until heated through, about 2 minutes, after adding cooked meat to vegetable mixture. **Serve:** with hot cooked rice.

Glazed Corned Beef

Prep time: 18 minutes **Cooking time:** 20 minutes
Serve: 1

Ingredients

4 ½ pounds corned beef, rinsed	1 cup apricot pre**Serve:**s
¼ cup brown sugar	1 cup water
	2 tablespoons soy sauce

Directions

Preheat the oven carefully to 350°F (175 degrees C). Spray a big skillet with nonstick cooking spray. Fill a dish halfway with water and add the corned meat.

Bake for 2 hours, carefully wrapped in aluminum foil; drain liquid. Combine the apricot pre**Serve:**s, brown sugar, and soy sauce in a small mixing dish. Evenly distribute the apricot mixture over the corned meat.

Bake uncovered at 350°F (175°C) for 25–30 minutes, or until the meat is cooked, basting periodically with pan drippings. **Serve:** corned beef slices against the grain.

Lengua (Beef Tongue)

Prep time: 20 minutes **Cooking time:** 20 minutes
Serve: 1

Ingredients

1 beef tongue	1 large onion, chopped, divided
2 cloves garlic	1 whole jalapeno pepper, stemmed
3 tablespoons salt	2 whole jalapeno peppers, stemmed
3 whole tomatoes	
2 tablespoons vegetable oil	

Directions

In a large saucepan, combine the tongue, half of the chopped onion, garlic cloves, 3 tablespoons salt, and 1 jalapeño pepper. Fill with enough water to cover the tongue by a few inches, then bring to a boil over high heat. Reduce heat to medium-low; cover and simmer for 3 to 4 hours, or until very tender. Allow the tongue to cool after removing it from the water. Keep the liquid aside. Peel off the rough outer skin of the tongue once it has cooled, then shred the flesh with two forks.

Over high heat, bring a large pot of water to a boil. Boil until the veggies are soft, then add the entire tomatoes and 2 jalapeno peppers. Put the veggies in a blender and purée them until smooth. In a large

skillet over medium heat, heat the vegetable oil. Cook, often stirring, until the onion has softened and turned translucent about 5 minutes.
Stir in the shredded beef tongue and tomato salsa once the onion has softened. Bring to a boil, stirring regularly, and then add 2 cups of the saved cooking liquid. Cook and stir for 20 minutes, or until the liquid evaporates, leaving juicy, delicious meat.

Slow Cooker Beef Barbacoa

Prep time: 15 minutes **Cooking time:** 20 minutes
Serve: 1

Ingredients

3 pounds boneless beef
chuck roast
½ teaspoon ground black
pepper, or to taste
1 (14 ounces) can tomato
sauce
2 tablespoons garlic
powder

3 bay leaves
1 onion, chopped
¼ cup distilled white
vinegar
¼ cup chili powder salt to
taste

Directions

In a slow cooker, combine the roast, onion, bay leaves,
black pepper, garlic powder, and vinegar, cover with
water fully. Cook, covered, on High for 4 hours, or
until the flesh is extremely soft and falling apart.

Take the meat out of the slow cooker and discard the
juices. Return the meat to the slow cooker and shred
with a fork and knife. Combine the shredded meat,
tomato sauce, chili powder, and salt in a mixing bowl.
Cook the beef and sauce for 2 hours on High,
covered.

Beef Martini

Prep time: 15 minutes **Cooking time:** 20 minutes
Serve: 1

Ingredients

½ onion, chopped
¼ cup gin
1 tablespoon green olive
brine
1 teaspoon dried basil
salt and pepper to taste

2 cloves garlic, crushed
1 tbsp dry vermouth
4 (1/2 pound) beef sirloin
steaks
1 cup barbecue sauce

Directions

Combine the onion, garlic, barbecue sauce, gin,
vermouth, olive brine, and basil in a medium mixing
bowl. Place each steak in a resealable sandwich bag and
season with salt and pepper. Divide the marinade evenly
among the bags and seal. Make certain that the marinade
is well dispersed across the steaks. Refrigerate for at least
2 hours and up to 24 hours.

Preheat the grill to medium-high heat and liberally oil
the   grill grate. Remove the steaks from the bags and
discard the marinade. Grill steaks for 7 to 8 minutes
per side, or until done to preference.

Bibimbap with Beef

Prep time: 15 minutes **Cooking time:** 25 minutes
Serve: 1

Ingredients

½ pound beef top sirloin
steak
2 teaspoons honey
2 teaspoons vegetable oil
1 carrot, thinly sliced
½ cup peeled and
matchstick-cut daikon
radish

ground black pepper to
taste

1 tablespoon sesame oil
2 tablespoons soy sauce
2 teaspoons dry sherry
1 ½ cups bean sprouts
4 cups hot cooked rice
¼ teaspoon salt
1 cup fresh spinach
⅛ teaspoon cayenne
pepper,
or to taste

Directions

Cut the steak into 2-inch-long, 1/4-inch-wide slices
across the grain. Stack the slices and cut them into
1/4-inch strips lengthwise. Combine soy sauce, sesame
oil, honey, and sherry in a mixing bowl.

Toss in the meat strips. Stir. Marinate for 15 minutes
at room temperature. Over high heat, heat a nonstick
wok. Cook and stir the steak and marinate for
approximately 2 minutes, or until the beef is slightly
browned.
Divide the rice among four individual serving dishes.
Distribute the meat mixture over the rice. Maintain
your body temperature.

In the same wok, heat the oil over medium-high heat.
Combine carrot, bean sprouts, daikon, salt, black
pepper, and cayenne pepper in a mixing bowl. Cook
and stir for 1 minute or until slightly tender. Mix in the
spinach. Cook for 1 minute or until wilted. Distribute
the vegetable
mixture on top of the meat and rice.

Hawaiian Beef Stew

Prep time: 20 minutes **Cooking time:** 25 minutes
Serve: 1

Ingredients

1 tablespoon vegetable oil	4 pounds stew beef
5 stalks celery	10 cups water
5 cloves garlic, minced	½ cup red wine
1 onion, cut into chunks	6 ounces can tomato paste
1 teaspoon ground black pepper	3 potatoes
2 tablespoons salt, or to taste	4 carrots
	3 bay leaves
¼ cup cornstarch	2 tablespoons white sugar
	¼ cup water

Directions

In a medium-high-heat saucepan, heat the oil. Cook and stir the meat for approximately 10 minutes or until browned. Cook for 2 to 3 minutes, or until the garlic is fragrant. Cook until the alcohol has cooked off, about 5 minutes. Cook until the celery and onions are soft, approximately 5 minutes.

Fill the saucepan with 10 glasses of water. Combine tomato paste, salt, sugar, bay leaves, and pepper in a mixing bowl. Bring the water to a boil. Reduce the heat to medium-low. Cook, covered, for 1 hour, or until meat is tender.

Cook until the carrots are slightly soft, about 10 minutes. Cook for 10 to 15 minutes, or until potatoes are soft. Combine the cornstarch and 1/4 cup water; add to the stew. Allow thickening for about 3 minutes.

Greek-Style Beef Pita

Prep time: 15 minutes **Cooking time:** 18 minutes
Serve: 1

Ingredients

1 pound beef sirloin tip steaks, cut 1/8 to 1/4-inch thick	3 teaspoons vegetable oil, divided
¾ cup plain or seasoned hummus	1 tbsp lemon pepper
	4 each whole-wheat pita bread, cut crosswise in half

Directions

Stack beef steaks and cut them half lengthwise, then crosswise into 1- inch broad strips. In a medium mixing dish, combine the beef and lemon pepper.

In a large nonstick pan, heat 2 teaspoons oil over medium-high heat until hot. Stir-fry 1/2 of the meat for 1 to 3 minutes, or until the outer surface of the beef is no longer pink. (Avoid overcooking.) Take out of the skillet. Repeat with the entire meat, adding the remaining 1 teaspoon oil to the skillet as needed.

Fill pita pockets equally with hummus. Fill with equal parts steak and preferred toppings.

Backyard Bourbon Beef Marinade

Prep time: 15 minutes **Cooking time:** 22 minutes
Serve: 1

Ingredients

1 cup Kikkoman Soy Sauce	¾ cup water
3 tablespoons bourbon	2 pounds beef flank steak
1 tbsp crushed garlic clove	2 tablespoons sugar
	1 tablespoon confectioners' sugar

Directions

Except for the beef flank steak, combine all Ingredients in a mixing bowl. Marinate the beef* in the marinade for 12 to 24 hours in the refrigerator. Grill using your preferred manner.

Grilled Beef Fajitas

Prep time: 18 minutes **Cooking time:** 20 minutes
Serve: 1

Ingredients

1 (1 ounces) package fajita seasoning mix	Reynolds Wrap® Heavy Duty Aluminum Foil
1-pound boneless beef top round steak	1 medium red or yellow bell pepper
1 medium green bell pepper, cut into strips	1 tablespoon vegetable oi
1 medium onion	l 8 (8 inches) flour tortillas
Salsa	

Directions

Prepare the fajita spice mix according to the package recommendations and pour over the meat. Marinate the steak for 1 to 2 hours in Reynolds Wrap® Heavy Duty Aluminum Foil.

Form two layers of foil around the outside of a 13x9x2inch baking pan to make a grill pan. Remove the foil and crimp the edges to make a tight rim, resulting in a pan with 1-inch sides. Place on a baking sheet.

Preheat the grill to high heat. Remove the steak from the marinade and discard the marinade. In a foil pan, combine the peppers, onion, and oil. Slide the foil pan from the cookie sheet onto the grill and set the steak next to it.
Grill on high for 8 to 10 minutes in a covered grill. After 5 minutes, stir the veggies and flip the steak. Remove the foil pan from the grill and place it on a cookie sheet. Thinly slice the grilled steak.

Wrap tortillas in foil and place them on the grill while carving meat. Wrap meat, peppers, and onions in warm tortillas and **Serve:** with salsa.

Asian Beef with Snow Peas

Prep time: 10 minutes **Cooking time:** 18 minutes
Serve: 1

Ingredients

3 tablespoons soy sauce	1 tablespoon brown sugar
½ teaspoon cornstarch	1 tablespoon vegetable oil
2 tablespoons rice wine	1 tablespoon minced garlic
1 tablespoon minced fresh ginger root	8 ounces snow peas
	1 pound beef round steak

Directions

Combine the soy sauce, rice wine, brown sugar, and cornstarch in a small bowl. Place aside. In a wok or pan, heat the oil over medium-high heat. For 30 seconds, stir-fry the ginger and garlic. Stir-fry the steak for 2 minutes, or until evenly browned. Stir in the snow peas for a further 3 minutes.

Bring the soy sauce mixture to a boil while continually stirring. Reduce the heat to low and cook until the sauce is thick and smooth. **Serve:** right away.

Beef Bourguignon Without the Burgundy

Prep time: 20 minutes **Cooking time:** 20 minutes
Serve: 1

Ingredients

1 (2 1/2 pound) boneless beef chuck roast	2 tablespoons vegetable oil
salt and freshly ground black pepper	1 onion, chopped
	2 cups Merlot wine
1 tablespoon butter	2 stalks celery
2 carrots, cut into 1-inch pieces	2 tablespoons flour
	4 sprigs of fresh thyme
1 bay leaf	2 cups beef broth

Directions

Season the meat well with salt and pepper. In a large Dutch oven, heat the oil over high heat. Cook and stir beef cubes in heated oil for 10 to 15 minutes or browned on both sides. Place the meat on a platter.

In a Dutch oven, cook and stir onion, butter, and a bit of salt until the onion begins to sweat. Next, cook and whisk the flour into the onion mixture for 3 to 4 minutes or until the onion softens.

Pour wine into the onion mixture; bring to a boil and cook for 10 minutes, or until wine is reduced by half. Return the steak to the Dutch oven, along with any collected juices. Combine the beef broth, carrots, celery, thyme sprigs, bay leaf, and salt in a large pot. Bring to a simmer, cover with a lid, and cook for 1 1/2 hours on low or until the meat is almost tender.

Remove the lid from the Dutch oven and continue to cook until the beef is cooked, and the stew is thick, about 30 minutes more. Season with salt and pepper to taste.

Butter Beef

Prep time: 15 minutes **Cooking time:** 25 minutes
Serve: 1

Ingredients

3 pounds cubed beef stew meat	½ cup butter
	1 (1 ounces) envelope dry onion soup mix

Directions

In a slow cooker, combine the meat and butter. Sprinkle with the onion soup mix. Cook on low for 8 hours or High for 4 to 5 hours, covered. Once or twice, stir the mixture.

Baked Spanish Rice and Beef

Prep time: 15 minutes **Cooking time:** 25 minutes
Serve: 1

Ingredients

1 (16 ounces) package ground beef	1 (28 ounces) can diced tomatoes
1 cup chopped onion	1 cup chopped green bell pepper
1 cup uncooked long-grain rice	1 teaspoon browning sauce
1 teaspoon salt	1 teaspoon chili powder
½ teaspoon ground black pepper	½ teaspoon dried thyme

Directions

Preheat the oven carefully to 350 degrees Fahrenheit (175 degrees C).

Preheat a 4- to 6-quart Dutch oven on medium-high. Cook and stir the beef in the heated skillet for 5 to 7 minutes, or until it is browned and crumbly. Remove and discard the grease. Combine the tomatoes, rice, onion, green bell pepper, browning sauce, salt, chili powder, pepper, and thyme in a mixing bowl. Cover.

Cook, tossing every 20 minutes until the rice is cooked, about 1 hour 10 minutes in a preheated oven.

Beef and Cheese Ball

Prep time: 15 minutes **Cooking time:** 20 minutes
Serve: 1

Ingredients
1 (8 ounces) package
cream cheese, softened
1 small finely chopped
green bell pepper
1 tablespoon
Worcestershire sauce

1 small white onion,
chopped
1 teaspoon onion juice
5 ounces dried beef

Directions

Combine cream cheese, 2/3 of the meat, onion, green
bell pepper, Worcestershire sauce, and onion juice in a
medium mixing bowl. Mix well and roll the mixture
into a ball. Coat the rest of the ball with the saved
meat.

Simple Beef Stroganoff

Prep time: 20 minutes **Cooking time:** 25 minutes
Serve: 1

Ingredients
1 (8 ounces) package egg
noodles
1 pound ground beef
½ cup sour cream
1 tablespoon garlic
powder

1 (10.75 ounces) can fat-
free condensed cream of
mushroom soup
salt and pepper to taste

Directions

Set aside the egg noodles after cooking them
according to package guidelines. Sauté the ground beef
in a separate large pan over medium heat for 5 to 10
minutes or browned. After draining the fat, add the
soup and garlic powder. Simmer, stirring periodically,
for 10 minutes.

Remove from the heat and toss in the meat mixture
and egg noodles. Stir in the sour cream and season
with salt and pepper to taste.

Corned Beef and Cabbage

Prep time: 15 minutes **Cooking time:** 20 minutes
Serve: 1

Ingredients
1 pound kosher salt
6 bay leaves
1 onion, chopped
8 pounds beef brisket
1 turnip, chopped
1-pound carrots, sliced

2 gallons water, divided
8 black peppercorns
1 medium head cabbage,
quartered
1 teaspoon chopped fresh
cilantro
8 potatoes - peeled and
cubed

Directions

Combine the salt, water, and beef in big stainless steel
or cast-iron kettle. Allow it remains in the refrigerator
for 7 days, covered. (Be aware that the brisket must be
immersed, so increase the salt and water as needed.)

Drain the brine after 7 days and replace it with 1
gallon of freshwater, bay leaves, and peppercorns.
Bring to a boil, then lower to a low/medium-low heat
and continue to cook for 3 to 3 1/2 hours.

Add the onion, cabbage, carrots, turnip, cilantro, and
potatoes during the last 45 minutes of simmering.
Continue to cook until all of the veggies are soft.

Corned Beef and Cabbage

Prep time: 15 minutes **Cooking time:** 18 minutes
Serve: 1

Ingredients
1 pound kosher salt
6 bay leaves
1 onion, chopped
8 pounds beef brisket
1 turnip, chopped
1-pound carrots, sliced

2 gallons water, divided
8 black peppercorns
1 medium head cabbage,
quartered
1 teaspoon chopped fresh
cilantro
8 potatoes - peeled and
cubed

Directions

Add salt, water, and beef in big stainless steel or cast-
iron saucepan. Refrigerate for 7 days, covered. (Note
Brisket must be totally immersed, so increase the salt
and water if required.)

After 7 days, remove the brine and replace it with 1
gallon of freshwater, bay leaves, and peppercorns.
Bring to a boil, then lower to a low/medium-low heat
and simmer for 3 to 3 1/2 hours.

Add the onion, cabbage, carrots, turnip, cilantro, and
potatoes in the last 45 minutes of simmering.
Continue to boil until all of the veggies are soft.

Easy Vegetable Beef Soup

Prep time: 15 minutes **Cooking time:** 22 minutes
Serve: 1

Ingredients

1 pound ground beef 2 quarts water	1 (14.5 ounces) can diced tomatoes
1 onion, chopped	4 potatoes, peeled cubed
1 (16 ounces) package frozen mixed vegetables	½ teaspoon ground black pepper
8 cubes beef bouillon, crumbled	

Directions

Cook beef until brown in a large saucepan over medium heat; drain.

Cooked meat, water, tomatoes, onion, potatoes, mixed veggies, bouillon, and pepper in a large saucepan over medium heat. Bring to a boil, lower to low heat, and cook for 45 minutes.

Stuffed Greek Leg of Lamb

Prep time: 15 minutes **Cooking time:** 25 minutes
Serve: 1

Ingredients

1 (3 1/2) pound leg of lamb olive oil	1 (12 ounces) jar marinated artichoke hearts
2 tablespoons chopped fresh basil	1 (8 ounces) package crumbled feta cheese
1 (6 ounces) jar sun-dried tomatoes packed in oil, drained, and chopped	salt and ground black pepper to taste
3 cloves garlic, minced	2 tablespoons chopped fresh oregano

Directions

Preheat the oven carefully to 350°F (175 degrees C). Place the leg of lamb on a chopping board, with the interior facing you. Drizzle olive oil over the lamb in an equal layer. Season the lamb with oregano and basil. Season the lamb with salt and pepper and top with artichoke hearts, feta cheese, sun-dried tomatoes, and garlic.

Wrap the lamb with the filling. To keep the lamb from unrolling, wrap it in kitchen twine. Next, wrap the lamb in foil and lay it in a baking dish.

Roast in a preheated oven for 90 minutes, or until done to your liking, or an internal temperature of 150 degrees F (70 degrees C) for medium. Set aside for 10 minutes in a warm place before slicing. Keep the pan juices aside for dishing.

Roasted Lamb Breast

Prep time: 10 minutes **Cooking time:** 18 minutes
Serve: 1

Ingredients

2 tablespoons olive oil	2 teaspoons ground cumin
1 teaspoon freshly ground black pepper	1 teaspoon ground coriander
1 teaspoon dried Italian herb seasoning	1 teaspoon paprika
4 pounds lamb breast, separated into two pieces	2 teaspoons salt
⅓ cup white wine vinegar, more as needed	½ cup chopped Italian flat-leaf parsley
1 lemon, juiced	2 cloves garlic, crushed
½ tbs red pepper flakes	1 teaspoon honey
	1 tbsp ground cinnamon
	1 pinch salt

Directions

Preheat the oven carefully to 300°F (150 degrees C). In a large mixing bowl, combine chopped parsley, vinegar, fresh lemon juice, garlic, honey, red pepper flakes, and salt. Set aside after thoroughly mixing.

Add olive oil, salt, cumin, black pepper, dried Italian herbs, cinnamon, coriander, and paprika in a large mixing bowl.
Coat each lamb breast in the olive oil and spice mixture and place fat side up in a roasting pan.

Cover the roasting pan tightly with aluminum foil and bake for 2 hours, or until the flesh is tender when probed with a fork. Take the lamb out of the oven and chop it into four pieces.
Raise the oven temperature to 450°F (230 degrees C).

Place the lamb on a baking sheet lined with aluminum foil. Brush the tops of each piece with the roasting pan fat drippings. Bake, the lamb for 20 minutes, or until the flesh is browned and the edges are crispy.

Turn the broiler too high and brown the lamb for 4 minutes. Then, take it out of the oven **Serve:** the lamb with parsley and vinegar sauce on the side.

Simple Grilled Lamb Chops

Prep time: 18 minutes **Cooking time:** 20 minutes
Serve: 1

Ingredients

¼ cup distilled white vinegar
1 tablespoon minced garlic
2 pounds lamb chops
½ teaspoon black pepper
2 teaspoons salt
2 tablespoons olive oil
1 onion, thinly sliced

Directions

In a large resealable bag, combine the vinegar, salt, pepper, garlic, onion, and olive oil until the salt is dissolved. Add the lamb, stir to coat, and place in the refrigerator for 2 hours to marinade. Preheat the grill to medium-high heat.

Remove the lamb from the marinade, leaving any onions stuck to the flesh. Any leftover marinade should be discarded.

Honey-Grilled Pork Chops

Prep time: 15 minutes **Cooking time:** 18 minutes
Serve: 1

Ingredients

½ cup honey
6 pork chops
6 tablespoons soy sauce
3 tablespoons lemon juice
2 teaspoons minced garlic

Directions

Combine the honey, soy sauce, lemon juice, and garlic in a mixing dish until the marinade is smooth. Pour the marinade into a resealable plastic bag, keeping about 1/4 cup in a bowl for basting. Then add the pork chops to the bag, coat with the marinade, compress the bag to remove excess air, and close the bag; marinate for at least 5 hours in the refrigerator.

Preheat the grill to medium-high heat and liberally oil the grill grate. Shake off any excess marinade from the pork chops. Discard any leftover marinade.
Grill the pork chops on a hot grill for 15 to 20 minutes, basting with the remaining marinade in the final few minutes, or until cooked through. In the center, an instant-read thermometer should register 145 degrees
F. (63 degrees C). Allow 3 minutes for the pork chops to rest before serving.

Chef John's Grilled Lamb with Mint Orange Sauce

Prep time: 20 minutes **Cooking time:** 20 minutes
Serve: 1

Ingredients

2 pounds lamb loin chops
2 tablespoons olive oil
1 teaspoon mixed herbs - Italian, Greek, or French blend
½ teaspoon ground coriander
¼ cup orange marmalade
1 tbs chopped fresh mint
3 cloves garlic, minced
1 tablespoon cumin
½ teaspoon black pepper
salt as needed
1 pinch hot chili flakes
¼ teaspoon cinnamon
1 pinch cayenne pepper
½ tablespoon rice vinegar

Directions

In a large mixing basin, combine the lamb chops. Season with the following Ingredients olive oil, garlic, cumin, mixed herbs, pepper, coriander, cinnamon, cayenne pepper, and salt. Toss until the oil and spices are well distributed. Refrigerate, covered. Allow at least 4 hours to marinate.

Preheat an outside grill to high heat and brush the grate gently with oil. Place the lamb chops on the grill. Season the chops with salt and pepper. Grill until the first side is seared, 4 to 7 minutes, depending on the size of the chops. Before rotating the chops, give them a half-turn on the grill for about a minute. Next, turn and grill the other side until done, 4 to 7 minutes more. An instant-read thermometer put into the middle should read 125 to 130 degrees F for medium-rare (54 degrees C). Cover loosely with foil and transfer to a serving dish.

Put the marmalade in a basin. Mix in the chili flakes, mint, and rice vinegar. Stir everything together completely. **Serve:** with the sauce brushed over the chops.

Chile Pork

Prep time: 15 minutes **Cooking time:** 20 minutes
Serve: 1

Ingredients

2 tablespoons chili powder	2 ½ teaspoons ground
1 teaspoon salt	cumin
1 tablespoon fresh cilantro	2 pounds pork tenderloin,
2 teaspoons minced garlic	cubed
	1 dash ground black
	pepper

Directions

Chili powder, salt, cumin, garlic, cilantro, and pepper should be combined. Refrigerate pork cubes for 45 minutes after coating with the mixture. Preheat the oven carefully to 225°F (107 degrees C). Bake for 2 hours, or until crispy.

Pork Marinade

Prep time: 20 minutes **Cooking time:** 25 minutes
Serve: 1

Ingredients

¼ cup dry mustard	1 ½ cups brown sugar
¾ cup chili sauce	¾ cup pineapple juice
2 teaspoons white sugar	

Directions

Chill dry mustard, brown sugar, chili sauce, pineapple juice, and sugar.

Basic Pork Brine

Prep time: 15 minutes **Cooking time:** 20 minutes
Serve: 1

Ingredients

2 cups water, more if	2 tablespoons kosher
needed	salt
3 cloves garlic, gently	3 slices fresh ginger, gently
crushed	crushed
1 cup brown sugar	

Directions

In a mixing dish, combine water, brown sugar, and salt until the sugar is dissolved. Mix in the garlic and ginger.

Jinx-Proof Braised Lamb Shanks

Prep time: 15 minutes **Cooking time:** 25 minutes
Serve: 1

Ingredients

5 ½ pounds lamb shanks	salt and freshly ground
2 tablespoons olive oil	black pepper
½ teaspoon dried	½ teaspoon dried thyme
rosemary	
1 tablespoon butter	1 onion, diced
1 rib celery, diced	1 large carrot, diced
1 ½ tablespoon all-	½ cup red wine
purpose flour	4 cloves garlic, minced
1 cup chicken broth 1 cup	1 tablespoon balsamic
water	vinegar
⅛ teaspoon ground	1 teaspoon minced fresh
cinnamon	rosemary leaves

Directions

Preheat the oven carefully to 450°F (230 degrees C). Drizzle olive oil over lamb shanks in a roasting pan; season with salt, black pepper, dried rosemary, and thyme. Toss the lamb shanks in the oil and spices to coat. Cook until the lamb is browned, about 30 minutes in a preheated oven.

Reduce the oven temperature to 325°F (165 degrees C). Melt butter in a saucepan over medium-high heat; cook and stir onion, celery, and carrot in the hot butter for 10 minutes, or until onion is browned. Combine flour and veggies in a mixing bowl; stir in garlic. Cook and stir for 1 minute more.

Pour red wine into vegetable mixture and whisk to incorporate. Add chicken stock, water, balsamic vinegar, and cinnamon and stir to combine. In the roasting pan, pour the sauce over the lamb shanks. Cover the roasting pan with aluminum foil, loosely closing the foil to allow the sauce to decrease somewhat while it cooks.

Bake the lamb shanks for 1 hour; turn the lamb shanks and replace the foil on the dish. Continue baking for another hour, or until a fork easily inserts into the flesh. Place the lamb shanks in a large mixing basin, cover with foil, and set aside for 10 minutes.

Pour braising liquid into a saucepan and bring to a boil over high heat for 10 minutes, scraping fat as it reduces and thickens slightly. Stir in the rosemary, taste for salt and pepper, and **Serve:** the lamb shanks with the pan sauce.

Tim's Smoked Pork Butt

Prep time: 15 minutes **Cooking time:** 22 minutes
Serve: 1

Ingredients

1 tablespoon garlic powder
8 pounds boneless pork butt
3 tablespoons applewood rub seasoning (such as McCormick® Grill Mates®)
2 tbsp smoked paprika
1 tablespoon ground black pepper

⅔ cup brown sugar substitute (such as Sukrin® Gold)
2 tablespoons onion powder
2 (12 fluid ounces) bottles of hard apple cider
1 tablespoon salt
2 (12 fluid ounces) cans or bottles of stout beer, divided

Directions

Season with brown sugar replacement, applewood rub, onion powder, smoked paprika, garlic powder, salt, and pepper in a mixing bowl.

Trim the butt of the pig but leave a layer of fat on one side. 1/2 cup seasoning blend should be applied to the entire pork butt. Refrigerate for three days, covered with plastic wrap. Set aside any leftover spice blend for another use.

Preheat, the smoker to 230°F (110 degrees C). Fill the smoker with your preferred wood chips or pellets. Place the pork butt onto the center rack, fat side up. In a drip pan, combine 12 ounces of stout and 12 ounces of cider.

Pork should be smoked for 4 hours. Add the rest of the stout and cider to the drip pan, along with more wood chips or pellets. Continue to smoke for another 3 hours. Remove the drip pan and save the drippings in a basin.
Continue to smoke the pork for 1 to 3 hours more, or until a meat thermometer reads 196 degrees F (91 degrees C). Then, allow for an hour of relaxation.

Using two forks, pull the pork apart. Pour as much of the con**Serve**d drippings as you like over the pulled pork. Serve

Simply the Easiest Beef Brisket

Prep time: 10 minutes **Cooking time:** 18 minutes
Serve: 1

Ingredients

1 (3 pounds) beef brisket, trimmed of fat
1 (12 fluid ounces) can of beer
¾ cup packed brown sugar

salt and pepper to taste
1 medium onion, thinly slice
1 (12 ounces) bottle tomato-based chili sauce

Directions

Preheat the oven carefully to 325 degrees Fahrenheit (165 degrees C).

Season the brisket with salt and pepper on all sides and set it in a glass baking dish. Add a layer of sliced onions on top. Combine the beer, chili sauce, and brown sugar in a medium mixing bowl. Pour the sauce over the roast. Wrap the dish in aluminum foil securely.

In a preheated oven, bake for 3 hours. Bake for a further 30 minutes after removing the aluminum foil. Allow the brisket to rest for a few minutes before slicing and returning to the dish. Reheat in the oven, spooning the sauce over the cut meat.

Best Ever Beef Marinade

Prep time: 18 minutes **Cooking time:** 20 minutes
Serve: 1

Ingredients

1 cup vegetable oil
½ cup lemon juice

¼ cup Dijon mustard
1 clove garlic, minced

¾ cup soy sauce
¼ cup Worcestershire sauce
salt and ground black pepper to taste

Directions

Combine the vegetable oil, soy sauce, lemon juice, Worcestershire sauce, Dijon mustard, and garlic in a mixing bowl. Season with salt and pepper to taste.

POULTRY

Festive Turkey with Chili Mayo

(**Ready in about** 45 minutes | **Servings:** 4)

Ingredients

3 teaspoons olive oil	1/2 tbsp garlic powder
1/2 teaspoon marjoram	1 teaspoon shallot powder
Coarse salt and ground black pepper, to taste	2 pounds turkey breast, boneless Chili mayo
1/4 cup mayonnaise	1/4 cup sour cream
1 tablespoon chili sauce	1/2 teaspoon stone-ground mustard
1 teaspoon basil	

Directions

Start by preheating your Air Fryer to 360 degrees F.

In a mixing bowl, thoroughly combine the olive oil with spices. Rub the turkey breast with the spice mixture until it is well coated on all sides. Air fry for 40 minutes, turning them over halfway through the cooking time.

Your instant-read thermometer should read 165 degrees.

Meanwhile, mix all of the Ingredients for the chili mayo. Place in your refrigerator until ready to **Serve:**.

Place the turkey breast skin-side up on a cutting board and slice it against the grain; **Serve:** with chili mayo and enjoy!

Garlic Butter Chicken Wings

(**Ready in about** 20 minutes | **Servings:** 3)

Ingredients

1 pound chicken wings	Salt black pepper, to taste
1 teaspoon garlic paste	2 tablespoons butter
1 lemon, cut into slices	

Directions

Pat dry the chicken wings with a kitchen towel and season all over with salt and black pepper. In a bowl, mix together butter and garlic paste. Rub the mixture all over the wings.

Cook in the preheated Air Fryer at 380 degrees F for 18 minutes. **Serve:** garnished with lemon slices. Bon appétit!

Homemade Chicken Burgers

(**Ready in about** 20 minutes | **Servings:** 4)

Ingredients

1 ¼ pounds chicken white meat, ground	1 teaspoon fresh garlic, finely chopped
1/2 white onion, finely chopped	1 teaspoon paprika
Sea salt and ground black pepper, to taste	4 burger buns
	1/2 cup cornmeal
1 ½ cups breadcrumbs	2 tablespoons ketchup
2 small pickles, sliced	4 lettuce leaves
	1 teaspoon yellow mustard

Directions

Thoroughly combine the chicken, onion, garlic, salt and black pepper in a mixing dish. Form the mixture into 4 equal patties. In a shallow bowl, mix paprika with cornmeal and breadcrumbs. Dip each patty in this mixture, pressing to coat well on both sides.

Spritz a cooking basket with a nonstick cooking spray. Air fry the burgers at 370 degrees F for about 11 minutes or to your desired degree of doneness.

Place your burgers on burger buns and **Serve:** with toppings. Bon appétit!

Italian-Style Turkey Meatballs

(**Ready in about** 20 minutes | **Servings:** 5)

Ingredients

1 ½ pounds ground turkey	1/2 cup parmesan cheese, grated
1/2 cup tortilla chips, crumbled	1 yellow onion, finely chopped
1 egg, beaten	2 cloves garlic, minced
2 tablespoons Italian parsley, finely chopped	1 tablespoon soy sauce
1 teaspoon Italian seasoning mix	1 teaspoon olive oil

Directions

Combine all of the Ingredients listed above until thoroughly combined. Form the mixture into 10 meatballs.

Spritz a nonstick cooking spray into a cooking basket. Cook at 360°F for about 10 minutes, or until done to your liking. Good appetite!

Hot Chicken Drumettes with Peppers

(**Ready in about** 45 minutes | **Servings:** 3)

Ingredients

1/2 cup all-purpose four
1/2 teaspoon dried basil
1/2 teaspoon dried oregano
1 tablespoon hot sauce
1/4 cup mayonnaise
1/4 cup milk

1 teaspoon shallot powder
1/2 teaspoon smoked paprika

1 pound chicken drumettes
2 bell peppers, sliced
1 teaspoon kosher salt

Directions

In a shallow bowl, mix the flour, salt, shallot powder, basil, oregano and smoked paprika.

In another bowl, mix the hot sauce, mayonnaise and milk.

Dip the chicken drumettes in the flour mixture, then, coat them with the milk mixture; make sure to coat well on all sides.

Cook in the preheated Air Fryer at 380 degrees F for 28 to 30 minutes; turn them over halfway through the cooking time. Reserve chicken drumettes, keeping them warm.

Then, cook the peppers at 400 degrees F for 13 to 15 minutes, shaking the basket once or twice. Eat warm.

Tortilla Chip-Crusted Chicken Tenders

(**Ready in about** 15 minutes | **Servings:** 3)

Ingredients

1 pound chicken tenders
1/2 tbsp shallot powder

1/2 tbs porcini powder

Sea salt black pepper to taste
1/3 cup tortilla chips,
1/2 tbs dried rosemary

Directions

Toss the chicken tenders with salt, pepper, shallot powder, porcini powder, dried rosemary and tortilla chips.

Spritz the cooking basket with a nonstick cooking spray. Cook in the preheated Air Fryer at 360 degrees F for 10 minutes, flipping them halfway through the cooking time.

Serve: warm with your favorite sauce for dipping. Enjoy!

Chicken Nuggets with Turnip Chips

(**Ready in about** 35 minutes | **Servings:** 3)

Ingredients

1 egg
1/4 teaspoon Romano cheese, grated
2 teaspoons canola oil
1 medium-sized turnip, trimmed and sliced
1/2 tbsp garlic powder

1/2 tbsp cayenne pepper
1 pound chicken breast, cut into slices
1/3 cup panko crumbs
Sea salt and ground black pepper, to taste

Directions

Beat the egg with the cayenne pepper until frothy. In another shallow bowl, mix the panko crumbs with the cheese until well combined.

Dip the chicken slices into the egg mixture; then, coat the chicken slices on all sides with the the panko mixture. Brush with 1 teaspoon of canola oil.

Season with salt and pepper to taste.

Cook in the preheated Air Fryer at 380 degrees F for 12 minutes, shaking the basket halfway through the cooking time; an instant-read thermometer should read 165 degrees F. Re**Serve:**, keeping them warm.

Drizzle the turnip slices with the remaining teaspoon of canola oil. Season with garlic powder, salt and pepper to taste.

Cook the turnips slices at 370 degrees F for about 20 minutes. **Serve:** with the warm chicken nuggets. Bon appétit!

Thanksgiving Turkey with Gravy

(**Ready in about** 55 minutes | **Servings:** 4)

Ingredients

1 ½ pound turkey breast
2 tablespoons butter, at room temperature
Sea salt and ground black pepper, to taste
2 cups vegetable broth

1 tbsp Dijon mustard
1/2 teaspoon garlic powder Gravy
1 tbsp cayenne pepper
1/4 cup all-purpose flour
Freshly ground black pepper, to taste

Directions

Brush Dijon mustard and butter all over the turkey breast. Season with salt, black pepper, cayenne pepper and garlic powder.

Cook in the preheated Air Fryer at 360 degrees F for about 50 minutes, flipping them halfway through the cooking time. Place the fat drippings from the cooked turkey in a sauté pan. Pour in 1 cup of broth and 1/8 cup of all-purpose flour; continue to cook, whisking continuously, until a smooth paste forms.

Add in the remaining Ingredients and continue to simmer until the gravy has reduced by half. Enjoy!

Chicken and Cheese Stuffed Mushrooms

(**Ready in about** 15 minutes | **Servings:** 4)

Ingredients

9 medium-sized button mushrooms, cleaned and steams removed
1 teaspoon soy sauce
2 ounces cheddar cheese, grated
1 teaspoon fresh garlic, finely chopped

2 ounces goat cheese, room temperature
1/2 pound chicken white meat, ground
2 tablespoons scallions, finely chopped
Sea salt and red pepper, to season

Directions

Set the mushrooms aside after patting them dry.

In a mixing bowl, thoroughly combine all Ingredients except the cheddar cheese. Stir everything together thoroughly before stuffing your mushrooms.

Bake for 5 minutes at 370°F in your Air Fryer. Top with cheddar cheese and continue to cook an additional 3 to 4 minutes or until the cheese melts. Good appetite!

Turkey and Bacon Casserole

(**Ready in about** 15 minutes | **Servings:** 5)

Ingredients

4 tablespoons bacon bits
1/2 cup sour cream
1 cup milk
1/2 teaspoon smoked paprika
1 cup Colby cheese, shredded

1 pound turkey sausage, chopped
5 eggs
Sea salt and ground black pepper, to your liking

Directions

Add the bacon bits and chopped sausage to a lightly greased baking dish.

In a mixing dish, thoroughly combine the sour cream, milk, eggs, paprika, salt and black pepper.

Pour the mixture into the baking dish.

Cook in your Air Fryer at 310 degrees F for about 10 minutes or until set. Top with Colby cheese and cook an additional 2 minutes or until the cheese is bubbly. Bon appétit!

Turkey Sausage Breakfast Cups

(**Ready in about** 20 minutes | **Servings:** 2)

Ingredients

1 smoked turkey sausage, chopped

4 tablespoons cheddar cheese, shredded
4 tablespoons fresh scallions, chopped
1/2 teaspoon garlic, minced

4 tablespoons cream cheese
4 eggs
1/4 teaspoon mustard seeds 1/4 teaspoon chili powder Salt and red pepper, to taste

Directions

Divide the sausage into four silicone baking cups.

In a mixing bowl, whisk together the eggs until pale and frothy. Then, add in the remaining Ingredients and thoroughly combine.

Fill the cups with the egg mixture.

Cook for 10 to 11 minutes in an Air Fryer at 330°F. Before unmolding, place the cups on wire racks to cool slightly. Enjoy.

Greek-Style Chicken Salad

(**Ready in about** 20 minutes | **Servings:** 2)

Ingredients

1/2 pound chicken breasts, boneless and skinless
2 bell peppers, deveined and chopped
2 tablespoons olives, pitted and sliced

1 cup baby spinach
2 tablespoons Greek-style yogurt 1 teaspoon lime juice
1/4 teaspoon red pepper flakes, crushed

1 Serrano pepper, deveined and chopped

1 red onion, sliced
1 cup arugula
1 cup grape tomatoes, halved
1 cucumber, sliced
1/4 cup mayonnaise
1/4 teaspoon oregano
1/4 teaspoon basil

Sea salt and ground black pepper, to taste

Directions

Spritz the chicken breasts with a nonstick cooking oil.

Cook in the preheated Air Fryer at 380 degrees F for 12 minutes. Transfer to a cutting board to cool slightly before slicing.

Cut the chicken into bite-sized strips and transfer them to a salad bowl.

Toss the chicken with the remaining Ingredients and place in your refrigerator until ready to **Serve:**. Enjoy!

Authentic Indian Chicken with Raita

(**Ready in about** 15 minutes | **Servings:** 2)

Ingredients

2 chicken fillets
2 teaspoons garam masala
1 teaspoon ground
turmeric 1/2 cup plain
yogurt
1 tablespoon fresh
cilantro, coarsely chopped
A pinch of ground
cinnamon

Sea salt and ground black
pepper, to taste
1 English cucumber,
shredded and drained

A pinch of grated nutmeg
1/2 red onion, chopped

Directions

Sprinkle the chicken fillets with salt, pepper, garam
masala and ground turmeric until well coated on all
sides.

Cook in the preheated Air Fryer at 380 degrees F for
12 minutes, turning them over once or twice.

Meanwhile, make traditional raita by mixing the
remaining

Ingredients in a bowl. Serve the chicken fillets with the
raita sauce on the side. Enjoy!

Asian-Style Chicken Drumettes

(**Ready in about** 15 minutes + marinating time |
Servings: 3)

Ingredients

1/4 cup soy sauce
2 tbsp tomato paste
2 tablespoons sesame oil
2 tablespoons rice vinegar

1 tbsp brown mustard
1 tablespoon brown sugar
1 teaspoon garlic paste
1 pound chicken
drumettes

Directions

Place the chicken drumettes and the other Ingredients
in a resalable bag; allow it to marinate for 2 hours.

Discard the marinade and transfer the chicken
drumettes to the Air Fryer cooking basket.

Cook at 400 degrees F for 12 minutes, shaking the
basket halfway through the **Cooking time:**to ensure
even cooking.

In the meantime, bring the re**Serve:**d marinade to a
boil in a small saucepan. Immediately turn the heat to
low and let it simmer until the sauce has reduced by
half.

Spoon the sauce over the chicken drumettes and **Serve:**
immediately.

Easy Chicken Taquitos

(**Ready in about** 20 minutes | **Servings:** 3)

Ingredients

1 pound chicken breast,
boneless
1/2 teaspoon onion
powder 1/2 teaspoon
garlic powder 1/2
teaspoon mustard powder

Sea salt and ground black
pepper, to taste
1/2 teaspoon cayenne
pepper
1 cup Cotija cheese,
shredded 6 corn tortillas

Directions

Salt, black pepper, cayenne pepper, onion powder,
garlic powder, and mustard powder season the chicken.

Cook for 12 minutes in a preheated Air Fryer at 380°F;
turn the chicken over halfway through the **Cooking
time:**to ensure even cooking.

Shred the chicken with two forks and place it on a
cutting board. Roll up your taquitos and fill them with
the chicken and Cotija cheese. Bake the taquitos for 5
to 6 minutes at 390°F; Serve immediately.

Huli-Huli Turkey

(**Ready in about** 35 minutes | **Servings:** 2)

Ingredients

2 turkey drumsticks
1 teaspoon paprika
1 teaspoon hot sauce
1 teaspoon olive oil
1/2 small pineapple, cut
into wedges

Sea salt and ground black
pepper, to season
1 teaspoon garlic paste
1/2 teaspoon rosemary
2 stalks scallions, sliced
1 teaspoon coconut oil,
melted

Directions

Toss the turkey drumsticks with salt, black pepper,
paprika, hot sauce, garlic paste, olive oil and rosemary.

Cook in the preheated Air Fryer at 360 degrees F for
25 minutes. Reserve.

Turn the temperature to 400 degrees F, place pineapple
wedges in the cooking basket and brush them with
coconut oil.

Cook your pineapple for 8 to 9 minutes. **Serve:** the
turkey drumsticks garnished with roasted pineapple and
scallions. Enjoy!

Keto Chicken Quesadillas

(**Ready in about** 25 minutes | **Servings:** 2)

Ingredients

1/2 pound chicken breasts, boneless and skinless	3 eggs
4 ounces Ricotta cheese	Salt to taste
1 teaspoon psyllium husk powder	Black pepper, to taste
	2 tablespoons flaxseed meal

Directions

Cook the chicken in the preheated Air Fryer at 380 degrees F for 12 minutes; turn the chicken over halfway through the cooking time. Salt to taste and slice into small strips.

In a mixing bowl, beat the eggs, cheese, flaxseed meal, psyllium husk powder and black pepper. Spoon the mixture into a lightly oiled baking pan.

Bake at 380 degrees F for 9 to 10 minutes.

Spoon the chicken pieces onto your quesadilla and fold in half. Cut your quesadilla into two pieces and **Serve:**.

Easy Hot Chicken Drumsticks

(**Ready in about** 40 minutes | **Servings:** 6)

Ingredients

6 chicken drumsticks	6 ounces hot sauce
Sauce	
3 tablespoons olive oil	3 tablespoons tamari sauce
1 teaspoon dried thyme	1/2 teaspoon dried oregano

Directions

Spritz the sides and bottom of the cooking basket with a nonstick cooking spray.

Cook the chicken drumsticks at 380 degrees F for 35 minutes, flipping them over halfway through.

Meanwhile, heat the hot sauce, olive oil, tamari sauce, thyme, and oregano in a pan over medium-low heat; re**Serve:**.

Drizzle the sauce over the prepared chicken drumsticks; toss to coat well and **Serve:**. Bon appétit!

Crispy Chicken Fingers

(**Ready in about** 15 minutes | **Servings:** 3)

Ingredients

1 pound chicken tenders	1/2 teaspoon cayenne pepper
1/2 teaspoon garlic powder	1/4 cup all-purpose flour
1/2 cup breadcrumbs	1 egg
Sea salt and ground black pepper, to taste	1/2 tbsp onion powder
1 tablespoon olive oil	

Directions

Pat dry the chicken with kitchen towels and cut into bite-sized pieces.

In a shallow bowl, mix the flour, onion powder, garlic powder, cayenne pepper, salt and black pepper. Dip the chicken pieces in the flour mixture and toss to coat well on all sides.

In the second bowl, place breadcrumbs.

In the third bowl, whisk the egg; now, dip the chicken in the beaten egg. Afterwards, roll each piece of chicken in the breadcrumbs until well coated on all sides.

Spritz the chicken fingers with olive oil. Cook in your Air Fryer at 360 degrees F for 8 to 10 minutes, turning it over halfway through the cooking time.

Serve with your favorite sauce for dipping. Enjoy!

Chicken Alfredo with Mushrooms

(**Ready in about** 15 minutes | **Servings:** 3)

Ingredients

1 pound chicken breasts, boneless	1 teaspoon butter, melted
12 ounces Alfredo sauce	1 medium onion, quartered
1/2 pound mushrooms, cleaned	Salt and black pepper, to taste

Directions

Start by preheating your Air Fryer to 380 degrees F. Then, place the chicken and onion in the cooking basket. Drizzle with melted butter.

Cook in the preheated Air Fryer for 6 minutes. Add in the mushrooms and continue to cook for 5 to 6 minutes more.

Slice the chicken into strips. Chop the mushrooms and onions; stir in the Alfredo sauce. Salt and pepper to taste.

Serve: with hot cooked fettuccine. Bon appétit!

Grandma's Chicken with Rosemary and Sweet Potatoes

(**Ready in about** 35 minutes | **Servings:** 2)

Ingredients

2 chicken legs, bone-in
2 garlic cloves, minced
1 teaspoon sesame oil
2 sprigs rosemary, leaves picked and crushed

Sea salt and ground black pepper, to taste
1/2 pound sweet potatoes

Directions

Begin by preheating your Air Fryer to 380°F. Rub the chicken legs with the garlic halves.

Drizzle the sesame oil over the chicken legs and sweet potatoes. Season with salt and rosemary. In the cooking basket, combine the chicken and potatoes.

Cook for 30 minutes in a preheated Air Fryer, or until the potatoes are tender. The chicken must be cooked until it reaches an internal temperature of 165 degrees F.

Serve: the chicken legs with the sweet potatoes on the side. Good appetite

Crunchy Munchy Chicken Tenders with Peanuts

(**Ready in about** 25 minutes | **Servings:** 4)

Ingredients

1 ½ pounds chicken tenderloins
Sea salt and ground black pepper, to taste
2 tablespoons peanut oil

2 tablespoons peanuts, roasted and roughly chopped

1/2 cup tortilla chips, crushed
1 teaspoon red pepper flakes
1/2 teaspoon garlic powder

Directions

Begin by preheating your Air Fryer to 360°F. Brush the chicken tenderloins on all sides with peanut oil.

Combine the crushed chips, salt, black pepper, garlic powder, and red pepper flakes in a mixing bowl. Dredge the chicken in the breading, shaking off any excess.

Place the tenderloins in the cooking basket. Cook for 12 to 13 minutes, or until the centre is no longer pink. Working in batches, an instant-read thermometer should read at least 165 degrees Fahrenheit.

Serve: garnished with roasted peanuts. Bon appétit!

Pretzel Crusted Chicken with Spicy Mustard Sauce

(**Ready in about** 20 minutes | **Servings:** 6)

Ingredients

1 eggs
1/2 cup crushed pretzels
2 tablespoons olive oil
1 teaspoon shallot powder
1 teaspoon paprika
1/2 cup vegetable broth
1 tablespoon cornstarch
3 tablespoons tomato paste
1 teaspoon yellow mustard
garlic cloves, chopped

1 ½ pound chicken breasts, boneless, skinless, cut into bite-sized chunks
Sea salt and ground black pepper, to taste
3 tablespoons Worcestershire sauce
1 tablespoon apple cider vinegar

1 jalapeno pepper, minced

Directions

Start by preheating your Air Fryer to 390 degrees F.

In a mixing dish, whisk the eggs until frothy; toss the chicken chunks into the whisked eggs and coat well.

In another dish, combine the crushed pretzels with shallot powder, paprika, salt and pepper. Then, lay the chicken chunks in the pretzel mixture; turn it over until well coated.

Place the chicken pieces in the air fryer basket. Cook the chicken for 12 minutes, shaking the basket halfway through. Meanwhile, whisk the vegetable broth with cornstarch, Worcestershire sauce, tomato paste, and apple cider vinegar.

Preheat a cast-iron skillet over medium flame. Heat the olive oil and sauté the garlic with jalapeno pepper for 30 to 40 seconds, stirring frequently.

Add the cornstarch mixture and let it simmer until the sauce has thickened a little. Now, add the air-fried chicken and mustard; let it simmer for 2 minutes more or until heated through. **Serve:** immediately and enjoy!

Farmhouse Roast Turkey

(**Ready in about** 50 minutes | **Servings:** 6)

Ingredients
2 pounds turkey
1 teaspoon sea salt
1/2 teaspoon ground
black pepper

1 tablespoon fresh
rosemary, chopped
1 celery stalk, chopped
1 onion, chopped

Directions

Start by preheating your Air Fryer to 360 degrees F. Spritz the sides and bottom of the cooking basket with a nonstick cooking spray.

Place the turkey in the cooking basket. Add the rosemary, salt, and black pepper. Cook for 30 minutes in the preheated Air Fryer.

Add the onion and celery and cook an additional 15 minutes. Bon appétit!

Chinese-Style Sticky Turkey Thighs

(**Ready in about** 35 minutes | **Servings:** 6)

Ingredients
1 tablespoon sesame oil
2 pounds turkey thighs
1 teaspoon pink
Himalayan salt
1 tablespoon Chinese rice
vinegar
1 tablespoon mustard

1 teaspoon Chinese Five-
spice powder
6 tablespoons honey
1/4 tbsp Sichuan pepper
1 tablespoon sweet chili
sauce
2 tablespoons soy sauce

Directions

Preheat your Air Fryer to 360 degrees F.

Brush the sesame oil all over the turkey thighs. Season them with spices.

Cook for 23 minutes, turning over once or twice. Make sure to work in batches to ensure even cooking

In the meantime, combine the remaining Ingredients in a wok (or similar type pan) that is preheated over medium-high heat. Cook and stir until the sauce reduces by about a third.

Add the fried turkey thighs to the wok; gently stir to coat with the sauce. Let the turkey rest for 10 minutes before slicing and serving. Enjoy!

Tarragon Turkey Tenderloins with Baby Potatoes

(**Ready in about** 50 minutes | **Servings:** 6)

Ingredients
2 pounds turkey
tenderloins
1 teaspoon smoked
paprika
1 pound baby potatoes,
rubbed

Salt and ground black
pepper, to taste
2 tbsp dry white wine
2 teaspoons olive oil
1 tablespoon fresh
tarragon leaves, chopped

Directions

Brush the turkey tenderloins with olive oil. Season with salt, black pepper, and paprika.

Afterwards, add the white wine and tarragon.

Cook the turkey tenderloins at 350 degrees F for 30 minutes, flipping them over halfway through. Let them rest for 5 to 9 minutes before slicing and serving.

After that, spritz the sides and bottom of the cooking basket with the remaining 1 teaspoon of olive oil.

Then, preheat your Air Fryer to 400 degrees F; cook the baby potatoes for 15 minutes. **Serve:** with the turkey and enjoy!

Paprika Chicken Legs with Brussels Sprouts

(**Ready in about** 30 minutes | **Servings:** 2)

Ingredients
2 chicken legs
1/2 teaspoon black pepper
1 pound Brussels sprouts

1/2 teaspoon paprika
1 teaspoon dill, fresh or
dried
1/2 teaspoon kosher salt

Directions

Start by preheating your Air Fryer to 370 degrees F.

Now, season your chicken with paprika, salt, and pepper. Transfer the chicken legs to the cooking basket. Cook for 10 minutes.

Flip the chicken legs and cook an additional 10 minutes. Re**Serve:**.

Add the Brussels sprouts to the cooking basket; sprinkle with dill. Cook at 380 degrees F for 15 minutes, shaking the basket halfway through.

Serve: with the re**Serve:**d chicken legs. Bon appétit!

Asian Chicken Filets with Cheese

(**Ready in about** 50 minutes | **Servings:** 2)

Ingredients

4 rashers smoked bacon
1 teaspoon garlic, minced
1/4 tbsp black pepper, preferably freshly ground
1 tbsp mild curry powder
1 tbsp black mustard seeds
1/2 cup Pecorino Romano cheese, freshly grated

1/2 tbsp coarse sea salt
1/2 cup coconut milk
1 (2-inch) piece ginger, peeled and minced
2 chicken filets
1/3 cup tortilla chips, crushed

Directions

Start by preheating your Air Fryer to 400 degrees F. Add the smoked bacon and cook in the preheated Air Fryer for 5 to 7 minutes. Re**Serve:**.

In a mixing bowl, place the chicken fillets, salt, black pepper, garlic, ginger, mustard seeds, curry powder, and milk. Let it marinate in your refrigerator about 30 minutes.

In another bowl, mix the crushed chips and grated Pecorino Romano cheese.

Dredge the chicken fillets through the chips mixture and transfer them to the cooking basket. Reduce the temperature to 380 degrees F and cook the chicken for 6 minutes.

Turn them over and cook for a further 6 minutes. Repeat the process until you have run out of Ingredients.

Serve: with re**Serve:**d bacon. Enjoy!

Roasted Citrus Turkey Drumsticks

(**Ready in about** 55 minutes | **Servings:** 3)

Ingredients

3 medium turkey drumsticks, bone-in
1 teaspoon cayenne pepper
1 teaspoon dried parsley flakes
Zest of one orange
1/4 cup orange juice

Sea salt and ground black pepper, to taste
1 teaspoon fresh garlic, minced
1 teaspoon onion powder
1/2 butter stick, melted

Directions

Rub all Ingredients onto the turkey drumsticks.

Preheat your Air Fryer to 400 degrees F. Cook the turkey drumsticks for 16 minutes in the preheated Air Fryer.

Loosely cover with foil and cook an additional 24 minutes.

Once cooked, let it rest for 10 minutes before slicing and serving. Bon appétit!

Turkey Bacon with Scrambled Eggs

(**Ready in about** 25 minutes | **Servings:** 4)

Ingredients

1/2 pound turkey bacon
2 tablespoons yogurt
1/2 teaspoon sea salt
2 green onions, finely chopped
4 eggs

1/3 cup milk
1 bell pepper, finely chopped
1/2 cup Colby cheese, shredded

Directions

Place the turkey bacon in the cooking basket.

Cook at 360 degrees F for 9 to 11 minutes. Work in batches. Re**Serve:** the fried bacon.

In a mixing bowl, thoroughly whisk the eggs with milk and yogurt. Add salt, bell pepper, and green onions.

Brush the sides and bottom of the baking pan with the re**Serve:**d 1 teaspoon of bacon grease.

Pour the egg mixture into the baking pan. Cook at 355 degrees F about 5 minutes. Top with shredded Colby cheese and cook for 5 to 6 minutes more. **Serve:** the scrambled eggs with the re**Serve:**d bacon and enjoy!

Chinese Duck (Xiang Su Ya)

(**Ready in about** 30 minutes + marinating time | **Servings:** 6)

Ingredients

2 pounds duck breast, boneless
1 teaspoon Chinese 5-spice powder
1 teaspoon Szechuan peppercorns
1 teaspoon coarse salt
1/4 cup molasses

1 tbsp light soy sauce
2 green onions, chopped
1/2 teaspoon ground black pepper Glaze
3 tablespoons Shaoxing rice wine
1 tablespoon soy sauce
3 tablespoons orange juice

Directions

In a ceramic bowl, place the duck breasts, green onions, light soy sauce, Chinese 5-spice powder, Szechuan peppercorns, and Shaoxing rice wine. Let it marinate for 1 hour in your refrigerator.

Preheat your Air Fryer to 400 degrees F for 5 minutes.

Now, discard the marinade and season the duck breasts with salt and pepper. Cook the duck breasts for 12 to 15 minutes or until they are golden brown.

Repeat with the other Ingredients.In the meantime, add the re**Serve:**d marinade to the saucepan that is preheated over medium-high heat. Add the molasses, orange juice, and 1 tablespoon of soy sauce. Bring to a simmer and then, whisk constantly until it gets syrupy. Brush the surface of duck breasts with glaze so they are completely covered. Place duck breasts back in the Air Fryer basket; cook an additional 5 minutes. Enjoy!

Italian Chicken and Cheese Frittata

(**Ready in about** 25 minutes | **Servings:** 4)

Ingredients

1 (1-pound) fillet chicken breast	Sea salt and ground black pepper, to taste
4 eggs	1/2 teaspoon cayenne pepper
1 tablespoon olive oil	
1/4 cup Asiago cheese, freshly grated	1/2 cup Mascarpone cream

Directions

Flatten the chicken breast with a meat mallet. Season with salt and pepper.

Heat the olive oil in a frying pan over medium flame. Cook the chicken for 10 to 12 minutes; slice into small strips, and re**Serve:**.

Then, in a mixing bowl, thoroughly combine the eggs, and cayenne pepper; season with salt to taste. Add the cheese and stir to combine.

Add the re**Serve:**d chicken. Then, pour the mixture into a lightly greased pan; put the pan into the cooking basket.

Cook in the preheated Air Fryer at 355 degrees F for 10 minutes, flipping over halfway through

Garden Vegetable and Chicken Casserole

(**Ready in about** 30 minutes | **Servings:** 4)

Ingredients

2 teaspoons peanut oil	2 pounds chicken drumettes
1/2 medium-sized leek, sliced 2 carrots, sliced	1 cup cauliflower florets
1 tbsp all-purpose flour	1 garlic clove, minced
1 thyme sprig	1/4 cup dry white wine
2 cups vegetable broth	1 rosemary sprig

Directions

Preheat your Air Fryer to 370 degrees F. Then, drizzle the chicken drumettes with peanut oil and cook them for 10 minutes. Transfer the chicken drumettes to a lightly greased pan.Add the garlic, leeks, carrots, and cauliflower.

Mix the remaining Ingredients in a bowl. Pour the flour mixture into the pan. Cook at 380 degrees F for 15 minutes. **Serve:** warm.

Thanksgiving Turkey Tenderloin with Gravy

(**Ready in about** 40 minutes | **Servings:** 4)

Ingredients

2 ½ pounds turkey tenderloin, sliced into pieces	1 dried marjoram
	1/2 head of garlic, peeled and halved
1 teaspoon cayenne pepper	
Sea salt and ground black pepper, to taste	Gravy
	1/3 cup all-purpose flour
3 cups vegetable broth	Sea salt and ground black pepper, to taste

Directions

Start by preheating your Air Fryer to 350 degrees F.

Rub the turkey tenderloins with garlic halves; add marjoram, salt, black pepper, and cayenne pepper.

Cook the turkey tenderloins at 350 degrees F for 30 minutes or until an instant-read thermometer inserted into the center of the breast reaches 165 degrees F; flip them over halfway through.

In a saucepan, place the drippings from the roasted turkey. Add 1 cup of broth and 1/6 cup of flour to the pan; whisk until it makes a smooth paste.

Once it gets a golden brown color, add the rest of the chicken broth and flour. Sprinkle with salt and pepper to taste.

Let it simmer over medium heat, stirring constantly for 6 to 7 minutes. **Serve:** with warm turkey tenderloin and enjoy!

Creole Turkey with Peppers

(**Ready in about** 35 minutes | **Servings:** 4)

Ingredients

2 pounds turkey thighs, skinless and boneless	2 bell peppers, deveined and sliced
1 habanero pepper, deveined and minced	1 tablespoon Creole seasoning mix
1 carrot, sliced	1 red onion, sliced
1 tablespoon fish sauce	2 cups chicken broth

Directions

Preheat your Air Fryer to 360° F. Using a nonstick cooking spray, spritz the bottom and sides of the casserole dish.

In the casserole dish, arrange the turkey thighs. Combine the onion, pepper, and carrot in a mixing bowl. Season with Creole seasoning. After that, stir in the fish sauce and chicken broth. Cook for 30 minutes in a preheated Air Fryer. **Serve:** immediately and enjoy!

Pesto Chicken

Prep time: 10 minutes **Cooking time:** 20 minutes
Serve: 2

Ingredients

4 chicken drumsticks	6 garlic cloves
1/2 jalapeno pepper	1 tbsp. ginger, sliced
2 tbsp. lemon juice	1/2 cup cilantro
2 tbsp. olive oil	1 tsp. salt

Directions

Add all the ingredients except chicken into the blender and blend until smooth. Pour blended mixture into the large bowl.

Add chicken and stir well to coat. Place in refrigerator for 2 hours. Spray air fryer basket with cooking spray. Place marinated chicken into the air fryer basket and cook at 390 F for 20 minutes. Turn halfway through. **Serve:** and enjoy.

Peanut Chicken and Pepper Wraps

(**Ready in about** 25 minutes | **Servings:** 4)

Ingredients

1 ½ pounds chicken breast, boneless and skinless	1 tablespoon sesame oil
	1/4 cup peanut butter
1 tablespoon soy sauce	
2 teaspoons rice vinegar	1 teaspoon fresh ginger, peeled and grated
1 teaspoon fresh garlic, minced	2 tablespoons lemon juice, freshly squeezed
4 tortillas	1 bell pepper, julienned
1 teaspoon brown sugar	

Directions

Start by preheating your Air Fryer to 380 degrees F.

Cook the chicken breasts in the preheated Air Fryer approximately 6 minutes. Turn them over and cook an additional 6 minutes.

Meanwhile, make the sauce by mixing the peanut butter, sesame oil, soy sauce, vinegar, ginger, garlic, sugar, and lemon juice.

Slice the chicken crosswise across the grain into 1/4-inch strips. Toss the chicken into the sauce.

Decrease temperature to 390 degrees F. Spoon the chicken and sauce onto each tortilla; add bell peppers and wrap them tightly. Drizzle with a nonstick cooking spray and bake about 7 minutes. **Serve:** warm.

Turkey Wings with Butter Roasted Potatoes

(**Ready in about** 55 minutes | **Servings:** 4)

Ingredients

4 large-sized potatoes, peeled and cut into 1-inch chunks	1 teaspoon rosemary
	1 tablespoon butter, melted
2 garlic cloves, minced	1/2 tbsp cayenne pepper
1 teaspoon garlic salt	1/2 teaspoon ground black pepper
1 ½ pounds turkey wings	
2 tablespoons olive oil	1 tbsp Dijon mustard

Directions

Add the potatoes, butter, rosemary, salt, and pepper to the cooking basket.

Cook at 400 degrees F for 12 minutes. Re**Serve:** the potatoes, keeping them warm.

Now, place the turkey wings in the cooking basket that is previously cleaned

and greased with olive oil. Add the garlic, mustard, and cayenne pepper. Cook in the preheated Air Fryer at 350 degrees f for 25 minutes. Turn them over and cook an additional 15 minutes.

Test for doneness with a meat thermometer. **Serve:** with warm potatoes.

Smoked Duck with Rosemary-Infused Gravy

(**Ready in about** 30 minutes | **Servings:** 4)

Ingredients

1 ½ pounds smoked duck breasts, boneless	2 tablespoons ketchup
	1 tbsp yellow mustard
1 teaspoon agave syrup	5 ounces chicken broth
12 pearl onions peeled	1 tablespoon flour
1 teaspoon rosemary, finely chopped	

Directions

Cook the smoked duck breasts in the preheated Air Fryer at 365 degrees F for 15 minutes.

Smear the mustard, ketchup, and agave syrup on the duck breast. Top with pearl onions. Cook for a further 7 minutes or until the skin of the duck breast looks crispy and golden brown.

Slice the duck breasts and re**Serve:**. Drain off the duck fat from the pan.

Then, add the re**Serve:**d 1 tablespoon of duck fat to the pan and warm it over medium heat; add flour and cook until your roux is dark brown.

Add the chicken broth and rosemary to the pan. Reduce the heat to low and cook until the gravy has thickened slightly. Spoon the warm gravy over the re**Serve:**d duck breasts. Enjoy!

Chicken with Golden Roasted Cauliflower

(**Ready in about** 30 minutes | **Servings:** 4)

Ingredients

2 pounds chicken legs
2 tablespoons olive oil
1 teaspoon sea salt
1 teaspoon dried marjoram
2 garlic cloves minced
1/3 cup Pecorino Romano cheese, freshly grated

1/2 teaspoon ground black pepper
1 tbsp smoked paprika
1 (1-pound) head cauliflower, broken into small florets
1/2 teaspoon dried thyme
Salt, to taste

Directions

Toss the chicken legs with the olive oil, salt, black pepper, paprika, and marjoram.

Cook in the preheated Air Fryer at 380 degrees F for 11 minutes. Flip the chicken legs and cook for a further 5 minutes.

Toss the cauliflower florets with garlic, cheese, thyme, and salt.

Increase the temperature to 400 degrees F; add the cauliflower florets and cook for 12 more minutes. **Serve:** warm.

Adobo Seasoned Chicken with Veggies

(**Ready in about** 1 hour 30 minutes | **Servings:** 4)

Ingredients

2 pounds chicken wings, rinsed and patted dry
1/2 teaspoon red pepper flakes, crushed
1 teaspoon granulated onion 1 teaspoon ground turmeric
2 cloves garlic, peeled but not chopped
2 tbsp tomato powder
2 bell peppers, seeded and sliced
4 carrots, trimmed and halved

1/4 teaspoon ground black pepper
1 teaspoon paprika
1 teaspoon coarse sea salt
1 tablespoon dry Madeira wine
2 stalks celery, diced
1 large Spanish onion, diced
1 teaspoon ground cumin
2 tablespoons olive oil

Directions

In a large mixing bowl, combine all of the Ingredients. Cover and place in the refrigerator for 1 hour.

Place the chicken wings in a baking dish.

Cook the chicken wings for 7 minutes in a preheated Air Fryer at 380 degrees F.

Cook for 15 minutes more after adding the vegetables, shaking the basket once or twice. **Serve:** hot.

Chicken and Brown Rice Bake

(**Ready in about** 50 minutes | **Servings:** 3)

Ingredients

1 cup brown rice
1 tablespoon butter, melted
Kosher salt and ground black pepper, to taste
1 onion, chopped
1 cup tomato puree

2 cups vegetable broth
2 garlic cloves, minced
1/2 cup water
3 chicken fillets
1 tbsp cayenne pepper
1 tablespoon fresh chives, chopped

Directions

Heat the brown rice, vegetable broth and water in a pot over high heat. Bring it to a boil; turn the stove down to simmer and cook for 35 minutes.

Grease a baking pan with butter.

Spoon the prepared rice mixture into the baking pan. Add the onion, garlic, salt, black pepper, cayenne pepper, and chicken. Spoon the tomato puree over the chicken.

Cook in the preheated Air Fryer at 380 degrees F for 12 minutes. **Serve:** garnished with fresh chives. Enjoy!

Sticky Exotic Chicken Drumettes

(**Ready in about** 25 minutes | **Servings:** 4)

Ingredients

2 tablespoons peanut oil
1 tablespoon yellow mustard
2 tablespoons honey
1/2 teaspoon sambal oelek
1/4 cup chicken broth
1 ½ pounds chicken drumettes, bone-in
Salt and ground white pepper, to taste

1 tablespoon tamari sauce
1 clove garlic, peeled and minced
2 tablespoons fresh orange juice

1/2 cup raw onion rings, for garnish

Directions

Start by preheating your Air Fryer to 380 degrees F.

Line the cooking basket with parchment paper. Lightly grease the parchment paper with 1 tablespoon of peanut oil. In a mixing bowl, thoroughly combine the remaining 1 tablespoon of oil honey, tamari sauce, mustard, garlic, orange juice, and sambal oelek. Whisk to combine well.

Arrange the chicken drumettes in the prepared cooking basket. Season with salt and white pepper.

Spread 1/2 of the honey mixture evenly all over each breast. Pour in the chicken broth. Cook for 12 minutes.

Turn them over, add the remaining 1/2 of the honey mixture, and cook an additional 10 minutes. Garnish with onion rings and **Serve:** immediately.

Spanish Chicken with Golden Potatoes

(**Ready in about** 25 minutes | **Servings:** 4)

Ingredients

2 tablespoons butter, melted

1 pound Yukon Gold potatoes, peeled and diced

1 teaspoon dried rosemary, crushed

1 teaspoon dried thyme, crushed

1/3 teaspoon freshly ground black pepper

4 chicken drumsticks bonein

1 teaspoon fresh garlic, minced

1 teaspoon cayenne pepper

1 lemon, 1/2 juiced, 1/2 cut into wedges

2 tablespoons sherry

Kosher salt, to taste

Directions

Start by preheating your Air Fryer to 370 degrees F. Then, grease a baking pan with the melted butter. Arrange the chicken drumsticks in the baking pan. Bake in the preheated Air Fryer for 8 minutes. Add the diced potatoes.

Drizzle chicken and potatoes with lemon juice. Sprinkle with garlic, rosemary, thyme, cayenne pepper, black pepper, and salt. Turn the temperature to 400 degrees F and cook for a further 12 minutes. Make sure to shake the basket once or twice. Remove from the Air Fryer basket and sprinkle sherry on top. **Serve:** with the lemon wedges. Enjoy

Pizza Spaghetti Casserole

(**Ready in about** 30 minutes | **Servings:** 4)

Ingredients

8 ounces spaghetti

2 tomatoes, pureed

1/2 cup Asiago cheese, shredded

3 tablespoons Romano cheese, grated

1 pound smoked chicken sausage, sliced

1 tablespoon Italian seasoning mix

1 tablespoon fresh basil leaves, chiffonade

Directions

Bring a large pot of lightly salted water to a boil. Cook your spaghetti for 10 minutes or until al dente; drain and re**Serve:**, keeping warm.

Stir in the chicken sausage, tomato puree, Asiago cheese, and Italian seasoning mix.

Then, spritz a baking pan with cooking spray; add the spaghetti mixture to the pan. Bake in the preheated Air Fryer at 325 degrees F for 11 minutes.

Top with the grated Romano cheese. Turn the temperature to 390 degrees F and cook an additional 5 minutes or until everything is thoroughly heated and the cheese is melted.

Garnish with fresh basil leaves. Bon appétit!

Turkey Breakfast Frittata

(**Ready in about** 50 minutes | **Servings:** 4)

Ingredients

1 tablespoon olive oil

3 tablespoons Greek yogurt

1/4 teaspoon red pepper flakes, crushed Himalayan salt, to taste

1 green bell pepper, seeded and sliced

1 pound turkey breasts, slices

3 tablespoons Cottage cheese, crumbled

1 red bell pepper, seeded and sliced

1/4 teaspoon ground black pepper

6 large-sized eggs

Directions

Grease the cooking basket with olive oil. Add the turkey and cook in the preheated Air Fryer at 350 degrees F for 30 minutes, flipping them over halfway through. Cut into bite-sized strips and re**Serve:**.

Now, beat the eggs with Greek yogurt, cheese, black pepper, red pepper, and salt. Add the bell peppers to a baking pan that is previously lightly greased with a cooking spray. Add the turkey strips; pour the egg mixture over all Ingredients. Bake in the preheated Air Fryer at 360 degrees F for 15 minutes. **Serve:** right away!

Nana's Turkey Chili

(**Ready in about** 1 hour | **Servings:** 4)

Ingredients

1/2 medium-sized leek, chopped

1 jalapeno pepper, seeded and minced

2 cups tomato puree

1 pound ground turkey, 85% lean 15% fat

1/2 teaspoon black peppercorns

1 teaspoon mustard seeds

2 garlic cloves, minced

1/2 red onion, chopped

2 tablespoons olive oil

1 bell pepper, seeded and chopped

2 cups chicken stock

Salt, to taste

1 teaspoon chili powder

1 teaspoon ground cumin

1 (12-ounce) can kidney beans, rinsed and drained

Directions

Start by preheating your Air Fryer to 365 degrees F.

Place the leeks, onion, garlic and peppers in a baking pan; drizzle olive oil evenly over the top. Cook for 4 to 6 minutes. Add the ground turkey. Cook for 6 minutes more or until the meat is no longer pink.

Now, add the tomato puree, 1 cup of chicken stock, black peppercorns, salt, chili powder, mustard seeds, and cumin to the baking pan. Cook for 24 minutes, stirring every 7 to 10 minutes. Stir in the canned beans and the remaining 1 cup of stock; let it cook for a further 9 minutes; make sure to stir halfway through. Bon appétit!

Authentic Chicken-Fajitas with Salsa

(**Ready in about** 30 minutes | **Servings:** 4)

Ingredients

1 pound chicken tenderloins, chopped
1 teaspoon fajita seasoning
1 teaspoon shallot powder
Salsa
4 flour tortillas
1 bunch fresh coriander, roughly chopped
1 lime
Sea salt and ground black pepper, to your liking
2 bell peppers, seeded and diced
1 ancho chili pepper, seeded and finely chopped
2 tablespoons extra-virgin olive oil
2 ripe tomatoes, crushed

Directions

Toss the chicken in a bowl with the salt, pepper, shallot powder, and fajita seasoning mix. 9 minutes in a preheated Air Fryer at 390 degrees F. Roast for an additional 8 minutes after adding the bell peppers

Combine the chilli, tomatoes, and coriander for the salsa. Squeeze 1 lime juice over the top; add olive oil and stir well to combine.

Warm the tortillas in your Air Fryer for 10 minutes at 200 degrees F. **Serve:** the chicken fajitas with tortillas and salsa on the side. Enjoy!

Vermouth Bacon and Turkey Burgers

(**Ready in about** 30 minutes | **Servings:** 4)

Ingredients

2 tablespoons vermouth
2 strips Canadian bacon, sliced
2 garlic cloves, minced 2 tablespoons fish sauce
4 soft hamburger rolls
1 tbsp red pepper flakes
4 (1-ounce) slices Cheddar cheese
1 tablespoon honey
1/2 shallot, minced
1 pound ground turkey
Sea salt and ground black pepper, to taste
4 tablespoons tomato ketchup
4 tablespoons mayonnaise
4 lettuce leaves

Directions

Start by preheating your Air Fryer to 400 degrees F.

Whisk the vermouth and honey in a mixing bowl; brush the Canadian bacon with the vermouth mixture.

Cook for 3 minutes. Flip the bacon over and cook an additional 3 minutes. Then, thoroughly combine the ground turkey, shallots, garlic, fish sauce, salt, black pepper, and red pepper. Form the meat mixture into 4 burger patties.

Bake in the preheated Air Fryer at 370 degrees F for 10 minutes. Flip them over and cook another 10 minutes.

Spread the ketchup and mayonnaise on the inside of the hamburger rolls and place the burgers on the rolls; top with bacon, cheese and lettuce; **Serve:** immediately.

Chicken Taquitos with Homemade

Guacamole

(**Ready in about** 35 minutes | **Servings:** 4)

Ingredients

1 tablespoon peanut oil
1 pound chicken breast
1 teaspoon chili powder
1 teaspoon garlic powder
1/2 cup sour cream
1 ripe avocado, pitted and peeled
1 tbs fresh cilantro, chopped
1 lime, juiced
1 tbs fresh garlic, minced
Seasoned salt and ground black pepper, to taste
1 cup Colby cheese, shredded 8 corn tortillas
Guacamole
1/2 onion, finely chopped
1 teaspoon ground cumin
1 tomato, crushed
1 chili pepper, seeded and minced
Sea salt black pepper to taste

Directions

Toss the chicken with the salt, pepper, shallot powder, and fajita seasoning mix in a mixing bowl.

9 minutes in a 390° F preheated Air Fryer. After adding the bell peppers, roast for an additional 8 minutes.

For the salsa, combine the chilli, tomatoes, and coriander. Squeeze 1 lime juice over the top, then drizzle with olive oil and mix well.

Warm the tortillas in an Air Fryer at 200°F for 10 minutes. With tortillas and salsa on the side, **Serve:** the chicken fajitas. Enjoy!

Fennel Chicken

Prep time: 10 minutes **Cooking time:** 15 minutes
Servings: 2

Ingredients

1/2 lb. chicken thighs, skinless, boneless, and cut each thigh into 3 pieces
1 tsp. garlic, minced
1 tsp. ginger, minced
1/4 tsp. garam masala
1/2 tsp. salt
1/2 tsp. paprika
1/2 tbsp. olive oil
1/2 onion, sliced
1/4 tsp. cayenne pepper
1/2 tsp. turmeric
1/2 tsp. ground fennel seeds

Directions

Add chicken into the bowl and toss with remaining ingredients to coat. Place in refrigerator for overnight. Place marinated chicken into the air fryer basket and cook at 360 F for 15 minutes. Turn halfway through. **Serve:** and enjoy.

Herb Chicken Roast

Prep time: 10 minutes **Cooking time:** 25 minutes
Serve: 2

Ingredients

10 oz. chicken breast	1 tbsp. butter
1/2 tsp. paprika	1/4 tsp. dried thyme
1/4 tsp. black pepper	1/4 tsp. garlic powder
1/4 tsp. salt	1/4 tsp. dried rosemary

Directions

Place turkey breast into the air fryer basket and cook at 25 F for 60 minutes. Turn turkey breast to another side halfway through. enjoy.

Thyme Butter Turkey Breast

Prep time: 10 minutes **Cooking time:** 60 minutes
Serve: 8

Ingredients

2 lbs. turkey breast	1/2 tsp. thyme leaves, chopped
1/4 tsp. pepper	
1/2 tsp. sage leaves, chopped	1 tsp. salt
	1 tbsp. butter

Directions

Spray air fryer basket with cooking spray.
Rub butter all over the turkey breast and season with pepper, sage, thyme, and salt.
Place turkey breast into the air fryer basket and cook at 25 F for 60 minutes. Turn turkey breast to another side halfway through.
Slice and **Serve:**.

Meatballs

Prep time: 10 minutes **Cooking time:** 10 minutes
Serve: 6

Ingredients

2 lbs. ground chicken breast	2 eggs, lightly beaten
1/4 cup fresh parsley, chopped	1/2 tsp. pepper
1/2 cup almond flour	1/2 cup ricotta cheese
	2 tsp. salt

Directions

Spray air fryer basket with cooking spray.
Add all ingredients into the large bowl and mix until well combined.
Make small balls from meat mixture and place in the air fryer basket and cook at 380 F for 10 minutes. Shake basket twice while cooking.
Serve: and enjoy.

Turkey Meatballs

Prep time: 10 minutes **Cooking time:** 12 minutes
Servings: 4

Ingredients

1lb. ground turkey	2 green onion, chopped
2garlic cloves, minced	1/4 cup celery, chopped
2tbsp. coconut flour	Pepper
Salt	1/4 cup carrots, grated
	1 egg, lightly beaten

Directions

Spray air fryer basket with cooking spray.

Preheat the air fryer to 400 F.

Add all ingredients into the large bowl and mix until well combined.

Make balls from meat mixture and place into the air fryer basket and cook for 12 minutes. Turn halfway through.

Serve: and enjoy.

Chicken Tenders

Prep time: 10 minutes **Cooking time:** 12 minutes
Servings: 4

Ingredients

1lb. chicken tenders	3/4 cup pecans, crushed
1 egg, lightly beaten	1/4 tsp. pepper
1/4 cup ground mustard	1/4 tsp. garlic powder
1/2 tsp. paprika	1/4 tsp. onion powder
	1 tsp. salt

Directions

Spray air fryer basket with cooking spray. Add chicken into the large bowl. Season with paprika, pepper, garlic powder, onion powder, and salt. Add mustard mix well.

In a separate bowl, add egg and whisk well. In a shallow bowl, add crushed pecans. Dip chicken into the egg then coats with pecans and place into the air fryer basket. Cook at 350 F for 12 minutes. **Serve:** and enjoy.

Chicken Coconut Meatballs

Prep time: 10 minutes **Cooking time:** 10 minutes
Servings: 4

Ingredients

1lb. ground chicken	1/2 tbsp. hoisin sauce
11/2 tsp. sriracha	1/2 tbsp. soy sauce
1/4 cup shredded coconut	1/2 cup fresh cilantro,
1 tsp. sesame oil	chopped
2green onions, chopped	Pepper
Salt	

Directions

Spray air fryer basket with cooking spray.
Attach all ingredients into the large bowl and merge until well combined.

Make small balls from meat mixture and set into the air fryer basket. Cook at 350 F for 10 minutes. Turn halfway through. **Serve:** and enjoy.

Cheese Herb Chicken Wings

Prep time: 10 minutes **Cooking time:** 15 minutes
Servings: 4

Ingredients

2 lbs. chicken wings	1/2 cup parmesan cheese,
1tsp. herb de Provence	grated
Salt	1 tsp. paprika

Directions

Preheat the air fryer to 350 F. In a small bowl, mix together cheese, herb de Provence, paprika, and salt. Spray air fryer basket with cooking spray.

Toss chicken wings with cheese mixture and place into the air fryer basket and cook for 15 minutes. Turn halfway through. **Serve:** and enjoy.

Tasty Caribbean Chicken

Prep time: 10 minutes **Cooking time:** 10 minutes
Servings: 8

Ingredients

3 lbs. chicken thigh,	3tbsp. coconut oil, melted
skinless and boneless	1/2 tsp. ground nutmeg
1tbsp. coriander powder	1/2 tsp. ground ginger
1 tbsp. cayenne Salt	1 tbsp. cinnamon Pepper

Directions

In a small bowl, mix together all spices and rub all over the chicken. Spray air fryer basket with cooking spray.

Place chicken into the air fryer basket and cook at 390 F for 10 minutes. **Serve:** and enjoy.

Delicious Chicken Tenderloins

Prep time: 10 minutes **Cooking time:** 15 minutes
Servings: 6

Ingredients

1egg, lightly beaten	1/4 cup heavy whipping
8 oz. chicken breast	cream
tenderloins	1 cup almond flour
1/4 tsp. garlic powder	1 tsp. salt
1 tsp. pepper	1/4 tsp. onion powder

Directions

Whisk egg, with garlic powder, onion powder, cream, pepper, and salt in a bowl. In a dish, add the almond flour.
Dip chicken in egg mixture then coats with almond flour mixture.

Spray air fryer basket with cooking spray.
Place chicken into the air fryer basket and cook at 450 F for 15 minutes. **Serve:** and enjoy.

Garlic Herb Chicken Breasts

Prep time: 10 minutes **Cooking time:** 15 minutes
Servings: 5

Ingredients

2 lbs. chicken breasts,	1/4 cup yogurt
skinless and boneless	4 garlic cloves, minced
1/4 cup mayonnaise	2 tsp. garlic herb
	seasoning
1/4 tsp. salt	1/2 tsp. onion powder

Directions

Preheat the air fryer to 380 F. In a small bowl, mix together mayonnaise, seasoning, onion powder, garlic, and yogurt.

Brush chicken with mayo mixture and season with salt.
Spray air fryer basket with cooking spray. Place chicken into the air fryer basket and cook for 15 minutes. **Serve:** and enjoy.

Chicken Kebab

Prep time: 10 minutes **Cooking time:** 6 minutes
Servings: 3

Ingredients

1lb. ground chicken
1green onion, chopped
3garlic cloves
1/3 cup fresh parsley, chopped
1/4 tsp. turmeric powder

1 tbsp. fresh lemon juice
1/4 cup almond flour
1 egg, lightly beaten
4oz. onion, chopped
1/2 tsp. pepper

Directions

Attach all ingredients into the food processor and process until well combined. Transfer chicken mixture to the bowl and place in the refrigerator for 1 hour.

Divide mixture into the 6 equal portions and roll around the soaked wooden skewers. Spray air fryer basket with cooking spray. Place skewers into the air fryer basket and cooks at 400 F for 6 minutes. **Serve:** and enjoy.

Mediterranean Chicken

Prep time: 10 minutes **Cooking time:** 35 minutes
Servings: 6

Ingredients

4 lbs. whole chicken, cut into pieces
2 tbsp. olive oil
1tsp. lemon zest

2 garlic cloves, minced
2 lemons, sliced
2tsp. kosher salt
2 tsp. ground sumac

Directions

Rub chicken with oil, sumac, lemon zest, and salt. Place in the refrigerator for 2-3 hours. Add lemon sliced into the air fryer basket top with marinated chicken. Cook at 350 for 35 minutes. **Serve:** and enjoy.

Asian Chicken Wings

Prep time: 10 minutes **Cooking time:** 30 minutes
Servings: 2

Ingredients

4 chicken wings
1 tsp. mixed spice Pepper
1tbsp. soy sauce

3/4 tbsp. Chinese spice
Salt

Directions

Add chicken wings into the bowl. Add remaining ingredients and toss to coat. Set chicken wings into the air fryer basket. Cook at 350 f for 15 minutes.

Turn chicken to another side and cook for 15 minutes more. **Serve:** and enjoy.

Delicious Chicken Fajitas

Prep time: 10 minutes **Cooking time:** 15 minutes
Servings: 4

Ingredients

4 chicken breasts
1 1/2 tbsp. fajita seasoning
2tbsp olive oil
1onion, sliced

1 bell pepper, sliced
3/4 cup cheddar cheese, shredded

Directions

Preheat the air fryer at 380 F. Coat chicken with oil and rub with seasoning. Place chicken into the air fryer baking dish and top with bell peppers and onion.

Cook for 15 minutes. Top with shredded cheese and cook for 1-2 minutes until cheese is melted. **Serve:** and enjoy.

Juicy and Spicy Chicken Wings

Prep time: 10 minutes **Cooking time:** 25 minutes
Servings: 4

Ingredients

2 lbs. chicken wings
12 oz. hot sauce
6 tbsp. butter, melted

1tsp. Worcestershire sauce
1 tsp. Tabasco

Directions

Spray air fryer basket with cooking spray. Add chicken wings into the air fryer basket and cook at 380 F for 25 minutes. Shake basket after every 5 minutes.

Meanwhile, in a bowl, mix together hot sauce, Worcestershire sauce, and butter. Set aside. Add chicken wings into the sauce and toss well. **Serve:** and enjoy.

Curried Drumsticks

Prep time: 10 minutes **Cooking time:** 22 minutes
Servings: 2

Ingredients

2 turkey drumsticks
1/4 tsp. cayenne pepper
2 tbsp red curry paste
1/4 tsp. pepper

11/2 tbsp. ginger, minced
1 tsp. kosher salt
1/3 cup coconut milk

Directions

Add all ingredients into the bowl and stir to coat. Place in refrigerator for overnight. Spray air fryer basket with cooking spray. Place marinated drumsticks into the air fryer basket and cook at 390 F for 22 minutes. **Serve:** and enjoy.

Indian Chicken Tenders

Prep time: 10 minutes **Cooking time:** 15 minutes
Servings: 4

Ingredients

1lb. chicken tenders, cut in half	1/2 tbsp. garlic, minced
1/4 cup parsley, chopped	1/2 tbsp. ginger, minced
3/4 tsp. paprika	1/4 cup yogurt
1/2 tsp. cayenne pepper	1 tsp. garam masala
1 tsp. turmeric	1 tsp. salt

Directions

Preheat the air fryer to 350 F. Attach all ingredients into the large bowl and mix well. Place in refrigerator for 30 minutes. Spray air fryer basket with cooking spray.

Add marinated chicken into the air fryer basket and cook for 10 minutes. Turn chicken to another side and cook for 5 minutes more. **Serve:** and enjoy.

Dijon Turkey Drumstick

Prep time: 10 minutes **Cooking time:** 28 minutes
Serve: 2

Ingredients

4 turkey drumsticks	1/3 cup sherry wine
1/3 tsp. paprika	1/3 cup coconut milk
1/2 tbsp. ginger, minced	Pepper and Salt
2 tbsp. Dijon mustard	

Directions

Attach all ingredients into the large bowl and stir to coat. Place in refrigerator for 2 hours. Spray air fryer basket with cooking spray.

Place marinated turkey drumsticks into the air fryer basket and cook at 380 F for 28 minutes. Turn halfway through.
Serve: and enjoy.

Korean Chicken Tenders

Prep time: 10 minutes **Cooking time:** 10 minutes
Servings: 3

Ingredients

12 oz. chicken tenders, skinless and boneless	3 garlic cloves, chopped
1tbsp ginger, grated	2 tbsp. green onion, chopped
2 tsp. sesame seeds, toasted	1/4 cup sesame oil
	1/4 tsp. pepper
	1/2 cup soy sauce

Directions

Slide chicken tenders onto the skewers. In a large bowl, mix together green onion, garlic, sesame seeds, ginger, sesame oil, soy sauce, and pepper. Add chicken skewers into the bowl and coat well with marinade. Place in refrigerator for overnight.

Preheat the air fryer to 390 F. Place marinated chicken skewers into the air fryer basket and cook for 10 minutes.

Air Fried Maple Chicken Thighs

Prep time: 10 minutes **Cooking time:** 25 minutes
Servings: 4

Ingredients

1 egg	Buttermilk 1 cup Maple syrup 1/2 cup Chicken garlic 1 tsp.
thighs 4 pieces	
Granulated	
All-purpose flour 1/2 cup	
Dry Mix	Granulated garlic 1/2 tsp.
Black pepper 1/4 teaspoon	Salt 1 tbsp.
Sweet paprika 1 tsp.	Cayenne pepper 1/4 teaspoon
Smoked paprika 1/2 tsp.	
Tapioca flour 1/4 cup	Granulated onion one tsp.
Honey powder 1/2 tsp.	

Directions

In a Ziploc bag, add egg, one tsp. of granulated garlic, buttermilk, and maple syrup, add in the chicken thighs and let it marinate for one hour or more in the refrigerator

In a mixing bowl, add sweet paprika, tapioca flour, granulated onion, half tsp. of granulated garlic, flour, cayenne pepper, salt, pepper, honey powder, and smoked
paprika mix it well. Let the air fry preheat to 380 F

Coat the marinated chicken thighs in the dry spice mix, shake the excess off. Bring the chicken skin side down in the air fryer Let it cook for 12 minutes. Flip thighs halfway through and cook for 13 minutes more.
Serve: with salad greens.

Mushroom Oatmeal

Prep time: 10 minutes **Cooking time:** 20 minutes
Servings: 4

Ingredients

1small yellow onion, chopped
1 cup steel-cut oats
1 and a half cup of canned chicken stock Thyme springs, chopped
1 cup mushroom, sliced

1 Garlic cloves, minced
1Tablespoons butter
1/2 cup of water
1Tablespoons extra virgin olive oil
1/2 cup gouda cheese,grated
Salt and black pepper to taste

Directions

Heat a pan over medium heat, which suits your air fryer with the butter, add onions and garlic, stir and cook for 4 minutes.

Add oats, sugar, salt, pepper, stock, and thyme, stir, place in the air fryer and cook for 16 minutes at 360 degrees F.

In the meantime, prepare a skillet over medium heat with the olive oil, add mushrooms, cook them for 3 minutes, add oatmeal and cheese, whisk, divide into bowls and **Serve:** for breakfast. Enjoy.

Bell Peppers Frittata

Prep time: 10 minutes **Cooking time:** 20 minutes
Servings: 4

Ingredients

2 Tablespoons olive oil
One sweet onion, chopped
1red bell pepper, chopped
Salt and black pepper to taste
1/2 cup mozzarella cheese, shredded
8 eggs, whisked

2 cups chicken sausage, casings removed and chopped
1 orange bell pepper, chopped
1 green bell pepper
1teaspoons oregano, chopped

Directions

Add 1 spoonful of oil to the air fryer, add bacon, heat to 320 degrees F, and brown for 1 minute. Remove remaining butter, onion, red bell pepper, orange and white, mix and simmer for another 2 minutes. Stir and cook for 15 minutes, add oregano, salt, pepper, and eggs.

Southwest Chicken in Air Fryer

Prep time: 20 minutes **Cooking time:** 30 minutes
Servings: 4

Ingredients

Avocado oil 1 tbsp.
Chili powder 1/2 tsp
Salt to taste Cumin 1/2 tsp.
Garlic powder 1/4 tsp.

4 cups of boneless, skinless, chicken breast .
Onion powder 1/4 tsp.

Lime juice 2 tbsp.

Directions

In a Ziploc bag, add chicken, oil, and lime juice. Add all spices in a bowl and rub all over the chicken in the Ziploc bag. Let it marinate in the fridge for ten minutes or more.

Take chicken out from the Ziploc bag and put it in the air fryer. Cook for 25 minutes at 400 F, flipping chicken halfway through until internal temperature reaches 165 degrees.

No-Breading Chicken Breast in Air Fryer

Prep time: 10 minutes **Cooking time:** 20 minutes
Servings: 2

Ingredients

Olive oil spray
teaspoon Salt 1/4 cup teaspoon
Smoked paprika 1/2 tsp.
Garlic powder 3/4 teaspoon

Chicken breasts 4 (boneless)
Salt 1/4 cup.
Dried parsley half tsp
1/8 tsp. of cayenne pepper

Directions

In a bowl, attach six cups of warm water; add salt (1/4 cup) and mix to dissolve. Put chicken breasts in the warm salted water and let it refrigerate for almost 2 hours. Remove from water and pat dry.

In a bowl, add all the spices with 3/4 tsp. of salt. Spray the oil all over the chicken and rub the spice mix all over the chicken. Let the air fryer heat at 380F. Put the chicken in the air fryer and cook for ten minutes. Flip halfway through and **Serve:** with salad green.

Air Fried Chicken Fajitas

Prep time: 10 minutes **Cooking time:** 20 minutes
Servings: 6

Ingredients

Chicken breasts 4 cups, cut into thin strips	Salt 1/2 tsp.
Bell peppers,	Cumin 1 tsp.
Garlic powder 1/4 tsp.	Chili powder 1/2 tsp.
	Lime juice 1 tbsp.

Directions

In a bowl, add seasonings, chicken and lime juice, and mix well. Then add sliced peppers and coat well.

Spray the air fryer with olive oil.Put the chicken and peppers in, and cook for 15 minutes at 400 F. flip halfway through. **Serve:** with wedges of lemons and enjoy.

Herb-Marinated Chicken Thighs

Prep time: 30 minutes **Cooking time:** 10 minutes
Servings: 4

Ingredients

Chicken thighs 8 skin-on, bone-in, Lemon juice 2 Tablespoon	Onion powder 1/2 teaspoon
Olive oil 1/4 cup	Garlic powder 2 teaspoon
Dried basil 1 teaspoon	Spike Seasoning 1 tbsp.
Dried oregano 1/2 teaspoon.	Black Pepper 1/4 tsp.

Directions

In a bowl, add dried oregano, olive oil, lemon juice, dried sage, garlic powder, Spike Seasoning, onion powder, dried basil, black pepper.

In a Ziploc bag, add the spice blend and the chicken and mix well. Marinate the chicken for six hours or more.

Preheat the air fryer to 360F. Set the chicken in the air fryer basket, cook for six-eight minutes, flip the chicken, and cook for six minutes more. Until the internal chicken temperature reaches 165F. Take out from the air fryer and **Serve:** with micro greens.

Air Fried Blackened Chicken Breast

Prep time: 10 minutes **Cooking time:** 20 minutes
Servings: 2

Ingredients

Paprika 2 teaspoons	Onion powder 1/2 tsp.
Ground thyme 1 teaspoon	Cumin 1 teaspoon
Black Pepper 1/2 tsp.	Cayenne
Salt 1/4 teaspoon	Pieces of chicken breast halves (without bones and skin)
Vegetable oil 2 teaspoons pepper 1/2 tsp.	

Directions

In a mixing bowl, add onion powder, salt, cumin, paprika, black pepper, thyme, and cayenne pepper. Mix it well.
Drizzle oil over chicken and rub.

Dip each piece of chicken in blackening spice blend on both sides. Let it rest for five minutes while the air fryer is preheating.

Preheat it for five minutes at 360F. Put the chicken in the air fryer and let it cook for ten minutes. Flip and then cook for another ten minutes.

After, let it sit for five minutes, then slice and **Serve:** with the side of greens.

Chicken with Mixed Vegetables

Prep time: 20 minutes **Cooking time:** 20 minutes
Servings: 2

Ingredients

1/2 onion diced	Chicken breast 4 cups, cubed pieces
1/2 zucchini chopped	Olive oil 2 tablespoons
Italian seasoning 1 tablespoon	1/2 teaspoon of chili powder, garlic powder, pepper, salt,
Bell pepper chopped 1/2 cup Clove of garlic pressed Broccoli florets 1/2 cup	

Directions

Let the air fryer heat to 400 F and dice the vegetables In a bowl, add the seasoning, oil and add vegetables, chicken and toss well

Place chicken and vegetables in the air fryer, and cook for ten minutes, toss half way through, cook in batches.
Make sure the veggies are charred and the chicken is cooked through. **Serve:** hot.

Garlic Parmesan Chicken Tenders

Prep time: 5 minutes **Cooking time:** 12 minutes
Servings: 4

Ingredients

1 egg
Olive oil
To coat
Black Pepper 1/4
teaspoon Garlic powder 1
teaspoon Parmesan cheese
1/4 cup Any dipping
Sauce

8 raw chicken tenders
Water 2 tablespoons
Panko breadcrumbs 1 cup
1/2 tsp. of salt
Onion powder 1/2
teaspoon

Directions

Add all the coating ingredients in a big bowl In another bowl, mix water and egg. Dip the chicken in the egg mix, then in the coating mix. Put the tenders in the air fry basket in a single layer.

Spray with the olive oil light Cook at 400 degrees for 12 minutes. Flip the chicken halfway through. **Serve:** with salad greens and enjoy.

Lemon-Garlic Chicken

Prep time: 2 hours **Cooking time:** 35 minutes
Servings: 4

Ingredients

Lemon juice 1/4 cup
1Tbsp. olive oil
1/8 tsp. black pepper
Chicken thighs Lemon
wedges

1 tsp. mustard Cloves of
garlic
1/4 tsp. salt

Directions

In a bowl, merge together the olive oil, lemon juice, mustard Dijon, garlic, salt, and pepper. Bring the chicken thighs in a large Ziploc bag. Spill marinade over chicken and seal bag, ensuring all chicken parts are covered. Cool for at least 2 hours.

Preheat a frying pan to 360 F (175 C). Remove the chicken with towels from the marinade, and pat dry. Place pieces of chicken in the air fryer basket, if necessary, cook them in batches. Fry till chicken is no longer pink on the bone and the juices run smoothly, 22 to 24 min. Upon serving, press a lemon slice across each piece.

Chicken Thighs Smothered Style

Prep time: 30 minutes **Cooking time:** 30 minutes
Servings: 4

Ingredients

8-ounce of chicken thighs
1tsp. paprika
Onions, roughly sliced

1 pinch salt Mushrooms
1/2 cup

Directions

Let the air fryer preheat to 400F
Chicken thighs season with paprika, salt, and pepper on both sides. Place the thighs in the air fryer and cook for 20 minutes. Meanwhile, sauté the mushroom and onion.

Buttermilk Chicken in Air-Fryer

Prep time: 30 minutes **Cooking time:** 20 minutes
Servings: 6

Ingredients

Chicken thighs 4 cups
skin-on, bone-in Marinade
Salt 2 tsp
Seasoned Flour
All-purpose flour 2 cups
Garlic powder 1 tbsp.

Buttermilk 2 cups
Black pepper 2 tsp.
Cayenne pepper 1 tsp.
Baking powder 1 tbsp.
Paprika powder 1 tbsp.
Salt 1 tsp.

Directions

Let the air fry heat at 180 C. With a paper towel, pat dry the chicken thighs. In a mixing bowl, add paprika, black pepper, salt mix well, and then add chicken pieces. Add buttermilk and coat the chicken well. Let it marinate.

In another bowl, add baking powder, salt, flour, pepper, and paprika. Put one by one of the chicken pieces and
coat in the seasoning mix.

Spray oil on chicken pieces and place breaded chicken skin side up in air fryer basket in one layer, cook for 8 minutes, then flip the chicken pieces' cook for another ten minutes Take out from the air fryer and **Serve:** right away.

Orange Chicken Wings

Prep time: 5 minutes **Cooking time:** 14 minutes
Servings: 2

Ingredients

Honey 1 tbsp.	Chicken Wings, 6 pieces
Worcestershire Sauce 1.5 tbsp.	Herbs (sage, rosemary, oregano, parsley, basil, thyme, and mint)
Black pepper to taste	
1 orange zest and juice	

Directions

Wash and pat dry the chicken wings In a bowl, add chicken wings, pour zest and orange juice Add the rest of the ingredients and rub on chicken wings. Let it marinate for at least half an hour. Let the Air fryer preheat at 180C

In an aluminum foil, wrap the marinated wings and put them in an air fryer, and cook for 20 minutes at 180 C
After 20 minutes, remove aluminum foil and brush the sauce over wings and cook for 15 minutes more. Then again, brush the sauce and cook for another ten minutes. Take out from the air fryer and **Serve:** hot.

Air Fryer Brown Rice Chicken Fried

Prep time: 10 minutes **Cooking time:** 20 minutes
Servings: 2

Ingredients

Olive Oil Cooking Spray	Chicken Breast 1 Cup, Diced and Cooked and White
Onion 1/4 cup chopped	
Cooked brown rice 4 Cups	
Celery 1/4 Cup chopped	Carrots 1/4 cup chopped

Directions

Place foil on the air fryer basket, make sure to leave room for air to flow, roll up on the sides Spray with olive oil, the foil. Mix all ingredients. On top of the foil, add all ingredients in the air fryer basket.

Give an olive oil spray on the mixture. Cook for five minutes at 390F. Open the air fryer and give a toss to the mixture Cook for five more minutes at 390F. Take out from air fryer and **Serve:** hot.

Chicken Cheesy Quesadilla in Air Fryer

Prep time: 4 minutes **Cooking time:** 7 minutes
Servings: 4

Ingredients

Precooked chicken 1 cup, diced Tortillas 2 pieces	Low-fat cheese 1 cup (shredded)

Directions

Spray oil the air basket and place one tortilla in it. Add cooked chicken and cheese on top. Add the second tortilla on top. Put a metal rack on top.

Cook for 6 minutes at 370 degrees; flip it halfway through so cooking evenly.Slice and **Serve:** with dipping sauce.

Delicious Chicken Pie

Prep time: 10 minutes **Cooking time:** 30 minutes
Servings: 2

Ingredients

Puff pastry 2 sheets	Chicken thighs 2 pieces, cut into cubes
One small onion, chopped	
Small potatoes 2, chopped	Light soya sauce 1 carrot, chopped
Mushrooms 1/4 cup	
Black pepper to taste	Italian mixed dried herbs
Worcestershire sauce to taste Salt to taste	Garlic powder a pinch
	Plain flour 2 tbsp.
Milk	

Directions

In a bowl, add light soya sauce and pepper add the chicken cubes, and coat well.

In a pan over medium heat, merge carrot, potatoes, and onion. Add some water, if required, to cook the vegetables. Add the chicken cubes and mushrooms and cook them too.

Stir in black pepper, salt, Worcestershire sauce, garlic powder, and dried herbs. When the chicken is cooked through, add some of the flour and mix well.

Add in the milk and let the vegetables simmer until tender. Place one piece of puff pastry in the baking tray of the air fryer, poke holes with a fork.

Add on top the cooked chicken filling and eggs and puff pastry on top with holes. Cut the excess pastry off. Glaze with oil spray or melted butter

Air fry at 180 F for six minutes, or until it becomes golden brown. **Serve:** right away and enjoy.

Air Fryer Vegetables and Italian Sausage

Prep time: 5 minutes **Cooking time:** 14 minutes
Servings: 4

Ingredients

1 bell pepper
1 small onion
¼ cup of mushrooms

Italian Sausage 4 pieces
spicy or sweet

Directions

Let the air fryer pre-heat to 400 F for three minutes. Put Italian sausage in a single layer in the air fryer basket and let it cook for six minutes.

Slice the vegetables while the sausages are cooking. After six minutes, reduce the temperature to 360 F. flip the sausage halfway through. Add the mushrooms, onions, and peppers in the basket around the sausage. Cook at 360 F for 8 minutes. After a 4-minute mix around the sausage and vegetables. With an instant-read thermometer, the sausage temperature should be 160 F. Cook more for few minutes if the temperature is not 160F. Take vegetables and sausage out and **Serve:** hot with brown rice.

Chicken Bites in Air Fryer

Prep time: 10 minutes **Cooking time:** 10 minutes
Servings: 3

Ingredients

Chicken breast 2 cups
cup Scallions 1/4 cup
1 Egg beat

Kosher salt and pepper to taste Smashed potatoes one
Whole wheat breadcrumbs 1 cup

Directions

Boil the chicken until soft. Batter the chicken with the help of a fork. Attach the smashed potatoes, scallions to the shredded chicken. Season with kosher salt and pepper.

Coat with egg and then in bread crumbs. Put in the air fryer, and cook for 8 minutes at 380F. Or until golden brown. **Serve:** warm.

Popcorn Chicken in Air Fryer

Prep time: 10 minutes **Cooking time:** 20 minutes
Servings: 4

Ingredients

For Marinade
1/2tsp ground black pepper.
Almond milk 2 cups
Dry Mix
Flour 3 cups
Salt 1 tsp.
Freshly ground black pepper 2 tsp.

8 cups, chicken tenders, cut into bite-size pieces
Paprika 1/2 tsp.
Salt 3 tsp.
Paprika 2 tsp.
Oil spray

Directions

In a bowl, attach all marinade ingredients and chicken. Mix well, and put it in a Ziploc bag and refrigerator for two hours for the minimum, or six hours.

In a large bowl, add all the dry ingredients. Coat the marinated chicken to the dry mix. Into the marinade again, then for the second time in the dry mixture. Set the air fryer basket with olive oil and place the breaded chicken pieces in one single layer. Spray oil over the chicken pieces too.

Cook at 370 degrees for 10 minutes, tossing halfway through. **Serve:** immediately with salad greens or dipping sauce.

Beer Glazed Ham Steak

Prep time: 10 minutes **Cooking time:** 30 minutes
Servings: 3

Ingredients

3 8-ounce ham steaks
tablespoons balsamic vinegar

1 tbsp Dijon mustard
2 12-ounce cans beer cup brown sugar

Directions

Place the ham steaks in a baking dish and pour 1 can of beer over top. Cover with plastic wrap and put in the refrigerator 3 hours to marinate.

When ready to make, start with the glaze. In another pan mix the brown sugar, Dijon and balsamic vinegar. Add 1/3 of the other can of beer and whisk well. Place 1 ham steak in the pan that fits into the air fryer and pour some glaze over top.

Place another ham steak on top and cover with glaze. Top with another steak and more glazes. Air fry at 380 degrees F until brown and gooey.

Asian Style Salt and Pepper Chops

Prep time: 10 minutes **Cooking time:** 20 minutes
Servings: 2

Ingredients

1egg white	1/2 teaspoon sea salt
1/4 teaspoon ground black pepper	3/4 cup potato starch (can use cornstarch) Oil in an
2to 3 boneless pork chops	oil mist bottle (I used peanut)
3tablespoons peanut oil	2 green onions,
2 jalapeno peppers, stems removed, seeded and	1/4 teaspoon ground black pepper
sliced 1 teaspoon sea salt	

Directions

Whisk the egg white, salt and pepper in a bowl until it is foamy. Cut the pork chops in pieces and place in the bowl making sure to coat each piece well.

Cover and refrigerate 20 minutes. Remove the chop pieces from the egg white bowl and drop into the potato starch. Coat evenly.Warmth the air fryer to 390 degrees F.
Spray the air fryer basket with the oil in the mist bottle and place the chop pieces in the basket. Spray them liberally with the oil as well.

Cook for 9 minutes shaking the basket frequently. Turn the chop pieces, spray with oil and put in for another 4 to 6 minutes or until brown and crispy. Heat up a wok on the stove and spray some oil into it. Sauté the onions, jalapenos, salt and pepper for about 1 minute.
Add the pork and sauté 2 to 3 minutes. **Serve:** with rice.

Paprika Pork Ribs

Prep time: 30 minutes **Cooking time:** 15 minutes
Servings: 2

Ingredients

1pound ribs, cut apart so they fit in the air fryer	21/2 tablespoons olive oil
1 1/2 tablespoons paprika	1 teaspoon salt

Directions

Place the ribs in a large bowl. Pour in the paprika, olive oil and salt and stir around or mix with your hands to make sure the ribs are all coated.

Set the basket of the air fryer with cooking spray and place the coated ribs in. Cook at 360 degrees F – Do not preheat the air fryer! Cook for 20 minutes, removing the basket and shaking the ribs around 2 times during those 20 minutes. They should be done and the meat should pull away from the bone.

Barbeque Pork Ribs-Finger Licking' Good

Prep time: 5 minutes **Cooking time:** 15 minutes
Servings: 2

Ingredients

1tablespoon dark brown sugar	1 teaspoon garlic powder
1 tablespoon paprika (sweet) 1 teaspoon poultry seasoning	1 teaspoon onion powder
	1/2 teaspoon prepared mustard powder
1/2 teaspoon ground black pepper	1 tablespoon kosher salt
	21/4-pounds St Louis-style pork spareribs

Directions

In a bowl, whisk the brown sugar, onion powder, garlic powder, paprika, poultry seasoning, mustard powder, salt and pepper. Rub this mixture into the ribs on both sides until it is completely covered.

Set the basket of the air fryer with cooking spray and place the ribs in on end leaning against the basket crossing each other.

Set the heat to 350 degrees F and cook 35 minutes. The ribs come out brown and crispy.

Garlic Butter Pork Chops

Prep time: 10 minutes **Cooking time:** 15 minutes
Servings: 4

Ingredients

2 teaspoons parsley	1/2 teaspoon kosher salt
1/4 teaspoon pepper	2 teaspoons grated garlic
1 tablespoon coconut butter	pork chops
1tablespoon coconut oil	

Directions

Mix the parsley, salt, pepper, garlic, coconut oil and coconut butter and mix with a rubber spatula squishing everything together so it is well mixed. Take your hands and rub the mixture in all pork chops on both sides.

Fold into aluminum foil and refrigerate at least 2 hours or overnight. When ready to cook, preheat the air fryer to 350 degrees F for 5 minutes. Unwrap the chops from the aluminum and place 2 of them in a pan that
fits inside of the air fryer that has been sprayed with cooking spray. Spread them out as well as possible. Cook 7 minutes, turn and cook another 8 minutes. Remove and repeat with the other two chops

Bacon Wrapped Pork Tenderloin

Prep time: 10 minutes **Cooking time:** 20 minutes
Servings: 4-6

Ingredients

1 to 2 tablespoons Dijon mustard
2 tablespoons butter, divided
2 to 3 Granny Smith apples, peeled, cored and cut in slices
1 cup vegetable broth

3 to 4 strips bacon
1 pork tenderloin
1 small onion, peeled and chopped
1 tablespoon flour
Garnish with fresh chopped rosemary
salt and pepper to taste

Directions

Preheat the air fryer to 360 for about 5 minutes. Spread the mustard onto the pork loin and wrap it with uncooked bacon.

Place it in the air fryer basket that has been treated with cooking spray and cook 15 minutes. Turn the roast and cook another 10 to 15 minutes until brown and crisp on the outside. Check that internal temperature is around 145 degrees F.

Heat 1 teaspoon of the butter in a saucepan and sauté the onions 1 to 2 minutes. Add the apple slices and sauté 3 to 5 minutes or until soft. Pour the onions and apples into a bowl and set it aside. Use the same pan and add the remaining butter, melting it. Stir in the flour to make a roux

Slowly add the broth while stirring until it is well combined and not lumpy. Let it come to a simmer with bubbles forming around the edges. It will thicken. Add the apple and onion mixture and stir in well. Slice the roast after it rests about 5 to 8 minutes and pour the gravy over top.

Almond-Crusted Chicken

Prep time: 15 minutes **Cooking time:** 25 minutes
Servings: 4

Ingredients

1/4 cup slivered almonds
2 tablespoons full-fat mayonnaise

2 (6-ounce) boneless, skinless chicken breasts
1 tablespoon Dijon mustard

Directions

Pulse the almonds in a food processor or chop until finely chopped. Place almonds evenly on a plate and set aside. Completely slice each chicken breast in half lengthwise. Mix the mayonnaise and mustard in a small bowl and then coat chicken with the mixture.

Lay each piece of chicken in the chopped almonds to fully coat. Carefully move the pieces into the device.

Brown Sugar Ham Steak

Prep time: 10 minutes **Cooking time:** 15 minutes
Servings: 8

Ingredients

1-8 ounce bone in fully cooked ham steak

5 tablespoons brown sugar
5 tbsp butter, in slices

Directions

Lay a piece of foil big enough to completely fold the ham steak in on a flat surface and place the steak in the middle.
Melt the butter (I do it in the microwave) and add the brown sugar. Stir until combined.

Spread half the thick butter/brown sugar spread on the ham steak and turn it over.

Spread the rest on the side of the ham steak.
Pre heat the air fryer to 380 degrees F for 4 minutes.
Fold the foil up and over the ham steak creating an envelope that will not leak over the steak.
Place the folded ham steak in the basket of the air fryer and cook for 8 minutes.

Remove from the air fryer and carefully unfold the foil watching for steam. The ham steak should be done and coated with the rich brown sugar and butter sauce.
If you are making more than one ham steak, be careful. It might not take as long to cook subsequent steaks because the air fryer will be hot.

Pepperoni and Chicken Pizza Bake

Prep time: 10 minutes **Cooking time:** 15 minutes
Servings: 4

Ingredients

2 cups cubed cooked chicken
20 slices pepperoni
1/4 cup grated Parmesan cheese

1 cup low-carb, sugar-free pizza sauce
1 cup shredded mozzarella cheese

Directions

In a 4-cup round baking dish add chicken, pepperoni, and pizza sauce. Stir so meat is completely covered with sauce.
Top with mozzarella and grated Parmesan. Place dish into the air fryer basket.

Adjust the temperature to 375F and set the timer for 15 minutes. Dish will be brown and bubbling when cooked. **Serve:** immediately.

Crispy Boneless Pork Chops

Prep time: 10 minutes **Cooking time:** 15 minutes
Servings: 4

Ingredients

6 pork chops with fat trimmed 1teaspoon kosher salt, divided 1/2 cup panko bread crumbs	1/2 teaspoon garlic powder 1/2 teaspoon onion powder 1 1/4 teaspoon paprika 1/3 cup crushed cornflake crumbs
1/4 teaspoon chili powder tablespoons grated Parmesan cheese Olive oil in a mist bottle	1 egg, beaten 1/8 teaspoon black pepper

Directions

Rub the chops with 1/2 teaspoon of the salt and set them aside. In a shallow bowl, combine the cornflakes, panko crumbs, garlic powder, onion powder, paprika, chili powder, Parmesan cheese, pepper and the remaining salt.

Mix well and set the bowl aside. Whisk the egg in another bowl and set it aside. Warmth the air fryer to 400 degrees F Soak the chops in the egg and then in the crumb mixture pressing it in on both sides.

Place three of the chops in and spray liberally with oil. Cook for 6 minutes, turn and spray with oil again and cook another 6 minutes. Repeat with other chops.

Mexican Taco Chicken Fingers

Prep time: 10 minutes **Cooking time:** 10 minutes
Servings: 4

Ingredients

1egg, whisked 1/2 cup tortilla chips crushed 1/2 teaspoon onion powder 1/2 teaspoon garlic powder 1 teaspoon red chili powder	1/2 cup parmesan cheese, preferably freshly grated 1 1/2 pounds chicken breasts, boneless skinless cut into strips

Directions

Whisk the egg in a shallow bowl. In a separate bowl, whisk the parmesan cheese, tortilla chips, onion powder, garlic powder, and red chili powder.

Dip the chicken pieces into the egg mixture. Then, roll the chicken pieces over the breadcrumb mixture. Cook the chicken at 380 degrees F for 12 minutes, turning them over halfway through the cooking time. Bon appétit!

Ham Steak with Pineapple Glaze

Prep time: 10 minutes **Cooking time:** 20 minutes
Servings: 4

Ingredients

3/4 cup brown sugar	1/2 cup apple cider vinegar
2 tablespoons Dijon mustard 1teaspoon ground black pepper	1 1/2-pound ham steak, cut in half to fit in the basket 1/2 cup maple syrup 2cups fresh pineapple, cubed

Directions

Mix in a bowl the brown sugar, vinegar, syrup, mustard and pepper to make a glaze. I use a whisk to get it smooth.

Set the air fryer to 400 degrees F for 5 minutes. Toss the pineapple cubes in the glaze and get just a little on each cube even if it is one side. You need to keep enough to glaze the ham steak too.

Place the cubes into a pan that fits inside the air fryer that has been sprayed with cooking spray. Cook for 2 minutes and shake the pan in the basket with tongs and cook 2 more minutes. Shake the pan again and cook for another 3 minutes. Shake the pan and cook 3 more minutes. Pour out the pineapple into a bowl, cover with foil and keep warm.

Place the ham steak into the same pan the pineapple was in sprayed with cooking spray. Spread half of what is left of the glaze on the side facing up and cook at 380 degrees F for 10 minutes.

Traditional Orange Duck

Prep time: 5 minutes **Cooking time:** 45 minutes
Servings: 4

Ingredients

1pound duck legs 1/4 cup orange sauce	Sea salt and red pepper flakes, crushed

Directions

Toss the duck legs with the remaining ingredients. Cook the duck legs at 400 degrees F for 40 minutes, turning them over halfway through the cooking time. Bon appétit!

Harvest Citrus and Honey Glazed Ham

Prep time: 10 minutes **Cooking time:** 20 minutes
Servings: 6-8

Ingredients

1/2 cup light brown sugar
2 tablespoons orange juice
2 tablespoons apple cider vinegar
2 teaspoon orange zest
1/4 cup honey
1/4 teaspoon salt

1/4 teaspoon pepper

1 tablespoons Dijon mustard
1/4 teaspoon ground ginger 1/4 teaspoon ground cloves 1/4 teaspoon ground cinnamon
1/4 tbsp smoked paprika
1/2-pound fully cooked boneless smoked ham

Directions

In a bowl combine the brown sugar, orange juice, honey, Dijon, vinegar, orange zest, ginger, cloves, cinnamon, paprika, salt and pepper and mix well.

Preheat the air fryer to 320 degrees F for 5 minutes. Remove the ham from the wrapper and pat it dry. Spray a pan that fits inside the air fryer with cooking spray and place the ham in it.

Drizzle about 1/4 cup of the glaze over top and spread it out with a brush. Cover the pan with foil and cook for 15 minutes.

Remove the pan from the air fryer and set on a heat resistant surface. Carefully remove the foil and brush the top of the ham with glaze.

Place the pan with the ham in the air fryer without the foil and cook another 5 minutes at 320 degrees F.

Open the drawer and brush with more glaze. Cook 5 more minutes. Do this two more times at 3 minute intervals. Remove the ham from the air fryer, let rest 5 minutes and **Serve:**.

Honey Pork Ribs

Prep time: 30 minutes **Cooking time:** 30 minutes
Servings: 2

Ingredients

1/2 tablespoon sugar
1/2 teaspoon ginger paste
1/2 teaspoon salt
1/4 teaspoon pepper
1 tablespoon warm water
1/2 tablespoon tomato sauce
1 teaspoon sugar
1 tbs garlic peeled chopped

1/8 teaspoon five spice powder
1 tablespoon teriyaki sauce, more if using fresh ginger
1 pound pork ribs,
1 tablespoon honey (2 works better for me)
1 teaspoon olive oil
1 tablespoon light soy sauce

Directions

Make the marinade by combining the sugar, five spice powder ginger paste, salt, and pepper and teriyaki sauce in a bowl. It should be like a thick paste.

Place the ribs in the bowl and stir around to coat all of them. Cover and put in the refrigerator overnight. When ready to cook, remove the ribs from the refrigerator. Set the basket of the air fryer with cooking spray, shake off excess marinade from each rib and set in the basket.
Cook at 320 degrees F for 8 minutes. You want them ever so slightly under cooked because you must warm them up again.

In a bowl, combine the tomatoes sauce, honey, water and sugar and whisk until well combined. In a large skillet over medium heat, sauté the garlic in the oil about 1 to 2 minutes. Add the soy sauce and all the sauce ingredients in the bowl. Bring to a low boil and add all the ribs stirring around to coat them all with the sauce. Cook until heated through and **Serve:**.

Italian Style Pork Roast

Prep time: 30 minutes **Cooking time:** 30 minutes
Servings: 4

Ingredients

tablespoons olive oil
1tablespoon dried
rosemary
salt and pepper to taste

1/4 to 1/2 cup fresh
grated Parmesan cheese

cloves garlic, peeled and
minced

2to 3 pound pork
tenderloin

Directions

Preheat the air fryer to 360 degrees F for 6 minutes.
In a bowl, merge together the olive oil, garlic,
rosemary, salt and pepper. It will be pasty. Spread this
on the top and sides of the tenderloin.

Set the basket of the air fryer with cooking spray and place
the roast in and cook 25 minutes. Check the temperature
of the roast. It should be about 140 degrees F or a little
less. If not, cook a little longer. Sprinkle the Parmesan
cheese over the roast and cook another 5 to 8 more
minutes but watch so the cheese does not burn. Let the
roast sit 5 minutes and then slice

Maple Glazed Ham

Prep time: 30 minutes **Cooking time:** 30 minutes
Servings: 6-8

Ingredients

4to 6 pound ham
1/4 teaspoon ground
nutmeg
1/4 teaspoon allspice

1 jar maraschino cherries

11/2 cups maple syrup
1/2 teaspoon ground
ginger 1 can pineapple
slices
16 whole cloves

Directions

Set the ham and stud it with the cloves and place it on
a dish. In a bowl, whisk together the maple syrup,
nutmeg, all spice and ginger. Pour the glaze over top
and let it sit at room temperature 1 hour, basting 4
times during that hour with the glaze that settles on
the plate.

Warmth the air fryer to 350 degrees F for 5 minutes.
Spray the basket with cooking spray. Place the ham in
the basket without the plate under it. Cook 1 hour or
until the internal temperature reaches 140 degrees F.

Decorate the top of the ham with drained pineapple
slices and drained cherries in the holes of the
pineapple slices.
Put back in the air fryer for 5 to 8 minutes just to
brown the pineapple. Let rest 5 minutes before slicing.

Parmesan Pork Chops

Prep time: 30 minutes **Cooking time:** 30 minutes
Servings: 6

Ingredients

3to 6 center cut pork
chops with bone
1tablespoon grated fresh
Parmesan cheese
1/2 teaspoon onion
powder
2large eggs, beaten

1/4 teaspoon pepper
1cup pork rind crumbs
1/4 teaspoon chili powder
1 teaspoon smoked
paprika
1/2 teaspoon salt

Directions

Preheat the air fryer to 400 degrees F for 8 minutes
and spray the basket with cooking spray. Flavor the
chops with salt and pepper on both sides and set
aside.

Grind the pork rinds in the food processor and pour
into a shallow bowl. Add the Parmesan cheese, onion
powder, chili powder and paprika and whisk in well.
Beat the eggs in another bowl.

Dip each chop in the eggs and then in the pork rind
mixture and press it in so it sticks. Place three chops in
the basket of the air fryer and cook 7 minutes, turn
and cook 8 more minutes. Repeat with other three
chops and **Serve:.**

The Best Marinated Chicken Ever

Prep time: 1 hour 15 minutes **Cooking time:** 25 minutes
Servings: 3

Ingredients

3/4 pound chicken
breasts, boneless, skinless
1 tablespoon Dijon
mustard
1teaspoon garlic, minced

1/2 cup red wine
1/4 cup hot sauce
Sea salt and cayenne
pepper, to taste

Directions

Place the chicken, garlic, red wine, hot sauce, and
mustard in a ceramic bowl. Cover the bowl and let the
chicken marinate for about 3 hours in your
refrigerator.

Discard the marinade and place the chicken breasts in
the Air Fryer cooking basket. Cook the chicken
breasts at 380 degrees F for 12 minutes, turning them
over halfway through the cooking time. Flavor the
chicken with the salt and cayenne pepper to taste. Bon
appétit!

Sesame Pork Ribs

Prep time: 30 minutes **Cooking time:** 15 minutes
Servings: 4

Ingredients

1/2 cup soy sauce
2 tablespoons sesame oil
2 cloves garlic, peeled and minced
1 inch fresh ginger, peeled and grated
Green onions, thinly sliced for garnish

2 tablespoons rice vinegar
2 tablespoons brown sugar
1 tablespoon cornstarch
2 pounds baby back ribs
2 tablespoons honey
1/4 cup cold water
Sesame seeds for garnish

Directions

Make the sauce in a saucepan by combining the soy sauce, rice vinegar, honey, sesame oil, brown sugar, garlic and ginger. Put it over medium heat and heat until it gets hot. Combine the water and cornstarch and add to the hot sauce. Whisk it in so that there are no lumps and bring it to a simmer. It should thicken and once it does remove it from the heat and set it aside.

Warmth the air fryer to 380 degrees F for 6 to 8 minutes. Cut the ribs to be able to fit them into the air fryer basket. Place the ribs in a large bowl with enough of the sauce to coat them well. (I use about 1 cup.)

Set the basket of the air fryer with cooking spray and put the ribs in. Cook 15 to 20 minutes or until the meat starts to pull away from the bones. Place the ribs on a platter and brush with a little more of the sauce. Garnish with onions and sesame seed.

Country-Style Turkey Drumsticks

Prep time: 20 minutes **Cooking time:** 45 minutes
Servings: 5

Ingredients

2 pounds turkey drumsticks, bone-in
2 tablespoons olive oil
1 teaspoon dried rosemary
1 teaspoon dried thyme

Kosher salt and freshly ground black pepper, to taste
1 teaspoon garlic, minced

Directions

Toss the turkey drumsticks with the remaining ingredients. Cook the turkey drumsticks at 400 degrees F for 40 minutes, turning them over halfway through the cooking time. Bon appétit!

Classic Turkey Schnitzel

Prep time: 10 minutes **Cooking time:** 15 minutes
Servings: 3

Ingredients

1 1/2 pounds turkey thighs, skinless, boneless
1/2 cup seasoned breadcrumbs
1 tablespoon olive oil

1/2 cup all-purpose flour
1 egg, beaten
1/2 teaspoon red pepper flakes, crushed
Sea salt and ground black pepper, to taste

Directions

Flatten the turkey thighs with a mallet. Whisk the egg in a shallow bowl. Place the flour in a second bowl.

Then, in a third shallow bowl, place the breadcrumbs, red pepper, salt, and black pepper. Soak the turkey first in the flour, then, in the beaten egg, and roll them in the breadcrumb mixture.

Place the breaded turkey thighs in the Air Fryer basket. Mist your schnitzel with the olive oil and transfer them to the cooking basket.

Cook the schnitzel at 380 degrees F for 22 minutes, turning them over halfway through the cooking time. Bon appétit!

Parsley Lemon Turkey

Prep time: 5 minutes **Cooking time:** 45 minutes
Servings: 5

Ingredients

2 pounds turkey wings
2 tablespoons olive oil

1 teaspoon poultry seasoning mix parsley, roughly chopped

1/2 teaspoon garlic powder 1/2 teaspoon onion powder
1 lemon, cut into slices
2 tablespoons fresh

Directions

Toss the turkey wings with the olive oil, garlic powder, onion powder, and poultry seasoning mix.
Cook the turkey wings at 400 degrees F for 40 minutes, turning them over halfway through the cooking time.
Let the turkey rest for 10 minutes before carving and serving. Garnish the turkey wings with the parsley and lemon slices. Bon appétit!

Southwestern Style Pork Loin

Prep time: 30 minutes **Cooking time:** 15 minutes
Servings: 4

Ingredients

1/2 cup vegetable oil	1/2 cup green onion tops, chopped
1/2 cup onion, peeled and chopped	1/2 cup cilantro, chopped
2 jalapenos, stemmed, seeded and chopped	1/2 teaspoon cumin
	1/2teaspoon chili powder
1 teaspoon garlic powder	1 teaspoon coriander
1 teaspoon paprika	1 pinch cayenne pepper
	3pound pork loin roast

Directions

Place the vegetable oil, green onions, regular onion, cilantro and jalapenos in the bowl of a food process and pulse until it creates a paste.

In a small bowl merge the chili powder, cumin, garlic powder, coriander, paprika and cayenne. Bring the roast in the middle of a square of foil that can be folded over the roast and sealed.

Rub the roast down with the chili powder seasoning mix on top and sides. Pour 3/4 cup of the paste over top and spread on the top of the roast.

Wrap the roast in the foil and put in the air fryer basket.
Set for 350 degrees F and cook for 10 minutes. Carefully fold the foil down to expose the very top of the roast.
Set for 300 degrees F and cook for 40 more minutes.

Check with a meat thermometer to make sure the roast has an internal temperature of 145 degrees F. Remove from the air fryer and carefully unwrap and watch for steam. Let it sit about 10 minutes and slice crosswise in 1/2- inch thick slices.

Crispy Chicken Wings

Prep time: 20 minutes **Cooking time:** 25 minutes
Servings: 2

Ingredients

3/4 pound chicken wings, boneless	1/2 teaspoon shallot powder
1/2 teaspoon garlic Powder	1tbs butter room temperature
1/2 teaspoon mustard powder	

Directions

Toss the chicken wings with the remaining ingredients. Cook the chicken wings at 380 degrees F for 18 minutes, turning them over halfway through the cooking time. Bon appétit!

Takeout Sweet and Sour Pork

Prep time: 30 minutes **Cooking time:** 15 minutes
Servings: 4

Ingredients

For the Sauce	Cup pineapple juice
1/2 cup light brown sugar	1 tablespoon canola or peanut oil
1tablespoon low sodium soy sauce	1/2 cup rice vinegar
1 red bell pepper, stemmed, seeded and cut in 1-inch chunks	1 green bell pepper, stemmed, seeded and cut into 1-inch chunks 1/2 yellow onion, peeled and cut into 1-inch chunks
1 tablespoon cornstarch	For Pork
1 cup pineapple chunks	1/4 teaspoon ground black pepper
1cup potato or corn starch	1 pinch Chinese Five Spice Powder
1/2 teaspoon sea salt	
2pounds pork, cut into bite size chunks	tablespoons canola or peanut oil, some in a mist bottle
1 teaspoon sesame oil large eggs	

Directions
for the Sauce

In a bowl, whisk the pineapple juice, vinegar, brown sugar, soy sauce and cornstarch until it is well combined and somewhat smooth. It will smooth out and thicken once you heat it up.Set the bowl aside for now.

In a skillet, warmth the oil and add the bell peppers, onion and pineapple. Stir fry for 2 to 3 minutes until tender crisp. Pour in the sauce and stir until thickened. Remove from heat and set aside

Directions for Pork

In a bowl, whisk together the potato or cornstarch, salt, pepper and five spice powders and set it aside. In another bowl, merge the eggs with the sesame oil and set it aside.

Coat the air fryer basket with the canola or peanut oil. Dip each piece of pork in the potato starch mixture and shake off excess. Dip next into the egg mixture and shake off excess. Dip back into the potato starch mixture and place in the air fryer basket.

Do each piece completely and only do what will fit in the air fryer at the time Spray the pork pieces with canola or peanut oil in a mist bottle.

Set for 340 degrees 4 minutes. Shake the basket and cook. Shake the basket again and cook another 2 to 4 minutes. It is done when the coating is browned and you can hear sizzling. Repeat with rest of pork. Heat up the sauce and **Serve:** over top.

Peppery Chicken Fillets

Prep time: 30 minutes **Cooking time:** 20 minutes
Servings: 4

Ingredients

1pound chicken fillets
2tablespoons butter
Sea salt and ground pepper, to taste
1 teaspoon garlic, minced

2bell peppers, seeded and sliced
1 teaspoon red pepper flakes

Directions

Toss the chicken fillets with the butter and place them in the Air Fryer basket. Top the chicken with bell peppers, garlic, and salt, black pepper, and red pepper flakes.

Cook the chicken and peppers at 380 degrees F for 15 minutes, tossing the basket halfway through the cooking time. **Serve:** warm and enjoy!

Chicken Dinner Rolls

Prep time: 5 minutes **Cooking time:** 20 minutes
Servings: 4

Ingredients

1pound chicken, ground
1 teaspoon dried parsley flakes
1 teaspoon cayenne pepper
1/2 teaspoon paprika

1/2 cup tortilla chips, crushed
1ounces cheddar cheese, grated

Kosher salt and ground black pepper, to taste
1/2dinner rolls

Directions

Mix the chicken, tortilla chips, cheese, and spices until everything is well combined. Now, roll the mixture into four patties.

Cook the burgers at 380 degrees F for about 17 minutes or until cooked through; make sure to turn them over halfway through the cooking time. **Serve:** your burgers in dinner rolls. Bon appétit!

Ham and Cheese Stuffed Chicken

Prep time: 5 minutes **Cooking time:** 25 minutes
Servings: 4

Ingredients

1pound chicken breasts, skinless, boneless and cut into 4 slices
1/2 teaspoon onion powder
1/4 cup all-purpose flour
1/2 teaspoon garlic powder

4 ounces ham, chopped
1 egg
4 ounces goat cheese, crumbled
1/4 cup parmesan cheese, grated

Directions

Flatten the chicken breasts with a mallet. Stuff each piece of chicken with cheese and ham. Roll them up and secure with toothpicks.

In a shallow bowl, mix the remaining ingredients until well combined. Dip the chicken rolls into the egg/flour mixture.

Place the stuffed chicken in the Air Fryer cooking basket. Cook the stuffed chicken breasts at 400 degrees F for about 22 minutes, turning them over halfway through the cooking time. Bon appétit!

Chicken Cutlets with Broccoli

Prep time: 5 minutes **Cooking time:** 15 minutes
Servings: 4

Ingredients

1pound chicken cutlets
1 pound broccoli florets
1 tablespoon olive oil

Sea salt and ground black pepper, to taste

Directions

Pat the chicken dry with kitchen towels. Place the chicken cutlets in a lightly greased Air Fryer basket. Cook the chicken cutlets at 380 degrees F for 6 minutes, turning them over halfway through the cooking time.

Creamed Chicken Salad

Prep time: 5 minutes **Cooking time:** 20 minutes
Servings: 4

Ingredients

1 pound chicken breasts, skinless and boneless	1/4 cup sour cream
1 tablespoon lemon juice	1/4 cup mayonnaise
1/2 cup celery, chopped	Sea salt and ground black pepper

Directions

Pat the chicken dry with paper towels. Place the chicken in a lightly oiled cooking basket. Cook the chicken breasts at 380 degrees F for 12 minutes, turning them over halfway through the cooking time. Shred the chicken breasts using two forks; transfer it to a salad bowl and add in the remaining ingredients. Toss to combine and **Serve:** well chilled. Bon appétit!

Tender Spicy Chicken

Prep time: 1 hour 15 minutes **Cooking time:** 20 minutes
Servings: 4

Ingredients

1 pound chicken breasts, boneless, skinless	1 tablespoon stone-ground mustard
1/2 cup rice wine	1 teaspoon garlic, minced
1 teaspoon black peppercorns, whole	1/4 teaspoon sea salt
	1 teaspoon chili powder

Directions

Place the chicken, wine, mustard, garlic, and whole peppercorns in a ceramic bowl. Seal the bowl and let the chicken marinate for about 3 hours in your refrigerator.
Discard the marinade and place the chicken breasts in the Air Fryer cooking basket.

Cook the chicken breasts at 380 degrees F for 12 minutes, turning them over halfway through the cooking time. Season the chicken with the chili powder and salt. **Serve:** immediately and enjoy!

Ranch Chicken Wings

Prep time: 1 hour 15 minutes **Cooking time:** 25 minutes
Servings: 3

Ingredients

1 pound chicken wings, boneless	1 teaspoon Ranch seasoning mix
2 tablespoons olive oil	
Kosher salt and ground pepper, to taste	

Directions

Pat the chicken dry with kitchen towels. Toss the chicken with the remaining ingredients. Cook the chicken wings at 380 degrees F for 22 minutes, turning them over halfway through the cooking time. Bon appétit!

Roasted Turkey Legs with Scallions

Prep time: 5 minutes **Cooking time:** 45 minutes
Servings: 4

Ingredients

1 1/2 pounds turkey legs	1 tablespoon butter, melted
1 teaspoon garlic, pressed	Sea salt and ground black pepper, to taste
1 teaspoon hot paprika	2 tablespoons scallions, chopped

Directions

Toss the turkey legs with the remaining ingredients, except for the scallions. Cook the turkey legs at 400 degrees F for 40 minutes, turning them

over halfway through the cooking time. Garnish the roasted turkey legs with the fresh scallions and enjoy!

Turkey and Avocado Sliders

Prep time: 15 minutes **Cooking time:** 25 minutes
Servings: 4

Ingredients

1 pound turkey, ground	1 avocado, peeled, pitted and chopped
1 tablespoon olive oil	
1 garlic cloves, minced	Kosher salt and ground pepper, to taste
1/2 cup breadcrumbs	
8 small rolls	

Directions

Mix the turkey, olive oil, avocado, garlic, breadcrumbs, salt, and black pepper until everything is well combined. Form the mixture into eight small patties.

Cook the patties at 380 degrees F for about 20 minutes or until cooked through; make sure to turn them over halfway through the cooking time. **Serve:** your patties in the prepared rolls and enjoy!

Chicken Salad Sandwich

Prep time: 15 minutes **Cooking time:** 20 minutes
Servings: 4

Ingredients

1pound chicken breasts, boneless and skinless	1 carrot, chopped
1 small onion, chopped	1 stalks celery, chopped
1 cup mayonnaise	Sea salt and ground black pepper, to taste
4 sandwich buns	

Directions

Pat the chicken dry with paper towels. Place the chicken in a lightly oiled cooking basket. Cook the chicken breasts at 380 degrees F for 12 minutes, turning them over halfway through the cooking time.

Shred the chicken breasts using two forks; transfer it to a salad bowl and add in the celery, carrot, onion, mayo, salt, and pepper. Toss to combine and **Serve:** in sandwich buns. Enjoy!

Italian-Style Chicken Drumsticks

Prep time: 15 minutes **Cooking time:** 25 minutes
Servings: 4

Ingredients

4 chicken drumsticks, bone-in 1 tablespoon butter	1/2 teaspoon cayenne pepper
Sea salt and ground pepper, to taste	1 teaspoon Italian herb mix

Directions

Rub the chicken drumsticks dry with paper towels. Toss the chicken drumsticks with the remaining ingredients.
Cook the chicken drumsticks at 370 degrees F for 20 minutes, turning them over halfway through the cooking time. Bon appétit!

Thai Hot Chicken Drumettes

Prep time: 5 minutes **Cooking time:** 25 minutes
Servings: 3

Ingredients

1pound chicken drumettes, bone-in	2tablespoons sesame oil
1/4 cup Thai hot sauces	1teaspoon tamari sauce
	salt and freshly ground pepper, to taste

Directions

Toss the chicken drumettes with the remaining ingredients. Cook the chicken drumettes at 380 degrees F for 22 minutes, turning them over halfway through the cooking time. Bon appétit!

Buttermilk Fried Chicken

Prep time: 30 minutes **Cooking time:** 25 minutes
Servings: 4

Ingredients

1pound chicken breast halves	1 cup all-purpose flour
1/2 teaspoon onion powder 1 teaspoon garlic powder	1 cup buttermilk
	1 teaspoon smoked paprika
	salt and ground black pepper, to taste

Directions

Toss together the chicken pieces, salt, and black pepper in a large bowl to coat. Stir in the buttermilk until the chicken is coated on all sides. Place the chicken in your refrigerator for about 6 hours.

In a shallow bowl, thoroughly combine the flour, onion powder, garlic powder, and smoked paprika. Then, dredge the chicken in the seasoned flour; shake off any excess and transfer them to a lightly oiled Air Fryer basket.

Cook the chicken breasts at 380 degrees F for 12 minutes, turning them over halfway through the cooking time.
Enjoy!

Crispy Chicken Wings

Prep time: 10 minutes **Cooking time:** 22 minutes
Serve: 4

Ingredients

1 ½ lbs. chicken wings	3 tbsp everything seasoning
Salt	
1 tbsp olive oil	¼ tsp garlic powder
	Pepper
	2 tbsp butter, melted

Directions

Preheat the air fryer to 400 F. In a mixing bowl, toss chicken wings with oil, garlic powder, pepper, and salt.

Place chicken wings into the air fryer basket and cook for 20 minutes. Transfer chicken wings into the mixing bowl and toss with everything seasoning and melted butter.

Return chicken wings into the air fryer basket and cook for 2 minutes more. **Serve:** and enjoy.

Chicken Liver Pate

Prep time: 15 minutes **Cooking time:** 15 minutes
Servings: 6

Ingredients

Small onion 1, peeled and quartered
Double cream 100ml
Chicken livers 450g, cleaned, sinews removed, patted dry

Garlic clove 1, peeled
Brandy or cognac 1 tbsp.
Butter 100g, divided
Ground black pepper Salt and freshly to taste
Dried thyme 1/2 tbsp.

Directions

In Precision Processor Bowl, mount the cutting blade. In a cup, add the garlic and onions, and choose CHOP.

Remove the blade and onion mixture cautiously from the cup, and rinse the bowl. Over medium heat, heat a frying pan, melt butter, put onions, and scatter over the thyme. Fry until the onions are tender, for many minutes.

Stir in some more butter and add the chicken liver and cook on either side for around 2-3 minutes. Stir in the cream and brandy, season to taste, and switching off the heat.

Enable to cool slightly with a chopping blade before applying back to the Precision Processor bowl. Choose PUREE. Move to six ramekins. Enable many hours to cool and chill before serving.

Jerk Chicken Wings

Prep time: 10 minutes **Cooking time:** 20 minutes
Serve: 2

Ingredients

1 lb. chicken wings
1 tbsp arrowroot Pepper
1 tsp canola oil

1 tbsp jerk seasoning
Salt

Directions

Preheat the air fryer to 380 F. Add chicken wings and remaining ingredients into the mixing bowl and toss well.
Arrange chicken wings into the air fryer basket and cook for 20 minutes. Turn halfway through. **Serve:** and enjoy.

Lemon and Paprika Roast Chicken with Fat Potatoes

Prep time: 20 minutes **Cooking time:** 60 minutes
Servings: 4

Ingredients

Gloves of garlic 6
1 Sprigs rosemary 5
Potatoes that are good for roasting 4 average (I used rooster)
Water 120ml
Sea salt

Lemons 2
Chicken approx. 1.2kg
Paprika 2 tbsp. (I recommend Hungarian or Spanish paprika)

Directions

Combine 120 ml of water, 1 tablespoon of sea salt, three sprigs of rosemary and garlic cloves, and pinch the lemons. Place it all in your Ninja pot.

On the skin and in the cavity, gently salt the chicken and place it in the Cook and Crisp Basket. Organize the pressure lid to maintain the closing location of the pressure release mechanism. On high, scheduled for 22 minutes.

Peel the potatoes, and slice them into 1cm chunks. Cover the squeezed lemons with water too.

Enable the pressure to relax naturally for 5 minutes when the chicken is done frying, and then rapidly release any residual pressure by transferring the pressure release to the vent.

Remove the cooker and crisp basket and brush the paprika on the skin of the chicken very softly. Throw the liquid away from the pot.

Placed the Cook and Crisp Basket back into the system and prepare to Air Crisp at 22 degrees C for 10 minutes. It ought to be golden and crisp then, so if you would prefer it to be crisper; you should press it for some minutes.
Remove the chicken and place it on a tray for serving. Cover it with parchment when you are cooking the potatoes and allow it to rest.

There'll be loads of beautiful chicken fat in the pot. Drain the potatoes, remove the lemons and place the chicken fat in the container with the potatoes. Apply the salt to a sprinkle and mix well. Add the leftover rosemary. Set for 10 minutes with Air Crisp, stirring softly halfway through.

Chicken Fajitas along with Spicy Potatoes

Prep time: 10 minutes **Cooking time:** 55 minutes
Servings: 4

Ingredients

Chicken breast 3
1 tbsp. Ground

Yellow pepper 1, (de-seeded and sliced)
Ground cumin 1 tbsp.
Red pepper 1, (de-seeded and sliced)
Peeled and sliced onion 1
Juice of lime 1
For spicy potatoes
Baby potatoes 1kg, cut in quarters
Smoked paprika 1 tbsp.
Chicken breasts

Tortillas medium 8
Smoked paprika coriander 1 tbsp.
Garlic powder 1 tbsp.
Dried chili flakes 1/2 tbsp.
Hot paprika 2 tbsp.
Dried oregano 1 tbsp.
Olive oil 4 tbsp.
Salt and freshly ground black pepper
Sea salt 1 tbsp.
Olive oil 3 tbsp.
Garlic powder 1 tbsp.

Directions

In a bowl, attach the spices, herbs, and oil, season to taste, and blend. Stir in the bits of chicken, onion and peppers, and blend until it is covered in the marinade.

In another cup, toss the oil and spices with the potatoes.
In both drawers, put a crisper plate. Put the chicken and veggies to the drawer of zone 1 and the potatoes to the drawer of zone 2 and put them in the machine.

Select zone 1, choose AIR FRY, set the temp to 200 C, and set the time to 20 minutes. Select zone 2 and ROAST, set the temp to 180 C, and set the time to 25 minutes. Click SYNC. To start, select START/STOP.

Give all drawers a shake/stir after 10 minutes. Repeat after 15 minutes. When the time in zone 1 is 0, verify that the chicken is fried. When the inner temp exceeds at least 75 C on a thermometer, the cooking is done.
Serve: with potatoes, chicken and veggies wrapped in tortillas.

Cesar Salad with Peri Peri Breasts of Chicken

Prep time: 15 minutes **Cooking time:** 33 minutes
Servings: 6

Ingredients

For the chicken
Chicken breasts (boneless, skinless) 6 (200-250g each)
For the salad
Peri-peri sauce 70ml
Mayonnaise 5 tbsp.
Small romaine lettuces 2
Parmesan shavings 50g, (plus extra to **Serve:**)

Vegetable oil 3 tbsp.
Black pepper salt and freshly ground to taste
Garlic clove 1, peeled and crushed
Small romaine lettuces 25g
Juice of lemon 1/2 (approximately 1 1/2 tablespoons)

Directions

In the machine, insert the grill plate and close the cover. Link a probe to a device. In the machine, put the pot and close the cover. Choose GRILL, set the MED temperature, and then pick PRESET. To cook the chicken to a temp (food-safe), the machine will switch to CHICKEN WELL on default. To commence preheating, click START/STOP.

Brush the each breast of chicken uniformly with a half tablespoon of veg oil when preheating the machine. Season with pepper and salt and insert the probe into the middle of one breast.

See Directions for positioning of the probe.Set the top side of the chicken down on the grill pan, in the tank, when the machine beeps to show it has preheated. Cover the probe cord's lid. Turn the chicken over, brushing with peri peri sauce when the device beeps to warn the chicken requires to be flipped,

While the salad is combined, put the garlic, lemon juice, mayonnaise, and parmesan in a cup. Dispose of the lettuce's outer leaves and tear the remainder over a pan, mixing with the dressing gently.

Remove the chicken from the machine when cooking is done, and leave to rest for five min before cutting on the leanings. **Serve:** hot or maybe cold over leaves of lettuce, drizzle with dressing, if needed, shave over extra Parmesan and sprinkle with croutons.

Cajun Grilled Chicken and Pepper Kebabs

Prep time: 75 minutes **Cooking time:** 85 minutes
Servings: 6

Ingredients

Ground cumin 2 tsp.
Sunflower oil 4 tbsp.
Lime juice 2 tbsp.
Oregano 1 tsp.
Green pepper 1, deseeded and cut in 2.5cm pieces, cut into quarters
Wooden skewers 6, soaked in water for 30 minutes
To taste, salt
Small red onions 2, (peeled and cut into 2.5cm pieces)

Yellow pepper 1, deseeded and cut in 2.5cm pieces, cut into quarters
Ground coriander 2 tsp.
Paprika 2 tsp.
Chicken thighs, cut into 2.5cm cubes 600g
Chili flakes 1/2 tsp.
freshly ground black pepper
Red pepper 1, deseeded and cut in 2.5cm pieces, cut into quarters

Directions

Combine the oil, cumin, lime juice, coriander, oregano, paprika, chili flakes, pepper, and salt in a bowl to taste. Insert the pieces of chicken and mix to cover them. Cover and allow marinating for at least an hour in the refrigerator.

In the machine, insert the grill plate and close the cover. Pick GRILL, set MED to set the temperature and set the time to ten minutes. To commence preheating, click START/STOP. Gather your skewers in the following manner when the machine is preheating until they are almost full chicken, onion, and pepper. Ensure that the products are nearly exclusively squeezed down at the bottom of the skewers. ReServe: some marinade for shaving.

Place kebabs on the grill plate until the machine has beeped to indicate it has preheated. Close the lid Open lid baste uncovered side of the kebabs with marinade when the machine beeps and the screen reads FLIP halfway into cooking. Flip the skewers and baste them again with silicone tongs. To finish cooking, close the lid. When the chicken achieves an internal temp of 75 ° C, cooking is done. Open the cover and cut the skewers off. On a tray, put the kebabs and **Serve:** with rice/salad.

Cheesy Chicken Fritters

Prep time: 10 minutes **Cooking time:** 10 minutes
Serve: 4

Ingredients

1 lb. ground chicken
1/2 tsp garlic powder
1/2 cup parmesan cheese, shredded
1/2 tsp onion powder
Salt

2 tbsp green onions, chopped
1/2 tbsp dill, chopped
1/2 cup almond flour
Pepper

Directions

Preheat the air fryer to 350 F. Add chicken and remaining ingredients into the large bowl and mix until well combined.

Make small patties from the mixture and place into the air fryer basket and cook for 10 minutes. Turn halfway through. **Serve:** and enjoy

Flavorful Turkey Patties

Prep time: 10 minutes **Cooking time:** 20 minutes
Serve: 4

Ingredients

1 lb. ground turkey
1 tbsp garlic, minced
1 tbsp olive oil

1 tsp Italian seasoning
4 oz feta cheese, crumbled
1 1/4 cup spinach, Pepper
Salt

Directions

Preheat the air fryer to 390 F. Add ground turkey and remaining ingredients into the bowl and mix until well combined. Make equal shapes of patties from the mixture and place into the air fryer basket and cook for 20 minutes. Turn halfway through. **Serve:** and enjoy.

Mustard-Rubbed Chicken with Roasted Veggies

Prep time: 10 minutes **Cooking time:** 55 minutes
Servings: 6

Ingredients

Chicken Mustard	Patch cooked chicken 1.8
Vegetables Roasted	kg whole chicken cut in
Sea salt 1 tbsp.	half or whole Dijon
Sea salt 1/2 tbsp.	mustard 90ml
Vegetable oil 90ml	Zest and juice 1/2 lemon
Ground black pepper 1/2	Mixture of root veggies
tsp.	800g (like parsnips,
Dried oregano 1 tbsp.	carrots, turnips and
Italian seasoning 1 tbsp	potatoes)
	Fresh leaves of thyme
	1 tbsp.

Directions

Mix all the ingredients excluding chicken in a bowl. Cover both sides of chicken with mustard rub and re**Serve:**.

Link a probe to a device. In the machine, put the pot and close the cover. Set the temperature to 180 °C, select ROAST, and then select PRESET. To cook at a food-safe temperature, the machine will switch to CHICKEN WELL by default. To commence preheating, click START/STOP.

Set the probe into the middle of the chicken breast while the device is preheated (see probe placement guidance). Place the chicken in the pot, skin-side down, when the machine beeps to show it has preheated. Cover the probe cord's lid. When the machine beeps to show that the chicken requires to be turned, switch the chicken over, cover with more rub and add vegetables, ensuring that the hot fat combination is covered. Using thyme leaves and sea salt to sprinkle. To finish cooking, close the lid. Using oven mitts to detach the probe from the chicken as the device beeps to indicate the chicken is finished cooking. Then move chicken to board of cutting and permit to rest covered for Ten minutes before serving. In the meanwhile, check whether the vegetables are properly prepared, pick ROAST, set the temperature to 180 C, and set the time to 10 minutes if not. To cancel, pick preheat. To commence, click START/STOP. **Serve:** with chicken until the veggies are cooked.

Flavors Chicken Thighs

Prep time: 10 minutes **Cooking time:** 20 minutes
Serve: 4

Ingredients

4 chicken thighs, bone-in	1/2 tsp oregano
& skin-on	1 tsp smoked paprika
3/4 tsp onion powder	3/4 tsp garlic powder
1/2 tsp kosher salt	1 tbsp canola oil

Directions

Preheat the air fryer to 380 F. Add chicken thighs and remaining ingredients into the large zip-lock bag. Seal bag and shake well. Add marinated chicken into the air fryer basket and cook for 20 minutes. Turn halfway through.
Serve: and enjoy.

Chicken Masala

Prep time: 15 minutes **Cooking time:** 36 minutes
Servings: 4

Ingredients

Rosemary (finely chopped)	Corn starch 3 tsp.
1 tbsp. Oil 2 tbsp.	Chicken breasts 4
Brown champignons	Baby potatoes (halved)
(sliced) 250g Chicken	500g Masala wine 200ml
stock 1 pot	
Shallots (finely chopped) 2	Salt and pepper
Water 400ml	

Directions

Set the temp to HIGH and pick SEAR/SAUTÉ. Click the START/STOP key and allow 5 minutes to preheat.
Put the potatoes, 1 tablespoon of oil, rosemary, pepper and salt and in a big dish. Toss until evenly flavored with the potatoes.

After preheating, put 1 tablespoon of oil and breasts of chicken in the pot, season with pepper and salt, and brown on both sides for around 2 to 3 minutes on either side. Detach the chicken from the pot and set it aside.
In the oven, put the mushrooms and shallots and sauté for 2 min. Then add the Masala wine and plan for a reduction time of 5 minutes.

Add the water, chicken stock and corn starch to the mixture. Once again, in the oven, put the chicken. To retain the higher position of the rack, place the rack that is reversible in the jar. Place it with potatoes that are seasoned.

Gather the pressure lid to pre**Serve:** the pressure release mechanism's SEAL position. Set to LOW and PRESSURE to pick. Use 10 minutes for clock scheduling. Select START/STOP to start. **Serve:** sweet.

Chicken Wings

Prep time: 20 minutes **Cooking time:** 30 minutes
Servings: 6

Ingredients

Ginger crushed 1 inch	Ground Cardamom 1/2
Plain Yoghurt 200g	tbsp. Paprika 2 tsp.
Garlic cloves crushed 3	Chili Powder 1/2 tbsp.
Ground Cumin 1 tbsp.	Salt 1 tbsp.
Garam masala Powder1	Lemon Juice 2 tbsp.
tbsp.	Ground Black Pepper 2
Ground Coriander 1 tbsp.	tbsp.

Directions

Put the basket of air fryer in and close the machine's door.
At 200 C, select an Air Fry. Set a timer of 20 minutes. Insert chicken wings to guarantee they don't really smoke and turn after 5 minutes.

Mix all ingredients in a bowl for marinade and whisk them together. Toss the wings into the marinade. Put the wings again to the air fryer on the grill set at 260 C for a minute or two.

Chicken, Mushroom, Leek, and Pie of Puff Pastry

Prep time: 25 minutes **Cooking time:** 65 minutes
Servings: 4

Ingredients

Light olive oil 2 tbsp.	Skinless, boneless chicken
Egg yolk 1	thighs 300g, cut into of 2cm
Chopped tarragon 1 1/2	Large leek 1, cut into 1
tbsp. Chestnut	1/2cm slices Chopped flat
mushrooms 300g	parsley 1 1/2 tbsp.
Sprigs thyme 4, leaves	Ready-made
picked	béchamel/white sauce
Chunky smoked bacon	275ml
pancetta lardoons 60g	Dijon mustard 2 tbsp.
Chopped chives 1 1/2	All-butter puff pastry 200g
tbsp.	(preferably in a block),
To taste, salt and pepper	kept fridge cold

Directions

Put the basket of air fryer in and close the machine's door.
At 200 C, select an Air Fry. Set a timer of 20 minutes. Insert chicken wings to guarantee they don't really smoke and turn after 5 minutes. Mix all ingredients in a bowl for marinade and whisk the together. Toss the wings into the marinade. Put the wings again to the air fryer on the grill setting at 260 C for a minute or two.

Chicken Couscous Bowl

Prep time: 10 minutes **Cooking time:** 25 minutes
Servings: 2

Ingredients

Water 120ml	Tomato purees 2 tbsp.
Couscous 120g	Vegetable stock cube 1/2
Sriracha sauce 1 tbsp.	Tomatoes 2, diced
Chicken breasts, sliced 2	Oil 1 tbsp.
Paprika 1 tsp.	Onion 1, peeled and diced
Garlic powder 1 tsp.	Salt and pepper
Bell pepper 1, deseeded	For garnishing parsley feta
and diced	and cheese

Directions

Boil 120 ml of water and transfer some of the vegetable stock. Stir until the stock dissolves. In a bowl put the couscous and pour over it with vegetable stock. Cover and set the bowl on the side. Ensure that a pot is placed, but remove the grill plate. Choose ROAST, set the temp to 200 ° C, and set the timer for 15 minutes. To commence preheating, click START/STOP.

Mix the chicken, paprika, oil, garlic powder, pepper, and salt together in a dish. Once the device beeps to signal that it has preheated, insert the seasoned chicken and close the lid to start cooking. Open the cover and put bell pepper, tomatoes and onion when 10 minutes are remaining on the timer. To keep cooking, close the lid. Insert Sriracha, tomato puree and already cooked couscous and mix well when there are 3 minutes left on the timer.

Juicy Turkey Breast

Prep time: 10 minutes **Cooking time:** 60 minutes
Serve: 8

Ingredients

4 lbs. turkey breast,	1/2 tsp cinnamon
boneless 1 tbsp canola oil	1 1/2 tsp paprika
1 1/2 tsp garlic powder	2 tsp salt
1/2 tsp pepper	

Directions

Preheat the air fryer to 350 F. In a small bowl, mix together paprika, garlic powder, cinnamon, pepper, and salt.

Brush turkey breast with oil and rub with spice mixture. Place turkey breast into the air fryer basket and cook for 60 minutes. Turn after 25 minutes. Slice and **Serve:**.

Turkey with Tabasco Sauce

Prep time: 15 minutes **Cooking time:** 22 minutes
Servings: 6

Ingredients

1 1/2 pounds (680g) ground turkey
6 whole eggs, well beaten
2 tablespoons sesame oil
½ tsp black pepper
3 cloves garlic, finely minced
1/3 teaspoon smoked paprika
2 egg whites, beaten
Tabasco sauce, for drizzling
2 leeks, chopped
1/2 teaspoon sea salt

Directions

Warmth the oil in a pan over moderate heat; then, sweat the leeks and garlic until tender; stir periodically. Next, grease 6 oven safe ramekins with pan spray. Divide the sautéed mixture among six ramekins.

In a bowl, beat the eggs and egg whites using a wire whisk. Stir in the smoked paprika, salt and black pepper; whisk until everything is thoroughly combined. Divide the egg mixture among the ramekins.

Air-fry approximately 22 minutes at 345F (174C). Drizzle Tabasco sauce over each portion and **Serve:**.

White Wine Chicken Breast

Prep time: 30 minutes **Cooking time:** 28 minutes
Servings: 4

Ingredients

1/2 teaspoon grated fresh ginger

3 medium-sized boneless chicken breasts, cut into small pieces
1/2 teaspoon fresh thyme leaves, minced
11/2 tablespoons sesame oil
1/2 teaspoon sea salt flakes
1/3 cup coconut milk
3 green garlic stalks, finely chopped
1/2 cup dry white wine
1/3 teaspoon freshly cracked black pepper

Directions

Warm the sesame oil in a deep sauté pan over a moderate heat. Then, sauté the green garlic until just fragrant.
Detach the pan from the heat and pour in the coconut milk and the white wine.

After that, add the thyme, sea salt, fresh ginger, and freshly cracked black pepper. Scrape this mixture into a baking dish.

Stir in the chicken chunks. Cook in the preheated Air Fryer for 28 minutes at 335F (168C). **Serve:** on individual plates and eat warm.

Easy Chicken Tenders

Prep time: 10 minutes **Cooking time:** 16 minutes
Serve: 4

Ingredients

1 lb. chicken tenders
1/2 tbsp onion powder
1/2 tbsp dried thyme
1 tbsp garlic powder
Pepper
1 tbsp smoked paprika
1/2 tsp cayenne
Salt

Directions

Preheat the air fryer to 370 F. Add chicken tenders and remaining ingredients into the mixing bowl and mix until well coated.

Place chicken tenders into the air fryer basket and cook for 16 minutes. Turn halfway through. **Serve:** and enjoy.

Delicious Chicken Breasts

Prep time: 10 minutes **Cooking time:** 10 minutes
Serve: 3

Ingredients

1/2 cup almond flour
12 oz chicken breasts, skinless and boneless
1/2 tsp pepper
¼ tsp paprika
1/2 tsp salt
1 egg, beaten

Directions

Preheat the air fryer to 330 F. In a bowl, add egg and whisk well. In a shallow dish, mix almond flour, paprika, pepper, and salt. Dip chicken breasts in egg and coat with almond flour mixture.

Place the coated chicken into the air fryer basket and cook for 10 minutes. Turn halfway through.**Serve:** and enjoy.

Chicken Kebab

Prep time: 10 minutes **Cooking time:** 15 minutes
Serve: 4

Ingredients

1 lb. chicken thighs, skinless, boneless, and cut into 4 pieces	1/2 tsp cinnamon
	1 tbsp canola oil
	1/2 tsp cayenne
1 tbsp tomato paste	1 tsp ground cumin
1 tbsp garlic, minced	1/2 tsp pepper
1 tsp salt	1/4 cup lemon juice
	1 tsp paprika

Directions

Preheat the air fryer to 370 F. Add chicken and remaining ingredients into the zip-lock bag. Seal bag and place in the refrigerator for 2 hours.

Arrange marinated chicken into the air fryer basket and cook for 15 minutes. Turn halfway through. **Serve:** and enjoy.

Air Fryer Buttermilk Fried Chicken

Prep time: 15 minutes **Cooking time:** 25 minutes
Serve: 1

Ingredients

1 ½ pound boneless, skinless chicken thighs	1 cup all-purpose flour
	2 cups buttermilk
1 tablespoon seasoned salt	½ tablespoon ground black pepper
1 cup panko breadcrumbs	
1 serving cooking spray	

Directions

In a shallow casserole dish, place the chicken thighs. Refrigerate the chicken for 4 hours or overnight in the buttermilk.

Preheat the air fryer carefully to 380°F (190 degrees C).
In a large gallon-sized resealable bag, combine the flour, seasoned salt, and pepper. Chicken thighs should be dredged in seasoned flour. Return to the buttermilk and coat with panko breadcrumbs.

Spray the air fryer basket with nonstick cooking spray. Place half of the chicken thighs in the basket, ensuring no contact. Cooking spray should be sprayed on the top of each chicken thigh.

Cook for 15 minutes in a preheated air fryer. Flip. Spray the tops of the birds once more. Cook for another 15 minutes. In the middle, an instant-read thermometer should read at least 165 degrees F. Rep with the remaining chicken

Marinated Chicken Thighs

Prep time: 10 minutes **Cooking time:** 20 minutes
Serve: 4

Ingredients

1 lb. chicken thighs, boneless and skinless	2 tsp ginger, minced
	1/2 cup coconut milk
2 tbsp curry paste	1 tbsp garlic, chopped
Salt	Pepper

Directions

Preheat the air fryer to 350 F. Add chicken and remaining ingredients into the zip-lock bag. Seal bag and place in the refrigerator for 1 hour.

Arrange marinated chicken into the air fryer basket and cook for 20 minutes. Turn halfway through. **Serve:** and enjoy.

Air Fryer Blackened Chicken Breast

Prep time: 20 minutes **Cooking time:** 20 minutes
Serve: 1

Ingredients

2 teaspoons paprika	1 teaspoon ground thyme
2 teaspoons vegetable oil	1 teaspoon cumin
½ teaspoon cayenne pepper	½ teaspoon onion powder
½ teaspoon black pepper	¼ teaspoon salt
2 (12 ounces) skinless, boneless chicken breast halves	

Directions

Combine paprika, onion powder, black pepper, thyme, cumin, cayenne pepper, and salt in a mixing bowl. Place the spice mixture on a flat dish.

Rub the oil all over each chicken breast until it is well covered. Roll each piece of chicken in the blackening spice mixture, pressing down, so the spice adheres to both sides. Allow resting for 5 minutes while the air fryer heats up. Preheat the air fryer carefully for 5 minutes at 360 degrees F (175 degrees C).

Cook the chicken in the air fryer basket for 10 minutes. Cook it for another 10 minutes on the other side. Place the chicken on a platter and let it aside for 5 minutes before serving.

Spicy Air Fryer Wings

Prep time: 15 minutes **Cooking time:** 25 minutes
Serve: 1

Ingredients

1 ½ pounds chicken wings and drumettes
1 tablespoon smoked paprika
1 ½ teaspoon ground cumin,
1½ tbs ground black pepper
2 teaspoons olive oil
1 tablespoon chili powder
1 ½ teaspoon garlic powder
1 ½ tbsp onion powder
1 ½ teaspoon kosher salt
1 teaspoon cayenne pepper

Directions

Rinse and pat dry the chicken. Toss in a large mixing basin with the oil to coat. In a small bowl, combine paprika, garlic powder, black pepper, salt, chili powder, cumin, onion powder, and cayenne. Sprinkle over chicken and toss to coat evenly. According to the manufacturer's instructions, preheat the air fryer carefully to 375°F (190°C).

Arrange the chicken in a single layer in the preheated air fryer basket, not touching. Cook, rotating halfway through until the meat is no longer pink at the bone and the juices run clear about 12 minutes. A thermometer near the bone should read 165 degrees F. (74 degrees C). Cook for an additional 2 to 3 minutes at 400 degrees F (200 degrees C) for crispier wings. Allow for a few minutes of rest before serving.

Air Fryer Keto Chicken Wings

Prep time: 20 minutes **Cooking time:** 25 minutes
Serve: 1

Ingredients

3 pounds chicken wings
2 teaspoons olive oil
1 tbsp taco seasoning mix

Directions

Combine the chicken wings, taco seasoning, and oil in a resealable plastic bag. Shake well to coat. Preheat the air fryer carefully for 2 minutes at 350 degrees F (175 degrees C). Cook the wings in the air fryer for 12 minutes, flipping after 6 minutes. **Serve:** right away.

Air Fryer Stuffing Balls

Prep time: 15 minutes **Cooking time:** 20 minutes
Serve: 1

Ingredients

1 tablespoon butter
½ cup finely chopped celery
1 teaspoon dried parsley
½ teaspoon poultry seasoning
¼ tbs ground black pepper
cooking spray
¼ cup finely chopped onion
5 cups stale bread, cut into cubes
½ teaspoon salt
1 egg, well beaten
¼ cup no-salt-added chicken broth

Directions

In a small pan over medium heat, melt the butter. Cook until the celery and onion are cooked, about 5 minutes.
Combine the bread, parsley, poultry seasoning, salt, and pepper in a mixing bowl. Incorporate the sautéed onion and celery. With one hand, slowly pour the egg into the bowl while mixing to ensure that the mixture is equally covered. Repeat with the chicken broth and stir everything together until fully blended. Divide the filling mixture into 8 equal amounts and roll it into balls on a platter. Refrigerate for at least 15 minutes before serving.
Preheat the air fryer carefully to 350°F (180 degrees C). Remove the stuffing balls from the refrigerator and gently coat them with cooking spray. Place the stuffing balls in the air fryer, sprayed side down, without touching. Lightly spray the opposite side. Cook for 5 minutes in a hot air fryer, then turn and cook for 2 minutes.

Air-Fried Buffalo Chicken

Prep time: 18 minutes **Cooking time:** 20 minutes
Serve: 1

Ingredients

¼ cup plain fat-free Greek yogurt
1 tablespoon hot sauce
1tbs garlic pepper seasoning
1 cup panko breadcrumbs
¼ cup egg substitute
1 tbsp cayenne pepper
1 tbsp sweet paprika
1 teaspoon hot sauce
1-pound skinless, boneless chicken breasts

Directions

Combine Greek yogurt, egg replacement, and 1 tablespoon + 1 teaspoon spicy sauce in a mixing dish. Combine the panko breadcrumbs, paprika, garlic pepper, and cayenne pepper in a separate bowl. Coat chicken strips with panko bread crumb mixture after dipping them in the yogurt mixture. In an air fryer, arrange coated chicken strips in a single layer. Cook for 10 minutes per side or until uniformly browned

Air Fryer Chicken Fajitas

Prep time: 20 minutes **Cooking time:** 25 minutes
Serve: 1

Ingredients

1 medium red bell pepper
1 large onion, slice petals
3 teaspoons olive oil, divided salt and pepper to taste
8 (6 inches) flour tortillas, warmed

1 medium green bell pepper, cut into thin strips
1 pound chicken tenders, cut into strips
2 teaspoons fajita seasoning

Directions

Combine the bell pepper strips and onion petals in a large mixing basin. Drizzle with 2 tablespoons olive oil and season with salt and pepper. Stir until everything is well blended. In a separate dish, toss the chicken strips with the fajita spice. Drizzle with the remaining 1 teaspoon olive oil and stir with your fingertips until evenly incorporated.

Preheat the air fryer carefully to 350 degrees Fahrenheit (175 degrees C). Cook for 12 minutes, shaking halfway through, with the chicken in the basket. Transfer to a platter and set aside while you prepare the veggies. Cook for 14 minutes, shaking halfway through, in the air fryer basket with the vegetable mixture. Distribute the chicken and veggie mixture among the tortillas.

Air Fryer Chimichangas

Prep time: 15 minutes **Cooking time:** 20 minutes
Serve: 1

Ingredients

1 tablespoon vegetable oil
2 cups shredded cooked chicken
¼ cup chicken broth
1 (4 ounces) can hot fire-roasted diced green chiles
½ teaspoon salt
1 cup shredded Mexican cheese blend

½ cup diced onion
½ (8 ounces) package Neufchatel cheese,
1 ½ tablespoons chicken taco seasoning mix
6 (10 inches) flour tortillas
¼ tbsp black pepper
avocado oil cooking spray

Directions

In a medium skillet, heat the oil. Cook until the onion is tender and transparent, 4 to 6 minutes. Combine the chicken, Neufchatel cheese, diced chiles, chicken broth, taco seasoning, salt, and pepper in a mixing bowl. Cook and stir until the mixture is fully mixed and the Neufchatel has softened.

Heat tortillas until soft and malleable in a big pan or directly on the grates of a gas burner. Fill each tortilla with a third of the chicken mixture and a heaping spoonful of Mexican cheese

Air Fryer Buffalo Chicken Wings

Prep time: 15 minutes **Cooking time:** 18 minutes
Serve: 1

Ingredients

2 ½ pounds chicken wings

½ cup butter
1 teaspoon garlic powder
1 tablespoon olive oil

⅔ cup cayenne pepper sauce
2 tablespoons vinegar
¼ teaspoon cayenne pepper

Directions

Preheat the air fryer carefully to 360°F (182 degrees C). Place the wings in a large mixing basin. Drizzle oil over the wings and massage until evenly covered. Cook for 25 minutes with half of the wings in the air fryer basket. Flip the wings with tongs and cook for another 5 minutes. Place the cooked wings in a large mixing dish. Rep with the remaining wings.

In a small saucepan over medium heat, mix hot pepper sauce, butter, vinegar, garlic powder, and cayenne pepper while the second batch is cooking. Keep stirring and heating until the wings are done. Toss cooked wings with sauce to coat.

Air Fryer Chicken Nuggets

Prep time: 15 minutes **Cooking time:** 22 minutes
Serve: 1

Ingredients

1 cup buttermilk
1 cup flour
1 tablespoon paprika
3 tablespoons grated Parmesan cheese
1 teaspoon ground black pepper
2 eggs

2 pounds chicken tenderloins, cut into nugget size
1 tablespoon parsley flakes
1 teaspoon salt
2 cups panko breadcrumbs
cooking spray

Directions

In a large mixing basin, combine the buttermilk and chicken and set aside while you make the seasoned flour.
Combine the flour, Parmesan cheese, paprika, parsley, salt, and pepper
in a large mixing bowl. Separately, beat the eggs. On a flat dish, spread out the breadcrumbs. Each chicken nugget should be dredged in flour, then in beaten egg, and finally in breadcrumbs.
Preheat the air fryer carefully to 400°F (200 degrees C). Cooking spray should be sprayed on the basket. Fill the basket with as many nuggets as you can without overflowing it. Spray the tops of the nuggets lightly with cooking spray.
The **Cooking time:**is 10 minutes. Cook for a further 2 minutes after flipping the chicken nuggets. Repeat with the remaining nuggets.

Air Fryer Popcorn Chicken

Prep time: 10 minutes **Cooking time:** 18 minutes
Serve: 1

Ingredients

1-pound boneless, skinless chicken breast halves	¾ teaspoon salt cooking spray
½ teaspoon paprika	¼ teaspoon black pepper
¼ teaspoon ground mustard	¼ teaspoon garlic powder
¼ teaspoon onion powder	⅛ teaspoon ground thyme
⅛ teaspoon dried basil	⅛ teaspoon dried oregano
⅛ teaspoon dried sage	3 tablespoons cornstarch

Directions

In a medium mixing dish, combine the chicken pieces. Combine salt, paprika, black pepper, mustard, garlic powder, onion powder, thyme, basil, oregano, and sage in a small bowl. 1 teaspoon of the spice combination should be set aside, and the remaining seasoning should be sprinkled on the chicken. To coat evenly, toss everything together.

In a resealable plastic bag, add cornstarch and reServe:d 1 teaspoon seasoning; shake to incorporate. Place the chicken in the bag, close it, and shake to coat evenly. Next, shake the chicken in a fine-mesh sieve to remove extra cornstarch. Allow to rest for 5 to 10 minutes, or until the cornstarch has begun to seep into the chicken.
Preheat the air fryer carefully to 390°F (200 degrees C).
Spray the air fryer basket with oil and arrange the chicken pieces inside, ensuring they do not overlap. Depending on the size of your air fryer, you may need to prepare two batches. Cooking spray should be sprayed on the chicken.
4 minutes in the oven. Shake the air fryer basket and re-spray the chicken with oil to ensure no dry or powdery parts. Cook until the chicken is no longer pink on the interior, 4 to 5 minutes more. **Serve:** right away.

Cornflake-Crusted Chicken Drumsticks in the Air Fryer

Prep time: 18 minutes **Cooking time:** 20 minutes
Serve: 1

Ingredients

1 egg	1 tablespoon water
½ cup cornflake crumbs	½ teaspoon garlic powder
½ teaspoon onion powder	½ teaspoon salt
¼ teaspoon Cajun seasoning	¼ teaspoon chili powder
¼ teaspoon paprika	6 large chicken drumsticks
1 serving no-stick cooking spray	salt to taste

Directions

In a small dish, combine the egg and water. In a separate shallow dish, combine cornflake crumbs, garlic powder, onion powder, 1/2 teaspoon salt, Cajun spice, chili powder, and paprika.

Preheat the air fryer carefully to 400°F (200 degrees C). Season both sides of the drumsticks gently with salt. Dip each drumstick into the egg mixture, then into the cornflake mixture, rolling and pushing down to cover all sides.

Cooking sprays the top of the chicken and lays it, sprayed side down, in the air fryer basket. Next, spray the tops of the drumsticks; depending on their size, you may need to turn them on their side.

Air-fry for 10 minutes, then carefully flip them. Reduce the temperature to 325°F (160 degrees C). Cook for another 10 minutes, or until the internal temperature of the chicken reaches 165 degrees F. (74 degrees C). After 5 minutes, check for doneness because the size of the drumsticks determines the time.

Honey-Sriracha Air Fryer Wings

Prep time: 15 minutes **Cooking time:** 20 minutes
Serve: 1

Ingredients

12 fresh chicken wing drumettes	½ teaspoon salt
½ teaspoon garlic powder	1 tablespoon butter
2 teaspoons rice vinegar	¼ cup honey
	1 tablespoon sriracha sauce

Directions

Preheat the air fryer carefully to 360°F (182 degrees C). Toss the chicken wings in a basin with the salt and garlic powder to coat. Fill the air fryer basket halfway with wings. Cook the wings for 25 minutes, shaking the basket every 7 to 8 minutes. When the timer goes off, switch off the air fryer and leave the wings in the basket for another 5 minutes. Meanwhile, in a small saucepan over medium heat, melt the butter. Bring butter, honey, rice vinegar, and sriracha sauce to a boil. Reduce the heat to medium-low and cook the sauce for 8 to 10 minutes, stirring regularly. Remove from fire and set aside; the sauce will thicken as it cools. In a mixing dish, combine the cooked wings and the sauce. Next, make the extra sauce to **Serve:** with the wings.

Healthier Bang Bang Chicken in the Air Fryer

Prep time: 15 minutes **Cooking time:** 25 minutes
Serve: 1

Ingredients

1 egg	½ cup milk
1 tbsp hot pepper sauce	½ cup flour
½ cup tapioca starch	1 ½ teaspoon seasoned salt
½ teaspoon cumin	1-pound boneless, skinless chicken breasts
1 teaspoon garlic granules	3 tablespoons sweet chili sauce
¼ cup plain Greek yogurt cooking spray	1 teaspoon hot sauce

Directions

Preheat the air fryer carefully to 380°F (190 degrees C).
Whisk together the egg, milk, and spicy sauce in a small bowl. Combine the flour, tapioca starch, salt, garlic, and cumin in a separate bowl. Dredge the chicken pieces in the dry mix first, then in the egg mixture, brushing off excess. Place the chicken in the air fryer basket in batches, be careful not to overcrowd it, and lightly spritz with oil.
Cook for about 10 minutes per batch, shaking the basket every 5 minutes until the chicken is no longer pink in the middle and the juices flow clear. Combine Greek yogurt, sweet chili sauce, and spicy sauce in a small bowl. **Serve:** the sauce beside the chicken.

Air Fryer Old Bay® Chicken Wings

Prep time: 20 minutes **Cooking time:** 20 minutes
Serve: 1

Ingredients

2 pounds chicken wings	2 tablespoons seafood seasoning
4 tablespoons butter	¼ tbsp freshly black pepper
½ cup cornstarch	
1 teaspoon seafood seasoning	

Directions

Preheat the air fryer carefully to 400°F (200 degrees C).
Toss the chicken wings with 2 tablespoons Old Bay® seasoning and black pepper in a large mixing dish. Toss the wings in the cornstarch until well covered. Shake each wing before placing it in the air fryer basket, making sure they don't contact; cook in batches if necessary.
Fry for 10 minutes in a hot air fryer, then shake the basket and cook for another 8 minutes. Fry the wings for 5 to 6 minutes longer, or until the chicken is cooked through and the juices flow clear.

Meanwhile, add butter and 1 teaspoon Old Bay® in seasoning for the sauce in a small saucepan. Bring to a boil, frequently stirring, over medium heat. Each wing should be dipped in the sauce. **Serve:** with any leftover sauce on the side.

Air Fryer Cornflake Chicken Fingers

Prep time: 15 minutes **Cooking time:** 20 minutes **Serve:** 1

Ingredients

1 pound chicken tenders	1 teaspoon poultry seasoning
1 teaspoon salt	1 cup corn flakes, crushed
½ teaspoon ground black pepper	1 large egg, beaten
1 serving avocado oil cooking spray	

Directions

Preheat the air fryer carefully to 375°F (190 degrees C).
Chicken tenders should be seasoned with poultry seasoning, salt, and black pepper. Dip in the egg, then in the crumbled cornflakes. Spray with avocado oil and place in the air fryer basket.

Cook for 7 to 8 minutes in an air fryer. Flip the chicken tenders, spritz with avocado oil again, and air fry for 3 to 5 minutes more. In the middle, an instant-read thermometer should read at least 165 degrees F. (74 degrees C).

Mexican-Style Air Fryer Stuffed Chicken Breasts

Prep time: 20 minutes **Cooking time:** 20 minutes
Serve: 1

Ingredients

4 extra-long toothpicks
salt and ground black
pepper to taste
4 teaspoons ground
cumin, divided
1 skinless, boneless
chicken breast

1 fresh jalapeno pepper,
sliced into thin strips
2 teaspoons corn oil

2 tbsp Mexican oregano
½ red bell pepper, sliced
into thin strips
½ onion, sliced into thin
strips
4 tbsp chili powder,
divided
2 teaspoons chipotle flakes
½ lime, juiced

Directions

Fill a small basin halfway with water and soak
toothpicks to protect them from burning during
cooking.

In a small dish, combine 2 teaspoons of chili powder
and 2 tablespoons of cumin. Preheat the air fryer
carefully to 400°F (200 degrees C).

Place the chicken breast on a flat work surface. Cut
horizontally through the center. Using a kitchen mallet
or rolling pin, pound each half until it is approximately
1/4-inch thick.

Sprinkle the remaining chili powder, cumin, chipotle
flakes, oregano, salt, and pepper evenly over each
breast half. In the middle of 1 breast half, place 1/2 of
the bell pepper, onion, and jalapeño. Roll the chicken
from the tapered end up and fasten with two
toothpicks. Repeat with the remaining breast, spices,
veggies, and fasten with toothpicks. Roll each roll-up
in the chili-cumin mixture in the shallow dish while
drizzling with olive oil until equally coated.

Place the roll-ups in the air fryer basket, toothpick side
up. Set a 6- minute timer.

Flip the roll-ups over. Cook for another 5 minutes in
the air fryer, or until the juices flow clear and an
instant-read thermometer put into the middle reads at
least 165 degrees F (74 degrees C). Before serving,
evenly drizzle the roll-ups with lime juice.

Air Fryer Chicken Thigh Schnitzel

Prep time: 15 minutes **Cooking time:** 25 minutes
Serve: 1

Ingredients

1-pound skinless, boneless
chicken thighs, trimmed of
fat
½ cup seasoned
breadcrumbs
avocado oil cooking spray

¼ cup flour
1 teaspoon salt
1 egg, beaten
½ teaspoon ground black
pepper

Directions

Place one chicken thigh between two pieces of
parchment paper and flatten with a mallet. Combine
breadcrumbs, salt, and black pepper in a small dish. In
a separate shallow bowl, place the flour, and in a third
shallow bowl, place the beaten egg. Dip the chicken
thighs in flour, then in the beaten egg, and finally in
the bread crumb mixture.

Preheat the air fryer carefully to 375°F (190 degrees
C).

Place the breaded thighs in the air fryer basket, not
touching; work in batches if required. Cook for 6
minutes after misting with avocado oil. Cook for
another 3 to 4 minutes after flipping each thigh.

Air Fryer Chicken Katsu

Prep time: 15 minutes **Cooking time:** 25 minutes
Serve: 1

Ingredients

1 large egg salt to taste
¾ pound chicken breast
cutlets avocado oil
cooking spray
1 tablespoon chopped
green onions (Optional)

1 cup panko breadcrumbs
1 tablespoon barbecue
sauce (Optional)

Directions

Preheat the air fryer carefully to 400°F (200°C)
according to the manufacturer's instructions.
Softly beat the egg and season with salt in a
shallow bowl or small casserole dish. On a dish,
spread out the panko breadcrumbs.
Allow extra egg mixture to drop back into the
bowl as you dip each cutlet. Turn the cutlets in
the panko breadcrumbs to cover both sides well,
carefully pushing the cutlets into the crumbs.
Place on a sheet of parchment paper. Spray each
side with cooking spray and set in an air fryer
basket.

Air Fryer Coconut Chicken

Prep time: 20 minutes **Cooking time:** 25 minutes
Serve: 1

Ingredients

½ cup canned coconut milk

½ cup pineapple juice

2 tablespoons brown sugar

1-pound boneless skinless chicken breasts

1 tablespoon soy sauce

1 teaspoon ground ginger

2 eggs

2 teaspoons Sriracha sauce

1 ½ teaspoons salt

cooking spray

1 cup sweetened shredded coconut

1 cup panko breadcrumbs

½ teaspoon ground black pepper

Directions

Combine the coconut milk, pineapple juice, brown sugar, soy sauce, Sriracha sauce, and ginger in a medium mixing bowl. Toss in the chicken strips to coat. Refrigerate for 2 hours or overnight, covered with plastic wrap. Preheat the air fryer carefully to 375°F (190 degrees C).

In a mixing dish, whisk together the eggs. Next, combine the shredded coconut, panko, salt, and pepper in a separate dish. Shake off any excess marinade from the chicken strips. Remove and discard the leftover marinade. Next, dip chicken strips in beaten egg, then in the coconut-panko mixture, then back in egg mixture, and finally in the coconut-panko mixture, dipping and coating each strip twice.

Cooking spray should be sprayed on the air fryer basket. Place the breaded chicken strips in the air fryer basket, not touching; work in batches if required. Cook for 6 minutes, rotate the strips, and cook for another 4 to 6 minutes, or gently browned and toasted

Air Fryer Chicken Kiev

Prep time: 15 minutes **Cooking time:** 20 minutes
Serve: 1

Ingredients

4 tablespoons butter, softened

2 tablespoons chopped fresh flat-leaf parsley

1 teaspoon salt

salt and ground black pepper to taste

1 clove garlic, minced

1 teaspoon paprika

2 sheets plastic wrap

8 ounces skinless, boneless chicken breast halves

½ cup all-purpose flour

1 egg, beaten

1 cup panko breadcrumbs

nonstick cooking spray

Directions

Combine the butter, parsley, garlic, and salt in a mixing dish until well blended. Place half of the herbed butter on a baking sheet. 10 minutes in the freezer

Season the chicken in a clean work area with salt and pepper. In the center of each pounded chicken breast, place 1/2 of the herbed butter. Gather the chicken's sides up around the butter mixture. Wrap each chicken ball in plastic wrap and twist to seal. Return to the baking sheet and place in the freezer for 30 minutes. Meanwhile, prepare an air fryer to 400°F (200 degrees C).

Combine the flour, the beaten egg, and the panko and paprika in one bowl. Remove the plastic from the chicken. Dredge each chicken breast in flour, then in beaten egg, and finally in panko breadcrumbs.

Place the breaded chicken in the air fryer basket. Coat the tops in cooking spray. 5 minutes in the air fryer. Cook for 5 minutes more after respraying with nonstick spray. Transfer to a chopping board and let aside for 5 minutes to rest.

Spicy Chicken Jerky in the Air Fryer

Prep time: 15 minutes **Cooking time:** 18 minutes
Serve: 1

Ingredients
2 (5 ounces) boneless chicken breasts, cut into strips

wooden skewers

½ cup mojo criollo marinade (such as Goya®)
2 teaspoons Cajun seasoning

Directions

Combine the chicken strips, marinade, and Cajun spice in a resealable plastic bag. Refrigerate for at least 8 hours and up to overnight. Skewers should be measured to fit across the air fryer basket, barely overlapping the edge. Remove any surplus length. Preheat the air fryer carefully for 10 minutes at 180 degrees F (80 degrees C).

While the air fryer is heating, thread chicken strips onto skewers, allowing space between each piece. 1 hour 15 minutes in the air fryer **Cooking time:** should be adjusted because most air fryers have a maximum of 32 minutes. During the reset time, rearrange the skewers. Increase the temperature to 200°F (95°C) and air fry for 15 minutes. Transfer the strips to a storage container lined with paper towels. Seal. Allow resting for at least an overnight before serving.

Crispy Keto Fried Chicken in the Air Fryer

Prep time: 15 minutes **Cooking time:** 22 minutes
Serve: 1

Ingredients
½ cup whole-milk plain kefir (such as Lifeway®)
2 (3.25 ounce) packages pork rinds, crushed
½ tbs sweet smoked paprika
¾ teaspoon Catanzaro herbs

1 ½ pounds chicken tenders
1 ½ teaspoon garlic powder
3 ounces finely grated Parmesan cheese
1 tablespoon hot sauce

Directions

In a small bowl, combine the kefir and spicy sauce. Marinate the chicken tenders for 30 minutes to an hour, or longer if desired.

Fill a small resealable container halfway with crumbled pork rinds. Combine the Parmesan cheese, garlic powder, Catanzaro herbs, and paprika in a mixing bowl.

Preheat the air fryer carefully to 390°F (200°C) for about 3 minutes. Remove the chicken from the kefir mixture and dredge it in the pork rind mixture. Air fried the chicken for 17 minutes in a preheated fryer, flipping halfway through.

Air Fryer Stuffed Chicken Breasts

Prep time: 10 minutes **Cooking time:** 18 minutes
Serve: 1

Ingredients
2 tbsp extra-virgin olive oil
½ cup crumbled feta cheese
1 teaspoon minced garlic
½ cup diced red bell pepper
½ cup chopped fresh spinach
1 pinch salt and ground black pepper
¾ cup grated Parmesan cheese

1 egg, beaten

½ cup diced red onion

4 boneless, skinless chicken breasts

½ cup diced fresh mushrooms
½ teaspoon dried Italian seasoning
12 toothpicks
4 slices prosciutto
¾ cup fine dry breadcrumbs 1 teaspoon dried parsley
1 serving avocado oil cooking spray

Directions

In a small pan over medium heat, heat the olive oil until hot. Cook and stir for 3 minutes, or until the onion is softened. Cook, stirring periodically, for 3 minutes more after adding the red bell pepper and mushrooms. Remove the skillet from the heat and toss in the chopped spinach and garlic. Continue to stir until the spinach has wilted somewhat. Allow cooling for 10 minutes after seasoning with Italian seasoning, salt, and pepper.

Mix in the feta cheese crumbles, breaking up any large pieces as you go. Place the chicken pieces on a secure cutting board and pat dry. Insert a knife into the thickest section of each breast and slice parallel to the cutting board, leaving about 1 inch at each tip. Be cautious not to cut through the breast's thinnest edge.

If the manufacturer recommends it, preheat the air fryer carefully to 370 degrees F (190 degrees C). Place the prosciutto slices on a clean prep surface. Place 2 tablespoons of the vegetable-feta mixture on top and twist up into an oblong bundle. Tuck one prosciutto-wrapped bundle into each cut chicken breast and secure with toothpicks.

Combine the Parmesan cheese, breadcrumbs, parsley, salt, and pepper on a dish. Dredge each filled chicken breast in the breadcrumb mixture after dipping it in the beaten egg. Use avocado oil spray to coat the pan.

Cook until browned in the air fryer basket, about 15 minutes on each side. In the middle, an instant-read thermometer should read at least 165 degrees F. (74 degrees C).

Air Fryer General Tso's Chicken

Prep time: 18 minutes **Cooking time:** 20 minutes **Serve:** 1

Ingredients

½ cup chicken broth
1 tablespoon hoisin sauce
1 tablespoon soy sauce
1-pound skinless, boneless chicken breasts
2 tablespoons cornstarch
1 teaspoon chopped scallions, or to taste
1 tablespoon sesame oil
1 tablespoon cornstarch
1 teaspoon minced garlic
1 tablespoon soy sauce
cooking spray
1 teaspoon Sriracha
1 teaspoon toasted sesame seeds

Directions

In a medium saucepan, combine broth, sesame oil, soy sauce, hoisin sauce, cornstarch, garlic, and Sriracha for the sauce. Whisk until the cornstarch is completely dissolved. Bring the water to a boil over medium-high heat. Turn down the heat to low.
Preheat the air fryer carefully to 400°F (200°C) according to the manufacturer's instructions.

Stir together the chicken, cornstarch, and soy sauce in a mixing dish until the chicken is equally covered. Place the chicken in the air fryer basket. Coat the pan with cooking spray.

Cook for 8 minutes in a hot air fryer. Shake the basket, breaking up any stuck-together bits, then respray with cooking spray. Cook for another 8 minutes, or until the chicken is no longer pink in the center.

Place the chicken in a large mixing basin. Toss the chicken in the sauce to coat. Garnish with onions and sesame seeds if desired.

Air Fryer Chicken Taquitos

Prep time: 15 minutes **Cooking time:** 25 minutes **Serve:** 1

Ingredients

1 teaspoon vegetable oil
2 tablespoons diced onion
6 each corn tortillas
1 clove garlic, minced
2 tablespoons chopped green chiles
2 tablespoons Neufchatel cheese
1 cup shredded rotisserie chicken
1 pinch salt and ground black pepper to taste
½ cup shredded Mexican cheese blend
2 tablespoons Mexican-style hot tomato sauce
1 serving avocado oil cooking spray

Directions

In a skillet, heat the oil. Cook until the onion is tender and transparent, 3 to 5 minutes. Cook until the garlic is aromatic, approximately 1 minute. Stir in the green chilies and Mexican tomato sauce. Combine the chicken, Neufchatel cheese, and Mexican cheese mixture in a bowl. Cook and stir for 3 minutes, or until the cheeses have melted and the mixture is well warmed. Season with salt and pepper to taste.

Heat tortillas in a pan or directly on the gas stove grates till warm and flexible. Fill each tortilla with 3 tablespoons of the chicken mixture. Roll into taquitos after folding over.
Preheat the air fryer carefully to 400°F (200 degrees C).
Place the taquitos in the air fryer basket without touching and spritz with avocado oil. If necessary, cook in batches. Cook for 6 to 9 minutes, or until golden brown and crispy. Turn the taquitos over, spray with avocado oil, and continue to air fry for 3 to 5 minutes.

Air Fryer Herb-Seasoned Chicken Wings

Prep time: 15 minutes **Cooking time:** 20 minutes
Serve: 1

Ingredients

1 cooking spray 8 chicken wings	1 tbs ground black pepper
1 teaspoon ground cumin	1 tbsp Hungarian paprika
1 teaspoon garlic powder	1 teaspoon herbs de Provence
½ teaspoon kosher salt	1 teaspoon onion powder

Directions

Preheat the air fryer carefully to 390°F (200°C) according to the manufacturer's instructions. Cooking spray should be sprayed on the basket. Rinse and pat dry the chicken wings. Combine black pepper, paprika, cumin, garlic powder, onion powder, herbs de Provence, and kosher salt in a mixing bowl. On both sides of the wings, sprinkle with the seasoning.

Place the wings in the fryer basket in a single layer, ensuring they don't touch. Fry for about 9 minutes per side, or until browned and no longer pink in the middle.

Air Fryer Chicken Thighs

Prep time: 15 minutes **Cooking time:** 20 minutes
Serve: 1

Ingredients

4 boneless chicken thighs	¾ teaspoon garlic powder
1 teaspoon smoked paprika	2 tbs extra-virgin olive oil
½ teaspoon salt	½ tbsp ground black pepper

Directions

Preheat the air fryer carefully to 400°F (200 degrees C). Dry the chicken thighs with a paper towel and brush the skin side with olive oil. Arrange the chicken thighs in a single layer on a platter, skin side down.

Combine the smoked paprika, garlic powder, salt, and pepper in a mixing dish. Sprinkle half of the seasoning mixture equally over the 4 chicken thighs. Turn the thighs over and equally sprinkle with the remaining spice mixture. Place the chicken thighs in a single layer in the air fryer basket, skin side up. Fry in a preheated air fryer for 18 minutes, or until the chicken is brown and the juices flow clear. In the middle, an instant-read thermometer should read at least 165 degrees F. (74 degrees C).

Air Fryer Chicken Fajita Taquitos

Prep time: 15 minutes **Cooking time:** 18 minutes
Serve: 1

Ingredients

2 (4 ounces) boneless, skinless chicken breasts, cut into strips	1 ¼ cups mojo criollo marinade
1 (14 ounces) package fire-roasted peppers and onion blend (such as Trader Joe's®), thawed cooking spray	1 pound corn tortillas 1 cup shredded Mexican cheese blend

Directions

Add the marinade to the chicken strips in a sealable container. Allow to marinade for 2 hours after sealing. Drain and discard marinade. Cook the chicken strips in a pan over medium-high heat until browned, 6 to 7 minutes. Cook for 2 to 3 minutes more after adding the thawed peppers and onions.

Place the chicken strips on a chopping board and cut them into smaller pieces. Return the chopped chicken to the peppers and onions and stir to mix. Preheat the air fryer carefully to 370 degrees Fahrenheit (187 degrees Celsius) for 5 minutes. Fill a tortilla bag halfway with tortillas. Microwave 5 tortillas for 30 seconds at a time. Place warmed tortillas on a cutting board and spray each side with about 1/2 teaspoon of oil. 1 to 2 tablespoons chicken filling on top, followed by 1 tablespoon cheese mixture. Taquitos should be firmly rolled.

Place the taquitos in the air fryer basket, seam side down, and cook for 5 minutes. Then, increase the temperature of the air fryer to 400 degrees F (200 degrees C) and continue to air fry for 5 minutes.

Air Fried Maple Chicken Thighs

Prep time: 15 minutes **Cooking time:** 22 minutes
Serve: 1

Ingredients

1 cup buttermilk	½ cup maple syrup
1 teaspoon granulated garlic	4 skin-on, bone-in chicken thighs
1 egg	
½ cup all-purpose flour	¼ cup tapioca flour
1 teaspoon sweet paprika	½ teaspoon smoked paprika
1 tablespoon salt	
¼ tbsp ground black pepper	¼ teaspoon cayenne pepper
½ teaspoon granulated garlic	½ teaspoon honey powder (such as Savory Spice®)
1 teaspoon granulated onion	

Directions

In a resealable bag, combine buttermilk, maple syrup, egg, and 1 teaspoon granulated garlic. Marinate the chicken thighs for at least 1 hour or overnight in the refrigerator.

In a shallow bowl, combine flour, granulated onion, pepper, tapioca flour, salt, sweet paprika, smoked paprika, cayenne pepper, 1/2 teaspoon granulated garlic, and honey powder. Preheat the air fryer carefully to 380°F (190 degrees C).

Remove the chicken thighs from the marinade and set them aside. Dredge the chicken in the flour mixture and brush off any excess. Cook the chicken for 12 minutes, skin side down, in a preheated air fryer. Fry the thighs for a further 13 minutes on the other side.

Crispy Ranch Air Fryer Nuggets

Prep time: 10 minutes **Cooking time:** 18 minutes
Serve: 1

Ingredients

1 pound chicken tenders, cut into 1.5 to 2-inch pieces 1 package dry ranch salad dressing mix	2 tablespoons flour
	1 egg, lightly beaten
	1 serving olive oil cooking spray
1 cup panko breadcrumbs	

Directions

Toss the chicken in a bowl with the ranch seasoning to mix. Allow for 5-10 minutes of resting time. Fill a resealable bag halfway with flour. Place the panko breadcrumbs on a dish and the egg in a small bowl. Preheat the air fryer carefully to 390°F (200 degrees C). Toss the chicken in the bag to coat. Dip the chicken in the egg mixture lightly, allowing excess to drain off. Roll the chicken in panko, pushing the crumbs into the meat.

Spray the air fryer basket with oil and arrange the chicken pieces inside, ensuring no overlap. Depending on the size of your air fryer, you may need to prepare two batches. Next, spray the chicken lightly with cooking spray. 4 minutes in the oven. Cook for 4 minutes more, or until the chicken is no longer pink on the inside. **Serve:** right away.

Air Fryer Bang-Bang Chicken

Prep time: 18 minutes **Cooking time:** 20 minutes **Serve:** 1

Ingredients

1 cup mayonnaise	½ cup sweet chili sauce
2 tbsp Sriracha sauce	⅓ cup flour
1 pound chicken breast tenderloins, cut into bite-size pieces	1 ½ cups panko breadcrumbs
	2 green onions, chopped

Directions

Combine the mayonnaise, sweet chili sauce, and Sriracha in a large mixing bowl. Set aside a third of a cup of the mixture. Fill a big resealable plastic bag halfway with flour. Close the bag and shake to coat the chicken. Stir the coated chicken pieces into the large mixing bowl with the mayonnaise mixture. In a separate big plastic resealable bag, place the panko breadcrumbs. Drop chicken pieces into breadcrumbs in batches, close, and shake to coat.

Preheat the air fryer carefully to 400°F (200 degrees C). Fill the air fryer basket with as many chicken pieces as you can without overflowing it. Cook for 10 minutes in a hot air fryer. Cook for 5 minutes more on the other side. Rep with the remaining chicken. Pour the saved sauce over the fried chicken in a large mixing bowl. Stir in the green onions and toss to coat. **Serve:** right away.

Air Fryer Chicken Strips

Prep time: 15 minutes **Cooking time:** 20 minutes
Serve: 1

Ingredients

1 cup all-purpose flour
1 tablespoon paprika
½ teaspoon ground black pepper
1 large egg
cooking spray

1 tablespoon parsley flakes
1 teaspoon seasoned salt
1 ½ pounds chicken tenderloins

Directions

Preheat the air fryer carefully to 400°F (200°C) according to the manufacturer's instructions. Combine the flour, paprika, parsley, seasoned salt, and pepper in a large mixing bowl. In a separate dish, beat the egg.

Dredge each chicken strip in seasoned flour, then in beaten egg, and last in seasoned flour.
Fill the basket with as many strips as you can without overflowing it. Spray the tops of the strips lightly with cooking spray. 8 minutes in the oven, turn the strips over, and sprinkle the tops gently with additional cooking spray. Cook for an additional 8 minutes. Rep with the rest of the strips.

Air Fryer Cornflake-Crusted Chicken Tenders

Prep time: 18 minutes **Cooking time:** 20 minutes
Serve: 1

Ingredients

1 egg
1 pinch salt
1 ounce finely shredded Parmesan cheese
½ teaspoon granulated garlic
1 pinch salt

1 tablespoon pesto
1 cup crushed cornflakes
½ teaspoon Catanzaro herbs
1 pound chicken tenders

Directions

Preheat the air fryer carefully to 400°F (200 degrees C). In a shallow bowl, combine the egg, pesto, and salt. Separately, combine cornflake crumbs, Parmesan cheese, Catanzaro herbs, garlic, and salt in a separate dish.

Dip each piece of chicken in the egg wash first, then in the cornflake mixture, brushing off excess breading. Finally, place the chicken in the air fryer basket.

After 5 minutes, rotate the chicken pieces and air fry until the center is no longer pink and the juices run clear, about 5 minutes more.

Air Fryer Chicken Cordon Bleu

Prep time: 15 minutes **Cooking time:** 25 minutes
Serve: 1

Ingredients

2 boneless, skinless chicken breasts salt and ground black pepper to taste
2 toothpicks
1 cup panko breadcrumbs
1 egg, beaten

4 slices deli Swiss cheese
4 slices of deli ham
1 tablespoon Dijon mustard
¼ cup all-purpose flour
⅓ cup grated Parmesan cheese cooking spray

Directions

1 chicken breast should be placed on a chopping board. Holding a sharp knife parallel to the cutting board and down one long edge of the chicken breast, cut it almost in half, leaving one side connected. Cover the breast with plastic wrap once it has been opened flat like a book.

Lightly pound to 1/4-inch thickness with the flat side of a
meat mallet. Rep with the remaining chicken breasts. Season both sides of each chicken breast with salt and pepper. On top, smear Dijon mustard. 1 piece of cheese on each breast, 2 slices of ham, and 1 slice of cheese on top of each. Each breast should be rolled up and secured with a toothpick.

In a small basin, combine the flour and salt. In a separate bowl, crack the egg. In a third bowl, combine panko breadcrumbs and grated Parmesan.
Preheat the air fryer carefully to 350°F (175 degrees C). Dip the chicken in flour first, then in egg, and then in the bread crumb mixture. Spray the chicken rolls with nonstick cooking spray and set aside for 5 minutes while the air fryer warms up.

Cook the chicken for 10 minutes in the prepared air fryer basket. Reapply nonstick spray to any chalky areas. Cook for 8 minutes more, or until the chicken is no longer pink in the center.

Air Fryer Honey-Cajun Chicken Thighs

Prep time: 20 minutes **Cooking time:** 20 minutes
Serve: 1

Ingredients

½ cup buttermilk
1 ½ pound skinless, boneless chicken thighs
⅓ cup tapioca flour
½ teaspoon garlic salt
¼ teaspoon ground paprika

1 teaspoon hot sauce
¼ cup all-purpose flour
4 teaspoons honey
2 ½ tbsp Cajun seasoning
½ teaspoon honey powder
⅛ teaspoon cayenne pepper

Directions

In a resealable plastic bag, combine buttermilk and spicy sauce. Marinate the chicken thighs for 30 minutes. Combine the flour, tapioca flour, Cajun spice, garlic salt, honey

powder, paprika, and cayenne pepper in a small mixing bowl. Remove the thighs from the buttermilk mixture and coat them in the flour mixture. Excess flour should be shaken off.

Preheat the air fryer carefully to 360°F (175 degrees C). Cook the chicken thighs in the air fryer basket for around 15 minutes. Cook until the chicken thighs are no longer pink in the middle and the juices run clear, about 10 minutes more. In the middle, an instant-read thermometer should read at least 165 degrees F. (74 degrees C). Remove the chicken thighs from the air fryer and sprinkle with 1 teaspoon honey on each thigh

.

Bacon-Wrapped Stuffed Chicken Breasts in the Air Fryer

Prep time: 15 minutes **Cooking time:** 25 minutes **Serve:** 1

Ingredients

3 breast half, bone, and skin removed
3 slices Monterey Jack cheese

1tbs lemonpepper seasoning
6 spears of fresh asparagus
9 slices bacon
12 each wooden toothpick

Directions

If the manufacturer recommends it, preheat the air fryer carefully to 350°F (175°C). Using paper towels, pat the chicken pieces dry. Slice horizontally down the center, starting at the thickest area and being cautious not to cut through to the other side with a sharp knife. Spread the two sides out as if they were a book.

Both sides should be seasoned with lemon-pepper spice. Next, 1 piece of cheese for each chicken breast Cut the asparagus spears in half and arrange four halves on top of the cheese. Then roll the chicken up and over the cheese and asparagus, maintaining the filling within each roll. Next, wrap three slices of bacon around each chicken breast, using wooden toothpicks to bind the bacon where it overlaps. Place each bacon-wrapped breast in the air fryer basket and cook for 15 minutes on high

Air Fryer Balsamic-Glazed Chicken Wings

Prep time: 20 minutes **Cooking time:** 25 minutes
Serve: 1

Ingredients

cooking spray
1 teaspoon paprika
1 ½ teaspoons salt
1 green onion, thinly sliced
2 pounds chicken wings
⅓ cup balsamic vinegar
2 tablespoons soy sauce
2 tablespoons honey
1 teaspoon water
3 tablespoons baking powder
1 ½ teaspoon freshly ground black pepper
⅓ cup water
2 tablespoons chili sauce (such as Heinz®)
2 cloves garlic, minced
¼ teaspoon cornstarch
¼ teaspoon toasted sesame seeds

Directions

Preheat the air fryer carefully to 380°F (190 degrees C). Cooking spray should be sprayed on the fryer basket.

Combine the baking powder, salt, pepper, and paprika in a small mixing bowl. Place some chicken wings in a bag with the baking powder mixture and shake to coat. Remove the wings from the bag, shake off any excess powder, and continue until all of the wings have been coated with the baking powder mixture.

Cook for 20 minutes, shaking and rotating the wings midway through, after lightly spraying them with frying spray and placing them in the preheated air fryer basket. Next, raise the heat to 400°F (200°C) and cook until the bacon is crispy, about 5 minutes longer. You may need to cook the wings in batches depending on the size of your air fryer.

Meanwhile, add 1/3 cup water, balsamic vinegar, soy sauce, honey, chili sauce, and garlic in a saucepan over medium heat. Bring to a low boil and simmer for 15 minutes, or until the sauce has reduced. Whisk together 1 teaspoon water and cornstarch; pour into the sauce and stir until thickened.

Toss crispy wings in a large mixing basin with sauce until fully covered. **Serve:** immediately, garnished with chopped green onion and sesame seeds.

Keto Lemon-Garlic Chicken Thighs in the Air Fryer

Prep time: 15 minutes **Cooking time:** 18 minutes
Serve: 1

Ingredients

¼ cup lemon juice
1 teaspoon Dijon mustard
⅛ teaspoon ground black pepper
4 skin-on, bone-in chicken thighs
2 tablespoons olive oil
¼ teaspoon salt
2 cloves garlic, minced
4 lemon wedges

Directions

Combine the lemon juice, olive oil, Dijon mustard, garlic, salt, and pepper in a mixing bowl. Set aside the marinade.

Fill a large resealable plastic bag halfway with chicken thighs. Pour marinade over chicken and close bag, ensuring that all chicken portions are covered. Refrigerate for at least 2 hours before serving. Preheat the air fryer carefully to 360°F (175 degrees C). Take the chicken out of the marinade and blot it dry with paper towels. Cook the chicken in batches if required in the air fryer basket.

Fry for 22 to 24 minutes, or until the chicken is no longer pink at the bone and the juices flow clear. A thermometer near the bone should read 165 degrees F. (74 degrees C). When serving, squeeze a lemon slice over each piece.

Air Fryer Bacon-Wrapped Chicken Thighs

Prep time: 15 minutes **Cooking time:** 22 minutes
Serve: 1

Ingredients

½ stick butter softened
¼ teaspoon dried thyme,
¼ teaspoon dried basil
⅓ pound thick-cut bacon
2 teaspoons minced garlic
½ clove minced garlic
⅛ teaspoon coarse salt
freshly black pepper
1 ½ pounds boneless skinless chicken thighs

Directions

Combine melted butter, garlic, thyme, basil, salt, and pepper in a mixing bowl. Place the butter on wax paper and roll it up tightly to produce a butter log. Refrigerate for 2 hours, or until firm.
One bacon strip should be placed flat on a sheet of wax paper. Sprinkle with garlic and place the chicken thigh on top of the bacon. Remove the chicken thigh. Place 1-2 tablespoons of the cool finishing butter in the center of each chicken thigh. Insert one end of the bacon into the center of the chicken thigh. Fold the bacon over the chicken thigh and wrap it around it. Repeat with the rest of the thighs and bacon.

Air Fryer Sesame Chicken Thighs

Prep time: 10 minutes **Cooking time:** 18 minutes
Serve: 1

Ingredients

2 tablespoons sesame oil	1 tablespoon sriracha
2 tablespoons soy sauce	sauce 1 teaspoon rice
	vinegar
2 pounds chicken thighs	2 tablespoons toasted
1 green onion, chopped	sesame seeds
1 tablespoon honey	

Directions

Combine sesame oil, soy sauce, honey, sriracha, and vinegar in a large mixing bowl. Stir in the chicken to mix. Refrigerate for at least 30 minutes, covered.
Preheat the air fryer carefully to 400°F (200 degrees C). Remove the chicken from the marinade.

Place them skin-side up chicken thighs in the air fryer basket. 5 minutes in the oven Cook for another 10 minutes on the other side.

Place the chicken on a platter and set it aside for 5 minutes before serving. Garnish with green onion and sesame seeds if desired.

Air Fryer Chicken Katsu with Homemade Katsu Sauce

Prep time: 15 minutes **Cooking time:** 25 minutes
Serve: 1

Ingredients

½ cup ketchup	2 tablespoons soy sauce
1 tablespoon brown sugar	1 tablespoon sherry
2 teaspoons	1-pound boneless skinless
Worcestershire sauce	chicken breast
1 teaspoon minced garlic	1 pinch salt and ground
1 serving cooking spray	black pepper
2 large eggs, beaten	1 ½ cups panko
	breadcrumbs

Directions

In a mixing bowl, combine ketchup, soy sauce, brown sugar, sherry, Worcestershire sauce, and garlic until the sugar is dissolved. Set aside the katsu sauce.
Preheat the air fryer carefully to 350°F (175 degrees C).

In the meantime, arrange the chicken pieces in a clean work area. Season with salt and pepper to taste.
On a flat plate, place the beaten eggs. Fill a second flat plate halfway with breadcrumbs. Dredge the chicken in the egg, then in the breadcrumbs. Repeat by dredging the chicken in egg and then breadcrumbs, pressing down to ensure that the breadcrumbs adhere to the chicken.

Place the chicken pieces in the air fryer basket that has been preheated. Nonstick cooking spray should be sprayed on the tops.

10 minutes in the air fryer. Flip the chicken pieces over and coat the tops with nonstick cooking spray using a spatula. Cook for an additional 8 minutes. Slice the chicken on a chopping board. Toss with katsu sauce and **Serve:**.

Air Fryer Chicken Kyiv Balls

Prep time: 20 minutes **Cooking time:** 20 minutes
Serve: 1

Ingredients

½ cup unsalted butter softened

1 (19.1 ounces) package ground chicken breast

2 eggs, beaten

1 teaspoon salt

½ tbsp ground black pepper

2 tablespoons chopped fresh flat-leaf parsley

1 cup panko breadcrumbs

1 teaspoon paprika

2 cloves garlic, crushed

cooking spray

Directions

Blend the butter, parsley, and garlic until well incorporated into a mixing dish. On a baking sheet, divide the mixture into 12 equal sections. Freeze for approximately 20 minutes or until solid.

Make 12 balls out of the ground chicken. In the middle of each ball, make a deep imprint. Place a slice of frozen herbed butter in the indentation and wrap the meat around it until it is completely enclosed. Rep with the remaining balls.

In a mixing dish, combine the beaten eggs. Next, combine panko, paprika, salt, and pepper in a separate bowl. 1 ground chicken ball should be dipped in the beaten eggs first, then in the seasoned breadcrumbs. Re-dunk the ball in the egg and then in the seasoned breadcrumbs. Rep with the remaining balls. Place on a baking sheet and place in the freezer for 10 minutes.

Preheat the air fryer carefully to 400°F (200 degrees C). Spray half of the balls with nonstick cooking spray and place them in the air fryer. 5 minutes in the oven with tongs, turn the balls over and re-spray with nonstick cooking spray. Cook for another 5 minutes. Repeat with the rest of the chicken balls.

Air Fryer Sweet and Sour Chicken Wings

Prep time: 15 minutes **Cooking time:** 25 minutes
Serve: 1

Ingredients

1 ½ pounds chicken wings, tips discarded

1 teaspoon ground black pepper

¼ cup pineapple juice

1 tablespoon brown sugar

1 teaspoon paprika

1 teaspoon sesame oil

1 tablespoon cornstarch

¾ teaspoon sesame seeds

1 stalk green onion, sliced

2 tablespoons baking powder

½ cup white vinegar

1 teaspoon salt

¼ cup ketchup

1 tablespoon reduced-sodium soy sauce

1 tablespoon water

1 teaspoon Sriracha sauce

Directions

Preheat the air fryer carefully to 380°F (190 degrees C). Coat the basket with cooking spray. Using a paper towel, pat dries the chicken wings. Combine baking powder, salt, pepper, and paprika in a resealable plastic bag. Place some chicken wings in the bag and shake vigorously until the wings are fully covered. Shake off any extra baking powder mixture, then repeat with the remaining wings until all of them are covered.

Cook the chicken wings in the air fryer basket for 22 to 23 minutes, turning halfway through. Meanwhile, add vinegar, pineapple juice, ketchup, brown sugar, soy sauce, Sriracha, and sesame oil in a small saucepan over medium heat. Bring to a boil, stirring constantly. For around 2 minutes, bring the water to a boil. Then, reduce the heat to a low simmer. In a small bowl, mix the cornstarch and water. Pour into the pot and stir vigorously until the sauce thickens about 1 minute. Thin the sauce with a little water if it's too thick.

Increase the temperature of the air fryer to 400 degrees F (200 degrees C) and cook the wings for another 2 minutes, or until they are cooked through and crispy brown.

Pour the sauce into a large mixing dish and toss in the cooked wings. Toss well to coat. **Serve:** immediately, garnished with sesame seeds and green onion.

VEGETABLES & SIDE DISHES

Roasted Broccoli and Cauliflower with Tahini Sauce

(**Ready in about** 15 minutes | **Servings:** 3)

Ingredients

1/2 pound broccoli, broken into florets
1/2 pound cauliflower, broken into florets
1 teaspoon onion powder
1 tablespoons tahini
Salt and chili flakes, to taste

1/2 teaspoon porcini powder 1/4 teaspoon cumin powder 1/2 teaspoon granulated garlic
1 teaspoon olive oil
2 tablespoons soy sauce
1 teaspoon white vinegar

Directions

Start by preheating your Air Fryer to 400 degrees F.

Now, toss the vegetables with the onion powder, porcini powder cumin powder, garlic and olive oil. Transfer your vegetables to the lightly greased cooking basket.

Air Fry your veggies in the preheated Air Fryer at 400 degrees F for 6 minutes. Remove the broccoli florets from the cooking basket. Continue to cook the cauliflower for 5 to 6 minutes more.

Meanwhile, make the tahini sauce by simply whisking the remaining Ingredients in a small bowl. Spoon the sauce over the warm vegetables and **Serve:** immediately. Bon appétit!

Sweet & Sticky Baby Carrots

(**Ready in about** 45 minutes | **Servings:** 3)

Ingredients

1 tablespoon coconut oil
1 pound baby carrots
2 lemongrasses, finely chopped
3 tablespoons honey

1 teaspoon fresh ginger, peeled and grated
1 teaspoon lemon thyme

Directions

Toss all Ingredients in a mixing bowl and let it stand for 30 minutes. Transfer the baby carrots to the cooking basket.

Cook the baby carrots at 380 degrees F for 15 minutes, shaking the basket halfway through the **Cooking time:**to ensure even cooking.

Serve: warm and enjoy!

Green Bean Salad with Goat Cheese and Almonds

(**Ready in about** 15 minutes | **Servings:** 3)

Ingredients

1 ½ pounds green beans, trimmed and cut into small chunks
1 teaspoon deli mustard
2 bell peppers, deseeded and sliced
1 tablespoon Shoyu sauce
Dressing
2 tbs extra-virgin olive oil

1 small-sized red onion, sliced
Sea salt black pepper to taste
1/4 cup almonds
1/2 cup goat cheese, crumbled
1 tbsp champagne vinegar
1 clove garlic, pressed

Directions

Season the green beans with salt and black pepper to your liking. Brush them with a nonstick cooking oil.

Place the green beans in the Air Fryer cooking basket. Cook the green beans at 400 degrees F for 5 minutes and transfer to a salad bowl. Stir in the onion and bell peppers.

Then, add the raw almonds to the cooking basket. Roast the almonds at 350 degrees F for 5 minutes, shaking the basket periodically to ensure even cooking.

In the meantime, make the dressing by blending all Ingredients until well incorporated. Dress your salad and top with goat cheese and roasted almonds. Enjoy!

Roasted Asparagus with Pecorino Romano Cheese

(**Ready in about** 10 minutes | **Servings:** 3)

Ingredients

1 pound asparagus spears, trimmed
1/2 tbsp shallot powder
1/4 tsp cumin powder
1/2 tsp dried rosemary
1 tbs sesame seeds, toasted

1/2 tbsp garlic powder
1 teaspoon sesame oil
Coarse sea salt and ground black pepper, to taste 4 tablespoons Pecorino Romano cheese, grated

Directions

Begin by preheating your Air Fryer to 400°F.

Toss the asparagus with the sesame oil, spices, and cheese before placing it in the Air Fryer cooking basket.

Cook the asparagus for 5 to 6 minutes in a preheated Air Fryer, shaking the basket halfway through to ensure even browning. **Serve:** warm, garnished with toasted sesame seeds. Good appetite!

Mediterranean-Style Roasted Broccoli

(**Ready in about** 10 minutes | **Servings:** 3)

Ingredients

1 pound broccoli florets
1 teaspoon butter, melted
Sea salt, to taste
1 tablespoon fresh lemon juice

1 teaspoon mixed peppercorns, crushed
1/4 cup mayonnaise
1 teaspoon deli mustard
2 cloves garlic, minced

Directions

Toss the broccoli florets with butter, salt and crushed peppercorns until well coated on all sides.

Cook in the preheated Air Fryer at 400 degrees F for 6 minutes until they've softened.

In the meantime, make your aioli by mixing the mayo, lemon juice, mustard and garlic in a bowl. **Serve:** the roasted broccoli with the sauce on the side. Enjoy!

Hot Cheesy Roasted Eggplants

(**Ready in about** 15 minutes | **Servings:** 2)

Ingredients

1 pound eggplants, sliced
1 teaspoon sesame oil
1/4 teaspoon chili flakes
1/2 teaspoon parsley flakes
1 teaspoon garlic, pressed

Sea salt and freshly ground black pepper, to taste
1/2 cup cream cheese, at room temperature

Directions

Brush the eggplants with sesame oil and season with salt and black pepper before placing them in the Air Fryer cooking basket. Cook your eggplants for 10 minutes at 400 degrees F. In the meantime, combine the remaining Ingredients to make the rub. Cook for 5 minutes more after topping the eggplants with the chilli cheese mixture.

Arrange the eggplants on a serving platter. Good appetite!

Roasted Cherry Tomato Pasta

(**Ready in about** 15 minutes | **Servings:** 3)

Ingredients

1 pound cherry tomatoes
1 teaspoon olive oil
1/2 teaspoon oregano
1 pound fettuccine pasta

Sea salt and ground black pepper, to taste
1/2 teaspoon dried basil

Directions

Toss the cherry tomatoes with the olive oil, salt, black pepper, oregano, and basil until well combined.

Cook for 4 minutes in a preheated Air Fryer at 400 degrees F, tossing the basket halfway through to ensure even cooking. Cook the pasta as directed on the package. Enjoy the roasted tomatoes over the hot pasta.

Stuffed and Baked Sweet Potatoes

(**Ready in about** 35 minutes | **Servings:** 2)

Ingredients

2 medium sweet potatoes
1 tablespoon butter, cold
2 tbs cilantro, chopped
Coarse sea salt and ground black pepper, to taste

6 ounces canned kidney beans 1/4 cup Cotija cheese, crumbled

Directions

Poke the sweet potatoes all over using a small knife; transfer them to the Air Fryer cooking basket.

Cook in the preheated Air Fryer at 380 degrees F for 20 to 25 minutes. Then, scrape the sweet potato flesh using a spoon; mix sweet potato flesh with kidney beans, cheese, butter, salt and pepper. Bake for a further 10 minutes until cooked through.

Place the sweet potatoes on serving plates. Garnish with cilantro and **Serve:**.

Spring Beet and Feta Cheese Salad

(**Ready in about** 45 minutes | **Servings:** 2)

Ingredients

2 medium beets, scrubbed and trimmed
2 scallions stalks, chopped
1 tablespoon maple syrup
1 tablespoon orange juice concentrate
1/2 tbsp Dijon mustard
Salt black pepper, to taste
2 ounces feta cheese, crumbled

6 ounces mixed greens
1 teaspoon olive oil
2 stalks green garlic, finely chopped
2 tablespoons extra-virgin olive oil
1/4 teaspoon ground cumin seeds
2 tablespoons white vinegar

Directions

Toss your beets with 1 teaspoon of olive oil. Cook your beets in the preheated Air Fryer at 400 degrees F for 40 minutes, turning them over once or twice to ensure even cooking.

Let your beets cool completely and then, slice them with a sharp knife. Place the beets in a salad bowl and add in the mixed greens, scallions and garlic.

In a small mixing dish, whisk the maple syrup, orange juice concentrate, vinegar, 2 tablespoons of extra-virgin olive oil, Dijon mustard, salt, black pepper and ground cumin.

Dress your salad, toss to combine and garnish with feta cheese. Bon appétit!

Roasted Chermoula Parsnip

(**Ready in about** 20 minutes | **Servings:** 3)

Ingredients

1 pound parsnip, trimmed, peeled and cut into 1/2 inch pieces
1/2 tbs saffron strands
2 garlic cloves
1 teaspoon ground cumin
1/2 tbsp ground coriander
1 tablespoon freshly squeezed lemon juice

1 tablespoon fresh cilantro leaves
1 tablespoon fresh parsley leaves
Salt and black pepper, to taste
4 tbso extra-virgin olive oil
1/2 tbs cayenne pepper

Directions

Place your parsnips in the Air Fryer cooking basket; spritz the parsnip with a nonstick cooking oil.

Cook the parsnip in the preheated Air Fryer at 380 degrees F for 15 minutes, shaking the basket halfway through the **Cooking time:**to ensure even browning.

Add the remaining Ingredients to a bowl of your food processor or blender. Blend until smooth and well combined.

Spoon the Chermoula dressing over roasted parsnip and **Serve:**. Bon appétit!

Mexican-Style Roasted Zucchini

(**Ready in about** 15 minutes | **Servings:** 3)

Ingredients

1 pound zucchini, sliced into thick rounds
1/2 teaspoon garlic powder 1/8 teaspoon cayenne pepper 1 teaspoon Mexican oregano
1 teaspoon chili oil
1 tablespoon fresh cilantro, roughly chopped

1/2 teaspoon red pepper flakes, crushed
Kosher salt and black pepper, to taste
1/2 cup Cotija cheese, crumbled

Directions

Toss your zucchini with the chili oil, red pepper flakes, garlic powder, cayenne pepper, Mexican oregano, salt and black pepper.

Transfer your zucchini to the Air Fryer cooking basket.

Cook your zucchini at 400 degrees F for 7 minutes. Turn over the slices of zucchini and top them with crumbled cheese.

Continue to cook for 5 minutes more. Garnish with cilantro and **Serve:**.

Mediterranean Herb-Crusted Cauliflower

(**Ready in about** 15 minutes | **Servings:** 3)

Ingredients

1 ½ pounds cauliflower, cut into florets
1 teaspoon garlic, minced
1 teaspoon lemon zest
1 teaspoon dried rosemary
1/2 teaspoon dried thyme
1/4 cup breadcrumbs
1 teaspoon olive oil

Sea salt and ground black pepper, to taste
1 tablespoon fresh Italian parsley, chopped
1/4 cup Parmesan cheese, grated
1/4 cup Kalamata olives

Directions

Toss the cauliflower florets with all Ingredients, except for the Kalamata olives.

Cook the cauliflower at 400 degrees F for 12 minutes, shaking the basket once or twice to ensure even browning.

Garnish the roasted cauliflower with Kalamata olives and **Serve:** immediately. Enjoy!

Creamed Sweet Potato Casserole

(**Ready in about** 30 minutes | **Servings:** 3)

Ingredients

1 cup heavy cream

1/2 teaspoon dried parsley flakes

1 ½ ponds sweet potatoes, peeled and thinly sliced

1/2 cup Colby cheese, grated

1/2 teaspoon garlic, minced

A pinch of freshly grated nutmeg

1 teaspoon rosemary

1 teaspoon basil

Direction

Begin by preheating your Air Fryer to 330°F. Brush nonstick cooking oil on the sides and bottom of a casserole dish.

Except for the cheese, thoroughly combine all Ingredients in a mixing bowl. Fill the casserole dish halfway with the mixture.

Bake for 25 minutes in a preheated Air Fryer. Bake for an additional 5 minutes after adding the cheese. Good appetite!

Classic Brussels Sprouts with Bacon

(**Ready in about** 20 minutes | **Servings:** 2)

Ingredients

3/4 pound Brussels sprouts, trimmed and halved

1/2 teaspoon smoked paprika 1 teaspoon garlic, minced

1 tablespoon white wine

3 ounces bacon, sliced

Sea salt and ground black pepper, to taste

1 teaspoon lemon juice, freshly squeezed

1 teaspoon butter, melted

Directions

Toss the Brussels sprouts with butter, salt, black pepper, paprika, garlic, lemon juice and wine. Transfer your Brussels sprouts to the Air Fryer cooking basket.

Top your Brussels sprouts with bacon and cook them at 380 degrees F for 15 minutes, shaking the basket once or twice to ensure even cooking.

Serve: warm and enjoy!

Cauliflower Tater Tots

(**Ready in about** 20 minutes | **Servings:** 3)

Ingredients

1 ½ pounds cauliflower

1 tablespoon corn flour

1 tablespoon butter

1 tbsp dried parsley flakes

1/2 teaspoon dried basil

2 tablespoons plain flour

1 teaspoon shallot powder

1/2 tbsp garlic powder

Sea salt and freshly ground black pepper, to taste

Directions

Blanch the cauliflower in salted boiling water for 4 minutes, or until al dente. Drain the cauliflower and pulse it in a food processor.

Place the cauliflower in a mixing bowl and set aside. Mix in the remaining Ingredients until well combined. To make bite-sized tots, roll the mixture into balls.

Cook for 16 minutes in a preheated Air Fryer at 375 degrees F, shaking the basket halfway through to ensure even browning. Good appetite!

Fried Peppers with Roasted Garlic Sauce

(**Ready in about** 50 minutes | **Servings:** 2)

Ingredients

4 bell peppers

Sea salt and black pepper to taste

1/4 cup mayonnaise

6 cloves garlic

1 teaspoon fresh lime juice

1 teaspoon olive oil

1 tablespoon fresh parsley, roughly chopped Dipping Sauce

1/4 cup sour cream

1/4 teaspoon paprika

Directions

Brush the peppers with olive oil and transfer them to the cooking basket.

Roast the peppers at 400 degrees F for 15 minutes, turning your peppers over halfway through the cooking time; roast the peppers until the skin blisters and turns black.

Transfer the peppers to a plastic bag until cool; the skins should peel away off of the peppers easily; season the peppers with salt and pepper and re**Serve:**.

To make the sauce, place the garlic on a sheet of aluminum foil and spritz with cooking spray. Wrap the garlic in the foil.

Cook in the preheated Air Fryer at 400 degrees for 12 minutes. Then, open the top of the foil and continue to cook for a further 10 minutes.

Let it cool for about 10 minutes; remove the cloves by squeezing them out of the skins; mash the garlic and combine it with the sour cream, mayonnaise, fresh lime juice and paprika.

Garnish the roasted peppers with parsley and **Serve:** with the sauce on the side and enjoy!

Greek-Style Air Grilled Tomatoes with Feta

(**Ready in about** 15 minutes | **Servings:** 3)

Ingredients

3 medium tomatoes, quartered, pat dry	1 teaspoon basil
3 ounces feta cheese, sliced	1 tablespoon extra-virgin olive oil
1 teaspoon oregano	1 teaspoon cilantro
1 teaspoon parsley	1/2 teaspoon rosemary
Sea salt and ground black pepper, to season	2 tablespoons Greek black olives, pitted and sliced

Directions

Brush your tomatoes with olive oil. Sprinkle them with spices until well coated on all sides. Now, transfer your tomatoes to the Air Fryer cooking basket

Cook your tomatoes at 350 degrees F for approximately 12 minutes, turning them over halfway through the cooking time.

Garnish with black olives and feta cheese and **Serve:**. Enjoy!

Rainbow Vegetable Croquettes

(**Ready in about** 15 minutes | **Servings:** 3)

Ingredients

1/3 canned green peas	1/3 pound zucchini, grated and squeezed
1/3 sweet corn kernels	
1/4 cup plain flour	1/4 cup chickpea flour
1/2 cup cheddar cheese, grated	1 teaspoon fresh coriander, chopped
1 egg	1 teaspoon fresh parsley, chopped
1/2 teaspoon fresh garlic, pressed	1/2 tbsp cayenne pepper
Kosher salt and freshly ground black pepper, to taste	1 tablespoon olive oil

Directions

In a mixing bowl, thoroughly combine the vegetables, flour, cheese, egg, coriander, parsley; sprinkle with all spices and stir until everything is well incorporated.

Shape the mixture into small patties and transfer them to the lightly oiled Air Fryer cooking basket.

Cook the vegetable croquettes in the preheated Air Fryer at 365 degrees F for 6 minutes. Turn them over and cook for a further 6 minutes

Serve: immediately and enjoy!

Sweet Potato Hash Browns

(**Ready in about** 50 minutes | **Servings:** 3)

Ingredients

1 pound sweet potatoes, grated	1 bell pepper, chopped
1/2 teaspoon garlic, finely chopped	1/2 cup scallion, chopped
1/4 teaspoon ground allspice 1 tablespoon peanut oil	Sea salt and ground black pepper, to your liking
	1 teaspoon peanut oil

Directions

Allow your sweet potatoes to soak in cold water for 25 minutes. Remove from the water and pat dry with a paper towel.

Stir in the remaining Ingredients until everything is thoroughly combined.

Cook for 25 minutes at 395°F in a preheated Air Fryer, turning halfway through the cooking time. Good appetite!

Authentic Japanese Vegetable Tempura

(**Ready in about** 15 minutes | **Servings:** 3)

Ingredients

1 cup plain flour 1 egg	1 cup ice-cold water
1 pound green beans	1 white onion, slice rings
2 tablespoons soy sauce	1 teaspoon dashi granules
1 tablespoon mirin	
Himalayan salt, to taste	

Directions

Sift the flour in a bowl. In another bowl, whisk the egg until pale and frothy; pour in the water.

Fold the sifted flour into the egg/water mixture and stir to combine. Dip the green beans and onion in the prepared tempura.

Cook your veggies in the preheated Air Fryer at 400 degrees F for 10

minutes, shaking the basket halfway through the cooking time; work with batches.

Meanwhile, whisk the dashi granules, soy sauce and mirin; salt to taste and set the sauce aside.

Serve: the vegetable tempura with the sauce on the side. **Serve:** immediately!

Spanish Patatas Bravas

(**Ready in about** 15 minutes | **Servings:** 3)

Ingredients

1 pound russet potatoes, cut into 1-inch cubes
1 cup tomatoes, crushed
1/2 teaspoon paprika
2 garlic cloves, crushed
A pinch of brown sugar
Salt and ground black pepper, to taste
1/2 teaspoon chili powder
2 teaspoons canola oil

Directions

Toss the potatoes with 1 teaspoon of oil, salt and black pepper. Transfer the potato chunks to the lightly oiled Air Fryer cooking basket.

Cook the potatoes in your Air Fryer at 400 degrees F for 12 minutes total, shaking the basket halfway through the cooking time.

In the meantime, heat the remaining teaspoon of oil in a saucepan over medium-high heat. Once hot, stir in the other Ingredients cook for 8 to 10 minutes until cooked through.

Spoon the sauce over roasted potatoes and **Serve:** immediately. Enjoy!

Vegetable Oatmeal Fritters

(**Ready in about** 20 minutes | **Servings:** 3)

Ingredients

1 cup rolled oats
1/2 teaspoon shallot powder 1/2 teaspoon porcini powder 1/2 teaspoon garlic powder
1/2 cup celery, grated
1/2 teaspoon mustard seeds
1 ½ cups water
2 tablespoons soy sauce
1 cup white mushrooms, chopped
1 carrot, grated

1/2 teaspoon cumin
2 tablespoons tomato ketchup

Directions

Start by preheating your Air Fryer to 380 degrees F.

Thoroughly combine all Ingredients. Shape the batter into equal patties and place them in the cooking basket. Spritz your patties with a nonstick cooking spray.

Cook the fritters in the preheated Air Fryer for 15 minutes, turning them over halfway through the cooking time.

Serve: with your favorite dipping sauce. Bon appétit!

Favorite Winter Bliss Bowl

(**Ready in about** 25 minutes | **Servings:** 3)

Ingredients

1 pound cauliflower florets
9 ounces frozen crab cakes
1 cup iceberg lettuce
1 red bell pepper, deseeded and sliced
2 tbsp fresh lemon juice
2 tbsp cilantro leaves, chopped
Sea salt and freshly ground black pepper, to taste
1 cup quinoa
1 cup baby spinach
1 tablespoon extra-virgin olive oil
1 teaspoon yellow mustard
1 teaspoon olive oil

Directions

Brush the cauliflower and crab cakes with olive oil; season them with salt and black pepper and transfer them to the cooking basket.

Cook the cauliflower at 400 degrees F for about 12 minutes total, shaking the basket halfway through the cooking time. Then, cook the crab cakes at 400 degrees F for about 12 minutes total, flipping them halfway through the cooking time.

In the meantime, rinse your quinoa, drain it and transfer to a soup pot with 2 cups of lightly salted water; bring to a boil.

Turn heat to a simmer and continue to cook, covered, for about 20 minutes; fluff with a fork and transfer to a serving bowl.

Add the cauliflower and crab cakes to the bowl. Add your greens and bell pepper to the bowl. In a small mixing dish, whisk the lemon juice, extra- virgin olive oil and yellow mustard.

Drizzle the dressing over all Ingredients, garnish with fresh cilantro and **Serve:** immediately. Bon appétit!

Mexican-Style Roasted Corn Salad

(**Ready in about** 15 minutes | **Servings:** 2)

Ingredients

2 ears of corn, husked
4 ounces Cotija cheese crumbled
1/2 red onion, chopped
1/2 teaspoon Mexican oregano
1 cup Mexican Escabeche
2 tablespoons extra-virgin olive oil
Fresh juice of 1 lime
Kosher salt and freshly ground black pepper, to taste

Directions

Start by preheating your Air Fryer to 390 degrees F.

Place the corn on the cob in the lightly greased cooking basket; cook the corn on the cob for 10 minutes, turning over halfway through the cooking time.

Once the corn has cooled, use a sharp knife to cut off the kernels into a salad bowl. Toss the corn kernels with the remaining Ingredients and **Serve:** immediately. Enjoy!

Traditional Indian Bhajiya

(**Ready in about** 20 minutes | **Servings:** 3)

Ingredients

1 cup carrot, grated	1 cup cabbage, shredded
1 small garlic clove, finely chopped	Himalayan salt and ground black pepper, to taste
1/2 cup chickpea flour	1 small onion, chopped
1 teaspoon Chaat masala	1 teaspoon coriander, minced
	1 teaspoon olive oil

Directions

Combine all Ingredients in a mixing bowl until well combined.

After that, spoon 2 tablespoons of the mixture into the cooking basket and flatten with a wide spatula.

Cook for 7 to 8 minutes at 350 degrees F, then flip and cook for another 8 minutes, or until golden brown on top. Warm up and enjoy!

Easy Sweet Potato Bake

(**Ready in about** 35 minutes | **Servings:** 3)

Ingredients

1 stick butter, melted	1 pound sweet potatoes, mashed
2 tablespoons honey	
2 eggs, beaten	1/3 cup coconut milk
1/2 cup fresh breadcrumbs	1/4 cup flour

Directions

Start by preheating your Air Fryer to 325 degrees F. Spritz a casserole dish with cooking oil.

In a mixing bowl, combine all Ingredients, except for the breadcrumbs and 1

tablespoon of butter. Spoon the mixture into the prepared casserole dish.

Top with the breadcrumbs and brush the top with the remaining 1 tablespoon of butter. Bake in the preheated Air Fryer for 30 minutes. Bon appétit!

Avocado Fries with Roasted Garlic Mayonnaise

(**Ready in about** 50 minutes | **Servings:** 4)

Ingredients

1/2 head garlic (6-7 cloves) 3/4 cup all-purpose flour	Sea salt and ground black pepper, to taste
2 eggs	1 cup tortilla chips, crushed Sauce
3 avocados, cut into wedges	
1/2 cup mayonnaise	1 teaspoon lemon juice
	1 teaspoon mustard

Directions

Place the garlic on a piece of aluminum foil and spritz with cooking spray. Wrap the garlic in the foil.

Cook in the preheated Air Fryer at 400 degrees for 12 minutes. Check the garlic, open the top of the foil and continue to cook for 10 minutes more.

Let it cool for 10 to 15 minutes; remove the cloves by squeezing them out of the skins; mash the garlic and re**Serve:**. In a shallow bowl, combine the flour, salt, and black pepper. In another shallow dish, whisk the eggs until frothy.

Place the crushed tortilla chips in a third shallow dish. Dredge the avocado wedges in the flour mixture, shaking off the excess. Then, dip in the egg mixture; lastly, dredge in crushed tortilla chips. Spritz the avocado wedges with cooking oil on all sides.

Cook in the preheated Air Fryer at 395 degrees F approximately 8 minutes, turning them over halfway through the cooking time.

Meanwhile, combine the sauce Ingredients with the smashed roasted garlic. To **Serve:**, divide the avocado fries between plates and top with the sauce. Enjoy!

Easy Sweet Potato Hash Browns

(**Ready in about** 50 minutes | **Servings:** 2)

Ingredients

1 pound sweet potatoes, peeled and grated	1/4 cup scallions, chopped
	1/4 tbsp ground allspice
1 tbs fresh garlic, minced	Sea salt and ground black pepper, to taste
1 tablespoon peanut oil	
1/2 teaspoon cinnamon	2 eggs, whisked

Directions

Allow the sweet potatoes to soak in cold water for 25 minutes. Drain the sweet potatoes and pat them dry with a kitchen towel. Stir in the remaining Ingredients until well combined. Cook for 20 minutes in a preheated Air Fryer at 395°F. Shake the basket a couple of times. With ketchup, of course.

Roasted Broccoli with Sesame Seeds

(**Ready in about** 15 minutes | **Servings:** 2)

Ingredients

1 pound broccoli florets	1/2 tbsp shallot powder
1/2 teaspoon porcini powder	Sea salt and ground black pepper, to taste
1/2 teaspoon cumin powder	2 tablespoons sesame seeds
1/4 teaspoon paprika	2 tablespoons sesame oil
1 teaspoon garlic powder	

Directions

Start by preheating the Air Fryer to 400 degrees F.

Blanch the broccoli in salted boiling water until al dente, about 3 to 4 minutes. Drain well and transfer to the lightly greased Air Fryer basket.

Add the sesame oil, shallot powder, porcini powder, garlic powder, salt, black pepper, cumin powder, paprika, and sesame seeds.

Cook for 6 minutes, tossing halfway through the cooking time. Bon appétit!

Corn on the Cob with Herb Butter

(**Ready in about** 15 minutes | **Servings:** 2)

Ingredients

2 ears fresh corn, shucked and cut into halves	1 teaspoon granulated garlic
1 tbsp fresh rosmary chopped	2 tablespoons butter, room temperature
1/2 teaspoon fresh ginger, grated	Sea salt and ground black pepper, to taste
1 tablespoon fresh basil, chopped	2 tablespoons fresh chives, roughly chopped

Directions

Spritz the corn with cooking spray. Cook at 395 degrees F for 6 minutes, turning them over halfway through the cooking time.

In the meantime, mix the butter with the granulated garlic, ginger, salt, black pepper, rosemary, and basil.

Spread the butter mixture all over the corn on the cob. Cook in the preheated Air Fryer an additional 2 minutes. Bon appétit!

Rainbow Vegetable Fritters

(**Ready in about** 20 minutes | **Servings:** 2)

Ingredients

1 zucchini, grated and squeezed	1/2 cup canned green peas
4 tbs all-purpose flour	1 cup corn kernels
1 tbsp cayenne pepper	2 tablespoons fresh shallots, minced
1 tablespoon peanut oil	Sea salt and ground black pepper, to taste
1 tbs fresh garlic, minced	

Directions

In a mixing bowl, thoroughly combine all Ingredients until everything is well incorporated.

Shape the mixture into patties. Spritz the Air Fryer basket with cooking spray.Cook in the preheated Air Fryer at 365 degrees F for 6 minutes. Turn them over and cook for a further 6 minutes**Serve:** immediately and enjoy!

Cheese Stuffed Roasted Peppers

(**Ready in about** 20 minutes | **Servings:** 2)

Ingredients

2 red bell peppers, tops and seeds removed	2 yellow bell peppers, tops and seeds removed
1 cup cream cheese	4 tablespoons mayonnaise
2 pickles, chopped	Salt and pepper, to taste

Directions

Arrange the peppers in the lightly greased cooking basket. Cook in the preheated Air Fryer at 400 degrees F for 15 minutes, turning them over halfway through the cooking time.Season with salt and pepper.

Then, in a mixing bowl, combine the cream cheese with the mayonnaise and chopped pickles. Stuff the pepper with the cream cheese mixture and **Serve:**. Enjoy!

Greek-Style Roasted Tomatoes with Feta

(**Ready in about** 20 minutes | **Servings:** 2)

Ingredients

3 medium-sized tomatoes, cut into four slices, pat dry	1 teaspoon dried oregano
1/4 teaspoon red pepper flakes, crushed	1 teaspoon dried basil
	3 slices Feta cheese
	1/2 teaspoon sea salt

Directions

Spritz the tomatoes with cooking oil and transfer them to the Air Fryer basket. Sprinkle with seasonings.

Cook at 350 degrees F approximately 8 minutes turning them over halfway through the cooking time.

Top with the cheese and cook an additional 4 minutes. Bon appétit!

American-Style Brussel Sprout Salad

(**Ready in about** 35 minutes | **Servings:** 4)

Ingredients

1 pound Brussels sprouts
1 apple, cored and diced
1/2 cup pomegranate seeds
1/4 cup olive oil
4 eggs, hardboiled and sliced Dressing
1 teaspoon honey

1/2 cup mozzarella cheese, crumbled
1 small red onion, chopped
2 tablespoons champagne vinegar
1 teaspoon Dijon mustard
Sea salt and ground black pepper, to taste

Directions

Start by preheating your Air Fryer to 380 degrees F.

Add the Brussels sprouts to the cooking basket. Spritz with cooking spray and cook for 15 minutes. Let it cool to room temperature about 15 minutes. Toss the Brussels sprouts with the apple, cheese, pomegranate seeds, and red onion.

Mix all Ingredients for the dressing and toss to combine well. **Serve:** topped with the hard-boiled eggs. Bon appétit!

The Best Cauliflower Tater Tots

(**Ready in about** 25 minutes | **Servings:** 4)

Ingredients

1 pound cauliflower florets
2 tbs scallions, chopped
1 garlic clove, minced
1/4 teaspoon dried dill weed
1/2 cup breadcrumbs
1 teaspoon paprika

1 tablespoon olive oil
1 cup Colby cheese, shredded
2 eggs

Sea salt and ground black pepper, to taste

Directions

Blanch the cauliflower for 3 to 4 minutes in salted boiling water, or until al dente. Drain thoroughly before pulsing in a food processor. Mix in the remaining Ingredients until well combined. Make bite-sized tots out of the cauliflower mixture.

Spritz the cooking spray into the Air Fryer basket.

Cook for 16 minutes, shaking, in a preheated Air Fryer at 375 degrees F. halfway through the cooking time. **Serve:** with your favorite sauce for dipping. Bon appétit!

Skinny Pumpkin Chips

(**Ready in about** 20 minutes | **Servings:** 2)

Ingredients

1 pound pumpkin, cut into sticks
1/2 teaspoon basil

1/2 teaspoon rosemary
1 tablespoon coconut oil
Salt black pepper, to taste

Directions

Start by preheating the Air Fryer to 395 degrees F. Brush the pumpkin sticks with coconut oil; add the spices and toss to combine. Cook for 13 minutes, shaking the basket halfway through the cooking time. **Serve:** with mayonnaise. Bon appétit!

Classic Onion Rings

(**Ready in about** 30 minutes | **Servings:** 2)

Ingredients

1 medium-sized onion, slice into rings
Coarse sea salt and ground black pepper, to your liking
3/4 cup bread crumbs

1 teaspoon baking powder
1 cup all-purpose flour
2 eggs, beaten
1/2 cup yogurt

1 teaspoon onion powder
1 teaspoon garlic powder
1/2 teaspoon celery seeds

Directions

Place the onion rings in the bowl with cold water; let them soak approximately 20 minutes; drain the onion rings and pat dry using a pepper towel.

In a shallow bowl, mix the flour, baking powder, salt, and black pepper. Add the yogurt and eggs and mix well to combine.

In another shallow bowl, mix the bread crumbs, onion powder, garlic powder, and celery seeds. Dip the onion rings in the flour/egg mixture; then, dredge in the breadcrumb mixture.

Spritz the Air Fryer basket with cooking spray; arrange the breaded onion rings in the basket.

Cook in the preheated Air Fryer at 400 degrees F for 4 to 5 minutes, turning them over halfway through the cooking time. Bon appétit!

Sweet Corn Fritters with Avocado

(**Ready in about** 20 minutes | **Servings:** 3)

Ingredients

2 cups sweet corn kernels

2 eggs, whisked
2 tablespoons fresh cilantro, chopped
Sea salt and ground black pepper, to taste
1 avocado, peeled, pitted and diced

1 small-sized onion, chopped
1 teaspoon baking powder
2 tablespoons sweet chili sauce
1 garlic clove, minced

Directions

In a mixing bowl, thoroughly combine the corn, onion, garlic, eggs, baking powder, cilantro, salt, and black pepper.

Shape the corn mixture into 6 patties and transfer them to the lightly greased Air Fryer basket.

Cook in the preheated Air Fry at 370 degrees for 8 minutes; turn them over and cook for 7 minutes longer.

Serve: the fritters with the avocado and chili sauce.

Cauliflower and Goat Cheese Croquettes

(**Ready in about** 30 minutes | **Servings:** 2)

Ingredients

1/2 pound cauliflower florets
Sea salt and ground black pepper, to taste

1 cup sour cream
1/2 teaspoon shallot powder

1 cup goat cheese, shredded
1/4 teaspoon cumin powder
2 garlic cloves, minced
1 teaspoon Dijon mustard

Directions

Place the cauliflower florets in a saucepan of water; bring to the boil; reduce the heat and cook for 10 minutes or until tender.

Mash the cauliflower using your blender; add the garlic, cheese, and spices; mix to combine well.

Form the cauliflower mixture into croquettes shapes.

Cook in the preheated Air Fryer at 375 degrees F for 16 minutes, shaking halfway through the cooking time.
Serve: with the sour cream and mustard. Bon appétit!

Greek-Style Vegetable Bake

(**Ready in about** 35 minutes | **Servings:** 4)

Ingredients

1 eggplant, peeled and sliced
1 red onion, sliced
1 teaspoon fresh garlic, minced
1 teaspoon dried oregano

Salt and ground black pepper, to taste
1 tomato, sliced

2 bell peppers, seeded and sliced

1 teaspoon mustard
4 tablespoons olive oil
1 teaspoon smoked paprika
6 ounces halloumi cheese, sliced lengthways

Directions

Start by preheating your Air Fryer to 370 degrees F. Spritz a baking pan with nonstick cooking spray.

Place the eggplant, peppers, onion, and garlic on the bottom of the baking pan. Add the olive oil, mustard, and spices. Transfer to the cooking basket and cook for 14 minutes.

Top with the tomatoes and cheese; increase the temperature to 390 degrees F and cook for 5 minutes more until bubbling. Let it sit on a cooling rack for 10 minutes before serving. Bon appétit!

Baked Cholula Cauliflower

(**Ready in about** 20 minutes | **Servings:** 4)

Ingredients

1/2 cup all-purpose flour
1/2 teaspoon ground black pepper

1/2 teaspoon cayenne pepper
1/4 cup Cholula sauce
2 tablespoons olive oil

Salt, to taste
1/2 teaspoon garlic powder
1/2 cup water
1 pound cauliflower, broken into small florets
1/2 teaspoon shallot powder

Directions

Start by preheating your Air Fryer to 400 degrees F. Lightly grease a baking pan with cooking spray.

In a mixing bowl, combine the flour, water, spices, and olive oil. Coat the cauliflower with the prepared batter; arrange the cauliflower on the baking pan.

Then, bake in the preheated Air Fryer for 8 minutes or until golden brown.

Brush the Cholula sauce all over the cauliflower florets and bake an additional 4 to 5 minutes. Bon appétit!

Fall Vegetables with Spiced Yogurt

(**Ready in about** 25 minutes | **Servings:** 2)

Ingredients

1 pound celeriac, cut into
1 1/2-inch pieces
2 carrots, cut into 1 1/2-
inch pieces
1 tablespoon sesame oil
1/2 teaspoon chili powder
Spiced Yogurt
1 tablespoon mayonnaise

2 red onions, cut into 1
1/2-inch pieces
1/2 teaspoon sea salt
1/2 tbsp mustard seeds
1/2 teaspoon ground
black pepper, to taste
1/4 cup Greek yogurt
1 tablespoon honey

Directions

Place the vegetables in a single layer in the lightly
greased cooking basket. Drizzle the sesame oil over
vegetables.

Sprinkle with black pepper and sea salt.

Cook at 390 degrees F for 20 minutes, shaking the
basket halfway through the cooking time.

Meanwhile, make the sauce by whisking all Ingredients.
Spoon the sauce over the roasted vegetables. Bon
appétit!

Sweet-and-Sour Mixed Veggies

(**Ready in about** 25 minutes | **Servings:** 4)

Ingredients

1/2 pound asparagus, cut
into 1 1/2-inch pieces
1/2 pound broccoli, cut
into 1 1/2-inch pieces
Some salt and white
pepper, to taste
2 tablespoon honey

2 tablespoons peanut oil
1/2 pound carrots, cut
into 1 1/2-inch pieces
1/2 cup water
4 tablespoons raisins
2 tablespoons apple cider
vinegar

Directions

Place the vegetables in a single layer in the lightly
greased cooking basket. Drizzle the peanut oil over the
vegetables.

Sprinkle with salt and white pepper.

Cook at 380 degrees F for 15 minutes, shaking the
basket halfway through the cooking time.

Add 1/2 cup of water to a saucepan; bring to a rapid
boil and add the raisins, honey, and vinegar. Cook for 5
to 7 minutes or until the sauce has reduced by half.

Spoon the sauce over the warm vegetables and **Serve:**
immediately. Bon appétit!

Roasted Corn Salad

(**Ready in about** 15 minutes + chilling time | **Servings:** 3)

Ingredients

2 ears of corn, husked
1 garlic clove, minced
1/4 cup plain yogurt
Pink salt and white
pepper, to your liking
1 shallot, chopped
2 tablespoons fresh
parsley, chopped

3 tablespoons sour cream
1 jalapeño pepper, seeded
and minced
2 bell peppers, seeded and
thinly sliced
1 tbsp fresh lemon juice
1/4 cup Queso Fresco,
crumbled

Directions

Start by preheating the Air Fryer to 390 degrees F.
Spritz the Air Fryer grill pan with cooking spray.

Place the corn on the grill pan and cook for 10
minutes, turning over halfway through the cooking
time. Set aside.

Once the corn has cooled to the touch, use a sharp
knife to cut off the kernels into a salad bowl.

While the corn is resting, whisk the sour cream, yogurt,
garlic, jalapeño pepper, fresh lemon juice, salt, and
white pepper. Add the shallot, pepper, and parsley to
the salad bowl and toss to combine well. Toss with the
sauce and **Serve:** topped with cheese. Enjoy!

Quick Shrimp and Vegetable Bake

(**Ready in about** 25 minutes | **Servings:** 4)

Ingredients

1 pound shrimp cleaned
and deveined
1 carrot, sliced
1 shallot, sliced
1 cup tomato paste
2 tablespoons sesame oil

1 cup cauliflower, cut into
florets
2 bell pepper, sliced
1 cup broccoli, cut into
florets

Directions

Begin by preheating your Air Fryer to 360°F. Coat the
baking dish with cooking spray.

Arrange the shrimp and vegetables in the baking dish
now. Then pour the sesame oil over the vegetables.
Over the vegetables, pour the tomato paste.

In a preheated Air Fryer, cook for 10 minutes. Cook
for another 12 minutes, stirring occasionally. **Serve:**
hot.

Rainbow Vegetable and Parmesan Croquettes

(**Ready in about** 40 minutes | **Servings:** 4)

Ingredients

1 pound potatoes, peeled
Salt and black pepper, to taste
1/2 cup mushrooms, chopped
1 clove garlic, minced
1/2 cup panko bread crumbs
1/2 cup all-purpose flour
2 eggs
1/4 cup broccoli, chopped
2 tablespoons butter
1 carrot, grated
4 tablespoons milk
1/2 teaspoon cayenne pepper
3 tablespoons scallions, minced
1/2 cup parmesan cheese, grated
2 tablespoons olive oil

Directions

In a large saucepan, boil the potatoes for 17 to 20 minutes. Drain the potatoes and mash with the milk, butter, salt, black pepper, and cayenne pepper.

Add the mushrooms, broccoli, carrots, garlic, scallions, and olive oil; stir to combine well. Shape the mixture into patties. In a shallow bowl, place the flour; beat the eggs in another bowl; in a third bowl, combine the breadcrumbs with the parmesan cheese.

Dip each patty into the flour, followed by the eggs, and then the breadcrumb mixture; press to adhere.

Cook in the preheated Air Fryer at 375 degrees F for 16 minutes, shaking halfway through the cooking time. Bon appétit!

Fried Asparagus with Goat Cheese

(**Ready in about** 15 minutes | **Servings:** 3)

Ingredients

1 bunch of asparagus, trimmed
1/4 teaspoon cracked black pepper, to taste
1/2 teaspoon dried dill weed
1/2 teaspoon kosher salt
1 tablespoon olive oil
1/2 cup goat cheese, crumbled

Directions

Place the asparagus spears in the lightly greased cooking basket. Toss the asparagus with the olive oil, salt, black pepper, and dill.

Cook in the preheated Air Fryer at 400 degrees F for 9 minutes. **Serve:** garnished with goat cheese. Bon appétit!

Tater Tot Vegetable Casserole

(**Ready in about** 40 minutes | **Servings:** 6)

Ingredients

1 tablespoon olive oil
1 red bell pepper, seeded and sliced
1 shallot, sliced
1 (28-ounce) bag frozen tater tots
Sea salt and ground black pepper, to your liking
1 cup Swiss cheese, shredded
2 cloves garlic, minced
1 yellow bell pepper, seeded and sliced
1 ½ cups kale
1 cup milk
6 eggs
4 tablespoons seasoned breadcrumbs

Directions

Heat the olive oil in a saucepan over medium-high heat. Sauté the shallot, garlic, and peppers for 2 to 3 minutes. Add the kale and cook until wilted.

Arrange the tater tots evenly over the bottom of a lightly greased casserole dish. Spread the sautéed mixture over the top.

In a mixing bowl, thoroughly combine the eggs, milk, salt, pepper, and shredded cheese. Pour the mixture into the casserole dish. Lastly, top with the seasoned breadcrumbs. Bake at 330 degrees F for 30 minutes or until top is golden brown. Bon appétit!

Roasted Brussels Sprout Salad

(**Ready in about** 35 minutes + chilling time | **Servings:** 2)

Ingredients

1/2 pound Brussels sprouts
1 tablespoon olive oil
2 ounces baby arugula

Lemon Vinaigrette
1 shallot, thinly sliced
1 teaspoon Dijon mustard
1 tablespoon honey
Coarse sea salt and ground black pepper, to taste

2 ounces pancetta, chopped
2 tablespoons extra virgin olive oil
2 tbsp fresh lemon juice

Directions

Start by preheating your Air Fryer to 380 degrees F.

Add the Brussels sprouts to the cooking basket. Brush with olive oil and cook for 15 minutes. Let it cool to room temperature about 15 minutes.

Toss the Brussels sprouts with the salt, black pepper, baby arugula, and shallot.

Mix all Ingredients for the dressing. Then, dress your salad, garnish with pancetta, and **Serve:** well chilled. Bon appétit!

Winter Bliss Bowl

(**Ready in about** 45 minutes | **Servings:** 3)

Ingredients

1 cup pearled barley
sea salt and ground black pepper, to taste
2 tablespoons champagne vinegar
4 tablespoons olive oil, divided
2 tablespoons cilantro leaves, chopped

1 (1-pound) head cauliflower, broken into small florets Coarse
1 teaspoon yellow mustard
4 tablespoons mayonnaise
10 ounces ounce canned sweet corn, drained

Directions

Cook the barley in a saucepan with salted water. Bring to a boil and cook approximately 28 minutes. Drain and re**Serve:**.

Start by preheating the Air Fryer to 400 degrees F.

Place the cauliflower florets in the lightly greased Air Fryer basket. Season with salt and black pepper; cook for 12 minutes, tossing halfway through the cooking time.

Toss with the re**Serve:**d barley. Add the champagne vinegar, mayonnaise, mustard, olive oil, and corn. Garnish with fresh cilantro. Bon appétit!

FISH & SEAFOOD

Colorful Salmon and Fennel Salad

(**Ready in about** 20 minutes | **Servings:** 3)

Ingredients

1 pound salmon
Sea salt and ground black pepper, to taste
1/2 teaspoon paprika
1 tablespoon lime juice
1 tablespoon sesame seeds, lightly toasted
1 cucumber, sliced
1 fennel, quartered
1 tablespoon balsamic vinegar
1 teaspoon olive oil
1 tablespoon extra-virgin olive oil
1 tomato, sliced

Directions

Toss the salmon and fennel with 1 teaspoon olive oil, salt, black pepper, and paprika in a mixing bowl.

Cook for 12 minutes in a preheated Air Fryer at 380 degrees F, shaking the basket once or twice.

Transfer the salmon to a salad bowl and cut it into bite-sized strips.

Combine the fennel, balsamic vinegar, lime juice, 1 tablespoon extra-virgin olive oil, tomato, and cucumber in a mixing bowl.

Toss well to combine and **Serve:** topped with lightly toasted sesame seeds. Enjoy!

Parmesan Chip-Crusted Tilapia

(**Ready in about** 15 minutes | **Servings:** 3)

Ingredients

1 ½ pounds tilapia, slice into 4 portions Sea salt and ground black pepper, to taste
1/4 cup parmesan cheese, preferably freshly grated
2 tablespoons buttermilk
1 teaspoon granulated garlic
1/4 cup almond flour
1/2 tbsp cayenne pepper
1 egg, beaten
1 cup tortilla chips, crushed

Directions

Generously season your tilapia with salt, black pepper and cayenne pepper.
Prepare a bread station. Add the granulated garlic, almond flour and parmesan cheese to a rimmed plate.
Whisk the egg and buttermilk in another bowl and place crushed tortilla chips in the third bowl.
Dip the tilapia pieces in the flour mixture, then in the egg/buttermilk mixture and finally roll them in the crushed chips, pressing to adhere well.
Cook in your Air Fryer at 400 degrees F for 10 minutes, flipping halfway through the cooking time. **Serve:** with chips if desired. Bon appétit!

Keto Cod Fillets

(**Ready in about** 15 minutes | **Servings:** 2)

Ingredients

2 cod fish fillets
1 teaspoon Old Bay seasoning 1 egg, beaten
1 teaspoon butter, melted
2 tablespoons coconut milk, unsweetened
1/3 cup coconut flour, unsweetened

Directions

Place the cod fish fillets, butter and Old Bay seasoning in a Ziplock bag; shake until the fish is well coated on all sides.

In a shallow bowl, whisk the egg and coconut milk until frothy.

In another bowl, place the coconut flour. Dip the fish fillets in the egg mixture, then, coat them with coconut flour, pressing to adhere.

Cook the fish at 390 degrees F for 6 minutes; flip them over and cook an additional 6 minutes until your fish flakes easily when tested with a fork. Bon appétit!

Easiest Lobster Tails Ever

(**Ready in about** 10 minutes | **Servings:** 2)

Ingredients

2 (6-ounce) lobster tails
1/2 teaspoon dried rosemary
1/2 teaspoon garlic, pressed
1 teaspoon deli mustard
1 teaspoon olive oil
1 teaspoon fresh cilantro, minced
Sea salt and ground black pepper, to taste

Directions

Toss the lobster tails with the other Ingredients until they are well coated on all sides.

Cook the lobster tails at 370 degrees F for 3 minutes. Then, turn them and cook on the other side for 3 to 4 minutes more until they are opaque.

Serve: warm and enjoy!

Grouper with Miso-Honey Sauce

(**Ready in about** 15 minutes | **Servings:** 2)

Ingredients

3/4 pound grouper fillets	Salt white pepper to taste
1 teaspoon water	1 teaspoon deli mustard or
1 tablespoon sesame oil	Dijon mustard
1 tablespoon mirin	1 tablespoon honey
1 tablespoon Shoyu sauce	1/4 cup white miso

Directions

Sprinkle the grouper fillets with salt and white pepper; drizzle them with a nonstick cooking oil.

Cook the fish at 400 degrees F for 5 minutes; turn the fish fillets over and cook an additional 5 minutes. Meanwhile, make the sauce by whisking the remaining. **Serve:** the warm fish with the miso-honey sauce on the side. Bon appétit!

Salmon Bowl with Lime Drizzle

(**Ready in about** 15 minutes | **Servings:** 3)

Ingredients

1 pound salmon steak	Sea salt pepper to taste
2 teaspoons sesame oil	1 lime, juiced
1/2 tbs coriander seeds	2 tablespoons reduced-
1 teaspoon honey	sodium soy sauce

Directions

Pat the salmon dry and drizzle it with 1 teaspoon of sesame oil. Season the salmon with salt, pepper and coriander seeds. Transfer the salmon to the Air Fryer cooking basket.

Cook the salmon at 400 degrees F for 5 minutes; turn the salmon over and continue to cook for 5 minutes more or until opaque.

Meanwhile, warm the remaining Ingredients in a small saucepan to make the lime drizzle. Slice the fish into bite-sized strips, drizzle with the sauce and **Serve:** immediately. Enjoy!

Seed-Crusted Codfish Fillets

(**Ready in about** 15 minutes | **Servings:** 2)

Ingredients

codfish fillets	1 teaspoon sesame oil
Sea salt and black pepper,	1 tablespoon chia seeds
to taste	1 teaspoon sesame seeds

Directions

Start by preheating your Air Fryer to 380 degrees F.

Add the sesame oil, salt, black pepper, sesame seeds and chia seeds to a rimmed plate. Coat the top of the codfish with the seed mixture, pressing it down to adhere.

Lower the codfish fillets, seed side down, into the cooking basket and cook for 6 minutes. Turn the fish fillets over and cook for a further 6 minutes. **Serve:** warm and enjoy.

Classic Crab Cakes

(**Ready in about** 15 minutes | **Servings:** 3)

Ingredients

1 egg, beaten	2 tablespoons milk
2 crustless bread slices	2 tablespoons scallions,
1 pound lump crabmeat	chopped
1 teaspoon deli mustard	1 teaspoon Sriracha sauce
Sea salt and ground black	1 garlic clove, minced
pepper, to taste	
4 lemon wedges, for	
serving	

Directions

Whisk the egg and milk until pale and frothy; add in the bread and let it soak for a few minutes.

Stir in the other Ingredients, except for the lemon wedges; shape the mixture into 4 equal patties. Place your patties in the Air Fryer cooking basket. Spritz your patties with a nonstick cooking spray.

Cook the crab cakes at 400 degrees F for 5 minutes. Turn them over and cook on the other side for 5 minutes.

Serve: warm, garnished with lemon wedges. Bon appétit!

Fish Sticks with Vidalia Onions

(**Ready in about** 12 minutes | **Servings:** 2)

Ingredients

1/2 pound fish sticks, frozen

1/2 pound Vidalia onions, halved

Sea salt and ground black pepper, to taste

4 tablespoons mayonnaise

1/4 teaspoon mustard seeds

1/2 teaspoon red pepper flakes

4 tablespoons Greek-style yogurt

1 teaspoon chipotle chili in adobo, minced

1 teaspoon sesame oil

Directions

Drizzle the fish sticks and Vidalia onions with sesame oil. Toss them with salt, black pepper and red pepper flakes.

Transfer them to the Air Fryer cooking basket.

Cook the fish sticks and onions at 400 degreed F for 5 minutes. Shake the basket and cook an additional 5 minutes or until cooked through.

Meanwhile, mix the mayonnaise, Greek-style yogurt, mustard seeds and chipotle chili.

Serve: the warm fish sticks garnished with Vidalia onions and the sauce on the side. Bon appétit!

Salmon Fillets with Herbs and Garlic

(**Ready in about** 15 minutes | **Servings:** 3)

Ingredients

1 pound salmon fillets

1 tablespoon olive oil

1 sprig thyme

1 lemon, sliced

Sea salt and ground black pepper, to taste

2 sprigs rosemary

2 cloves garlic, minced

Directions

Pat the salmon fillets dry and season them with salt and pepper; drizzle salmon fillets with olive oil and place in the Air Fryer cooking basket.

Cook the salmon fillets at 380 degrees F for 7 minutes; turn them over, top with thyme, rosemary and garlic and continue to cook for 5 minutes more.

Serve: topped with lemon slices and enjoy!

Moroccan Harissa Shrimp

(**Ready in about** 10 minutes | **Servings:** 3)

Ingredients

1 pound breaded shrimp, frozen

Sea salt and ground black pepper, to taste

1 teaspoon coriander seeds

1 teaspoon crushed red pepper

1 teaspoon caraway seeds

1 teaspoon fresh garlic, minced

1 teaspoon extra-virgin olive oil

Directions

Toss the breaded shrimp with olive oil and transfer to the Air Fryer cooking basket.

Cook in the preheated Air Fryer at 400 degrees F for 5 minutes; shake the basket and cook an additional 4 minutes. Meanwhile, mix the remaining Ingredients until well combined. Taste and adjust seasonings. Toss the warm shrimp with the harissa sauce and **Serve:** immediately. Enjoy!

Classic Old Bay Fish with Cherry Tomatoes

(**Ready in about** 15 minutes | **Servings:** 3)

Ingredients

1 pound swordfish steak

1 tbs Old Bay seasoning

Salt black pepper, to season

1 pound cherry tomatoes

2 teaspoon olive oil

1/2 cup cornflakes, crushed

Directions

Toss the swordfish steak with cornflakes, Old Bay seasoning, salt, black pepper and 1 teaspoon of olive oil.

Cook the swordfish steak in your Air Fryer at 400 degrees F for 6 minutes. Now, turn the fish over, top with tomatoes and drizzle with the remaining teaspoon of olive oil. Continue to cook for 4 minutes. **Serve:** with lemon slices if desired. Bon appétit!

Classic Pancetta-Wrapped Scallops

(**Ready in about** 10 minutes | **Servings:** 3)

Ingredients

1 pound sea scallops
1/4 teaspoon shallot powder
1/4 teaspoon garlic powder
1/2 teaspoon dried dill
2 tablespoons soy sauce

1 tablespoon deli mustard
Sea salt and ground black pepper, to taste
4 ounces pancetta slices

Directions

Pat dry the sea scallops and transfer them to a mixing bowl. Toss the sea scallops with the deli mustard, soy sauce, shallot powder, garlic powder, dill, salt and black pepper.

Wrap a slice of bacon around each scallop and transfer them to the Air Fryer cooking basket.

Cook in your Air Fryer at 400 degrees F for 4 minutes; turn them over and cook an additional 3 minutes.

Serve: with hot sauce for dipping if desired. Bon appétit!

Fish Cakes with Bell Pepper

(**Ready in about** 15 minutes | **Servings:** 3)

Ingredients

1 pound haddock
2 tablespoons milk
2 stalks fresh scallions, minced
1/2 teaspoon fresh garlic, minced
1/4 teaspoon celery seeds

1 egg
1 bell pepper, deveined and finely chopped
1/2 teaspoon cumin seeds
Sea salt and ground black pepper, to taste
1/2 cup breadcrumbs
1 teaspoon olive oil

Directions

Except for the breadcrumbs and olive oil, thoroughly combine all Ingredients until well combined.

Roll the mixture into three patties and coat with breadcrumbs, pressing to adhere. Drizzle olive oil over the patties and place them in the cooking basket of an Air Fryer.

Cook the fish cakes for 5 minutes at 400 degrees F, then flip them over and cook for another 5 minutes, or until cooked through. Good appetite!

Greek Sardeles Psites

(**Ready in about** 40 minutes | **Servings:** 2)

Ingredients

4 sardines, cleaned
Sea salt and ground black pepper, to taste
1/4 cup sweet white wine
1/2 teaspoon fresh garlic, minced
1 tomato, crushed
1/4 cup baby capers, drained

1/4 cup all-purpose flour
1/2 red onion, chopped
4 tablespoons extra-virgin olive oil
1 tablespoon fresh coriander, minced
1/4 teaspoon chili paper flakes

Directions

Coat the sardines in all-purpose flour until they are evenly coated on all sides. Arrange your sardines in the cooking basket and season with salt and black pepper. Cook for 35 to 40 minutes at 325 degrees F in your Air Fryer, or until the skin is crispy.

Meanwhile, in a frying pan over medium heat, heat the olive oil. Now, begin to sauté 4 to 5 minutes, or until the onion and garlic are tender and aromatic

Stir in the remaining Ingredients, cover, and cook for 15 minutes, or until the sauce has thickened and reduced. **Serve:** the sauce immediately over the warm sardines. Enjoy!

Thai-Style Jumbo Scallops

(**Ready in about** 40 minutes | **Servings:** 2)

Ingredients

8 jumbo scallops
Sea salt and red pepper flakes, to season
1 tablespoon coconut oil
1 tablespoon oyster sauce
1 tablespoon soy sauce
1/4 cup coconut milk

1 teaspoon sesame oil
1 Thai chili, deveined and minced
1 teaspoon garlic, minced
2 tablespoons fresh lime juice

Directions

Pat the jumbo scallops dry and toss them with 1 teaspoon of sesame oil, salt and red pepper.

Cook the jumbo scallops in your Air Fryer at 400 degrees F for 4 minutes; turn them over and cook an additional 3 minutes. While your scallops are cooking, make the sauce in a frying pan. Heat the coconut oil in a pan over medium-high heat.

Once hot, cook the Thai chili and garlic for 1 minute or so until just tender and fragrant. Add in the oyster sauce, soy sauce and coconut milk and continue to simmer, partially covered, for 5 minutes longer.

Lastly, stir in fresh lime juice and stir to combine well. Add the warm scallops to the sauce and **Serve:** immediately.

Southwestern Prawns with Asparagus

(**Ready in about** 10 minutes | **Servings:** 3)

Ingredients

1 pound prawns, deveined
1 teaspoon butter, melted

1/4 teaspoon oregano
1/2 cup chunky-style salsa
1 ripe avocado
Salt, to taste

1/2 pound asparagus
spears, cut into1-inch
chinks
1/2 teaspoon mixed
peppercorns, crushed
1 lemon, sliced

Directions

Toss your prawns and asparagus with melted butter,
oregano, salt and mixed peppercorns. Cook the prawns and
asparagus at 400 degrees F for 5 minutes, shaking the
basket halfway through the cooking time. Divide the
prawns and asparagus between serving plates and garnish
with avocado and lemon slices. **Serve:** with the salsa on the
side. Bon appétit!

Haddock Steaks with Decadent Mango Salsa

(**Ready in about** 15 minutes | **Servings:** 2)

Ingredients

2 haddock steaks
Sea salt and ground black
pepper, to taste Mango
salsa
1/4 cup red onion,
chopped
1 teaspoon cilantro,
chopped

1 teaspoon butter, melted
1/2 mango, diced
1 tbs white wine

1 chili pepper, deveined
and minced
2 tbsp fresh lemon juice

Directions

Toss the haddock with butter, wine, salt and black
pepper. Cook the haddock in your Air Fryer at 400
degrees F for 5 minutes. Flip the haddock and cook on
the other side for 5 minutes more. Meanwhile, make
the mango salsa by mixing all Ingredients. **Serve:** the
warm haddock with the chilled mango salsa and enjoy!

Crispy Tilapia Fillets

(**Ready in about** 20 minutes | **Servings:** 5)

Ingredients

5 tbs all-purpose flour
Sea salt and white pepper,
to taste
1/2 cup cornmeal

2 tablespoons extra virgin
olive oil
1 teaspoon garlic paste
5 tilapia fillets, slice into
halves

Directions

Combine the flour, salt, white pepper, garlic paste, olive oil, and
cornmeal in a Ziploc bag. Add the fish fillets and shake to coat
well.

Spritz the Air Fryer basket with cooking spray. Cook in
the preheated Air Fryer at 400 degrees F for 10
minutes; turn them over and cook for 6 minutes more.
Work in batches.

Serve: with lemon wedges if desired. Enjoy!

Homemade Fish Fingers

(**Ready in about** 15 minutes | **Servings:** 2)

Ingredients

3/4 pound tilapia
4 tablespoons chickpea
flour

1/4 cup pork rinds
1 egg

2 tablespoons milk
1/2 cup breadcrumbs
1/2 tbsp red chili flakes

Coarse sea salt and black
pepper, to season

Directions

Rinse the tilapia and pat it dry using kitchen towels.
Then, cut the tilapia into strips.

Then, whisk the egg, milk and chickpea flour in a
rimmed plate.

Add the pork rinds and breadcrumbs to another plate;
stir in red chili flakes, salt and black pepper and stir to
combine well.

Dip the fish strips in the egg mixture, then, roll them
over the breadcrumb mixture. Transfer the fish fingers
to the Air Fryer cooking basket and spritz them with a
nonstick cooking spray.

Cook in the preheated Air Fryer at 400 degrees F for
10 minutes, shaking the basket halfway through to
ensure even browning. **Serve:** warm and enjoy!

Ahi Tuna with Peppers and Tartare Sauce

(**Ready in about** 15 minutes | **Servings:** 2)

Ingredients

2 ahi tuna steaks	2 Spanish peppers, quartered
2 tbs white onion, minced	Salt and freshly ground
1/2 teaspoon garlic powder	black pepper, to taste
4 tablespoons mayonnaise	1 tablespoon baby capers, drained
2 tablespoons sour cream	1 tablespoon gherkins, drained and chopped
Tartare sauce	
1 teaspoon olive oil	

Directions

Pat the ahi tuna dry using kitchen towels.

Toss the ahi tuna and Spanish peppers with olive oil, garlic powder, salt and black pepper.

Cook the ahi tuna and peppers in the preheated Air Fryer at 400 degrees F for 10 minutes, flipping them halfway through the cooking time.

Meanwhile, whisk all the sauce Ingredients until well combined. Plate the ahi tuna steaks and arrange Spanish peppers around them. **Serve:** with tartare sauce on the side and enjoy!

Fried Oysters with Kaffir Lime Sauce

(**Ready in about** 10 minutes | **Servings:** 2)

Ingredients

8 fresh oysters, shucked	1 egg
3/4 cup breadcrumbs	1/2 teaspoon Italian seasoning mix
1/3 cup plain flour	1 lime, freshly squeezed
1 habanero pepper, minced	
1 teaspoon coconut sugar	1 kaffir lime leaf, shredded
1 teaspoon olive oil	

Directions

Clean the oysters and set them aside. Add the flour to a rimmed plate. Whisk the egg in another rimmed plate. Mix the breadcrumbs and Italian seasoning mix in a third plate.

Dip your oysters in the flour, shaking off the excess. Then, dip them in the egg mixture and finally, coat your oysters with the breadcrumb mixture.

Spritz the breaded oysters with a nonstick cooking spray.

Cook your oysters in the preheated Air Fryer at 400 degrees F for 2 to 3 minutes, shaking the basket halfway through the cooking time.

Meanwhile, blend the remaining Ingredients to make the sauce. **Serve:** the warm oysters with the kaffir lime sauce on the side. Bon appétit

Tuna Steak with Roasted Cherry Tomatoes

(**Ready in about** 15 minutes | **Servings:** 2)

Ingredients

1 pound tuna steak	1 cup cherry tomatoes
1 teaspoon extra-virgin olive oil	2 sprigs rosemary, leaves picked and crushed
1 teaspoon garlic, finely chopped	1 tablespoon lime juice
	Sea salt and red pepper flakes, to taste

Directions

Toss the tuna steaks and cherry tomatoes with olive oil, rosemary leaves, salt, black pepper and garlic.

Place the tuna steaks in a lightly oiled cooking basket; cook tuna steaks at 440 degrees F for about 6 minutes.

Turn the tuna steaks over, add in the cherry tomatoes and continue to cook for 4 minutes more. Drizzle the fish with lime juice and **Serve:** warm garnished with roasted cherry tomatoes!

Salmon Filets with Fennel Slaw

(**Ready in about** 15 minutes | **Servings:** 3)

Ingredients

1 pound salmon filets	1 teaspoon Cajun spice mix
Sea salt and ground black pepper, to taste Fennel Slaw	1 pound fennel bulb, thinly sliced
1 Lebanese cucumber, sliced	1/2 red onion, thinly sliced
1 tablespoon soy sauce	2 tablespoons tahini
1/2 ounce tarragon	2 tablespoons lemon juice

Directions

Rinse the salmon filets and pat them dry with a paper towel. Then, toss the salmon filets with the Cajun spice mix, salt and black pepper.

Cook the salmon filets in the preheated Air Fryer at 380 degrees F for 6 minutes; flip the salmon filets and cook for a further 6 minutes.

Meanwhile, make the fennel slaw by stirring fennel, cucumber, red onion and tarragon in a salad bowl. Mix the remaining Ingredients to make the dressing.

Dress the salad and transfer to your refrigerator until ready to **Serve:**. **Serve:** the warm fish with chilled fennel slaw. Bon appétit!

Scallops with Pineapple Salsa and Pickled Onions

(**Ready in about** 15 minutes | **Servings:** 3)

Ingredients

12 scallops
1/4 teaspoon dried rosemary
1/2 teaspoon dried tarragon
1/2 cup pickled onions, drained
1 cup pineapple, diced
1 jalapeño, deveined and minced

1 small-sized red onion, minced
Sea salt and ground black pepper, to taste

1 teaspoon sesame oil
1/4 teaspoon red pepper flakes, crushed Coarse sea salt and black pepper, to taste Pineapple Salsa

2 tablespoons fresh cilantro, roughly chopped
1/2 teaspoon coconut sugar
1 teaspoon ginger root, peeled and grated
1/2 teaspoon dried basil

Directions

Toss the scallops sesame oil, rosemary, tarragon, basil, red pepper, salt and black pepper.

Cook in the preheated Air Fryer at 400 degrees F for 6 to 7 minutes, shaking the basket once or twice to ensure even cooking.

Meanwhile, process all the salsa Ingredients in your blender; cover and place the salsa in your refrigerator until ready to **Serve:**.

Serve: the warm scallops with pickled onions and pineapple salsa on the side. Bon appétit!

Tuna Steaks with Pearl Onions

(**Ready in about** 20 minutes | **Servings:** 4)

Ingredients

4 tuna steaks
1 teaspoon dried rosemary
1 teaspoon dried marjoram
1/2 teaspoon sea salt
1 lemon, sliced
4 teaspoons olive oil

1 pound pearl onions
1 tablespoon cayenne pepper

1/2 teaspoon black pepper, preferably freshly cracked

Directions

Place the tuna steaks in the lightly greased cooking basket. Top with the pearl onions; add the olive oil, rosemary, marjoram, cayenne pepper, salt, and black pepper.

Bake in the preheated Air Fryer at 400 degrees F for 9 to 10 minutes. Work in two batches.

Serve: warm with lemon slices and enjoy!

English-Style Flounder Fillets

(**Ready in about** 20 minutes | **Servings:** 2)

Ingredients

1 flounder fillets
1/2 teaspoon Worcestershire sauce

1/2 teaspoon coarse sea salt 1/4 teaspoon chili powder

1/4 cup all-purpose flour
1/2 teaspoon lemon pepper
1 egg
1/2 cup bread crumbs

Directions

The flounder fillets should be rinsed and patted dry. In a large saucepan, combine the flour and salt.

In a shallow bowl, whisk together the egg and Worcestershire sauce. Separately, combine the bread crumbs, lemon pepper, salt, and chilli powder in a separate bowl.

Dredge the fillets in the flour and shake off any excess. After that, dip them in the egg mixture. Finally, coat the fish fillets in the breadcrumb mixture, coating all sides.

Spritz with cooking spray before placing in the Air Fryer basket. Cook for 7 minutes at 390°F.

Turn them over, spritz the other side with cooking spray, and cook for another 5 minutes. Good appetite!

Cod and Shallot Frittata

(**Ready in about** 20 minutes | **Servings:** 3)

Ingredients

2 cod fillets
1/2 cup milk
2 garlic cloves, minced
1/2 teaspoon red pepper

6 eggs
1 shallot, chopped
Sea salt and ground black pepper, to taste

Directions

Bring a pot of salted water to a boil. Boil the cod fillets for 5 minutes or until it is opaque. Flake the fish into bite-sized pieces. In a mixing bowl, whisk the eggs and milk. Stir in the shallots, garlic, salt, black pepper, and red pepper flakes. Stir in the re**Serve:**d fish.

Pour the mixture into the lightly greased baking pan.

Cook in the preheated Air Fryer at 360 degrees F for 9 minutes, flipping over halfway through. Bon appétit!

Saucy Garam Masala Fish

(**Ready in about** 25 minutes | **Servings:** 2)

Ingredients

2 teaspoons olive oil
1 teaspoon Garam masala
1/4 cup coconut milk
1/4 cup coriander, chopped
1 garlic clove, minced

1/2 tbs cayenne pepper
1/4 teaspoon Kala namak (Indian black salt)
1/2 tbsp fresh ginger, grated
2 catfish fillets

Directions

Preheat your Air Fryer to 390 degrees F. Then, spritz the baking dish with a nonstick cooking spray.

In a mixing bowl, whisk the olive oil, milk, cayenne pepper, Garam masala, Kala namak, ginger, and garlic.

Coat the catfish fillets with the Garam masala mixture. Cook the catfish fillets in the preheated Air Fryer approximately 18 minutes, turning over halfway through the cooking time.

Shrimp Kabobs with Cherry Tomatoes

(**Ready in about** 30 minutes | **Servings:** 4)

Ingredients

1 ½ pounds jumbo shrimp, cleaned, shelled and
1 tablespoons Sriracha sauce
1/2 teaspoon dried basil
1/2 teaspoon marjoram
1/2 tbsp dried oregano

2 tablespoons butter, melted
1 pound cherry tomatoes
Sea salt and ground black pepper, to taste
1 tbsp dried parsley flakes
1/2 teaspoon mustard seeds

Directions

Toss all Ingredients in a mixing bowl until the shrimp and tomatoes are covered on all sides. Soak the wooden skewers in water for 15 minutes. Thread the jumbo shrimp and cherry tomatoes onto skewers

Grilled Salmon Steaks

(**Ready in about** 45 minutes | **Servings:** 4)

Ingredients

2 cloves garlic, minced

Sea salt and ground black pepper, to taste
1 teaspoon smoked paprika
4 salmon steaks

4 tablespoons butter, melted
1/2 teaspoon onion powder
1 tablespoon lime juice
1/4 cup dry white wine

Directions

Place all Ingredients in a large ceramic dish. Cover and let it marinate for 30 minutes in the refrigerator.

Arrange the salmon steaks on the grill pan. Bake at 390 degrees for 5 minutes, or until the salmon steaks are easily flaked with a fork. Flip the fish steaks, baste with the re**Serve:**d marinade, and cook another 5 minutes. Bon appétit!

Delicious Snapper en Papillote

(**Ready in about** 20 minutes | **Servings:** 2)

Ingredients

1 snapper fillets
1 bell pepper, sliced
2 garlic cloves, halved
1 tablespoon olive oil
1 tomato, sliced
Sea salt, to taste 2 bay leaves

1 shallot, peeled and sliced
1 small-sized serrano pepper, sliced
1/4 teaspoon freshly ground black pepper
1/2 teaspoon paprika

Directions

Place two parchment sheets on a working surface. Place the fish in the center of one side of the parchment paper.

Top with the shallot, garlic, peppers, and tomato. Drizzle olive oil over the fish and vegetables. Season with black pepper, paprika, and salt. Add the bay leaves

Fold over the other half of the parchment. Now, fold the paper around the edges tightly and create a half moon shape, sealing the fish inside.

Cook in the preheated Air Fryer at 390 degrees F for 15 minutes. **Serve:** warm.

Cajun shrimp

Prep time: 5 minutes **Cooking time:** 10 minutes
Servings: 4-6

Ingredients

Olive oil (1 tablespoon)
Smoked paprika (0.25 tsp.)
Cayenne pepper (0.25 tsp.)
Salt (1 pinch)

Old Bay seasoning (0.5 tsp.) Tiger shrimp (1.25 lbs. or 16-20)

Directions

Heat the air fryer to 390 Fahrenheit / 199 Celsius. Combine each of the fasteners and coat the shrimp with the oil and spices. Put the shrimp in the basket and fry for five minutes. Enjoy shrimp with a portion of rice.

Halibut Cakes with Horseradish Mayo

(**Ready in about** 20 minutes | **Servings:** 4)

Ingredients

Halibut Cakes
2 tablespoons olive oil
2 tablespoons cilantro, chopped
1 shallot, chopped
1/2 cup Romano cheese, grated
1 tablespoon Worcestershire sauce
Mayo Sauce
1/2 cup mayonnaise

1 pound halibut
1/2 tbs cayenne pepper
2 garlic cloves, minced
1/4 teaspoon black pepper Salt, to taste
1 egg, whisked
1/2 cup breadcrumbs
1 teaspoon horseradish, grated

Directions

Begin by preheating your Air Fryer to 380°F. Cooking oil should be sprayed into the Air Fryer basket.

In a mixing bowl, combine all of the

Ingredients for the halibut cakes; knead with your hands until everything is well combined.

Make equal-sized patties out of the mixture. Place the patties in the Air Fryer basket. Cook the fish patties for 10 minutes, flipping halfway through. Combine the horseradish and mayonnaise in a mixing bowl. With the horseradish mayo, **Serve:** the halibut cakes. Good appetite!

Dilled and Glazed Salmon Steaks

(**Ready in about** 20 minutes | **Servings:** 2)

Ingredients

2 salmon steaks Coarse sea salt, to taste
2 tablespoons honey
1 tablespoon fresh lemon juice
1 teaspoon garlic, minced
1/2 teaspoon dried dill

1/4 teaspoon freshly ground black pepper
1 tablespoon sesame oil
1/2 teaspoon smoked cayenne pepper
Zest of 1 lemon

Directions

Preheat your Air Fryer to 380 degrees F. Pat dry the salmon steaks with a kitchen towel.

In a ceramic dish, combine the remaining Ingredients until everything is well whisked.

Add the salmon steaks to the ceramic dish and let them sit in the refrigerator for 1 hour. Now, place the salmon steaks in the cooking basket. Re**Serve:** the marinade.

Cook for 12 minutes, flipping halfway through the cooking time.

Meanwhile, cook the marinade in a small sauté pan over a moderate flame. Cook until the sauce has thickened. Pour the sauce over the steaks and **Serve:** with mashed potatoes if desired. Bon appétit!

Easy Prawns alla Parmigiana

(**Ready in about** 20 minutes | **Servings:** 4)

Ingredients

2 egg whites
1 cup Parmigiano-Reggiano, grated
1/2 cup fine breadcrumbs
1 teaspoon garlic powder
1/2 teaspoon ground black pepper
1 ½ pounds prawns, deveined

1 cup all-purpose flour
1/2 teaspoon celery seeds
1/2 teaspoon porcini powder
1/2 tbsp onion powder
1/2 teaspoon sea salt
1/2 teaspoon dried rosemary

Directions

To make a breading station, whisk the egg whites in a shallow dish. In a separate dish, place the all-purpose flour.

In a third dish, thoroughly combine the Parmigiano-Reggiano, breadcrumbs,

and seasonings; mix to combine well.

Dip the prawns in the flour, then, into the egg whites; lastly, dip them in the parm/breadcrumb mixture. Roll until they are covered on all sides.

Cook in the preheated Air Fryer at 390 degrees F for 5 to 7 minutes or until golden brown. Work in batches. **Serve:** with lemon wedges if desired.

Indian Famous Fish Curry

(**Ready in about** 25 minutes | **Servings:** 4)

Ingredients

2 tablespoons sunflower oil	2 red chilies, chopped
1 tablespoon coriander powder	1 cup coconut milk
Salt and white pepper, to taste 1/2 teaspoon fenugreek seeds 1 shallot, minced	1/2 pound fish, chopped
	1 garlic clove, minced
	1 ripe tomato, pureed
	1 teaspoon curry paste

Directions

Preheat your Air Fryer to 380 degrees F; brush the cooking basket with 1 tablespoon of sunflower oil.

Cook your fish for 10 minutes on both sides. Transfer to the baking pan that is previously greased with the remaining tablespoon of sunflower oil.

Add the remaining Ingredients and reduce the heat to 350 degrees F. Continue to cook an additional 10 to 12 minutes or until everything is heated through. Enjoy!

Snapper Casserole with Gruyere Cheese

(**Ready in about** 25 minutes | **Servings:** 4)

Ingredients

2 tablespoons olive oil	1 ½ pounds snapper fillets
2 garlic cloves, minced	1 shallot, thinly sliced
Sea salt and ground black pepper, to taste	1/2 teaspoon dried basil
1 teaspoon cayenne pepper	1/2 cup tomato puree
1 cup Gruyere cheese, shredded	1/2 cup white wine

Directions

Heat 1 tablespoon of olive oil in a saucepan over medium-high heat. Now, cook the shallot and garlic until tender and aromatic.

Preheat your Air Fryer to 370 degrees F.

Grease a casserole dish with 1 tablespoon of olive oil. Place the snapper fillet in the casserole dish. Season with salt, black pepper, and cayenne pepper.

Add the sautéed shallot mixture.

Add the basil, tomato puree and wine to the casserole dish. Cook for 10 minutes in the preheated Air Fryer.

Top with the shredded cheese and cook an additional 7 minutes. **Serve:** immediately.

Monkfish Fillets with Romano Cheese

(**Ready in about** 15 minutes | **Servings:** 2)

Ingredients

2 monkfish fillets	1 teaspoon garlic paste
2 tablespoons butter, melted	1/2 teaspoon Aleppo chili powder
1/2 tbs dried rosemary	
1/4 teaspoon cracked black pepper	1/2 teaspoon sea salt
4 tablespoons Romano cheese, grated	

Directions

Start by preheating the Air Fryer to 320 degrees F. Spritz the Air Fryer basket with cooking oil.

Spread the garlic paste all over the fish fillets.

Brush the monkfish fillets with the melted butter on both sides. Sprinkle with the chili powder, rosemary, black pepper, and salt. Cook for 7 minutes in the preheated Air Fryer.

Top with the Romano cheese and continue to cook for 2 minutes more or until heated through. Bon appétit!

Grilled Hake with Garlic Sauce

(**Ready in about** 20 minutes | **Servings:** 3)

Ingredients

3 hake fillets	6 tablespoons mayonnaise
1 tablespoon fresh lime juice 1 cup panko crumbs	Salt, to taste
	1 teaspoon Dijon mustard
1/4 teaspoon ground black pepper, or more to taste	1/4 cup Greek-style yogurt
2 tablespoons olive oil	Garlic Sauce
2 cloves garlic, minced	1/2 teaspoon tarragon leaves, minced

Directions

Pat dry the hake fillets with a kitchen towel.

In a shallow bowl, whisk together the mayo, mustard, and lime juice. In another shallow bowl, thoroughly combine the panko crumbs with salt, and black pepper.

Spritz the Air Fryer grill pan with non-stick cooking spray. Grill in the preheated Air Fry at 395 degrees F for 10 minutes, flipping halfway through the cooking time. **Serve:** immediately.

Grilled Tilapia with Portobello Mushrooms

(**Ready in about** 20 minutes | **Servings:** 2)

Ingredients

2 tilapia fillets
1/2 teaspoon red pepper flakes, crushed
1/2 teaspoon dried sage, crushed
1 tsp dried parsley flakes

1 tablespoon avocado oil
1/4 teaspoon lemon pepper 1/2 teaspoon sea salt
A few drizzles of liquid smoke
4 medium-sized Portobello mushrooms

Directions

Toss all Ingredients in a mixing bowl; except for the mushrooms.

Transfer the tilapia fillets to a lightly greased grill pan. Preheat your Air Fryer to 400 degrees F and cook the tilapia fillets for 5 minutes.

Now, turn the fillets over and add the Portobello mushrooms. Continue to cook for 5 minutes longer or until mushrooms are tender and the fish is opaque. **Serve:** immediately.

Authentic Mediterranean Calamari Salad

(**Ready in about** 15 minutes | **Servings:** 3)

1 pound squid, cleaned, sliced into rings
2 tablespoons sherry wine
1/2 teaspoon ground black pepper
1 cup grape tomatoes
1 teaspoon yellow mustard
1/3 cup Kalamata olives, pitted and sliced
1/2 cup mayonnaise

1/2 teaspoon granulated garlic Salt, to taste
1/2 teaspoon basil
1/2 teaspoon dried rosemary
1 small red onion, thinly sliced
1/2 cup fresh flat-leaf parsley leaves, coarsely chopped

Directions

Start by preheating the Air Fryer to 400 degrees F. Spritz the Air Fryer basket with cooking oil.

Toss the squid rings with the sherry wine, garlic, salt, pepper, basil, and rosemary. Cook in the preheated Air Fryer for 5 minutes, shaking the basket halfway through the cooking time.

Work in batches and let it cool to room temperature. When the squid is cool enough, add the remaining **Ingredients**.

Gently stir to combine and **Serve:** well chilled. Bon appétit!

Filet of Flounder Cutlets

(**Ready in about** 15 minutes | **Servings:** 2)

Ingredients

1 egg
1/2 cup Pecorino Romano cheese, grated
2 flounder fillets
1 teaspoon dried parsley flakes

1/2 cup cracker crumbs
1/2 teaspoon cayenne pepper
Sea salt and white pepper, to taste

Directions

To make a breading station, whisk the egg until frothy.

In another bowl, mix the cracker crumbs, Pecorino Romano cheese, and spices.

Dip the fish in the egg mixture and turn to coat evenly; then, dredge in the cracker crumb mixture, turning a couple of times to coat evenly.

Cook in the preheated Air Fryer at 390 degrees F for 5 minutes; turn them over and cook another 5 minutes. Enjoy!

King Prawns with Lemon Butter Sauce

(**Ready in about** 15 minutes | **Servings:** 4)

Ingredients

King Prawns
2 cloves garlic, minced
1/2 cup Pecorino Romano cheese, grated
1 teaspoon garlic powder
1 teaspoon mustard seeds
2 tablespoons olive oil

2 tbs fresh lemon juice
1/2 teaspoon Worcestershire sauce

1 ½ pounds king prawns, peeled and deveined
Sea salt and ground white pepper, to your
2 tablespoons butter liking
1/2 teaspoon onion powder
1/4 teaspoon ground black pepper
Sauce

Directions

All Ingredients for the king prawns should be thoroughly combined in a plastic closeable bag; shake to combine well.

Place the coated king prawns in the Air Fryer basket that has been lightly greased.

Cook for 6 minutes at 390°F in a preheated Air Fryer, shaking the basket halfway through. Working in batches is recommended.

Meanwhile, melt the butter in a small saucepan over medium heat and add the remaining Ingredients.

Reduce the heat to low and whisk for 2 to 3 minutes, or until thoroughly heated. Pour the sauce over the hot king prawns. Good appetite!

Crusty Catfish with Sweet Potato Fries

(**Ready in about** 50 minutes | **Servings:** 2)

Ingredients

1/2 pound catfish	1/4 cup parmesan cheese, grated
1/2 cup bran cereal	1 teaspoon garlic powder
Sea salt and ground black pepper, to taste	1 tbsp smoked paprika
1/4 tbs ground bay leaf	2 tablespoons butter, Melted
4 sweet potatoes, cut French fries	1 egg

Directions

Pat the catfish dry with a kitchen towel. Combine the bran cereal with the parmesan cheese and all spices in a shallow bowl. Whisk the egg in another shallow bowl.

Dip the fish in the egg mixture and turn to coat evenly; then, dredge in the bran cereal mixture, turning a couple of times to coat evenly. Spritz the Air Fryer basket with cooking spray. Cook the catfish in the preheated Air Fryer at 390 degrees F for 10 minutes; turn them over and cook for 4 minutes more. Then, drizzle the melted butter all over the sweet potatoes; cook them in the preheated Air Fryer at 380 degrees F for 30 minutes, shaking occasionally. **Serve:** over the warm fish fillets. Bon appétit!

Crunchy Topped Fish Bake

(**Ready in about** 20 minutes | **Servings:** 4)

Ingredients

1 tablespoon butter, melted	1 medium-sized leek, thinly sliced
1 tablespoon dry white wine	1/2 teaspoon red pepper flakes, crushed
1 pound tuna	1 tbsp chicken stock
Sea salt and ground black pepper, to taste	1/2 teaspoon dried basil
1/2 teaspoon dried thyme	1/2 tbs dried rosemary
2 ripe tomatoes, pureed	1/4 cup Parmesan cheese, grated
1/4 cup breadcrumbs	

Directions

Melt 1/2 tablespoon of butter in a sauté pan over medium-high heat. Now, cook the leek and garlic until tender and aromatic. Add the stock and wine to deglaze the pan.

Preheat your Air Fryer to 370 degrees F.

Grease a casserole dish with the remaining 1/2 tablespoon of melted butter. Place the fish in the casserole dish. Add the seasonings. Top with the sautéed leek mixture. Add the tomato puree. Cook for 10 minutes in the preheated Air Fryer. Top with the breadcrumbs and cheese; cook an additional 7 minutes until the crumbs are golden. Bon appétit!

Creamed Trout Salad

(**Ready in about** 20 minutes | **Servings:** 2)

Ingredients

1/2 pound trout fillets, skinless	2 tablespoons horseradish, prepared, drained
1 tablespoon fresh lemon juice	Salt and ground white pepper, to taste
6 ounces chickpeas, canned and drained	1 cup Iceberg lettuce, torn into pieces
1 red onion, thinly sliced	1/4 cup mayonnaise
1 teaspoon mustard	

Directions

Spritz the Air Fryer basket with cooking spray.

Cook the trout fillets in the preheated Air Fryer at 395 degrees F for 10 minutes or until opaque. Make sure to turn them halfway through the cooking time.

Break the fish into bite-sized chunks and place in the refrigerator to cool. Toss your fish with the remaining Ingredients. Bon appétit!

Quick Thai Coconut Fish

(**Ready in about** 20 minutes + marinating time | **Servings:** 2)

Ingredients

1 cup coconut milk	2 tablespoons lime juice
2 tablespoons Shoyu sauce	1/2 Thai Bird's Eye chili, seeded and finely chopped
Salt and white pepper, to taste 1 teaspoon turmeric powder	1 pound tilapia
2 tablespoons olive oil	1/2 teaspoon ginger powder

Directions

In a mixing bowl, thoroughly combine the coconut milk with the lime juice, Shoyu sauce, salt, pepper, turmeric, ginger, and chili pepper. Add tilapia and let it marinate for 1 hour.

Brush the Air Fryer basket with olive oil. Discard the marinade and place the tilapia fillets in the Air Fryer basket.

Cook the tilapia in the preheated Air Fryer at 400 degrees F for 6 minutes; turn them over and cook for 6 minutes more. Work in batches.

Serve: with some extra lime wedges if desired. Enjoy!

Double Cheese Fish Casserole

(**Ready in about** 30 minutes | **Servings:** 4)

Ingredients

1 tablespoon avocado oil	1 teaspoon garlic powder
Sea salt and ground white pepper, to taste	1 bell pepper, seeded and chopped
2 tablespoons shallots, chopped	1 pound hake fillets
1/2 cup Cottage cheese	1/2 cup sour cream
1 teaspoon yellow mustard	1 egg, well whisked
1 tablespoon lime juice	1/2 cup Swiss cheese, shredded

Directions

Brush the bottom and sides of a casserole dish with avocado oil. Add the hake fillets to the casserole dish and sprinkle with garlic powder, salt, and pepper.

Add the chopped shallots and bell peppers.

In a mixing bowl, thoroughly combine the Cottage cheese, sour cream, egg, mustard, and lime juice. Pour the mixture over fish and spread evenly.

Cook in the preheated Air Fryer at 370 degrees F for 10 minutes.

Top with the Swiss cheese and cook an additional 7 minutes. Let it rest for 10 minutes before slicing and serving. Bon appétit!

Rosemary-Infused Butter Scallops

(**Ready in about** 1 hour 10 minutes | **Servings:** 4)

Ingredients

2 pounds sea scallops	4 tablespoons butter
2 sprigs rosemary, only leaves	Sea salt and freshly cracked black pepper, to taste
1/2 cup beer	

Directions

In a ceramic dish, mix the sea scallops with beer; let it marinate for 1 hour.

Meanwhile, preheat your Air Fryer to 400 degrees F. Melt the butter and add the rosemary leaves. Stir for a few minutes.

Discard the marinade and transfer the sea scallops to the Air Fryer basket. Season with salt and black pepper.

Cook the scallops in the preheated Air Fryer for 7 minutes, shaking the basket halfway through the cooking time. Work in batches. Bon appétit!

Snapper with Coconut Milk Sauce

(**Ready in about** 20 minutes + marinating time | **Servings:** 2)

Ingredients

½ cup full-fat coconut milk	1 tbs fresh ginger, grated
2 snapper fillets	1 tablespoon olive oil
1 tablespoon cornstarch	Salt and white pepper, to taste
2 tablespoons lemon juice	

Directions

In a glass bowl, combine the milk, lemon juice, and ginger; add the fish and marinate for 1 hour.

Placed the fish in the Air Fryer basket after removing it from the milk mixture. Drizzle olive oil over the fillets of fish. Cook for 15 minutes in a preheated Air Fryer at 390 degrees F.

Meanwhile, bring the milk mixture to a rapid boil over medium-high heat, stirring constantly. Reduce to a simmer and add the cornstarch, salt, and pepper; cook for another 12 minutes. **Serve:** the sauce over the warm snapper fillets right away. Good appetite

Creamy Salmon

Prep time: 15 minutes **Cooking time:** 20 minutes
Servings: 2

Ingredients

Chopped dill (1 tablespoon) Salt (1 pinch) Sour cream (3 tablespoons) Salmon (0.75 lb./340 g - 6 pieces)	Olive oil (1 tablespoon) Natural yogurt (1.75 oz. / 49 g)

Directions

Heat the air fryer to 285 Fahrenheit / 141 Celsius. Shake the salt over the salmon and add it to the basket with a spritz of olive oil. Set the timer to air fry for ten minutes.

Quick Paella

Prep time: 7 minutes **Cooking time:** 17 minutes
Servings: 4

Ingredients

1 (10-ounce) package frozen cooked rice, thawed
1/2 teaspoon turmeric
1/2 teaspoon dried thyme
1/4 cup vegetable broth
1 tomato, diced

1 (6-ounce) jar artichoke hearts, drained and chopped
1 cup frozen cooked small shrimp
1/2 cup frozen baby peas

Directions

In a 6-by-6-by-2-inch pan, combine the rice, artichoke hearts, vegetable broth, turmeric, and thyme, and stir gently. Set in the air fryer and bake for 8 to 9 minutes or until the rice is hot.

Remove from the air fryer and gently stir in the shrimp, peas, and tomato. Cook for 5 to 8 minutes or until the shrimp and peas are hot and the paella is bubbling.

Substitution tip If you like intensely flavored food, try using marinated artichoke hearts in this recipe. Be sure you taste the marinade first! For even more flavor, use the liquid in the jar of artichokes in place of the vegetable broth.

Crab Ratatouille

Prep time: 15 minutes **Cooking time:** 14 minutes
Servings: 4

Ingredients

11/2 cups peeled, cubed eggplant
1 onion, chopped
1/2 teaspoon dried thyme
11/2 cups cooked crabmeat, picked over

1 red bell pepper, chopped
2 large tomatoes, chopped
1 tablespoon olive oil
Freshly black pepper
1/2 teaspoon dried basil
Pinch salt

Directions

Combine the eggplant, onion, bell pepper, tomatoes, olive oil, thyme, and basil in a 6-inch metal bowl. Sprinkle with salt and pepper. Roast for 9 minutes, then remove the bowl from the air fryer and stir. Add the crabmeat and roast for 2 to 5 minutes or until the ratatouille is bubbling and the vegetables are tender.
Serve: immediately.

Air Fried Dragon Shrimp

Prep time: 10 minutes **Cooking time:** 20 minutes
Servings: 2

Ingredients

Shrimp (0.5 lb./230 g)
Ginger (1 pinch)
Soy sauce (0.5 cup)
Eggs (2)

Chopped onions (1 cup)
Almond flour (.25 cup)
Olive oil (2 tablespoons)

Directions

Heat the air fryer unit to 390 Fahrenheit. Boil the shrimp for about five minutes. Make a paste from the mixture of onion puree and ginger. Beat the eggs.

Seafood Tacos

Prep time: 15 minutes **Cooking time:** 12 minutes
Servings: 4

Ingredients

1 pound white fish fillets, such as snapper
1/2 cup salsa
3 tablespoons lemon juice, divided

1 tablespoon olive oil
2 avocados, peeled chopped
1/3 cup sour cream 6 soft flour tortillas
11/2 cups chopped red cabbage

Directions

Garnish the fish with olive oil and sprinkle with 1 tablespoon of the lemon juice. Place in the air fryer basket and air-fry for 9 to 12 minutes or until the fish just flakes when tested with a fork.

Meanwhile, combine remaining 2 tablespoons lemon juice, cabbage, salsa, and sour cream in a medium bowl.

When the fish is cooked, remove from the air fryer basket and break into large pieces.

Let everyone assemble their own taco combining the fish, tortillas, cabbage mixture, and avocados.

Crispy Herbed Salmon

Prep time: 5 minutes **Cooking time:** 12 minutes
Servings: 4

Ingredients

4 (6-ounce) skinless salmon fillets	1/2 teaspoon dried thyme
1/4 cup panko bread crumbs 1/3 cup crushed potato chips	1/2 teaspoon dried basil
	2 tablespoons olive oil
	3 tablespoons honey mustard

Directions

Place the salmon on a plate. In a small bowl, merge the mustard, thyme, and basil, and spread evenly over the salmon.

In another small bowl, merge the bread crumbs and potato chips and

mix well. Toss in the olive oil and mix until combined. Place the salmon in the air fryer basket and gently but firmly press the bread crumb mixture onto the top of each fillet.

Bake until the salmon reaches at least 145F on a meat thermometer and

the topping is browned and crisp.

Asian Steamed Tuna

Prep time: 10 minutes **Cooking time:** 10 minutes
Servings: 4

Ingredients

4 small tuna steaks	2 tablespoons low-sodium soy sauce
2 teaspoons sesame oil	
2 teaspoons rice wine vinegar 1 teaspoon grated fresh ginger	1 stalk lemongrass, bent in half
3 tablespoons lemon juice	1/8 teaspoon pepper

Directions

Place the tuna steaks on a plate.

In a small bowl, merge the soy sauce, sesame oil, rice wine vinegar, and ginger, and mix well. Pour this mixture over the tuna and marinate for 10 minutes.

Rub the soy sauce mixture gently into both sides of the tuna. Sprinkle with the pepper.

Place the lemongrass on the air fryer basket and top with the steaks. Put the lemon juice and 1 tablespoon water in the pan below the basket.

Steam the fish until the tuna registers at least 145°F.

Discard the lemongrass and **Serve:** the tuna.

Tuna Veggie Stir-Fry

Prep time: 15 minutes **Cooking time:** 12 minutes
Servings: 4

Ingredients

1 tablespoon olive oil	1 red bell pepper, chopped
1 cup green beans, divide into 2-inch pieces	2 cloves garlic, sliced
	1 onion, sliced
2 tablespoons low-sodium soy sauce	1/2 pound fresh tuna, cubed
	1 tablespoon honey

Directions

In a 6-inch metal bowl, combine the olive oil, pepper, green beans, onion, and garlic.

Cook in the air fryer for 4 to 6 minutes, stirring once, until crisp and tender. Add soy sauce, honey, and tuna, and stir.

Cook for another 3 to 6 minutes, stirring once, until the tuna is cooked as desired. Tuna can be **Serve:**d rare or medium-rare, or you can cook it until well done.

Scallops and Spring Veggies

Prep time: 10 minutes **Cooking time:** 10 minutes
Servings: 4

Ingredients

1/2 pound asparagus, ends trimmed, cut into 2-inch pieces	1 pound sea scallops
	1 cup sugar snap peas
1 tablespoon lemon juice	2 teaspoons olive oil
Freshly ground black pepper	1/2 teaspoon dried thyme
	Pinch salt Pinch salt

Directions

Set the asparagus and sugar snap peas in the air fryer basket. Cook for 2 to 3 minutes or until the vegetables are just starting to get tender.

Meanwhile, check the scallops for a small muscle attached to the side,

and pull it off and discard.

In a medium bowl, toss the scallops with the lemon juice, olive oil, thyme, salt, and pepper. Place into the air fryer basket on top of the vegetables.

Steam for 5 to 7 minutes, tossing the basket once during cooking time,

until the scallops are just firm when tested with your finger and are opaque in the center, and the vegetables are tender. **Serve:** immediately.

Snapper Scampi

Prep time: 5 minutes **Cooking time:** 10 minutes
Servings: 4

Ingredients

4 (6-ounce) skinless snapper or arctic char fillets
1 tablespoon olive oil
Pinch salt

2 cloves garlic, minced

3 tablespoons lemon juice, divided
1/2 teaspoon dried basil

Freshly ground black pepper
2 tablespoons butter

Directions

Massage the fish fillets with olive oil and 1 tablespoon of the lemon juice. Sprinkle with the basil, salt, and pepper, and place in the air fryer basket.
Grill the fish for 7 to 8 minutes or until the fish just flakes when tested
with a fork. Remove the fish from the basket and put on a serving plate. Cover to keep warm.
In a 6-by-6-by-2-inch pan, combine the butter, remaining 2 tablespoons
lemon juice, and garlic. Cook in the air fryer for 1 to 2 minutes or until the garlic is sizzling. Pour this mixture over the fish and **Serve:**.

Coconut Shrimp

Prep time: 15 minutes **Cooking time:** 7 minutes
Servings: 4

Ingredients

1 (8-ounce) can crushed pineapple

2/3 cup cornstarch
1/2 cup sour cream

1 pound uncooked large shrimp, thawed if frozen, deveined and shelled

1/4 cup pineapple pre**Serve:**s
2 egg whites
2/3 cup sweetened coconut
1 cup panko bread crumbs
Olive oil for misting

Directions

Rinse the crushed pineapple well, reserving the juice. In a small bowl, combine the pineapple, sour cream, and pre**Serve:**s, and merge well. Set aside.
In a bowl, beat the egg whites with 2 tablespoons of the re**Serve:**d
pineapple liquid. Set the cornstarch on a plate. Merge the coconut and bread crumbs on another plate.
Soak the shrimp into the cornstarch, shake it off, then dip into the egg
white mixture and finally into the coconut mixture.
Place the shrimp in the air fryer basket and mist with oil. Air-fry for 5 to 7 minutes or until the shrimp are crisp and golden brown.

Crispy Air Fried Halibut

Prep time: 10 minutes **Cooking time:** 40 minutes
Servings: 4

Ingredients

Fresh chives (.25 cup)
Fresh parsley (0.5 cup)
Fresh dill (.25 cup)
Lemon zest (1 tablespoon)
Halibut fillets (4)

Black pepper and sea salt (to taste)
Pork rinds (.75 cup)
Olive oil (1 tablespoon)

Directions

Heat the air fryer to reach 390 Fahrenheit / 199 Celsius.
Chop the chives, dill, and parsley. Prepare the lemon zest until it is finely grated. Combine all the dry Ingredients parsley, pork rinds, chives, lemon zest, dill, black pepper, sea salt, and olive oil.
Rinse the halibut thoroughly and drain it on a layer of absorbent paper.
Prepare a baking sheet that fits into the pot. Pour the peel over the fish and press well.
Add the prepared fillets to the fryer basket to cook for 1/2 hour to **Serve:**.

Air Fried Shrimp

Prep time: 5 minutes **Cooking time:** 15 minutes
Servings: 4

Ingredients

Egg white (3 tablespoons or 1 egg)
Panko Breadcrumbs (.75 cup)
McCormick's Grill Mates Montreal Chicken Seasoning Cooking oil spray (if needed)
Sriracha (2 tablespoons)

AP flour (0.5 cup)
Raw shrimp (1 lb./450 g)
Pepper and salt (to taste)

For the sauce
Paprika (1 tsp.)
Sweet Chili Sauce (.25 cup)
Low-fat Greek yogurt (0.33 cup)

Directions

Heat the air fryer to 400 Fahrenheit / 204 Celsius. Peel and remove the prawns. Add the toppings. Use three bowls for the breadcrumbs, egg whites, and flour.

Dip the shrimp in the flour, egg and breadcrumbs. Lightly spray the prawns and add them to the fryer basket for four minutes. Turn over the shrimp over and cook for another four minutes. Watch the last few minutes to prevent it from burning. Assemble the sauce toppings and **Serve:** with the prawns.

Cod Steaks with Ginger

Prep time: 15 minutes **Cooking time:** 30 minutes
Servings: 2

Ingredients

Large cod steaks (2 slices)
Turmeric powder (0.25 tsp.) Salt and pepper (1 pinch) Powdered ginger (0.5 tsp.)
Slices of ginger (to taste)

Flour topped with Kentucky kernels (+) cornmeal (1 part of each)
Garlic powder (0.5 tsp.)
Plum sauce (1 tablespoon)

Directions

Dry the cod steaks with several paper towels. Put the cod in a marinade for a few minutes (based on pepper, salt, ginger powder and turmeric powder). Lightly coat each of the steaks with the cornmeal and Kentucky mixture. Set the temperature in the air fryer to 356 Fahrenheit / 180 Celsius.

Airs fry them for 15 minutes. Increase the temperature setting to 400 Fahrenheit / 204 Celsius for five minutes. Prepare the sauce in a wok. Brown the ginger slices and places the pan on a cold stove. Stir in the plum sauce. Dilute the sauce (just enough) with a little water. **Serve:** the steaks with a drizzle of sauce.

Sole covered with crumbs

Prep time: 15 minutes **Cooking time:** 20 minutes
Servings: 4

Ingredients

Reduced fat mayonnaise (3 tablespoons)
Mustard seeds (2 tsp.)
Sole fillets (4 -6 oz./170 g each)
Ground mustard (1/2 tsp.)

Pepper (1/2 tsp.)
Grated Parmesan - divided (3 tablespoons)
Green onion (1)
Soft breadcrumbs (1 cup)
Melted butter (2 tsp.)

Directions

Set the air fryer temperature to 375 Fahrenheit / 191 Celsius. Lightly grease a baking sheet.

Finely chop the onion. Combine the mayonnaise, two tablespoons of cheese, mustard seeds and pepper. Spread the mixture on the tops of the fillets.

Place the fish on the baking tray and put it in the fryer basket. Cook them until the fish flakes easily with a fork (3-5 min).

Season the breadcrumbs with the ground mustard, onion, and remaining cheese (1 tablespoon) in a container to mix. Add the butter. Lay it on the fillets, gently tapping to adhere and spray with cooking spray. Cook until golden brown (2-3 min.). Sprinkle with a few more green onions for serving.

Chips and fish

Prep time: 15 minutes **Cooking time:** 25 minutes
Servings: 4

Ingredients

Fillets of catfish or similar fish (2)
Bag of Tortilla Chips (0.88 ounces / 25g)
Parsley (1 tablespoon)

Whole meal bread for breadcrumbs (3 slices)
Pepper and salt (to taste)
Medium beaten egg (1)
Lemon (1 - juice and zest)

Directions

Heat the air fryer to reach 356 Fahrenheit / 180 Celsius.
Cut the fillets into four pieces. Season each with the juice and set them aside for now.

Use a food processor to crumble and mix the tortillas, breadcrumbs, parsley, pepper, and lemon zest.

Cover each piece of fish with the egg mixture. Then dip it into the crumb mixture. Arrange them on a baking sheet and cook until crispy (15 minutes). **Serve:** to taste.

Oregano Clams

Prep time: 15 minutes **Cooking time:** 8-10 minutes
Servings: 4

Ingredients

Shelled clams (2 dozen)
Unseasoned breadcrumbs (1 cup)
Chopped garlic cloves (3)
Grated Parmesan (.25 cup)

Dried oregano (1 tsp.)
Chopped parsley (.25 cup)
Melted butter (4 tbs)
Sea salt (1 cup)
For the pan

Directions

Heat the air fryer to 400 Fahrenheit / 204 Celsius while you prepare the fixings. In a medium bowl, mix the breadcrumbs with the oregano, parsley, Parmesan, and melted butter.

Using a heaping spoonful of the crumb mixture and mix it with the clams. Fill the insert with salt and arrange the clams inside. Air fry for three minutes. Brush with lemon wedges and fresh parsley for serving.

Popcorn Shrimp Tacos with Cabbage Slaw

Prep time: 15 minutes **Cooking time:** 30 minutes
Servings: 4

Ingredients

Coleslaw mix (2 cups)
Lime juice (2 tablespoons)
Salt (1/4tsp.)
Optional jalapeno pepper
(1) Large eggs (2)
Garlic powder (1
tablespoon) Panko
Breadcrumbs (1.5 cups)
Corn tortillas (8 - 6 inches
/ 15 cm - reheated)
Ripe avocado (1 medium)

Chopped fresh cilantro
(1/4 cup)
Honey (2 tablespoons)
2% milk (2 tablespoons)
AP flour (0.5 cup)
Raw Jumbo Shrimp (1
pound / 450g)
Ground cumin (1 tbs)
Cooking spray (if needed)

Directions

Preheat the air fryer unit to 375 Fahrenheit / 191 Celsius. Remove the seeds and chop the jalapeño. Mix the kale salad with cilantro, honey, lime juice, salt, and jalapeno. Set aside. Peel and remove the prawns. Peel and slice the avocado. Use a shallow bowl to beat the eggs with the milk.

Measure and incorporate the flour into a separate shallow baking dish. In a third shallow container, mix the panko with the cumin and garlic powder. Dip the shrimp in the flour, shaking off the excess. Drag the shrimp into the egg mixture and pat to help the coating adhere to the panko mixture.

In batches, set the shrimp in a single layer in the fryer basket greased with a spritz of cooking spray. Air fry until golden brown (2-3 minutes.). Turn and spray with a little spray cooking oil. Cook until the prawns are golden and pink (2-3 minutes). **Serve:** the shrimp in the tortillas with the coleslaw and avocado mix.

Lobster Tails with Green Olives

Prep time: 10 Minutes **Cooking time:** 7 Minutes
Servings: 5

Ingredients

2 pounds (907 g) fresh
lobster tails, cleaned and
halved, in shells
1 cup of green olives

One teaspoon cayenne
pepper
Two garlic cloves, minced
One tbs onion powder

Directions

Warm the air fryer to 390F (199C) and spray the basket with cooking spray. Put all the Ingredients except for the green olives in a sealable plastic bag. Seal the bag and shake until the lobster tails are coated completely.

Arrange the coated lobster tails in the greased basket. Cook in batches in the preheated air fryer for 6 to 7 minutes, shaking the basket halfway through. Remove from the basket and **Serve:** with green olives.

Simple Salmon

Prep time: 10 minutes **Cooking time:** 12 minutes
Servings: 4

Ingredients

4 (6-oz.) salmon fillets

Salt & ground black
pepper

Directions

Flavor the salmon fillets with salt and black pepper evenly.
Choose "Power Button" of Air Fry Oven and set the dial to select the "Air Broil" mode.

Choose the Time button and again turn the dial to set the **Cooking time:**to 12 minutes. Press "Start/Pause" button to start. When the unit beeps to show that it is preheated, open the lid. Arrange the fish fillets over the greased "Wire Rack" and insert in the oven.**Serve:** hot.

Buttered Salmon

Prep time: 10 minutes **Cooking time:** 10 minutes
Servings: 2

Ingredients

2 (6-oz.) salmon fillets
1 tablespoon butter,
melted

Salt and ground black
pepper, as required

Direction

Flavor each salmon fillet with salt and black pepper and then, coat with the butter. Choose "Power Button" of Air Fry Oven and turn the dial to select the "Air Fry" mode.

Choose the Time button and again turn the dial to set the **Cooking time:**to 10 minutes. Now press the Temp button and rotate the dial to set the temperature at 360 degrees F.
Press "Start/Pause" button to start.
When the unit beeps to show that it is preheated, open the lid. Arrange the salmon fillets in greased "Air Fry Basket" and insert in the oven. **Serve:** hot.

Spicy Salmon

Prep time: 10 minutes **Cooking time:** 11 minutes
Servings: 2

Ingredients

1 teaspoon smoked paprika
1 teaspoon onion powder
Salt and ground black pepper, as required
2 teaspoons olive oil
1 teaspoon garlic powder
1 teaspoon cayenne pepper
2 (6-oz.) (11/2-inch thick) salmon fillets

Directions

Add the spices in a bowl and mix well. Drizzle the salmon fillets with oil and then, rub with the spice mixture. Choose "Power Button" of Air Fry Oven and turn the dial to select the "Air Fry" mode.

Choose the Time button and again turn the dial to set the **Cooking time:**to 11 minutes. Now press the Temp button and rotate the dial to set the temperature at 390 degrees F.
Press "Start/Pause" button to start.

When the unit beeps to show that it is preheated, open the lid. Arrange the salmon fillets in greased "Air Fry Basket" and insert in the oven. **Serve:** hot.

Lemony Salmon

Prep time: 10 minutes **Cooking time:** 8 minutes
Servings: 3

Ingredients

11/2 lbs. salmon
1 lemon, cut into slices
Salt and ground black pepper, as required
1/2 teaspoon red chili powder
1 tablespoon fresh dill, chopped

Directions

Season the salmon with chili powder, salt, and black pepper. Choose "Power Button" of Air Fry Oven and turn the dial to select the "Air Fry" mode.

Choose the Time button and again turn the dial to set the **Cooking time:**to 8 minutes. Now press the Temp button and rotate the dial to set the temperature at 375 degrees F.

Press "Start/Pause" button to start. When the unit beeps to show that it is preheated, open the lid. Arrange the salmon fillets in greased "Air Fry Basket" and insert in the oven. Garnish with fresh dill and **Serve:** hot.

Honey Glazed Salmon

Prep time: 10 minutes **Cooking time:** 8 minutes
Servings: 2

Ingredients

2 (6-oz.) salmon fillets
Salt, as required
2 tablespoons honey

Directions

Sprinkle the salmon fillets with salt and then, coat with honey. Choose "Power Button" of Air Fry Oven and turn the dial to select the "Air Fry" mode.

Choose the Time button and again turn the dial to set the **Cooking time:**to 8 minutes. Now press the Temp button and rotate the dial to set the temperature at 355 degrees F.

Press "Start/Pause" button to start. When the unit beeps to show that it is preheated, open the lid. Arrange the salmon fillets in greased "Air Fry Basket" and insert in the oven. **Serve:** hot.

Sweet and Sour Glazed Salmon

Prep time: 12 minutes **Cooking time:** 20 minutes
Servings: 2

Ingredients

1/3 cup soy sauce
3 teaspoons rice wine vinegar
1 teaspoon water
1/3 cup honey
4 (31/2-oz.) salmon fillets

Directions

In a small bowl, merge together the soy sauce, honey, vinegar, and water. In another small bowl, re**Serve:** about half of the mixture.

Add salmon fillets in the remaining mixture and coat well.
Cover the bowl and refrigerate to marinate for about 2 hours.

Choose "Power Button" of Air Fry Oven and turn the dial to select the "Air Fry" mode. Choose the Time button and again turn the dial to set the cooking time to 12 minutes.

Now press the Temp button and rotate the dial to set the temperature at 355 degrees F. Press "Start/Pause" button to start. When the unit beeps to show that it is preheated, open the lid.

Arrange the salmon fillets in greased "Air Fry Basket" and insert in the oven. Flip the salmon fillets once halfway through and coat with the re**Serve:**d marinade after every 3 minutes. **Serve:** hot.

Salmon Parcel

Prep time: 15 minutes **Cooking time:** 23 minutes
Servings: 2

Ingredients

2 (4-oz.) salmon fillets
6 asparagus stalks
1/4 cup champagne

1/4 cup white sauce
1 teaspoon oil
Salt and ground black pepper, as required

Directions

In a bowl, merge together all the Ingredients. Divide the salmon mixture over 2 pieces of foil evenly. Seal the foil around the salmon mixture to form the packet.

Choose "Power Button" of Air Fry Oven and turn the dial to select the "Air Fry" mode. Choose the Time button and again turn the dial to set the **Cooking time:** to 13 minutes.

Now press the Temp button and rotate the dial to set the temperature at 355 degrees F. Press "Start/Pause" button to start.

When the unit beeps to show that it is preheated, open the lid. Arrange the salmon parcels in "Air Fry Basket" and insert in the oven. **Serve:** hot.

Ranch Tilapia

Prep time: 15 minutes **Cooking time:** 13 minutes
Servings: 4

Ingredients

3/4 cup cornflakes, crushed
2 1/2 tbsp vegetable oil
2 eggs

1 (1-oz.) packet dry ranch-style dressing mix

4 (6-oz.) tilapia fillets

Directions

In a shallow bowl, beat the eggs. In another bowl, add the cornflakes, ranch dressing, and oil and mix until a crumbly mixture form.

Dip the fish fillets into egg and then, coat with the breadcrumb's mixture.

Choose "Power Button" of Air Fry Oven and turn the dial to select the "Air Fry" mode. Choose the Time button and again turn the dial to set the cooking time to 13 minutes.

Now press the Temp button and rotate the dial to set the temperature at 356 degrees F. Press "Start/Pause" button to start. When the unit beeps to show that it is preheated, open the lid.

Arrange the tilapia fillets in greased "Air Fry Basket" and insert in the oven. **Serve:** hot.

Salmon with Broccoli

Prep time: 15 minutes **Cooking time:** 12 minutes
Servings: 2

Ingredients

11/2 cups small broccoli florets
Salt and ground black pepper, as required
1 teaspoon light brown sugar
1 scallion, thinly sliced
1/4 teaspoon cornstarch

2 tablespoons vegetable oil, divided
1 tablespoon soy sauce
1 teaspoon rice vinegar
2 (6-oz.) skin-on salmon fillets
1 (1/2-inch) piece fresh ginger, grated

Directions

In a bowl, merge together the broccoli, 1 tablespoon of oil, salt, and black pepper. In another bowl, mix well the ginger, soy sauce, vinegar, sugar, and cornstarch.

Coat the salmon fillets with remaining oil and then with the ginger mixture. Choose "Power Button" of Air Fry Oven and turn the dial to select the "Air Fry" mode.

Choose the Time button and again turn the dial to set the **Cooking time:** to 12 minutes. Now press the Temp button and rotate the dial to set the temperature at 375 degrees F.
Press "Start/Pause" button to start.

When the unit beeps to show that it is preheated, open the lid. Arrange the broccoli florets in greased "Air Fry Basket" and top with the salmon fillets. Insert the basket in the oven. **Serve:** hot.

Sesame-Crusted Tuna Steak

Prep time: 5 minutes **Cooking time:** 8 minutes **Servings:** 2

Ingredients

2 (6-ounce) tuna steaks
1/2 teaspoon garlic powder
2 teaspoons white sesame seeds

1 tablespoon coconut oil, melted

2 teaspoons black sesame seeds

Directions

Brush each tuna steak with coconut oil and sprinkle with garlic powder. In a large bowl, mix sesame seeds and then press each tuna steak into them, covering the steak as completely as possible. Place tuna steaks into the air fryer basket.

Adjust the temperature to 400F and set the timer for 8 minutes. Flip the steaks halfway through the cooking time. Steaks will be well-done at 145F internal temperature. **Serve:** warm.

Salmon with Prawns and Pasta

Prep time: 20 minutes **Cooking time:** 18 minutes
Servings: 4

Ingredients

14 oz. pasta (of your choice) 4 (4-oz.) salmon steaks	2 tablespoons olive oil
1/2 lb. cherry tomatoes, chopped	4 tablespoons pesto, divided
2 tablespoons fresh thyme, chopped	8 large prawns, peeled and deveined
	2 tablespoons fresh lemon juice

Directions

Set a large pan of salted boiling water, add the pasta and cook for about 8-10 minutes or until desired doneness. Meanwhile, in the bottom of a baking pan, spread 1 tablespoon of pesto.

Place salmon steaks and tomatoes over pesto in a single layer and drizzle with the oil. Arrange the prawns on top in a single layer. Drizzle with lemon juice and sprinkle with thyme.

Choose "Power Button" of Air Fry Oven and turn the dial to select the "Air Fry" mode. Choose the Time button and again turn the dial to set the **Cooking time:** to 8 minutes. Now press the Temp button and rotate the dial to set the temperature at 390 degrees F.

Press "Start/Pause" button to start. When the unit beeps to show that it is preheated, open the lid. Arrange the baking pan in "Air Fry Basket" and insert in the oven. Rinse the pasta and transfer into a large bowl. Add the remaining pesto and toss to coat well. Divide the pasta onto serving plate and top with salmon mixture. **Serve:** immediately.

Salmon in Papillote with Orange

Prep time: 20 Minutes **Cooking time:** 30 Minutes
Servings: 4

Ingredients

600g salmon fillet	2 cloves of garlic
4 oranges	Chives to taste
1 lemon	

Directions

Pour the freshly squeezed orange juice, the lemon juice, the zest of the two oranges into a bowl. Add two tablespoons of oil, salt, and garlic. Dip the previously washed salmon fillet and leave it in the marinade for one hour, preferably in the refrigerator Place the steak and part of your marinade on a sheet of foil. Salt and sprinkle with chives and a few slices of orange.

Set to 160C. Simmer for 30 minutes. Open the sheet let it evaporate, and **Serve:** with a nice garnish of fresh orange.

Salmon Burgers

Prep time: 20 minutes **Cooking time:** 22 minutes
Servings: 6

Ingredients

3 large russet potatoes, peeled and cubed	1 egg
3/4 cup frozen vegetables (of your choice), parboiled and drained	6-oz. cooked salmon fillet
Salt and ground black pepper, as required	1 teaspoon fresh dill, chopped
1/4 cup olive oil	2 tbsp parsley, chopped
	1 cup breadcrumbs

Directions

In a pan of the boiling water, cook the potatoes for about 10 minutes. Drain the potatoes well. Set the potatoes into a bowl and mash with a potato masher.

Set aside to cool completely. In another bowl, add the salmon and flake with a fork. Add the cooked potatoes, egg, parboiled vegetables, parsley, dill, salt and black pepper and mix until well combined.

Make 6 equal-sized patties from the mixture. Coat patties with breadcrumb evenly and then drizzle with the oil evenly. Choose "Power Button" of Air Fry Oven and turn the dial to select the "Air Fry" mode.

Choose the Time button and again turn the dial to set the **Cooking time:** to 12 minutes. Now press the Temp button and rotate the dial to set the temperature at 355 degrees F.

Press "Start/Pause" button to start. When the unit beeps to show that it is preheated, open the lid. Arrange the patties in greased "Air Fry Basket" and insert in the oven.
Flip the patties once halfway through. **Serve:** hot.

Shrimp, Zucchini and Cherry Tomato Sauce

Prep time: 10 Minutes **Cooking time:** 30 Minutes
Servings: 4

Ingredients

2 zucchinis	300 shrimp
7 cherry tomatoes	1 clove garlic
Salt to taste	

Directions

Pour the oil, add the garlic clove, and diced zucchini. Cook for 15 minutes at 150C.

Add the shrimp and the pieces of tomato, salt, and spices.
Cook for another 5 to 10 minutes or until the shrimp water evaporates.

Seasoned Catfish

Prep time: 15 minutes **Cooking time:** 23 minutes
Servings: 4

Ingredients

4 (4-oz.) catfish fillets
1 tablespoon olive oil
Salt and ground black
pepper, as required

2 tablespoons Italian
seasoning
1 tablespoon fresh parsley,
chopped

Directions

Rub the fish fillets with seasoning, salt and black pepper generously and then, coat with oil. Choose "Power Button" of Air Fry Oven and turn the dial to select the "Air Fry" mode.
Choose the Time button and again turn the dial to set the **Cooking time:** to 20 minutes.

Now press the Temp button and rotate the dial to set the temperature at 400 degrees F. Press "Start/Pause" button to start.

When the unit beeps to show that it is preheated, open the lid.
Arrange the fish fillets in greased "Air Fry Basket" and insert in the oven. Flip the fish fillets once halfway through. **Serve:** hot with the garnishing of parsley.

Raba's

Prep time: 5 Minutes **Cooking time:** 12 Minutes
Servings: 4

Ingredients

16 abas
Salt, pepper, sweet
paprika

1 egg Breadcrumbs

Directions

Put the rabas boil for 2 minutes. Remove and dry well. Beat the egg and season to taste. You can put salt, pepper, and sweet paprika, place in the egg.

Bread with breadcrumbs. Place in sticks. Place in the fryer for 5 minutes at 1600C. Remove Spray with a cooking spray and place five more minutes at 2000C.

Monkfish with Olives and Capers

Prep time: 20 Minutes **Cooking time:** 45 Minutes
Servings: 4

Ingredients

1 monkfish
5 capers

10 cherry tomatoes
50 g cailletier olives

Directions

Spread aluminum foil inside the basket and place the monkfish clean and skinless. Add chopped tomatoes, olives, capers, oil, and salt.

Set the temperature to 160C. Cook the monkfish for around 40 minutes.

Chinese Cod

Prep time: 15 minutes **Cooking time:** 15 minutes
Servings: 2

Ingredients

2 (7-oz.) cod fillets
1/4 teaspoon sesame oil
1 cup water
5 tablespoons light soy
sauce 1 teaspoon dark soy
sauce
3 tablespoons olive oil
5 ginger slices

Salt and ground black
pepper, as required
5 little squares rock sugar
2 scallions (green part),
sliced 1/4 cup fresh
cilantro, chopped

Directions

Season each cod fillet evenly with salt, and black pepper and drizzle with sesame oil. Set aside at room temperature for about 15-20 minutes.

Dip the fish fillets into egg and then, coat with the breadcrumb's mixture. Choose "Power Button" of Air Fry Oven and turn the dial to select the "Air Fry" mode. Choose the Time button and again turn the dial to set the **Cooking time:** to 12 minutes. Now press the Temp button and rotate the dial to set the temperature at 355 degrees F.

Press "Start/Pause" button to start. When the unit beeps to show that it is preheated, open the lid. Arrange the cod fillets in greased "Air Fry Basket" and insert in the oven. Meanwhile, in a small pan, attach the water and bring it to a boil.

Add the rock sugar and both soy sauces and cook until. sugar is dissolved, stirring continuously. Remove from the heat and set aside. Remove the cod fillets from oven and transfer onto serving plates.

Top each fillet with scallion and cilantro. In a small frying pan, warmth the olive oil over medium heat and sauté the ginger slices for about 2-3 minutes. Remove the frying pan from heat and discard the ginger slices. Carefully, pour the hot oil evenly over cod fillets. Top with the sauce mixture and **Serve:**.

Cod Parcel

Prep time: 20 minutes **Cooking time:** 15 minutes
Servings: 2

Ingredients

2 tablespoons butter, melted
1/2 teaspoon dried tarragon
Salt and ground black pepper, as required
1/2 cup red bell peppers,
2 (5-oz.) frozen cod fillets, thawed

1 tablespoon fresh lemon juice

1/2 cup carrots, peeled and julienned
1/2 cup fennel bulbs, julienned
1 tablespoon olive oil

Directions

In a large bowl, merge together the butter, lemon juice, tarragon, salt, and black pepper. Add the bell pepper, carrot, and fennel bulb and generously coat with
the mixture. Arrange 2 large parchment squares onto a smooth surface.

Coat the cod fillets with oil and then, sprinkle evenly with salt and black pepper. Arrange 1 cod fillet onto each parchment square and top each evenly with the vegetables.

Top with any remaining sauce from the bowl. Fold the parchment paper and crimp the sides to secure fish and vegetables. Choose "Power Button" of Air Fry Oven and turn the dial to select the "Air Fry" mode.

Choose the Time button and again turn the dial to set the **Cooking time:**to 15 minutes. Now press the Temp button and rotate the dial to set the temperature at 350 degrees F. Press "Start/Pause" button to start.

When the unit beeps to show that it is preheated, open the lid. Arrange the cod parcels in "Air Fry Basket" and insert in the oven. **Serve:** hot.

Salted Marinated Salmon

Prep time: 10 Minutes **Cooking time:** 30 Minutes
Servings: 2

Ingredients

500g salmon fillet

1 kg of coarse salt

Directions

Place the baking paper on the basket and the salmon on top (skin side up) covered with coarse salt.

Set the air fryer to 150C. Cook everything for 25 to 30 minutes. At the end of cooking, remove the salt from the fish and **Serve:** with a drizzle of oil.

Cod Burgers

Prep time: 15 minutes **Cooking time:** 7 minutes
Servings: 6

Ingredients

1/2 lb. cod fillets
1/2 egg
1/2 teaspoon red chili paste Salt, to taste
3 tablespoons coconut, grated and divided

1/2 teaspoon fresh lime zest, grated finely
1/2 tablespoon fresh lime juice
1 tablespoon fresh parsley, chopped
1 small scallion, chopped

Directions

In a food processor, add cod filets, lime zest, egg, chili paste, salt and lime juice and pulse until smooth. Transfer the cod mixture into a bowl.

Add 1 1/2 tablespoons coconut, scallion and parsley and mix until well combined. Make 6 equal-sized patties from the mixture.

In a shallow dish, place the remaining coconut. Coat the patties in coconut evenly. Choose "Power Button" of Air Fry Oven and turn the dial to select the "Air Fry" mode.

Choose the Time button and again turn the dial to set the **Cooking time:**to 7 minutes. Now press the Temp button and rotate the dial to set the temperature at 375 degrees F.

Press "Start/Pause" button to start. When the unit beeps to show that it is preheated, open the lid. Arrange the patties in greased "Air Fry Basket" and insert in the oven. **Serve:** hot.

Stuffed Cuttlefish

Prep time: 20 Minutes **Cooking time:** 30 Minutes
Servings: 4

Ingredients

small cuttlefish
Garlic to taste
1 egg

50g of breadcrumbs
Parsley to taste

Directions

Clean the cuttlefish, cut, and separate the tentacles. In a blender, pour the breadcrumbs, the parsley (without the branches), the egg, the salt, a drizzle of olive oil, and the sepia tentacles. Blend until you get a dense mixture. Fill the sepia with the mixture obtained. Place the cuttlefish in the bowl.

Spicy Catfish

Prep time: 15 minutes **Cooking time:** 13 minutes
Servings: 2

Ingredients

2 tablespoons almond flour
1 teaspoon red chili powder
2 (6-oz.) catfish fillets
1/2 teaspoon paprika

1/2 teaspoon garlic powder Salt, as required

1 tablespoon olive oil

Directions

In a bowl, merge together the flour, paprika, garlic powder and salt. Add the catfish fillets and coat with the mixture evenly. Now, coat each fillet with oil. Choose "Power Button" of Air Fry Oven and turn the dial to select the "Air Fry" mode.

Choose the Time button and again turn the dial to set the **Cooking time:**to 13 minutes. Now press the Temp button and rotate the dial to set the temperature at 400 degrees F. Press "Start/Pause" button to start. When the unit beeps to show that it is preheated, open the lid.

Arrange the fish fillets in greased "Air Fry Basket" and insert in the oven. Flip the fish fillets once halfway through. **Serve:** hot.

Fried Catfish with Fish Fry

Prep time: 5 Minutes **Cooking time:** 13 Minutes
Servings: 4

Ingredients

4 catfish fillets rinsed and patted dry
1 tablespoon olive oil

1 tablespoon chopped parsley
1/4 cup seasoned fish fry

Directions

Warm the air fryer to 400F (205C).
Put the fillets and seasoned fish fry in a Ziploc bag. Cover the bag and shake well until the fish is nicely coated. Brush both sides of each piece of fish with olive oil. Put the fillets in the air fryer basket.

Cook in the preheated air fryer for 13 minutes. Flip the fillets once during cooking or until the fish is cooked through. Remove from the basket and garnish with chopped parsley.

Crispy Catfish

Prep time: 15 minutes **Cooking time:** 15 minutes
Servings: 5

Ingredients

5 (6-oz.) catfish fillets
1 cup milk
1/2 cup cornmeal
2 tbs dried parsley flakes
1/4 ybs cayenne pepper

Salt and ground black pepper, as required

2 tbs fresh lemon juice
1/2 cup yellow mustard
1/4 cup all-purpose flour
1/4 tbs red chili powder
1/4 teaspoon onion powder
Olive oil cooking spray
1/4 teaspoon garlic powder

Directions

In a large bowl, place the catfish, milk, and lemon juice and refrigerate for about 15 minutes. In a shallow bowl, add the mustard. In another bowl, mix together the cornmeal, flour, parsley flakes, and spices. Remove the catfish fillets from milk mixture and with paper towels, pat them dry. Coat each fish fillet with mustard and then, roll into cornmeal mixture. Then, spray each fillet with the cooking spray.

Choose "Power Button" of Air Fry Oven and turn the dial to select the "Air Fry" mode. Choose the Time button and again turn the dial to set the **Cooking time:**to 15 minutes. Now press the Temp button and rotate the dial to set the temperature at 400 degrees F.

Press "Start/Pause" button to start. When the unit beeps to show that it is preheated, open the lid. Arrange the catfish fillets in greased "Air Fry Basket" and insert in the oven. After 10 minutes of cooking, flip the fillets and spray with the cooking spray. **Serve:** hot.

Salmon with Pistachio Bark

Prep time: 20 Minutes **Cooking time:** 30 Minutes
Servings: 4

Ingredients

600 g salmon fillet
50g pistachios

Salt to taste

Directions

Place the parchment paper on the bottom of the basket and place the salmon fillet in it (it can be cooked whole or already divided into four portions). Cut the pistachios into thick pieces; grease the top of the fish, salt (little because the pistachios are already salted), and cover everything with the pistachios. Set the air fryer to 180C and simmer for 25 minutes.

Cornmeal Coated Catfish

Prep time: 15 minutes **Cooking time:** 14 minutes
Servings: 4

Ingredients

2 tablespoons cornmeal

1/2 tbs garlic powder Salt
1 tablespoon olive oil

2 teaspoons Cajun seasoning
2 (6-oz.) catfish fillets
1/2 teaspoon paprika

Directions

In a bowl, mix together the cornmeal, Cajun seasoning, paprika, garlic powder, and salt. Add the catfish fillets and coat with the mixture. Now, coat each fillet with oil.

Choose "Power Button" of Air Fry Oven and turn the dial to select the "Air Fry" mode. Choose the Time button and again turn the dial to set the cooking time to 14 minutes. Now press the Temp button and rotate the dial to set the temperature at 400 degrees F.

Press "Start/Pause" button to start. When the unit beeps to show that it is preheated, open the lid. Arrange the catfish fillets in greased "Air Fry Basket" and insert in the oven. After 10 minutes of cooking, flip the fillets and spray with the cooking spray. **Serve:** hot

Breaded Flounder

Prep time: 15 minutes **Cooking time:** 12 minutes
Servings: 3

Ingredients

1 egg
3 (6-oz.) flounder fillets
1/4 cup vegetable oil

1 cup dry breadcrumbs
1 lemon, sliced

Directions

In a bowl, beat the egg In another bowl, attach the breadcrumbs and oil and merge until crumbly mixture is formed. Dip flounder fillets into the beaten egg and then, coat with the breadcrumb mixture.

Choose "Power Button" of Air Fry Oven and turn the dial to select the "Air Fry" mode. Choose the Time button and again turn the dial to set the **Cooking time:**to 12 minutes. Now press the Temp button and rotate the dial to set the temperature at 356 degrees F. Press "Start/Pause" button to start.

When the unit beeps to show that it is preheated, open the lid. Arrange the flounder fillets in greased "Air Fry Basket" and insert in the oven. Season with the lemon slices and **Serve:** hot.

Roasted Salmon with Vegetables

Prep time: 15 Minutes **Cooking time:** 14 Minutes
Servings: 2

Ingredients

1 large carrot, peeled and sliced

2 (5-ounce / 142-g) salmon fillets

1 small onion, thinly sliced
1/4 cup low-fat sour cream
1 fennel bulb, thinly sliced

Directions

Preheat the air fryer to 400F (205C).
In a bowl, mix the carrot, fennel bulb, and onion. Toss well.
Transfer the vegetable mixture to a 6-inch metal pan, and then put the pan in the air fryer basket.

Roast in the preheated air fryer for 4 minutes, or until the vegetables are fork-tender. Remove the pan from the air fryer. Add the sour cream to the pan and season with ground pepper, and then spread the salmon fillets on top.

Set the pan to the air fryer and roast for an additional 10 minutes or until the fish flakes easily when tested with a fork.
Let the salmon and vegetables cool for 5 minutes before serving.

Quick Coconut Shrimp

Prep time: 10 Minutes **Cooking time:** 8 Minutes
Servings: 4

Ingredients

1/4 cup all-purpose flour
1 egg
1 pound (454 g) raw shrimp, peeled, deveined, and patted dry

1/3 cup shredded unsweetened coconut
1/4 cup panko bread crumbs

Directions

Heat the air fryer to 400F (20°C). On a plate, place the flour. In a small bowl, toss the egg until frothy.

In a separate bowl, mix the coconut, bread crumbs, salt, and pepper. Dredge the shrimp in the flour, shake off any excess, dip them in the egg, and finally coat them in the coconut-bread mixture.

Set the air fryer basket with cooking spray. Put the breaded shrimp in the basket and spray with cooking spray.

Cook in the warmed air fryer for 8 minutes, flipping the shrimp once during cooking, or until the shrimp are opaque and crisp. Remove from the basket and **Serve:** on a plate.

Lemon-Pepper Tilapia Fillets

Prep time: 5 Minutes **Cooking time:** 15 Minutes
Servings: 4

Ingredients
4 tilapia fillets
1 teaspoon dried basil
1 teaspoon paprika

1 teaspoon garlic powder
Lemon-pepper seasoning,
to taste

Directions

Heat the air fryer to 400F (205C). Add the olive oil, garlic powder, paprika, basil, lemon-pepper seasoning, fillets to a large bowl, and toss well to coat the fillets thoroughly.

Transfer the coated fillets to the air fryer basket. Cook in the warmed air fryer for 8 minutes. Flip the fillets and cook for 7 minutes more until the fish flakes easily with a fork. Divide the fillets among four serving plates and **Serve:** hot.

Blackened Shrimp with Lemon Juice

Prep time: 5 Minutes **Cooking time:** 10 Minutes
Servings: 4

Ingredients
1 pound (454 g) raw
shrimp, peeled, deveined,
and patted dry

1/2 tbs cayenne pepper
1/2 teaspoon dried
oregano
Juice of 1/2 lemon
One teaspoon paprika

Directions

Heat the air fryer to 400F (205C). Put the shrimp in a sealable plastic bag. Add the paprika, cayenne pepper, oregano, lemon juice, salt, and pepper to the shrimp. Lid the bag and shake to coat the shrimp with the spices evenly.

Set the air fryer basket with cooking spray. Arrange the shrimp in the basket. Cook in the warmed air fryer for 7 minutes, shaking the basket once during cooking, or until the shrimp is blackened. Let the shrimp cool for 5 minutes and **Serve:** warm.

Air-Fried Sardines

Prep time: 10 Minutes **Cooking time:** 12 Minutes
Servings: 4

Ingredients
11/2 pounds (680 g)
sardines, rinsed and patted
dry

1 tablespoon Italian
seasoning mix
1 tablespoon lemon juice

Directions

Warm the air fryer to 350F (180C). In a large bowl, merge the sardines with olive oil, lemon juice, Italian seasoning mix, soy sauce, salt, and pepper. Let the sardines marinate for 30 minutes. Put the marinated sardines in the air fryer basket and air fry for about 12 minutes until flaky, flipping the fish halfway through. Transfer to a plate and **Serve:** hot.

Pecan-Crusted Catfish Fillets

Prep time: 5 Minutes **Cooking time:** 12 Minutes
Servings: 4

Ingredients
1/2 cup pecan meal
Pecan halves, for garnish
(optional)

4 (4-ounce / 113-g) catfish
fillets, rinsed and patted
dry Fresh oregano, for
garnish

Directions

Warm the air fryer to 375F (190C). Grease the air fryer basket with half of the avocado oil and set aside. Stir together the pecan meal, salt, and pepper in a large bowl. Roll the fillets with the mixture, pressing, so the fish is well coated.

Brush the fillets with the remaining avocado oil and transfer to the air fryer basket. Cook in the preheated air fryer for 12 minutes, flipping the fillets halfway through, or until the fish flakes easily with a fork. Remove from the basket to a large plate. Sprinkle the oregano and pecan halves on top for garnish, if desired.

Fish Fillets with Parmesan Cheese

Prep time: 5 Minutes **Cooking time:** 10 to 12 Minutes
Servings: 4

Ingredients

1 cup Parmesan cheese, grated
4 white fish fillets
1 teaspoon garlic powder
1/2 tbsp shallot powder
1 egg whisked

Directions

Preheat the air fryer to 370F (188C). In a shallow dish, put the Parmesan cheese. Mix the whisked egg, garlic powder, and shallot powder in a bowl, and stir to combine. On a clean surface, season the fillets generously with salt and pepper.

Dredge the fillets into the egg mixture, and then roll over the cheese until thickly coated. Assemble the fillets in the air fryer basket and air fry until golden brown, about 10 to 12 minutes. Let the fish fillets cool for 5 minutes before serving.

Garlicky Shrimp

Prep time: 5 Minutes **Cooking time:** 3 to 4 Minutes
Servings: 4

Ingredients

11/2 pounds (680 g) shrimp, shelled and deveined
3 cloves garlic, minced
1/2 tablespoon fresh basil leaves, chopped
1 teaspoon smoked cayenne pepper
1/2 tbsp ginger freshly grated

Directions

Warm the air fryer to 390F (199C). Merge all the Ingredients in a large bowl and toss until well incorporated. Let the shrimp sit for 30 minutes.

Put it in the basket and air fry for 3 to 4 minutes, or until the shrimp are opaque. **Serve:** hot.

Tuna Steaks with Red Onions

Prep time: 10 Minutes **Cooking time:** 10 Minutes
Servings: 4

Ingredients

4 tuna steaks
1 teaspoon dried rosemary
1 tbs cayenne pepper
1/2 pound (227 g) red onions
1 lemon, sliced

Directions

Warm the air fryer to 400F (205C) and spray the basket with cooking spray. Place the tuna steaks in the basket and scatter the onions all over. Sprinkle with the olive oil and sprinkle with rosemary, cayenne pepper, salt, and black pepper.

Bake in batches in the preheated air fryer for 10 minutes until cooked through. Garnish with the lemon slices and **Serve:** warm.

Parmesan Haddock Fillets

Prep time: 5 Minutes **Cooking time:** 11 to 13 Minutes
Servings: 2

Ingredients

1/2 cup Parmesan cheese, freshly grated
1/4 tbs cayenne pepper
1 egg
1 tbs dried parsley Flake
2 haddock fillets patted dry

Directions

Warm the air fryer to 360F (182C). Stir together the Parmesan cheese and parsley flakes in a shallow dish. Beat the egg with the cayenne pepper, sea salt, and pepper in a bowl.

Dunk the haddock fillets into the egg, and then roll over the Parmesan mixture until fully coated on both sides. Handover the fillets to the air fryer basket and drizzle with the olive oil Cook in the preheated air fryer for 11 to 13 minutes, or until the flesh is opaque.

Shrimp Skewers with Vermouth

Prep time: 10 Minutes **Cooking time:** 5 Minutes
Servings: 4

Ingredients

11/2 pounds (680 g) shrimp	2 cloves garlic, crushed
1 lemon, cut into wedges	1/4 cup vermouth

Directions

Warm the air fryer to 400F (205C).
Toss the shrimp with the vermouth, olive oil, garlic, salt, and pepper in a bowl and then set it in the fridge to marinate for 1 hour.

Remove the shrimp from the refrigerator and discard the marinade. Skewer the shrimp by piercing through the center and transfer to the basket.

Cook in the warmed air fryer for 5 minutes, flipping the shrimp halfway through. Relish with the lemon wedges and **Serve:** hot.

Fish Sticks

Prep time: 15 minutes **Cooking time:** 12 minutes
Servings: 4

Ingredients

4 (4 ounces) fillets of frozen cod or tilapia thawed	1/4 cup of whole wheat flour
1 tsp. of garlic powder	1 tsp. of salt plus more for sprinkling after air frying
1/2 tsp. of pepper	
2 large eggs	1 large lemon juiced, plus more for serving after air frying
1 cup of panko breadcrumbs	
2 tsp. of old bay	1 tsp. of paprika
	Tarter sauce (recommended for serving)

Directions

Firstly, on your Air-fryer. Then preheat at 400F and set the timer to 10 to 12 minutes.

Then press "Start", the Air-fryer will notify at you when it's finished preheating.
Once warmth set the basket with cooking spray and place in approximately 6 pieces of fish and make sure they aren't touching.

After 5 minutes, carefully flip each piece of fish, and then continue cooking for the remaining 5 minutes.

Remove from Air-fryer, sprinkle with more salt (if necessary) and a generous squeeze of lemon. Repeat with remaining fish. **Serve:** and enjoy with tarter sauce!

Zesty Ranch Fish Fillets

Prep time: 5 minutes **Cooking time:** 12 minutes
Servings: 2 - 4

Ingredients

3/4 cup of bread crumbs or panko	130g packet of dry ranch-style dressing mix
2 eggs beaten	4 tilapia salmon or other fish fillets
2 1/2 tbsp. of vegetable oil	
	Lemon wedges to garnish

Directions

Preheat your Air-fryer at 180C.Merge the panko/breadcrumbs and the ranch dressing mix together. Attach in the oil and keep stirring until the mixture becomes loose and crumbly.

After that, soak the fish fillets into the egg, letting the excess drip off, dip the fish fillets into the crumb mixture, making sure they are coated evenly and thoroughly. Now place fish fillets into your Air-fryer carefully and cook for 12 to 13 minutes, depending on the thickness of the fillets. Remove and **Serve:** immediately. Press the lemon wedges over the fish if desired.

Fish and Chips

Prep time: 5 minutes **Cooking time:** 10 minutes
Servings: 2 - 4

Ingredients

1 lb. of cod fillet cut into strips	2 tsp. paprika
	1/2 cup of all-purpose flour
1/2 tsp. of garlic powder	1/4 tsp. of black pepper
1/4 tsp. of salt	Large egg beaten
2 cups of panko breadcrumbs Tartar sauce for serving	Lemon wedges for serving

Directions

Mix-up flour with the paprika, garlic powder and salt in a small bowl. Set the egg in another bowl and the panko breadcrumbs in a third bowl.

Set the fish dry using a paper towel. After that, dredge the fish in the flour mixture, then the egg and finally the panko breadcrumbs.

Press it down lightly until the crumbs sticks. Then spray both sides with oil. Now Air-fry at 400F for about for 10 to 12 minutes, turning halfway through cooking until it's crispy and lightly golden. **Serve:** immediately with fries and tartar sauce, and enjoy!

Crispy Fish Tacos with Slaw

Prep time: 15 minutes **Cooking time:** 18 minutes
Servings: 2 - 4

Ingredients

1 serving nonstick of cooking spray
4 cups of cabbage slaw mix
1 tbsp. of olive oil
1/4 cup of all-purpose flour
1/4 tsp. of ground black pepper
1/4 tsp. of ground cayenne pepper
1 pound of cod fillets, cut into bite-sized pieces
1 tbsp. of chopped fresh jalapeno pepper
1 tbsp. of lime juice
1 tbsp. of apple cider vinegar
1/4 cup of yellow cornmeal
2 tbsp. of taco seasoning mix
8 (6 inch) corn tortillas
1/2 tsp. of salt

Directions

Preheat an air fryer to 400 F and spray the basket of the Air-fryer with cooking spray. Merge cabbage slaw, jalapeno pepper, lime juice, olive oil, vinegar, salt, pepper, and cayenne pepper in a large bowl. Then mix until evenly combined and set it aside.

Merge together flour, cornmeal, and taco seasoning in a separate bowl. Attach fish pieces and toss until evenly coated, discarding any remaining seasoning mix. Set in the prepared Air-fryer basket and mist lightly with cooking spray.

Cook fish in the preheated air fryer and shake the basket, then cook until fish is crispy and flakes easily with a fork, for about 5 minutes more.

Crumbed Fish

Preparation 10 minutes **Cooking time:** 12 minutes
Servings: 2 - 4

Ingredients

1 cup of dry bread crumbs
1/4 cup of vegetable oil
1 sliced lemon
4 each of flounder fillets
1 egg, beaten

Directions

Preheat your Air-fryer at 350F in a bowl, mix bread crumbs and oil together and stir until mixture. Soak fish fillets into the egg; shake off any excess. Dip fillets into the

bread crumb mixture; coat evenly and fully. Set coated fillets gently in the preheated air fryer and cook for about 12 minutes until fish flakes easily with a fork. Garnish with lemon slices. **Serve:** and enjoy!

Healthy White Fish with Garlic and Lemon

Prep time: 5 minutes **Cooking time:** 12 minutes
Servings: 2 - 4

Ingredients

12 oz. of tilapia filets or 2 filets (6 oz. each)
1/2 tsp. of garlic powder (2.5 ml)
Kosher salt or sea salt , to taste
Fresh chopped parsley
1/2 tsp. of lemon pepper seasoning (2.5 ml)
1/2 tsp. of onion powder (optional)
Lemon wedges
Fresh cracked black pepper , to taste

Directions

Pre-heat your Air-fryer at 360F for 5 minutes. Wash and pat dry the fish filets. Cover or coat with olive oil spray and season with garlic powder,

lemon pepper, and/or onion powder, salt and pepper. Lay perforated Air-fryer baking paper inside base of air fryer and lightly spray the paper. If you are not using a liner, spray enough olive oil spray at the base of the Air-fryer basket to make sure fish does not stick.

Set the fish on top of the paper and add a few lemon wedges next to fish. Line with Parchment Paper.

After that, Air-Fry at 360F for about 6 to12 minutes. Sprinkle with chopped parsley and **Serve:** warm with the toasted lemon wedges.

Southern Fried Catfish Nuggets

Prep time: 5 minutes **Cooking time:** 17 minutes
Servings: 2

Ingredients

2 pounds of catfish nuggets 1/4 cup of oil
10 ounces box of fish fry mix

Directions

Firstly, wash fish and set aside. Whisk half the box of fish fry mix into a large Ziploc bag.

Attach the Catfish Nuggets into the bag with the fish fry mix. Secure the bag and shake well to coat. Using the tongs, detach the nuggets one at a time, shaking off excess batter. Attach the catfish nuggets to the basket of the Air-fryer. Check the Directions of your Air-fryer for filling the basket in case it requires no over filling of basket.

Toss the oil into a small bowl, dip your basting brush into the oil and baste a small amount of oil onto the top of each catfish nugget. Set your Air-fryer on to 380F and set timer for 17 minutes. Start checking at about 12 minutes.
Detach from basket when done and drain on paper toweling. Attach the next batch to the basket and repeat. **Serve:** when ready and enjoy!

Beer Battered Fish

Prep time: 10 minutes **Cooking time:** 12 minutes
Servings: 5

Ingredients

1 cup of all-purpose flour	1/2 tsp. of baking soda 6
2 tbsp. of cornstarch	oz. of beer
1 egg beaten	3/4 cup of all flour
1 tsp. of salt	1/4 tsp. of ground black
1/2 tsp. of paprika	pepper
11/2 lb. of cod cut into 4	Vegetable oil
or 5 pieces	Pinch of cayenne pepper

Directions

Merge the 1 cup of flour, cornstarch and baking soda in a large bowl and add the beer and egg, stir until it's smooth. Seal the bowl of batter with plastic wrap and refrigerate for at least 20 minutes. Combine the 3/4 cup of flour, paprika, salt, black pepper and cayenne pepper in a shallow dredging pan.

Set the cod fish fillets dry with a paper towel. Now dip the fish into the batter, coating all sides and allow the excess batter to drip off and then coat each fillet with the seasoned flour.

Whisk any leftover flour on the fish fillets and pat gently to adhere the flour to the batter. After that, pre-heat your air fryer at 390F. Air-fry for 12 minutes at 390F. **Serve:** with lemon wedges, malt vinegar and tartar sauce.

Breaded Sea Scallops

Prep time: 10 minutes **Cooking time:** 5 minutes
Servings: 2 - 4

Ingredients

1/2 cup of finely crushed	1/2 tsp. of seafood
buttery crackers	seasoning
1 lb. of sea scallops, patted	1 serving cooking spray
dry	1/2 tsp. of garlic powder
2 tbsp. of butter, melted	

Directions

Preheat the Air-fryer to 390F. Merge cracker crumbs, garlic powder, and seafood seasoning together in a bowl.
Place dissolved butter in a second bowl. Then start to dip each scallop in the melted butter and roll in the breading until it's completely coated.

Bring on a plate and repeat with the remaining scallops. Set the air fryer basket with cooking spray. Set scallops in the prepared basket so that they don't touching each other. You may require working in batches. Cook in the preheated air-fryer. Turn scallops over gently with a small spatula and cook.

Crab Cakes

Prep time: 15 minutes **Cooking time:** 10 minutes
Servings: 4 - 5

Ingredients

1 large egg, beaten	2 tbsp. of mayonnaise
1 tsp. of Worcestershire	1 tsp. of seafood
sauce	seasoning 1/2 tsp. of hot
	pepper sauce
2 tbsp. of finely chopped	1 lb. of lump crabmeat,
green onion	drained and picked over
1 pinch of salt and black	3 tbsp. of milk
pepper to taste	4 wedges lemon
11 crackers saltine	1 serving olive oil cooking
crackers, crushed	spray
1 tsp. of baking powder	1 tsp. of Dijon mustard

Directions

Mix-up egg, mayonnaise, Worcestershire sauce, mustard, seafood seasoning, and hot pepper sauce in a small mixing bowl and stir in green onion and set aside.

Set crab meat in a medium bowl and break up with a fork. Then add milk, salt, and pepper and toss to coat. Attach crushed saltines and baking powder and toss lightly to combine. Attach to the egg mixture, stirring gently and being careful not to break apart the crab lumps.
Spoon crab with a 1/3-cup measure and form into 8 patties. Set patties on a plate, cover, and refrigerate for about 1 hour or until its firm.

Preheat your Air-fryer at 400F then spray crab cakes on both sides with cooking spray and place them in the air fryer basket. Cook and then gently turn the cakes over, and cook 5 minutes longer until it turns crispy brown. **Serve:** immediately!

Lemon Pepper Shrimp

Prep time: 5 minutes **Cooking time:** 10 minutes
Servings: 2 -4

Ingredients

1 tbsp. of olive oil	1 tsp. of lemon pepper
1 lemon, juiced	1/4 tsp. of paprika
1/4 tsp. of garlic powder	12 oz. of uncooked
	medium shrimp, peeled
	and deveined 1 Lemon,
	sliced

Directions

Preheat your Air-fryer to 400F. Then mix olive oil, lemon juice, lemon pepper, paprika, and garlic powder in a bowl. Add shrimp and toss until it's coated.

Set shrimp in the air fryer and cook until it turns pink and firm for about 6 to 10 minutes. **Serve:** with lemon slices.

Lobster Tails with Lemon-Garlic Butter

Prep time: 10 minutes **Cooking time:** 10 minutes
Servings: 2 - 4

Ingredients

4 oz. of lobster tails
1 clove of garlic, grated
4 tbsp. of butter
2 wedges lemon
1 tsp. of lemon zest
1 pinch of salt and ground pepper
1 tsp. of chopped fresh parsley

Directions

Butterfly lobster tails by cutting lengthwise through the centers of the hard top shells and meat with kitchen shears.

Cut the bottoms of the shells. Scatter the tail halves apart.
Then place tails in the Air-fryer basket with lobster meat facing up.
Dissolve butter in a small saucepan over medium heat. Attach lemon zest and garlic and heat until garlic is tender for about 30 seconds. Set 2 tablespoons of butter mixture to a small bowl and brush onto lobster tails, discard any remaining brushed butter to avoid contamination from uncooked lobster.

Flor lobster with salt and pepper then cook for 5 to 7 minutes in an air fryer at 380F until lobster meat is opaque. Spoon re**Serve:**d butter from the saucepan over lobster meat. Set with parsley and **Serve:** with lemon wedges.

Cajun Salmon

Prep time: 10 minutes **Cooking time:** 10 minutes
Servings: 2

Ingredients

6 oz. of skin-on salmon fillets
1 tsp. of brown sugar
1 tbsp. of Cajun seasoning
1 serving cooking spray

Directions

Preheat the Air-fryer to 390F. Wash and dry salmon fillets with a paper towel. Mist fillets with cooking spray and merge Cajun seasoning and brown sugar in a small bowl.
Sprinkle onto a plate and press flesh sides of fillets into the seasoning mixture.

Spray the basket of the Air-fryer with cooking spray and place salmon fillets skin-side down. Mist salmon again lightly with cooking spray. Cook for 8 minutes then remove from Air-fryer and let rest for 2 minutes before serving.**Serve:** and enjoy!

Golden Cod with Mayo

Prep time: 10 minutes **Cooking time:** 9 minutes
Servings: 4

Ingredients

1 pound (454 g) cod fillets
2 tbsp Old Bay seasoning
1/2 teaspoon paprika
1 large egg, beaten
1/4 cup sugar-free mayonnaise (homemade, here, or store-bought)
Elevated Tartar Sauce, for serving
11/2 cups finely ground blanched almond flour
Sea salt, freshly ground pepper, to taste
Avocado oil spray

Directions

Cut the fish into 3/4-inch-wide strips. In a bowl, merge together the almond flour, Old Bay seasoning, paprika, and salt and pepper to taste. In another shallow bowl, whisk together the mayonnaise and egg. Dip the cod strips in the egg mixture, then the almond flour, gently pressing with your fingers to help adhere the coating.

Place the coated fish on a parchment paper–lined baking sheet and freeze for 30 minutes. Spray the air fryer basket with oil. Set the air fryer to 400F (205C). Place the fish in the basket in a single layer, and spray each piece with oil.
Cook for 5 minutes. Flip and spray with more oil.
Cook for 4 minutes more, until the internal temperature reaches 140F (60C). **Serve:** with the tartar sauce.

Crisp Catfish

Prep time: 10 minutes **Cooking time:** 12 minutes
Servings: 4

Ingredients

1- pound (907-g) catfish fillet
1 teaspoon salt
2 eggs, beaten
1/2 cup almond flour
1 teaspoon avocado oil

Directions

Sprinkle the catfish fillet with salt and dip in the eggs. Then coat the fish in the almond flour and put in the air fryer basket. Sprinkle the fish with avocado oil. Cook the fish for 6 minutes per side at 380F (193C).

Cod Fillet with Turmeric

Prep time: 10 minutes **Cooking time:** 7 minutes
Servings: 2

Ingredients

12 ounces (340 g) cod fillet	1 tablespoon coconut oil, melted
1 teaspoon ground turmeric	
1/2 teaspoon salt	1 teaspoon chili flakes

Directions

Mix coconut oil with ground turmeric, chili flakes, and salt. Then mix cod fillet with ground turmeric and put in the air fryer basket. Cook the cod at 385F (196C) for 7 minutes.

Lemon Cod

Prep time: 20 minutes **Cooking time:** 10 minutes
Servings: 2

Ingredients

2 medium-sized cod fillets	1/2 tablespoon fresh lemon juice
1 1/2 tablespoons olive oil	
1/2 tablespoon whole-grain mustard	1/2 cup coconut flour
	Sea salt and ground pepper
2 eggs	

Directions

Set your Air Fryer to cook at 355F (181C). Thoroughly combine olive oil and coconut flour in a shallow bowl.
In another shallow bowl, whisk the egg. Drizzle each cod fillet with lemon juice and spread with mustard. Then, sprinkle each fillet with salt and ground black pepper.

Dip each fish fillet into the whisked egg; now, roll it in the olive oil mixture. Set in a single layer in the Air Fryer cooking basket. Cook for 10 minutes, working in batches, turning once or twice. **Serve:**.

Crab Bun

Prep time: 15 minutes **Cooking time:** 20 minutes
Servings: 2

Ingredients

5 ounces (142 g) crab meat, chopped	2 tablespoons coconut flour 1/4 teaspoon baking powder
2 eggs, beaten	
1/2 teaspoon ground black pepper	1 tablespoon coconut oil, softened
	1/2 teaspoon coconut aminos

Directions

In the mixing bowl, mix crab meat with eggs, coconut flour, baking powder, coconut aminos, ground black pepper, and coconut oil.

Knead the smooth dough and cut it into pieces. Make the buns from the crab mixture and put them in the air fryer basket. Cook the crab buns at 365F (185C) for 20 minutes.

Lemony Snapper

Prep time: 5 minutes **Cooking time:** 7 minutes
Servings: 4

Ingredients

1 pound (454 g) snapper, grouper, or salmon fillets	1 tablespoon avocado oil
1/4 cup sugar-free mayonnaise (homemade, here, or store-bought)	1/4 cup sour cream
	1 tablespoon freshly squeezed lemon juice
2 tablespoons fresh dill, chopped,	Sea salt, freshly ground pepper
1/2 teaspoon grated lemon zest	

Directions

Set the fish dry with paper towels and season well with salt and pepper. Brush with the avocado oil.
Set the air fryer to 400F (205C). Place the fillets in the air fryer basket and cook for 1 minute.

Lower the air fryer temperature to 325F and continue cooking for 5 minutes. Turn over the fish and cook until an instant-read thermometer reads 145F (63C). (If using salmon, cook it to 125F (52C) for medium-rare.)

While the fish is cooking, make the sauce by combining the sour cream, mayonnaise, dill, lemon juice, and lemon zest in a medium bowl. Flavor with salt and pepper and stir until combined. Refrigerate until ready to **Serve:**.
Serve: the fish with the sauce, garnished with the remaining dill.

Salmon Patties

Prep time: 10 minutes **Cooking time:** 8 minutes
Servings: 2

Ingredients

2 (5-ounce) pouches cooked pink salmon

2 tablespoons full-fat mayonnaise

1/4 cup ground pork rinds
1 large egg
1 teaspoon chili powder
2 teaspoons sriracha

Directions

Merge all Ingredients in a bowl and form into four patties. Place patties into the air fryer basket. Adjust the temperature to 400F and set the timer for 8 minutes.

Carefully flip each patty halfway through the cooking time. Patties will be crispy on the outside when fully cooked.

Firecracker Shrimp

Prep time: 10 minutes **Cooking time:** 7 minutes
Servings: 4

Ingredients

1 pound medium shelled and deveined shrimp
1/2 tbsp Old Bay seasoning
2 tablespoons sriracha
1/4 cup full-fat mayonnaise
1/8 teaspoon ground black pepper

2 tablespoons salted butter, melted
1/4 teaspoon garlic powder
1/4 teaspoon powdered Erythritol

Directions

In a large bowl, toss shrimp in butter, Old Bay seasoning, and garlic powder. Place shrimp into the air fryer basket.
Adjust the temperature to 400F and set the timer for 7 minutes.
Flip the shrimp halfway through the cooking time. Shrimp will be bright pink when fully cooked.
In another large bowl, mix sriracha, powdered Erythritol, mayonnaise, and pepper. Toss shrimp in the spicy mixture and **Serve:** immediately.

Crab Legs

Prep time: 5 minutes **Cooking time:** 15 minutes
Servings: 4

Ingredients

1/4 cup salted butter, melted and divided

Juice of 1/2 medium lemon

1/4 teaspoon garlic powder
3 pounds crab legs

Directions

In a bowl, merge 2 tablespoons butter over crab legs. Set crab legs into the air fryer basket.
Adjust the temperature to 400F and set the timer for 15 minutes.
Shake the air fryer basket to merge the crab legs halfway through the cooking time. In a small bowl, mix remaining butter, garlic powder, and lemon juice. To **Serve:**, crack open crab legs and remove meat. Dip in lemon butter.

Foil-Packet Lobster Tail

Prep time: 15 minutes **Cooking time:** 12 minutes
Servings: 2

Ingredients

2 (6-ounce) lobster tails, halved
1/2 tbsp Old Bay seasoning
1 teaspoon dried parsley

2 tablespoons salted butter, melted
Juice of 1/2 medium lemon

Directions

Place the two halved tails on a sheet of aluminum foil. Drizzle with butter, Old Bay seasoning, and lemon juice.
Seal the foil packets, completely covering tails. Place into the air fryer basket.
Adjust the temperature to 375F and set the timer for 12 minutes.
Once done, sprinkle with dried parsley and **Serve:** immediately.

Tuna Zoodle Casserole

Prep time: 15 minutes **Cooking time:** 15 minutes
Servings: 4

Ingredients

2 tablespoons salted butter
1/4 cup diced white onion
1/2 cup heavy cream
1/2 cup vegetable broth
2 stalks celery, finely chopped
1/2 teaspoon red pepper flakes
2 (5-ounce) cans albacore tuna

1/4 cup chopped white mushrooms
2 tablespoons full-fat mayonnaise
1/4 teaspoon xanthan gum
1 ounce pork rinds, finely ground
2 medium zucchini, spiralized

Directions

In a skillet, dissolve the butter. Add onion, mushrooms, and celery and sauté until fragrant, about 3–5 minutes.
Pour in heavy cream, vegetable broth, mayonnaise, and xanthan gum.

Reduce heat and continue cooking an additional 3 minutes, until the mixture begins to thicken. Add red pepper flakes, zucchini, and tuna. Turn off heat and stir until zucchini noodles are coated.

Pour into 4-cup round baking dish. Top with ground pork rinds and cover the top of the dish with foil. Place into the air fryer basket. Adjust the temperature to 370F and set the timer for 15 minutes. When 3 minutes remain, remove the foil to brown the top of the casserole. **Serve:** warm

Shrimp Scampi

Prep time: 10 minutes **Cooking time:** 8 minutes
Servings: 4

Ingredients

4 tablespoons salted butter
1/2 medium lemon
1/4 cup whipping cream
1/4 teaspoon red pepper flakes

1 teaspoon minced roasted garlic
1/4 tbsp xanthan gum
1 pound medium peeled and deveined shrimp
1 tbs chopped parsley

Directions

In a saucepan over medium heat, melt butter. Zest the lemon, and then squeeze juice into the pan. Add garlic. Pour in the cream, xanthan gum, and red pepper flakes. Whisk until the mixture begins to thicken, about 2–3 minutes.

Place shrimp into a 4-cup round baking dish. Pour the cream sauce over the shrimp and cover with foil. Place the dish into the air fryer basket. Adjust the temperature to 400F and set the timer for 8 minutes. Stir twice during cooking. When done, garnish with parsley and **Serve:** warm.

Fried Tuna Salad Bites

Prep time: 10 minutes **Cooking time:** 7 minutes
Servings: 12

Ingredients

1 (10-ounce) can tuna, drained
1 medium avocado, peeled, pitted, and mashed
1/4 cup full-fat mayonnaise

1 stalk celery, chopped
1/2 cup blanched finely ground almond flour, divided
2 teaspoons coconut oil

Directions

In a large bowl, mix tuna, mayonnaise, celery, and mashed avocado. Form the mixture into balls. Roll balls in almond flour and spritz with coconut oil. Place balls into the air fryer basket.

Adjust the temperature to 400F and set the timer for 7 minutes. Gently turn tuna bites after 5 minutes. **Serve:** warm.

Fish Taco Bowl with Jalapeño Slaw

Prep time: 10 minutes **Cooking time:** 10 minutes
Servings: 2

Ingredients

1 cup shredded cabbage
1/4 cup full-fat sour cream
1/4 cup chopped pickled jalapeños
1 teaspoon chili powder
1/4 teaspoon garlic powder
1/2 medium lime

2 tablespoons full-fat mayonnaise
2 (3-ounce) cod fillets
1 teaspoon cumin
1/2 teaspoon paprika
1 medium avocado, peeled, pitted, and sliced

Directions

In a large bowl, place cabbage, sour cream, mayonnaise, and jalapeños. Mix until fully coated. Let sit for 20 minutes in the refrigerator.

Sprinkle cod fillets with chili powder, cumin, paprika, and garlic powder. Place each fillet into the air fryer basket. Adjust the temperature to 370F and set the timer for 10 minutes. Turn over the fillets halfway through the cooking time. When fully cooked, fish should have an internal temperature of at least 145F.

To **Serve:**, divide slaw mixture into two serving bowls, break cod fillets into pieces and spread over the bowls, and top with avocado. Squeeze lime juice over each bowl. **Serve:** immediately.

Hot Crab Dip

Prep time: 10 minutes **Cooking time:** 8 minutes
Servings: 4

Ingredients

8 ounces full-fat cream cheese, softened
1/4 cup full-fat mayonnaise
1/4 cup chopped pickled jalapeños
1/4 cup sliced green onion
1/4 cup full-fat sour cream 1tablespoon lemon juice
1/2 teaspoon hot sauce
2 (6-ounce) cans lump crabmeat
1/2 cup shredded Cheddar cheese

Directions

Place all Ingredients into a 4-cup round baking dish and stir until fully combined. Place dish into the air fryer basket. Adjust the temperature to 400F and set the timer for 8 minutes. Dip will be bubbling and hot when done. **Serve:** warm.

Almond Pesto Salmon

Prep time: 5 minutes **Cooking time:** 12 minutes
Servings: 2

Ingredients

1/4 cup pesto
2 tbsp unsalted butter, melted
2 (11/2"-thick) salmon fillets (about 4 ounces each)
1/4 cup sliced almonds, roughly chopped

Directions

Garnish each fillet with butter and place half of the pesto mixture on the top of each fillet. Place dish into the air
fryer basket. Set the temperature to 390F.

Salmon will easily flake when fully cooked and reach an internal temperature of at least 145°F. **Serve:** warm.
In a bowl, merge pesto and almonds. Set aside. Set fillets into a 6" round baking dish.

Tender & Flaky Salmon

Prep time: 10 minutes **Cooking time:** 8 minutes
Serve: 2

Ingredients

2 salmon fillets
2 tsp olive oil
1/8 tsp garlic powder
2 tsp brown sugar Pepper
¼ tsp lemon pepper seasoning
Salt

Directions

Preheat the air fryer to 400 F. In a small bowl, mix together lemon pepper seasoning, garlic powder, sugar, pepper, and salt.

Brush salmon fillets with oil and rub with spice mixture.
Place salmon fillets into the air fryer basket and cook for 6-8 minutes. **Serve:** and enjoy

Spicy Prawns

Prep time: 10 minutes **Cooking time:** 8 minutes **Serve:** 2

Ingredients

6 prawns
1 tsp chili powder
1/4 tsp pepper
1 tsp chili flakes, crushed
1/4 tsp salt

Directions

Preheat the air fryer to 350 F. In a bowl, toss shrimp with remaining Ingredients. Transfer prawns into the air fryer basket and cook for 6-8 minutes. **Serve:** and enjoy.

Shrimp Skewers

Prep time: 10 minutes **Cooking time:** 8 minutes **Serve:** 2

Ingredients

1 cup raw shrimp
¼ tsp paprika
Salt
1 garlic clove, minced
1 tbsp parsley, minced
1 fresh lime juice Pepper

Directions

Preheat the air fryer to 350 F. In a bowl, mix shrimp with remaining Ingredients. Thread shrimp onto the skewers and place skewers into the air fryer basket and cook for 8 minutes. **Serve:** and enjoy.

Chipotle Lime Shrimp

Prep time: 10 minutes **Cooking time:** 8 minutes
Serve: 4

Ingredients

1 1/2 lbs. shrimp, peeled and deveined	1/4 tsp ground cumin
4 tbsp fresh lime juice	2 tsp chipotle in adobo
Salt	2 tbsp canola oil Pepper

Directions

Preheat the air fryer to 350 F. Add shrimp and remaining Ingredients in a zip-lock bag. Seal bag and place in the refrigerator for 30 minutes.

Thread marinated shrimp onto skewers and place skewers into the air fryer basket and cook for 8 minutes. Turn halfway through. **Serve:** and enjoy.

Lemon Garlic Shrimp

Prep time: 10 minutes **Cooking time:** 6 minutes
Serve: 4

Ingredients

1 lb. shrimp	1 tbsp parsley, chopped
2 tsp Canola oil	2 tsp fresh lemon juice
1 tsp lemon zest, grated	Salt
1 tsp steak seasoning	1/4 tsp red pepper flakes
1 tsp garlic, minced	
Pepper	

Directions

Preheat the air fryer to 400 F. Add shrimp and remaining Ingredients into the bowl and toss well. Transfer shrimp into the air fryer basket and cook for 6 minutes. **Serve:** and enjoy.

Creole Shrimp

Prep time: 10 minutes **Cooking time:** 7 minutes
Serve: 2

Ingredients

1/2 lb. shrimp, deveined and shelled	1/4 tsp paprika
1 tsp Creole seasoning	1 tbsp canola oil
Salt	1 tsp vinegar
	1/8 tsp cayenne Pepper

Directions

Preheat the air fryer to 400 F. Add shrimp and remaining Ingredients into the bowl and mix well. Add marinated shrimp into the air fryer basket and cook for 5-7 minutes. **Serve:** and enjoy.

Lemon Scallops

Prep time: 10 minutes **Cooking time:** 12 minutes
Serve: 2

Ingredients

8 scallops, cleaned and pat dry	1/4 cup canola oil
1/2 tsp garlic, chopped	2 tbsp parsley, chopped
1/4 tsp pepper	1/8 tsp salt
	1 tsp lemon zest, grated
	2 tsp capers, chopped

Directions

Preheat the air fryer to 400 F.
Add scallops and remaining Ingredients into the bowl and mix well. Add scallops into the air fryer basket and cook for 12 minutes. Turn halfway through. **Serve:** and enjoy.

Asian Salmon

Prep time: 10 minutes **Cooking time:** 8 minutes
Serve: 4

Ingredients

4 salmon fillets	1 tsp sesame seeds, toasted
2 tsp soy sauce	1 tbsp honey
Pepper	Salt

Directions

Preheat the air fryer to 375 F. Brush salmon with soy sauce and season with pepper and salt. Place salmon into the air fryer basket and cook for 8 minutes. Brush salmon with honey and sprinkle with sesame seeds. **Serve:** and enjoy.

Herb Salmon

Prep time: 10 minutes **Cooking time:** 15 minutes
Serve: 4

Ingredients

1 lb. salmon fillets	1/2 tbsp dried rosemary
1/4 tsp dried basil	Pepper
1 tbsp canola oil	1 tbsp dried chives
Salt	

Directions

Preheat the air fryer to 400 F. In a small bowl, mix oil, basil, rosemary, and chives and brush over salmon.

Place salmon fillets into the air fryer basket and cook for 15 minutes. Turn halfway through. **Serve:** and enjoy.

Honey Garlic Salmon

Prep time: 10 minutes **Cooking time:** 20 minutes
Serve: 2

Ingredients

2 salmon fillets
1/4 cup butter, melted
1/2 tbsp garlic, minced
Salt

1 fresh lime juice
Pepper
2 tbsp honey

Directions

Preheat the air fryer to 350 F. In a small bowl, mix honey, garlic, pepper, lime juice, butter, and salt. Brush salmon with honey mixture and place into the air fryer basket and cook for 12-15 minutes. **Serve:** and enjoy.

Wonderful Fried Fish Tacos

Prep time: 15 minutes **Cooking time:** 25 minutes
Serve: 1

Ingredients

1 cup dark beer
½ teaspoon salt
1 lime, cut into wedges
20 (6 inches) corn tortillas
5 cups shredded cabbage
1 cup mayonnaise

1 cup all-purpose flour
1 ½ pounds cod fillets, cubed
¼ cup salsa
1-quart vegetable oil for frying

Directions

Whisk together the beer, flour, and salt in a small basin.
Rinse and pat dry the fish. Cut each piece into ten equal pieces. 1-inch oil, heated to 360 degrees F in a big saucepan (168 degrees C).

Coat the fish in batter with a fork. Drop coated fish into heated oil; adjust heat to maintain oil temperature. Fry for about 2 minutes, or until golden.

Remove with a slotted spoon and quickly drain on paper towels; keep heated. Fry the remaining fish in the same manner. 2 tortillas stacked Fill the tortillas with a salmon and 1/2 cup cabbage. Garnish with mayonnaise, lime wedges, and salsa if desired.

Marinated Fried Fish

Prep time: 20 minutes **Cooking time:** 20 minutes
Serve: 1

Ingredients

2 (4 ounces) fillets flounder
2 tablespoons lemon juice
1 teaspoon paprika
1 teaspoon dried dill weed
1 egg, beaten
1 tablespoon water
2 teaspoons ground cumin

2 tablespoons chopped garlic
½ cup all-purpose flour
¼ teaspoon cayenne pepper, or to taste
1 cup vegetable oil for frying

Directions

Fillets of flounder should be placed in a small glass dish. Combine lemon juice, garlic, cumin, and paprika; pour over flounder fillets. Cover the dish with plastic wrap and place the flounder in the refrigerator for 2 hours to marinade.

On a piece of waxed paper, combine the flour, dill weed, and cayenne pepper. In a large mixing basin, combine the egg and water.

In a large skillet over medium heat, heat the oil. To coat the flounder fillets, gently press them into the flour mixture; shake to remove excess flour. Dip into the
beaten egg to coat, then back into the flour mixture to coat.

Fry flounder in heated oil for 5 minutes per side, or until the fish flakes readily with a fork.

Easy Baked Fish with Lemon

Prep time: 15 minutes **Cooking time:** 20 minutes
Serve: 1

Ingredients

1 serving cooking spray
1 cup dry seasoned breadcrumbs
2 tablespoons dried parsley
¼ cup melted butter

2 pounds tilapia fillets, cut into serving-sized pieces
2 teaspoons lemon zest
½ teaspoon garlic powder

Directions

Preheat the oven carefully to 350 degrees Fahrenheit (175 degrees C). Coat a baking dish with nonstick cooking spray.

Place the fish in the prepared baking dish. Combine breadcrumbs, parsley, lemon zest, and garlic powder in a small mixing bowl. Mix in the melted butter and sprinkle over the fish fillets.

Bake for 15 minutes in a preheated oven or until the tilapia flakes easily with a fork.

Air Fryer Blackened Fish Tacos

Prep time: 20 minutes **Cooking time:** 25 minutes
Serve: 1

Ingredients
1 (15 ounces) can
seasoned black beans,
rinsed, and drained
½ teaspoon salt
1 teaspoon Louisiana-style
hot sauce (Optional)
¼ cup blackened
seasoning
4 (6 inches) corn tortillas

1 tablespoon olive oil
1 tablespoon lime juice
2 ears corn, kernels
1 pound tilapia fillets
cooking spray
1 lime, cut into wedges

Directions

Preheat the oven carefully to 400 degrees Fahrenheit
(200 degrees C). Combine black beans, corn, olive oil,
lime juice, and salt in a mixing dish. Set aside after
gently stirring until the beans and corn are uniformly
covered.

Place the fish fillets on a clean work area and pat with
paper towels to dry. Spray each fillet lightly with
cooking spray and sprinkle with ½ of the blackened
seasoning. Turn the fillets over, spray with cooking
spray, and season with the rest of the spice.

Place the fish in the air fryer basket in a single layer,
working in batches if required. 2 minutes in the oven,
cook for 2 minutes more on the other side before
transferring to a platter. Cook for 10 minutes, stirring
halfway through, in the bean and corn mixture, in the
air fryer basket.

Fill corn tortillas with fish and top with bean and corn
mixture. **Serve:** with lime wedges and spicy sauce on
the side.

Baked Fish Fillets

Prep time: 15 minutes **Cooking time:** 25 minutes
Serve: 1

Ingredients
1 tablespoon vegetable oil,
or to taste
⅛ tbsp ground black
pepper
2 tablespoons lemon juice

1 teaspoon salt
2 pounds mackerel fillets
¼ cup butter, melted

⅛ teaspoon ground
paprika

Directions

Preheat the oven carefully to 350°F (175 degrees C).
Vegetable oil should be used to grease a baking pan.
Season the mackerel fillets in the baking pan with salt
and pepper.

Combine the butter, lemon juice, and paprika in a

mixing dish. **Serve:** with mackerel fillets. Cook in a
preheated oven for 20 to 25 minutes or until the
mackerel flakes easily with a fork.

Tamarind Sauce Fish Curry

Prep time: 15 minutes **Cooking time:** 20 minutes
Serve: 1

Ingredients
2 pounds white carp
1 tablespoon vegetable oil
1 cup warm water
1 ½ teaspoons salt
½ teaspoon cumin seeds
1 large onion, minced

2 tablespoons red chili
powder
2 tablespoons ground
coriander

¼ cup oil
1 tablespoon red chili
powder
¼ cup tamarind pulp
1 ½ tablespoon garlic
paste
1 pinch salt to taste
1 tablespoon chopped
fresh coriander
1 tbs ground turmeric

Directions

Place the fish in a bowl and toss with 1 tablespoon
vegetable oil, 1 tablespoon chili powder, turmeric, and
1 1/2 teaspoons salt for about 10 minutes. Pour warm
water over the tamarind pulp in a dish.

To obtain the juice from the tamarind, squeeze it. In a
pan over medium heat, heat 1/4 cup oil; add cumin
seeds and stir. Cook, constantly stirring, until the
onion is transparent, 5 to 10 minutes. Cook for 3
minutes after adding the garlic paste.

Cover the skillet and cook the carp for 5 minutes.
Bring the fish mixture to a boil with the tamarind
juice. Turn the carp pieces over and season with 2
teaspoons red chili powder, coriander, and salt. Cook
over low heat for 10 minutes or until the sauce
thickens and the oil separates. Garnish with coriander
leaves if desired.

Baja Sauce for Fish or Shrimp Tacos

Prep time: 15 minutes **Cooking time:** 25 minutes
Serve: 1

Ingredients
¼ cup sour cream
1 teaspoon lime juice
¾ teaspoon seafood
seasoning (such as Old
Bay®)

¼ cup mayonnaise
1 tbsp chopped cilantro
¼ teaspoon ground ancho
chili pepper

Directions

Combine the sour cream, mayonnaise, lime juice,
cilantro, seafood seasoning, and ancho chili pepper in
a mixing bowl. Refrigerate for at least 1 hour, covered
with plastic wrap.

Poached Fish with Cucumbers

Prep time: 15 minutes **Cooking time:** 18 minutes
Serve: 1

Ingredients

1 teaspoon salt
1 cup whipping cream
2 tablespoons prepared mustard
2 cups white wine salt to taste
2 (3 ounces) fresh tilapia fillets

2 cucumbers, peeled, halved lengthwise, seeded, and chopped
2 teaspoons chopped fresh tarragon
1 bay leaf

Directions

Allow the cucumber chunks to rest for 1 hour after sprinkling with salt. Cucumber liquid should be strained.
In a saucepan over medium heat, combine the whipping cream, mustard, and tarragon; add the cucumbers and cook for 8 minutes.

In a large skillet over medium heat, pour in the wine. Season with salt and pepper, then add the bay leaf. Bring the wine to a boil in a saucepan. Place the tilapia in the skillet, decrease the heat to medium- low, and cook for 8 to 10 minutes, or until the fish flakes easily with a fork. Cucumbers should be **Serve:**d on the side with the fish.

Air-Fried Crumbed Fish

Prep time: 15 minutes **Cooking time:** 22 minutes
Serve: 1

Ingredients

1 cup dry breadcrumbs
1 egg, beaten
4 flounder fillets

¼ cup vegetable oil
1 lemon, sliced

Directions

Preheat an air fryer to 350°F (180 degrees C).
In a mixing dish, combine breadcrumbs and oil. Stir until the mixture is loose and crumbly. Shake off any excess egg before dipping the fish fillets. Then, coat the fillets evenly and completely in the bread crumb mixture.

Place the coated fillets in the preheated air fryer. Cook for 12 minutes, or until the salmon flakes easily with a fork. Garnish with lemon slices if desired.

Whole Fish Fried with Basil and Chiles

Prep time: 18 minutes **Cooking time:** 20 minutes
Serve: 1

Ingredients

1 whole (10 ounces) tilapia, or more as desired
oil for deep frying
5 large red chili peppers, sliced
2 tablespoons light soy sauce
¼ cup chopped fresh cilantro, or to taste

1 tablespoon vegetable oil, or as desired
1 yellow onion, chopped
2 tablespoons fish sauce
5 cloves garlic, chopped
¼ cup Thai basil leaves, or to taste

Directions

Make multiple angled incisions down the fish's body, all the way to the rib bones. Next, cut two lateral slits down the fish's back, one on each side of the dorsal fin, from head to tail. These slices are designed to cook quickly and crisply.

Heat the frying oil to 350 degrees F. (175 degrees C) in a deep-fryer or big saucepan. Place the fish in the heated oil and cook until crispy, about 3 to 4 minutes on each side. Remove the fish from the oil and drain it on a dish lined with paper towels.

In a wok or large pan, heat 1 tablespoon vegetable oil over medium heat; sauté and stir onion, red chili peppers and garlic until gently browned, 5 to 10 minutes. Remove the wok from the heat and add the fish sauce and soy sauce. Stir basil and cilantro into sauce quickly. Place the fish on a large serving plate and drizzle with the sauce.

Seasoned Swai Fish Fillet

Prep time: 10 minutes **Cooking time:** 18 minutes
Serve: 1

Ingredients

cooking spray
2 tablespoons margarine
1 tablespoon lemon juice
1 teaspoon minced garlic
1 teaspoon salt
1 teaspoon paprika

4 fillets swai fish
¼ cup dry white wine
1 tablespoon chopped fresh cilantro (optional)
1 teaspoon ground black pepper

Directions

Preheat the oven carefully to 350°F (175 degrees C). Coat a shallow baking dish or baking sheet with cooking spray. Fillets of fish should be placed in the preheated pan. In a saucepan over medium heat, melt the margarine.

In a small saucepan, combine the melted margarine, white wine, lemon juice, cilantro, garlic, salt, and black pepper; cook for 2 minutes. Spoon sauce generously over fish fillets. Season the fillets with paprika. Bake for 10 to 12 minutes, or until the salmon flakes easily with a fork.

Beth's Baked Fish

Prep time: 10 minutes **Cooking time:** 18 minutes
Serve: 1

Ingredients

¼ cup unsalted butter, melted

½ teaspoon dried dill weed

2 (4 ounces) fillets cod fillets

½ teaspoon seasoned salt

¼ teaspoon garlic powder

Directions

Preheat the oven carefully to 350°F (175 degrees C). Combine the melted butter, seasoned salt, dill weed, and garlic powder in a small mixing bowl. Fill a large baking dish halfway with the mixture. Turn the fish fillets to cover both sides.

Cook in a preheated oven for 20 to 30 minutes or until the cod flakes easily with a fork.

Portuguese Cod Fish Casserole

Prep time: 15 minutes **Cooking time:** 25 minutes
Serve: 1

Ingredients

2 pounds salted codfish

3 large onions, sliced

¾ cup olive oil

1 tablespoon chopped fresh parsley

3 tablespoons tomato sauce

5 large potatoes, peeled and sliced

2 cloves garlic, minced

1 ½ teaspoon crushed red pepper flakes

1 teaspoon paprika

Directions

Soak salted fish in cold water for several hours or overnight. Drain the water and repeat. Bring a big saucepan of water to a boil. Cook the fish for 5 minutes before draining and cooling it in big slices. Place aside.
Preheat the oven carefully to 375°F (190 degrees C).

Layer half of the potato pieces, the fish, and all of the onions in an 8x11 casserole dish. Finish with the remaining potato slices. Combine the olive oil, garlic, parsley, pepper flakes, paprika, and tomato sauce in a small mixing bowl. Distribute evenly over casserole. Bake for 45 minutes, or until potatoes are cooked, in a preheated oven.

Indian Fish Curry

Prep time: 20 minutes **Cooking time:** 20 minutes
Serve: 1

Ingredients

2 teaspoons Dijon mustard

½ teaspoon salt

1 onion, coarsely chopped

4 white fish fillets

5 cashew halves

1 tablespoon canola oil

½ teaspoon ground turmeric

1 teaspoon ground cumin

1 teaspoon white sugar

¼ cup vegetable broth

1 tbsp ground black pepper

2 tablespoons canola oil

4 cloves garlic, roughly chopped

1 (1 inch) piece ginger root

2 tbsp cayenne pepper,

1 teaspoon ground coriander

1 teaspoon salt

½ cup chopped tomato

¼ cup chopped fresh cilantro

Directions

Combine the mustard, pepper, 1/2 teaspoon salt, and 2 tablespoons canola oil in a small dish. Pour in the fish fillets and flip to coat. Refrigerate the salmon for 30 minutes to allow it to marinate.

In a blender or food processor, combine the onion, garlic, ginger, and cashews and pulse until the mixture forms a paste. Preheat the oven carefully to 350°F (175 degrees C).

In a skillet over medium-low heat, heat 1 tablespoon canola oil. Cook and stir for a minute or two after adding the prepared paste. Combine the cayenne pepper, turmeric, cumin, coriander, 1 teaspoon salt, and sugar in a mixing bowl. Cook and stir for another five minutes. Combine the chopped tomato and vegetable broth in a mixing bowl. Place the fish fillets in a baking tray and discard any excess marinade.

Top the fish with the sauce, cover the baking dish, and bake for 30 minutes, or until the fish flakes easily with a fork. Garnish with cilantro, if desired.

Parchment-Cooked Fish with Morels, Spring Garlic, and Thyme

Prep time: 20 minutes **Cooking time:** 25 minutes
Serve: 1

Ingredients

1-pound fresh morel mushrooms
 salt and ground black pepper to taste
½ cup chopped garlic scapes
4 12x20-inch pieces of parchment paper

1 ½ teaspoons butter
4 (6 ounces) Pacific halibut fillets
1 tablespoon canola oil
5 sprigs fresh thyme, leaves stripped

Directions

Preheat the oven carefully to 350°F (175 degrees C). In a dry skillet over medium heat, season morel mushrooms with salt and black pepper. Cook, often stirring, for 5 minutes, or until the mushrooms release their juice and the liquid evaporates.

Season both sides of the halibut fillets with salt and black pepper. Cook the halibut fillets in a large pan with butter over medium-low heat until golden brown on the exterior, about 2 minutes on each side. Remove the fish from the skillet and put it aside.
In the same skillet used to cook the fish, sauté, and stir garlic scapes until fragrant, about 1 minute. Remove the pan from the heat and add the morel mushrooms, thyme, and garlic scapes.

Crosswise fold a piece of parchment paper in half. Cut a giant valentine-like heart form out of the folded paper with scissors, as large as possible. Rep with the remaining sheet to create four huge heart shapes. Brush the right sides of the hearts with canola oil after opening the heart forms. 1/4 morel mushroom combination should be placed on each heart's left (unoiled) side. Arrange a halibut fillet on top of the mushroom mixture. Season the fish with salt and black pepper to taste.

Fold the right side of the slippery heart over the fish. Starting at the rounded end, fold about 1/4 inch of parchment paper over and work your way down to the tip, folding as you go. Fold the edge over a second time to surround the fish and mushrooms in a double-folded, sealed bundle. Allow roughly a quarter inch of the bottom point to be unfurled. Blow air into the bundle using a straw put into the open bottom to make it puff out like a little balloon. Twist the bottom shut to seal in the air. Place the parchment bundles on two baking pans, ensuring they don't touch.

Bake in a preheated oven for 15 minutes or until the fish is no longer transparent in the center. To **Serve:**, gently rip apart the paper and plate each slice to reveal the fish, mushrooms, and liquids. When the bundle is opened, heated steam will be released.

Easy Elegant Baked Fish

Prep time: 15 minutes **Cooking time:** 18 minutes
Serve: 1

Ingredients

2 pounds swai fish
¼ tbs garlic powder

1 lemon, thinly sliced

¼ cup butter, melted
¼tbs garlic pepper seasonin
1 tablespoon capers

Directions

Preheat the oven carefully to 350°F (175 degrees C). Place the fish in a baking dish and sprinkle with melted butter, season with garlic powder, garlic pepper spice, and salt. Garnish the fish with lemon wedges and capers. Bake for 15 to 20 minutes, or until the salmon flakes easily with a fork.

Crispy Beer Batter Fish & Chips

Prep time: 15 minutes **Cooking time:** 20 minutes
Serve: 1

Ingredients

1 cup self-rising flour

2 tablespoons rice flour, or as needed salt to taste
vegetable oil for frying

¼ teaspoon baking powder
4 (6 ounces) cod fillets
1 cup lager-style beer
2 tablespoons rice flour

Directions

Combine self-rising flour, rice flour, and baking powder in a mixing bowl. Place in the freezer until ready to use.
Pat the fish dry as much as possible. Cut each piece lengthwise to make eight 1-inch-thick strips. Season rice flour with salt and spread it out on a platter. Shake off any excess mixture before gently dusting the fish. Cover a dish with crinkled foil to create a rapid drying rack, then set the fish on top.

Heat the oil in a deep fryer to 375°F (190 degrees C). Pour the beer into the flour mixture and stir until the batter is the consistency of the thick pancake batter. Dip the fish pieces into the batter to coat them, pull them out and allow the excess drip off.

Fry the fish in batches until golden brown, 3 to 4 minutes, dipping periodically if necessary. Using paper towels, drain. **Serve:** right away.

Easy Elegant Baked Fish

Prep time: 15 minutes **Cooking time:** 18 minutes
Serve: 1

Ingredients

2 pounds swai fish	¼ cup butter, melted
¼ tbs garlic powder	¼tbs garlic pepper seasonin
1 lemon, thinly sliced	1 tablespoon capers

Directions

Preheat the oven carefully to 350°F (175 degrees C). Place the fish in a baking dish and sprinkle with melted butter, season with garlic powder, garlic pepper spice, and salt. Garnish the fish with lemon wedges and capers. Bake for 15 to 20 minutes, or until the salmon flakes easily with a fork.

Crunchy Fish Tacos

Prep time: 15 minutes **Cooking time:** 22 minutes
Serve: 1

Ingredients

9 each Old El Paso® taco shells	2 teaspoons Old El Paso
½ cup sour cream	8 (6 inches) Old El Paso
1 pound tilapia fillets	1 cup Pico de Gallo salsa

Directions

Preheat the oven carefully to 425°F. Line a cookie sheet with aluminum foil. Fill a 1-gallon resealable food-storage plastic bag halfway with taco shells. Seal the bag and crush the shells with a rolling pin. Shake in taco seasoning mix until thoroughly combined.

Tilapia fillets, cut into 3x1-inch chunks. Place the fillet pieces in the bag and press the crumbs onto them to coat. Place on a baking sheet. Bake for 15 minutes, flipping halfway through. Place two slices of each on a tortilla. Toppings are optional. Roll the tortillas up.

Mexican Baked Fish

Prep time: 15 minutes **Cooking time:** 25 minutes
Serve: 1

Ingredients

1 ½ pounds cod	1 cup shredded sharp Cheddar cheese
1 cup salsa	1 avocado - peeled, pitted, and sliced
½ cup coarsely crushed corn chips	
¼ cup sour cream	

Directions

Preheat the oven carefully to 400°F (200 degrees C). Grease one 8x12 inch baking dish lightly.
Fish fillets should be rinsed under cold water and patted dry with paper towels. Place the fillets in the prepared baking dish side by side. Pour the salsa over the top, then equally sprinkle with the shredded cheese. Crush the corn chips on top.
Bake for 15 minutes, uncovered, in a preheated oven, or until the fish is opaque and flakes with a fork.
Serve:

Cerveza and Lime Marinade for Shrimp and Fish

Prep time: 20 minutes **Cooking time:** 25 minutes
Serve: 1

Ingredients

2 cups minced onion	½ cup chopped cilantro
½ cup seeded, minced jalapeno pepper	¼ cup minced garlic
¾ cup fresh lime juice	1 cup oil
1 tbs ground black pepper	½ cup Mexican beer
	½ tablespoon ground cumin
	2 tablespoons tequila

Directions

In a blender, combine the onion, cilantro, jalapeño pepper, garlic, oil, lime juice, beer, tequila, black pepper, and cumin until smooth.

Quick and Easy Baked Fish Fillet

Prep time: 18 minutes **Cooking time:** 20 minutes
Serve: 1

Ingredients

1 pound flounder fillets ground black pepper to taste	½ teaspoon salt
	2 teaspoons melted butter
1 teaspoon minced onion	1 tablespoon lemon juice

Directions

Preheat the oven carefully to 400°F (200 degrees C). Season the flounder in a baking dish with salt and pepper. Combine lemon juice, butter, and onion; pour over flounder.

Chicken-Cheese-Fish

Prep time: 18 minutes **Cooking time:** 20 minutes
Serve: 1

Ingredients

2 pounds skinless, boneless chicken breast halves	1 cup shredded Swiss cheese
	4 cups shred Cheddar cheese
4 (3 ounces) cans of tuna packed in olive oil	2 cups heavy whipping cream 4 eggs, beaten
2 cups crumbled feta	1 cup shredded mozzarella cheese
2 cups ricotta cheese	
1 (8 ounces) package cream cheese, softened	3 cups Italian seasoned breadcrumbs
2 eggs, beaten	2 (16 ounces) cans pink salmon, drained
2 tbs butter, cut small pieces	

Directions

Preheat the oven carefully to 350°F (175 degrees C). Fill a large baking dish halfway with chicken breasts. Sprinkle with Cheddar and Swiss cheeses. Layer the tuna and salmon on the cheese in an equal layer. In a mixing bowl, combine the whipped cream and the 4 beaten eggs; pour over the top of the dish.

In a mixing dish, combine the feta, mozzarella, and ricotta cheeses; distribute over the fish. Next, combine the cream cheese, 2 beaten eggs, and breadcrumbs; spread evenly over the cheese. Finally, arrange little slices of butter evenly throughout the entire dish. Wrap with aluminum foil. Bake for 1 1/2 hours, or until cooked through and golden brown on top, in a preheated oven.

Fish Batter with Newcastle™ Brown Ale

Prep time: 15 minutes **Cooking time:** 25 minutes
Serve: 1

Ingredients

1-quart vegetable oil for frying	½ cup flour
½ cup cornmeal	1 pound cod fillets, cut into pieces
½ teaspoon garlic powder	1 teaspoon garlic salt
1 cup brown ale (such as Newcastle™ brown ale)	½ tbsp ground cinnamon

Directions

Heat the oil in a deep fryer to 325°F (165 degrees C). Combine the flour, cornmeal, garlic salt, garlic powder, and cinnamon in a large mixing bowl. Mix in the beer until there are no dry lumps left. Dip the fish into the batter, allowing some of the excess to run out before gently placing it in the deep fryer. Cook for 8 minutes, or until the fish is golden brown and crispy on the exterior and easily flaked. To prevent overcrowding the deep fryer, cook the fish in batches.

Classic Fish and Chips

Prep time: 20 minutes **Cooking time:** 20 minutes
Serve: 1

Ingredients

4 large potatoes, peeled and cut into strips	1 cup all-purpose flour
	1 teaspoon baking powder
1 teaspoon ground black pepper	1 cup milk
	1 teaspoon salt
1 egg	1-quart vegetable oil for frying
1 ½ pounds cod fillets	

Directions

Place the potatoes in a medium dish of cool water. In a medium-sized mixing basin, combine the flour, baking powder, salt, and pepper separately. Whisk in the milk and egg and continue to stir until the mixture is smooth. Allow the mixture to stand for 20 minutes.

Preheat the oil to 350°F in a big pot or electric skillet (175 degrees C). Fry the potatoes until they are soft in heated oil. They should be drained on paper towels.

Dredge the fish in the batter, one piece at a time, and fry in heated oil. Fry the fish till golden brown. Increase the heat as needed to keep the temperature at 350 degrees F (175 degrees C). Drain well on paper towels. Fry the potatoes for another 1 to 2 minutes to enhance crispness.

Fish and Things Teriyaki Marinade

Prep time: 15 minutes **Cooking time:** 25 minutes
Serve: 1

Ingredients

2 cups soy sauce	¾ cup brown sugar, divided
1 cup honey	
¾ cup white sugar, divided	1 clove garlic, chopped
	4 slices fresh ginger root
8 green onions	

Directions

In a 2-quart saucepan, combine soy sauce, 1/2 cup brown sugar, 1/2 cup white sugar, green onions, ginger, and garlic. Bring the mixture to a simmer. Reduce the heat to low and continue to cook for 15 minutes.

Pour in the remaining whites and brown sugar, as well as the honey. Bring the water to a boil. When the mixture rises and foams and doubles in size, take it from the fire and set it aside to cool.

Fish Tacos from Reynolds Wrap

Prep time: 15 minutes **Cooking time:** 20 minutes
Serve: 1

Ingredients

Reynolds Wrap® Non-Stick Aluminum Foil
1 teaspoon olive oil
1 tablespoon fresh lime juice
½ teaspoon salt
1 clove garlic, minced
Mango salsa

4 (4 ounces) tilapia fillets, fresh or frozen (thawed)
1 teaspoon seafood seasoning
⅛ teaspoon red pepper flakes
Sliced avocado

Directions

Preheat the oven carefully to 400°F. Line a 13x9x2-inch baking sheet with Reynolds Wrap® Nonstick Foil, nonstick (dull) side up.

Place the tilapia in a pan lined with foil. Combine lime juice, olive oil, seafood seasoning, garlic, salt, and red pepper flakes in a medium mixing bowl. Pour over the fish. Bake for 18 to 20 minutes, or until the salmon flakes easily with a fork. Fill each tortilla with 1/2 fillet, lettuce, salsa, and avocado.

Corn Crusted Red Fish

Prep time: 15 minutes **Cooking time:** 20 minutes
Serve: 1

Ingredients

1 ½ cups fresh corn kernels
1 tbsp red onion, chopped
1 tablespoon cornstarch
1 cup all-purpose flour
1 teaspoon Creole seasoning, or to taste
1 tablespoon vegetable oil

1 tablespoon red bell pepper, chopped
4 (5 ounces) red snapper fillets
3 egg whites, lightly beaten

Directions

Preheat the oven carefully to 350°F (175 degrees C). In a mixing dish, combine corn kernels, bell pepper, onion, and cornstarch; put aside.

Season the red snapper with the Creole seasoning. Dip the fish in the flour, then in the egg whites. Coat both sides of the fish with the corn mixture by pushing it into the egg whites.

In an oven-safe skillet, heat the vegetable oil over medium-high heat. Fry the fillets in the pan until brown, about 5 minutes per side. Place the pan in the preheated oven and cook for another 5 minutes, or until the fish flakes easily with a fork.

Halibut Fish Tacos

Prep time: 15 minutes **Cooking time:** 18 minutes
Serve: 1

Ingredients

1 lime, juiced
¼ cup chopped cilantro
1 jalapeno pepper, diced
¼ teaspoon ground cumin
½ pound halibut fillets
8 corn tortillas
1 cup shredded pepper Jack cheese

¼ cup olive oil
1 tablespoon ground ancho chili powder
salt and black pepper to taste
2 cups shredded cabbage
1 (8 ounces) jar salsa
1 avocado, sliced

Directions

In a large mixing bowl or resealable zip-top bag, combine lime juice, olive oil, cilantro, jalapeño, chili powder, cumin, salt, and pepper. Marinade the halibut for 20 to 25 minutes. Do not over marinate the fish since the lime juice will begin to 'cook' it.

Preheat an outside grill to medium heat and brush the grate gently with oil. Drain marinade and cook fillets for 5 minutes on each side. Cook for another 2 minutes, or until the salmon flakes easily with a fork.

Warm the tortillas on the grill or in the oven. Top tortillas with fish, cabbage, salsa, pepper Jack cheese, and avocado.

Beer Batter for Fish

Prep time: 15 minutes **Cooking time:** 22 minutes
Serve: 1

Ingredients

3 eggs, ¾ cup beer
4 cups pastry flour
½ teaspoon baking soda
.063 teaspoon garlic powder
2 quarts of vegetable oil for frying

1 ½ cups milk
1 tablespoon baking powder
ground black pepper to taste
1 ½ pounds cod fillets
2 tablespoons cornstarch
salt to taste

Directions

Combine flour, baking powder, baking soda, and cornstarch in a medium mixing basin. In a large mixing basin, combine eggs and milk. Pour in the beer.

Mix in the flour mixture. Season with salt, pepper, and garlic powder to taste. Heat the oil to 375 degrees F in an electric deep fryer or a heavy saucepan (190 degrees C).

Coat the fish with batter and place it in the heated oil. Fry for 4 to 5 minutes, or until golden brown. **Serve:.**

Twice Fried Fish

Prep time: 10 minutes **Cooking time:** 18 minutes
Serve: 1

Ingredients

1 tablespoon hoisin sauce	1 tablespoon canned
1 tablespoon dry sherry	tomato sauce
1 teaspoon ground black	1 teaspoon white sugar
pepper	1 teaspoon salt
1 ½ pounds cod fillets	3 tablespoons vegetable oil
2 tbs dark soy sauce	1 tablespoon lard
1 teaspoon cornstarch	4 tablespoons water

Directions

Mix hoisin sauce, tomato sauce, sherry, pepper, soy sauce, sugar, and salt in a mixing bowl. Allow for a 20-minute resting period.

1 tablespoon of oil should be rubbed into the filets of fish. Heat the remaining 2 tablespoons of oil in a large pan. Fry the fish for 2 minutes on both sides, then drain on paper towels.

Remove the skillet's oil and replace it with 1 tablespoon of lard. Melt over medium heat and toss in the soy sauce mixture. Dissolve the cornstarch in the water and pour it into the skillet, continually swirling. Cook until the sauce thickens.

Return the fish to the skillet and cook for another minute on each side.

Grilled Tuna Fish Steaks

Prep time: 20 minutes **Cooking time:** 20 minutes
Serve: 1

Ingredients

8 (3 ounces) fillets fresh tuna steaks, 1 inch thick	½ cup soy sauce
	1 tablespoon fresh lime juice
⅓ cup sherry	¼ cup vegetable oil
1 clove garlic, minced	

Directions

In a shallow baking dish, place the tuna steaks. Combine the soy sauce, sherry, vegetable oil, fresh lime juice, and garlic in a medium mixing bowl. Turn the tuna steaks in the soy sauce mixture to coat. Refrigerate for at least one hour, covered.

Preheat the grill to high. Grease the grill grate lightly. Place the tuna steaks on the grill and discard the marinade. Grill for 3 to 6 minutes per side, or until done to preference.

Baked Fish Croquettes

Prep time: 15 minutes **Cooking time:** 25 minutes
Serve: 1

Ingredients

2 cups leftover cooked steelhead trout	1 cup soft breadcrumbs
½ sweet onion, minced	½ cup mayonnaise
½ cup sour cream	½ lemon, juiced
½ teaspoon Worcestershire sauce	½ teaspoon seasoned salt, or more to taste
½ teaspoon garlic powder	½ cup panko
ground black pepper to taste	breadcrumbs, or as needed

Directions

Preheat the oven carefully to 425°F (220 degrees C). Then, using parchment paper or aluminum foil, line a baking pan.

Remove the skin, bones, and crust from the trout and flake it with a fork. In a mixing bowl, combine flaked fish, soft breadcrumbs, onion, mayonnaise, sour cream, lemon juice, Worcestershire sauce, salt, garlic powder, and black pepper. Form the mixture into balls, then roll each one in the panko. Place the balls on the baking sheet that has been prepared.

Bake for 15 to 20 minutes, or until the croquettes are gently browned and crispy.

Accidental Fish

Prep time: 15 minutes **Cooking time:** 20 minutes
Serve: 1

Ingredients

4 ounces fillets Mahi Mahi	½ cup salted butter
2 drops Louisiana-style hot sauce	1 Roma tomato, seeded and chopped
1 tablespoon lemon juice	1 clove garlic, minced
1 green onion, chopped	2 teaspoons olive oil

Directions

Preheat the oven carefully to 450°F (230 degrees C). Place the mahi-mahi fillets on a baking dish and brush with olive oil. Bake for 20 minutes in a preheated oven or until the fish flakes easily with a fork. Melt the butter in a skillet over medium heat while the mahi-mahi bakes.

Simmer the garlic, lemon juice, and spicy sauce in the melted butter for 1 minute. Cook and stir the tomato and green onion into the butter mixture until heated. To **Serve:**, spoon the sauce over the cooked fish.

Easy-Bake Fish

Prep time: 20 minutes **Cooking time:** 25 minutes
Serve: 1

Ingredients
3 tablespoons honey	3 tbs Dijon mustard
4 (6 ounces) salmon steaks	½ teaspoon pepper
1 teaspoon lemon juice	

Directions

Preheat the oven carefully to 325°F (165 degrees C). Combine the honey, mustard, and lemon juice in a small bowl. Distribute the mixture evenly over the salmon steaks. Season with pepper to taste. In a medium baking dish, arrange the Ingredients.

Coconut Fish Curry

Prep time: 15 minutes **Cooking time:** 20 minutes
Serve: 1

Ingredients
1 ½ teaspoon curry powder	½ teaspoon ground ginger
¼ teaspoon ground turmeric	¼ teaspoon olive oil
3 cloves garlic, minced	4 ¼ ounces coconut milk, divided
1 onion, chopped	
4 ¼ ounces water, divided	3 ½ ounces cod, cut into bite-size pieces
1 large tomato, diced	

Directions

Combine the curry powder, powdered ginger, and ground turmeric; roast the spices over medium heat until browned, about 5 minutes. Stir the olive oil and garlic into the spice mixture to produce a paste.

Cook and toss the onion into the spice mixture for 5 to 7 minutes, or until it is soft. Stir in half of the coconut milk and half of the water to the onion mixture; cook for 5 minutes. Cook until the fish is firm, about 5 minutes, after adding it to the mixture. Cook until the tomato is softened, approximately 5 minutes, with the remaining coconut milk and water in the pan.

Lemony Steamed Fish

Prep time: 15 minutes **Cooking time:** 18 minutes
Serve: 1

Ingredients
6 (6 ounces) halibut fillets	1 tablespoon dried dill weed
2 teaspoons dried parsley	¼ teaspoon paprika
1 seasoned pinch salt, or more to taste	1 pinch garlic powder
	1 tablespoon onion powder
2 tablespoons lemon juice	1 pinch lemon pepper

Directions

Preheat the oven carefully to 375°F (190 degrees C). Make 6 foil squares, one for each fillet.

Sprinkle dill weed, onion powder, parsley, paprika, seasoned salt, lemon pepper, and garlic powder on top of the fillets. Each fillet should be sprayed with lemon juice. Fold the foil over the fillets to form a pocket, then fold the edges close. Spread the wrapped packages out on a baking sheet.

Bake for 30 minutes in a preheated oven or until the fish flakes easily with a fork.

Freda's Fabulous Fish

Prep time: 15 minutes **Cooking time:** 22 minutes
Serve: 1

Ingredients
1 pound cod fillets	½ cup butter, melted
¼ cup soy-based steak marinade	1 tbs ground black pepper
1 teaspoon salt	1 teaspoon cayenne pepper
	2 small tomatoes, thinly sliced
1 lemon, quartered	

Directions

Preheat the oven carefully to 375°F (190 degrees C). Put the fish in a 13x9 baking dish or pan.
Spread the butter, marinade, salt, and pepper all over the fish. Squeeze the lemon juice over the fish. Place tomato slices on top of the fish 30 minutes in the oven, or until the fish is flaky.

Pretzel Coated Fried Fish1-quart oil for frying

Prep time: 15 minutes **Cooking time:** 20 minutes
Serve: 1

Ingredients

1-quart oil for frying	¾ cup all-purpose flour
½ tbs ground black pepper	¾ cup crushed pretzels
1-pound frozen cod fillets, thawed	1 teaspoon salt
	2 eggs

Directions

Heat the oil in a deep fryer to 350°F (175 degrees C). In a large resealable plastic bag, combine the flour, salt, and pepper. Place the cod in the bag and shake gently to coat. Separate the eggs and crumbled pretzels into two small bowls. Coat the fish in eggs, then with broken pretzels.

Fry coated fish in hot oil for 10 minutes, rotating once, until golden brown and readily flaked with a fork.

Fiery Fish Tacos with Crunchy Corn Salsa

Prep time: 10 minutes **Cooking time:** 18 minutes
Serve: 1

Ingredients

2 cups cooked corn kernels	½ cup diced red onion
1 cup peeled, diced jicama	½ cup diced red bell pepper, 1 cup cilantro leaves chopped
1 lime, juiced, and zested	
2 tablespoons olive oil	
2 tablespoons cayenne pepper, or to taste	2 tbs salt, or to taste
1 tbso ground black pepper	6 (4 ounces) fillets of tilapia
	2 tbs sour cream, or to taste
12 corn tortillas, warmed	

Directions

Preheat the grill to high. Combine corn, red onion, jicama, red bell pepper, and cilantro in a medium mixing bowl. Mix in the lime juice and zest. Combine cayenne pepper, ground black pepper, and salt in a small bowl. Brush each fillet with olive oil and season with salt and pepper to taste. Place the fillets on the grill grate and cook for 3 minutes on each side. Top two corn tortillas with fish, sour cream, and corn salsa for each spicy fish taco.

Spicy Fish Soup

Prep time: 18 minutes **Cooking time:** 20 minutes
Serve: 1

Ingredients

½ onion, chopped	1 clove garlic, minced
1 tablespoon chili powder	1 ½ cups chicken broth
1 (4 ounces) can canned green chili peppers, chopped	1 ½ cups canned peeled and diced tomatoes
½ cup chopped green bell pepper	½ cup shrimp
	1 teaspoon ground cumin
½ pound cod fillets	¾ cup plain nonfat yogurt

Directions

Over medium-high heat, coat a large pot with vegetable cooking spray. Sauté the onions for about 5 minutes, stirring often. Cook for 2 minutes more after adding the garlic and chili powder.

Then, add the chicken broth, chili peppers, and cumin while stirring constantly. Bring to a boil, then lower to low heat, cover, and leave to simmer for 20 minutes.

Add the tomatoes, green bell pepper, prawns, and fish next. Return to a boil, lower to low heat, cover, and continue cooking for 5 minutes. Stir in the yogurt gradually until it is cooked completely.

Air Fryer Fish Sticks

Prep time: 15 minutes **Cooking time:** 25 minutes
Serve: 1

Ingredients

1 pound cod fillets	¼ cup all-purpose flour,
½ cup panko breadcrumbs	¼ cup grated Parmesan cheese
1 egg	
1 teaspoon paprika	½ teaspoon black pepper
1 tablespoon parsley flakes	cooking spray

Directions

Preheat an air fryer to 400°F (200 degrees C).
Pat the fish dry using paper towels before slicing it into 1x3-inch pieces.
In a small bowl, combine the flour and salt. In a separate shallow dish,
beat the egg. In a third shallow dish, combine panko, Parmesan cheese, parsley, paprika, and pepper.
Each fish stick should be coated in flour, then dipped in beaten egg, and then coated in seasoned panko mixture.
Spray the air fryer basket with nonstick cooking spray. Arrange half of
the sticks in the basket, ensuring none of them is a contact. Cooking spray should be sprayed on the top of each stick.
Cook for 5 minutes in a hot air fryer. Cook for a further 5 minutes after
flipping the fish sticks. Rep with the rest of the fish sticks.

Easy Baked Fish

Prep time: 20 minutes **Cooking time:** 20 minutes
Serve: 1

Ingredients

cooking spray
¼ cup butter
½ teaspoon dried basil
¼ teaspoon ground black pepper
1 ⅓ cups instant rice
1 red bell pepper, chopped
1 cup frozen peas
1 lemon, quartered

½ cup chicken broth
2 tbs dry white wine
½ teaspoon salt
1 red onion, chopped
1 tablespoon fresh lemon juice
2 cloves garlic, chopped
1-pound sole fillets
2 plum (Roma) tomatoes, thinly sliced

Directions

Preheat the oven carefully to 450°F (230 degrees C). Coat a 9x13-inch baking dish with nonstick cooking spray.
In a saucepan over medium heat, combine the chicken broth, butter, wine, lemon juice, basil, salt, and black pepper until the butter has melted, about 5 minutes.

Combine rice, onion, bell pepper, peas, and garlic in a prepared baking dish. Arrange sole fillets on the rice mixture, followed by tomato slices. Distribute the butter mixture over the fish, rice, and veggies. Wrap aluminum foil around the baking dish.

Cook in a preheated oven for 20 to 25 minutes, or until the fish flakes easily with a fork and soft rice. With lemon slices, **Serve:**.

Easy Mediterranean Fish

Prep time: 20 minutes **Cooking time:** 25 minutes
Serve: 1

Ingredients

4 (6 ounces) fillets of halibut
1 large tomato, chopped
1 onion, chopped
salt and pepper to taste
¼ cup capers
1 tablespoon lemon juice

1 tablespoon Greek seasoning

1 (5 ounces) jar pitted kalamata olives
¼ cup olive oil

Directions

Preheat the oven carefully to 350°F (175 degrees C). Season the halibut fillets with Greek seasoning and place them on a wide piece of aluminum foil.
Combine the tomato, onion, olives, capers, olive oil, lemon juice, salt, and pepper in a mixing bowl.

Distribute the tomato mixture over the halibut. To make a huge packet, carefully seal all of the foil's edges. Spread the package out on a baking sheet. 30 to 40 minutes in a preheated oven until the salmon flakes easily with a fork.

Fish on a Plank

Prep time: 15 minutes **Cooking time:** 25 minutes
Serve: 1

Ingredients

1 cedar plank
2 mangos - peeled, seeded, and diced
1 cup bottled teriyaki sauce
1 tablespoon chopped fresh cilantro
salt and pepper to taste
2 teaspoons olive oil
1 teaspoon fresh lime juice
1 teaspoon lemon juice
1 teaspoon hot-pepper sauce

5 ounces mahi-mahi fillets
½ red bell pepper, seeded and chopped
4 green onions, chopped
1 jalapeno pepper, seeded and chopped
½ teaspoon garlic powder
1 teaspoon chipotle seasoning
1 teaspoon red pepper flakes

Directions

Combine the mangos, green onion, cilantro bell pepper, and jalapeño pepper in a medium mixing bowl. Season with garlic powder, salt & pepper, and lime juice to taste. Stir together, then cover and chill until ready to **Serve:** to mix the flavors.

Soak the plank in water for at least 2 hours, preferably longer. In a shallow dish, coat the mahi-mahi fillets with teriyaki sauce. Cover and set aside for at least 1 hour to marinate. Prepare an indirect-heat grill. Arrange and fire the coals beneath one- half of the grill if using charcoal. Season the fish fillets with lemon juice, chipotle spice, red pepper flakes, and hot pepper sauce. Lay the fillets out on the plank.

Place the board over direct heat on the grill. Cook for 10 minutes, covered. Cook for 10 minutes more, or until the fish can be flaked with a fork, on the plank with the fish over indirect heat (the colder area of the grill). **Serve:** the fillets with mango salsa on the side.

Homemade Fish Stock

Prep time: 15 minutes **Cooking time:** 20 minutes
Serve: 1

Ingredients

3 pounds fish heads,
bones, and trimmings
2 tablespoons unsalted
butter
1 rib celery, chopped
1 cup dry white wine
10 whole black
peppercorns

2 leeks, white part only,
thinly sliced
1 carrot, chopped

2 ½ quarts water
1 bouquet garni
3 thick slices of lemon

Directions

Fish should be washed in cold water and thoroughly
drained. Melt the butter in a saucepan over low heat.
Cook until the leeks, carrots, and celery are cooked, 5
to 7 minutes. Bring the fish portions, wine, and water
to a boil for about 5 minutes. Residuum should be
skimmed and discarded. After adding the bouquet
garni, peppercorns, and lemon, return to a boil.

Sexy Fish Stew

Prep time: 15 minutes **Cooking time:** 18 minutes
Serve: 1

Ingredients

2 tablespoons butter
salt and pepper to taste
½ cup sliced shallots salt
1 ¼ cups chicken
broth
1 pound baby red
potatoes, trimmed
½ cup heavy whipping
cream
1 tbs chopped fresh
tarragon

1 large leek, cleaned and
thinly sliced
¾ cup white wine
½ cup thinly sliced fennel
bulb
1 pinch cayenne
pepper
1-pound boneless rockfish
filets, cut into 1-inch
pieces

Directions

In a large saucepan over medium-low heat, melt the
butter. Cook and stir the leek, shallots, and 1/2
teaspoon salt in the melted butter for 10 to 15
minutes, or until softened. Stir the wine into the leek
mixture, turn the heat up to medium and cook for 2
minutes. Bring the chicken broth to a boil. Stir in the
fennel and potatoes and cook, occasionally turning,
until the potatoes are nearly cooked about 10 minutes.
Season with salt, pepper, and cayenne pepper to taste.
Stir in the cream to mix.
Cover and heat for 3 minutes after adding the fish and
tarragon to the soup. Reduce heat to medium-low, stir
gently, and cook until fish flakes easily with a fork,
about 6 minutes. Season with salt and black pepper to
taste.

Fish and Chips Sliders

Prep time: 15 minutes **Cooking time:** 22 minutes
Serve: 1

Ingredients

cooking spray
3 egg whites
1 tbs. apple cider vinegar
1 pound cod fillets
2 green onions, chopped
1 pinch salt and ground
black pepper 8 slider buns

1 (8.5 ounces) bag malt
vinegar-and-sea salt chips
½ teaspoon celery seed
⅓ cup plain Greek yogurt
2 tbs honey mustard
3 cups coleslaw mix

Directions

Preheat the oven carefully to 450 degrees Fahrenheit
(230 degrees C). Spray a wire rack with cooking spray
and place it on a rimmed baking sheet.
Blend the chips in batches until they have the
consistency of breadcrumbs. Place the chips on a flat
platter.
In a mixing basin, combine egg whites. Place a piece
of fish on the prepared rack after dipping it in egg
white and coating it with chip crumbs. Rep with the
leftover fish. Coat the fish with frying spray. Bake for
15 minutes in a preheated oven. Turn on the broiler
and broil
the salmon for 5 minutes, or until it is golden and
crispy.
In a large mixing bowl, combine coleslaw mix and
green onions while the fish is cooking. Combine the
yogurt, honey mustard, vinegar, celery seed, salt, and
pepper in a separate dish. Toss the coleslaw mix with
the dressing to blend.

Cod Fish Cakes

Prep time: 18 minutes **Cooking time:** 20 minutes
Serve: 1

Ingredients

2 large potatoes, peeled
and halved
1 tablespoon grated onion
1 egg

1 tablespoon butter
1 pound cod fillets, cubed
1 tbs chopped fresh
parsley
3 tablespoons oil for
frying

Directions

Put the potatoes in a large saucepan of water and
bring to a boil. Allow the potatoes to simmer until
almost tender.
Add the fish to the saucepan and boil until both the
fish and the potatoes are tender. Drain well and place
the potatoes and fish in a large mixing dish.
Mash together the butter, onion, parsley, and egg in mixing
dish

Fort Worth Fish Tacos

Prep time: 10 minutes **Cooking time:** 18 minutes
Serve: 1

Ingredients

8 (3 ounces) fillets tilapia
2 tb hot pepper sauce
2 small limes, quartered
2 tbsp chopped fresh cilantro
1 (5.3 ounces) container plain Greek yogurt
1 teaspoon salt
1 cup dark beer
¼ teaspoon ground black pepper

¼ medium head cabbage, finely shredded

2 teaspoons salt
4 ounces cream cheese softened
½ cup mayonnaise
1 tablespoon lime juice
1 cup flour
8 (8 inches) flour tortillas
1 teaspoon garlic powder
cayenne pepper to taste
3 cups peanut oil for frying
(8 ounces) jar prepared salsa
¼ cup chopped fresh cilantro

Directions

Place the tilapia fillets on a platter and season with salt and spicy sauce; cover and chill while creating the cilantro cream sauce. In a small or large measuring cup, combine cream cheese, 2 tablespoons cilantro, mayonnaise, and yogurt; stir well. Mix the lime juice into the cream sauce. Refrigerate, covered.

In a mixing basin, add flour, salt, garlic powder, cayenne pepper, and pepper; stir in beer to produce a smooth batter. Heat the oil in a big, deep-frying pan to 375°F (190 degrees C).

Remove the fish from the refrigerator, dip it in the beer batter, and cook it three times in the heated oil, flipping it until golden (approximately 2 minutes on each side, depending on the thickness). Drain the fish on paper towels and place it on a covered platter to keep warm. Rep with the remaining fillets.

Wrap tortillas in a clean kitchen towel and microwave for 20 seconds or warm. Assemble tacos by laying a heated tortilla on top of a fish fillet. Shredded cabbage properly, a dollop of cilantro cream sauce, a teaspoon of salsa, and a sprinkling of chopped cilantro complete the dish. Each taco should be **Serve:**d with a lime quarter for squeezing.

SNACKS & APPETIZERS

Root Vegetable Chips with Dill Mayonnaise

(**Ready in about** 40 minutes | **Servings:** 4)

Ingredients

1/2 pound red beetroot, julienned
1/2 pound golden beetroot, julienned
1/2 cup mayonnaise
Sea salt and ground black pepper, to taste
1 teaspoon olive oil
1/4 pound carrot
1 teaspoon garlic, minced
1/4 teaspoon dried dill weed

Directions

Toss your veggies with salt, black pepper and olive oil.

Arrange the veggie chips in a single layer in the Air Fryer cooking basket.

Cook the veggie chips in the preheated Air Fryer at 340 degrees F for 20 minutes; tossing the basket occasionally to ensure even cooking. Work with two batches.

Meanwhile, mix the mayonnaise, garlic and dill until well combined.

Serve: the vegetable chips with the mayo sauce on the side. Bon appétit!

Parmesan Squash Chips

(**Ready in about** 20 minutes | **Servings:** 3)

Ingredients

3/4 pound butternut squash, cut into thin rounds
1 teaspoon butter
1/2 cup ketchup
Sea salt and ground black pepper, to taste
1 teaspoon Sriracha sauce
1/2 cup Parmesan cheese, grated

Directions

Toss the butternut squash with Parmesan cheese, salt, black pepper and butter.

Transfer the butternut squash rounds to the Air Fryer cooking basket.

Air Fryer at 400 degrees F for 12 minutes. Shake the Air Fryer basket periodically to ensure even cooking. Work with batches.

While the parmesan squash chips are baking, whisk the ketchup and sriracha and set it aside.

Serve: the parmesan squash chips with Sriracha ketchup and enjoy!

Mexican Crunchy Cheese Straws

(**Ready in about** 15 minutes | **Servings:** 3)

Ingredients

1/2 cup almond flour
1/4 teaspoon shallot powder 1/4 teaspoon garlic powder
1 ounce Manchego cheese, grated
1/4 teaspoon xanthan gum 1/4 teaspoon ground cumin
1 egg yolk, whisked
2 ounces Cotija cheese, grated

Directions

Mix all Ingredients until everything is well incorporated.

Twist the batter into straw strips and place them inside your Air Fryer on a baking mat.

Cook the cheese straws in your Air Fryer at 360°F for 5 minutes, then flip them over and cook for another 5 minutes.

Before serving, allow the cheese straws to cool. Enjoy!

Greek-Style Zucchini Rounds

(**Ready in about** 15 minutes | **Servings:** 3)

Ingredients

1/2 pound zucchini, cut into thin rounds
1/2 teaspoon oregano
Coarse sea salt and ground black pepper, to taste
Greek dipping sauce
1/2 teaspoon fresh lemon juice
2 tablespoons mayonnaise
1/2 teaspoon dried sage, crushed
1/4 tbs ground bay leaf
1/2 cup Greek yogurt
1 teaspoon extra-virgin olive oil
1/2 teaspoon garlic, pressed

Directions

Toss the zucchini rounds with olive oil and spices and place them in the Air Fryer cooking basket.

Cook in the preheated Air Fryer at 400 degrees F for 10 minutes; shaking the basket halfway through the cooking time.

Let it cool slightly and cook an additional minute or so until crispy and golden brown.

Meanwhile, make the sauce by whisking all the sauce Ingredients; place the sauce in the refrigerator until ready to **Serve:**.

Serve: the crispy zucchini rounds with Greek dipping sauce on the side. Enjoy!

Paprika and Cheese French Fries

(**Ready in about** 15 minutes | **Servings:** 2)

Ingredients

8 ounces French fries, frozen	1/2 cup Monterey-Jack cheese, grated
Sea salt, to taste	1 teaspoon paprika

Directions

Cook the French fries in your Air Fryer at 400 degrees F for about 7 minutes. Shake the basket and continue to cook for a further 6 minutes.

Top the French fries with cheese, paprika and salt cheese. Continue to cook for 1 minute more or until the cheese has melted. **Serve:** warm and enjoy!

Beer-Battered Vidalia Onion Rings

(**Ready in about** 15 minutes | **Servings:** 2)

Ingredients

1/2 cup all-purpose flour 1	1/4 tbsp cayenne pepper
1/4 teaspoon dried oregano	Kosher salt and ground black pepper, to taste
/2 teaspoon baking powder	
1/4 cup beer	1 cup crushed tortilla chips
1/2 pound Vidalia onions, cut into rings	1 large egg, beaten

Directions

In a mixing bowl, thoroughly combine the flour, baking powder, cayenne pepper, oregano, salt, black pepper, egg and beer; mix to combine well.

In another shallow bowl, place the crushed tortilla chips.

Dip the Vidalia rings in the beer mixture; then, coat the rings with the crushed tortilla chips, pressing to adhere.

Transfer the onion rings to the Air Fryer cooking basket and spritz them with a nonstick spray. Cook the onion rings at 380 degrees F for about 8 minutes, shaking the basket halfway through the **Cooking time:**to ensure even browning. Bon appétit!

Cinnamon Pear Chips

(**Ready in about** 10 minutes | **Servings:** 2)

Ingredients

1 large pear, cored and sliced	1 teaspoon apple pie spice blend
1 teaspoon honey	1 teaspoon coconut oil

Directions

Toss the pear slices with the spice blend, coconut oil and honey. Then, place the pear slices in the Air Fryer cooking basket and cook at 360 degrees F for about 8 minutes.

Shake the basket once or twice to ensure even cooking. Pear chips will crisp up as it cools

Italian-Style Tomato Chips

(**Ready in about** 20 minutes | **Servings:** 2)

Ingredients

2 tomatoes, cut into thick rounds	Sea salt and fresh ground pepper, to taste
1 teaspoon Italian seasoning mix	1 teaspoon extra-virgin olive oil
1/4 cup Romano cheese, grated	

Directions

Start by preheating your Air Fryer to 350 degrees F.

Toss the tomato sounds with remaining Ingredients. Transfer the tomato rounds to the cooking basket without overlapping.

Cook your tomato rounds in the preheated Air Fryer for 5 minutes. Flip them over and cook an additional 5 minutes. Work with batches. Bon appétit!

Bacon Chips with Chipotle Dipping Sauce

(**Ready in about** 15 minutes | **Servings:** 3)

Ingredients

6 ounces bacon, cut into strips	6 tablespoons sour cream
Chipotle Dipping Sauce	1/2 teaspoon chipotle chili powder

Directions

Place the bacon strips in the Air Fryer cooking basket.

Cook the bacon strips at 360 degrees F for 5 minutes; turn them over and cook for another 5 minutes.

Meanwhile, make the chipotle dipping sauce by whisking the sour cream and chipotle chili powder; re**Serve:**.

Serve: the bacon chips with the chipotle dipping sauce and enjoy!

Sea Scallops and Bacon Kabobs

(**Ready in about** 10 minutes | **Servings:** 2)

Ingredients

10 sea scallops, frozen
1 teaspoon paprika
4 ounces bacon, diced

1 teaspoon garlic powder
Sea salt and ground black
pepper, to taste

Directions

Assemble the skewers alternating sea scallops and
bacon. Sprinkle the garlic powder, paprika, salt and
black pepper all over your kabobs. Bake your kabobs in
the preheated Air Fryer at 400 degrees F for 6 minutes.
Serve: warm with your favorite sauce for dipping.
Enjoy!

Hot Cheesy Mushrooms Bites

(**Ready in about** 10 minutes | **Servings:** 3)

Ingredients

1 teaspoon butter, melted
4 ounces cheddar cheese,
grated
4 tablespoons tortilla
chips, crushed
12 button mushrooms,
stalks removed and
chopped

1 teaspoon fresh garlic,
finely minced
1/2 teaspoon hot sauce
1 tablespoon fresh
coriander, chopped
Sea salt and ground black
pepper, to taste

Directions

In a mixing bowl, thoroughly combine the butter,
garlic, cheddar cheese, tortilla chips, coriander, hot
sauce and chopped mushrooms.

Divide the filling among mushroom caps and transfer
them to the air Fryer cooking basket; season them with
salt and black pepper.

Cook your mushrooms in the preheated Air Fryer at
400 degrees F for 5 minutes. Transfer the warm
mushrooms to a serving platter and **Serve:** at room
temperature. Bon appétit!

Pecorino Romano Meatballs

(**Ready in about** 15 minutes | **Servings:** 2)

Ingredients

1/2 pound ground turkey
1 egg, beaten
1 teaspoon stone-ground
mustard
2 tablespoons scallions,
chopped
1/2 teaspoon red pepper
flakes, crushed

2 tablespoons tomato
ketchup
1/4 Pecorino-Romano
cheese, grated
1 garlic clove, minced
Sea salt and ground black
pepper, to taste

Directions

In a mixing bowl, thoroughly combine all Ingredients.

Shape the mixture into 6 equal meatballs. Transfer the
meatballs to the Air Fryer cooking basket that is
previously greased with a nonstick cooking spray.

Cook the meatballs at 360 degrees F for 10 to 11
minutes, shaking the basket occasionally to ensure
even cooking. An instant thermometer should read
165 degrees F.

Bon appétit!

Crunchy Roasted Chickpeas

(**Ready in about** 20 minutes | **Servings:** 2)

Ingredients

1 tablespoon extra-virgin
olive oil
8 ounces can chickpeas,
drained
1/2 teaspoon smoked
paprika

1/2 teaspoon ground
cumin 1/2 teaspoon garlic
powder Sea salt, to taste

Directions

Drizzle olive oil over the drained chickpeas and
transfer them to the Air Fryer cooking basket.

Cook your chickpeas in the preheated Air Fryer at 395
degrees F for 13 minutes. Turn your Air Fryer to 350
degrees F and cook an additional 6 minutes.

Toss the warm chickpeas with smoked paprika, cumin,
garlic and salt. Bon appétit!

Pork Crackling with Sriracha Dip

(**Ready in about** 40 minutes | **Servings:** 3)

Ingredients

1/2 pound pork rind	Sea salt and ground black
1/2 cup tomato sauce	pepper, to taste
1 teaspoon Sriracha sauce	½ tbs stone-ground mustard

Directions

Rub sea salt and pepper on the skin side of the pork rind. Allow it to sit for 30 minutes.

Then, cut the pork rind into chunks using kitchen scissors.

Roast the pork rind at 380 degrees F for 8 minutes; turn them over and cook for a further 8 minutes or until blistered. Meanwhile, mix the tomato sauce with the Sriracha sauce and mustard. **Serve:** the pork crackling with the Sriracha dip and enjoy!

Fish Sticks with Honey Mustard Sauce

(**Ready in about** 10 minutes | **Servings:** 3)

Ingredients

10 ounces fish sticks	2 tbsp yellow mustard
2 teaspoons honey	1/2 cup mayonnaise

Directions

Add the fish sticks to the Air Fryer cooking basket; drizzle the fish sticks with a nonstick cooking spray.

Cook the fish sticks at 400 degrees F for 5 minutes; turn them over and cook for another 5 minutes. Meanwhile, mix the mayonnaise, yellow mustard and honey until well combined. **Serve:** the fish sticks with the honey mustard sauce for dipping. Enjoy.

Easy Mexican Elote

(**Ready in about** 10 minutes | **Servings:** 2)

Ingredients

2 ears of corn, husked	4 tbsp Mexican crema
4 tablespoons Mexican cheese blend, crumbled	Sea salt and chili powder, to taste
1 tbsp cilantro chopped	1 tbsp fresh lime juice

Directions

Cook the corn for about 6 minutes in a 390°F preheated Air Fryer. In a mixing bowl, combine the Mexican crema, Mexican cheese blend, lime juice, salt, and chilli powder.

After that, insert a wooden stick into the core to **Serve:** as a handle. Rub the topping mixture over each ear of corn. Garnish with fresh cilantro, if desired. **Serve:** right away.

Prosciutto Stuffed Jalapeños

(**Ready in about** 15 minutes | **Servings:** 2)

Ingredients

8 fresh jalapeño peppers, deseeded and cut in half lengthwise	1/4 teaspoon cayenne pepper
½ tbs granulated garlic	4 ounces Ricotta cheese
	8 slices prosciutto, chopped

Directions

Place the fresh jalapeño peppers on a clean surface.

Mix the remaining Ingredients in a bowl; divide the filling between the jalapeño peppers. Transfer the peppers to the Air Fryer cooking basket. Cook the stuffed peppers at 400 degrees F for 15 minutes. **Serve:** and enjoy!

Salmon, Cheese and Cucumber Bites

(**Ready in about** 15 minutes | **Servings:** 3)

Ingredients

1/2 pound salmon	1 tbsp extra-virgin olive oil
1/4 teaspoon cumin powder 1 teaspoon granulated garlic	Sea salt and ground black pepper, to taste
2 ounces cream cheese	
1/2 teaspoon onion powder	1 English cucumber, cut into 1-inch rounds

Directions

Pat the salmon dry and drizzle it with olive oil. Season the salmon with onion powder, cumin, granulated garlic, salt and black pepper. Transfer the salmon to the Air Fryer cooking basket.

Cook the salmon at 400 degrees F for 5 minutes; turn the salmon over and continue to cook for 5 minutes more or until opaque. Cut the salmon into bite-sized pieces. Spread 1 teaspoon of cream cheese on top of each cucumber slice; top each slice with a piece of salmon. Insert a tiny party fork down the center to keep in place. Bon appétit!

Classic Jiaozi (Chinese Dumplings)

(**Ready in about** 15 minutes | **Servings:** 3)

Ingredients

1/2 pound ground pork
2 scallion stalks, chopped
1 ounce bamboo shoots, shredded
1/2 teaspoon garlic paste
1 teaspoon honey
Sauce
1 tablespoon ketchup
1 teaspoon sesame seeds, lightly toasted

1 cup Napa cabbage, shredded
1 teaspoon fresh ginger, peeled and grated
8 ounces round wheat dumpling
2 tablespoons rice vinegar
1 teaspoon deli mustard
1/4 cup soy sauce

Directions

Cook the pork in a wok that is preheated over medium-high heat; cook until no longer pink and stir in the Napa cabbage, scallions, bamboo shoots, garlic paste and ginger; salt to taste and stir to combine well.

Divide the pork mixture between dumplings. Moisten the edge of each dumpling with water, fold the top half over the bottom half and press together firmly.

Place your dumplings in the Air Fryer cooking basket and spritz them with cooking spray. Cook your dumplings at 400 degrees F for 8 minutes. Work with batches.

While your dumplings are cooking, whisk the sauce Ingredients. **Serve:** the warm dumplings with the sauce for dipping. Enjoy!

Eggplant Parm Chips

(**Ready in about** 30 minutes | **Servings:** 2)

Ingredients

1/2 pound eggplant, cut into rounds
1/2 teaspoon porcini powder 1/2 teaspoon garlic powder 1/4 teaspoon cayenne pepper

Kosher salt and ground black pepper, to taste
1/2 cup Parmesan cheese, grated
1/2 teaspoon shallot powder

Directions

Toss the eggplant rounds with the remaining Ingredients until well coated on both sides.

Bake the eggplant chips at 400 degrees F for 15 minutes; shake the basket and continue to cook for 15 minutes more.

Let cool slightly, eggplant chips will crisp up as it cools. Bon appétit!

Apple Chips with Walnuts

(**Ready in about** 35 minutes | **Servings:** 2)

Ingredients

1 apples, peeled, cored and sliced

1/4 cup walnuts

1 teaspoon cinnamon
1/2 teaspoon ground cloves

Directions

Toss the apple slices with ground cloves and cinnamon.

Place the apple slices in the Air Fryer cooking basket and cook at 360 degrees F for 10 minutes or until crisp. Re**Serve:**.

Then, toast the walnuts at 300 degrees F for 10 minutes; now, shake the basket and cook for another 10 minutes.

Chop the walnuts and scatter them over the apple slices. Bon appétit!

Sticky Glazed Wings

(**Ready in about** 30 minutes | **Servings:** 2)

Ingredients

1/2 pound chicken wings

1 tablespoon Worcestershire sauce
1 tablespoon hot sauce

2 tablespoons brown sugar
1 tablespoon balsamic vinegar
1 tablespoon sesame oil

Directions

Brush the chicken wings with sesame oil and transfer them to the Air Fryer cooking basket.

Cook the chicken wings at 370 degrees F for 12 minutes; turn them over and cook for a further 10 minutes.

Meanwhile, bring the other Ingredients to a boil in a saucepan; cook for 2 to 3 minutes or until thoroughly cooked.

Toss the warm chicken wings with the sauce and place them on a serving platter. **Serve:** and enjoy!

Barbecue Little Smokies

(**Ready in about** 20 minutes | **Servings:** 6)

Ingredients
1 pound beef cocktail wieners

10 ounces barbecue sauce

Directions

Start by preheating your Air Fryer to 380 degrees F.

Prick holes into your sausages using a fork and transfer them to the baking pan.

Cook for 13 minutes. Spoon the barbecue sauce into the pan and cook an additional 2 minutes.

Serve: with toothpicks. Bon appétit!

Greek-Style Deviled Eggs

(**Ready in about** 20 minutes | **Servings:** 2)

Ingredients
4 eggs
2 tablespoons Kalamata olives, pitted and chopped
1 tablespoon Greek-style yogurt

1 tbs chives, chopped
1 teaspoon habanero pepper, seeded and chopped
1 tablespoon parsley, chopped

Sea salt and crushed red pepper flakes, to taste

Directions

Place the wire rack in the Air Fryer basket and lower the eggs onto the rack. Cook the eggs at 260 degrees F for 15 minutes.

Transfer the eggs to an ice-cold water bath to stop cooking. Peel the eggs

under cold running water; slice them into halves, separating the whites and yolks.

Mash the egg yolks with the remaining Ingredients and mix to combine. Spoon the yolk mixture into the egg whites and **Serve:** well chilled. Enjoy!

Mini Plantain Cups

(**Ready in about** 10 minutes | **Servings:** 3)

Ingredients
2 blackened plantains, chopped
1/2 cup milk
1 teaspoon fresh ginger, peeled and minced

1/2 cup cornmeal
1/4 cup all-purpose flour
1 tablespoon coconut oil
A pinch of ground cinnamon
A pinch of salt

Directions

In a mixing bowl, thoroughly combine all Ingredients until everything is well incorporated.

Spoon the batter into a greased mini muffin tin.

Bake the mini plantain cups in your Air Fryer at 330 degrees F for 6 to 7 minutes or until golden brown. Bon appétit.

Baby Carrots with Asian Flair

(**Ready in about** 20 minutes | **Servings:** 3)

Ingredients
1 pound baby carrots
1/2 teaspoon Szechuan pepper

1 large garlic clove, crushed
1 tablespoon honey

2 tablespoons sesame oil
1 teaspoon Wuxiang powder (Five-spice powder)
1 (1-inch) piece fresh ginger root, peeled and grated
2 tablespoons tamari sauce

Directions

Start by preheating your Air Fryer to 380 degrees F.

Toss all Ingredients together and place them in the Air Fryer basket. Cook for 15 minutes, shaking the basket halfway through the cooking time. Enjoy!

Sweet Potato Fries with Spicy Dip

(**Ready in about** 50 minutes | **Servings:** 3)

Ingredients

3 medium sweet potatoes, cut into 1/3-inch sticks
Spicy Dip
1/4 teaspoon Dijon mustard
1 teaspoon kosher salt
2 tablespoons olive oil
1/4 cup mayonnaise
1/4 cup Greek yogurt
1 teaspoon hot sauce

Directions

Soak the sweet potato for 30 minutes in icy cold water. Drain and pat the sweet potatoes dry with paper towels. Toss the sweet potatoes in a bowl with the olive oil and salt.

Place in a cooking basket that has been lightly oiled. Cook for 14 minutes in a preheated Air Fryer at 360°F. Cook in small batches.

While the sweet potatoes are cooking, whisk together the remaining Ingredients for the spicy dip. Keep refrigerated until ready to **Serve:**. Enjoy!

Puerto Rican Tostones

(**Ready in about** 15 minutes | **Servings:** 2)

Ingredients

1 ripe plantain, sliced
A pinch of kosher salt
1 tablespoon sunflower oil
A pinch of grated nutmeg

Directions

In a mixing bowl, combine the plantains, oil, nutmeg, and salt.

Cook for 10 minutes in a preheated Air Fryer at 400 degrees F, shaking the cooking basket halfway through.

Season with salt and pepper to taste, and **Serve:** immediately.

Crunchy Broccoli Fries

(**Ready in about** 15 minutes | **Servings:** 4)

Ingredients

1 pound broccoli florets
1/2 teaspoon cayenne pepper
4 tbs parmesan cheese, preferably freshly grated
1 tsp granulated garlic
Sea salt and ground black pepper, to taste
2 tablespoons sesame oil
1/2 tbsp onion powder

Directions

Start by preheating the Air Fryer to 400 degrees F. Blanch the broccoli in salted boiling water until al dente, about 3 to 4 minutes. Drain well and transfer to the lightly greased Air Fryer basket.

Add the onion powder, garlic, cayenne pepper, salt, black pepper, and sesame oil. Cook for 6 minutes, tossing halfway through the cooking time. Bon appétit!

Kale Chips with Tahini Sauce

(**Ready in about** 15 minutes | **Servings:** 4)

Ingredients

5 cups kale leaves, torn into 1-inch pieces
1/2 teaspoon shallot powder
1 ½ tablespoons sesame oil
1 teaspoon garlic powder
1/4 tbs porcini powder
1/2 teaspoon mustard seeds
1 teaspoon salt
1/3 cup tahini (sesame butter)
1 tbs fresh lemon juice
2 cloves garlic, minced

Directions

Toss the kale with the sesame oil and seasonings.

Bake in the preheated Air Fryer at 350 degrees F for 10 minutes, shaking the cooking basket occasionally.

Bake until the edges are brown. Work in batches. Meanwhile, make the sauce by whisking all Ingredients in a small mixing bowl.**Serve:** and enjoy!

Classic Deviled Eggs

(**Ready in about** 20 minutes | **Servings:** 3)

Ingredients

5 eggs
2 tablespoons sweet pickle relish Sea salt, to taste
2 tablespoons mayonnaise
1/2 teaspoon mixed peppercorns, crushed

Directions

Place the wire rack in the Air Fryer basket; lower the eggs onto the wire rack. Cook at 270 degrees F for 15 minutes.

Transfer them to an ice-cold water bath to stop the cooking. Peel the eggs under cold running water; slice them into halves. Mash the egg yolks with the mayo, sweet pickle relish, and salt; spoon yolk mixture into egg whites. Arrange on a nice serving platter and garnish with the mixed peppercorns. Bon appétit!

Famous Blooming Onion with Mayo Dip

(**Ready in about** 25 minutes | **Servings:** 3)

Ingredients

1 large Vidalia onion
1/2 cup all-purpose flour
1 teaspoon salt

1/2 teaspoon dried thyme
2 eggs

1/4 cup milk Mayo Dip
3 tablespoons sour cream
Kosher salt and freshly
ground black pepper, to
taste

1/2 teaspoon ground
black pepper
1 teaspoon cayenne
pepper
1/2 teaspoon dried
oregano 1/2 teaspoon
ground cumin
3 tablespoons mayonnaise
1 tablespoon horseradish

Directions

Cut off the top 1/2 inch of the Vidalia onion; peel your onion and place it cut- side down. Starting 1/2 inch from the root, cut the onion in half. Make a second cut that splits each half in two. You will have 4 quarters held together by the root.

Repeat these cuts, splitting the 4 quarters to yield eighths; then, you should split them again until you have 16 evenly spaced cuts. Turn the onion over and gently separate the outer pieces using your fingers.

In a mixing bowl, thoroughly combine the flour and spices. In a separate bowl, whisk the eggs and milk. Dip the onion into the egg mixture, followed by the flour mixture.

Spritz the onion with cooking spray and transfer to the lightly greased cooking basket. Cook for 370 degrees F for 12 to 15 minutes.

Meanwhile, make the mayo dip by whisking the remaining Ingredients. **Serve:** and enjoy!

Parsnip Chips with Spicy Citrus Aioli

(**Ready in about** 20 minutes | **Servings:** 4)

Ingredients

1 pound parsnips, peel
long strips
1 teaspoon red pepper
flakes, crushed
Spicy Citrus Aioli
1 tablespoon fresh lime
juice
1 clove garlic, smashed
2 tablespoons sesame oil

Sea salt and ground black
pepper, to taste
1/2 teaspoon mustard
seeds
1/4 cup mayonnaise
Salt and black pepper, to
taste
1/2 teaspoon curry
powder

Directions

Start by preheating the Air Fryer to 380 degrees F.

Toss the parsnip chips with the sesame oil, salt, black pepper, red pepper, curry powder, and mustard seeds.

Cook for 15 minutes, shaking the Air Fryer basket periodically. Meanwhile, make the sauce by whisking the mayonnaise, lime juice, garlic, salt, and pepper. Place in the refrigerator until ready to use. Bon appétit!

Cajun Cheese Sticks

(**Ready in about** 15 minutes | **Servings:** 4)

Ingredients

1/2 cup all-purpose flour
2 eggs
1 tablespoon Cajun
seasonings
8 cheese sticks, kid-
friendly

1/2 cup parmesan cheese,
grated
1/4 cup ketchup

Directions

To begin, set up your breading station. Place the all-purpose flour in a shallow dish. In a separate dish, whisk the eggs. Finally, mix the parmesan cheese and Cajun seasoning in a third dish.

Start by dredging the cheese sticks in the flour; then, dip them into the egg. Press the cheese sticks into the parmesan mixture, coating evenly.

Place the breaded cheese sticks in the lightly greased Air Fryer basket. Cook at 380 degrees F for 6 minutes.

Serve: with ketchup and enjoy!

The Best Calamari Appetizer

(**Ready in about** 20 minutes | **Servings:** 6)

Ingredients

1 ½ pounds calamari tubes, cleaned, cut into rings
1/4 cup buttermilk
1 cup cornmeal
1 egg, whisked

2 tablespoons lemon juice
Sea salt and ground black pepper, to taste

1 cup all-purpose flour
1 teaspoon paprika

Directions

Preheat your Air Fryer to 390 degrees F. Rinse the calamari and pat it dry. Season with salt and black pepper. Drizzle lemon juice all over the calamari.

Now, combine the cornmeal, flour, and paprika in a bowl; add the whisked egg and buttermilk.

Dredge the calamari in the egg/flour mixture. Arrange them in the cooking basket. Spritz with cooking oil and cook for 9 to 12 minutes, shaking the basket occasionally. Work in batches.

Serve: with toothpicks. Bon appétit

Roasted Parsnip Sticks with Salted Caramel

(**Ready in about** 25 minutes | **Servings:** 4)

Ingredients

1 pound parsnip, trimmed, scrubbed, cut into sticks
2 tablespoon avocado oil
2 tablespoons butter

2 tablespoons granulated sugar
1/2 teaspoon coarse salt
1/4 teaspoon ground allspice

Directions

Toss the parsnip with the avocado oil; bake in the preheated Air Fryer at 380 degrees F for 15 minutes, shaking the cooking basket occasionally to ensure even cooking.

Then, heat the sugar and 1 tablespoon of water in a small pan over medium heat. Cook until the sugar has dissolved; bring to a boil.

Keep swirling the pan around until the sugar reaches a rich caramel color. Pour in 2 tablespoons of cold water. Now, add the butter, allspice, and salt. The mixture should be runny.

Afterwards, drizzle the salted caramel over the roasted parsnip sticks and enjoy!

Greek-Style Squash Chips

(**Ready in about** 25 minutes | **Servings:** 4)

Ingredients

1/2 cup seasoned breadcrumbs
1/4 teaspoon oregano
1/2 cup Parmesan cheese, grated
1 garlic clove, minced
1/2 cup Greek-style yogurt
Freshly ground black pepper, to your liking

Sea salt and ground black pepper, to taste
2 yellow squash, cut into slices
2 tablespoons grapeseed oil Sauce
1 tbsp fresh cilantro, chopped

Directions

In a shallow bowl, thoroughly combine the seasoned breadcrumbs, Parmesan, salt, black pepper, and oregano.

Dip the yellow squash slices in the prepared batter, pressing to adhere.

Brush with the grapeseed oil and cook in the preheated Air Fryer at 400 degrees F for 12 minutes. Shake the Air Fryer basket periodically to ensure even cooking. Work in batches.

While the chips are baking, whisk the sauce Ingredients; place in your refrigerator until ready to **Serve:**. Enjoy!

Romano Cheese and Broccoli Balls

(**Ready in about** 25 minutes | **Servings:** 4)

Ingredients

1/2 pound broccoli
2 garlic cloves, minced
1 shallot, chopped
2 tablespoons butter, at room temperature
Sea salt and ground black pepper, to taste

1/2 cup Romano cheese, grated
4 eggs, beaten
1/4 teaspoon dried basil
1/2 teaspoon paprika

Directions

Add the broccoli to your food processor and pulse until the consistency resembles rice.

Stir in the remaining Ingredients; mix until everything is well combined. Shape the mixture into bite-sized balls and transfer them to the lightly greased cooking basket.

Cook in the preheated Air Fryer at 375 degrees F for 16 minutes, shaking halfway through the cooking time. **Serve:** with cocktail sticks and tomato ketchup on the side.

Summer Meatball Skewers

(**Ready in about** 20 minutes | **Servings:** 6)

Ingredients

1/2 pound ground pork
1 teaspoon fresh garlic, minced
Salt and black pepper, to taste
1 red pepper, 1-inch pieces
1/2 cup barbecue sauce
1 tbsp dried onion flakes
1 cup pearl onions
1/2 pound ground beef
1 teaspoon dried parsley flakes

Directions

Mix the ground meat with the onion flakes, garlic, parsley flakes, salt, and black pepper. Shape the mixture into 1-inch balls.

Thread the meatballs, pearl onions, and peppers alternately onto skewers. Microwave the barbecue sauce for 10 seconds.

Cook in the preheated Air Fryer at 380 degrees for 5 minutes. Turn the skewers over halfway through the cooking time. Brush with the sauce and cook for a further 5 minutes. Work in batches.

Serve: with the remaining barbecue sauce and enjoy!

Italian-Style Tomato-Parmesan Crisps

(**Ready in about** 20 minutes | **Servings:** 4)

Ingredients

4 Roma tomatoes, sliced
2 tablespoons olive oil
1 teaspoon Italian seasoning mix
Sea salt and white pepper, to taste
4 tablespoons Parmesan cheese, grated

Directions

Begin by preheating your Air Fryer to 350°F. Grease the Air Fryer basket generously with nonstick cooking oil.

Toss the remaining Ingredients with the sliced tomatoes. Place them in the cooking basket without overlapping them.

Cook for 5 minutes in a preheated Air Fryer. Cook for an additional 5 minutes after shaking the cooking basket. Working in batches is recommended.

If desired, **Serve:** with Mediterranean aioli for dipping. Good appetite!

Loaded Tater Tot Bites

(**Ready in about** 20 minutes | **Servings:** 6)

Ingredients

24 tater tots, frozen
6 tablespoons Canadian bacon, cooked and chopped
1 cup Swiss cheese, grated
1/4 cup Ranch dressing

Directions

Spritz the silicone muffin cups with non-stick cooking spray. Now, press the tater tots down into each cup. Divide the cheese, bacon, and Ranch dressing between tater tot cups.

Cook in the preheated Air Fryer at 395 degrees for 10 minutes. **Serve:** in paper cake cups. Bon appétit!

Crunchy Roasted Chickpeas

(**Ready in about** 25 minutes | **Servings:** 4)

Ingredients

1 (15-ounce) can chickpeas, drained and patted dry
1/4 teaspoon mustard powder
1/2 teaspoon shallot powder
1/2 teaspoon red pepper flakes, crushed
1/8 cup Romano cheese, grated
1 teaspoon coriander, minced
1 tablespoon sesame oil
1/2 teaspoon garlic powder
Coarse sea salt and ground black pepper, to taste

Directions

Toss all Ingredients in a mixing bowl.

Roast in the preheated Air Fryer at 380 degrees F for 10 minutes, shaking the basket halfway through the cooking time. Work in batches. Bon appétit!

Southern Cheese Straws

(**Ready in about** 30 minutes | **Servings:** 6)

Ingredients

1 cup all-purpose flour
1/4 teaspoon smoked paprika
1/2 teaspoon celery seeds
1 sticks butter

Sea salt and ground black pepper, to taste

4 ounces mature Cheddar, cold, freshly grated

Directions

Start by preheating your air Fryer to 330 degrees F. Line the Air Fryer basket with parchment paper.

In a mixing bowl, thoroughly combine the flour, salt, black pepper, paprika, and celery seeds.

Then, combine the cheese and butter in the bowl of a stand mixer. Slowly stir in the flour mixture and mix to combine well.

Then, pack the dough into a cookie press fitted with a star disk. Pipe the long ribbons of dough across the parchment paper. Then cut into six-inch lengths.

Bake in the preheated Air Fryer for 15 minutes.

Repeat with the remaining dough. Let the cheese straws cool on a rack. You can store them between sheets of parchment in an airtight container. Bon appétit!

Sea Scallops and Bacon Skewers

(**Ready in about** 50 minutes | **Servings:** 6)

Ingredients

1/2 pound sea scallops
1/2 cup coconut milk
6 ounces orange juice
1 shallot, diced
1 tablespoon vermouth

Sea salt and ground black pepper, to taste 1/2 pound bacon, diced
1 teaspoon garlic powder
1 teaspoon paprika

Directions

In a ceramic bowl, place the sea scallops, coconut milk, orange juice, vermouth, salt, and black pepper; let it marinate for 30 minutes.

Assemble the skewers alternating the scallops, bacon, and shallots. Sprinkle garlic powder and paprika all over the skewers.

Bake in the preheated air Fryer at 400 degrees F for 6 minutes. **Serve:** warm and enjoy!

Blue Cheesy Potato Wedges

(**Ready in about** 20 minutes | **Servings:** 4)

Ingredients

2 Yukon Gold potatoes, peeled and cut into wedges
1/2 cup blue cheese, crumbled

Kosher salt, to taste
2 tablespoons ranch seasoning

Directions

Sprinkle the potato wedges with the ranch seasoning and salt. Grease generously the Air Fryer basket.

Place the potatoes in the cooking basket.

Roast in the preheated Air Fryer at 400 degrees for 12 minutes. Top with the cheese and roast an additional 3 minutes or until cheese begins to melt. Bon appétit!

Cocktail Sausage and Veggies on a Stick

(**Ready in about** 25 minutes | **Servings:** 4)

Ingredients

16 cocktail sausages, halved 16 pearl onions
1 green bell pepper, cut into
1 ½-inch pieces
Salt and cracked black pepper, to taste

1 red bell pepper, cut into
1 ½-inch pieces
1/2 cup tomato chili sauce

Directions

Thread the cocktail sausages, pearl onions, and peppers alternately onto skewers. Sprinkle with salt and black pepper.

Cook in the preheated Air Fryer at 380 degrees for 15 minutes, turning the skewers over once or twice to ensure even cooking.

Serve: with the tomato chili sauce on the side. Enjoy!

The Best Party Mix Ever

(**Ready in about** 15 minutes | **Servings:** 10)

Ingredients

2 cups mini pretzels
1 cup mini crackers
1 cup peanuts

1 tablespoon Creole seasoning
2 tablespoons butter, melted

Directions

Toss all Ingredients in the Air Fryer basket.

Cook in the preheated Air Fryer at 360 degrees F approximately 9 minutes until lightly toasted. Shake the basket periodically. Enjoy

Yakitori (Japanese Chicken Skewers)

(**Ready in about** 2 hours 15 minutes | **Servings:** 4)

Ingredients

1/2 pound chicken tenders, cut bite-sized pieces
Sea salt and ground pepper, to taste
1 tablespoon fresh lemon juice
1 teaspoon sesame oil

1 teaspoon coriander seeds
1 clove garlic, minced

2 tablespoons sake
2 tablespoons Shoyu sauce

Directions

Place the chicken tenders, garlic, coriander, salt, black pepper, Shoyu sauce, sake, and lemon juice in a ceramic dish; cover and let it marinate for 2 hours.

Then, discard the marinade and tread the chicken tenders onto bamboo skewers.

Place the skewered chicken in the lightly greased Air Fryer basket. Drizzle sesame oil all over the skewered chicken.

Cook at 360 degrees for 6 minutes. Turn the skewered chicken over; brush

with the re**Serve:**d marinade and cook for a further 6 minutes. Enjoy!

Paprika Zucchini Bombs with Goat Cheese

(**Ready in about** 20 minutes | **Servings:** 4)

Ingredients

1 cup zucchini, grated, juice squeezed out
1/2 cup all-purpose flour
1/2 cup cornbread crumbs
1/2 cup goat cheese, grated Salt and black pepper, to taste 1 teaspoon paprika

1 garlic clove, minced
1 egg
1/2 cup parmesan cheese, grated

Directions

Start by preheating your Air Fryer to 330 degrees F. Spritz the cooking basket with nonstick cooking oil.

Mix all Ingredients until everything is well incorporated. Shape the zucchini mixture into golf sized balls and place them in the cooking basket.

Cook in the preheated Air Fryer for 15 to 18 minutes, shaking the basket periodically to ensure even cooking.

Garnish with some extra paprika if desired and **Serve:** at room temperature. Bon appétit!

Cauliflower Bombs with Sweet & Sour Sauce

(**Ready in about** 25 minutes | **Servings:** 4)

Ingredients

Cauliflower Bombs
2 ounces Ricotta cheese
1 egg
2 tablespoons olive oil
1 red bell pepper, jarred
1 clove garlic, minced

Salt and black pepper, to taste

1/2 pound cauliflower
1/3 cup Swiss cheese
1 tablespoon Italian seasoning mix Sweet & Sour Sauce
1 teaspoon sherry vinegar
1 tablespoon tomato puree

Directions

Blanch the cauliflower in salted boiling water about 3 to 4 minutes until al dente. Drain well and pulse in a food processor.

Add the remaining Ingredients for the cauliflower bombs; mix to combine well.

Bake in the preheated Air Fryer at 375 degrees F for 16 minutes, shaking halfway through the cooking time.

In the meantime, pulse all Ingredients for the sauce in your food processor until combined. Season to taste. **Serve:** the cauliflower bombs with the Sweet & Sour Sauce on the side. Bon appétit!

Classic Zucchini Chips

Prep time: 5 minutes **Cooking time:** 35 minutes
Servings: 6

Ingredients
3 zucchinis thinly sliced   1 teaspoon salt

Directions

Put the zucchini in the air fryer and sprinkle with salt. Cook them at 350F for 35 minutes. Shake the zucchini every 5 minutes.

Seaweed Crisps

Prep time: 10 minutes **Cooking time:** 5 minutes
Servings: 4

Ingredients
3 nori sheets   1 teaspoon nutritional
2 tablespoons water   yeast

Directions

Cut the nori sheets roughly and put in the air fryer basket.
Sprinkle the nori sheets with water and nutritional yeast and cook at 375F for 5 minutes.

Avocado Sticks

Prep time: 10 minutes **Cooking time:** 14 minutes
Servings: 4

Ingredients
1 avocado, pitted, halves   1 tablespoon coconut
1 egg, beaten   shred

Directions

Cut the avocado halves into 4 wedges and dip in the egg.
Then coat the avocado in coconut shred and put in the air fryer. Cook the avocado sticks at 375F for 7 minutes per side.

Mozzarella Sticks

Prep time: 10 minutes **Cooking time:** 4 minutes
Servings: 4

Ingredients
1 egg, beaten   4 tbsp almond flour
9 oz. Mozzarella, cut into
sticks

Directions

Dip the mozzarella sticks in the egg and they coat in the almond flour. Then put the mozzarella sticks in the air fryer basket and cook at 400F for 4 minutes.

Lettuce Wraps

Prep time: 10 minutes **Cooking time:** 4 minutes
Servings: 12

Ingredients
12 bacon strips   12 lettuce leaves
1 tablespoon mustard   1 tablespoon apple cider
                         vinegar

Directions

Set the bacon in the air fryer in one layer and cook at 400f for 2 minutes per side.

Then sprinkle the bacon with mustard and apple cider vinegar and put on the lettuce. Wrap the lettuce into rolls.

Carrot Chips

Prep time: 10 minutes **Cooking time:** 13 minute
Servings: 8

Ingredients
3 carrots, thinly sliced   1 teaspoon avocado oil

Directions

Set the carrots in the air fryer basket, sprinkle with avocado oil. Cook the carrot chips for 30 minutes at 355F. Shake the carrot chips every 5 minutes.

Crunchy Bacon

Prep time: 5 minutes **Cooking time:** 8 minutes
Servings: 4

Ingredients
8 bacon slices   1 teaspoon Erythritol
Directions

Sprinkle the bacon with Erythritol and put in the air fryer basket in one layer. Cook it for 4 minutes per side or until the bacon is crunchy.

Keto Granola

Prep time: 10 minutes **Cooking time:** 12 minutes
Servings: 4

Ingredients
1 teaspoon monk fruit   1 teaspoon pumpkin pie
2 teaspoons coconut oil   spices
3 pecans, chopped   1 tbsp coconut shred
3 oz. almonds, chopped   1 tablespoon flax seeds

Directions

In the mixing bowl, mix all Ingredients from the list above. Make the small balls from the mixture and put them in the air fryer. Cook the granola for 6 minutes per side at 365F. Cool the cooked granola.

Bacon Pickles

Prep time: 5 minutes **Cooking time:** 6 minutes
Servings: 4

Ingredients
4 pickled cucumbers   4 bacon slices

Directions

Preheat the air fryer to 400F and put the bacon inside. Cook it for 3 minutes per side. Then cool the bacon and wrap pickled cucumbers in the bacon.

Smokies

Prep time: 10 minutes **Cooking time:** 10 minutes
Servings: 10

Ingredients
12 oz. pork smokies   1 teaspoon cayenne
                             pepper

1 teaspoon keto tomato   1 tablespoon coconut oil
paste

Directions

Mix pork smokies with cayenne pepper, coconut oil, and tomato paste.
Set them in the air fryer basket and cook for 5 minutes per side at 375F.

Avocado and Pork Rinds Balls

Prep time: 10 minutes **Cooking time:** 5 minutes
Servings: 4

Ingredients
1 avocado, peeled, pitted   2 oz. pork rinds
and mashed   1 tablespoon cream cheese
1 teaspoon dried oregano

Directions

Preheat the air fryer to 360F and put the pork rinds inside. Cook them for 5 minutes. Then mix the pork rinds with dried oregano, cream cheese, and mashed avocado. Make the balls from the mixture.

Chicken Skin

Prep time: 10 minutes **Cooking time:** 10 minutes
Servings: 3

Ingredients
6 oz. chicken skin   1 teaspoon avocado oil
1/2 teaspoon ground
black pepper

Directions

Chop the chicken skin roughly and mix it with avocado oil and ground black pepper.

Put the chicken skin in the air fryer basket and cook at 375F for 10 minutes. Shake the chicken skin every 3 minutes to avoid burning.

Seafood Balls

Prep time: 15 minutes **Cooking time:** 15 minutes
Servings: 4

Ingredients
1-pound salmon fillet,   3 tablespoons coconut,
minced   shredded
1 tablespoon avocado oil   1 teaspoon dried basil
1/2 cup almond flour   1 egg, beaten

Directions

In the mixing bowl, mix minced salmon fillet, egg, coconut, almond flour, and dried basil.

Make the balls from the fish mixture and put them in the air fryer basket. Sprinkle the balls with avocado oil and cook at 365F for 15 minutes.

Popcorn Balls

Prep time: 10 minutes **Cooking time:** 12 minutes
Servings: 6

Ingredients
2 cups ground chicken   1 tbs Italian seasonings
1/4 cup coconut flour   1 tablespoon avocado oil
1 egg, beaten

Directions

Mix the ground chicken with Italian seasonings, egg, and coconut flour. Make the small balls from the chicken mixture (popcorn) and put in the air fryer in one layer.
Sprinkle the popcorn balls with avocado oil and cook at 365F for 6 minutes per side.

Parsley Balls

Prep time: 10 minutes **Cooking time:** 8 minutes
Servings: 6

Ingredients
4 pecans, grinded
1 egg, beaten
1 teaspoon onion powder
3 tablespoons dried parsley
2 oz. Parmesan, grated

Directions

In the mixing bowl, mix pecans with dried basil, onion powder, egg, and Parmesan. Make the balls and put them in the air fryer in one layer. Cook them at 375F for 8 minutes (4 minutes per side).

Chicken Pies

Prep time: 15 minutes **Cooking time:** 10 minutes
Servings: 6

Ingredients
1-pound chicken fillet, boiled
1 egg, beaten
6 wonton wraps
1 teaspoon chili powder
1 teaspoon garlic powder
1 tablespoon avocado oil
1 tablespoon cream cheese

Directions

Shred the chicken fillet and mix it with cream cheese, chili powder, garlic powder, and egg. Then put the chicken mixture on the wonton wraps and roll them. Sprinkle the chicken pies with avocado oil and bake in the air fryer at 375F for 10 minutes.

Salmon Bites

Prep time: 5 minutes **Cooking time:** 10 minutes
Servings: 6

Ingredients
1- pound salmon fillet, roughly chopped
1 tbsp ground black pepper
1 teaspoon dried basil
1 tablespoon avocado oil

Directions

Mix chopped salmon with dried basil and ground black pepper. Put the fish pieces in the air fryer basket and sprinkle with

Eggplant Bites

Prep time: 10 minutes **Cooking time:** 25 minutes
Servings: 4

Ingredients
1 eggplant, sliced
1/2 teaspoon salt
1 teaspoon nutritional yeast

Directions

Sprinkle the sliced eggplant with salt and nutritional yeast.
Set it in the air fryer and cook at 360F for 25 minutes.

Cilantro Meatballs

Prep time: 15 minutes **Cooking time:** 20 minutes
Servings: 6

Ingredients
2 cups ground beef
1 teaspoon ground black pepper
1 tablespoon dried cilantro
Cooking spray
1 egg, beaten

Directions

Set the air fryer basket with cooking spray. Then mixes all remaining Ingredients and make the meatballs. Put them in the air fryer and cook at 365F for 20 minutes.

Bacon Rolls

Prep time: 10 minutes **Cooking time:** 8 minutes
Servings: 5

Ingredients
5 bacon slices
3 tablespoons mascarpone
1 teaspoon dried oregano

Directions

Preheat the air fryer to 400F. Put the bacon slices inside in one layer and cook for 4 minutes per side. Then cool the bacon slices little and sprinkle with dried oregano. Spread the mascarpone over the bacon slices and roll them.

Air Fryer Fried Pickles

Prep time: 5 minutes **Cooking time:** 15 minutes
Servings: 4

Ingredients

1/2 cup crushed pork rinds	3 tablespoons parmesan cheese, finely grated
16 sliced dill pickles	
1/2 cup almond flour	1 large free-range egg, beaten
1 teaspoon olive oil	

Directions

Preheat the air fryer to 370F. Mix the pork and parmesan properly in a shallow bowl. Whisk eggs together properly in another bowl. In another bowl, add the almond flour. Dip the pickle in the almond flour, then the egg, then the pork and parmesan. Cook for 6 minutes. **Serve:** and enjoy.

Bacon and Cream Cheese Stuffed Jalapeno Poppers

Prep time: 5 minutes **Cooking time:** 15 minutes
Servings: 5

Ingredients

10 fresh jalapenos, sliced in half horizontally	2 slices bacon
1/4 cup shredded cheddar cheese	6 oz. cream cheese, softened in the microwave

Directions

Preheat your air fryer to 370F. Mix the cream cheese, bacon and shredded cheese in a medium-sized bowl.

Fill the jalapenos with the cheese mixture. Cook for 10-15 minutes in the air fryer. **Serve:** and enjoy.

Cauliflower Buffalo Wings

Prep time: 5 minutes **Cooking time:** 20 minutes
Servings: 4

Ingredients

1 head cauliflower, cut into pieces	1 tablespoon butter
Salt and pepper, to taste	1/2 cup buffalo sauce

Directions

Preheat the air fryer to 400F. Mix the butter, buffalo sauce, and salt and pepper to taste in a medium- sized bowl.

Cook the cauliflower into the air fryer for 7 minutes. Add the butter mixture to the cooked cauliflower, mix well to coat properly. Cook for 7 minutes in the air fryer again. **Serve:** and enjoy.

Healthy French Fries

Prep time: 5 minutes **Cooking time:** 30 minutes
Servings: 4

Ingredients

3 medium russet potatoes, cut into 1/4" fries	2 tablespoons finely chopped fresh parsley
2 tablespoons Parmesan cheese	1 tablespoon olive oil
	Salt, to taste

Directions

Preheat the air fryer to 360F. Stir cheese, herbs and oil in a large bowl. Cook for 20 minutes in the air fryer, overturning often. **Serve:** and enjoy.

Healthy Zucchini Corn Fritters

Prep time: 5 minutes **Cooking time:** 22 minutes
Servings: 4

Ingredients

2 medium zucchinis, shredded	1 medium potato, cooked and smashed
1 cup corn kernels	2 tablespoons chickpea flour
2-3 garlic finely minced	Salt and pepper, to taste
1-2 teaspoon olive oil	Ketchup or Yogurt tahini sauce
To **Serve:**"	

Directions

Preheat the air fryer to 360F. Attach all the Ingredients to a large bowl. Stir well to combine. Form flat shapes with the paste and place in the air fryer. Cook for 12-15 minutes, flipping often.

Serve: with any condiment of your choice. For example, ketchup or yoghurt tahini sauce.

Tortilla Snack Chips

Prep time: 10 minutes **Cooking time:** 15 minutes
Servings: 1-2

Ingredients

1 x 8 pack tortillas of choice Cooking spray	Salt to taste

Directions

Heat your air fryer to 350F. Slice the tortillas into rounds using a cookie cutter. Spray the tortillas with oil and sprinkle with salt. Cook for 2-3 minutes. **Serve:** and enjoy.

Eggplant Parmesan

Prep time: 10 minutes **Cooking time:** 40 minutes
Servings: 4

Ingredients

1 large eggplant,	1/2 cup whole wheat
1 free-range egg	bread crumbs
3 tablespoons finely grated	1 teaspoon Italian
parmesan cheese	seasoning mix
Salt, to taste	3 tbsp whole wheat flour
1 tbsp water Olive oil	1 cup marinara sauce
spray	
1/4 cup grated mozzarella	Fresh parsley or basil to
cheese	garnish

Directions

Set your air fryer to 360F. Merge the flour, egg and water in a large bowl. Add the breadcrumbs, parmesan, Italian seasoning and salt in a shallow bowl. Mix properly to combine.

Put the eggplant into the egg mixture, drip off any excess, place into the breadcrumbs and coat evenly. Cook in the air fryer until perfectly cooked.

Roasted Brussels Sprouts with Garlic and Thyme

Prep time: 5 minutes **Cooking time:** 20 minutes
Servings: 4

Ingredients

1 lb. Brussels sprouts,	1 teaspoon dried parsley
cleaned and trimmed	4 cloves garlic, crushed
1/2 teaspoon dried thyme	1/4 teaspoon salt
2 teaspoons oil (opt.)	

Directions

Heat your air fryer to 390F. Merge all the Ingredients in a bowl and Stir well to combine. Cook in the air fryer until perfect. **Serve:** and enjoy.

Special Cauliflower Rice

Prep time: 5 minutes **Cooking time:** 30 minutes
Servings: 3

Ingredients

For the tofu	1/2 extra firm tofu,
1/2 cup frozen peas	crumbled
2 tablespoons soy sauce	2 carrots, diced
1 teaspoon turmeric	For the rice
3 cups riced cauliflower	2 tablespoons reduced-
1 tablespoon rice vinegar	sodium soy sauce
1/2 cup diced onion	1 1/2 tbsp toasted sesame
2 cloves garlic, minced	oil, opt.
1 tablespoon minced	1/2 cup finely chopped
ginger	
	broccoli

Directions

Heat the air fryer to 370F. Mix the tofu to the rest of the tofu Ingredients. Stir well to combine.

Set in the air fryer and cook for 10 minutes. Add the remaining Ingredients to another bowl. Stir well. Set into the air fryer and cook for another 10 minutes. **Serve:** and enjoy.

Baked Sweet Potato Cauliflower Patties

Prep time: 10 minutes **Cooking time:** 35 minutes
Servings: 1

Ingredients

1 medium to large sweet	1 green onion, chopped.
potato	1 teaspoon minced garlic
2 tablespoon ranch	1/2 teaspoon chili powder
seasoning mix or paleo	1/4 teaspoon cumin
ranch seasoning	2 cups cauliflower florets
2 tablespoons arrowroot	1/4 cup sunflower seeds
powder	1/4 cup ground flaxseed
Salt and pepper, to taste	To **Serve:**
Dipping sauce of choice	1 cup packed cilantro

Directions

Heat the oven to 400F. Add the sweet potato, cauliflower, onion and garlic to a food processor. Blend until smooth.

Add the remaining Ingredients to the blend Ingredients. Blend again until smooth. Shape into patties using your hands and place onto an oiled baking sheet.
Place in a freezer for 10 minutes.

Remove from the freezer and place the patties into the air fryer. Cook for 20 minutes, overturning frequently.

Cheese Sticks

Prep time: 15 minutes **Cooking time:** 17 minutes
Servings: 8

Ingredients

8 regular cheese sticks	1/2 cup grated parmesan
1 large free-range egg	cheese
1/4 cup almond flour	1 teaspoon Italian
	seasoning
1 teaspoon garlic powder	1/4 tbsp ground rosemary

Directions

Whisk the egg properly in a bowl. Add the almond flour, parmesan, Italian seasoning, and rosemary and garlic powder in another bowl. Mix well to combine properly.

Coat the cheese sticks with the egg by dipping it in the egg, drip off any excess and dip in the almond flour. Line a baking pan with a baking sheet. Place the cheese sticks in the pan and place in the freezer for 10 minutes.
Heat the air fryer to 370F.

Set out the cheese sticks from the freezer then place in the air fryer. Cook for 10 minutes, then **Serve:** and enjoy.

Sweets and Treats

Prep time: 10 minutes **Cooking time:** 20 minutes
Servings: 6-8

Ingredients

2 free-range eggs	1 1/2 teaspoon vanilla
1 1/2 cups milk	extract
1/2 cup Monk Fruit	1/2 cup coconut flour
sweetener	1/4 cup butter
1 cup shredded coconut	

Directions

Heat the air fryer to 350F and oil a 6 inches pie plate with any oil of your choice. Set aside.

Attach all the Ingredients to a large bowl. Mix properly to combine. Pour the mixture into the pie plate and place in your air fryer. Let it cook properly for 10-12 minutes. **Serve:** and enjoy!

Cinnamon Donuts

Prep time: 5 minutes **Cooking time:** 15 minutes
Servings: 10

Ingredients

For the donuts	1/2 cup sour cream
1/4 cup heavy whipping	1 teaspoon vanilla extract
cream	1/2 cup coconut flour
1/4 teaspoon nutmeg	1/4 teaspoon baking soda
4 large free-range eggs	1/4 cup Erythritol
Pinch of salt	For the cinnamon coating
1/4 cup Erythritol	1 teaspoon cinnamon 1/4
	cup of coconut oil.

Directions

Heat your air fryer to 360F. Get a pan that fits into your air fryer. Grease the pan with any oil of your choice.
Stir the sour cream, whipping cream, eggs and vanilla in a large bowl.

Add the dry Ingredients into the bowl, mix well. Add the coconut flour, nutmeg, baking soda, Erythritol and salt, mix well again to combine.
Pour the mix into the donut tin. Cook for 15 minutes in the air fryer until perfectly done. **Serve:** and enjoy.

Gluten-Free Chocolate Lava Cake

Prep time: 10 minutes **Cooking time:** 15 minutes
Servings: 1

Ingredients

1 free-range egg	2 tablespoons cocoa
	powder
2 tablespoons Erythritol	1 tablespoon golden flax
1/8 teaspoon Stevia	meal
1 tablespoon coconut oil,	1/2 teaspoon aluminum-
melted	free baking powder
Pinch of Himalayan salt	Dash of vanilla extract
2 tablespoons water	

Directions

Heat your air fryer to 350F. Merge all the Ingredients. Stir well to combine. Pour the mix into a 2-cup glass ramekin.
Cook in the air fryer. **Serve:** and enjoy.

Brazilian Grilled Pineapple

Prep time: 5 minutes **Cooking time:** 20 minutes
Servings: 6

Ingredients

1 small pineapple cut into spears	2 teaspoons ground cinnamon
3 tablespoons melted butter	1/2 cup sweetener

Directions

Heat up your air fryer to 400F. Add the sugar and cinnamon to a large bowl. Mix well to combine. Brush the melted butter on the surface of the pineapple, then sprinkle with sugar and then place into the air fryer.
Cook for 6-10 minutes. **Serve:** and enjoy.

Fried Cheesecake Bites

Prep time: 5 minutes **Cooking time:** 45 minutes
Servings: 16

Ingredients

8 oz. cream cheese, at room temp	1/2 cup + 2 tbsp Erythritol
	1/2 teaspoon vanilla extract
4 tablespoons cream, divided	1/2 cup almond flour

Directions

Add the cream cheese, 1/2 cup Erythritol, vanilla and 2 tablespoons of the heavy cream in a large bowl. Stir to combine.

Whisk with a wooden spoon until smooth.
Scoop out the batter and place in a lined baking sheet. Place in the freezer for 30 minutes. Warm-up your air fryer to 350F.

Merge the almond flour with the rest of the Erythritol in a bowl and stir together In another bowl add the remaining cream.

Dip the batter into the cream, and then roll up in the almond flour. Cook for 2-3 minutes in the air fryer. **Serve:** and enjoy.

Chocolate Almond Cupcakes

Prep time: 15 minutes **Cooking time:** 25-30 minutes
Servings: 3

Ingredients

3 tablespoons butter	2 tablespoons real maple syrup
1/2 cup almond flour	1/3 cup chocolate chips
1/8 teaspoon salt	1/2 teaspoon vanilla
1 free-range egg, beaten	

Directions

Heat up the air fryer to 320F then prepare your silicone cake liners.

Combine the chocolate chips, butter, and honey in a large bowl. Mix well to combine properly. Fill water in a pan. Set over medium heat and bring to the boil then

place the bowl on top of the hot water. Continuously stir until the chocolate melts. Remove from the bowl and add the remaining Ingredients to the melted chocolate. Stir well again.

Transfer the mix into the silicone cake dish then place into the air fryer. Cook for 15-20 minutes.
After cooking, allow to cool then sprinkle with icing sugar if you want. **Serve:** and enjoy!

Spiced Apples

Prep time: 5 minutes **Cooking time:** 15 minutes
Servings: 4

Ingredients

4 small apples, sliced	2 tablespoons coconut oil, melted
2 tablespoons sweetener	
1 teaspoon apple pie spice	

Directions

Heat the air fryer to 350F. Put the apples inside a medium-sized bowl. Whisk in the melted coconut oil and mix well to coat.

Dust the sugar and spice on the apples. Mix properly to coat. Pierce the apple with a fork then place into your air fryer for 10 minutes. **Serve:** and enjoy.

Flourless Chocolate Brownies

Prep time: 5 minutes **Cooking time:** 45 minutes
Servings: 6

Ingredients

1/2 cup sugar-free chocolate chips	3 free-range eggs
1 teaspoon vanilla extract	1/4 cup sweetener
	1/2 cup butter

Directions

Heat your air fryer to 350F and grease a spring form tin with an oil of your choice. Add the butter and chocolate to a microwaveable bowl. Place the mix in the microwave and warm up for a minute until perfectly melted. Mix well and place aside.

Whisk eggs, sweetener and vanilla all together in a medium-sized bowl until frothy.

Add the melted chocolate and butter and stir well to combine. Whisk the mix into the tin and cook for 30 minutes. **Serve:** and enjoy.

Air Fried Mushroom

Prep time: 10 minutes **Cooking time:** 10 minutes
Servings: 4

Ingredients

8 ounces (227 g) Cremini mushrooms, halved	1/4 teaspoon salt
	2 tablespoons salted butter, melted
1/4 teaspoon ground black pepper	

Directions

In a medium bowl, merge mushrooms with butter, and then sprinkle with salt and pepper. Place into ungreased air fryer basket. Adjust the temperature to 400°F (205°C) and set the timer for 10 minutes, shaking the basket halfway through cooking. Mushrooms will be tender when done. **Serve:** warm.

Sticky Glazed Wings

Prep time: 10 minutes **Cooking time:** 15 minutes
Servings: 2

Ingredients

1/2 pound chicken wings	2 tbsp brown sugar
1 tbs Worcestershire sauce	1 tbs balsamic vinegar
1 tablespoon hot sauce	1 tablespoon sesame oil

Directions

Brush the chicken wings with sesame oil and transfer them to the Air Fryer cooking basket. Cook the chicken wings at 370 degrees F for 12 minutes; turn them over and cook for a further 10 minutes. Meanwhile, bring the other Ingredients to a boil in a saucepan; cook for 2 to 3 minutes or until thoroughly cooked.

Toss the warm chicken wings with the sauce and place them on a serving platter. **Serve:** and enjoy!

Asian Twist Chicken Wings

Prep time: 10 minutes **Cooking time:** 10 minutes
Servings: 6

Ingredients

1 1/2 pounds chicken wings	salt and ground black pepper, to taste
2 teaspoons sesame oil	
1 tablespoon rice vinegar	2 tablespoons honey
2 garlic clove, minced	2 tablespoons tamari sauce
2 sun-dried tomatoes, minced	

Directions

Toss the chicken wings with the sesame oil, salt, and pepper. Add chicken wings to a lightly greased baking pan. Roast the chicken wings in the preheated Air Fryer at 390 degrees F for 7 minutes. Set them over once or twice to ensure even cooking.

In a mixing dish, thoroughly combine the tamari sauce, vinegar, garlic, honey, and sun-dried tomatoes. Pour the sauce all over the chicken wings; bake an additional 5 minutes. **Serve:** warm.

Quick and Easy Popcorn

Prep time: 10 minutes **Cooking time:** 10 minutes
Servings: 4

Ingredients

2 tablespoons dried corn
kernels
1 tbs red pepper flakes

Kosher salt, to taste
1 teaspoon safflower oil

Directions

Add the dried corn kernels to the Air Fryer basket;
brush with safflower oil. Cook at 395 degrees F for 15
minutes, shaking the basket every 5 minutes. Sprinkle
with salt and red pepper flakes. Enjoy!

Beer-Battered Vidalia Onion Rings

Prep time: 5 minutes **Cooking time:** 10 minutes
Servings: 2

Ingredients

1/2 cup all-purpose flour
1/2 teaspoon baking
powder
salt and ground black
pepper, to taste
1 cup crushed tortilla
chips

1/4 teaspoon cayenne
pepper 1/4 teaspoon dried
oregano
1/4 cup beer
1 large egg, beaten
1/2 pound Vidalia onions,
cut into rings

Directions

In a mixing bowl, merge the flour, baking powder,
cayenne pepper, oregano, salt, black pepper, egg and
beer; mix to combine well. In another shallow bowl,
place the crushed tortilla chips. Dip the Vidalia rings in
the beer mixture; then, coat the rings with the crushed
tortilla chips, pressing to adhere. Transfer the onion
rings to the Air Fryer cooking basket and spritz them
with a nonstick spray.
Cook the onion rings at 380 degrees F for about 8
minutes, shaking the basket halfway through the
Cooking time:to ensure even browning. **Serve:** and
enjoy!

Coconut Banana Chips

Prep time: 5 minutes **Cooking time:** 5 minutes
Servings: 2

Ingredients

1 large banana, peeled and
sliced
1 teaspoon coconut oil

1/4 tbs ground cinnamon
A pinch of coarse salt
2 tbs coconut flakes

Directions

Toss the banana slices with the coconut oil, cinnamon and
salt. Transfer banana slices to the Air Fryer cooking basket.
Cook the banana slices at 375 degrees F for about 8
minutes, shaking the basket every 2 minutes. Scatter
coconut flakes over the banana slices and let banana
chips cool slightly before serving. Enjoy!

Eggplant Pram Chips

Prep time: 10 minutes **Cooking time:** 15 minutes
Servings: 2

Ingredients

1/2 pound eggplant, cut
into rounds
salt black pepper, to taste
1/2 cup Parmesan cheese,

Grated

1/2 teaspoon porcini
powder
1/2 teaspoon garlic
powder 1/4 tbs cayenne
pepper
1/2 tbs shallot powder

Directions

Toss the eggplant rounds with the remaining
Ingredients until well coated on both sides. Bake the
eggplant chips at 400 degrees F for 15 minutes; shake
the basket and continue to cook for 15 minutes more.
Let cool slightly, eggplant chips will crisp up as it
cools.Enjoy!

Mexican Crunchy Cheese Straws

Prep time: 5 minutes **Cooking time:** 10 minutes
Servings: 3

Ingredients

1/2 cup almond flour
1/4 teaspoon shallot
powder 1/4 teaspoon
garlic powder
1 ounce Manchego cheese,
grated

1/4 teaspoon xanthan
gum 1/4 teaspoon ground
cumin
1 egg yolk, whisked
2 ounces Cotija cheese,
grated

Directions

Merge all Ingredients until everything is well
incorporated. Twist the batter into straw strips and
place them on a baking mat inside your Air Fryer.
Cook the cheese straws in your Air Fryer at 360
degrees F for 5 minutes; turn them over and cook an
additional 5 minutes. Let the cheese straws cool before
serving. Enjoy!

Greek-Style Deviled Eggs

Prep time: 5 minutes **Cooking time:** 10 minutes
Servings: 2

Ingredients

3 eggs

2 tablespoons Kalamata olives, pitted and chopped

1 tablespoon Greek-style yogurt

Sea salt and red pepper flakes,

1 tbsp chives, chopped

1 teaspoon habanero pepper, seeded and chopped

1 tablespoon parsley, chopped

Directions

Set the wire rack in the Air Fryer basket and lower the eggs onto the rack. Cook the eggs at 260 degrees F for 15 minutes.

Transfer the eggs to an ice-cold water bath to stop cooking. Skin the eggs under cold running water; slice them into halves, separating the whites and yolks. Press the egg yolks with the remaining Ingredients and mix to combine. Spoon the yolk mixture into the egg whites and **Serve:** well chilled. Enjoy!

Puerto Rican Tostones

Prep time: 5 minutes **Cooking time:** 10 minutes
Servings: 2

Ingredients

1 ripe plantain, sliced

A pinch of grated nutmeg

1 tablespoon sunflower oil

A pinch of kosher salt

Directions

Toss the plantains with the oil, nutmeg, and salt in a bowl. Cook in the preheated Air Fryer at 400 degrees F for 10 minutes, shaking the cooking basket halfway through the cooking time. Set the seasonings to taste and **Serve:** immediately.

Green Bean Crisps

Prep time: 10 minutes **Cooking time:** 10 minutes
Servings: 4

Ingredients

1 egg, beaten

1/4 cup parmesan, grated

1 teaspoon sea salt

2 tablespoons grape seed oil

1/4 cup cornmeal

1/2 teaspoon red pepper flakes, crushed

1 pound green beans

Directions

Ina mixing bowl, combine together the egg, cornmeal, parmesan, salt, and red pepper flakes; mix to combine well. Dip the green beans into the batter and transfer them to the cooking basket. Brush with the grape seed oil.

Cook in the preheated Air Fryer at 390 degrees F for 4 minutes. Shake the basket and cook for a further 3 minutes. Work in batches. Taste, adjust the seasonings and **Serve:** warm.

Homemade Ranch Tater Tots

Prep time: 10 minutes **Cooking time:** 5 minutes
Servings: 2

Ingredients

1/2 pound potatoes, peeled and shredded

1 teaspoon Ranch seasoning mix

Sea salt and ground black pepper, to flavor

1/2 teaspoon dried marjoram

2 tablespoons Colby cheese, finely grated about 1/3 cup 1 tbsp butter, melted

1/2 teaspoon hot paprika

Directions

In a mixing bowl, merge all Ingredients until everything is well incorporated. Transfer your tater tots to a lightly greased Air Fryer cooking basket. Cook your tater tots in the preheated Air Fryer at 400 degrees F for 12 minutes to ensure even browning. **Serve:** and enjoy!

Barbecue Little Smokies

Prep time: 10 minutes **Cooking time:** 10 minutes
Servings: 6

Ingredients

1 pound beef cocktail wieners

10 ounces barbecue sauce

Directions

Set by preheating your Air Fryer to 380 degrees F. Prick holes into your sausages using a fork and transfer them to the baking pan. Cook for 13 minutes. Spoon the barbecue sauce into the pan and cook an additional 2 minutes. **Serve:** with toothpicks. Enjoy!

Baby Carrots with Asian Flair

Prep time: 10 minutes **Cooking time:** 10 minutes
Servings: 3

Ingredients

1 pound baby carrots	2 tablespoons sesame oil
1/2 teaspoon Szechuan pepper	1 tablespoon honey
	1 teaspoon Wuxiang powder
1 large garlic clove, crushed	1 1-inch piece fresh ginger root
5-spice powder	2 tablespoons tamari sauce

Directions

Begin by preheating your Air Fryer to 380 degrees F. Toss all Ingredients together and place them in the Air Fryer basket. Cook for 15 minutes, shaking the basket halfway through the cooking time.
Enjoy!

Greek-Style Squash Chips

Prep time: 10 minutes **Cooking time:** 15 minutes
Servings: 4

Ingredients

1/2 cup seasoned breadcrumbs	Sea salt and ground black pepper, to flavor
1/2 cup Parmesan cheese	1/4 teaspoon oregano
2 yellow squash, cut into slices	2 tablespoons grape seed oil
	1 garlic clove, minced
Sauce	1/2 cup Greek-style yogurt
1 tablespoon fresh cilantro, chopped	Freshly ground black pepper, to your liking

Directions

In a shallow bowl, thoroughly combine the seasoned breadcrumbs, Parmesan, salt, black pepper, and oregano.
Dip the yellow squash slices in the prepared batter, pressing to adhere. Brush with the grape seed oil and cook in the preheated Air Fryer at 400 degrees F for 12 minutes.

Shake the Air Fryer basket periodically to ensure even cooking. Work in batches. While the chips are baking, whisk the sauce Ingredients; place in your refrigerator until ready to **Serve:**. Enjoy!

Zucchini Chips

Prep time: 5 minutes **Cooking time:** 25 minutes
Servings: 4

Ingredients

2 Zucchini	1 Teaspoon Olive Oil
	1 tbs Paprika Sea Salt to Taste

Directions

Preheat your air fryer to 370, and then slice your zucchini. Sprinkle your salt and paprika over the zucchini. Sprinkle them down with oil, and then cook for thirteen minutes.

Cajun Cheese Sticks

Prep time: 5 minutes **Cooking time:** 10 minutes
Servings: 4

Ingredients

1/2 cup all-purpose flour	1/2 cup parmesan cheese, grated
2 eggs	
1 tbsp Cajun seasonings	8 cheese sticks, kid-friendly
1/4 cup ketchup	

Directions

To begin, set up your breading station. Set the all-purpose flour in a shallow dish. In a separate dish, whisk the eggs. Finally, mix the parmesan cheese and Cajun seasoning in a third dish. Start by dredging the cheese sticks in the flour; then, dip them into the egg. Press the cheese sticks into the parmesan mixture, coating evenly. Place the breaded cheese sticks in the lightly greased Air Fryer basket. Cook at 380 degrees F.
Serve: with ketchup and enjoy!

Kale Chips with White Horseradish Mayo

Prep time: 5 minutes **Cooking time:** 5 minutes
Servings: 1

Ingredients

2 cups loosely packed kale	Sea salt and ground black pepper, to flavor
1 teaspoon sesame oil	
1 ounce mayonnaise	1 teaspoon prepared white horseradish
1 teaspoon sesame seeds, lightly toasted	

Directions

Toss the kale pieces with sesame oil, salt and black pepper. Cook the kale pieces at 370 degrees F for 2 minutes; shake the basket and continue to cook for 2 minutes more. Meanwhile, make the horseradish mayo by whisking the mayonnaise and prepared horseradish. Let cool slightly, kale chips will crisp up as it cools. Sprinkle toasted sesame seeds over the kale chips.
Serve: the kale chips with the horseradish mayo.
Enjoy!

Mexican Cheesy Zucchini Bites

Prep time: 15 minutes **Cooking time:** 10 minutes
Servings: 4

Ingredients

1 large-sized zucchini, thinly sliced
1/2 cup tortilla chips, crushed
1/2 cup Queso Añejo, grated

1/4 cup yellow cornmeal
1 egg, whisked
Salt and cracked pepper, to taste
1/2 cup flour

Directions

Pat dry the zucchini slices with a kitchen towel. Mix the remaining Ingredients in a shallow bowl; mix until everything is well combined. Dip each zucchini slice in the prepared batter. Cook in the preheated Air Fryer at 400 degrees F for 12 minutes.

Homemade Apple Chips

Prep time: 5 minutes **Cooking time:** 15 minutes
Servings: 4

Ingredients

2 cooking apples, cored and thinly sliced
1 teaspoon peanut oil
1 tablespoon smooth peanut butter

1/4 teaspoon ground cloves 1/4 teaspoon ground cinnamon

Directions

Toss the apple slices with the peanut oil. Bake at 350 degrees F for 5 minutes; shake the basket to ensure even cooking and continue to cook an additional 5 minutes.

Spread each apple slice with a little peanut butter and sprinkle with ground cloves and cinnamon. **Serve:** and enjoy!

Toasted Nuts

Prep time: 5 minutes **Cooking time:** 15 minutes
Servings: 4

Ingredients

1/2 Cup Macadamia Nuts
1/2 Cup Pecans
1 Tablespoon Olive Oil

1/4 Cup Walnuts
1/4 Cup Hazelnuts
1 Teaspoon Sea Salt, Fine

Directions

Start by turning your air fryer to 32, and then place your nuts in your air fryer. Cook your nuts for eight minutes, and then stir. Cook for another four minutes.

Sprinkle them with oil and salt before shaking them. Cook for one more minute before serving.

Easy and Delicious Pizza Puffs

Prep time: 5 minutes **Cooking time:** 10 minutes
Servings: 6

Ingredients

6 ounces crescent roll dough
3 ounces pepperoni
3 ounces mushrooms, chopped
1/4 cup Marina sauce, for dipping

1/2 cup mozzarella cheese, shredded

1 teaspoon garlic powder
1 teaspoon oregano

Directions

Unroll the crescent dough. Set out the dough using a rolling pin; cut into 6 pieces. Place the cheese, pepperoni, and mushrooms in the center of each pizza puff.
Sprinkle with oregano and garlic powder. Fold each corner over the filling using wet hands. Press together to cover the filling entirely and seal the edges. Now, spritz the bottom of the Air Fryer basket with cooking oil.
Lay the pizza puffs in a single layer in the cooking basket. Work in batches. Bake at 370 degrees F for 5 to 6 minutes or until golden brown. **Serve:** with the marinara sauce for dipping.

Parmesan Sticks

Prep time: 10 minutes **Cooking time:** 15 minutes
Servings: 3

Ingredients

1/4 Teaspoon Black Pepper
4 Tablespoons Almond Flour
8 Ounces Parmesan Cheese

1/2 Cup Heavy Cream
1 Egg

Directions

Crack your egg into a bowl, beating it. Add in your almond flour and cream, mixing well. Sprinkle your cream mixture with black pepper, whisking well.

Cut your cheese into short, thick sticks, and then dip it in the cream mixture. Place these sticks in a plastic bag and place them in the freezer. Let them freeze.

Turn your air fryer to 400, and then place your frozen sticks on the air fryer rack, and then cook for eight minutes.

Party Greek Keftedes

Prep time: 10 minutes **Cooking time:** 10 minutes
Servings: 6

Ingredients

Greek Keftedes
1/2 pound pork sausage, chopped
1 teaspoon granulated garlic
1 teaspoon dried rosemary
2 tablespoons cornbread crumbs
1 Lebanese cucumbers, grated, juice squeezed out
1 cup full-fat Greek yogurt
1 tablespoon extra-virgin olive oil

1/2 pound mushrooms, chopped
1 teaspoon shallot powder
1 teaspoon dried oregano
2 eggs

Tzatziki Dip
1 teaspoon dried basil
1 tablespoon fresh lemon juice
1 garlic clove, minced
1/2 teaspoon salt

Directions

In a mixing bowl, merge all Ingredients for the Greek keftedes. Shape the meat mixture into bite-sized balls.

Cook in the preheated Air Fryer at 380 degrees for 10 minutes, shaking the cooking basket once or twice to ensure even cooking. Meanwhile, make the tzatziki dip by mixing all Ingredients.

Serve: the keftedes with cocktail sticks and tzatziki dip on the side. Enjoy!

Garlic Mozzarella Sticks

Prep time: 5 minutes **Cooking time:** 1 hour 15 minutes
Servings: 4

Ingredients

1 Tablespoon Italian Seasoning
1 Cup Parmesan Cheese

8 Strings Cheeses, Diced
2 Eggs, Beaten
1 Clove Garlic, Minced

Directions

Start by combining your parmesan, garlic and Italian seasoning in a bowl. Dip your cheese into the egg, and mix well. Roll it into your cheese crumbles, and then press the crumbs into the cheese.

Place them in the fridge for an hour, and then preheat your air fryer to 375. Spray your air fryer down with oil, and then arrange the cheese strings into the basket. Cook for eight to nine minutes at 365. Allow them to cool for at least five minutes before serving.

Bacon Biscuits

Prep time: 5 minutes **Cooking time:** 25 minutes
Servings: 6

Ingredients

3 Tablespoons Butter
1 Tablespoon Apple Cider Vinegar
1 Cup Almond Flour

1 Egg

4 tbs Heavy Cream
1/2 Teaspoon Baking Soda
4 Ounces Bacon, Cooked
1 Teaspoon Oregano

Directions

Start by cracking your eggs in a bowl, whisking well. Chop your bacon, adding it into your egg, sprinkling with apple cider vinegar and baking soda.

Add in your oregano and heavy cream, stirring well. Add in your almond flour and butter next, and mix well. Once your batter is smooth, and then preheats your air fryer to 400. Pour your batter into muffin molds, and then cook for ten minutes. Allow them to cool to room temperature before serving.

Pork Bacon Bites

Prep time: 5 minutes **Cooking time:** 30 minutes
Servings: 6

Ingredients

1 Teaspoon Olive Oil
1/2 Teaspoon Red Pepper
1 Teaspoon Turmeric
6 Ounces Bacon, Sliced

1 Tablespoon Apple Cider Vinegar
1 Teaspoon Sea Salt, Fine
1 lb. Pork Brisket

Directions

Start by cutting your pork into bite size pieces, and then place your pork bites into a mixing bowl. Sprinkle with red pepper, apple cider vinegar, turmeric and salt and mix well. Allow this to marinate for ten minutes, and then wrap each one in a slice of bacon. Secure them with toothpicks, and then heat your air fryer to 370.

Beef Jerky

Prep time: 5 minutes **Cooking time:** 3 hours **Servings:** 6

Ingredients

14 Ounces Beef Flank Steak
1 Teaspoon Chili Pepper
1 Teaspoon Black Pepper
1 Teaspoon Garlic Powder
1 Teaspoon Onion Powder
3 Tablespoons Apple Cider Vinegar
1/4 Teaspoon Liquid Smoke

Directions

Slice your beefsteak before tenderizing it. Get out a bowl and combine your black pepper, onion powder, apple cider vinegar, garlic and liquid smoke.

Wisk well, and then transfer our beef into it. Stir well, and allow it to marinate for up eight hours. You have to let at least it marinate for ten minutes. Cook your beef jerky at 150 for two and a half hours. Allow it to cool before serving.

Chicken Poppers

Prep time: 5 minutes **Cooking time:** 20 minutes **Servings:** 5

Ingredients

1 Teaspoon Garlic Powder
1 Teaspoon Black Pepper
1 Teaspoon Chili Flakes
1 Tablespoon Canola Oil
11 Ounces Chicken Breast, Boneless and Skinless
1/2 Cup Coconut Flour

Direction

Start by cubing your chicken, and then place it in a bowl. Sprinkle your chicken cubes with black pepper, garlic, and chili flakes. Stir well, and then sprinkle your almond flour over it. Sake the bowl so that the meat is coated properly, and preheat your air fryer to 365.

Sprinkle your air fryer down with your canola oil, and then cook your chicken for ten minutes. Turn them over, cooking for another five minutes. **Serve:** warm.

Pork Rinds

Prep time: 10 minutes **Cooking time:** 18 minutes **Servings:** 8

Ingredients

1/2 Teaspoon Black Pepper
1 Teaspoon Chili Flakes
1 Teaspoon Olive Oil
1 lb. Pork Rinds
1/2 Teaspoon Sea Salt, Fine

Directions

Start by heating your air fryer to 365, and then spray it down with olive oil.

Place your pork rinds in your air fryer basket, and sprinkle with your seasoning. Mix well, and then cook for seven minutes.

Shake gently, and then **Serve:** cooled.

Chicken Skin Crisps

Prep time: 10 minutes **Cooking time:** 16 minutes **Servings:** 6

Ingredients

1 lb. Chicken Skin
1/2 Teaspoon Chili Flakes
1 Teaspoon Butter
1/2 Teaspoon Black Pepper
1/2 Teaspoon Sea Salt, Fine
1 Teaspoon Dill

Directions

Slice your chicken skin roughly, and then sprinkle it with your seasoning. Mix you're the chicken skin, and melt your butter before adding it.

Preheat your air fryer to 360, and then place your chicken skin in your air fryer basket. Cook for three minutes per side, and then **Serve:** warm or room temperature.

Rosemary Potato Wedges

Prep time: 10 minutes **Cooking time:** 25 minutes
Serve: 4

Ingredients

3 potatoes, cut into wedges	3 tbsp olive oil
1 tsp garlic powder	1 tbsp fresh rosemary, chopped Pepper
1 tbsp parsley, chopped	
Salt	

Directions

Preheat the air fryer to 390 F. Soak potato wedges into the water for 30 minutes. Drain well and pat dry with paper towels.

In a mixing bowl, toss potato wedges with parsley, oil, garlic powder, rosemary, pepper, and salt.
Place potato wedges into the air fryer basket and cook for 15 minutes. Stir well and cook for 10 minutes more. **Serve:** and enjoy.

Healthy Mixed Nuts

Prep time: 10 minutes **Cooking time:** 9 minutes
Serve: 4

Ingredients

1/4 cup hazelnuts	1/2 cup macadamia nuts
1/2 cup pecans	1 tbsp olive oil
1/4 cup walnuts	1 tsp salt

Directions

Preheat the air fryer to 320 F. In a bowl, toss nuts with oil and salt. Add nuts into the air fryer basket and cook for 9 minutes. Stir halfway through. **Serve:** and enjoy.

Stuff Mushrooms

Prep time: 10 minutes **Cooking time:** 5 minutes
Serve: 6

Ingredients

9 oz mushrooms, cut stems	1 tsp dried parsley
6 oz mozzarella cheese, shredded	1 tbsp butter
1/2 tsp salt	

Directions

Preheat the air fryer to 400 F. In a small bowl, mix together cheese, butter, parsley, and salt until well combined. Stuff cheese mixture into the mushroom caps and place in the air fryer basket and cook for 5 minutes.
Serve: and enjoy.

Crispy Broccoli Popcorn

Prep time: 10 minutes **Cooking time:** 6 minutes
Serve: 4

Ingredients

4 eggs yolks	2 cups broccoli florets
1/4 cup butter, melted	2 cups coconut flour Pepper
Salt	

Directions

Preheat the air fryer to 400 F. In a small bowl, whisk egg yolks with butter, pepper, and salt. In a separate bowl, add coconut flour.

Dip each broccoli floret with egg mixture and coat with coconut flour. Place coated broccoli florets into the air fryer basket and cook for 6 minutes. **Serve:** and enjoy.

Zucchini Bites

Prep time: 10 minutes **Cooking time:** 10 minutes
Serve: 6

Ingredients

1 egg, lightly beaten	1 tsp Italian seasoning
4 zucchinis, grated and squeezed	1/2 cup parmesan cheese, grated Pepper
Salt	1 cup shredded coconut

Directions

Preheat the air fryer to 400 F. Add all Ingredients into the bowl and mix until well combined.

Make small balls from the zucchini mixture and place into the air fryer basket and cook for 10 minutes. Turn halfway through. **Serve:** and enjoy.

Air Fryer Almonds

Prep time: 5 minutes **Cooking time:** 6 minutes **Serve:** 6

Ingredients

1 cup almonds	1/4 tsp cumin
1 tsp chili powder	2 tsp olive oil
1/4 tsp paprika Salt	

Directions

Preheat the air fryer to 320 F.
Add almond and remaining Ingredients into the bowl and toss to coat.
Transfer almonds into the air fryer basket and cook for 6 minutes.
Serve: and enjoy.

Tasty Broccoli Nuggets

Prep time: 10 minutes **Cooking time:** 15 minutes
Serve: 4

Ingredients

2 egg whites	2 cups broccoli florets,
1/4 cup almond flour	cooked & mashed
1 cup mozzarella cheese,	1/8 tsp salt
shredded	

Directions

Preheat the air fryer to 325 F. Add all Ingredients to the bowl and mix well to combine.
Make nuggets from broccoli mixture and place into the air fryer basket and cook for 15 minutes.
Serve: and enjoy.

Curried Sweet Potato Fries

Prep time: 10 minutes **Cooking time:** 20 minutes
Serve: 2

Ingredients

2 small, sweet potatoes,	1/2 tsp curry powder
peel and cut into fry's	1/4 tsp coriander Pepper
shape	
2 tbsp olive oil	
Salt	

Directions

Preheat the air fryer to 370 F.
Add sweet potato slices and remaining Ingredients into the mixing bowl and toss well.
Transfer sweet potato slices into the air fryer basket and cook for 20 minutes. Stir after every 5 minutes.
Serve: and enjoy.

Asparagus Fries

Prep time: 10 minutes **Cooking time:** 10 minutes
Serve: 6

Ingredients

4 eggs, lightly beaten	1 lb. asparagus, trimmed &
1/4 tsp baking powder	poke using a fork
1 cup parmesan cheese,	3/4 cup almond flour
grated	1/4 tsp cayenne
Pepper	Salt

Directions

Preheat the air fryer to 400 F. Season asparagus spears with pepper and salt. In a shallow dish, mix together parmesan cheese, almond flour, and cayenne. In a separate shallow dish, add eggs and whisk well. Dip each asparagus spear in eggs then coat with cheese mixture.

Place coated asparagus spears into the air fryer basket and cook for 10 minutes. Turn halfway through. **Serve:** and enjoy.

Savory Walnuts

Prep time: 10 minutes **Cooking time:** 5 minutes
Serve: 6

Ingredients

2 cups walnuts	1/4 tsp garlic powder
1 tsp olive oil	1/8 tsp paprika Pepper
Salt	

Directions

Preheat the air fryer to 350 F. In a bowl, add walnuts, oil, paprika, garlic powder, pepper, and salt and toss well.
Add walnuts into the air fryer basket and cook for 4-5 minutes. **Serve:** and enjoy.

Air Fryer Zucchini Curly Fries

Prep time: 15 minutes **Cooking time:** 25 minutes **Serve:** 1

Ingredients

1 zucchini	1 egg, beaten
1 cup panko breadcrumbs	½ cup grated Parmesan
cooking spray	cheese
	1 teaspoon Italian
	seasoning nonstick

Directions

Preheat an air fryer carefully to 400°F (200 degrees C). Spiralize zucchini with a spiralizer fitted with the big shredding blade. In a shallow dish, place the egg. In a large resealable plastic bag, combine breadcrumbs, Parmesan cheese, and Italian seasoning. 1/2 of the spiralized zucchini should be dipped in the beaten egg before being placed in the bag to be coated with the bread crumb mixture. Coat the air fryer basket with cooking spray. Arrange the breaded zucchini fries in the prepared basket, being careful not to overcrowd them. Coat the tops in cooking spray.

Air Fryer Rib-Eye Steak

Prep time: 20 minutes **Cooking time:** 20 minutes
Serve: 1

Ingredients

2 rib-eye steaks, cut 1
1/2- inch thick
¼ cup olive oil

4 teaspoons grill seasoning
(such as Montreal Steak
Seasoning®)
½ cup reduced-sodium soy
sauce

Directions

Combine the steaks, soy sauce, olive oil, and spice in a
large resealable bag. Marinate the meat for at least 2
hours before cooking. Take the steaks out of the bag
and discard the marinade. Next, remove any extra oil
from the steaks.

To prevent the air fryer pan from smoking throughout
the cooking process, add roughly 1 tablespoon of
water to the bottom. Preheat the air fryer carefully to
400°F (200 degrees C). Cook the steaks in the air fryer
for 7 minutes. Cook for another 7 minutes, or until
the steaks are medium-rare. Increase the overall cook
time to 16 minutes for a medium steak, turning after 8
minutes.

Remove the steaks from the pan, keep warm, and set
aside for 4 minutes before serving.

Air Fryer Roasted Broccoli and Cauliflower

Prep time: 15 minutes **Cooking time:** 25 minutes
Serve: 1

Ingredients

3 cups broccoli florets
½ teaspoon garlic powder
¼ teaspoon paprika
2 tablespoons olive oil

3 cups cauliflower florets
¼ teaspoon sea salt
⅛ teaspoon ground black
pepper

Directions

Heat an air fryer to 400°F (200°C) according to the
manufacturer's instructions. In a large microwave-safe dish,
combine broccoli florets. Cook for 3 minutes on high
power in the microwave. Any collected liquid should be
drained.

Combine the cauliflower, olive oil, garlic powder, sea salt,
paprika, and black pepper in the same bowl as the
broccoli. To blend, mix everything thoroughly. Fill the air
fryer basket halfway with the mixture. Cook for 12
minutes, turning the veggies halfway through to ensure
equal browning.

Air Fryer Roasted Cauliflower

Prep time: 15 minutes **Cooking time:** 20 minutes
Serve: 1

Ingredients

3 cloves garlic
½ teaspoon salt

1 tablespoon peanut oil
½ teaspoon smoked
paprika
4 cups cauliflower florets

Directions

Preheat an air fryer carefully to 400°F (200 degrees C).
Cut the garlic in half and pound it with a knife blade.

Air Fryer Lemon Pepper Shrimp

Prep time: 20 minutes **Cooking time:** 25 minutes **Serve:**
1

Ingredients

1 tablespoon olive oil
¼ teaspoon paprika
12 ounces uncooked
medium shrimp, peeled
and deveined
1 lemon, sliced

1 teaspoon lemon pepper
¼ teaspoon garlic powder
1 lemon, juiced

Directions

Preheat an air fryer carefully to 400 degrees F. (200
degrees C). Cut the garlic in half and smash it with the
blade of a knife. Combine in a bowl with the oil, salt,
and paprika. Add the cauliflower and toss to coat.
Place the coated cauliflower in the air fryer bowl and
cook until crisp, about 15 minutes total, shaking every
5 minutes.

Air Fryer Bacon

Prep time: 20 minutes **Cooking time:** 20 minutes
Serve: 1

Ingredients

½ (16 ounces) package
bacon

Directions

Preheat an air fryer carefully to 390°F (200 degrees C).
Lay the bacon in a single layer in the air fryer basket;
little overlap is OK. Cook for 8 minutes. Cook for
another 7 minutes, or until the bacon is crisp. Place
fried bacon on a dish lined with paper towels to
absorb extra fat.

Air Fryer Baby Back Ribs

Prep time: 15 minutes **Cooking time:** 20 minutes
Serve: 1

Ingredients

1 rack baby back ribs	1 tablespoon liquid smoke
1 tablespoon olive oil	flavoring
½ teaspoon salt	½ teaspoon ground black
1 tablespoon brown sugar	pepper
½ teaspoon garlic powder	½ teaspoon onion powder
½ teaspoon chili powder	1 cup BBQ sauce

Directions

Remove the membrane off the back of the ribs and pat dry with a paper towel. Cut the rack into four parts. In a small dish, combine the olive oil and liquid smoke and apply them on both sides of the ribs. Combine brown sugar, garlic powder, onion powder, salt, pepper, and chili powder in a mixing bowl. Season both sides of the ribs well with the seasoning mixture. Allow the ribs to rest for 30 minutes to allow the taste to develop.
Preheat an air fryer carefully to 375°F (190 degrees C). Place the ribs in the air fryer basket, bone side down, ensure they don't touch; cook in batches if required. The **Cooking time:** is 15 minutes. Cook for 10 minutes more after flipping the ribs (meat-side down). Remove the ribs from the air fryer and brush the bone-side with 1/2 cup BBQ sauce. Return the basket to the air fryer and cook for 5 minutes. Cook for a further 5 minutes, or until desired char is obtained, after flipping the ribs over and brushing the meat side with the remaining 1/2 cup BBQ sauce.

Roasted Rainbow Vegetables in the Air Fryer

Prep time: 15 minutes **Cooking time:** 18 minutes
Serve: 1

Ingredients

1 red bell pepper	1 yellow summer squash,
1 zucchini cut in pieces	cut into 1-inch pieces
4 ounces fresh	½ sweet onion, cut into 1-
mushrooms, cleaned and	inch wedges
halved	
salt and pepper to taste	1 tbsp extra-virgin olive
	oil

Directions

Preheat an air fryer carefully according to the manufacturer's instructions.
Combine the red bell pepper, summer squash, zucchini, mushrooms, and onion in a large bowl. Toss in the olive oil, salt, and black pepper to taste.
In the air fryer basket, arrange the vegetables in an even layer. Cook until the veggies are roasted, approximately 20 minutes, stirring halfway through.

Air Fryer Flour Tortilla Bowls

Prep time: 15 minutes **Cooking time:** 22 minutes
Serve: 1

Ingredients

1 (8 inches) flour tortilla	1 (4 1/2-inch) souffle dish

Directions

Preheat the air fryer carefully to 375°F (190 degrees C).
Heat the tortilla in a big pan or directly on the gas stove grates until warm and malleable. Place the tortilla in the souffle dish, smoothing it down and fluting it up the sides.
4 to 5 minutes in the air fryer until the tortilla becomes golden brown.
Place the tortilla bowl upside down in the basket after removing it from the souffle dish. 1 to 2 minutes more air fry until golden brown.

Air Fryer Steak and Cheese Melts

Prep time: 10 minutes **Cooking time:** 18 minutes
Serve: 1

Ingredients

1 pound beef rib-eye	1 tablespoon reduced-
steak, thinly sliced	sodium soy sauce
1 medium onion, sliced	4 ounces sliced baby
into petals	portobello mushrooms
½ green bell pepper,	½ teaspoon salt
thinly sliced	2 tablespoons
1 tablespoon olive oil	Worcestershire sauce
½ teaspoon ground	¼ teaspoon ground black
mustard	pepper
4 hoagie rolls	
4 slices Provolone cheese	

Directions

Combine the steak, Worcestershire sauce, and soy sauce in a mixing bowl. Refrigerate for 4 hours to overnight. Remove from the refrigerator and set aside for 30 minutes to come to room temperature.
Preheat the air fryer carefully to 380°F (190 degrees C).
Combine the onion, mushrooms, and bell pepper in a large mixing basin. Stir in the olive oil, salt, ground mustard, and pepper to coat. Place the hoagie rolls in the air fryer basket and toast for about 2 minutes. Then, place the rolls on a platter.
Place the steak in the air fryer basket and cook for 3 minutes. Cook for 1 minute more after stirring. Place on a platter.
Cook for 5 minutes in the air fryer basket with the veggie mix. Cook until softened, approximately 5 minutes more.
Incorporate the meat into the veggie mixture. Place somewhat overlapping cheese slices on top. Cook for 3 minutes, or until the cheese is melted and bubbling.
Serve: immediately on toasted buns with the mixture.

Air Fryer Mini Pizza Calzones

Prep time: 18 minutes **Cooking time:** 20 minutes
Serve: 1

Ingredients

1 (13.8 ounces) package refrigerated pizza dough (such as Pillsbury®)
4 ½ tablespoons shredded mozzarella cheese avocado oil cooking spray

1 (1.75 ounces) package pepperoni (such as Hormel®)
9 teaspoons pizza sauce

Directions

On a lightly floured board, roll out the pizza dough. Then, using a 2 1/8-inch biscuit cutter, cut out 9 circles. Each circular should be rolled into a 4 1/2-inch disc. 1 teaspoon pizza sauce, 3 slices pepperoni, and 1/2 tablespoon mozzarella cheese in each disc. Fold over, seal the edges by folding, and crimp with fork tines.
Preheat an air fryer carefully to 375°F (190 degrees C). Spray the air fryer basket with avocado oil after lining it with parchment paper. Mist a batch of calzones with avocado oil and place them in the basket. Cook for 6 to 8 minutes in an air fryer. Turn the calzones over, spritz
with avocado oil, and air fry for another 2 to 3 minutes, or

Air Fryer Pumpkin Seeds

Prep time: 15 minutes **Cooking time:** 25 minutes
Serve: 1

Ingredients

1 ¾ cups pumpkin seeds
2 teaspoons avocado oil
1 teaspoon salt

1 teaspoon smoked paprika

Directions

Rinse the pumpkin seeds well in a small colander.
On a plate, place two sheets of paper towels. Cover two additional paper towels after placing the pumpkin seeds on the towels. Press down to get rid of the majority of the water. Allow at least 15 minutes for drying.
Preheat the air fryer carefully to 350°F (180 degrees C). Place the seeds in a medium mixing basin. Mix in the avocado oil, paprika, and salt. Mix with a medium spoon. Cook for 35 minutes, stirring the basket periodically, in the air fryer basket with the seeds. Keep an eye on the pumpkin seeds for the last 5 minutes; they may easily go from nicely cooked to burnt.

Air Fryer Spanish Potato Wedges

Prep time: 15 minutes **Cooking time:** 25 minutes
Serve: 1

Ingredients

1 ½ pounds russet potatoes, unpeeled cooking spray,
½ teaspoon paprika
¼ teaspoon garlic powder
2 tablespoons vegetable oil

1 teaspoon chili powder,
1 teaspoon ground cumin
½ tbs ground coriander
⅛ teaspoon ground cinnamon salt to taste

Directions

To avoid breaking, cut potatoes into 8 equal wedges less than 5 inches long.
Soak potato wedges in a dish of boiling tap water for about 10 minutes.
Take the potatoes out of the water, rinse them, and wipe them dry with a paper towel.
Preheat an air fryer carefully to 375°F (190 degrees C). Cooking oil spray should be sprayed on the air fryer basket.
Drizzle oil over the potatoes in a large mixing basin. Combine chili powder, cumin, paprika, coriander, garlic powder, and cinnamon; sprinkle over potatoes and mix thoroughly. Place the potatoes in the air fryer basket without crowding them. If necessary, cook in two batches.
10 minutes in the air fryer. Open the air fryer and delicately turn the wedges with tongs. Cook for another 10 to 15 minutes, or until crispy and golden brown. Season with salt and pepper and **Serve:** immediately.

Air Fryer Oreos

Prep time: 20 minutes **Cooking time:** 25 minutes
Serve: 1

Ingredients

½ cup complete pancake mix
9 chocolate sandwich cookies (such as Oreo®)

⅓ cup water cooking spray
1 tablespoon confectioners' sugar, or to taste

Directions

In a mixing bowl, combine the pancake mix and water. Line an air fryer basket with parchment paper. On parchment paper, apply the nonstick cooking spray. After dipping each cookie in the pancake mixture, place it in the basket. Make sure they don't touch and, if necessary, cook in batches.
Preheat the air fryer to 400°F on a low setting (200 degrees C). Cook for 4 to 5 minutes on one side, then turn and cook for another 2 to 3 minutes on the other side, or until golden brown. On top, confectioners' sugar is strewn.

Stuffed Air Fryer Potatoes

Prep time: 15 minutes **Cooking time:** 20 minutes
Serve: 1

Ingredients

4 baking potatoes, peeled and halved	½ cup Cheddar cheese, divided
½ yellow onion diced fine	3 teaspoons olive oil, divided
2 slices bacon	

Directions

Preheat the air fryer carefully to 350°F (175 degrees C).

Brush potatoes lightly with 1 teaspoon oil; place in the air fryer basket and cook for 10 minutes. Brush potatoes with 1 teaspoon more oil and cook in the air fryer for 10 minutes. Cook until soft, approximately 10 minutes more, after coating with the remaining oil. Cooked potatoes should be cut in half. Spoon the insides into a mixing basin; stir in 1/4 cup Cheddar cheese.

In a pan, sauté the onion and bacon over medium-high heat, rotating periodically until the bacon is uniformly browned, about 10 minutes.

Stuff potato-Cheddar cheese mixture, onion, bacon into the skins. Top with the remaining cheese. Return the filled potatoes to the air fryer and cook for 6 minutes

Air Fryer Blueberry Muffins

Prep time: 15 minutes **Cooking time:** 20 minutes
Serve: 1

Ingredients

1 cup self-rising flour	2 ½ tablespoons white sugar
¼ teaspoon ground cinnamon	⅓ cup milk
3 tablespoons melted butter	1 egg
½ cup blueberries	2 teaspoons vanilla extract

Directions

Preheat the air fryer carefully for 5 minutes at 340 degrees F (170 degrees C).

In a mixing basin, combine the flour, sugar, and cinnamon. Combine the milk, melted butter, egg, and vanilla essence in a mixing bowl. Blend until everything is properly incorporated. Blueberries should be folded in. Fill silicone cupcake liners 3/4 full of the mixture, using a tiny scoop. Carefully place in the air fryer basket. Muffins should be cooked in the oven for 14 minutes.

Air Fryer Sourdough Bread

Prep time: 15 minutes **Cooking time:** 18 minutes
Serve: 1

Ingredients

1 cup bread flour	½ cup spelled flour
½ cup sourdough starter	1 tbsp extra-virgin olive oil
½ teaspoon fine sea salt	½ cup water

Directions

In the bowl of a stand mixer, combine bread flour, spelled flour, sourdough starter, oil, and salt. Begin kneading with the dough hook. Add water until all Ingredients come together and start to pull together; you may not need all of the water. Knead for 5 minutes at low speed.

Form the dough into a ball by folding it in half. Place in a baking dish that can be used in an air fryer. Cover with plastic wrap and set aside for 5 hours to overnight to double in volume. Preheat the air fryer carefully to 390°F (200 degrees C). Remove the plastic wrap off the bread and score it.

Place the baking dish in the air fryer and cook for 20 minutes, or until the loaf is golden. In the middle, an instant-read thermometer should read at least 190 degrees F. (88 degrees C). Allow cooling completely before slicing.

Air Fryer Asparagus Tots

Prep time: 15 minutes **Cooking time:** 22 minutes
Serve: 1

Ingredients

12 ounces asparagus, trimmed and diced	½ cup panko breadcrumbs
¼ cup finely shredded Parmesan cheese	1 serving cooking spray

Directions

Over medium-high heat, bring a saucepan of salted water to a boil. Cook the asparagus for 5 minutes. Drain in a colander and set aside to cool for 5 minutes, or until easily handled.

Combine the asparagus, breadcrumbs, and Parmesan cheese in a large mixing dish. Knead the Ingredients with your hands until it resembles dough. 1 tablespoon of the mixture should be formed into a tot. **Serve:** on a platter. Repeat with the rest of the mixture. Freeze the tater tots for 30 minutes.

Preheat the air fryer carefully to 400°F (200 degrees C).

Spray the air fryer basket with nonstick cooking spray. Next, spray the tops of the tots with cooking spray before placing them in the basket. Fry for 10 minutes, shaking once halfway through.

Air Fryer Cinnamon-Sugar Doughnuts

Prep time: 10 minutes **Cooking time:** 18 minutes
Serve: 1

Ingredients

¼ cup butter, melted
¼ cup brown sugar
¼ teaspoon ground
nutmeg (optional)

½ cup white sugar
1 tbs ground cinnamon
1 (16.3 ounces) package
refrigerated flaky biscuit
dough (such as Pillsbury™
Grands! ™ Flaky Layers)

Directions

Melt the butter in a basin. Combine the white sugar,
brown sugar, cinnamon, and nutmeg in a separate
dish.

Separate the biscuit dough into individual biscuits and
use a biscuit cutter to cut out the centers to make a
doughnut shape. Fill the air fryer basket halfway with
doughnuts.

4 to 6 minutes in an air fryer at 350°F (175°C) until
golden brown. Cook for a further 1 to 3 minutes after
flipping the doughnuts.

Take the doughnuts out of the air fryer. Dip each
doughnut into melted butter (coating top, bottom, and
sides), then into the sugar-cinnamon mixture until
completely coated. **Serve:** right away.

Rosemary Potato Wedges for the Air Fryer

Prep time: 18 minutes **Cooking time:** 20 minutes
Serve: 1

Ingredients

2 russet potatoes, sliced
into 12 wedges, each with
skin on
1 tablespoon finely
chopped fresh rosemary

2 teaspoons seasoned salt
1 tbsp extra-virgin olive oil

Directions

Preheat an air fryer carefully to 380°F (190 degrees C).
Toss the potatoes with the olive oil in a large mixing
basin. Toss with the seasoned salt and rosemary to
mix.

Once the air fryer is heated, place the potatoes in a
uniform layer in the fryer basket; you may need to
cook them in batches.

Air fried the potatoes for 10 minutes before flipping
them with tongs. Continue air frying until the potato
wedges are done to your liking, about 10 minutes
longer.

Air Fryer Fried Green Tomatoes

Prep time: 15 minutes **Cooking time:** 25 minutes
Serve: 1

Ingredients

2 green tomatoes, cut into
1/4-inch slices
½ cup buttermilk
1 cup plain panko
breadcrumbs
½ teaspoon paprika

⅓ cup all-purpose flour
salt and black pepper
2 eggs, lightly beaten
1 teaspoon garlic powder
1 cup yellow cornmeal
1 tablespoon olive oil, or
as needed

Directions

Season the tomato slices properly with salt and pepper to
taste. Set up a breading station with three shallow dishes
flour in the first, buttermilk and eggs in the second, and
breadcrumbs, cornmeal, garlic powder, and paprika in the
third.

Dredge tomato slices in flour and shake off excess.
Dip the tomatoes into the egg mixture, then the bread
crumb mixture, coating both sides.

Preheat the air fryer carefully to 400°F (200 degrees
C). Brush olive oil into the frying basket. Place the
breaded tomato slices in the fryer basket, making sure
they don't touch; cook in batches if required. Brush
olive oil over the tops of the tomatoes. Cook for 12
minutes, then turn the tomatoes and spray with olive
oil one more. 3 to 5 minutes more, or until crisp and
golden brown. To keep the tomatoes crisp, place them
on a rack lined with paper towels. Rep with the
remaining tomatoes.

Air Fryer French Toast Sticks

Prep time: 15 minutes **Cooking time:** 25 minutes
Serve: 1

Ingredients

2 large eggs
1 tablespoon butter,
melted
4 slices of day-old bread,
cut into thirds
1 teaspoon vanilla extract

⅓ cup milk
1 tbs ground cinnamon
1 teaspoon confectioners'
sugar, or to taste

Directions

Combine the eggs, milk, butter, vanilla essence, and
cinnamon in a mixing dish. Using parchment paper,
line an air fryer basket. Place each slice of bread in the
basket after dipping it in the milk mixture. Make sure
they are not touching and, if required, cook in batches.

Preheat the air fryer carefully to 370°F (188 degrees
C). Fry the bread for 6 minutes in the basket, then
flips and cook for another 3 minutes. Confectioners'
sugar should be sprinkled on each stick.

Air Fryer To stones

Prep time: 20 minutes **Cooking time:** 20 minutes
Serve: 1

Ingredients

2 green (unripe) plantains olive oil cooking spray	3 cups water, or as needed, salt to taste

Directions

Preheat an air fryer carefully to 400°F (200 degrees C). Remove the plantain tips. Make a vertical cut from end to end in the skin, careful not to cut through the thick skin and into the plantain flesh. Plantain, still in its peel, should be cut into 1-inch segments. Peel the skin off each portion, beginning with the slit you formed.

Spray the plantain pieces with olive oil spray and place them in the air fryer basket. 5 minutes in the air fryer. Prepare a dish of salted water in the meantime.

Using tongs, remove the plantain pieces from the air fryer. Using a Costanera, pound to a thickness of about 1/2-inch (plantain smasher). While the remainder of the two stones is being broken, soak them in a dish of salted water.
After removing the two stones from the salted water, blot them dry using a paper towel.

Return to stones to the air fryer in batches, each time filling the basket with a single layer. Season the tops with salt and coat with olive oil spray; air fry for 5 minutes. With tongs, flip the pan over and coat the opposite side with olive oil spray. Season with salt and pepper. 4 to 5 minutes longer air fry until golden brown and crunchy.

Air Fryer Rosemary Garlic Baby Potatoes

Prep time: 15 minutes **Cooking time:** 18 minutes
Serve: 1

Ingredients

1 ½ pounds multi-colored new potatoes, halved	2 cloves garlic, minced
1 teaspoon finely chopped fresh rosemary	2 tablespoons olive oil
½ teaspoon lemon zest	½ teaspoon kosher salt

Directions

Preheat the air fryer carefully to 400°F (200 degrees C).
Combine the potatoes, oil, garlic, rosemary, and salt in a large mixing basin. Arrange the potatoes in the air fryer basket in a single layer, not overcrowded; work in batches if required. Cook for 20 minutes, or until potatoes are golden brown and soft. Before serving, sprinkle with lemon zest.

Air Fryer Zesty Cheddar Biscuits

Prep time: 15 minutes **Cooking time:** 20 minutes
Serve: 1

Ingredients

1 cup self-rising flour	¾ cup freshly shredded sharp Cheddar cheese
1 pinch white sugar	¾ teaspoon taco seasoning mix
½ cup milk,	2 tbsp taco seasoning mix
2 tablespoons canned chopped green chili peppers	
¾ teaspoon garlic powder	¼ teaspoon ground cumin
1 serving cooking spray	¼ cup salted butter, melted

Directions

Preheat an air fryer carefully for 5 minutes at 350 degrees F (175 degrees C).
Combine the flour, Cheddar cheese, milk, green chili peppers, taco seasoning, garlic powder, cumin, and sugar in a medium mixing bowl. Combine all of the Ingredients in a mixing bowl until a dough forms. Line the air fryer basket with a ring of parchment paper. Coat the pan with nonstick cooking spray. Using a spring-hinged scoop, place dough in the basket. 12 minutes in the air fryer
Meanwhile, make the taco spice topping by combining melted butter and seasoning mix. Brush biscuits with taco-seasoned butter after separating them. **Serve:** right away.

Air Fryer Sriracha-Honey Shrimp

Prep time: 15 minutes **Cooking time:** 25 minutes
Serve: 1

Ingredients

1 tablespoon Sriracha sauce	½ tablespoon lime juice
½ tablespoon soy sauce	½ teaspoon minced garlic
½ pound large raw tail-on shrimp	2 green onions, chopped
	1 tablespoon honey

Directions

According to the manufacturer's instructions, preheat the air fryer carefully to 400°F (200°C). Combine the Sriracha, honey, lime juice, soy sauce, and garlic in a large mixing bowl. Stir in the shrimp until evenly coated.

Place the shrimp in the air fryer basket with tongs and cook for 3 minutes. Return the shrimp to the sauce and toss to combine. Return the shrimp to the basket and cook for 3 minutes more. Garnish with green onions, if desired.

Tex-Mex Air Fryer Hash Browns

Prep time: 20 minutes **Cooking time:** 25 minutes
Serve: 1

Ingredients

1 ½ pounds potatoes	½ teaspoon olive oil
½ teaspoon taco seasoning mix	½ teaspoon ground cumin
1 red bell pepper, seeded and cut into 1-inch pieces	1 tablespoon olive oil
	1 jalapeno, seeded and cut into 1-inch rings
1 pinch salt and ground black pepper to taste	1 small onion, cut into 1-inch pieces

Directions

Soak potatoes for 20 minutes in cold water. Preheat the air fryer carefully to 320°F (160 degrees C). Drain the potatoes, dry them with a clean towel, and place them in a large mixing basin. Toss the potatoes with 1 tablespoon olive oil to coat. Place them in the air fryer basket that has been warmed. Make a timer for 18 minutes.

In the previously used basin for the potatoes, combine bell pepper, onion, and jalapeño. Add 1/2 teaspoon olive oil, taco seasoning, ground cumin, salt, and pepper to taste. To coat, toss everything together. Remove the potatoes from the air fryer and place them in the bowl with the veggie mixture. Return the empty basket to the air fryer and heat it to 356 degrees F. (180 degrees C).

Toss the dish's contents quickly to combine the potatoes, veggies, and bspices evenly. Place the mixture in the basket. Cook for 6 minutes, then shake the basket and cook for another 5 minutes, or until the potatoes are

Air Fryer Rosemary Garlic Baby Potatoes

Prep time: 15 minutes **Cooking time:** 22 minutes
Serve: 1

Ingredients

1 ½ pounds multi-colored new potatoes, halved	2 cloves garlic, minced
1 teaspoon finely chopped fresh rosemary	2 tablespoons olive oil
½ teaspoon lemon zest	½ teaspoon kosher salt

Directions

Preheat the air fryer carefully to 400 degrees F. (200 degrees C).
In a large mixing basin, combine potatoes, oil, garlic, rosemary, and salt. Arrange the potatoes in a single layer in the air fryer basket, not overcrowded; work in batches if required. Cook until the potatoes are golden brown and soft, about 20 minutes. Before serving, top with lemon zest.

Perfect Turkey Breast Roast in the Air Fryer

Prep time: 15 minutes **Cooking time:** 20 minutes
Serve: 1

Ingredients

1 (3 pounds) frozen turkey breast roast	⅓ cup kosher salt
	2 cups water
⅓ cup brown sugar	ground black pepper to taste
2 tablespoons butter, or as needed	1 seasoned pinch salt, or to taste (such as Texas Roadhouse®)

Directions

Refrigerate frozen turkey breast for roughly 24 hours to thaw.
Bring the water to a boil, then add the kosher salt, brown sugar, and pepper. Remove the brine from the heat and set it aside for 30 minutes to cool fully.
Remove the turkey breast from the wrapping, leaving the netting in place if feasible. Place the turkey in a container and cover with the cooled brine; add extra water as needed to completely cover, stirring to ensure the brine is combined with the water. Allow the turkey to brine in the refrigerator for 8 hours or overnight.
Preheat an air fryer carefully to 390°F (200°C) according to the manufacturer's instructions.
Remove the turkey from the brine and set it aside. Pat the turkey dry. Rub with butter and season with salt and pepper.
Cook the turkey for 15 minutes in a preheated air fryer; flip, remove the netting, and season again. Next, reduce the temperature to 360°F (182 degrees C). Cook for another 20 minutes, rotating after 15 minutes. Then, raise the temperature to 390°F (200°C), flip, and cook until the center is no longer pink, about 15 minutes more. Finally, remove the turkey from the oven and set it aside for 5 minutes before slicing and serving.

Air Fryer Triple-Chocolate Oatmeal Cookies

Prep time: 15 minutes **Cooking time:** 18 minutes
Serve: 1

Ingredients

3 cups quick-cooking oatmeal	1 ½ cups all-purpose flour
¼ cup cocoa powder	3.4 ounces package instant chocolate pudding mix
1 teaspoon baking soda	1 cup butter, softened
1 teaspoon salt	¾ cup white sugar
¾ cup brown sugar	1 cup chopped walnuts (optional)
1 teaspoon vanilla extract	2 eggs
2 cups chocolate chips	
nonstick cooking spray	

Directions

Preheat an air fryer carefully to 350°F (175°C) according to the manufacturer's instructions. Nonstick cooking spray should be sprayed on the air fryer basket.
Combine the oats, flour, cocoa powder, pudding mix, baking soda, and
salt in a mixing dish. Place aside.
Cream together the butter, brown sugar, and white sugar in a separate dish using an electric mixer.
Combine the eggs and vanilla essence in a mixing bowl. Mix in the oatmeal mixture well. Finally, combine the chocolate chips and walnuts in a mixing bowl.
Place dough in the air fryer; level out and allow approximately 1 inch between each cookie.
Cook for 6 to 10 minutes, or until gently browned. Allow cooling on a wire rack before serving.

Air Fryer Teriyaki Snap Peas and Mushrooms

Prep time: 20 minutes **Cooking time:** 20 minutes
Serve: 1

Ingredients

1 (8 ounces) package fresh sugar snap peas	½ (8 ounces) package mushrooms, sliced
2 teaspoons olive oil	3 tablespoons teriyaki sauce

Directions

Preheat an air fryer carefully to 400°F (200 degrees C). Add snap peas, mushrooms, teriyaki sauce, and olive oil; toss until equally mixed. Fill the air fryer basket halfway with the veggie mixture. Cook for 12 minutes in an air fryer, shaking halfway through.

Air Fryer Mini Peppers Stuffed with Cheese and Sausage

Prep time: 15 minutes **Cooking time:** 22 minutes
Serve: 1

Ingredients

8 ounces bulk Italian sausage	1 (16 ounces) package miniature multi-colored sweet peppers
2 tbs olive oil, divided	½ cup shredded Cheddar cheese
1 (8 ounces) package cream cheese, softened	1 clove garlic, minced
2 tablespoons crumbled blue cheese (Optional)	1 tablespoon finely chopped fresh chives
2 tbs. panko breadcrumbs	
¼ teaspoon ground black pepper	

Directions

Melt the butter in a large nonstick pan over medium-high heat. Cook and stir sausage in a heated pan for 5 to 7 minutes or browned and crumbled. Set away grease after draining and discarding it.

Preheat an air fryer carefully to 350°F (175 degrees C). Cut a slit in one side of each sweet pepper, from stem to tip, lengthwise. Place the peppers in the air fryer basket and brush with 1 tablespoon olive oil.

Cook for 3 minutes in a hot air fryer. Shake the basket and continue to cook until the peppers begin to brown and soften, about 3 minutes longer. Remove the peppers from the air fryer and set aside until cool enough to handle. While the peppers are cooling, combine the sausage, cream cheese, Cheddar cheese, blue cheese, chives, garlic, and black pepper in a medium mixing bowl. Combine the breadcrumbs and the remaining 1 tablespoon olive oil in a separate dish. Fill each pepper with cheese mixture and top with bread crumb mixture. Place the filled peppers in the air fryer basket, working in batches if required, and cook for 4 to 5 minute

Air Fryer Cheese-Stuffed Mini Italian Meatloaves

Prep time: 10 minutes **Cooking time:** 18 minutes
Serve: 1

Ingredients

⅓ cup milk
1 egg, lightly beaten
2 ounces small fresh mozzarella balls
2 tablespoons purchased basil pesto
¼ teaspoon ground black pepper
1 pound 90% lean ground beef
⅓ cup Italian-seasoned panko breadcrumbs
½ cup marinara sauce, warmed
1 clove garlic, minced
8 slices pepperoni
1 tablespoon chopped fresh basil

Directions

Combine the milk, pesto, egg, garlic, and pepper in a medium mixing bowl. Next, combine the ground beef and breadcrumbs, being careful not to overmix. Divide the meat mixture into four equal halves. Make a well in the center of each section, leaving a 1/2-inch border around the edge. Fill each well with 2 slices of pepperoni, overlapping to span the whole length of the well. Top with a quarter of the mozzarella balls. Enclose the filling by pressing the meat mixture around it; shape each chunk into an oblong loaf shape. Loaves should be placed in the air fryer basket in batches.

Cook in the air fryer at 370°F (190°C) for 15 minutes, or until an instant-read thermometer inserted into the thickest part of the meat registers 165°F (75°C).

Serve: the meatloaves with warm marinara sauce and fresh basil on top.

Air Fryer Mahi Mahi with Brown Butter

Prep time: 15 minutes **Cooking time:** 25 minutes
Serve: 1

Ingredients

4 (6 ounces) mahi-mahi fillets
⅔ cup butter
salt and ground black pepper
to taste cooking spray

Directions

Preheat an air fryer carefully to 350°F (175 degrees C). Season the mahi-mahi fillets with salt and pepper and coat both sides with cooking spray. Place the fillets in the air fryer basket, leaving space between them.

Cook for 12 minutes, or until the fish flakes easily with a fork and has a golden tint.

Melt butter in a small saucepan over medium-low heat while the fish cooks. Bring the butter to a boil and cook for 3 to 5 minutes, or until it becomes foamy and deep brown. Turn off the heat.

Place the fish fillets on a platter and top with brown butter.

Air Fryer Black Garlic-Cauliflower Patties

Prep time: 18 minutes **Cooking time:** 20 minutes
Serve: 1

Ingredients

1 medium head cauliflower, cut into florets
¼ cup Italian-seasoned breadcrumbs
½ teaspoon ground black pepper to taste

½ teaspoon dried parsley
½ teaspoon dried rosemary
½ teaspoon onion powder cooking spray
½ cup all-purpose flour
2 eggs, beaten
1 teaspoon salt
4 solo black garlic bulbs
½ teaspoon dried basil
2 teaspoons baking powder
½ teaspoon dried oregano
½ tbs red pepper flakes

4 slices Swiss cheese, torn into 4 pieces each

Directions

Combine cauliflower and black garlic; process until finely "riced." Transfer to a mixing basin. In a large mixing bowl, combine the flour, eggs, breadcrumbs, baking powder, salt, black pepper, basil, parsley, oregano, rosemary, red pepper flakes, and onion powder. Stir until everything is completely blended. Preheat an air fryer carefully to 400°F (200 degrees C). Spray the air fryer basket with cooking spray and line it with parchment paper.

Using a big cookie scoop, drop the cauliflower mixture onto the parchment paper and flatten gently with your fingertips.

Cook for 4 to 6 minutes in the air fryer, turn with a spatula, and continue cooking until patties are set, about 1 minute more. Remove each burger from the air fryer and top with 1/4 slice Swiss cheese. Return to the air fryer and cook for 30 to 40 seconds more, or until the cheese is melted.

Air Fryer Tajin Apple Chips

Prep time: 10 minutes **Cooking time:** 18 minutes
Serve: 1

Ingredients

1 apple, cored
½ tablespoon chili-lime seasoning (such as Tajin®), or more to taste

Directions

Preheat the air fryer carefully to 180°F (82 degrees C).

Using a mandolin, thinly slice the apple.

Place as many apple slices as you can in the air fryer basket, ensuring they don't touch.

Cook for 12 minutes in the air fryer, working in batches as required. Remove the basket and heat until the apple slices are gently browned on the other side, 8 to 12 minutes longer. Sprinkle with chili-lime seasoning right away.

Air Fryer Bang Bang Tofu

Prep time: 20 minutes **Cooking time:** 20 minutes
Serve: 1

Ingredients

1 (14 ounces) package
extra-firm tofu
½ cup sweet chili sauce
1 ½ cups panko
breadcrumbs

1 cup mayonnaise
2 tbs. toasted sesame oil
1 ½ tbs. Sriracha sauce
1 green onion, chopped

Directions

Place the tofu on a dish lined with paper towels. Cover with additional paper towels and a second plate. Press the tofu for 30 minutes with a 3- to 5-pound weight on top. Drain and discard any remaining liquid, then cut the tofu into 1/2-inch pieces.

Toss the cubed tofu in a dish with the sesame oil. Allow for a 20- minute resting period after gently stirring.

Meanwhile, create the bang bang sauce by whisking together the mayonnaise, sweet chili sauce, and Sriracha sauce until smooth. Then, in a separate dish, combine the panko.

Preheat the air fryer carefully to 400°F (200 degrees C).

Tofu should be mixed with 1/2 cup bang bang sauce until evenly incorporated. Coat the tofu in the panko breadcrumbs and set it in the air fryer basket, ensuring the tofu pieces do not overlap. You may need to perform this in batches depending on the size of your air fryer.

5 minutes in the oven. Cook for 3 minutes more after shaking. **Serve:** with the leftover bang bang sauce and garnished with green onion.

Air Fryer Butternut Squash Home Fries

Prep time: 15 minutes **Cooking time:** 25 minutes
Serve: 1

Ingredients

1 pound butternut squash
2 teaspoons bagel
seasoning (such as Trader
Joe's Everything but the
Bagel Sesame Seasoning
Blend)

1 tbs. extra-virgin olive oil
1 teaspoon chopped fresh
rosemary

Directions

Preheat an air fryer carefully to 400°F (200 degrees C). Toss the butternut squash with the olive oil in a large mixing basin. Place the squash pieces in the air fryer basket. Cook until gently browned, approximately 22 minutes total, stirring every 3 to 4 minutes.

Transfer to a dish or serving plate and evenly sprinkle with the spice blend. Garnish with fresh rosemary if desired.

Air Fryer Lobster Tails with Lemon-Garlic Butter

Prep time: 15 minutes **Cooking time:** 20 minutes
Serve: 1

Ingredients

2 (4 ounces) lobster tails
1 teaspoon lemon zest
1 clove garlic, grated
2 wedges lemon

4 tablespoons butter
salt and ground black
pepper to taste
1 teaspoon chopped fresh
parsley

Directions

Butterfly lobster tails by using kitchen shears to cut longitudinally through the hard upper shells and flesh. Cut to the bottoms of the shells, but not all the way through. Separate the tail halves. Place the lobster tails in the air fryer basket, lobster flesh facing up.

In a small saucepan over medium heat, melt the butter. Heat the lemon zest and garlic for 30 seconds, or until the garlic is soft. Brush 2 tablespoons of the butter mixture onto the lobster tails; remove any excess brushed butter to avoid contamination with raw lobster. Season the lobster with salt and pepper to taste. Cook for 5 to 7 minutes in an air fryer at 380°F (195°C) until lobster flesh is opaque.

Spicy Homemade Breakfast Sausage in the Air Fryer

Prep time: 15 minutes **Cooking time:** 25 minutes
Serve: 1

Ingredients

1 pound ground pork
1 teaspoon crushed red
pepper

½ teaspoon onion powder
¼ teaspoon dried thyme

1 teaspoon rubbed sage
½ teaspoon dried
marjoram
1 teaspoon sea salt
½ teaspoon ground black
pepper

Directions

Preheat an air fryer carefully to 400°F (200 degrees C). In a large mixing bowl, combine ground pork, sea salt, sage, red pepper, marjoram, onion powder, pepper, and thyme. Mix thoroughly with your hands until everything is equally incorporated. Make 8 patties out of the mixture.

Cook for 5 minutes with 4 patties in the air fryer basket. Cook for 5 minutes longer after carefully flipping the burgers. Repeat with the remaining patties on a plate lined with paper towels.

Air Fryer Dry-Rubbed Pork Tenderloin with Broccoli

Prep time: 20 minutes **Cooking time:** 25 minutes
Serve: 1

Ingredients

2 tablespoons brown sugar
1 teaspoon salt
1 teaspoon ground mustard
¼ teaspoon garlic powder
1 tablespoon olive oil
1 (1 1/2 pound) pork tenderloin
1 tablespoon olive oil

1 tablespoon smoked paprika
½ teaspoon ground black pepper
¼ teaspoon ground cayenne pepper (Optional)
salt and ground black pepper to taste
4 cups chopped broccoli florets

Directions

In a small mixing bowl, add brown sugar, paprika, ground mustard, salt, black pepper, garlic powder, and cayenne pepper until equally blended.
Brush the pork tenderloin with olive oil until it is evenly covered. Rub the spice mixture all over the tenderloin and set aside for 5 minutes.
Preheat an air fryer carefully to 400°F (200 degrees C). Place the tenderloin in the air fryer basket and cook for 20 minutes, undisturbed, in the preheated air fryer. In the meantime, arrange the broccoli in a microwave-safe bowl.
Microwave on high for 3 minutes, or until tender. Season with salt and pepper after adding the olive oil.
Place the tenderloin on a cutting board and set it aside for 10 minutes before slicing.
Place the broccoli in the air fryer basket while the tenderloin is resting. Cook for 10 minutes, shaking the basket halfway during the cooking time.

Air Fryer Apple Fritters

Prep time: 15 minutes **Cooking time:** 20 minutes
Serve: 1

Ingredients

cooking spray
¼ cup white sugar
1 egg
2 tablespoons white sugar
1 pinch salt
1 apple - peeled, cored, and chopped
½ teaspoon caramel extract

1 cup all-purpose flour
¼ cup milk
1 ½ tbs baking powder
½ teaspoon ground cinnamon
½ cup confectioners' sugar
1 tablespoon milk
¼ tbs ground cinnamon

Directions

Preheat an air fryer carefully to 350°F (175 degrees C). Insert a round of parchment paper into the bottom of the air fryer. Coat the pan with nonstick cooking spray.
Combine the flour, 1/4 cup sugar, milk, egg, baking powder, and salt in a small mixing bowl. Stir until everything is mixed.
Combine 2 tablespoons sugar and cinnamon; sprinkle over apples until evenly covered. Combine the apples and flour in a mixing bowl. Place the cakes in the bottom of the air fryer basket using a cookie scoop. Air-fry for 5 minutes in a preheated fryer. Cook until the cakes are golden brown, approximately 5 minutes more.
Meanwhile, combine the confectioners' sugar, milk, caramel essence, and cinnamon in a mixing dish.
Drizzle the glaze over the cakes and set them aside to cool.

Air Fryer Sweet and Spicy Roasted Carrots

Prep time: 20 minutes **Cooking time:** 25 minutes
Serve: 1

Ingredients

1 serving cooking spray
1 tablespoon hot honey
½ pound baby carrots
1 teaspoon grated orange zest

1 tbsp butter, melted
½ tbs ground cardamom
1 tablespoon freshly squeezed orange juice
1 pinch salt and ground black pepper

Directions

Preheat an air fryer carefully to 400°F (200 degrees C). Nonstick cooking spray should be sprayed on the basket.
Combine the butter, honey, orange zest, and cardamom in a mixing dish. Set aside 1 tablespoon of the sauce in a separate dish. Toss the carrots in the remaining sauce until evenly covered. Place the carrots in the air fryer basket.
Toss carrots every 7 minutes for 15 to 22 minutes, or until

Air Fryer Bacon-Wrapped Scallops with Sriracha Mayo

Prep time: 10 minutes **Cooking time:** 18 minutes
Serve: 1

Ingredients

½ cup mayonnaise	2 tablespoons Sriracha sauce
1 pound bay scallops (about 36 small scallops),	12 slices bacon, cut into thirds
1 pinch coarse salt	1 pinch cracked black pepper
1 serving olive oil	cooking spray

Directions

In a small bowl, combine mayonnaise and Sriracha sauce. Refrigerate the Sriracha mayonnaise until ready to use. Preheat the air fryer carefully to 390°F (200 degrees C). Spread the scallops on a plate or cutting board and wipe dry with a paper towel. Season with salt and pepper to taste. Wrap a third of a slice of bacon around each scallop and fasten with a toothpick.

Cooking spray should be sprayed on the air fryer basket. Place the bacon-wrapped scallops in a single layer in the basket; if required, divide them into two groups.

Cook for 7 minutes in the air fryer. Check for doneness; the scallops should be opaque and the bacon crispy. Cook for an additional 1 to 2 minutes, checking every minute. With tongs, carefully remove the scallops and lay them on a paper towel-lined dish to soak any extra oil from the bacon. Toss with Sriracha mayonnaise and **Serve:**.

Air Fryer Prosciutto and Mozzarella Grilled Cheese

Prep time: 15 minutes **Cooking time:** 20 minutes
Serve: 1

Ingredients

2 tbs unsalted butter	2 slices sourdough bread
2 ounces prosciutto	3 ounces fresh mozzarella

Directions

Preheat the oven to 360° F. (180 degrees C). Butter one side of a slice of bread and set it greased side down on a platter. Top with prosciutto and mozzarella slices in an even layer. Butter the second slice of bread and set it on top, buttered side out. Place in the air fryer and cook for 8 minutes, or until gently browned and toasted.

Air Fryer Beignets

Prep time: 18 minutes **Cooking time:** 20 minutes
Serve: 1

Ingredients

cooking spray	½ cup all-purpose flour
¼ cup white sugar	⅛ cup water
1 large egg, separated	1 ½ teaspoon melted butter
½ teaspoon baking powder	½ teaspoon vanilla extract
2 tablespoons confectioners' sugar, or to taste	1 pinch salt

Directions

Preheat the air fryer carefully to 370°F (185 degrees C). Nonstick cooking sprays a silicone egg-bite mold. Combine the flour, sugar, water, egg yolk, butter, baking powder, vanilla extract, and salt in a large mixing basin. To blend, stir everything together.

In a small mixing basin, beat the egg white with an electric hand mixer on medium speed until soft peaks form. Incorporate into the batter. Transfer the batter to the prepared mold using a tiny, hinged ice cream scoop.

Fill the silicone mold and place it in the air fryer basket.

Fry for 10 minutes in a hot air fryer. Carefully remove the mold from the basket; pop the beignets out and flip them onto a parchment paper circle.

Return the parchment round containing the beignets to the air fryer basket. Cook for another 4 minutes. Remove the beignets from the air fryer basket and sprinkle them with confectioners' sugar.

Air-Fryer Potato-Skin Wedges

Prep time: 15 minutes **Cooking time:** 20 minutes **Serve:** 1

Ingredients

4 medium russet potatoes	3 tablespoons canola oil
1 cup water	1 teaspoon paprika
¼ teaspoon ground black pepper	¼ teaspoon salt

Directions

Fill a big saucepan halfway with salted water and bring to a boil. Reduce the heat to medium-low and cook until the potatoes are fork- tender, about 20 minutes. Drain. Refrigerate in a bowl for 30 minutes or until totally cold.

Combine the oil, paprika, black pepper, and salt in a mixing dish. Toss the quartered cold potatoes into the mixture.

Preheat an air fryer carefully to 400°F (200 degrees C). Place half of the potato wedges in the air fryer basket, skin side down, being careful not to overcrowd.

13 to 15 minutes, or until golden brown. Rep with the remaining wedges.

Air Fryer Salt and Vinegar Chickpeas

Prep time: 15 minutes **Cooking time:** 18 minutes
Serve: 1

Ingredients

1 (15 ounces) can of chickpeas	1 tablespoon olive oil
½ teaspoon sea salt	1 cup white vinegar

Directions

In a small saucepan, combine the chickpeas and vinegar and bring to a boil. Turn off the heat. Allow for a 30-minute resting period.

Remove any loose skins from the chickpeas before draining. Preheat an air fryer carefully to 390°F (198 degrees C). In the basket, distribute the chickpeas equally. Cook for 4 minutes or until the mixture is dry.

Place chickpeas in a heat-resistant bowl and drizzle with oil and sea salt. To coat, toss everything together. Return chickpeas to air fryer and cook for 8 minutes, shaking basket every 2 to 3 minutes, until gently toasted. **Serve:** right away

Fried Green Tomatoes in the Air Fryer

Prep time: 15 minutes **Cooking time:** 22 minutes
Serve: 1

Ingredients

cooking spray	½ cup cornmeal
⅓ cup self-rising flour	⅓ cup panko breadcrumbs
1 egg, beaten	1 teaspoon salt
½ teaspoon ground black pepper	2 green tomatoes, sliced

Directions

Preheat an air fryer carefully to 400°F (200 degrees C).
Coat the air fryer basket with cooking spray.
Place the egg in a small dish. Combine cornmeal, flour, panko, salt, and pepper in a second shallow dish.
Dip each tomato slice in the egg, then in the cornmeal mixture on both sides.
Place the tomato slices in the prepared basket in a single layer and gently sprinkle the tops with cooking spray.
Cook for 8 minutes in a hot air fryer. Cooking spray should be sprayed on any dry parts after flipping the tomatoes. Cook for 4 minutes more before transferring to a dish lined with paper towels. Repeat with the rest of the tomato slices.

Air Fryer Cajun Crab Cakes

Prep time: 18 minutes **Cooking time:** 20 minutes
Serve: 1

Ingredients

¾ cup panko breadcrumbs	¼ cup mayonnaise 1 egg
2 teaspoons Worcestershire sauce	¾ teaspoon Cajun seasoning
	1 teaspoon Dijon mustard
½ teaspoon salt	¼ teaspoon cayenne pepper
¼ teaspoon ground white pepper (Optional)	3 tablespoons remoulade sauce, or to taste
3 brioche slider buns (Optional)	4 ounces fresh lump crabmeat

Directions

According to the manufacturer's instructions, preheat an air fryer carefully to 370°F (188°C).
In a small mixing bowl, combine breadcrumbs, mayonnaise, egg, Worcestershire sauce, mustard, Cajun spice, salt, cayenne pepper, and pepper. Gently fold in the crabmeat.
Using a biscuit cutter, cut out three equal-sized crab cakes. Place the
cakes on a parchment-lined baking sheet and place them in the air fryer basket.
Cook for 6 minutes in a hot air fryer. Cook until browned on the other
side, approximately 6 minutes longer. **Serve:** on slider buns with remoulade sauce.

DESSERTS

Homemade Chelsea Currant Buns

(**Ready in about** 50 minutes | **Servings:** 4)

Ingredients

1/2 pound cake flour	1 tablespoons granulated sugar
1 teaspoon dry yeast	
A pinch of sea salt	4 tablespoons butter
1/2 cup milk, warm	1/2 cup dried currants
1 egg, whisked	1 ounce icing sugar

Directions

Mix the flour, yeast, sugar and salt in a bowl; add in milk, egg and 2 tablespoons of butter and mix to combine well. Add lukewarm water as necessary to form a smooth dough.

Knead the dough until it is elastic; then, leave it in a warm place to rise for 30 minutes.

Roll out your dough and spread the remaining 2 tablespoons of butter onto the dough; scatter dried currants over the dough.

Cut into 8 equal slices and roll them up. Brush each bun with a nonstick

cooking oil and transfer them to the Air Fryer cooking basket.

Cook your buns at 330 degrees F for about 20 minutes, turning them over halfway through the cooking time.

Dust with icing sugar before serving. Bon appétit!

Old-Fashioned Pinch-Me Cake with Walnuts

(**Ready in about** 20 minutes | **Servings:** 4)

Ingredients

1 (10-ounces) can crescent rolls	1/2 cup caster sugar
	1/2 stick butter
1 teaspoon pumpkin pie spice blend	1/2 cup walnuts, chopped
	1 tablespoon dark rum

Directions

Start by preheating your Air Fryer to 350 degrees F.

Roll out the crescent rolls. Spread the butter onto the crescent rolls; scatter the sugar, spices and walnuts over the rolls. Drizzle with rum and roll them up.

Using your fingertips, gently press them to seal the edges.

Bake your cake for about 13 minutes or until the top is golden brown. Bon appétit!

Authentic Swedish Kärleksmums

(**Ready in about** 20 minutes | **Servings:** 3)

Ingredients

2 tablespoons Swedish butter, at room temperature	1 egg
	4 tablespoons brown sugar
1 tablespoon lingonberry jam	2 tablespoons cocoa powder A pinch of grated nutmeg
5 tbs all-purpose flour	1/2 tbs baking powder
A pinch of coarse sea salt	

Directions

Using an electric mixer, cream the butter and sugar together. Fold in the egg and lingonberry jam until well combined. Mix in the flour, baking powder, cocoa powder, grated nutmeg, and salt until well combined. Pour the batter into a baking dish that has been lightly buttered.

Bake your cake for about 15 minutes, or until a tester inserted into the centre comes out dry and clean. Good appetite!

Air Grilled Peaches with Cinnamon-Sugar Butter

(**Ready in about** 25 minutes | **Servings:** 2)

Ingredients

2fresh peaches pitted halved	2 tablespoons caster sugar
1/4 tbsp ground cinnamon	1 tablespoon butter

Directions

Mix the butter, sugar and cinnamon. Spread the butter mixture onto the peaches and transfer them to the Air Fryer cooking basket. Cook your peaches at 320 degrees F for about 25 minutes or until the top is golden.

Serve: with vanilla ice cream, if desired. Bon appétit!

Chocolate Mug Cake

(**Ready in about** 10 minutes | **Servings:** 2)

Ingredients

1/2 cup self-rising flour
5 tablespoons coconut milk
4 tablespoons unsweetened cocoa powder
2 eggs
6 tablespoons brown sugar
4 tablespoons coconut oil
A pinch of grated nutmeg
A pinch of salt

Directions

Mix all the Ingredients together; divide the batter between two mugs. Place the mugs in the Air Fryer cooking basket and cook at 390 degrees F for about 10 minutes. Bon appétit!

Easy Plantain Cupcakes

(**Ready in about** 10 minutes | **Servings:** 4)

Ingredients

1 teaspoon baking powder
1/4 teaspoon ground cloves
1 cup all-purpose flour
2 ripe plantains, peeled and mashed with a fork
1 egg, whisked
1/4 cup brown sugar
1/4 tbs ground cinnamon
A pinch of salt
2 tablespoons raisins, soaked
4 tablespoons coconut oil, room temperature
4 tablespoons pecans, roughly chopped

Directions

In a mixing bowl, thoroughly combine all Ingredients until everything is well incorporated. Spoon the batter into a greased muffin tin.

Bake the plantain cupcakes in your Air Fryer at 350 degrees F for about 10 minutes or until golden brown on the top. Bon appétit!

Strawberry Dessert Dumplings

(**Ready in about** 10 minutes | **Servings:** 3)

Ingredients

9 wonton wrappers
1/3 strawberry jam
2 ounces icing sugar

Directions

Start by laying out the wonton wrappers. Divide the strawberry jam between the wonton wrappers. Fold the wonton wrapper over the jam; now, seal the edges with wet fingers.

Cook your wontons at 400 degrees F for 8 minutes; working in batches. Bon appétit!

Crunchy French Toast Sticks

(**Ready in about** 10 minutes | **Servings:** 3)

Ingredients

1 egg
1 tablespoon brown sugar
1/4 teaspoon ground cloves
1/4 vanilla paste
1/4 cup milk
1/4 cup double cream
1/4 teaspoon ground cinnamon
3 thick slices of brioche bread, cut into thirds
1 cup crispy rice cereal

Directions

Thoroughly combine the egg, cream, milk, sugar, ground cloves, cinnamon and vanilla.

Dip each piece of bread into the cream mixture and then, press gently into the cereal, pressing to coat all sides.

Arrange the pieces of bread in the Air Fryer cooking basket and cook them at 380 degrees F for 2 minutes; flip and cook on the other side for 2 to 3 minutes longer.

Bon appétit!

Old-Fashioned Apple Crumble

(**Ready in about** 35 minutes | **Servings:** 4)

Ingredients

2 baking apples, peeled, cored and diced
1/4 teaspoon grated nutmeg 1/4 teaspoon ground cloves 1/2 teaspoon ground cinnamon
1/2 teaspoon vanilla essence
1/4 cup coconut oil
1 tablespoon cornstarch
2 tablespoons brown sugar
1/2 cup quick-cooking oats 1/4 cup self-rising flour
1/4 cup brown sugar
1/4 cup apple juice
1/2 teaspoon baking powder

Directions

Toss the apples with 2 tablespoons brown sugar and 2 tablespoons cornstarch. Place the apples in a baking pan that has been lightly greased with nonstick cooking spray. Spray with cooking spray.

Combine the remaining topping Ingredients in a mixing bowl. Over the apple layer, sprinkle the topping Ingredients.

Bake your apple crumble for 35 minutes in a preheated Air Fryer at 330 degrees F. Good appetite!

Blueberry Fritters with Cinnamon Sugar

(**Ready in about** 20 minutes | **Servings:** 4)

Ingredients

1/2 cup plain flour	1/2 tbs baking powder
A pinch of grated nutmeg	1/4 teaspoon ground star
1 teaspoon brown sugar	anise
1 cup fresh blueberries	A pinch of salt
1 egg	1/4 cup coconut milk
1 tablespoon coconut oil, melted	4 tablespoons cinnamon sugar

Directions

Combine the flour, baking powder, brown sugar, nutmeg, star anise and salt.

In another bowl, whisk the eggs and milk until frothy. Add the wet mixture to the dry mixture and mix to combine well. Fold in the fresh blueberries.

Carefully place spoonfuls of batter into the Air Fryer cooking basket. Brush them with melted coconut oil.

Cook your fritters in the preheated Air Fryer at 370 degrees for 10 minutes, flipping them halfway through the cooking time. Repeat with the remaining batter.

Dust your fritters with the cinnamon sugar and **Serve:** at room temperature. Bon appétit!

Cinnamon-Streusel Coffeecake

(**Ready in about** 30 minutes | **Servings:** 4)

Ingredients

Cake	1/2 cup unbleached white
1/4 cup yellow cornmeal	flour
1 teaspoon baking powder	1 tablespoon unsweetened
3 tablespoons white sugar	cocoa powder
A pinch of kosher salt	3 tablespoons coconut oil
1 egg Topping	2 tablespoons polenta
1/4 cup brown sugar	1 teaspoon ground
1/4 cup milk	cinnamon
2 tablespoons coconut oil	1/4 cup pecans, chopped

Directions

In a large bowl, combine together the cake Ingredients. Spoon the mixture into a lightly greased baking pan.

Then, in another bowl, combine the topping Ingredients. Spread the topping Ingredients over your cake.

Bake the cake at 330 degrees F for 12 to 15 minutes until a tester comes out dry and clean. Allow your cake to cool for about 15 minutes before cutting and serving. Bon appétit!

Air Grilled Apricots with Mascarpone

(**Ready in about** 30 minutes | **Servings:** 2)

Ingredients

6 apricots, halved and pitted	1 tbs coconut oil, melted
2 ounces mascarpone cheese	1/2 teaspoon vanilla extract
A pinch of sea salt	1 tbs confectioners' sugar

Directions

Place the apricots in the Air Fryer cooking basket. Drizzle the apricots with melted coconut oil.

Cook the apricots at 320 degrees F for about 25 minutes or until the top is golden. In a bowl, whisk the mascarpone, vanilla extract, confectioners' sugar by hand until soft and creamy.

Remove the apricots from the cooking basket. Spoon the whipped mascarpone into the cavity of each apricot. Sprinkle with coarse sea salt and enjoy!

Chocolate Chip Banana Crepes

(**Ready in about** 30 minutes | **Servings:** 2)

Ingredients

1 small ripe banana	1/8 tbs baking powder
1 egg, whisked	1/4 cup chocolate chips

Directions

Mix all Ingredients until creamy and fluffy. Let it stand for about 20 minutes. Spritz the Air Fryer baking pan with cooking spray. Pour 1/2 of the batter into the pan using a measuring cup.

Cook at 230 degrees F for 4 to 5 minutes or until golden brown. Repeat with another crepe. Bon appétit!

Classic Flourless Cake

(**Ready in about** 2 hours | **Servings:** 4)

Ingredients

Crust
1 tablespoon flaxseed meal
1/3 cup almond meal
2 tablespoons powdered sugar
6 ounces cream cheese
1 teaspoon butter
1 teaspoon pumpkin pie spice
1 tbsp caster sugar Filling
1 egg
1/2 tbs pure vanilla extract

Directions

Mix all theIngredients for the crust and then, press the mixture into the bottom of a lightly greased baking pan.

Bake the crust at 350 degrees F for 18 minutes. Transfer the crust to the freezer for about 25 minutes.

Now, make the cheesecake topping by mixing the remaining Ingredients. Spread the prepared topping over the cooled crust.

Bake your cheesecake in the preheated Air Fryer at 320 degrees F for about 30 minutes; leave it in the Air Fryer to keep warm for another 30 minutes.

Serve: well chilled. Bon appétit!

Old-Fashioned Baked Pears

(**Ready in about** 10 minutes | **Servings:** 2)

Ingredients

2 large pears, halved and cored
1/2 cup rolled oats
1 teaspoon apple pie spice mix
2 teaspoons coconut oil
1 teaspoon lemon juice
1/4 cup walnuts, chopped
1/4 cup brown sugar

Directions

Drizzle the pear halves with lemon juice and coconut oil. In a mixing bowl, thoroughly combine the rolled oats, walnuts, brown sugar and apple pie spice mix.

Cook in the preheated Air Fryer at 360 degrees for 8 minutes, checking them halfway through the cooking time.

Dust with powdered sugar if desired. Bon appétit!

Lemon-Glazed Crescent Ring

(**Ready in about** 25 minutes | **Servings:** 6)

Ingredients

8 ounces refrigerated crescent dough
1 tablespoon coconut oil, at room temperature
1/3 cup powdered sugar
2 ounces caster sugar
1 tablespoon full-fat coconut milk
2 ounces mascarpone cheese, at room temperature
Glaze
1/2 teaspoon vanilla paste
1 tablespoon fresh lemon juice

Directions

Separate the crescent dough sheet into 8 triangles. Then, arrange the triangles in a sunburst pattern so it should look like the sun. Mix the mascarpone cheese, vanilla, coconut oil and caster sugar in a bowl.

Place the mixture on the bottom of each triangle; fold triangle tips over filling and tuck under base to secure.

Bake the ring at 360 degrees F for 20 minutes until dough is golden.

In small mixing dish, whisk the powdered sugar, lemon juice and coconut milk. Drizzle over warm crescent ring and garnish with grated lemon peel. Bon appétit!

Fluffy Chocolate Chip Cookies

(**Ready in about** 20 minutes | **Servings:** 6)

Ingredients

1/2 cup butter, softened
1/2 cup granulated sugar
1 cup quick-cooking oats
1 large egg
1/2 teaspoon vanilla paste
6 ounces dark chocolate chips
1/2 teaspoon coconut extract
1/2 cup all-purpose flour
1/2 teaspoon baking powder

Directions

Start by preheating your Air Fryer to 330 degrees F.

In a mixing bowl, beat the butter and sugar until fluffy. Beat in the egg, coconut extract and vanilla paste.

In a second mixing bowl, whisk the oats, flour and baking powder. Add the flour mixture to the egg mixture. Fold in the chocolate chips and gently stir to combine.

Drop 2-tablespoon scoops of the dough onto the parchment paper and transfer it to the Air Fryer cooking basket. Gently flatten each scoop to make a cookie shape.

Cook in the preheated Air Fryer for about 10 minutes. Work in batches. Bon appétit!

Authentic Spanish Churros

(**Ready in about** 20 minutes | **Servings:** 4)

Ingredients

1/2 cup water
1 tablespoon granulated sugar A pinch of ground cinnamon
1/2 teaspoon lemon zest
2 ounces dark chocolate
1/2 cup milk

1/4 cup butter, cut into cubes A pinch of salt
1/2 cup plain flour

1 egg Chocolate Dip
1 teaspoon ground cinnamon

Directions

Boil the water in a saucepan over medium-high heat; now, add the butter, sugar, cinnamon, salt and lemon zest; cook until the sugar has dissolved.

Next, remove the pan from the heat. Gradually stir in the flour, whisking continuously until the mixture forms a ball; let it cool slightly.

Fold in the egg and continue to beat using an electric mixer until everything comes together.

Pour the dough into a piping bag with a large star tip. Squeeze 4-inch strips of dough into the greased Air Fryer pan.

Cook your churros at 380 degrees F for about 10 minutes, shaking the basket halfway through the cooking time.

In the meantime, melt the chocolate and milk in a saucepan over low heat. Add in the cinnamon and cook on low heat for about 5 minutes. **Serve:** the warm churros with the chocolate dip and enjoy!

Classic Brownie Cupcakes

(**Ready in about** 25 minutes | **Servings:** 3)

Ingredients

1/3 cup all-purpose flour
1/4 teaspoon baking powder
1/2 teaspoon rum extract
1/3 cup caster sugar
3 tablespoons cocoa powder

2 ounces butter, room temperature
1 large egg
A pinch of ground cinnamon A pinch of salt

Directions

In a mixing bowl, combine the dry Ingredients. Combine the wet Ingredients in a separate bowl. Stir in the wet Ingredients gradually into the dry mixture.

Divide the batter evenly among the muffin cups and place them in the Air Fryer cooking basket.

Bake the cupcakes at 330°F for 15 minutes, or until a tester comes out dry and clean. Allow your cupcakes to cool for 10 minutes on a wire rack before unmolding. Good appetite!

Baked Fruit Salad

(**Ready in about** 15 minutes | **Servings:** 2)

Ingredients

1 banana, peeled
1 tablespoon freshly squeezed lemon juice
1/2 teaspoon ground star anise
1/2 teaspoon granulated ginger

1 cooking pear, cored
1/4 teaspoon ground cinnamon
1 cooking apple, cored
1/4 cup brown sugar
1 tablespoon coconut oil, melted

Directions

Toss your fruits with lemon juice, star anise, cinnamon, ginger, sugar and coconut oil.

Transfer the fruits to the Air Fryer cooking basket.

Bake the fruit salad in the preheated Air Fryer at 330 degrees F for 15 minutes.

Serve: in individual bowls, garnished with vanilla ice cream. Bon appétit

Red Velvet Pancakes

(**Ready in about** 35 minutes | **Servings:** 3)

Ingredients

1 cup all-purpose flour

1/8 teaspoon sea salt
1/2 teaspoon baking soda
1/2 cup powdered sugar

1 small-sized egg, beaten
1/2 cup milk
2 ounces cream cheese, softened
1 tablespoon butter, softened

1 teaspoon granulated sugar
1/8 teaspoon freshly grated nutmeg
2 tablespoons ghee, melted
1 teaspoon red paste food color

Directions

Thoroughly combine the flour, baking soda, granulated sugar, salt and nutmeg in a large bowl.

Gradually add in the melted ghee, egg, milk and red paste food color, stirring into the flour mixture until moistened. Allow your batter to rest for about 30 minutes.

Spritz the Air Fryer baking pan with cooking spray. Pour the batter into the pan using a measuring cup. Set the pan into the Air Fryer cooking basket.

Cook at 330 degrees F for about 5 minutes or until golden brown. Repeat with the other pancakes.

Meanwhile, mix the remaining Ingredients until creamy and fluffy. Decorate your pancakes with cream cheese topping. Bon appétit!

Apricot and Almond Crumble

(**Ready in about** 35 minutes | **Servings:** 3)

Ingredients

1 cup apricots, pitted and diced
4 tablespoons granulated sugar
1/2 teaspoon ground cinnamon
1 tbs crystallized ginger
1/3 cup self-raising flour
1/4 cup flaked almonds
2 tablespoons butter
1/2 teaspoon ground cardamom

Directions

Place the sliced apricots and almonds in a baking pan that is lightly greased with a nonstick cooking spray.

In a mixing bowl, thoroughly combine the remaining Ingredients. Sprinkle this topping over the apricot layer.

Bake your crumble in the preheated Air Fryer at 330 degrees F for 35 minutes. Bon appétit!

Easy Monkey Rolls

(**Ready in about** 25 minutes | **Servings:** 4)

Ingredients

8 ounces refrigerated buttermilk biscuit dough
1/4 teaspoon grated nutmeg 1/2 tbs ground cinnamon
4 ounces butter, melted
1/2 cup brown sugar
1/4 teaspoon ground cardamom

Directions

Spritz 4 standard-size muffin cups with a nonstick spray. Thoroughly combine the brown sugar with the melted butter, nutmeg, cinnamon and cardamom.

Spoon the butter mixture into muffins cups.

Separate the dough into biscuits and divide your biscuits between muffin cups.

Bake the Monkey rolls at 340 degrees F for about 15 minutes or until golden brown. Turn upside down just before serving. Bon appétit!

Sherry Roasted Sweet Cherries

(**Ready in about** 35 minutes | **Servings:** 4)

Ingredients

2 cups dark cherries
3 tablespoons sherry
A pinch of sea salt
1/4 cup granulated sugar
A pinch of grated nutmeg
1 tablespoon honey

Directions

Arrange your cherries in the bottom of a lightly greased baking dish. Whisk the remaining Ingredients; spoon this mixture into the baking dish. Air fry your cherries at 370 degrees F for 35 minutes. Bon appétit!

Greek Roasted Figs with Yiaourti me Meli

(**Ready in about** 20 minutes | **Servings:** 3)

Ingredients

1 teaspoon coconut oil, melted
1/4 teaspoon ground cloves 1/4 tbs ground cinnamon
3 tablespoon honey
1/4 teaspoon ground cardamom
1/2 cup Greek yogurt
6 medium-sized figs

Directions

Drizzle the melted coconut oil all over your figs. Sprinkle cardamom, cloves and cinnamon over your figs.

Roast your figs in the preheated Air Fryer at 330 degrees F for 15 to 16

minutes, shaking the basket occasionally to promote even cooking.

In the meantime, thoroughly combine the honey with the Greek yogurt to make the yiaourti me meli.

Divide the roasted figs between 3 serving bowls and **Serve:** with a dollop of yiaourti me meli. Enjoy!

Chocolate Lava Cake

(**Ready in about** 20 minutes | **Servings:** 4)

Ingredients

4 ounces butter, melted
4 ounces dark chocolate
2 eggs, lightly whisked
1 teaspoon baking powder
4 tablespoons granulated sugar
2 tablespoons cake flour
1/2 tbs ground cinnamon
1/4 tbs ground star anise

Directions

Begin by preheating your Air Fryer to 370 degrees F. Spritz the sides and bottom of a baking pan with nonstick cooking spray.

Melt the butter and dark chocolate in a microwave-safe bowl. Mix the eggs and sugar until frothy.

Pour the butter/chocolate mixture into the egg mixture. Stir in the flour, baking powder, cinnamon, and star anise. Mix until everything is well incorporated.

Scrape the batter into the prepared pan. Bake in the preheated Air Fryer for 9 to 11 minutes.

Let stand for 2 minutes. Invert on a plate while warm and **Serve:**. Bon appétit!

Banana Chips with Chocolate Glaze

(**Ready in about** 20 minutes | **Servings:** 2)

Ingredients

2 banana, cut into slices
1/4 teaspoon lemon zest

1 tablespoon coconut oil, melted

1 tablespoon cocoa powder
1 tablespoon agave syrup

Directions

Toss the bananas with the lemon zest and agave syrup. Transfer your bananas to the parchment-lined cooking basket.

Bake in the preheated Air Fryer at 370 degrees F for 12 minutes, turning them over halfway through the cooking time.

In the meantime, melt the coconut oil in your microwave; add the cocoa powder and whisk to combine well.

Serve: the baked banana chips with a few drizzles of the chocolate glaze. Enjoy!

Grandma's Butter Cookies

(**Ready in about** 25 minutes | **Servings:** 4)

Ingredients

8 ounces all-purpose flour
A pinch of grated nutmeg
A pinch of coarse salt
1 stick butter, room temperature
1 teaspoon vanilla extract
1 teaspoon baking powder
1 large egg, room temperature.
2 ½ ounces sugar

Directions

Mix the flour, sugar, baking powder, grated nutmeg, and salt in a bowl. In a separate bowl, whisk the egg, butter, and vanilla extract.

Stir the egg mixture into the flour mixture; mix to combine well or until it forms a nice, soft dough.

Roll your dough out and cut out with a cookie cutter of your choice.

Bake in the preheated Air Fryer at 350 degrees F for 10 minutes. Decrease the temperature to 330 degrees F and cook for 10 minutes longer. Bon appétit!

Cinnamon Dough Dippers

(**Ready in about** 20 minutes | **Servings:** 6)

Ingredients

1/2 pound bread dough
1/2 cup caster sugar
1/2 cup cream cheese, softened
1 cup powdered sugar
1 tablespoon cinnamon
1/4 cup butter, melted
1/2 teaspoon vanilla
2 tablespoons milk

Directions

Roll the dough into a log; cut into 1-1/2 inch strips using a pizza cutter. Mix the butter, sugar, and cinnamon in a small bowl. Use a rubber spatula to spread the butter mixture over the tops of the dough dippers.

Bake at 360 degrees F for 7 to 8 minutes, turning them over halfway through the cooking time. Work in batches.

Meanwhile, make the glaze dip by whisking the remaining Ingredients with a hand mixer. Beat until a smooth consistency is reached. **Serve:** at room temperature and enjoy!

Chocolate Apple Chips

(**Ready in about** 15 minutes | **Servings:** 2)

Ingredients

1 large Pink Lady apple, cored and sliced	A pinch of kosher salt
2 teaspoons cocoa powder	1 tbs light brown sugar
	2 tablespoons lemon juice

Directions

Toss the apple slices in with the remaining Ingredients. Bake at 350°F for 5 minutes, then shake the basket to ensure even cooking and cook for another 5 minutes. Good appetite!

Favorite Apple Crisp

(**Ready in about** 40 minutes | **Servings:** 4)

Ingredients

4 cups apples, peeled, cored and sliced	1 tablespoon honey
1 tablespoon cornmeal	1/2 cup brown sugar
1/2 teaspoon ground cinnamon	1/4 teaspoon ground cloves 1/4 cup water
1/2 cup quick-cooking oats 1/2 cup all-purpose flour	1/2 cup caster sugar
	1/2 tbs baking powder
	1/3 cup coconut oil, melted

Directions

Toss the sliced apples with the brown sugar, honey, cornmeal, cloves, and cinnamon. Divide between four custard cups coated with cooking spray.

In a mixing dish, thoroughly combine the remaining Ingredients. Sprinkle over the apple mixture.

Bake in the preheated Air Fryer at 330 degrees F for 35 minutes. Bon appétit!

Cocktail Party Fruit Kabobs

(**Ready in about** 10 minutes | **Servings:** 6)

Ingredients

1 pears, diced into bite-sized chunks	2 mangos, diced into bite sized chunks
2 apples, diced into bite-sized chunks	1 teaspoon vanilla essence
1 tbs fresh lemon juice	1/2 tbsp ground cloves
1 tbs ground cinnamon	2 tablespoons maple syrup

Directions

Toss all Ingredients in a mixing dish. Tread the fruit pieces on skewers. Cook at 350 degrees F for 5 minutes.

Bon appétit!

Peppermint Chocolate Cheesecake

(**Ready in about** 40 minutes | **Servings:** 6)

Ingredients

1 cup powdered sugar	1 cup mascarpone cheese, at room temperature
1/2 cup all-purpose flour	4 ounces semisweet chocolate, melted
1/2 cup butter	
2 drops peppermint extract	
1 teaspoon vanilla extract	

Directions

In a mixing bowl, combine the sugar, flour, and butter. Press the mixture into the bottom of a baking pan that has been lightly greased.

Bake for 18 minutes at 350 degrees F. Set it in the freezer for 20 minutes. Then, combine the remaining Ingredients to make the cheesecake topping.

Place this topping on top of the crust and place it in the freezer for another 15 minutes to cool. Chill before serving.

Baked Coconut Doughnuts

(**Ready in about** 20 minutes | **Servings:** 6)

Ingredients

1 ½ cups all-purpose flour	A pinch of freshly grated nutmeg
1 teaspoon baking powder	1/2 cup white sugar
A pinch of kosher salt	2 tablespoons full-fat coconut milk
2 eggs	1/4 tbs ground cinnamon
1/4 tbs ground cardamom	1/2 teaspoon vanilla essence
2 tbsp coconut oil, melted	
1 teaspoon coconut essence	
1 cup coconut flakes	

Directions

In a mixing bowl, thoroughly combine the all-purpose flour with the baking powder, salt, nutmeg, and sugar.

In a separate bowl, beat the eggs until frothy using a hand mixer; add the coconut milk and oil and beat again; lastly, stir in the spices and mix again until everything is well combined.

Then, stir the egg mixture into the flour mixture and continue mixing until a dough ball forms. Try not to over-mix your dough. Transfer to a lightly floured surface.

Roll out your dough to a 1/4-inch thickness using a rolling pin. Cut out the doughnuts using a 3-inch round cutter; now, use a 1-inch round cutter to remove the center.

Bake in the preheated Air Fryer at 340 degrees F approximately 5 minutes or until golden. Repeat with remaining doughnuts. Decorate with coconut flakes and **Serve:**.

Coconut Pancake Cups

(**Ready in about** 30 minutes | **Servings:** 4)

Ingredients

1/2 cup flour
1 tablespoon coconut oil, melted
1/2 cup coconut chips
1 teaspoon vanilla

1/3 cup coconut milk
A pinch of ground cardamom
2 eggs

Directions

Mix the flour, coconut milk, eggs, coconut oil, vanilla, and cardamom in a large bowl.

Let it stand for 20 minutes. Spoon the batter into a greased muffin tin.

Cook at 230 degrees F for 4 to 5 minutes or until golden brown. Repeat with the remaining batter.

Decorate your pancakes with coconut chips. Bon appétit!

Classic Vanilla Mini Cheesecakes

(**Ready in about** 40 minutes + chilling time | **Servings:** 6)

Ingredients

1/2 cup almond flour
1 tablespoon white sugar
1 (8-ounce) package cream cheese, softened
1 egg, at room temperature Topping
3 tablespoons white sugar

1 ½ tablespoons unsalted butter, melted
1/2 teaspoon vanilla paste
1/4 cup powdered sugar
1 ½ cups sour cream
1 teaspoon vanilla extract
1/4 cup maraschino cherries

Directions

Thoroughly combine the almond flour, butter, and sugar in a mixing bowl. Press the mixture into the bottom of lightly greased custard cups.

Then, mix the cream cheese, 1/4 cup of powdered sugar, vanilla, and egg using an electric mixer on low speed. Pour the batter into the pan, covering the crust.

Bake in the preheated Air Fryer at 330 degrees F for 35 minutes until edges are puffed and the surface is firm.

Mix the sour cream, 3 tablespoons of white sugar, and vanilla for the topping; spread over the crust and allow it to cool to room temperature.

Transfer to your refrigerator for 6 to 8 hours. Decorate with maraschino cherries and **Serve:** well chilled.

Bakery-Style Hazelnut Cookies

(**Ready in about** 20 minutes | **Servings:** 6)

Ingredients

1 ½ cups all-purpose flour
1 stick butter
1 teaspoon baking soda
2 eggs, at room temperature

1 teaspoon fine sea salt
1 cup brown sugar
2 teaspoons vanilla
1 cup hazelnuts, coarsely chopped

Directions

Begin by preheating your Air Fryer to 350 degrees F. Mix the flour with the baking soda, and sea salt.

In the bowl of an electric mixer, beat the butter, brown sugar, and vanilla until creamy.

Fold in the eggs, one at a time, and mix until well combined. Slowly and gradually, stir in the flour mixture. Finally, fold in the coarsely chopped hazelnuts.

Divide the dough into small balls using a large cookie scoop; drop onto the prepared cookie sheets. Bake for 10 minutes or until golden brown, rotating the pan once or twice through the cooking time.

Work in batches and cool for a couple of minutes before removing to wire racks. Enjoy!

Sunday Banana Chocolate Cookies

(**Ready in about** 20 minutes | **Servings:** 8)

Ingredients

1 stick butter, at room temperature
1 teaspoon vanilla paste
1 ½ teaspoons baking powder
1/4 tbs ground cinnamon
1 ½ cups chocolate chips

2 ripe bananas, mashed
1 ¼ cups caster sugar
1 2/3 cups all-purpose flour
1/3 cup cocoa powder
1/4 teaspoon crystallized ginger

Directions

In a mixing dish, beat the butter and sugar until creamy and uniform. Stir in the mashed bananas and vanilla.

In another mixing dish, thoroughly combine the flour, cocoa powder, baking powder, cinnamon, and crystallized ginger. Add the flour mixture to the banana mixture; mix to combine well. Afterwards, fold in the chocolate chips.

Drop by large spoonfuls onto a parchment-lined Air Fryer basket. Bake at 365 degrees F for 11 minutes or until golden brown on the top. Bon appétit!

Rustic Baked Apples

(**Ready in about** 25 minutes | **Servings:** 4)

Ingredients

4 Gala apples
2 tablespoons honey
1 teaspoon cinnamon
powder 1/2 teaspoon
ground cardamom
1/2 teaspoon ground
cloves

1/4 cup rolled oats
1/3 cup walnuts, chopped
2/3 cup water
1/4 cup sugar

Directions

Use a paring knife to remove the stem and seeds from the apples, making deep holes.

In a mixing bowl, combine together the rolled oats, sugar, honey, walnuts, cinnamon, cardamom, and cloves.

Pour the water into an Air Fryer safe dish. Place the apples in the dish.

Bake at 340 degrees F for 17 minutes. **Serve:** at room temperature. Bon appétit!

The Ultimate Berry Crumble

(**Ready in about** 40 minutes | **Servings:** 6)

Ingredients

18 ounces cherries
1/4 teaspoon ground star
anise
1/2 teaspoon ground
cinnamon
1/2 teaspoon baking
powder

1/2 cup granulated sugar
1 cup demerara sugar
2 tablespoons cornmeal
2/3 cup all-purpose flour
1/3 cup rolled oats
1/2 stick butter, cut into
small pieces

Directions

Combine the cherries, granulated sugar, cornmeal, star anise, and cinnamon in a mixing bowl. Divide the mixture among six custard cups that have been sprayed with cooking spray.

Combine the remaining Ingredients in a mixing bowl. Sprinkle the berry mixture on top.

35 minutes in a preheated Air Fryer at 330 degrees F. Good appetite!

Mocha Chocolate Espresso Cake

(**Ready in about** 40 minutes | **Servings:** 8)

Ingredients

1 ½ cups flour
1/4 teaspoon salt
1/2 cup hot strongly
brewed coffee
1/4 cup flour
1/2 cup sugar
1 teaspoon ground
cinnamon 3 tablespoons
coconut oil

1 teaspoon baking powder
1 stick butter, melted
1 egg Topping
2/3 cup sugar
1/2 teaspoon ground
cardamom
1/2 teaspoon vanilla

Directions

Mix all dry Ingredients for your cake; then, mix in the wet Ingredients. Mix until everything is well incorporated.

Spritz a baking pan with cooking spray. Scrape the batter into the baking pan. Then make the topping by mixing all Ingredients. Place on top of the cake.

Smooth the top with a spatula.

Bake at 330 degrees F for 30 minutes or until the top of the cake springs back when gently pressed with your fingers. **Serve:** with your favorite hot beverage. Bon appétit!

Baked Peaches with Oatmeal Pecan Streusel

(**Ready in about** 20 minutes | **Servings:** 3)

Ingredients

2 tablespoons old-
fashioned rolled oats
1 egg
3 tablespoons golden
caster sugar
3 large ripe freestone
peaches, halved and pitted

1/2 teaspoon ground
cinnamon
2 tablespoons cold salted
butter, cut into pieces
3 tbsp pecans, chopped

Directions

Mix the rolled oats, sugar, cinnamon, egg, and butter until well combined. Add a big spoonful of prepared topping to the center of each peach. Pour 1/2 cup of water into an Air Fryer safe dish. Place the peaches in the dish.

Top the peaches with the roughly chopped pecans. Bake at 340 degrees F for 17 minutes. **Serve:** at room temperature. Bon appétit!

Favorite New York Cheesecake

(**Ready in about** 40 minutes + chilling time | **Servings:** 8)

Ingredients

1 ½ cups digestive biscuits crumbs	1 ounce demerara sugar
1/2 stick butter, melted	2 ounces white sugar
1/2 cup heavy cream	32 ounces full-fat cream cheese
1 ¼ cups caster sugar	3 eggs, at room temperature
1 tablespoon vanilla essence	1 teaspoon grated lemon zest

Directions

Coat the sides and bottom of a baking pan with a little flour. In a mixing bowl, combine the digestive biscuits, white sugar, and demerara sugar. Add the melted butter and mix until your mixture looks like breadcrumbs.

Press the mixture into the bottom of the prepared pan to form an even layer. Bake at 330 degrees F for 7 minutes until golden brown. Allow it to cool completely on a wire rack. Meanwhile, in a mixer fitted with the paddle attachment, prepare the filling by mixing the soft cheese, heavy cream, and caster sugar; beat until creamy and fluffy.

Crack the eggs into the mixing bowl, one at a time; add the vanilla and lemon zest and continue to mix until fully combined. Pour the prepared topping over the cooled crust and spread evenly.

Bake in the preheated Air Fryer at 330 degrees F for 25 to 30 minutes; leave it in the Air Fryer to keep warm for another 30 minutes.

Cover your cheesecake with plastic wrap. Place in your refrigerator and allow it to cool at least 6 hours or overnight. **Serve:** well chilled

Authentic Indian Gulgulas

(**Ready in about** 20 minutes | **Servings:** 3)

Ingredients

1 banana, mashed	1 egg
1/2 teaspoon vanilla essence 1/4 teaspoon ground cardamom	1/2 milk
	1/4 cup sugar
	1/4 teaspoon cinnamon
3/4 cup all-purpose flour	1 teaspoon baking powder

Directions

In a mixing bowl, whisk the mashed banana with the sugar and egg; add the vanilla, cardamom, and cinnamon and mix to combine well. Gradually pour in the milk and mix again. Stir in the flour and baking powder. Mix until everything is well incorporated.

Drop a spoonful of batter onto the greased Air Fryer pan. Cook in the preheated Air Fryer at 360 degrees F for 5 minutes, flipping them halfway through the cooking time.

Repeat with the remaining batter and **Serve:** warm. Enjoy!

English-Style Scones with Raisins

(**Ready in about** 20 minutes | **Servings:** 6)

Ingredients

1 ½ cups all-purpose flour	1 teaspoon baking powder
1/4 cup brown sugar	1/2 cup double cream
1/4 teaspoon sea salt	1/4 teaspoon ground cloves
1/2 teaspoon ground cardamom	6 tablespoons butter, cooled and sliced
1 teaspoon ground cinnamon	1/2 cup raisins
2 eggs, lightly whisked	1/2 teaspoon vanilla essence

Directions

In a mixing bowl, thoroughly combine the flour, sugar, baking powder, salt, cloves, cardamom cinnamon, and raisins. Mix until everything is combined well.

Add the butter and mix again.

In another mixing bowl, combine the double cream with the eggs and vanilla; beat until creamy and smooth.

Stir the wet Ingredients into the dry mixture. Roll your dough out into a circle and cut into wedges.

Bake in the preheated Air Fryer at 360 degrees for 11 minutes, rotating the pan halfway through the cooking time. Bon appétit!

Red Velvet Pancakes

(**Ready in about** 35 minutes | **Servings:** 3)

Ingredients

1/2 cup flour
2 tablespoons white sugar
1/2 teaspoon cinnamon
1 egg
1 teaspoon vanilla
Topping
1/4 teaspoon salt
3/4 cup powdered sugar

1 teaspoon baking powder
1 teaspoon red paste food color
1/2 cup milk
2 ounces cream cheese, softened
2 tablespoons butter, softened

Directions

In a large mixing bowl, combine the flour, baking powder, salt, sugar, cinnamon, and red paste food colour.

Add the egg and milk in a steady stream, whisking constantly, until well combined.

Allow it to stand for 20 minutes.

Coat the baking pan of the Air Fryer with cooking spray. Using a measuring cup, pour the batter into the pan.

Cook for 4 to 5 minutes, or until golden brown, at 230°F. Repeat with the rest of the batter.

Meanwhile, make your topping by combining all of the Ingredients and mixing until creamy and fluffy. Make a topping for your pancakes. Good appetite!

Spanish-Style Doughnut Tejeringos

(**Ready in about** 20 minutes | **Servings:** 4)

Ingredients

3/4 cup water
1/4 teaspoon grated nutmeg 1/4 teaspoon ground cloves
6 tablespoons butter

1 tablespoon sugar
3/4 cup all-purpose flour
2 eggs
1/4 teaspoon sea salt

Directions

To make the dough, boil the water in a pan over medium-high heat; now, add the sugar, salt, nutmeg, and cloves; cook until dissolved.

Add the butter and turn the heat to low. Gradually stir in the flour, whisking continuously, until the mixture forms a ball.

Remove from the heat; fold in the eggs one at a time, stirring to combine well.

Pour the mixture into a piping bag with a large star tip. Squeeze 4-inch strips of dough into the greased Air Fryer pan.

Cook at 410 degrees F for 6 minutes, working in batches. Bon appétit!

Salted Caramel Cheesecake

(**Ready in about** 1 hour + chilling time | **Servings:** 10)

Ingredients

1 cup granulated sugar
2 tablespoons butter
1/3 cup water
1/3 cup salted butter, melted
1 ½ cups graham cracker crumbs
20 ounces cream cheese, softened
1 cup granulated sugar
1/4 teaspoon ground star anise

3/4 cup heavy cream
1 teaspoon vanilla extract
1/2 teaspoon coarse sea salt Crust

2 tablespoons brown sugar
Topping
1 cup sour cream
3 eggs
1 teaspoon vanilla essence

Directions

To make the caramel sauce, cook the sugar in a saucepan over medium heat; shake it to form a flat layer.

Add the water and cook until the sugar dissolves. Raise the heat to medium- high, and continue to cook your caramel for a further 10 minutes until it turns amber colored.

Turn the heat off; immediately stir in the heavy cream, butter, vanilla extract, and salt. Stir to combine well.

Let the salted caramel sauce cool to room temperature.

Beat all Ingredients for the crust in a mixing bowl. Press the mixture into the bottom of a lightly greased baking pan.

Bake at 350 degrees F for 18 minutes. Place it in your freezer for 20 minutes. Then, make the cheesecake topping by mixing the remaining Ingredients.

Pour the prepared topping over the cooled crust and spread evenly.

Bake in the preheated Air Fryer at 330 degrees F for 25 to 30 minutes; leave it in the Air Fryer to keep warm for another 30 minutes.

Refrigerate your cheesecake until completely cool and firm or overnight. Prior to serving, pour the salted caramel sauce over the cheesecake. Bon appétit!

Banana Crepes with Apple Topping

(**Ready in about** 40 minutes | **Servings:** 2)

Ingredients

Banana Crepes	1 large banana, mashed
1/4 teaspoon baking powder 1 shot dark rum	1/2 teaspoon vanilla extract
	2 eggs, beaten
1 teaspoon butter, melted	2 apples, peeled, cored,
2 tablespoons brown sugar	and chopped
Topping	2 tablespoons sugar
1/2 teaspoon cinnamon	3 tablespoons water

Directions

Mix all Ingredients for the banana crepes until creamy and fluffy. Let it stand for 15 to 20 minutes.

Spritz the Air Fryer baking pan with cooking spray. Pour the batter into the pan using a measuring cup.

Cook at 230 degrees F for 4 to 5 minutes or until golden brown. Repeat with the remaining batter.

To make the pancake topping, place all Ingredients in a heavy-bottomed skillet over medium heat. Cook for 10 minutes, stirring occasionally. Spoon on top of the banana crepes and enjoy!

Apricot and Walnut Crumble

(**Ready in about** 40 minutes | **Servings:** 8)

Ingredients

2 pounds apricots, pitted and sliced	2 tablespoons cornstarch
	1 cup brown sugar
Topping	1 ½ cups old-fashioned
1/2 cup brown sugar	rolled oats
2 tablespoons agave nectar	1 teaspoon crystallized
1/2 teaspoon ground	ginger cardamom
1 stick butter, cut into	A pinch of salt
pieces 1/2 cup dried	1/2 cup walnuts, chopped
cranberries	

Directions

Toss the sliced apricots with the brown sugar and cornstarch. Place in a baking pan lightly greased with nonstick cooking spray.

In a mixing dish, thoroughly combine all the topping Ingredients. Sprinkle the topping Ingredients over the apricot layer.

Bake in the preheated Air Fryer at 330 degrees F for 35 minutes. Bon appétit!

Pear Fritters with Cinnamon and Ginger

(**Ready in about** 20 minutes | **Servings:** 4)

Ingredients

1 pears, peeled, cored and sliced	1 teaspoon baking powder
	A pinch of fine sea salt
1 ½ cups all-purpose flour	1 tbsp coconut oil, melted
A pinch of freshly grated nutmeg	1/2 teaspoon ginger
	1 teaspoon cinnamon
2 eggs	4 tablespoons milk

Directions

In a shallow bowl, combine all Ingredients except the pears. Dip each pear slice in the batter until thoroughly coated.

Cook for 4 minutes at 360 degrees Fahrenheit in a preheated Air Fryer, flipping halfway through. Rep with the rest of the Ingredients.

If desired, dust with powdered sugar. Good appetite!

Old-Fashioned Plum Dumplings

(**Ready in about** 40 minutes | **Servings:** 4)

Ingredients

1 (14-ounce) box pie crusts	2 tablespoons granulated sugar
2 cups plums, pitted	
2 tablespoons coconut oil	1/4 teaspoon ground
1/2 teaspoon ground cinnamon	cardamom
	1 egg white, slightly beaten

Directions

Place the pie crust on a work surface. Roll into a circle and cut into quarters.

Place 1 plum on each crust piece. Add the sugar, coconut oil, cardamom, and cinnamon. Roll up the sides into a circular shape around the plums.

Repeat with the remaining Ingredients. Brush the edges with the egg white. Place in the lightly greased Air Fryer basket.

Bake in the preheated Air Fryer at 360 degrees F for 20 minutes, flipping them halfway through the cooking time. Work in two batches, decorate and **Serve:** at room temperature. Bon appétit!

Almond Chocolate Cupcakes

(**Ready in about** 20 minutes | **Servings:** 6)

Ingredients
3/4 cup self-raising flour
1 cup powdered sugar
1/4 teaspoon salt

2 ounces butter, softened
2 tablespoons almond milk
1/2 teaspoon vanilla
extract

1/4 teaspoon nutmeg,
preferably freshly grated
1 tablespoon cocoa
powder
1 egg, whisked
1 ½ ounces dark chocolate
chunks
1/2 cup almonds,
chopped

Directions

In a mixing bowl, combine the flour, sugar, salt, nutmeg, and cocoa powder. Mix to combine well.

In another mixing bowl, whisk the butter, egg, almond milk, and vanilla.

Now, add the wet egg mixture to the dry Ingredients. Then, carefully fold in the chocolate chunks and almonds; gently stir to combine.

Scrape the batter mixture into muffin cups. Bake your cupcakes at 350 degrees F for 12 minutes until a toothpick comes out clean.

Decorate with chocolate sprinkles if desired. **Serve:** and enjoy!

White Chocolate Rum Molten Cake

(**Ready in about** 20 minutes | **Servings:** 4)

Ingredients
2 ½ ounces butter, at
room temperature
1/2 cup powdered sugar
1/3 cup self-rising flour
1 teaspoon rum extract

2 eggs, beaten
3 ounces white chocolate
1 teaspoon vanilla extract

Directions

Begin by preheating your Air Fryer to 370 degrees F. Spritz the sides and bottom of four ramekins with cooking spray.

Melt the butter and white chocolate in a microwave-safe bowl. Mix the eggs and sugar until frothy.

Pour the butter/chocolate mixture into the egg mixture. Stir in the flour, rum extract, and vanilla extract. Mix until everything is well incorporated.

Scrape the batter into the prepared ramekins. Bake in the preheated Air Fryer for 9 to 11 minutes.

Let stand for 2 to 3 minutes. Invert on a plate while warm and **Serve:**. Bon appétit!

Summer Fruit Pie with Cinnamon Streusel

(**Ready in about** 40 minutes | **Servings:** 4)

Ingredients
1 (14-ounce) box pie
crusts Filling
1/3 cup all-purpose flour
1/2 tbs ground cinnamon
1/2 cup brown sugar
1/3 cup cold salted butter
2 cups apricots, pitted and
sliced peeled
2 cups peaches, pitted and
sliced peeled Streusel

1/3 cup caster
sugar
1/4 teaspoon ground
cardamom
1 teaspoon pure vanilla
extract
1 cup all-purpose flour
1 teaspoon ground
cinnamon

Directions

Place the pie crust in a lightly greased pie plate.

In a mixing bowl, thoroughly combine the caster sugar, 1/3 cup of flour, cardamom, cinnamon, and vanilla extract. Add the apricots and peaches and mix until coated. Spoon into the prepared pie crust.

Make the streusel by mixing 1 cup of flour, brown sugar, and cinnamon. Cut in the cold butter and continue to mix until the mixture looks like coarse crumbs. Sprinkle over the filling.

Bake at 350 degrees F for 35 minutes or until topping is golden brown. Bon appétit!

Keto Deviled Eggs

Prep time: 5 minutes **Cooking time:** 30 minutes
Servings: 4

Ingredients
6 eggs
1/3 cup sugar-free
mayonnaise

1tbsp. green Tabasco
Salt to taste

Directions

Place eggs in a pot with boiling salted water. Cook over medium heat for 10 minutes. Remove to an ice bath to cool. Peel and slice. Whisk Tabasco, mayonnaise, and salt in a bowl. Top the eggs with mayo mixture and **Serve:**.

Spicy Pistachio Dip

Prep time: 5 minutes **Cooking time:** 5 minutes
Servings: 4

Ingredients

Salt and cayenne pepper to taste	3 oz. toasted pistachios
1/2 tsp. smoked paprika	3 tbsp. coconut cream
1/2 lemon, juiced	1/2 cup olive oil

Directions

Pour pistachios, coconut cream, 1/4 cup water, lemon juice, paprika, cayenne pepper, and salt in a food processor. Puree until smooth. Mix in olive oil. Spoon into bowls, garnish with pistachios, and **Serve:** with celery and carrots.

Mozzarella in Prosciutto Blanket

Prep time: 5 minutes **Cooking time:** 30 minutes
Servings: 6

Ingredients

18 mozzarella cheese ciliegine	18 basil leaves
	6 thin prosciutto slices

Directions

Cut the prosciutto slices into three strips. Place basil leaves at the end of each strip. Top with mozzarella. Wrap the mozzarella in prosciutto. Secure with toothpicks. **Serve:**.

Chili Avocado-Chimichurri Appetizer

Prep time: 5 minutes **Cooking time:** 30 minutes
Servings: 4

Ingredients

4 zero carb bread slices	2 tbsp. red wine vinegar
1/4 cup + 2 tbsp. olive oil	1lemon, juiced
Salt and black pepper to taste	1/2 tsp. red chili flakes
1/2 cup chopped fresh parsley	1/2 tsp. dried oregano
	2avocados, cubed
	2garlic cloves, minced

Directions

Cut bread slices in half, brush both sides with 2 tbsp. of the olive oil, and arrange on a baking sheet. Place under the broiler and toast for 1-2 minutes per side.
In a bowl, mix 1/4 cup olive oil, vinegar, lemon juice, salt, pepper,
garlic, red chili flakes, oregano, and parsley. Fold in avocado. Spoon the mixture onto the bread and **Serve:**

Crispy Squash Nacho Chips

Prep time: 5 minutes **Cooking time:** 30 minutes
Servings: 4

Ingredients

1yellow squash, sliced Salt to season	1/2 cup coconut oil
1 tbsp. taco seasoning	

Directions

Heat coconut oil in a skillet over medium heat. Add in squash slices and fry until crispy and golden brown. Remove to a paper towel-lined plate. Sprinkle the slices with taco seasoning and salt and **Serve:**.

Mixed Seed Crackers

Prep time: 5 minutes **Cooking time:** 15 minutes
Servings: 6

Ingredients

1/3 cup sesame seed flour	1/3 cup chia seeds
1/3 cup sesame seeds	1/3 cup pumpkin seeds
1tbsp psyllium husk powder 1 tsp. salt	1/4 cup butter, melted
	1/3 cup sunflower seeds

Directions

Preheat oven to 300 F. Combine sesame seed flour with pumpkin, chia and sunflower seeds, psyllium husk powder, and salt. Pour in butter and 1 cup of boiling water and mix until a dough forms with a gel-like consistency.

Line a baking sheet with parchment paper and place the dough on the sheet. Cover with another parchment paper and with a rolling pin to flatten into the baking sheet. Remove the parchment paper on top. Bake for 25 minutes. Turn off and allow the crackers to cool and dry in the oven, 10 minutes. Break and **Serve:**.

Chorizo Stuffed Cabbage Rolls

Prep time: 5 minutes **Cooking time:** 30 minutes
Servings: 4

Ingredients

1/4 cup coconut oil
1 onion, chopped
1 cup canned tomato
sauce 1 tsp dried oregano
Salt black pepper to taste

3 cloves garlic, minced
1 cup crumbled chorizo
1 tsp. dried basil
1 cup cauliflower rice
8 green cabbage leaves

Directions

Heat coconut oil in a saucepan and sauté onion, garlic, and chorizo for 5 minutes. Stir in cauli rice, season with salt and pepper, and cook for 4 minutes; set aside. In the saucepan, pour tomato sauce, oregano, and basil. Add 1/4 cup water and simmer for 10 minutes.

Lay cabbage leaves on a flat surface and spoon chorizo mixture into the middle of each leaf. Roll the leaves to secure the filling. Put the cabbage rolls in tomato sauce and cook for 10 minutes.

All Seed Flapjacks

Prep time: 5 minutes **Cooking time:** 25 minutes
Servings: 4

Ingredients

4 tbsp. dried goji berries,
chopped
6 tbsp. salted butter
1 tbsp. poppy seeds
3 tbsp. sesame seeds
3 tbsp. sunflower seeds

8 tbsp. sugar-free maple
syrup
8 tbsp. swerve brown
sugar
3 tbsp. hemp seeds
3 tbsp. chia seeds

Directions

Preheat oven to 350 F. Place butter, maple syrup, and maple syrup in a saucepan over low heat, stir in swerve sugar until dissolved. Remove and stir all seeds along with goji berries. Spread into a lined with wax paper baking sheet and bake for 20 minutes. Slice flapjacks into strips.

No Bake and Egg Balls

Prep time: 5 minutes **Cooking time:** 30 minutes
Servings: 35

Ingredients

Salt and crushed red
pepper flakes, to taste
2 eggs, cooked and
chopped
1/2 cup butter, softened

3 tbsp. mayonnaise
2 tbsp. flax seeds
8 black olives, chopped
1 oz. salami, chopped

Directions

Throw the eggs, olives, pepper flakes, mayonnaise, butter, and salt in a food processor, and blitz until everything is combined

Pesto Mushroom Pinwheels

Prep time: 15 minutes **Cooking time:** 30 minutes
Servings: 4

Ingredients

1/4 cup almond flour
3 tbsp. coconut flour
1/2 tsp. xanthan gum
1/4 cup butter, cold
1 1/2 tsp. vanilla extract
1 whole egg, beaten
2 cups baby spinach
3 whole eggs

4 tbsp. cream cheese,
softened
1/4 tsp. yogurt
3 tbsp. Erythritol
1 cup mushrooms,
chopped 1 cup basil pesto
Salt and black pepper to
taste
1 cup grated cheddar
cheese
1 egg, beaten for brushing

Directions

In a bowl, mix almond and coconut flours, xanthan gum, and 1/2 tsp. salt. Add in yogurt, cream cheese, and butter; mix until crumbly. Add in Erythritol and vanilla extract until mixed. Pour in 3 eggs one after another while mixing until formed into a ball. Flatten the dough on a clean flat surface, cover in plastic wrap, and refrigerate for 1 hour.

Dust a clean flat surface with almond flour, unwrap the dough, and roll out into 15x12 inches. Spread pesto on top with a spatula, leaving a 2- inch border on one end. In a bowl, combine baby spinach and mushrooms, season with salt and pepper, and spread the mixture over the pesto. Sprinkle with cheddar cheese and roll up as tightly as possible from the shorter end. Refrigerate for 10 minutes.

Preheat oven to 380 F. Remove the pastry onto a flat surface and use a sharp knife to cut into 24 slim discs. Arrange on the baking sheet, brush with the remaining egg, and bake for 25 minutes until golden. Let cool.

Cheddar and Halloumi Sticks

Prep time: 5 minutes **Cooking time:** 10 minutes
Servings: 6

Ingredients
1/3 cup almond flour	1 lb. halloumi, cut into
2 tsp. smoked paprika	strips 1/2 cup grated
2 tbsp. chopped parsley	cheddar cheese
1/2 tsp. cayenne powder	

Directions

Preheat oven to 350 F. In a bowl, mix almond flour with paprika and lightly dredge in the halloumi cheese strips. Arrange them on a greased baking sheet. In a bowl, combine parsley, cheddar cheese, and cayenne powder.

Sprinkle the mixture on the cheese and grease with cooking spray. Bake for 10 minutes until golden brown. **Serve:**.

Pecorino Pork Rind Bread

Prep time: 5 minutes **Cooking time:** 30 minutes
Servings: 4

Ingredients
8 oz. cream cheese	2 cups grated mozzarella
1/4 cup grated Pecorino chees	1cup crushed pork rinds
1tbsp Italian mixed herbs	3 large eggs
	1 tbsp. baking powder

Directions

Preheat oven to 380 F. Line a baking sheet with parchment paper. Microwave cream and mozzarella cheeses for 1 minute or until melted.

Whisk in baking powder, pork rinds, eggs, Pecorino Romano cheese, and Italian mixed herbs. Spread the mixture on the baking sheet and bake for 20 minutes until lightly brown. Let cool, slice, and **Serve:**.

Chili Eggplant and Almond Roast

Prep time: 5 minutes **Cooking time:** 30 minutes
Servings: 4

Ingredients
2 tbsp. butter	2 large eggplant
1 tsp. red chili flakes	4 oz. raw ground almonds

Directions

Preheat oven to 380 F. Cut off the head of the eggplants and slice the body into rounds. Arrange on a parchment paper-lined baking sheet.

Drop thin slices of butter on each eggplant slice, sprinkle with chili flakes, and bake for 20 minutes. Slide out and sprinkle with almonds. Roast further for 5 minutes. **Serve:** with arugula salad.

Blackberry and Prosciutto Appetizer

Prep time: 5 minutes **Cooking time:** 30 minutes
Servings: 4

Ingredients
1cup fresh blackberries	1 cup crumbled goat cheese
3/4 cup balsamic vinegar	1/4 tsp. dry Italian seasoning
1 tbsp. Erythritol	
4 zero carb bread slices	1tbsp almond milk
4 thin prosciutto slices	

Directions

Slice the bread into 3 pieces each and arrange on a baking sheet. Place under the broiler and toast for 1-2 minutes on each side or until golden brown; set aside. In a saucepan, add balsamic vinegar and stir in Erythritol until dissolved. Boil the mixture over medium heat until reduced by half, 5 minutes. Turn the heat off and carefully stir in the blackberries.

Make sure they do not break open. Set aside. In a bowl, add goat cheese, Italian seasoning, and almond milk. Mix until smooth. Brush one side of the toasted bread with the balsamic reduction and top with the cheese mixture. Cut each prosciutto slice into 3 pieces and place on the bread. Top with some of the whole blackberries from the balsamic mixture. **Serve:** immediately.

Bell Peppers Stuffed with Tofu and Cheese

Prep time: 5 minutes **Cooking time:** 30 minutes
Servings: 4

Ingredients

2 tbsp. melted butter
1 cup cream cheese
2 red bell peppers
1 tbsp. fresh parsley, chopped

1 cup grated Parmesan
1 tbsp. chili paste, mild
1oz tofu, chopped

Directions

Preheat oven to 380 F. Cut bell peppers into two, lengthwise and remove the core and seeds. In a bowl, mix tofu with parsley, cream cheese, chili paste, and melted butter until smooth. Spoon the cheese mixture into the bell peppers.

Arrange peppers on a greased sheet. Sprinkle Parmesan on top and bake for 20 minutes.

Cauliflower Crackers with Cheese Dip

Prep time: 5 minutes **Cooking time:** 30 minutes
Servings: 6

Ingredients

3/4 cup dried cranberries, chopped
1head cauliflower, cut into florets

1tbsp flax seeds
4 tbsp. chia seeds
1tbsp lemon zest

1/2 cup toasted pecans, chopped
1 1/2 tbsp. almond flour
8 oz. cream cheese, softened
2 tbsp. sugar-free maple syrup

Directions

Preheat oven to 360 F. Pour cauliflower and 2 cups salted water in a pot and bring to a boil for 5 minutes. Drain and transfer to a food processor; pulse until smooth. Pour into a bowl and stir in flour. Mix in flax seeds and 1 tbsp. chia seeds.

Line a baking sheet with parchment paper and spread in the batter. Cover with a plastic wrap and use a rolling pin to flatten and level the mixture. Take off the plastic wrap and cut chip-size squares on the batter. Bake for 20 minutes. Let cool for 5 minutes and transfer to a serving bowl. In a bowl, mix cream cheese with maple syrup. Add in cranberries, pecans, remaining chia seeds, and lemon juice; mix well.
Serve: the dip with cauli chips.

Twisted Deviled Eggs

Prep time: 5 minutes **Cooking time:** 15 minutes
Servings: 6

Ingredients

2 tbsp. crumbled feta cheese
1 tsp. Dijon mustard
1 tsp. white wine vinegar
1/4 tsp. turmeric powder
1 tbsp. chopped parsley

6 large eggs

1tbsp smoked paprika
1 red chili, minced
3 tbsp. mayonnaise

Directions

Place the eggs in boiling salted water in a pot over medium heat and boil them for 10 minutes. Transfer to an ice water bath. Let cool for 5 minutes, peel, and slice in half. Remove the yolks to a bowl and put the whites on a plate.

Mash yolks with a fork and mix in mustard, mayonnaise, vinegar, feta, turmeric, and chili until evenly combined. Spoon the mixture into a piping bag and fill into the egg whites. Garnish with parsley and paprika.

Chocolate and Nut Mix Bars

Prep time: 5 minutes **Cooking time:** 15 minutes
Servings: 4

Ingredients

1/4 cup walnuts
1/4 cup coconut chips
1/4 cup almonds
1/4 cup hemp seeds
Salt to taste

1/4 cup cashew nuts
1 egg, beaten
1/2 cup butter, melted
1cup mixed dried berries
1/4 cup dark chocolate chips

Directions

Preheat oven to 350 F. Line a baking sheet with wax paper. In a food processor, pulse nuts until roughly chopped. Place in a bowl and stir in chocolate chips, egg, butter, hemp seeds, salt, and berries. Spread the mixture on the sheet and bake for 18 minutes. Let cool and cut into bars.

Herby Cheesy Nuts

Prep time: 5 minutes **Cooking time:** 30 minutes
Servings: 4

Ingredients

1egg white	4 tsp. yeast extract
1 tsp. swerve brown sugar	1/2 cup sunflower seeds
Salt and black pepper to taste	3 tbsp. grated Parmesan
1/2 tsp. dried mixed herbs	1 1/2 cups mixed nuts

Directions

Preheat oven to 350 F. In a bowl, beat egg white, yeast extract, and swerve brown sugar. Add in mixed nuts and sunflower seeds; combine and spread onto a lined baking sheet. Bake for 10 minutes. In a bowl, mix salt, pepper, Parmesan cheese, and herbs.

Remove the nuts and toss with the cheese mixture. Bake for 5 minutes until sticky and brown. Let cool for 5 minutes and **Serve:**.

Tasty Keto Snicker doodles

Prep time: 5 minutes **Cooking time:** 25 minutes
Servings: 4

Ingredients

2 cups almond flour	1/2 cup butter, softened
3/4 cup sweetener	1/2 tsp. baking soda
2 tbsp. Erythritol sweetener	1tsp cinnamon

Directions

Preheat oven to 350 F. Combine almond flour, baking soda, sweetener, and butter in a bowl. Make 16 balls out of the mixture. Flatten them with your hands.

Combine the cinnamon and Erythritol in a bowl. Dip in the cookies and arrange on a lined cookie sheet. Bake for 15 minutes.

Banana-Choco Brownies

Prep time: 5 minutes **Cooking time:** 30 minutes
Serving 12

Ingredients

2cups almond flour	1over-ripe banana 3large eggs
2teaspoons baking powder	1/2 teaspoon baking powder
1/2 teaspoon baking soda	
1/2 teaspoon salt	1/3 cup almond flour
1/2 teaspoon stevia powder 1/4 cup of coconut oil	1tablespoon vinegar
1/3 cup cocoa powder	

Directions

Preheat the air fryer oven for 5 minutes. Combine all ingredients in a food processor and pulse until well-combined.

Pour into a baking dish that will fit in the air fryer. Place in the air fryer basket and cook for 30 minutes at 350°F or if a toothpick inserted in the middle comes out clean.

Chocolate Donuts

Prep time: 5 minutes **Cooking time:** 20 minutes
Serving 8-10

Ingredients

(8-ounce) can jumbo biscuits Cooking oil	Chocolate sauce, such as Hershey's

Directions

Separate the biscuit dough into eight biscuits and place them on a flat work surface. Use a small circle cookie cutter or a biscuit cutter to cut a hole in each biscuit center. You can also cut the holes using a knife.

Spray the air fryer basket with cooking oil. Place four donuts in the air fryer oven. Do not stack. Spray with cooking oil. Set temperature to 350F. Cook for 4 minutes.

Open the air fryer and flip the donuts. Cook for an additional 4 minutes.Remove the cooked donuts from the air fryer oven, and then repeat for the remaining four donuts.

Drizzle chocolate sauce over the donuts and enjoy while warm.

Easy Air Fryer Donuts

Prep time: 5 minutes **Cooking time:** 5 minutes Serving 8

Ingredients

Pinch of allspice
1/3 C. granulated
sweetener 3tbsp. melted
coconut oil

4tbsp. dark brown sugar
1/2 - 1 tsp. cinnamon
1can of biscuits

Directions

Mix allspice, sugar, sweetener, and cinnamon. Take out biscuits from can and with a circle cookie cutter, cut holes from centers, and place into the air fryer.

Cook 5 minutes at 350 degrees. As batches are cooked, use a brush to coat with melted coconut oil and dip each into sugar mixture. **Serve:** warm!

Chocolate Soufflé for Two

Prep time: 5minutes **Cooking time:** 14 minutes Serving 2

Ingredients

2tbsp. Almond flour
1/2 tsp. vanilla
3ounces of semi-sweet
chocolate, chopped

1/4 C. melted coconut oil
3tbsp. sweetener
2separated eggs

Directions

Brush coconut oil and sweetener onto ramekins. Melt coconut oil and chocolate together. Beat egg yolks well, adding vanilla and sweetener. Stir in flour and ensure there are no lumps.

Preheat the air fryer oven to 330 degrees. Whisk egg whites till they reach peak state and fold them into chocolate mixture. Pour batter into ramekins and place them into the air fryer oven. Cook 14 minutes. **Serve:** with powdered sugar dusted on top.

Mini Maraschino Cherry Pies

Prep time: 10 minutes **Cooking time:** 25 minutes Serving 6

Ingredients

1/2 cup Maraschino
cherries, pitted
1/2 cup granulated sugar
1 tbsp hazelnuts, chopped

1/2 tbs ground cardamom
2 tbs pure vanilla extract
12 ounces refrigerated
flaky cinnamon rolls

Directions

Toss the cherries with the sugar, cardamom, vanilla, and hazelnuts. Spray muffin cups with a nonstick cooking spray. Separate the dough into 6 rolls and press them into the prepared muffin cups. Spoon the filling into each dough-lined cup.

Bake the mini pies at 350 degrees F for 20 minutes or until the top is golden brown. Bon appétit!

Fried Bananas with Chocolate Sauce

Prep time: 10 minutes **Cooking time:** 10 minutes Serving 2

Ingredients

1large egg
1/4 cup plain bread
crumbs 3bananas halved
crosswise Cooking oil

1/4 cup cornstarch
Chocolate sauce

Directions

In a small bowl, beat the egg. In another bowl, place the cornstarch. Place the breadcrumbs in a third bowl. Dip the bananas in the cornstarch, then the egg, and then the breadcrumbs.

Spray the air fryer basket with cooking oil. Place the bananas in the basket and spray them with cooking oil. Set temperature to 360F and cook for 5 minutes. Open the air fryer and flip the bananas—Cook for an additional 2 minutes. Transfer the bananas to plates.

Drizzle the chocolate sauce over the bananas and **Serve:**. You can make your chocolate sauce using two tablespoons of milk and 1/4 cup chocolate chips. Heat a saucepan over medium-high heat. Add the milk and stir for 1 to 2 minutes. Add the chocolate chips. Stir for 2 minutes, or until the chocolate has melted.

Chocolaty Banana Muffins

Prep time: 5 minutes **Cooking time:** 25 minutes Serving 12

Ingredients

3/4 cup whole wheat flour
3/4 cup plain flour
1teaspoon baking soda
1/4 teaspoon salt
1cup sugar
1/3 cup canola oil
1egg
1cup mini chocolate chips

1/4 cup of cocoa powder
1/4 teaspoon baking powder
2large bananas, peeled and mashed
1/2 teaspoon vanilla essence

Directions

In a large bowl, mix flour, cocoa powder, baking powder, baking soda, and salt. In another bowl, add bananas, sugar, oil, egg, and vanilla extract and beat till well combined. Slowly, add flour mixture to egg mixture and mix till just combined.

Fold in chocolate chips. Preheat the air fryer oven to 345 degrees F. Grease 12 muffin molds. Transfer the mixture into prepared muffin molds evenly and cooks for about 20-25 minutes or till a toothpick inserted in the center comes out clean.

Remove the Air fryer's muffin molds and keep on a wire rack to cool for about 10 minutes. Carefully turn on a wire rack to cool completely before serving.

Air Fryer Oreos

Prep time: 5 minutes **Cooking time:** 14 minutes Serving 4

Ingredients

1/2 cup total pancake mixture
9 chocolate sandwich cookies (like Oreo®)

cooking spray
1/3 cup water
1tbsp confectioners' sugar or to flavor

Directions

Mix pancake mix and water until well blended. Using parchment paper, Line-up the air fryer basket. Spray parchment paper with non-stick cooking spray.

Dip each cookie into the pancake mix and put it in the jar.
Be sure they're not touching; cook in batches if needed.
Preheat the air fryer to 400 degrees F (200 degrees C).

Insert basket and cook 4 to 5 minutes; reverse and cook till golden brown, 2-3 minutes longer. Sprinkle with confectioners' sugar.

Air Fryer Churros

Prep time: 8 minutes **Cooking time:** 15 minutes Serving 4

Ingredients

1/4 cup butter
1/2 cup milk
2eggs
1/2 teaspoon ground cinnamon

1/4 cup white sugar
1pinch salt
1/2 cup flour

Directions

Melt butter in a saucepan over medium-high water. Pour milk and then add salt. Reduce heat to mild and carry to a boil, still stirring with a wooden spoon. Instantly add flour all at one time. Keep mixing until the dough comes together.

Remove from heat and let cool for 5 to 7 minutes. Mix in eggs together with the wooden spoon till choux pastry comes together. Spoon dough to a pastry bag fitted with a large star tip—pipe dough into pieces directly into the air fryer bowl.

Air fry churros in 340 degrees F (175 degrees C) for 5 minutes. Meanwhile, blend sugar and cinnamon in a small bowl and then pour on a shallow plate. Eliminate fried churros from the air fryer and roll from the cinnamon- sugar mix.

Fluffy Blueberry Fritters

Prep time: 5minutes **Cooking time:** 15 minutes Serving 4

Ingredients

3/4 cup all-purpose flour
1teaspoon baking powder
A pinch of sea salt
2tablespoons melted butter

1 egg
1/2 cup coconut milk 2 tbsp coconut sugar
2 ounces fresh blueberries

Directions

In a mixing bowl, thoroughly combine all the Ingredients.
Drop a spoonful of batter onto the greased Air Fryer pan. Cook in the preheated Air Fryer at 360 degrees F for 10 minutes, flipping them halfway through the cooking time.
Repeat with the remaining batter and **Serve:** warm. Enjoy!

Cranberry Chocolate Cupcakes

Prep time: 5minutes **Cooking time:** 20 minutes
Serving 6

Ingredients Cupcakes

3/4 cup self-rising flour	A pinch of grated nutmeg
A pinch of sea salt	3/4 cup caster sugar
1/2 cup buttermilk	1/4 cup cocoa powder
2 eggs, whisked	1/2 stick butter, melted
2 ounces dried cranberries	Frosting
1/2 cup butter, room temperature	4tablespoons heavy whipping cream
1teaspoon vanilla extract	3ounces chocolate chips, melted

Directions

Start by preheating your Air Fryer to 330 degrees F. Mix all the Ingredients for the cupcakes. Scrape the batter into silicone baking molds; place them in the Air Fryer basket.

Bake your cupcakes for about 15 minutes or until a tester comes out dry and clean. Beat all the Ingredients for the frosting using an electric mixer. Pipe the frosting onto the cupcakes. Bon appétit!

Indian-Style Unnakai Malabar

Prep time: 5minutes **Cooking time:** 10 minutes
Serving 1

Ingredients

1plantain, peeled	1/4 cup coconut flakes
1/4 teaspoon cardamom powder	1/4 teaspoon cinnamon powder
1 tablespoon ghee	2tablespoons brown sugar

Directions

Preheat your Air Fryer to 390 degrees F. Toss the plantain with the remaining Ingredients. Bake the prepared plantain in the preheated Air Fryer approximately 13 minutes, flipping it halfway through the cooking time.
Bon appétit!

Squash Fried Cake

Prep time: 5minutes **Cooking time:** 10 minutes
Serving 4

Ingredients

2 cups butternut squash, shredded	2 eggs, beaten
1 tbs pumpkin pie spice mix	1tablespoon coconut oil
	1/2 cup all-purpose flour

Directions

In a mixing bowl, thoroughly combine all the Ingredients.
Drop a spoonful of batter onto the greased Air Fryer pan. Cook in the preheated Air Fryer at 360 degrees F for 10 minutes, flipping them halfway through the cooking time.
Repeat with the remaining batter and **Serve:** warm. Enjoy!

Honey and Coconut Apricots

Prep time: 5minutes **Cooking time:** 20 minutes
Serving 4

Ingredients

8 apricots, halved and pitted	1tablespoons honey
1 teaspoon ground cinnamon	2tablespoon coconut oil, melted
2ounces mascarpone cheese	1 tablespoon coconut flakes

Directions

Toss the apricots with the coconut oil, honey, and cinnamon. Place the apricots in a lightly oiled Air Fryer cooking basket.

Cook the apricots at 340 degrees F for 16 minutes. Top the fried apricots with mascarpone cheese and coconut flakes. Bon appétit!

Danish Cinnamon Rolls

Prep time: 5minutes **Cooking time:** 20 minutes
Serving 4

Ingredients
9 ounces refrigerated crescent rolls
1 teaspoon ground cinnamon

4 tablespoons caster sugar
1tablespoon coconut oil

Directions

Separate the dough into rectangles. Mix the remaining
Ingredients until well combined. Spread each rectangle with the cinnamon mixture; roll them up tightly.

Place the rolls in the Air Fryer cooking basket. Bake the rolls at 300 degrees F for about 5 minutes; turn them over and bake for a further 5 minutes.
Bon appétit!

Festive Rum Fritters

Prep time: 5minutes **Cooking time:** 25 minutes
Serving 4

Ingredients
3/4 cup all-purpose flour
3/4 cup water
1 banana, mashed
1/4 teaspoon grated nutmeg

4 tablespoons butter
1tablespoon rum
1 tablespoon caster sugar
1/4 teaspoon salt

Directions

In a mixing bowl, thoroughly combine all the Ingredients.
Drop a spoonful of batter onto the greased Air Fryer pan. Cook in the preheated Air Fryer at 360 degrees F for 10 minutes, flipping them halfway through the cooking time.
Repeat with the remaining batter and **Serve:** warm. Enjoy!

Vanilla Mug Cake

Prep time: 5minutes **Cooking time:** 25 minutes
Serving 1

Ingredients
2 tbs all-purpose flour
2 tablespoons almond flour
1/4 tbs baking powder
A pinch of kosher salt
2tablespoons coconut oil, at room temperature

2 tablespoons cocoa powder, unsweetened
2 tablespoons agave nectar
A pinch of grated nutmeg
1 tbsp pure vanilla extract
2tablespoons full-fat milk

Directions

Start by preheating your Air Fryer to 350 degrees F. Thoroughly combine all the Ingredients; mix until well combined.

Spoon the mixture into a mug and place it in the Air Fryer cooking basket. Airs fry the mug cake for approximately 20 minutes. Bon appétit!

Grandma's Fried Banana

Prep time: 5minutes **Cooking time:** 20 minutes
Serving 1

Ingredients
1banana, peeled and sliced
1 tablespoon coconut oil
1/2 teaspoon ground cinnamon

2tablespoons granulated sugar
1/2 teaspoon ground cloves

Directions

Preheat your Air Fryer to 390 degrees F. Toss banana slices with the remaining Ingredients. Bake the prepared banana slices in the preheated

Air Fryer approximately 13 minutes, flipping them halfway through the cooking time. Bon appétit!

Almond Butter Cookie Balls

Prep time: 5minutes **Cooking time:** 10 minutes
Serving 10

Ingredients

1 cup almond butter	1 teaspoon vanilla extract
1/4 cup low-carb protein powder	1/4 cup shredded unsweetened coconut
1/4 cup powdered Erythritol	1 large egg
	1/4 cup low-carb, sugar-free chocolate chips
1/2 tbs ground cinnamon	

Directions

In a large bowl, mix almond butter and egg. Add in vanilla, protein powder, and Erythritol. Fold in coconut, chocolate chips, and cinnamon. Roll into 1" balls. Place balls into 6" round baking pan and put into the air fryer basket.
Adjust the temperature to 320°F and set the timer for 10 minutes. Allow to cool completely. Store in an airtight container in the refrigerator up to 4 days.

Peanuts Almond Biscuits

Prep time: 20 minutes **Cooking time:** 35 minutes
Servings: 6

Ingredients

4 oz. peanuts, chopped	2 tablespoons peanut butter
1/2 tbs apple cider vinegar	6 oz. almond flour
1/4 cup of coconut milk	1 egg, beaten
2 tbs Erythritol	1 teaspoon vanilla extract
Cooking spray	

Directions

In the bowl mix up peanut butter, apple cider vinegar, egg, almond flour, coconut milk, Erythritol, and vanilla extract. When the mixture is homogenous, add peanuts and knead the smooth dough. Then spray the cooking mold with cooking spray and place the dough inside.

Preheat the air fryer to 350F. Put the mold with biscuits in the air fryer and cook it for 25 minutes. Then slice the cooked biscuits into pieces and return back in the air fryer. Cook them for 10 minutes more. Cool the cooked biscuits completely.

Walnuts and Almonds Granola

Prep time: 4 minutes **Cooking time:** 8 minutes
Servings: 6

Ingredients

1cup avocado, peeled, pitted and cubed	2tablespoons ghee, melted
	1/4 cup walnuts, chopped
1/2 cup coconut flakes	1/4 cup almonds, chopped
1tablespoons stevia	

Directions

In a pan that fits your air fryer, mix all the Ingredients, toss, put the pan in the fryer and cook at 320 degrees F for 8 minutes. Divide into bowls and **Serve:** right away.

Hazelnut Vinegar Cookies

Prep time: 25 minutes **Cooking time:** 11 minutes
Servings: 6

Ingredients

1 tablespoon flaxseeds	1/2 cup coconut flour
1/2 teaspoon baking powder	1 teaspoon apple cider vinegar
1 oz. hazelnuts, chopped	3 tablespoons coconut cream
1/4 cup flax meal	
1 tbs butter, softened	3 teaspoons Splenda
Cooking spray	

Directions

Put the flax meal in the bowl. Add flax seeds, coconut flour, baking powder, apple cider vinegar, and Splenda. Stir the mixture gently with the help of the fork and add butter, coconut cream, hazelnuts, and knead the non-sticky dough. If the dough is not sticky enough, add more coconut cream. Make the big ball from the dough and put it in the freezer for 10-15 minutes. After this, preheat the air fryer to 365F. Make the small balls (cookies) from the flax meal dough and press them gently. Spray the air fryer basket with cooking spray from inside.

Arrange the cookies in the air fryer basket in one layer (cook 3-4 cookies per one time) and cook them for 11 minutes. Then transfer the cooked cookies on the plate and cool them completely. Repeat the same
steps with remaining uncooked cookies. Store the cookies in the glass jar with the closed lid.

Clove Crackers

Prep time: 20 minutes **Cooking time:** 33 minutes
Servings: 8

Ingredients
1 cup almond flour	1 teaspoon xanthan gum
1 teaspoon flax meal	1/2 teaspoon salt
1 teaspoon baking powder	1 egg, beaten
2 tablespoons Erythritol	1 teaspoon lemon juice
3 tbs coconut oil, softened	1/2 tbsp ground clove

Directions

In the mixing bowl mix up almond flour, xanthan gum, flax meal, salt, baking powder, and ground clove. Add Erythritol, lemon juice, egg, and coconut oil. Stir the mixture gently with the help of the fork. Then knead the mixture till you get a soft dough. Line the chopping board with parchment. Put the dough on the parchment and roll it up in a thin layer. Cut the thin dough into squares (crackers). Preheat the air fryer to 360F.

Line the air fryer basket with baking paper. Put the prepared crackers in the air fryer basket in one layer and cook them for 11 minutes or until the crackers are dry and light brown. Repeat the same steps with remaining uncooked crackers.

Sage Cream

Prep time: 5 minutes **Cooking time:** 30 minutes
Servings: 4

Ingredients
7 cups red currants	1 cup water
6 sage leaves	1 cup swerve

Directions

In a pan that fits your air fryer, mix all the Ingredients, toss, put the pan in the fryer and cook at 330 degrees F for 30 minutes. Discard sage leaves, divide into cups and **Serve:** cold.

Currant Vanilla Cookies

Prep time: 5 minutes **Cooking time:** 30 minutes
Servings: 6

Ingredients
2 cups almond flour	2 teaspoons baking soda
1/2 cup ghee, melted	1/2 cup swerve
1 teaspoon vanilla extract	
1/2 cup currants	

Directions

In a bowl, mix all the Ingredients and whisk well. Spread this on a baking sheet lined with parchment paper put the pan in the air fryer and cooks at 350 degrees F for 30 minutes. Cool down, cut into rectangles and **Serve:**.

Chocolate Fudge

Prep time: 15 minutes **Cooking time:** 30 minutes
Servings: 8

Ingredients
1/2 cup butter, melted	1 oz. dark chocolate,
2 tbsp cocoa powder	chopped, melted
3 tbsp coconut flour	2 eggs, beaten
3 tablespoons Splenda	Cooking spray
1 teaspoon vanilla extract	

Directions

In the bowl mix up melted butter and dark chocolate. Then add vanilla extract, eggs, and cocoa powder. Stir the mixture until smooth and add Splenda, and coconut flour. Stir it again until smooth. Then preheat the air fryer to 325F.

Line the air fryer basket with baking paper and spray it with cooking spray. Pour the fudge mixture in the air fryer basket; flatten it gently with the help of the spatula. Cook the fudge for 30 minutes. Then cut it on the serving squares and cool the fudge completely.

Cranberries Pudding

Prep time: 5 minutes **Cooking time:** 20 minutes
Servings: 6

Ingredients
1 cup cauliflower rice	1 teaspoon vanilla extract
1/2 cup cranberries	2 cups almond milk

Directions

In a pan that fits your air fryer, mix all the Ingredients, whisk a bit, put the pan in the fryer and cook at 360 degrees F for 20 minutes. Stir the pudding, divide into bowls and **Serve:** cold.

Merengues

Prep time: 15 minutes **Cooking time:** 65 minutes
Servings: 6

Ingredients
2 egg whites	1 tbs lime zest, grated
4 tablespoons Erythritol	1 teaspoon lime juice

Directions

Whisk the egg whites until soft peaks. Then add Erythritol and lime juice and whisk the egg whites until you get strong peaks. After this, add lime zest and carefully stir the egg white mixture. Preheat the air fryer to 275F.

Line the air fryer basket with baking paper. With the help of the spoon make the small merengues and put them in the air fryer in one layer. Cook the dessert for 65 minutes.

Lemon Coconut Bars

Prep time: 10 minutes **Cooking time:** 20 minutes
Servings: 12

Ingredients

1 cup coconut cream	1/4 cup cashew butter, soft
1 egg, whisked Juice of 1 lemon	1 teaspoon lemon peel, grated
1 teaspoon baking powder	3/4 cup swerve

Directions

In a bowl, combine all the Ingredients gradually and stir well. Spoon balls this on a baking sheet lined with parchment paper and flatten them. Put the sheet in the fryer and cook at 350 degrees F for 20 minutes. Cut into bars and **Serve:** cold.

Orange Cinnamon Cookies

Prep time: 15 minutes **Cooking time:** 24 minutes
Servings: 10

Ingredients

3 tablespoons cream cheese	1 teaspoon vanilla extract
1/2 teaspoon ground cinnamon	1 egg, beaten
3 tablespoons Erythritol	1 cup almond flour
1/2 tbs baking powder	1 teaspoon butter, softened
	1/2 tbs orange zest, grated

Directions

Put the cream cheese and Erythritol in the bowl. Add vanilla extract, ground cinnamon, and almond flour. Stir the mixture with the help of the spoon until homogenous. Then add egg, almond flour, baking powder, and butter. Add orange zest and stir the mass until homogenous. Then knead it with the help of the fingertips.

Roll up the dough with the help of the rolling pin. Then make the cookies with the help of the cookies cutter. Preheat the air fryer to 365F. Line the air fryer basket with baking paper. Put the cookies on the baking paper and cook them for 8 minutes. The time of cooking depends on the cooking size.

Mini Almond Cakes

Prep time: 10 minutes **Cooking time:** 20 minutes
Servings: 4

Ingredients

3 ounces dark chocolate, melted	2 tablespoons swerve
	1/4 cup coconut oil, melted
2 eggs, whisked	1/4 teaspoon vanilla extract Cooking spray
1 tablespoon almond flour	

Directions

In bowl, combine all the Ingredients except the cooking spray and whisk really well. Divide this into 4 ramekins greased with cooking spray, put them in the fryer and cook at 360 degrees F for 20 minutes. **Serve:** warm.

Chia Bites

Prep time: 15 minutes **Cooking time:** 8 minutes
Servings: 2

Ingredients

1/2 scoop of protein powder	3 tbsp almond flour
1 oz. hazelnuts, grinded	1 egg, beaten
1 tablespoon flax meal	1 teaspoon butter, softened 1 teaspoon chia seeds, dried
1/4 teaspoon ground clove	1 teaspoon Splenda

Directions

In the mixing bowl mix up protein powder, almond flour, grinded hazelnuts, flax meal, chia seeds, ground clove, and Splenda. Then add egg and butter and stir it with the help of the spoon until you get a homogenous mixture.

Espresso Cinnamon Cookies

Prep time: 5 minutes **Cooking time:** 15 minutes
Servings: 12

Ingredients

tablespoons ghee, melted	1/4 cup brewed espresso
1 cup almond flour	1/4 cup swerve
1/2 tablespoon cinnamon powder	2 eggs, whisked
	2 teaspoons baking powder

Directions

In a bowl, mix all the Ingredients and whisk well. Spread medium balls on a cookie sheet lined parchment paper, flatten them, put the cookie sheet in your air fryer and cook at 350 degrees F for 15 minutes. **Serve:** the cookies cold.

Turmeric Almond Pie

Prep time: 20 minutes **Cooking time:** 35 minutes
Servings: 4

Ingredients

4 eggs, beaten	1 tablespoon poppy seeds
1 teaspoon ground	1 teaspoon baking powder
turmeric 1 teaspoon	1 teaspoon lemon juice
vanilla extract	
1 cup almond flour	2 tablespoons heavy cream
1 teaspoon avocado oil	1/4 cup Erythritol

Directions

Put the eggs in the bowl. Add vanilla extract, baking powder, lemon juice, almond flour, heavy cream, and Erythritol.

Then add avocado oil and poppy seeds. Add turmeric. With the help of the immersion blender, blend the pie batter until it is smooth. Line the air fryer cake mold with baking paper. Pour the pie batter in the cake mold. Flatten the pie surface with the help of the spatula if needed. Then preheat the air fryer to 365F.

Put the cake mold in the air fryer and cook the pie for 35 minutes. When the pie is cooked, cool it completely and remove it from the cake mold. Cut the cooked pie into the **Servings:**.

Sponge Cake

Prep time: 5 minutes **Cooking time:** 30 minutes
Servings: 8

Ingredients

1cup ricotta, soft	1 cup almond flour
1/3 swerve	3eggs, whisked
7 tablespoons ghee, melted	1 teaspoon baking powder
Cooking spray	

Directions

In a bowl, combine all the Ingredients except the cooking spray and stir them very well. Grease a cake pan that fits the air fryer with the cooking spray and pour the cake mix inside. Put the pan in the fryer and cook at 350 degrees F for 30 minutes. Cool the cake down, slice and **Serve:**.

Strawberry Cups

Prep time: 5 minutes **Cooking time:** 10 minutes
Servings: 8

Ingredients

16 strawberries, halved	2 tablespoons coconut oil
2 cups chocolate chips	

Directions

In a pan that fits your air fryer, mix the strawberries with the oil and the melted chocolate chips, toss gently, put the pan in the air fryer and cook at 340 degrees F for 10 minutes. Divide into cups and **Serve:** cold.

Pecan Brownies

Prep time: 10 minutes **Cooking time:** 20 minutes
Servings: 6

Ingredients

1/2 cup blanched finely ground almond flour	2 tablespoons unsweetened cocoa powder
1/2 cup powdered Erythritol	1/2 teaspoon baking powder
1/4 cup unsalted butter, softened	1/4 cup chopped pecans
1 large egg	1/4 cup low-carb, sugar-free chocolate chips

Directions

In a large bowl, mix almond flour, Erythritol, cocoa powder, and baking powder. Stir in butter and egg.
Fold in pecans and chocolate chips. Scoop mixture into 6" round baking pan. Place pan into the air fryer basket.

Adjust the temperature to 300°F and set the timer for 20 minutes. When fully cooked a toothpick inserted in center will come out clean. Allow 20 minutes to fully cool and firm up.

Chocolate Banana Packets

Prep time: 5 minutes **Cooking time:** 15 minutes
Servings: 1

Ingredients

Miniature marshmallows
(2 tablespoons)
Banana, peeled (1 piece)
Chocolate chips, semi-
sweet (2 tablespoons)

Cereal, cinnamon,
crunchy, slightly crushed
(2 tablespoons)

Directions

Preheat air fryer to 390 degrees Fahrenheit. Slightly
open banana by cutting lengthwise. Place on sheet of
foil. Fill sliced banana with chocolate chips and
marshmallows. Close foil packet. Air-fry for fifteen to
twenty minutes.
Open packet and top banana with crushed cereal.

Creamy Strawberry Mini Wraps

Prep time: 10 minutes **Cooking time:** 15 minutes
Servings: 12

Ingredients

Cream cheese, softened (4
ounces)
Powdered sugar (1/3 cup)

Pie crust, refrigerated (1
box)
Strawberry jam (12 tbs)

Directions

Preheat air fryer to 350 degrees Fahrenheit. Roll out
pie crusts and cut out 12 squares. Beat together
powdered sugar and cream cheese.

Shape each dough square into a diamond before filling
with cream cheese mixture (1 tablespoon). Top each
with strawberry jam (1 teaspoon) and cover with
dough sides. Place mini wraps on baking sheet and air-
fry for fifteen minutes.

Tasty Shortbread Cookies

Prep time: 25 minutes **Cooking time:** 1 hour 35 minutes
Servings: 4

Ingredients

Powdered sugar (3/4 cup)
Butter softened (1 cup)
Vanilla (1 teaspoon)

Flour all purpose (2 1/2
cups)

Directions

Preheat air fryer to 325 degrees Fahrenheit. Combine
butter, vanilla and powdered sugar with flour to form
a soft dough. Roll out dough and cut out 4 circles.
Place on cookie sheet. Air-fry for fourteen to sixteen
minutes.

Heavenly Butter Cake Bars

Prep time: 15 minutes **Cooking time:** 35 minutes
Servings: 12

Ingredients

Butter, melted (1/2 cup)
Cream cheese (8 ounces)
Vanilla (1 teaspoon)
Powdered sugar (1 pound)

Cake mix, super moist,
French vanilla (15 1/4
ounces)
Eggs (3 pieces)

Directions

Preheat air fryer to 325 degrees Fahrenheit. Use
parchment to line baking dish. Combine cake mix with
egg and melted butter to form soft dough. Press into
baking dish. Beat together 2 eggs, cream cheese,
vanilla, and sugar. Spread on top of cake mix layer.
Air-fry for forty-five minutes. Let cool before slicing.

Air-Fried Mini Pies

Prep time: 20 minutes **Cooking time:** 55 minutes
Servings: 4

Ingredients

Pie filling (4 cups)
Egg, whisked (1 piece)

Pie crusts, refrigerated (2
packages)

Directions

Preheat air fryer to 325 degrees Fahrenheit.
Mist cooking spray onto 12 muffin cups.
Roll out pie crust and cut out twelve 4-inch circles.
Press each onto bottom of a muffin cup. Cut
remaining dough into thin strips. Add pie filling (1/4
cup) to each dough cup. Cover each with dough strips
laid in a lattice pattern. Brush whisked egg on tops of
pies and air-fry for thirty to forty minutes.

Pumpkin Pie Minis

Prep time: 25 minutes **Cooking time:** 20 minutes
Servings: 12

Ingredients

Nutmeg (1/4 teaspoon)
Brown sugar (3/8 cup)
Heavy cream (1
tablespoon) Egg, large (1
piece)

Pie crust, refrigerated (1
package)
Pumpkin puree (1 cup)
Cinnamon (1/2 teaspoon)

Directions

Preheat air fryer to 325 degrees Fahrenheit.
Combine pumpkin, heavy cream, spices, and brown
sugar. Unroll dough pieces and cut out twenty-four
2.5-inch circles. Place 12 circles on sheet of
parchment. Top each with pie filling (1 tablespoon)
and cover with another circle. Press to seal and brush
all mini pies with whisked egg (1 piece). Dust all over
with mixture of cinnamon and sugar. Air-fry for
twenty minutes.

Mouthwatering Walnut Apple Pie Bites

Prep time: 10 minutes **Cooking time:** 15 minutes
Servings: 8

Ingredients

Brown sugar (4 tablespoons) Butter, melted (1 tbsp)
Cinnamon (3 teaspoons)
Crescent rolls, refrigerated (1 can)

Apple, tart juicy, red, washed, sliced into 8 portions, skin on (1 piece)

Walnuts, chopped finely (1 ounce)

Directions

Preheat air fryer to 325 degrees Fahrenheit.
Roll out crescent rolls onto baking sheet misted with cooking spray. Brush melted butter on rolls before sprinkling with cinnamon and brown sugar. Add 3/4 of finely chopped walnuts on top; press gently to adhere. Top each of wide ends with a slice of apple, and then roll up. Brush melted butter on top of rolls before sprinkling with cinnamon and remaining 1/4 of finely chopped walnuts. Air-fry for fifteen minutes.

Gooey Apple Pie Cookies

Prep time: 15 minutes **Cooking time:** 20 minutes
Servings: 12

Ingredients

Egg, slightly beaten (1 piece) Caramel sauce (1 jar)
Cinnamon sugar (3 tablespoons)

Flour, all purpose (2 tablespoons)
Pie crusts, refrigerated (1 package)
Apple pie filling (1 can)

Directions

Preheat air fryer to 325 degrees Fahrenheit. Roll out dough and spread thinly with caramel sauce. Chop up apple pie filling and spread over caramel sauce.

Cover with strips from other rolled out dough, laid to form a lattice pattern. Cut out 3-inch cookies and arrange on baking sheet. Air-fry for twenty to twenty-five minutes.

Apple Pie with Cinnamon Roll Crust

Prep time: 15 minutes **Cooking time:** 55 minutes
Servings: 16

Ingredients

Crust
Egg, beaten (1 piece) + water (1 teaspoon)—to make egg
Pie
wash Pie crust, refrigerated (1 package)
Apples, Granny Smith, small, peeled, cored, sliced thinly (7 pieces)
Granulated sugar
Vanilla (1/4 teaspoon)
Milk (2 teaspoons)
Powdered sugar (1/2 cup)

Butter, unsalted, melted (1 tablespoon)
Cinnamon, ground (2 teaspoons)
Butter, unsalted, at room temp. (1 stick)
Flour, all purpose, unbleached (1 cup)
Sugar, light brown (1 cup)
Icing
Cinnamon, ground (1/4 teaspoon)

Directions

Preheat air fryer to 375 degrees Fahrenheit. Unroll pie crust; brush top with butter before sprinkling with cinnamon. Roll up and slice into half-inch rounds. Press mini rolls into pie plate and brush tops with egg wash.

Top with sliced apples. Cover with crumbly mixture of flour, brown sugar, and butter. Sprinkle with granulated sugar.

Air-fry for forty to forty-five minutes.
Finish by icing with whisked mixture milk, powdered sugar, cinnamon, and vanilla.

Sugar Cookie Cake

Prep time: 5 minutes **Cooking time:** 35 minutes
Servings: 16

Ingredients

Condensed milk, sweetened (14 ounces)
Cinnamon, ground (1 tbsp)
Sugar cookie mix, prepared (17 1/2 ounces)

Butter, salted, melted (3/4 cup)
Cookie butter (14 ounces)
Eggs (3 pieces)

Directions

Preheat air fryer to 325 degrees Fahrenheit. Mist cooking spray onto baking dish. Combine cookie butter with eggs, cinnamon, and condensed milk.

Spread on baking dish and top with even layer of fry cookie mix. Drizzle melted butter on top and air-fry for thirty-five minutes. Let cool before slicing and serving.

Apple Hand Pies

Prep time: 5 minutes **Cooking time:** 8 minutes
Servings: 6

Ingredients

15-ounces no-sugar-added apple pie filling

1 store-bought crust

Directions

Lay out pie crust and slice into equal-sized squares. Place 2 tbsp. filling into each square and seal crust with a fork.

Pour into the Oven rack/basket. Place the Rack on the middle-shelf of the Air fryer oven. Set temperature to 390F, and set time to 8 minutes until golden in color.

Sweet Cream Cheese Wontons

Prep time: 5 minutes **Cooking time:** 5 minutes
Servings: 16

Ingredients

1 egg with a little water
Wonton wrappers

1/2 C. powdered Erythritol
8 ounces softened cream cheese Olive oil

Directions

Mix sweetener and cream cheese together. Lay out 4 wontons at a time and cover with a dish towel to prevent drying out. Place 1/2 of a teaspoon of cream cheese mixture into each wrapper.

Dip finger into egg/water mixture and fold diagonally to form a triangle. Seal edges well. Repeat with remaining Ingredients.

Place filled wontons into the air fryer oven and cook 5 minutes at 400 degrees, shaking halfway through cooking.

French Toast Bites

Prep time: 5 minutes **Cooking time:** 15 minutes
Servings: 8

Ingredients

Almond milk Cinnamon
Sweetener

3 eggs
4 pieces wheat bread

Directions

Preheat the air fryer oven to 360 degrees. Whisk eggs and thin out with almond milk. Mix 1/3 cup of sweetener with lots of cinnamon. Tear bread in half, ball up pieces and press together to form a ball.

Soak bread balls in egg and then roll into cinnamon sugar, making sure to coat thoroughly. Place coated bread balls into the air fryer oven and bake 15 minutes.

Cinnamon Sugar Roasted Chickpeas

Prep time: 5 minutes **Cooking time:** 10 minutes
Servings: 2

Ingredients

1 tbsp. sweetener tbsp. cinnamon

1 C. chickpeas

Directions

Preheat air fryer oven to 390 degrees. Rinse and drain chickpeas. Mix all Ingredients together and add to air fryer.

Pour into the Oven rack/basket. Place the Rack on the middle-shelf of the Air fryer oven. Set temperature to 390F, and set time to 10 minutes.

Tangy Mango Slices

Prep time: 10 minutes **Cooking time:** 12 hours
Servings: 6

Ingredients

4 mangoes, peel and cut into 1/4-inch slices

1 tbsp. honey
1/4 cup fresh lemon juice

Directions

In a big bowl, combine together honey and lemon juice and set aside.

Add mango slices in lemon-honey mixture and coat well.
Arrange mango slices on instant vortex air fryer rack and dehydrate at 135 F for 12 hours.

Brownie Muffins

Prep time: 10 minutes **Cooking time:** 10 minutes
Servings: 12

Ingredients

1package Betty Crocker fudge brownie mix	Egg
1/3 cup vegetable oil	1/4 cup walnuts, chopped
	2 teaspoons water

Directions

Grease 12 muffin molds. Set aside. In a bowl, put all Ingredients together. Place the mixture into the prepared muffin molds. Press "Power Button" of Air Fry Oven and turn the dial to select the "Air Fry" mode. Press the Time button and again turn the dial to set the **Cooking time:**to 10 minutes.

Now push the Temp button and rotate the dial to set the temperature at 300 degrees F. Press "Start/Pause" button to start. When the unit beeps to show that it is preheated, open the lid. Arrange the muffin molds in "Air Fry Basket" and insert in the oven. Place the muffin molds onto a wire rack to cool for about 10 minutes. Carefully, invert the muffins onto the wire rack to completely cool before serving.

Chocolate Mug Cake

Prep time: 15 minutes **Cooking time:** 13 minutes
Servings: 1

Ingredients

1/4 cup self-rising flour	5 tablespoons caster sugar
3tablespoons coconut oil	3tablespoons whole milk
1tablespoon cocoa powder	

Directions

In a shallow mug, add all the Ingredients and mix until well combined. Press "Power Button" of Air Fry Oven and turn the dial to select the "Air Fry" mode.

Press the Time button and again turn the dial to set the **Cooking time:**to 13 minutes. Now push the Temp button and rotate the dial to set the temperature at 392 degrees F.

Press "Start/Pause" button to start. When the unit beeps to show that it is preheated, open the lid. Arrange the mug in "Air Fry Basket" and insert in the oven. Place the mug onto a wire rack to cool slightly before serving.

Grilled Peaches

Prep time: 10 minutes **Cooking time:** 10 minutes
Servings: 2

Ingredients

2 peaches, cut into wedges and remove pits	1/4 cup brown sugar
1/4 cup graham cracker crumbs	1/4 cup butter, diced into pieces

Directions

Arrange peach wedges on air fryer oven rack and air fry at 350 F for 5 minutes. In a bowl, put the butter, graham cracker crumbs, and brown sugar together.

Turn peaches skin side down. Spoon butter mixture over top of peaches and air fry for 5 minutes more.
Top with whipped cream and **Serve:**.

Simple and Delicious Spiced Apples

Prep time: 10 minutes **Cooking time:** 10 minutes
Servings: 4

Ingredients

4 apples, sliced	1tsp apple pie spice
2tbsp. ghee, melted	2tbsp. sugar

Directions

Add apple slices into the mixing bowl.
Add remaining Ingredients on top of apple slices and toss until well coated.
Transfer apple slices on instant vortex air fryer oven pan and air fry at
350 F for 10 minutes.
Top with ice cream and **Serve:**.

Peanut Butter Cookies

Prep time: 10 minutes **Cooking time:** 5 minutes
Servings: 24

Ingredients

1egg, lightly beaten	1 cup of sugar
1 cup creamy peanut butter	

Directions

In a big bowl, combine sugar, egg, and peanut butter together until well mixed. Spray air fryer oven tray with cooking spray.

Using ice cream scooper scoop out cookie onto the tray and flattened them using a fork. Bake cookie at 350 F for 5 minutes. Cook remaining cookie batches using the same temperature. **Serve:** and enjoy.

Delicious Apple Crisps

Prep time: 10 minutes **Cooking time:** 25 minutes
Serve: 2

Ingredients
For filling	1 apple, diced
½ tbsp fresh lime juice	½ tbsp maple syrup
½ tsp cinnamon For	½ tsp cinnamon
1 tsp whole wheat flour	topping
1 tbsp maple syrup	1/3 cup rolled oats
1 tbsp butter, melted	

Directions

Mix together apple, lime juice, maple syrup, and cinnamon and divide into two ramekins. Mix together topping Ingredients and spread on top of the apple mixture.

Cover ramekin with foil and place into the air fryer basket and cook at 350 F for 15 minutes. Remove foil and cook for 10 minutes more. **Serve:** and enjoy.

Moist Orange Muffins

Prep time: 10 minutes **Cooking time:** 15 minutes
Serve: 12

Ingredients
4 eggs	3 cups almond flour
1 orange zest	1 orange juice
1/2 cup butter, melted	1 tsp baking soda

Directions

Preheat the air fryer to 350 F. Add all Ingredients into the mixing bowl and mix until well combined. Spoon mixture into the silicone muffin molds. Place muffin molds into the air fryer basket and cook for 12-15 minutes. **Serve:** and enjoy.

Sliced Apples

Prep time: 10 minutes **Cooking time:** 10 minutes
Serve: 6

Ingredients
4 small apples sliced	2 tbsp butter melted
1 tsp apple pie spice	1/2 cup erythritol

Directions

Preheat the air fryer to 350 F. In a mixing bowl, toss apple slices with butter, apple pie spice, and sweetener. Transfer apple slices into the baking dish. Place baking dish into the air fryer basket and cook for 10 minutes.**Serve:** and enjoy.

Baked Pears

Prep time: 10 minutes **Cooking time:** 10 minutes
Serve: 4

Ingredients
2 medium pears, cut in half & cored	2 tbsp butter, melted
	1 tbsp honey
½ tsp cinnamon	1 tbsp sugar

Directions

Mix together sugar and cinnamon and sprinkle over pears.
Place pears into the air fryer basket and cook at 370 F for 10 minutes.Drizzle butter and honey over pears and **Serve:**.

Gooey Chocolate Cake

Prep time: 10 minutes **Cooking time:** 10 minutes
Serve: 4

Ingredients
2 eggs	1 ½ tbsp self-rising flour
1 cup dark chocolate chips	7 tbsp butter
3 ½ tbsp sugar	

Directions

Add butter and chocolate chips into the bowl and microwave for 30 seconds or until butter and chocolate chips melted. Stir well. In a separate bowl, whisk eggs and sugar. Add melted chocolate mixture and flour and stir until smooth. Spoon batter into the four greased ramekins.

Chocolate Brownies

Prep time: 10 minutes **Cooking time:** 12 minutes
Serve: 4

Ingredients
1 egg	¼ cup cocoa powder
¼ cup butter, melted	½ tsp vanilla
½ cup sugar	¼ tsp salt
6 tbsp flour	

Directions

In a bowl, beat eggs with vanilla, sugar, and salt until light.
Add butter and mix well. Add cocoa powder and flour and stir until well combined. Pour batter into the greased air fryer baking dish. Place baking dish into the air fryer basket and cook at 330 F for 12 minutes. Slice and **Serve:**.

Sweet Caramel Pineapple

Prep time: 10 minutes **Cooking time:** 12 minutes
Serve: 4

Ingredients
2 cups pineapple slices	2 tbsp maple syrup
1 tbsp butter, melted	1 tsp cinnamon

Directions

Preheat the air fryer to 380 F. In a mixing bowl, mix together pineapple slices, butter, maple syrup, and cinnamon until well coated. Place pineapple slices into the air fryer basket and cook for 12 minutes. Turn halfway through. **Serve:** and enjoy.

Blueberry Cobbler

Prep time: 10 minutes **Cooking time:** 15 minutes
Serve: 2

Ingredients
6 oz blueberries	1 tbsp fresh lemon juice
For topping	¼ cup milk
½ tsp baking powder	¼ cup all-purpose flour
2 tbsp sugar	1 tbsp sugar
½ tsp salt	

Directions

Add blueberries, sugar, and lemon juice into the two ramekins and mix well. In a bowl, mix together topping Ingredients and pour over blueberry mixture. Place ramekins into the air fryer basket and cook at 320 F for 12-15 minutes. **Serve:** and enjoy.

Apple Pecan Carrot Muffins

Prep time: 10 minutes **Cooking time:** 10 minutes
Serve: 12

Ingredients
1 egg	1 ½ cups all-purpose flour
½ cup pecans, chopped	½ cup raisins
1 cup apples, shredded	2/3 cup honey
1 cup carrots, shredded	2 tsp vanilla
½ cup yogurt	1/3 cup applesauce
¼ tsp nutmeg	½ tsp ginger
2 tsp cinnamon	2 tsp baking powder
½ tsp salt	

Directions

Preheat the air fryer to 350 F. In a mixing bowl, mix together flour, ginger, nutmeg, cinnamon, baking powder, and salt. Add egg, vanilla, honey, yogurt, and applesauce and mix until just combined. Add pecans, raisins, apples, and carrots and fold well.
Spoon batter into the silicone muffin molds. Place muffin molds into the air fryer basket and cook for 10 minutes. **Serve:** and enjoy.

Blueberry Muffins

Prep time: 10 minutes **Cooking time:** 12 minutes
Serve: 8

Ingredients
1 egg	¾ cup blueberries
3 tbsp butter, melted	1/3 cup unsweetened
2 tsp vanilla	almond milk
¼ tsp cinnamon	¼ cup sugar
1 cup self-rising flour	

Directions

Preheat the air fryer to 340 F. In a mixing bowl, whisk egg with sugar, vanilla, butter, and almond milk.

Add flour and cinnamon and stir until well combined.
Add blueberries and fold well.

Spoon batter into the silicone muffin molds. Place muffin molds into the air fryer basket and cook for 12-14 minutes. **Serve:** and enjoy.

Air Fryer Kale Chips with Parmesan

Prep time: 15 minutes **Cooking time:** 25 minutes
Serve: 1

Ingredients
1 bunch kale	1 tablespoon olive oil
salt and ground black	1 ½ teaspoon chili-lime
pepper to taste	seasoning
2 tablespoons grated	
Parmesan cheese	

Directions

Carefully to 280°F (138°C) according to the manufacturer's instructions. Wash the kale and separate the leaves from the ribs. Dry the kale leaves
fully before tearing them into pieces. Ribs should be discarded.

In a large mixing bowl, combine the kale leaves and olive oil; toss with your hands until the kale is uniformly and lightly coated. Season with salt and pepper to taste. Mix in the chili-lime seasoning until equally distributed.

Place some kale in the hot air fryer in batches without overlapping. 5 minutes in the oven Shake the basket and continue to air-fry for 3 minutes. Sprinkle with Parmesan cheese to coat, shake, and air-fry for
another 2 minutes, or until crispy. Repeat with the remaining batches, keeping an eye on the air fryer and keeping the temperature low.

Air Fryer Pear Crisp for Two

Prep time: 20 minutes **Cooking time:** 20 minutes
Serve: 1

Ingredients

2 large pear (approx. 2 per lb.) spears - peeled, cored, and diced
1 teaspoon lemon juice
1 tablespoon all-purpose flour
1 tablespoon brown sugar

¾ teaspoon ground cinnamon, divided
2 tablespoons quick-cooking oats
1 tablespoon salted butter, softened

Directions

Preheat the air fryer carefully to 360°F (180 degrees C). Combine the pears, lemon juice, and 1/4 teaspoon cinnamon in a medium mixing dish. Toss to coat, then divide between two ramekins.

Combine the oats, flour, brown sugar, and the remaining 1/2 tsp cinnamon in a small mixing bowl. Stir in the softened butter using a fork until the mixture is crumbly. Sprinkle on top of the pears.

Place the ramekins in the air fryer basket and cook for 18 to 20 minutes, or until the pears are tender and bubbly.

Air Fryer Turkey Breakfast Sausage Links

Prep time: 15 minutes **Cooking time:** 20 minutes
Serve: 1

Ingredients

1 (9.6 ounces) package turkey breakfast sausage link

Directions

Preheat the air fryer carefully to 350°F (175 degrees C).
Place all 12 links in the air fryer basket in a single layer. 6 minutes in the oven

Air Fryer Mini Blueberry Scones

Prep time: 15 minutes **Cooking time:** 25 minutes
Serve: 1

Ingredients

1 cup all-purpose flour
1 ½ tbs baking powder
⅛ teaspoon salt
1 egg
½ teaspoon vanilla extract

4 tbsp white sugar, divided
⅛ teaspoon baking soda
2 tablespoons butter
¼ cup buttermilk
¼ cup fresh blueberries
2 teaspoons orange zest

Directions

Preheat the air fryer carefully to 360°F (180 degrees C). In a medium mixing basin, combine the flour, 2 tablespoons sugar, baking powder, baking soda, and salt with 2 knives or a pastry blender. Cut in the butter until the mixture resembles coarse crumbs.

In a small bowl, beat the egg with a fork. Set aside 2 tablespoons of the egg in a separate small dish. Whisk the remaining egg, buttermilk, and vanilla extract with a fork until incorporated. Stir until slightly moistened with the flour mixture. Stir in the blueberries gently.

Place the dough on a lightly floured surface. Gently knead the dough for 8 to 10 strokes, or until it is no longer sticky. Make a 6-inch round out of the dough. Without separating, cut into 8 wedges, soaking the knife in flour between cuts.

Combine the remaining 2 tablespoons of sugar and orange zest in a separate dish. Brush the top of the dough with the saved egg, then sprinkle with the sugar mixture.

Separate the dough wedges and gently put them in a single layer in the fryer basket, in batches if required, using a little broad spatula. Cook the scones for 6 minutes, or until golden brown.
Serve: hot.

Air Fryer Garlic and Parsley Baby Potatoes

Prep time: 20 minutes **Cooking time:** 25 minutes
Serve: 1

Ingredients

1 pound baby potatoes,
cut into quarters
½ teaspoon granulated
garlic
¼ teaspoon salt
1 tablespoon avocado oil
½ teaspoon dried parsley

Directions

Carefully to 350°F (175 degrees C). Toss the potatoes in a basin with the oil to coat. Toss in 1/4 teaspoon granulated garlic and 1/4 teaspoon parsley to coat. Rep with the rest of the garlic and parsley. Place the potatoes in the air fryer basket.

Place the basket in the air fryer and cook, stirring regularly, for 20 to 25 minutes, or until golden brown.

Air Fryer Salmon Cakes with Sriracha Mayo

Prep time: 15 minutes **Cooking time:** 20 minutes
Serve: 1

Ingredients

¼ cup mayonnaise
1-pound skinless salmon
fillets
1 ½ teaspoon seafood
seasoning
1 green onion, coarsely
chopped cooking spray
1 tablespoon Sriracha
⅓ cup almond flour
1 egg, lightly beaten
1 pinch seafood seasoning
(such as Old Bay®)
(Optional)

Directions

In a small mixing dish, combine mayonnaise and sriracha. 1 tablespoon Sriracha mayo in a food processor; chill the remainder until ready to use To the Sriracha mayo, add the salmon, almond flour, egg, 1 ½ teaspoons seafood spice, and green onion; pulse quickly for 4 to 5 seconds, or until Ingredients are barely mixed but tiny bits of salmon remains. (Be careful not to overprocess the mixture, or it will turn mushy.)

Line a plate with waxed paper and squirt cooking spray on your hands. Transfer the salmon mixture to a dish and shape it into 8 tiny patties. Refrigerate for 15 minutes or until cool and stiff. Preheat the air fryer carefully to 390°F (200 degrees C). Cooking spray should be sprayed on the air fryer basket. Take the salmon cakes out of the refrigerator. Spray both sides with frying spray and place in the air fryer basket, working in batches as required to minimize congestion. Cook for 6 to 8 minutes in a preheated air fryer. **Serve:** with the remaining Sriracha mayo and a small dusting of Old Bay seasoning, if preferred, on a serving dish.

Air Fryer Spicy Dill Pickle Fries

Prep time: 15 minutes **Cooking time:** 18 minutes
Serve: 1

Ingredients

1 ½ (16 ounces) jars spicy
dill pickle spears
¼ cup milk
1 cup panko breadcrumbs
cooking spray
½ teaspoon paprika
1 cup all-purpose flour
1 egg, beaten

Directions

Drain and pat dry the pickles. In a mixing dish, combine the flour and paprika. In a separate dish, whisk together the milk and the beaten egg. In a third bowl, combine the panko.

Carefully to 400°F (200°C) according to the manufacturer's instructions. Place a pickle on a dish after dipping it in the flour mixture, then the egg mixture, and finally the breadcrumbs. Rep with the remaining pickles. Lightly spray the covered pickles with cooking spray.
Place the pickles in the air fryer basket in a single layer; cook in batches if required to avoid overflowing the fryer. Set a timer for 14 minutes and flip the pickles halfway through.

Air Fryer Brown Sugar and Pecan Roasted Apples

Prep time: 15 minutes **Cooking time:** 22 minutes
Serve: 1

Ingredients

2 tablespoons coarsely
chopped pecans

¼ teaspoon apple pie
spice 2 medium apples
1 teaspoon all-purpose
flour
1 tablespoon brown sugar
1 tablespoon butter

Directions

Preheat the air fryer carefully to 360°F (180 degrees C).

Combine pecans, brown sugar, flour, and apple pie spice in a small mixing bowl. In a medium mixing bowl, combine apple wedges and drizzle with butter, tossing to coat. Arrange the apples in the air fryer basket in a single layer and top with the pecan mixture.

Cook in a hot air fryer for 10 to 15 minutes, or until apples are soft.

Air Fryer Hard-Boiled Eggs

Prep time: 10 minutes **Cooking time:** 18 minutes
Serve: 1

Ingredients
6 eggs

Directions

Carefully to 250°F (120 degrees C). Fill the air fryer basket halfway with eggs. The **Cooking time:**for eggs is 15 minutes. Then, remove the eggs and immerse them in a cold-water bath for 8 to 10 minutes or completely cool.

Air Fryer Soy-Ginger Shishito Peppers

Prep time: 18 minutes **Cooking time:** 20 minutes
Serve: 1

Ingredients

6 ounces shishito peppers
1 teaspoon vegetable oil
1 teaspoon honey
1 tablespoon fresh lime juice

1 tablespoon reduced-sodium soy sauce
½ teaspoon grated fresh ginger

Directions

Carefully to 390°F (199 degrees C). Tossing the peppers with the oil to coat in a medium mixing basin. Fill the air fryer basket halfway with peppers. 6 to 7 minutes, shaking the basket halfway through until blistered and tender.

Meanwhile, add the soy sauce, lime juice, honey, and ginger to the medium bowl. Toss in the cooked peppers to coat. **Serve:** hot.

Air Fryer Tilapia with Fresh Lemon Pepper

Prep time: 15 minutes **Cooking time:** 25 minutes
Serve: 1

Ingredients

4 (6 ounces) tilapia fillets
2 tablespoons lemon zest
2 tablespoons olive oil
2 cloves garlic, minced
1 pinch paprika
4 wedges lemon

1 ½ teaspoon coarsely ground black peppercorns
cooking spray,
1 sprig parsley, chopped
½ teaspoon salt

Directions

Preheat the air fryer carefully for 3 minutes at 400 degrees F (200 degrees C). While the fryer is heating up, rinse the tilapia fillets and blot them dry with a paper towel.

Combine the lemon zest, olive oil, pepper, salt, and garlic in a mixing bowl. Rub the spice mixture on top of the fish. Lightly sprinkle with paprika. Coat the fillets with cooking spray and set them in the air fryer basket, coated side up. Air fried the fish for 7 to 10 minutes, or until it can be flaked with a fork. Do not overcrowd the fish filets

Air Fryer Breaded Sea Scallops

Prep time: 20 minutes **Cooking time:** 20 minutes **Serve:** 1

Ingredients

½ cup finely crushed buttery crackers (such as Ritz®)
½ teaspoon seafood seasoning (such as Old Bay®)

½ teaspoon garlic powder
2 tablespoons butter, melted
1 pound sea scallops, patted dry
1 serving cooking spray

Directions

Preheat the air fryer carefully to 390°F (198 degrees C).

Combine the cracker crumbs, garlic powder, and seafood seasoning in a small bowl. In a second shallow dish, place the melted butter.

Dip each scallop in the melted butter, then roll in the breading until well covered. Place the scallops on a platter and repeat with the remaining scallops.

Coat the air fryer basket lightly with cooking spray. Arrange the scallops in the prepared basket to don't touch; you may need to work in batches.

Cook for 2 minutes in a preheated air fryer. Cook until the scallops are opaque, approximately 2 minutes more, using a small spatula.

Easy Air Fryer French Toast Sticks

Prep time: 15 minutes **Cooking time:** 25 minutes
Serve: 1

Ingredients

4 slices of slightly stale thick bread, such as Texas toast parchment paper
¼ cup milk

2 eggs, lightly beaten
1 teaspoon cinnamon
1 pinch ground nutmeg
1 teaspoon vanilla extract

Directions

To make sticks, cut each slice of bread into thirds. Then, to fit the bottom of the air fryer basket cut a piece of parchment paper.

Preheat the air fryer carefully to 360°F (180 degrees C).
Combine the eggs, milk, vanilla extract, cinnamon, and nutmeg in a mixing dish until thoroughly blended. Dip each slice of bread into the egg mixture, ensuring sure it is well immersed. Shake each breadstick to remove extra liquid before placing it in the air fryer basket in a single layer. If necessary, cook in batches to avoid overflowing the fryer.

Fry for 5 minutes, then flip the bread slices and cook for another 5 minutes.

Air Fryer Pull-Apart Pepperoni-Cheese Bread

Prep time: 15 minutes **Cooking time:** 20 minutes
Serve: 1

Ingredients

cooking spray
1tbs grated Parmesan cheese
1-ounce sliced turkey pepperoni
dried oregano to taste
1 teaspoon melted butter
½ cup shredded mozzarella cheese

1 ½ pound fresh pizza dough

ground red pepper to taste
garlic
salt to taste

Directions

To fit the bottom of your air fryer, shape a big piece of aluminum foil into a pan with 2-inch-high edges. Coat the pan with nonstick cooking spray. Preheat the air fryer carefully to 390°F (200°C) for 15 minutes.

Roll the pizza dough into 1-inch balls and set them in an aluminum foil pan in a single layer. Season with pepperoni, oregano, red pepper flakes, and garlic salt to taste. Brush with melted butter, then top with Parmesan cheese. Cook for 15 minutes with the pan at the bottom of the air fryer. Cook until the mozzarella cheese is melted and bubbling on the bread, about 2 minutes longer. Remove from the air fryer by pulling the sides of the pan up and out of the machine using tongs.

Air Fryer Asian-Inspired Deviled Eggs

Prep time: 20 minutes **Cooking time:** 25 minutes
Serve: 1

Ingredients

6 large eggs
1 ½ tbs sriracha sauce
1 tbs low-sodium soy sauce
1 teaspoon Dijon mustard
toasted sesame seeds

2 tablespoons mayonnaise
1 ½ tbs sesame oil
1 tbs finely grated ginger root
1 teaspoon rice vinegar
1 green onion, thinly sliced

Directions

Place the eggs on an air fryer rack or trivet, leaving enough room between them for air to circulate. Set the air fryer to 260 degrees Fahrenheit (125 degrees Celsius) and the timer for 15 minutes. The air fryer should be closed. Place the eggs in a dish of cold water for 10 minutes after being removed from the air fryer. Then, remove the eggs from the water, peel them, and cut them half. Scoop out the yolks and set them in a tiny food processor. In a mixing bowl, combine the mayonnaise, sriracha, sesame oil, low-sodium soy sauce, Dijon mustard, ginger root, and rice vinegar. Process until the mixture is well blended and creamy, mousse-like consistency. Fill a piping bag halfway with the yolk mixture and evenly spread it into the egg white halves until they are overflowing full; you can also do this with a spoon. Garnish with sesame seeds and green onion, if desired.

Air Fryer Steak Tips and Portobello Mushrooms

Prep time: 15 minutes **Cooking time:** 18 minutes
Serve: 1

Ingredients

¼ cup olive oil
½ teaspoon garlic powder
2 strip steaks
4 ounces portobello mushrooms, quartered

1 tbs coconut aminos
2 teaspoons Montreal steak seasoning

Directions

Combine the olive oil, coconut aminos, steak seasoning, and garlic powder in a small bowl. Mix well, then add the steak pieces and marinate for 15 minutes.

Carefully to 390°F (200 degrees C). The perforated parchment paper should line the bottom of the air fryer basket. Remove the meat from the marinade. Fill the air fryer basket halfway with steak and quartered portobello mushrooms.

Cook for 5 minutes in a hot air fryer. Remove the basket, stir the steak and mushrooms around, and cook for 4 minutes.

Air Fryer Chocolate Chip Cookie Bites

Prep time: 15 minutes **Cooking time:** 20 minutes
Serve: 1

Ingredients

½ cup butter softened	½ cup packed brown sugar
¼ cup white sugar	½ teaspoon baking soda
½ teaspoon salt,	1 ½ teaspoons vanilla extract
1 egg	
1 cup miniature semisweet chocolate chips	⅓ cup finely chopped pecans, toasted
1 ⅓ cups all-purpose flour	

Directions

To fit an air fryer basket, cut a piece of parchment paper.

In a large mixing basin, beat the butter for 30 seconds on medium to high-speed using an electric mixer. Mix in the brown sugar, white sugar, baking soda, and salt for 2 minutes on medium speed, scraping the bowl regularly. Mix in the egg and vanilla essence until well mixed. Mix in as much flour as possible. Combine the remaining flour, chocolate chips, and pecans in a mixing bowl.

Drop the dough by teaspoonfuls onto the parchment paper, 1 inch apart. Transfer the parchment paper to the air fryer basket with care.

Preheat the air fryer carefully to 300°F (150°C) and cook until golden

brown and firm, about 8 minutes. Cool the parchment paper on a wire rack. Repeat with the rest of the cookie dough.

Chocolate Cake in an Air Fryer

Prep time: 20 minutes **Cooking time:** 20 minutes
Serve: 1

Ingredients

cooking spray	¼ cup white sugar
3 ½ tablespoons butter, softened	1 tablespoon apricot jam
	1 egg
6 tablespoons all-purpose flour	1 tablespoon unsweetened cocoa powder salt to taste

Directions

Carefully to 320°F (160 degrees C). Coat a small, fluted tube pan with nonstick cooking spray. In a mixing bowl, beat the sugar and butter with an electric mixer until light and fluffy. Mix in the egg and jam until well mixed. Sift in the flour, cocoa powder, and salt and thoroughly combine.

Crispy Air Fryer Cod

Prep time: 15 minutes **Cooking time:** 22 minutes
Serve: 1

Ingredients

1 pound cod, about 1-inch thick	¼ cup all-purpose flour
1 ½ tbs seafood seasoning	¼ cup polenta
½ tbsp paprika olive oil	cooking spray
1 ½ teaspoon garlic salt	½ teaspoon ground black pepper
1 teaspoon onion powder	

Directions

Carefully to 380°F (195 degrees C). Using paper towels, pat the codpieces dry. Combine the polenta, flour, seafood seasoning, garlic salt, onion powder, pepper, and paprika in a shallow dish. Coat each piece of cod with the breading mixture, pressing the breading into each side of the fish until well coated.

Spray the air fryer basket with olive oil cooking spray. Arrange the cod in the basket, leaving enough space between each piece to allow air to flow. Cooking spray should be sprayed on the top of each piece of fish. 8 minutes in the oven cook for 4 minutes longer after turning each piece and spraying with cooking spray.

Air Fryer Fried Mushrooms

Prep time: 10 minutes **Cooking time:** 18 minutes
Serve: 1

Ingredients

3 eggs	1 cup all-purpose flour
½ cup plain breadcrumbs	½ cup panko breadcrumbs
½ tablespoon kosher salt	1 teaspoon ground black pepper
1 teaspoon onion powder	
1 teaspoon garlic powder	1 teaspoon paprika
1 teaspoon seafood seasoning (such as Old Bay®)	1 serving nonstick cooking spray
1-pound small cremini mushrooms	

Directions

Preheat the air fryer carefully to 400°F (200 degrees C). In a mixing dish, whisk together the eggs. Then, combine the flour, breadcrumbs, kosher salt, onion powder, garlic powder, pepper, paprika, and seafood seasoning in a separate bowl.

Dip the mushrooms in the eggs first, then in the seasoned flour. Dip into the eggs again, then into the seasoned flour. **Serve:** on a platter. Place a batch of mushrooms in the air fryer basket, being careful not to overlap them. Coat the pan with nonstick cooking spray. 6 minutes in the oven Shake the basket and apply nonstick cooking spray on chalky places. Cook for another 6 minutes. Rep with the remaining mushrooms

Air Fryer One-Bite Roasted Potatoes

Prep time: 18 minutes **Cooking time:** 20 minutes
Serve: 1

Ingredients

½ pound mini potatoes
2 teaspoons dry Italian-style salad dressing mix

2 tbs extra-virgin olive oil
salt and ground black pepper to taste

Directions

Preheat the air fryer carefully to 400°F (200 degrees C).
Wash and pat dry the potatoes. Trim the edges so that both ends have a level surface.

Combine the extra-virgin olive oil and salad dressing mix in a large mixing bowl. Toss in the potatoes until they are completely covered. Fill the air fryer basket in a single layer. If necessary, cook in batches.

5 to 7 minutes in the air fryer until golden brown the potatoes. Flip the potatoes and continue to air fry for 2 to 3 minutes. Season with salt and pepper to taste.

Air Fryer Keto Garlic Cheese 'Bread.'

Prep time: 15 minutes **Cooking time:** 25 minutes
Serve: 1

Ingredients

1 cup shredded mozzarella cheese
½ teaspoon garlic powder

¼ cup grated Parmesan cheese
1 large egg

Directions

Wrap a piece of parchment paper around the air fryer basket. In a mixing dish, combine mozzarella cheese, Parmesan cheese, egg, and garlic powder; stir well. Form a spherical circle on the parchment paper in the air fryer basket.

Preheat the air fryer carefully to 350°F (175 degrees C). Toast the bread for 10 minutes. Remove. Warm, but not hot, garlic cheese bread

Air Fryer Italian Sausages, Peppers, and Onions

Prep time: 15 minutes **Cooking time:** 25 minutes
Serve: 1

Ingredients

2 small onions
2 tablespoons olive oil
1 small yellow bell pepper, thinly sliced
4 each lightly toasted buns

¾ teaspoon salt

1-pound sweet Italian sausage links

1 small red bell pepper, thinly sliced
1 teaspoon Italian seasoning
1 small orange bell pepper, thinly sliced
½ tbs ground black pepper
4 slices provolone cheese

Directions

Preheat the air fryer carefully to 350°F (180 degrees C).
Cut the onions in half from root to stem, then into thirds. In a medium mixing dish, combine the onions and bell peppers. Toss in the olive oil, Italian seasoning, salt, and pepper. Place the veggies in the air fryer basket and place the sausage links on top, not touching.

Cook for 15 minutes in an air fryer. Air fried the sausages for another 10 minutes. Top each sausage with veggies and provolone cheese in a bun.

Air Fryer Shrimp a la Bang Bang

Prep time: 15 minutes **Cooking time:** 20 minutes
Serve: 1

Ingredients

½ cup mayonnaise
1 tablespoon sriracha sauce
1 cup panko breadcrumbs
1 head loose-leaf lettuce
2 green onions, chopped

¼ cup sweet chili sauce
¼ cup all-purpose flour

1-pound raw shrimp, peeled and deveined

Directions

Carefully to 400°F (200 degrees C). In a mixing bowl, combine mayonnaise, chili sauce, and sriracha sauce until smooth. If preferred, keep some bang bang sauce in a separate dish for dipping. On a dish, spread out the flour. Then, on a separate plate, place the panko.

Coat the shrimp with flour first, then with the mayonnaise mixture, and last with panko. Next, place the shrimp on a baking sheet that has been coated. Place the shrimp in the air fryer basket without crowding them. 12 minutes in the oven Rep with the remaining shrimp. **Serve:** in lettuce wraps with green onions on top.

Air Fryer Fried Pickles

Prep time: 20 minutes **Cooking time:** 25 minutes
Serve: 1

Ingredients

½ cup mayonnaise	2 tablespoons sriracha sauce
1 (16 ounces) jar dill pickle chips	2 tablespoons milk
½ cup all-purpose flour	1 egg
½ teaspoon seasoned salt	½ cup cornmeal
¼ teaspoon garlic powder	¼ teaspoon paprika
	⅛ teaspoon ground black pepper cooking spray

Directions

In a small bowl, combine mayonnaise and sriracha sauce. Place in the refrigerator until ready to **Serve:**.
Carefully to 400°F (200 degrees C).
Drain the pickles and pat them dry with paper towels.
In a mixing dish, combine the egg and milk. Next, combine the flour, cornmeal, seasoned salt, paprika, garlic powder, and black pepper in a separate bowl.
Dip pickle chips first in the egg mixture, then in the flour mixture,
coating both sides and lightly pushing the flour mixture into the chips.
Cooking spray should be sprayed on the air fryer basket. Place pickle chips in a single layer in the basket; if required, divide them into two batches.
Cook for 4 minutes before gently flipping the chips. Cook until the desired brownness is achieved, about 4 minutes more. **Serve:** with sriracha mayonnaise.

Air Fryer Sweet Potato Tots

Prep time: 15 minutes **Cooking time:** 20 minutes
Serve: 1

Ingredients

2 sweet potatoes, peeled sea salt to taste	½ teaspoon Cajun seasoning olive oil cooking spray

Directions

Bring a saucepan of water to a boil before adding the sweet potatoes. Boil for 15 minutes, or until potatoes can be pierced with a fork but are still firm. If you overcook them, they will be difficult to grate. Allow cooling after draining.
Using a box grater, shred sweet potatoes into a bowl. Mix in the Cajun spice with care. Form the mixture into cylinders in the shape of tots.
Use olive oil spray to coat the air fryer basket. Place the tots in the basket in a single row, not touching one other or the basket's sides. Toss tots in olive oil spray and season with sea salt.
Preheat the air fryer carefully to 400°F (200°C) and cook the tots for 8 minutes. Turn, re-spray with olive oil spray, then top with additional sea salt. Cook for an additional 8 minutes.

Air Fryer Cauliflower Tots

Prep time: 15 minutes **Cooking time:** 18 minutes
Serve: 1

Ingredients

1 serving nonstick cooking spray	1 (16 ounces) package frozen cauliflower tots (such as Green Giant® Cauliflower Veggie Tots)

Directions

Preheat the air fryer carefully to 400°F (200 degrees C). Nonstick cooking spray should be sprayed on the air fryer basket. Place as many cauliflower tots as you can in the basket, ensure they don't touch and cook in batches if required.

Cook for 6 minutes in a hot air fryer. Remove the basket, flip the tots over, and cook for another 3 minutes, or until browned and cooked through.

Air Fryer Souffle Egg Cups

Prep time: 15 minutes **Cooking time:** 22 minutes
Serve: 1

Ingredients

2 eggs	¼ cup frozen pepper and onion stir fry mix
⅛ teaspoon garlic salt	¼ teaspoon taco seasoning mix
¼ cup shredded mild Cheddar cheese	

Directions

Preheat the air fryer carefully for 5 minutes at 370 degrees F (190 degrees C). In a mixing bowl, whisk the eggs until they are light and fluffy. Combine the Cheddar cheese, veggie mix, taco seasoning, and garlic salt in a mixing bowl. Fill silicone baking cups with the batter and place them in the air fryer basket. 5 minutes in the air fryer. **Serve:** right away.

Air Fryer BBQ Baby Back Ribs

Prep time: 10 minutes **Cooking time:** 18 minutes
Serve: 1

Ingredients

1 tablespoon brown sugar	3 pounds babyback porkribs
1 tablespoon white sugar	1 teaspoon smoked paprika
1 teaspoon sweet paprika	
½ tbs ground black pepper	½ teaspoon ground cumin
½ tbs granulated onion	1 tbsp granulated garlic
⅓ cup barbeque sauce	¼ teaspoon Greek seasoning (Optional)

Directions

Preheat the air fryer carefully to 350°F (175 degrees C).

Remove the membrane off the rear of the ribs and cut the ribs into four equal pieces. Combine brown sugar, white sugar, sweet paprika, smoked paprika, granulated garlic, pepper, cumin, onion, and Greek seasoning in a small mixing bowl. Rub the spice mixture all over the ribs before placing them in the air fryer basket.

Air Fryer Peanut Butter & Jelly S'mores

Prep time: 15 minutes **Cooking time:** 25 minutes
Serve: 1

Ingredients

1 chocolate-covered peanut butter cup	2 chocolate graham cracker squares, divided
1 teaspoon seedless raspberry jam	1 large marshmallow

Directions

Preheat the air fryer carefully to 400°F (200 degrees C).

Place 1 graham cracker square on top of a peanut butter cup. **Serve:** with jelly and marshmallows on top. Place in the air fryer basket with care.

Cook for 1 minute in a hot air fryer until marshmallow is lightly browned and melted. Top with the remaining graham cracker square right away.

Air Fryer Jerk Pork Skewers with Black Bean and Mango Salsa

Prep time: 18 minutes **Cooking time:** 20 minutes
Serve: 1

Ingredients

2 tablespoons white sugar	4 ½ teaspoons onion powder
1 tbsp ground allspice	1 tablespoon ground black pepper
4 ½ teaspoons dried thyme, crushed	
1 ½ tbsp cayenne pepper	1 ½ teaspoons salt
¾ teaspoon ground nutmeg	¼ teaspoon ground cloves
¼ cup shredded coconut	1 (1 pound) pork tenderloin, cut into 1 1/2-inch cube
1 tablespoon vegetable oil	
4 each bamboo skewers, soaked in water for 30m	1 mango - peeled, seeded, and chopped
½ (15 ounces) can black beans	¼ cup finely chopped red onion
2 tablespoons fresh lime juice	1 tbs chopped fresh cilantro
¼ teaspoon salt	1 tablespoon honey
	⅛ tbs ground black pepper

Directions

In a small bowl, combine the sugar, onion powder, thyme, allspice, black pepper, cayenne pepper, salt, nutmeg, and cloves for the seasoning mix. Transfer the rub to a small airtight container, leaving 1 tablespoon in a separate bowl for the pork. Stir in the coconut and the remaining 1 tablespoon spice. Preheat the air fryer carefully to 350°F (175 degrees C). Thread the skewers with the pork slices. Brush the pork with oil and spice combination on all sides before placing it in the air frying basket.

Cook for 5 to 7 minutes in a preheated air fryer until an instant-read thermometer put into the thickest section of the meat reads 145 degrees F (63 degrees C). Meanwhile, in a medium mixing bowl, mash 1/3 of the mango. Add the remaining mango, black beans, red onion, lime juice, honey, cilantro, salt, and pepper to taste. **Serve:** with pork skewers and salsa.

Air Fryer Mini Bean and Cheese Tacos

Prep time: 20 minutes **Cooking time:** 20 minutes
Serve: 1

Ingredients

1 (16 ounces) can refried beans
cooking spray

1 (1 ounce) envelope taco seasoning mix
12 slices American cheese, cut in half 12 (6 inches) flour tortillas

Directions

Preheat the air fryer carefully to 400°F (200 degrees C).
In a bowl, combine the refried beans. Stir in taco seasoning until evenly blended.

1 slice of cheese in the centèr of a tortilla 1 spoonful of the bean mixture should be spooned over the cheese. On top of the beans, place another piece of cheese. To seal the taco, fold the tortilla over and press down. Continue with the remaining tortillas, beans, and cheese.

Nonstick frying spray should be sprayed on all sides of the tacos. Place tacos in the air fryer basket, ensuring sure none overlap. 3 minutes in the oven cook for 3 minutes longer after flipping the tacos. Rep with the remaining tacos.

Sweet Potato Chips in the Air Fryer

Prep time: 15 minutes **Cooking time:** 25 minutes
Serve: 1

Ingredients

1 teaspoon avocado oil
½ teaspoon Creole seasoning

1 medium sweet potato, peeled and sliced crossways into 1/8-inch slices

Directions

Preheat the air fryer carefully to 400°F (200 degrees C).
In a large mixing basin, combine the sweet potato pieces. Mix with the avocado oil, covering each piece equally.

Stir in the Creole seasoning until well combined. Spread the slices on the bottom of the air fryer basket in a thin layer.

Cook for 7 minutes in a preheated air fryer. Shake and flip the slices to ensure consistent frying. Cook for another 6 minutes, or until the desired crispness is attained. Allow the potato slices to cool on a rack.

Skinny Air Fryer Funnel Cakes

Prep time: 15 minutes **Cooking time:** 20 minutes
Serve: 1

Ingredients

nonstick cooking spray
1 tablespoon almond flour
4 tablespoons erythritol confectioners' sweetener
1 ½ teaspoons baking powder
1 teaspoon ground cinnamon

1 teaspoon vanilla extract
1 cup almond flour
1 cup nonfat plain Greek yogurt
½ teaspoon salt

Directions

Carefully to 325°F (165°C) according to the manufacturer's instructions. Line the basket with parchment paper and sprinkle it with nonstick cooking spray.
Combine almond flour, Greek yogurt, 2 tablespoons sweetener, baking powder, cinnamon, vanilla extract, and salt in a mixing dish. Make the dough come together by kneading it with your hands.
Flour your work surface, divide the dough into four equal pieces, and form into balls. Using a bench scraper, cut each ball into 8 equal pieces. Roll each piece in flour and roll into a long, thin rope between your palms. Place all 8 ropes, one by one, into the preheated air fryer basket in a circular mound. Repeat with the rest of the dough balls. Cooking spray should be sprayed on each funnel cake.
5 to 6 minutes in the air fryer until golden brown. Flip each funnel cake over, coat with cooking spray, and continue to air fry for 3 to 4 minutes. Finish with the remaining 2 teaspoons of sweetener.

Air-Fried Jalapeno Poppers

Prep time: 20 minutes **Cooking time:** 25 minutes
Serve: 1

Ingredients

6 medium jalapeno peppers, halved and seeded
3 slices salami, dry or hard, pork, beef
6 slices bacon, cut in half lengthwise

1-ounce shredded Cheddar cheese
6 ounces cream cheese, softened

Directions

Carefully to 390°F (199°C) according to the manufacturer's instructions.
Fill each half of jalapeño with cream cheese and Cheddar cheese. If
desired, place 1/2 a slice of salami on top of each pepper, wrap with bacon, and fasten with a toothpick.
Layer the jalapeño poppers in the preheated air fryer and cook for 10 to 12 minutes, or until the bacon is browned and the cheese is melted.

Air Fryer Frog Legs

Prep time: 15 minutes **Cooking time:** 20 minutes
Serve: 1

Ingredients

1 pound frog legs
2 cups milk
2 tablespoons seafood seasoning
2 cups yellow cornmeal
1 cup all-purpose flour
cooking spray

Directions

Pour milk over the top of the frog legs in a dish. Refrigerate for 1 hour, covered. Carefully to 400°F (200°C) according to the manufacturer's instructions. Meanwhile, add cornmeal, flour, and seafood seasoning in a gallon- sized resealable plastic bag. To blend, seal the container and shake it vigorously. Remove 1 frog leg from the milk, allowing the excess to drip into the
dish. Shake the bag with the seasoned cornmeal mixture to coat. Return the frog legs to the cornmeal mixture after dipping them back in the milk. Shake again to coat, then transfer to a dish. Rep with the remaining frog legs.
Cooking sprays the air fryer basket and puts as many frog legs as you can without overlapping. Coat the tops in cooking spray. If necessary, work in bunches. 5 minutes in the air fryer. Cooking spray should be used to remove any chalky patches. Cook for another 3 minutes, or until the bacon is crispy. Repeat with the remaining batches on a platter.

Air Fryer Churros

Prep time: 15 minutes **Cooking time:** 25 minutes **Serve:** 1

Ingredients

¼ cup butter
2 eggs
½ cup all-purpose flour
½ teaspoon ground cinnamon
½ cup milk
1 pinch salt
¼ cup white sugar

Directions

In a saucepan over medium-high heat, melt the butter. Pour in the milk and season with salt. Reduce the heat to medium and bring to a boil, constantly stirring with a wooden spoon. Add the flour all at once. Continue to whisk until the dough comes together.
Remove from the fire and set aside for 5 to 7 minutes to cool. With a wooden spoon, mix the eggs until the pastry comes together. Fill a pastry bag with a big star tip with the dough. Pipe dough strips directly into the air fryer basket. For 5 minutes, air-fried churros at 340 degrees F (175 degrees C).

Air Fryer Hush Puppies

Prep time: 15 minutes **Cooking time:** 18 minutes
Serve: 1

Ingredients

nonfat cooking spray
1 ½ teaspoons baking powder
¼ teaspoon cayenne pepper, or more to taste
2 tablespoons minced onion
¾ cup low-fat buttermilk
¾ cup all-purpose flour
½ teaspoon salt
1 cup yellow cornmeal
¼ teaspoon garlic powder
2 tablespoons minced green bell pepper
1 large egg

Directions

Carefully to 390°F (198°C) according to the manufacturer's instructions. Spray the bottom of the air fryer basket with nonfat cooking spray and line with aluminum foil. In a large mixing bowl, combine cornmeal, flour, baking powder, salt, cayenne pepper, and garlic powder. Next, combine the onion and bell pepper.

In a separate dish, whisk together the buttermilk and egg. Mix into the cornmeal mixture. Allow the mixture to sit for 5 minutes. Using a 2-tablespoon cookie scoop, scoop the cornmeal mixture into the foil-lined basket, making sure not to overlap. Coat the pan with nonfat cooking spray.
9 to 10 minutes in a preheated air fryer, until golden brown, crispy, and cooked through. **Serve:** immediately.

Chinese Five-Spice Air Fryer Butternut Squash Fries

Prep time: 20 minutes **Cooking time:** 20 minutes **Serve:** 1

Ingredients

1 large butternut squash
2 tablespoons olive oil
2 teaspoons sea salt
1 tablespoon minced garlic
1 tablespoon Chinese five-spice powder
2 teaspoons black pepper

Directions

Preheat the air fryer carefully to 400°F (200 degrees C).
In a large mixing basin, combine the chopped squash. Toss in the oil, five-spice powder, garlic, salt, and black pepper to coat. Cook butternut squash fries in a preheated air fryer for 15 to 20
minutes, shaking every 5 minutes, until crisp. Remove the fries and season with sea salt to taste.

Air-Fried Ratatouille, Italian-Style

Prep time: 15 minutes **Cooking time:** 22 minutes
 Serve: 1

Ingredients

½ small eggplant, cut into cubes	1 medium tomato, cut into cubes
½ large yellow bell pepper, cut into cubes	½ large red bell pepper, cut into cubes
½ onion, cut into cubes	1 fresh cayenne pepper, diced
1 zucchini, cut into cubes	2 sprigs of fresh oregano, stemmed and chopped
5 sprigs fresh basil, stemmed and chopped	1 tablespoon white wine
salt and ground black pepper to taste	1 clove garlic, crushed
1 teaspoon vinegar	1 tablespoon olive oil

Directions

Carefully to 400°F (200 degrees C).
Combine the eggplant, zucchini, tomato, bell peppers, and onion in a mixing dish. Next, combine the cayenne pepper, basil, oregano, garlic, salt, and pepper in a mixing bowl. To ensure that everything is distributed equally, combine all **Ingredients** in a mixing bowl. Drizzle in the oil, wine, and vinegar and toss to cover all veggies.
Place the vegetable mixture in a baking dish and place it in the air fryer basket. 8 minutes in the oven cook for another 8 minutes, stirring occasionally. Stir once more and simmer until tender, 10 to 15 minutes more, stirring every 5 minutes. Turn off the air fryer but leave the dish inside. Allow for a 5-minute pause before serving.

Air-Fried Cauliflower with Almonds and Parmesan

Prep time: 20 minutes **Cooking time:** 25 minutes
Serve: 1

Ingredients

3 cups cauliflower florets	3 teaspoons vegetable oil, divided
1 clove garlic, minced	¼ cup chopped almonds
⅓ cup finely shredded Parmesan cheese	½tsp dried thyme, crushed
¼ cup panko breadcrumbs	

Directions

In a medium mixing basin, combine cauliflower florets, 2 tablespoons oil, and garlic; toss to coat. Place in an air fryer basket in a single layer.
Cook for 10 minutes in the air fryer at 360°F (180°C), shaking the
basket halfway through.
Toss the cauliflower with the remaining 1 teaspoon oil in the basin. Toss in the Parmesan cheese, almonds, breadcrumbs, and thyme to coat. Return cauliflower mixture to air fryer basket and cook for another 5 minutes, or until crisp and golden

Air Fryer Corn Dogs

Prep time: 18 minutes **Cooking time:** 20 minutes
Serve: 1

Ingredients

parchment paper	6 bamboo skewers
1 (6.5 ounces) package cornbread mix	⅔ cup milk
	1 egg
1 teaspoon white sugar	8 hot dogs, cut in half

Directions

Divide the soaking bamboo skewers into thirds. To properly fit the bottom of the air fryer basket, cut a piece of parchment paper.
Preheat the air fryer carefully to 400°F (200 degrees C).
In a mixing bowl, combine cornbread mix, milk, egg, and sugar until blended; pour into a tall glass.
Insert a skewer into the center of each hot dog piece. Remove the air fryer basket and lay the cut parchment paper on the bottom of the basket. Dip four hot dogs in the batter and set them on top of the parchment paper, alternating the direction of the stick ends.
Cook for 8 minutes in a preheated air fryer without turning, or until desired brownness. Repeat with the remaining hot dogs on a dish.

Air Fryer Salt and Vinegar Fries for One

Prep time: 15 minutes **Cooking time:** 20 minutes
Serve: 1

Ingredients

1 large Yukon Gold potato 1 cup distilled white vinegar	½ tablespoon light vegetable oil
salt and ground black pepper to taste	

Directions

Peel the potato and cut it into 1/2-inch sticks lengthwise. For a few seconds, rinse the potato sticks under cold running water. Transfer to a large mixing bowl. Pour in just enough water to cover the potatoes with vinegar. Allow for a 30-minute soak.
Preheat the air fryer carefully to 320°F (160 degrees C).
Drain and pat dry the potatoes. Toss in a bowl with the oil, salt, and pepper and place in the air fryer basket.
Cook for 16 minutes in a hot air fryer until soft but not browned. Shake
the basket and heat it to 355 degrees Fahrenheit (180 degrees C). 6 minutes in the air fryer, shake, and check for doneness. Cook for another 6 minutes, or until the outsides of the fries are crispy and golden

Air Fryer Eggplant Parmesan Mini Pizzas

Prep time: 10 minutes **Cooking time:** 18 minutes
Serve: 1

Ingredients

1 medium eggplant, sliced into 1/2- inch rounds
1 tablespoon water
¼ cup freshly grated
1 (2.25 ounces) can slice ripe olives, drained
8 ounces shredded mozzarella cheese

1 egg, beaten
salt to taste
1 cup Italian breadcrumbs
4 ounces pizza sauce
1 tablespoon chopped fresh basil for garnish
Parmesan cheese cooking spray

Directions

Arrange the eggplant rounds on a broad chopping board and season lightly on both sides. Allow for a 10-minute rest. Then, using paper towels, pat dry. Preheat the oven to 250 degrees Fahrenheit (120 degrees C). Meanwhile, in a mixing dish, combine the egg and water. On a flat dish, combine breadcrumbs and Parmesan cheese. Line a rimmed baking sheet with foil and set a cooling rack on top.

Each eggplant round should be dipped in beaten egg and then coated in a bread crumb mixture.

Carefully to 400°F (200 degrees C). Nonstick cooking spray should be sprayed on the basket.

Fill your basket with as many eggplant rounds as space permits without

overloading. Coat the tops in cooking spray. The **Cooking time:**is 10 minutes. Place the rounds on a cooling rack and keep warm in a preheated oven. Rep with the leftover eggplant.

Spread pizza sauce on top of each eggplant circle. Cover with olive

slices and mozzarella cheese.

Preheat the oven's broiler to high and position the oven rack about 6 inches from the heat source.

Broil the eggplant slice pizzas for 4 minutes or until the cheese melts. Garnish with basil if desired.

Air Fryer Mustard-Crusted Pork Tenderloin with Potatoes and Green Beans

Prep time: 15 minutes **Cooking time:** 25 minutes
Serve: 1

Ingredients

¼ cup Dijon mustard
1 teaspoon dried parsley flakes
¼ teaspoon salt

1 ¼ pound pork tenderloin
1 (12 ounces) package fresh green beans, trimmed
1 tablespoon olive oil

2 tablespoons brown sugar
½ teaspoon dried thyme
¼ tbs ground black pepper
¾ pound small potatoes (such as The Little Potato® Company), halved

salt and ground black pepper to taste

Directions

Carefully to 400°F (200°C) according to the manufacturer's instructions.

Combine mustard, brown sugar, parsley, thyme, salt, and pepper in a large mixing bowl. Roll the tenderloin in the mustard mixture until uniformly coated on both sides.

Combine the potatoes, green beans, and olive oil in a separate bowl. Season with salt and pepper to taste and mix well. Place aside.

Place the tenderloin in the basket of a prepared air fryer and cook, undisturbed, for 20 minutes or until the middle is slightly pink. In the middle, an instant-read thermometer should read at least 145 degrees F. (63 degrees C). Transfer to a chopping board and set aside for 10 minutes to rest.

Meanwhile, cook the green beans and potatoes in the air fryer basket for 10 minutes, shaking halfway through.

Serve: tenderloin with potatoes and green beans.
. Before serving, taste and adjust the salt.

Air Fryer Breakfast Toad-in-the-Hole Tarts

Prep time: 15 minutes **Cooking time:** 20 minutes
Serve: 1

Ingredients

1 sheet frozen puff pastry, thawed
4 eggs
4 tablespoons diced cooked ham
4 tablespoons shredded Cheddar cheese
1 tablespoon chopped fresh chives

Directions

Preheat the air fryer carefully to 400°F (200 degrees C). Unfold the pastry sheet and cut it into 4 squares on a level surface.

Cook 6 to 8 minutes with 2 pastry squares in the air fryer basket. Remove the basket from the air fryer. To make an indentation, lightly push each square with a metal tablespoon. Fill each hole with 1 tablespoon Cheddar cheese and 1 tablespoon ham, then top with 1 egg.

Return the basket to the air fryer. Cook until done, about 6 minutes more. Remove tarts from the basket and set them aside for 5 minutes to cool. Rep with the rest of the pastry squares, cheese, ham, and eggs. Tarts should be garnished with chives.

Air Fryer Roasted Brussels Sprouts with Maple-Mustard Mayo

Prep time: 15 minutes **Cooking time:** 18 minutes
Serve: 1

Ingredients

2 tablespoons maple syrup, divided
¼ teaspoon ground black pepper
⅓ cup mayonnaise
1 tablespoon olive oil - ¼ teaspoon kosher salt
1 pound Brussels sprouts, trimmed and halved
1 tablespoon stone-ground mustard

Directions

Preheat the air fryer carefully to 400°F (200 degrees C).
In a large mixing bowl, combine 1 tablespoon maple syrup, olive oil, salt, and pepper. Toss in the Brussels sprouts to coat. Arrange Brussels sprouts in an air fryer basket in a single layer, without overcrowded; work in batches if required. 4 minutes in the oven cook until the sprouts are deep golden brown and tender, 4 to 6 minutes longer.

Meanwhile, combine mayonnaise, the remaining 1 tablespoon maple syrup, and mustard in a small mixing dish. Toss the sprouts in a little sauce combination and **Serve:** as a dipping sauce.

Air Fryer Onion Bhaji

Prep time: 15 minutes **Cooking time:** 22 minutes **Serve:** 1

Ingredients

1 small red onion, thinly sliced
1 jalapeno pepper, seeded and minced
1 tablespoon salt
1 teaspoon ground turmeric
4 tbs water, or as needed cooking spray
1 small yellow onion, thinly sliced
1 clove garlic, minced
1 teaspoon coriander
1 teaspoon chili powder
½ teaspoon cumin
⅔ cup chickpea flour (bean)

Directions

In a large mixing bowl, combine red onion, yellow onion, salt, jalapeño, garlic, coriander, chili powder, turmeric, and cumin. Stir until everything is well blended. Mix in the chickpea flour and water. To make a thick batter, put all
Ingredients in a mixing bowl. If required, add extra water. Allow the mixture to settle for 10 minutes.

Preheat the air fryer carefully to 350°F (175 degrees C).
Nonstick cooking spray should be sprayed on the air fryer basket. Flatten 2 tablespoons of batter into the basket. Repeat as many times as your basket permits without touching the bhajis.

Cook for 6 minutes in a hot air fryer. Cooking spray should be sprayed on the tops of each bhaji. Cook for 6 minutes more on the other side. Transfer to a plate lined with paper towels. Rep with the remaining batter.

RICE & GRAINS

Aromatic Seafood Pilaf

(**Ready in about** 45 minutes | **Servings:** 2)

Ingredients

1 cup jasmine rice	Salt and black pepper, to taste
1 small yellow onion, chopped	1 small garlic clove, finely chopped
1 bay leaf	1 teaspoon butter, melted
4 tablespoons cream of mushroom soup	1/2 pound shrimp, divined and sliced

Directions

Bring 2 cups of a lightly salted water to a boil in a medium saucepan over medium-high heat. Add in the jasmine rice, turn to a simmer and cook, covered, for about 18 minutes until water is absorbed.

Let the jasmine rice stand covered for 5 to 6 minutes; fluff with a fork and transfer to a lightly greased Air Fryer safe pan.

Stir in the salt, black pepper, bay leaf, yellow onion, garlic, butter and cream of mushroom soup; stir until everything is well incorporated.

Cook the rice at 350 degrees F for about 13 minutes. Stir in the shrimp and continue to cook for a further 5 minutes.

Check the rice for softness. If necessary, cook for a few minutes more. Bon appétit!

Easy Pizza Margherita

(**Ready in about** 15 minutes | **Servings:** 1)

Ingredients

6-inch dough	2 tablespoons tomato sauce
1 teaspoon extra-virgin olive oil Coarse sea salt, to taste	2-3 fresh basil leaves
	2 ounces mozzarella

Directions

Start by preheating your Air Fryer to 380 degrees F.

Stretch the dough on a pizza peel lightly dusted with flour. Spread with a layer of tomato sauce.

Add mozzarella to the crust and drizzle with olive oil. Salt to taste.

Bake in the preheated Air Fryer for 4 minutes. Rotate the baking tray and bake for a further 4 minutes. Garnish with fresh basil leaves and **Serve:** immediately. Bon appétit!

Famous Greek Tyrompiskota

(**Ready in about** 45 minutes | **Servings:** 3)

Ingredients

1 cup all-purpose flour	1 tablespoon flaxseed meal
1 teaspoon baking powder	1/2 stick butter
1/2 cup halloumi cheese, grated	1 teaspoon Greek spice blend Salt to taste
1 egg	

Directions

Combine the flour, flaxseed meal, and baking powder in a mixing bowl. In a separate bowl, combine the butter, cheese, and egg. Incorporate the cheese mixture into the dry flour mixture.

Mix with your hands, then stir in the Greek spice blend; season with salt and stir again to combine thoroughly.

Form the batter into a log, wrap in cling film, and place in the refrigerator for about 30 minutes.

Using a sharp knife, cut the chilled log into thin slices. Cook your biscuits for 15 minutes in a preheated Air Fryer at 360 degrees F. Make use of batches.

Good appetite!

Bacon and Cheese Sandwich

(**Ready in about** 15 minutes | **Servings:** 1)

Ingredients

2 slices whole-wheat bread	1/2 teaspoon Dijon mustard
2 ounces bacon, sliced	1 ounce cheddar cheese, sliced
1 tablespoon ketchup	

Directions

Spread the ketchup and mustard on a slice of bread. Add the bacon and cheese and top with another slice of bread.

Place your sandwich in the lightly buttered Air Fryer cooking basket.

Now, bake your sandwich at 380 degrees F for 10 minutes or until the cheese has melted. Make sure to turn it over halfway through the cooking time.

Bon appétit!

Autumn Pear Beignets

(**Ready in about** 15 minutes | **Servings:** 3)

Ingredients

1 medium-sized pear, peeled, cored and chopped

1/4 teaspoon ground cloves 1/2 teaspoon vanilla paste

5 ounces refrigerated buttermilk biscuits

2 tablespoons walnuts, ground

1/4 teaspoon ground cinnamon

2 tablespoons coconut oil, at room temperature

1/4 cup powdered sugar

Directions

In a mixing bowl, thoroughly combine the pear, sugar, walnuts, cloves, vanilla and cinnamon.

Separate the dough into 3 biscuits and then, divide each of them into 2 layers. Shape the biscuits into rounds.

Divide the pear mixture between the biscuits and roll them up. Brush the biscuits with coconut oil and transfer them to the Air Fryer cooking basket.

Cook your beignets at 330 degrees F for about 13 minutes, turning them over halfway through the cooking time. **Serve:** with some extra powdered sugar if desired. Bon appétit!.

Festive Crescent Ring

(**Ready in about** 25 minutes | **Servings:** 3)

Ingredients

1/2 (8-ounce) can crescent dough sheet

1/2 teaspoon dried basil

2 ounces capocollo, sliced

4 tablespoons tomato sauce

1 teaspoon dried oregano

1 ounces bacon, sliced

3 slices Colby cheese, cut half

1/3 teaspoon dried rosemary

Directions

Separate the crescent dough sheet into 8 triangles. Then, arrange the triangles in a sunburst pattern so it should look like the sun.

Place the cheese, bacon, capocollo and tomato sauce on the bottom of each triangle. Sprinkle with dried herbs.

Now, fold the triangle tips over the filling and tuck under the base to secure.

Bake the ring at 360 degrees F for 20 minutes until the dough is golden and the cheese has melted. Bon appétit!

Mediterranean Mini Monkey Bread

(**Ready in about** 15 minutes | **Servings:** 3)

Ingredients

6 ounces refrigerated crescent rolls

1/2 cup provolone cheese, shredded

1/2 teaspoon dried basil

1/4 cup pesto sauce

1/4 cup ketchup

1/2 teaspoon dried oregano

2 cloves garlic, minced

1/2 teaspoon dried parsley flakes

Directions

Begin by preheating your Air Fryer to 350°F.

Make crescent rolls. Roll up the crescent rolls with the Ingredients inside. Gently press the edges together with your fingertips to seal them.

Bake the mini monkey bread for 12 minutes, or until golden brown on top. Good appetite!

Oatmeal Pizza Cups

(**Ready in about** 25 minutes | **Servings:** 3)

Ingredients

1 egg

1/2 teaspoon baking soda

1/4 teaspoon salt

2 tablespoons butter, melted

1 cup rolled oats

3 ounces mozzarella cheese, shredded

1/2 cup oat milk

1/8 teaspoon ground black pepper

3 ounces smoked ham, chopped

4 tablespoons ketchup

Directions

In a mixing bowl, beat the egg and milk until pale and frothy.

In a separate bowl, mix the rolled oats, baking soda, salt, pepper and butter; mix to combine well.

Fold in the smoked ham and mozzarella; gently stir to combine and top with ketchup.

Spoon the mixture into a lightly greased muffin tin.

Bake in the preheated Air Fryer at 330 degrees F for 20 minutes until a toothpick inserted comes out clean. Bon appétit!

Traditional Italian Arancini

(**Ready in about** 35 minutes | **Servings:** 3)

Ingredients

3 cups vegetable broth
1 ounce Ricotta cheese, at room temperature
1 large egg
1 tablespoon fresh cilantro, chopped

2 ounces Colby cheese, grated
Sea salt and ground black pepper, to taste
1 cup white rice
1/2 cup Italian seasoned breadcrumbs

Directions

Bring the vegetable broth to a boil in a saucepan over medium-high heat. Stir in the rice and reduce the heat to simmer; cook about 20 minutes.

Add in the cheese and cilantro. Season with salt and pepper and shape the mixture into bite-sized balls.

Beat the egg in a shallow bowl; in another shallow bowl, place the seasoned breadcrumbs.

Dip each rice ball into the beaten egg, then, roll in the seasoned breadcrumbs, gently pressing to coat well.

Bake the rice balls in the preheated Air Fryer at 350 degrees F for about 10 minutes, shaking the basket halfway through the **Cooking time:**to ensure even browning. Bon appétit!

Basic Air Grilled Granola

(**Ready in about** 20 minutes | **Servings:** 3)

Ingredients

1 cup rolled oats
1/4 teaspoon ground cinnamon
1/4 cup walnuts, chopped
1 tablespoon honey

A pinch of grated nutmeg
1 tablespoon coconut oil
A pinch of salt
1 tablespoon sunflower seeds
1 tablespoon pumpkin seeds

Directions

In a mixing bowl, thoroughly combine the rolled oats, salt, nutmeg, cinnamon, honey and coconut oil.

Spread the mixture into an Air Fryer baking pan and bake at 330 degrees F for about 15 minutes.

Stir in the walnuts, sunflower seeds and pumpkin seeds. Continue to cook for a further 5 minutes.

Store your granola in an airtight container for up to 2 weeks. Enjoy!

Fluffy Pancake Cups with Sultanas

(**Ready in about** 30 minutes | **Servings:** 3)

Ingredients

1/2 cup all-purpose flour
1/2 cup coconut flour
1/3 cup coconut milk
1/2 teaspoon vanilla
1/4 teaspoon cardamom

1 tablespoon dark rum
2 eggs
1/3 cup carbonated water
1/2 cup Sultanas, soaked for 15 minutes

Directions

In a mixing bowl, thoroughly combine the dry Ingredients; in another bowl, mix the wet Ingredients.

Then, stir the wet mixture into the dry mixture and stir again to combine well. Let the batter sit for 20 minutes in your refrigerator. Spoon the batter into a greased muffin tin. Bake the pancake cups in your Air Fryer at 330 degrees F for 6 to 7 minutes or until golden brown. Repeat with the remaining batter. Bon appétit!

Apple Cinnamon Rolls

(**Ready in about** 20 minutes | **Servings:** 4)

Ingredients

1 (10-ounces) can buttermilk biscuits

1 teaspoon cinnamon

1/4 cup powdered sugar
1 apple, cored and chopped
1 tbs coconut oil, melted

Directions

Line the bottom of the Air Fryer cooking basket with a parchment paper Separate the dough into biscuits and cut each of them into 2 layers. Mix the remaining Ingredients in a bowl.

Divide the apple/cinnamon mixture between biscuits and roll them up. Brush the biscuits with coconut oil and transfer them to the Air Fryer cooking basket.

Cook the rolls at 330 degrees F for about 13 minutes, turning them over halfway through the cooking time. Bon appétit!

Healthy Oatmeal Cups

(**Ready in about** 15 minutes | **Servings:** 2)

Ingredients

1 large banana, mashed
1 tablespoon agave syrup
1 egg, well beaten

1 cup cooking steel cut oats
3 ounces mixed berries
1 cup coconut milk

Directions

In a mixing bowl, thoroughly combine the banana, oats, agave syrup, beaten egg and coconut milk.

Spoon the mixture into an Air Fryer safe baking dish.

Bake in the preheated Air Fryer at 395 degrees F for about 7 minutes. Top with berries and continue to bake an additional 2 minutes. Spoon into individual bowls and **Serve:** with a splash of coconut milk if desired. Bon appétit!

Traditional Japanese Onigiri

(**Ready in about** 30 minutes | **Servings:** 3)

Ingredients

3 cups water
1 egg, beaten
1/2 cup cheddar cheese, grated
1/2 teaspoon coriander seeds
1/2 teaspoon cumin seeds

1 cup white Japanese rice
1 teaspoon dashi granules
1 tablespoon fish sauce
1/2 teaspoon kinako
1 teaspoon sesame oil
1/4 cup shallots, chopped
Sea salt, to taste

Directions

Bring the vegetable broth to a boil in a saucepan over medium-high heat. Stir in the rice and reduce the heat to simmer; cook about 20 minutes and fluff with a fork.

Mix the cooked rice with the remaining Ingredients and stir until everything is well incorporated.

Then, shape and press the mixture into triangle-shape cakes.

Bake the rice cakes in the preheated Air Fryer at 350 degrees F for about 10 minutes, turning them over halfway through the cooking time.

Serve: with seasoned nori, if desired. Bon appétit!

Italian-Style Fried Polenta Slices

(**Ready in about** 35 minutes | **Servings:** 3)

Ingredients

9 ounces pre-cooked polenta roll
1 teaspoon Italian seasoning blend

2 ounces prosciutto, chopped
1 teaspoon sesame oil

Directions

Cut the pre-cooked polenta roll into nine equal slices. Brush them with sesame oil on all sides. Then, transfer the polenta slices to the lightly oiled Air Fryer cooking basket.

Cook the polenta slices at 395 degrees F for about 30 minutes; then, top them with chopped prosciutto and Italian seasoning blend.

Continue to cook for another 5 minutes until cooked through. **Serve:** with marinara sauce, if desired. Bon appétit!

Last Minute German Franzbrötchen

(**Ready in about** 15 minutes | **Servings:** 6)

Ingredients

6 slices white bread

1 tablespoon ground cinnamon Glaze
1/2 teaspoon vanilla paste

1 tablespoon butter, melted
1/2 cup icing sugar
1/4 cup brown sugar
1 tablespoon milk

Directions

Flatten the bread slices to 1/4-inch thickness using a rolling pin. In a small mixing bowl, thoroughly combine the butter, brown sugar and ground cinnamon.

Spread the butter mixture on top of each slice of bread; roll them up.

Bake the rolls at 350 degrees F for 10 minutes, flipping them halfway through the cooking time.

Meanwhile, whisk the icing sugar, vanilla paste and milk until everything is well incorporated. Drizzle the glaze over the top of the slightly cooled rolls.

Let the glaze set before serving. Bon appétit!

Mexican-Style Bubble Loaf

(**Ready in about** 20 minutes | **Servings:** 4)

Ingredients

1 (16-ounce) can flaky buttermilk biscuits
1/2 teaspoon granulated garlic
4 tablespoons olive oil, melted
1 teaspoon chili pepper flakes

1/2 cup Manchego cheese, grated
1 tablespoon fresh cilantro, chopped
1/2 teaspoon Mexican oregano
Kosher salt and ground black pepper, to taste

Directions

Open a can of biscuits and cut each biscuit into quarters. Brush each piece of biscuit with the olive oil and begin layering in a lightly greased Bundt pan.

Cover the bottom of the pan with one layer of biscuits.

Next, top the first layer with half of the cheese, spices and granulated garlic. Repeat for another layer.

Finish with a third layer of dough.

Cook your bubble loaf in the Air Fryer at 330 degrees for about 15 minutes until the cheese is bubbly. Bon appétit!

Mediterranean Monkey Bread

(**Ready in about** 20 minutes | **Servings:** 6)

Ingredients

1 can refrigerated buttermilk biscuits
1/4 cup black olives, pitted and chopped
4 tablespoons basil pesto
1 tablespoon Mediterranean herb mix

1 cup Provolone cheese, grated
1/4 cup pine nuts, chopped
3 tablespoons olive oil

Directions

Separate your dough into the biscuits and cut each of them in half; roll them into balls. Dip each ball into the olive oil and begin layering in a nonstick Bundt pan.

Cover the bottom of the pan with one layer of dough balls.

Prepare the coating mixtures. In a shallow bowl, place the provolone cheese and olives, add the basil pesto to a second bowl and add the pine nuts to a third bowl.

Roll the dough balls in the coating mixtures; then, arrange them in the Bundt pan so the various coatings are alternated. Top with Mediterranean herb mix Cook the monkey bread in the Air Fryer at 320 degrees for 13 to 16 minutes. Bon appétit!

Cinnamon Breakfast Muffins

(**Ready in about** 20 minutes | **Servings:** 4)

Ingredients

1 cup all-purpose flour
2 eggs
1 teaspoon cinnamon powder
1 teaspoon vanilla paste
4 tablespoons butter, melted

1 teaspoon baking powder
1 tablespoon brown sugar
1/4 cup milk

Directions

Start by preheating your Air Fryer to 330 degrees F. Now, spritz the silicone muffin tins with cooking spray.

Thoroughly combine all Ingredients in a mixing dish. Fill the muffin cups with batter.

Cook in the preheated Air Fryer approximately 13 minutes. Check with a toothpick; when the toothpick comes out clean, your muffins are done.

Place on a rack to cool slightly before removing from the muffin tins. Enjoy!

Hibachi-Style Fried Rice

(**Ready in about** 30 minutes | **Servings:** 2)

Ingredients

1 ¾ cups leftover jasmine rice
2 eggs, beaten
1 cup snow peas
1 tablespoon Shoyu sauce
1 tablespoon sake
2 teaspoons butter, melted

Sea salt and freshly ground black pepper
2 scallions, white and green parts separated
2 tablespoons Kewpie Japanese mayonnaise

Directions

Thoroughly combine the rice, butter, salt, and pepper in a baking dish.

Cook at 340 degrees F about 13 minutes, stirring halfway through the cooking time.

Pour the eggs over the rice and continue to cook about 5 minutes. Next, add the scallions and snow peas and stir to combine. Continue to cook 2 to 3 minutes longer or until everything is heated through.

Meanwhile, make the sauce by whisking the Shoyu sauce, sake, and Japanese mayonnaise in a mixing bowl.

Divide the fried rice between individual bowls and **Serve:** with the prepared sauce. Enjoy!

Basic Air Fryer Granola

(**Ready in about** 45 minutes | **Servings:** 12)

Ingredients

1/2 cup rolled oats	1 cup walnuts, chopped
3 tablespoons sunflower seeds	2 tablespoons honey
1 teaspoon coarse sea salt	3 tablespoons pumpkin seeds

Directions

Combine all of the Ingredients thoroughly and spread the mixture onto the Air Fryer trays. Spritz with nonstick cooking spray and set aside.

Bake at 230°F for 25 minutes, then rotate the trays and bake for another 10 to 15 minutes.

This granola will keep for up to 2 weeks in an airtight container. Enjoy

Taco Stuffed Bread

(**Ready in about** 15 minutes | **Servings:** 4)

Ingredients

1 loaf French bread	1 teaspoon garlic, minced
1/2 pound ground beef	1 package taco seasoning
1 ½ cups Queso Panela, sliced	Salt and ground black pepper, to taste
1 onion, chopped	3 tbs tomato paste
2 tbsp fresh cilantro leaves	

Directions

Cut the top off of the loaf of bread; remove some of the bread from the middle creating a well and re**Serve:**.

In a large skillet, cook the ground beef with the onion and garlic until the beef is no longer pink and the onion is translucent.

Add the taco seasoning, cheese, salt, black pepper, and tomato paste. Place the taco mixture into your bread.

Bake in the preheated Air Fryer at 380 degrees F for 5 minutes. Garnish with fresh cilantro leaves. Enjoy!

New York-Style Pizza

(**Ready in about** 15 minutes | **Servings:** 4)

Ingredients

1 pizza dough	1 cup tomato sauce
14 ounces mozzarella cheese, freshly grated	2 ounces parmesan, freshly grated

Directions

Stretch your dough on a pizza peel lightly dusted with flour. Spread with a layer of tomato sauce.

Top with cheese. Place on the baking tray.

Bake in the preheated Air Fryer at 395 degrees F for 5 minutes. Rotate the baking tray and bake for a further 5 minutes. **Serve:** immediately.

Favorite Cheese Biscuits

(**Ready in about** 30 minutes | **Servings:** 4)

Ingredients

1 ½ cups all-purpose flour	1/3 cup butter, room temperature
1 teaspoon baking powder	
1 teaspoon baking soda	1/2 cup buttermilk
1 cup Swiss cheese, shredded	2 eggs, beaten

Directions

In a mixing bowl, thoroughly combine the flour and butter. Gradually stir in the remaining Ingredients.

Divide the mixture into 12 balls.Bake in the preheated Air Fryer at 360 degrees F for 15 minutes. Work in two batches. **Serve:** at room temperature. Bon appétit!

Pretzel Knots with Cumin Seeds

(**Ready in about** 25 minutes | **Servings:** 6)

Ingredients

1 package crescent refrigerator rolls	2 eggs, whisked with 4 tablespoons of water
	1 teaspoon cumin seeds

Directions

Roll the dough out into a rectangle. Slice the dough into 6 pieces.

Roll each piece into a log and tie each rope into a knot. Cover and let it rest for 10 minutes.

Brush the top of the pretzel knots with the egg wash; sprinkle with the cumin seeds. Arrange the pretzel knots in the lightly greased Air Fryer basket.

Bake in the preheated Air Fryer at 340 degrees for 7 minutes until golden brown. Bon appétit!

Ciabatta Bread Pudding with Walnuts

(**Ready in about** 45 minutes | **Servings:** 4)

Ingredients

4 cups ciabatta bread cubes	1 cup milk
2 tablespoons butter	4 tablespoons honey
1 teaspoon vanilla extract	1/2 teaspoon ground cinnamon
1/2 teaspoon ground cloves	A pinch of salt
2 eggs, slightly beaten	
A pinch of grated nutmeg	
1/3 cup walnuts, chopped	

Directions

Place the ciabatta bread cubes in a lightly greased baking dish. In a mixing bowl, thoroughly combine the eggs, milk, butter, honey, vanilla, ground cloves, cinnamon, salt, and nutmeg.

Pour the custard over the bread cubes. Scatter the chopped walnuts over the top of your bread pudding.

Let stand for 30 minutes, occasionally pressing with a wide spatula to submerge.

Cook in the preheated Air Fryer at 370 degrees F degrees for 7 minutes; check to ensure even cooking and cook an additional 5 to 6 minutes. Bon appétit!

Sunday Glazed Cinnamon Rolls

(**Ready in about** 15 minutes | **Servings:** 4)

Ingredients

1 can cinnamon rolls	1 cup powdered sugar
1 teaspoon vanilla extract	2 tablespoons butter
3 tablespoons hot water	

Directions

Place the cinnamon rolls in the Air Fryer basket.

Bake at 300 degrees F for 10 minutes, flipping them halfway through the cooking time.

Meanwhile, mix the butter, sugar, and vanilla. Pour in water, 1 tablespoon at a time, until the glaze reaches desired consistency.

Spread over the slightly cooled cinnamon rolls. Bon appétit!

Rich Couscous Salad with Goat Cheese

(**Ready in about** 45 minutes | **Servings:** 4)

Ingredients

1/2 cup couscous	4 teaspoons olive oil
1/2 lemon, juiced, zested	Sea salt and freshly ground black pepper
1 tablespoon honey	1/2 English cucumber, thinly sliced
1 red onion, thinly sliced	2 tablespoons pine nuts
2 tomatoes, sliced	2 ounces goat cheese, crumbled
1 teaspoon ghee	
1/2 cup loosely packed Italian parsley, finely chopped	

Directions

Put the couscous in a bowl; now, pour the boiling water over it. Cover and set aside for 5 to 8 minutes; fluff with a fork.

Place the couscous in a cake pan. Transfer the pan to the Air Fryer basket and cook at 360 digress F about 20 minutes. Make sure to stir every 5 minutes to ensure even cooking.

Meanwhile, in a small mixing bowl, whisk the olive oil, lemon juice and zest, honey, salt, and black pepper. Toss the couscous with this dressing.

Add the tomatoes, red onion, English cucumber, and goat cheese; gently stir to combine.

Rub the ghee in the pine nuts, using your hands and place them in the Air Fryer basket. Roast for 4 minutes; give the nuts a good toss. Put the cooking basket back again and roast for a further 3 to 4 minutes.

Scatter the toasted nuts over your salad and garnish with parsley. Enjoy

Crème Brûlée French Toast

(**Ready in about** 10 minutes | **Servings:** 2)

Ingredients

4 slices bread, about 1-inch thick	1 teaspoon ground cinnamon
A pinch of sea salt	2 tbs butter, softened
2 ounces brown sugar	1/2 teaspoon vanilla paste
2 ounces Neufchâtel cheese, softened	

Directions

In a mixing dish, combine the butter, cinnamon, brown sugar, vanilla, and salt. Spread the cinnamon butter on both sides of the bread slices.

Arrange in the cooking basket. Cook at 390 degrees F for 2 minutes; turn over and cook an additional 2 minutes.

Serve: with softened Neufchâtel cheese on individual plates. Bon appétit!

The Best Fish Tacos Ever

(**Ready in about** 25 minutes | **Servings:** 3)

Ingredients

1 tablespoon mayonnaise
1 teaspoon Dijon mustard
1 tablespoon sour cream
Sea salt, to taste
2 bell peppers, seeded and sliced
1 tablespoon water
1/4 cup parmesan cheese, grated
1 halibut fillets, cut into 1-inch strips
6 mini flour taco shells

1/2 teaspoon fresh garlic, minced
1/4 teaspoon red pepper flakes
1 egg
1 shallot, thinly sliced
1 tablespoon taco seasoning mix
1/3 cup tortilla chips
6 lime wedges, for serving

Directions

Thoroughly combine the mayonnaise, mustard, sour cream, garlic, red pepper flakes, and salt. Add the bell peppers and shallots; toss to coat well. Place in your refrigerator until ready to **Serve:**.

Line the Air Fryer basket with a piece of parchment paper. In a shallow bowl, mix the egg, water, and taco seasoning mix. In a separate shallow bowl, mix the crushed tortilla chips and parmesan.

Dip the fish into the egg mixture, then coat with the parmesan mixture, pressing to adhere.

Bake in the preheated Air Fryer at 380 degrees F for 13 minutes, flipping halfway through the cooking time.

Divide the creamed pepper mixture among the taco shells. Top with the fish, and **Serve:** with lime wedges. Enjoy!

Savory Cheese and Herb Biscuits

(**Ready in about** 30 minutes | **Servings:** 3)

Ingredients

1 cup self-rising flour
1/2 stick butter, melted
1/2 teaspoon honey
1/4 teaspoon kosher salt
1 teaspoon dried parsley

1/2 tbs baking powder
1/2 cup Colby cheese, grated
1 teaspoon dried rosemary
1/2 cup buttermilk

Directions

Preheat your Air Fryer to 360° F. Wrap a piece of parchment paper around the cooking basket.

Combine the flour, baking powder, honey, and butter in a mixing bowl. Stir in the remaining Ingredients gradually.

Bake for 15 minutes in a preheated Air Fryer.

Working in batches is recommended. At room temperature, **Serve:**. Good appetite!

Puff Pastry Meat Strudel

(**Ready in about** 40 minutes | **Servings:** 8)

Ingredients

1 tablespoon olive oil
1 small onion, chopped
2 garlic cloves, minced

Sea salt and ground black pepper, to taste
2 cans (8-ounces) refrigerated crescent rolls
1 egg, whisked with
1 tablespoon of water

2 tablespoons tomato puree
2 tablespoons matzo meal
1/3 pound ground beef
1/4 tbsp dried marjoram
2 tsp sesame seeds
1/2 cup marinara sauce
1 cup sour cream
1/2 tbsp cayenne pepper
1/3 pound ground pork

Directions

Heat the oil in a heavy skillet over medium flame. Sauté the onion just until soft and translucent. Add the garlic and sauté for 1 minute more.

Add the ground beef and pork and continue to cook for 3 minutes more or until the meat is no longer pink. Remove from the heat.

Add the tomato puree and matzo meal.

Roll out the puff pastry and spread the meat mixture lengthwise on the dough. Sprinkle with salt, black pepper, cayenne pepper, and marjoram.

Fold in the sides of the dough over the meat mixture. Pinch the edges to seal. Place the strudel on the parchment lined Air Fryer basket. Brush the strudel with the egg wash; sprinkle with sesame seeds.

Bake in the preheated Air Fryer at 330 degrees F for 18 to 20 minutes or until the pastry is puffed and golden and the filling is thoroughly cooked.

Allow your strudel to rest for 5 to 10 minutes before cutting and serving. **Serve:** with the marinara sauce and sour cream on the side. Bon appétit!

Paella-Style Spanish Rice

(**Ready in about** 35 minutes | **Servings:** 2)

Ingredients

2 cups water
1 cube vegetable stock
1 chorizo, sliced
2 cloves garlic, finely
1/2 teaspoon fresh ginger, ground
1/2 cup tomato sauce
Kosher salt and ground black pepper, to taste

1 cup white rice, rinsed and drained
2 cups brown mushrooms, cleaned and sliced
1/4 cup dry white wine
1 long red chili, minced
1 tsp smoked paprika
1 cup green beans

Directions

In a medium saucepan, bring the water to a boil. Add the rice and vegetable stock cube. Stir and reduce the heat. Cover and let it simmer for 20 minutes.

Then, place the chorizo, mushrooms, garlic, ginger, and red chili in the baking pan. Cook at 380 degrees F for 6 minutes, stirring periodically.

Add the prepared rice to the casserole dish. Add the remaining Ingredients and gently stir to combine.

Cook for 6 minutes, checking periodically to ensure even cooking. **Serve:** in individual bowls and enjoy!

Beef and Wild Rice Casserole

(**Ready in about** 50 minutes | **Servings:** 3)

Ingredients

3 cups beef stock
1/2 pound steak, cut into strips
1 carrot, chopped
2 garlic cloves, minced
1 chili pepper, minced

1 cup wild rice, rinsed well
1 medium-sized leek, chopped
1 tablespoon olive oil
Kosher salt and ground black pepper, to your liking

Directions

Place beef stock and rice in a saucepan over medium-high heat.

Cover and bring it to a boil. Reduce the heat and let it simmer about 40 minutes. Drain the excess liquid and re**Serve:**.

Heat the olive oil in a heavy skillet over moderate heat. Cook the steak until no longer pink; place in the lightly greased baking pan.

Add carrot, leek, garlic, chili pepper, salt, and black pepper. Stir in the re**Serve:**d wild rice. Stir to combine well.

Cook in the preheated Air Fryer at 360 degrees for 9 to 10 minutes. **Serve:** immediately and enjoy!

Baked Tortilla Chips

(**Ready in about** 15 minutes | **Servings:** 3)

Ingredients

1/2 package corn tortillas
1 teaspoon salt

1/2 teaspoon chili powder
1 tablespoon canola oil

Directions

Using a cookie cutter, cut the tortillas into small rounds.

Canola oil should be applied to the rounds. Season with chilli powder and salt. Bake at 360°F for 5 minutes, shaking the basket halfway through, in a lightly greased Air Fryer basket. Working in batches, bake the chips until they are crisp.

Serve: with salsa or guacamole if desired. Enjoy

Golden Cornbread Muffins

(**Ready in about** 30 minutes | **Servings:** 4)

Ingredients

1/2 cup sorghum flour
1/2 cup yellow cornmeal
A pinch of grated nutmeg
1/4 cup white sugar
4 tablespoons butter, melted

2 teaspoons baking powder A pinch of salt
2 eggs, beaten
1/2 cup milk
4 tablespoons honey

Directions

Start by preheating your Air Fryer to 370 degrees F. Then, line the muffin cups with the paper baking cups.

In a mixing bowl, combine the flour, cornmeal, sugar, baking powder, salt, and nutmeg. In a separate bowl, mix the eggs, milk, and butter.

Pour the egg mixture into the dry cornmeal mixture; mix to combine well. Pour the batter into the prepared muffin cups. Bake for 15 minutes. Rotate the pan and bake for 10 minutes more. Transfer to a wire rack to cool slightly before cutting and serving. **Serve:** with honey and enjoy!

Cheese and Bacon Ciabatta Sandwich

(**Ready in about** 10 minutes | **Servings:** 2)

Ingredients

2 ciabatta sandwich buns, split
4 slices Canadian bacon
2 teaspoons Dijon mustard
2 tablespoons butter
4 slices Monterey cheese

Directions

Place the bottom halves of buns, cut sides up in the parchment lined Air Fryer basket.

Spread the butter and mustard on the buns. Top with the bacon and cheese Bake in the preheated Air Fryer at 400 degrees F for 3 minutes. Flip the sandwiches over and cook for 3 minutes longer or until the cheese has melted.

Serve: with some extra ketchup or salsa sauce. Bon appétit!

Caprese Mac and Cheese

(**Ready in about** 25 minutes | **Servings:** 3)

Ingredients

1/2 pound cavatappi
2 cups mozzarella cheese, grated
1/2 teaspoon Italian seasoning
2 tomatoes, sliced
1 cup cauliflower florets
Salt and ground black pepper, to taste
1 cup milk
1 tablespoon fresh basil leaves
1 cup Parmesan cheese, grated

Directions

Bring a pot of salted water to a boil over high heat; turn the heat down to medium and add the cavatappi and cauliflower.

Let it simmer about 8 minutes. Drain the cavatappi and cauliflower; place them in a lightly greased baking pan.

Add the milk and mozzarella cheese to the baking pan; gently stir to combine. Add the Italian seasoning, salt, and black pepper.

Top with the tomatoes and parmesan cheese.

Bake in the preheated Air Fryer at 360 degrees F for 15 minutes. **Serve:** garnished with fresh basil leaves. Bon appétit!

Buckwheat and Potato Flat Bread

(**Ready in about** 20 minutes | **Servings:** 4)

Ingredients

4 potatoes, medium-sized
1 cup buckwheat flour
1/2 teaspoon salt
1/2 teaspoon red chili powder
1/4 cup honey

Directions

Put the potatoes into a large saucepan; add water to cover by about 1 inch. Bring to a boil. Then, lower the heat, and let your potatoes simmer about 8 minutes until they are fork tender.

Mash the potatoes and add the flour, salt, and chili powder. Create 4 balls and flatten them with a rolling pin

Bake in the preheated Air Fryer at 390 degrees F for 6 minutes. **Serve:** warm with honey.

Couscous and Black Bean Bowl

(**Ready in about** 35 minutes | **Servings:** 4)

Ingredients

1 cup couscous
1 tablespoon fresh cilantro, chopped
1 bell pepper, sliced
1 red onion, sliced
1 teaspoon lemon juice
1 teaspoon lemon zest
4 tablespoons tahini
1 cup canned black beans, drained and rinsed
2 tomatoes, sliced
2 cups baby spinach
Sea salt and ground black pepper, to taste
1 tablespoon olive oil

Directions

Put the couscous in a bowl; pour the boiling water to cover by about 1 inch. Cover and set aside for 5 to 8 minutes; fluff with a fork.

Place the couscous in a lightly greased cake pan. Transfer the pan to the Air Fryer basket and cook at 360 digress F about 20 minutes. Make sure to stir

Mediterranean Pita Pockets

(**Ready in about** 25 minutes | **Servings:** 4)

Ingredients

1 teaspoon olive oil
1 onion
3/4 pound ground turkey
1 clove garlic, minced
4 small pitas Tzatziki
Sea salt, to taste
1/2 cucumber, peeled
1/4 teaspoon dried oregano

2 garlic cloves, minced
1/2 tsp mustard seeds
Salt and ground black pepper, to taste
1/2 cup Greek-style yogurt
2 tablespoons fresh lemon juice

Directions

Mix the olive oil, onion, garlic, turkey, salt, black pepper, and mustard seeds;

shape the mixture into four patties.

Cook in the preheated Air Fryer at 370 degrees F for 10 minutes, turning them over once or twice.

Meanwhile, mix all Ingredients for the tzatziki and place in the refrigerator until ready to use.

Warm the pita pockets in the preheated Air Fryer at 360 degrees F for 4 to 5 minutes or until thoroughly heated.

Spread the tzatziki in pita pockets and add the turkey patties. Enjoy!

Grilled Garlic and Avocado Toast

(**Ready in about** 15 minutes | **Servings:** 2)

Ingredients

4 slices artisan bread
1 garlic clove, halved
2 tablespoons olive oil
1/4 tbs ground black pepper

1 avocado, seeded, peeled and mashed
1/2 teaspoon sea salt

Directions

Rub 1 side of each bread slice with garlic. Brush with olive oil. Place the bread slices on the Air Fryer grill pan. Bake in the preheated Air Fryer at 400 degrees F for 3 to 4 minutes. Slather the mashed avocado on top of the toast and season with salt and pepper. Enjoy!

Stuffed French Toast

(**Ready in about** 15 minutes | **Servings:** 3)

Ingredients

6 slices of challah bread, without crusts
1/4 cup butter, melted
1 egg
1/2 teaspoon grated nutmeg 1 tbs ground cinnamon

3 tablespoons fig jam
1/4 cup Mascarpone cheese
4 tablespoons milk
1/2 cup brown sugar
1/2 teaspoon vanilla paste

Directions

Spread the three slices of bread with the mascarpone cheese, leaving 1/2-inch border at the edges.

Spread the three slices of bread with 1/2 tablespoon of fig jam; then, invert them onto the slices with the cheese in order to make sandwiches. Mix the egg, milk, nutmeg, cinnamon, and vanilla in a shallow dish. Dip your sandwiches in the egg mixture. Cook in the preheated Air Fryer at 340 degrees F for 4 minutes. Dip in the melted butter, then, roll in the brown sugar. **Serve:** warm.

Almost Famous Four-Cheese Pizza

(**Ready in about** 15 minutes | **Servings:** 4)

Ingredients

1 (11-ounce) can refrigerated thin pizza crust
1/4 cup Parmesan cheese, grated
1 cup mozzarella cheese.
1/2 cup tomato pasta sauce

2 tablespoons scallions, chopped
1 tablespoon olive oil
4 slices cheddar cheese
1 cup provolone cheese, shredded

Directions

Stretch the dough on a work surface lightly dusted with flour. Spread with a layer of tomato pasta sauce.

Top with the scallions and cheese. Place on the baking tray that is previously greased with olive oil. Bake in the preheated Air Fryer at 395 degrees F for 5 minutes. Rotate the baking tray and bake for a further 5 minutes. **Serve:** immediately.

Crispy Pork Wontons

(**Ready in about** 20 minutes | **Servings:** 3)

Ingredients

1 tablespoon olive oil
3/4 pound ground pork
1 green bell pepper, seeded and chopped
Salt and ground black pepper, to taste

6 wonton wrappers

1 red bell pepper, seeded and chopped
3 tablespoons onion, finely chopped
1 teaspoon dried thyme
1 habanero pepper, minced
1/2 teaspoon dried parsley flakes

Directions

Heat the olive oil in a heavy skillet over medium heat. Cook the ground pork, peppers, and onion until tender and fragrant or about 4 minutes.

Add the seasonings and stir to combine.

Lay a piece of the wonton wrapper on your palm; add the filling in the middle of the wrapper. Then, fold it up to form a triangle; pinch the edges to seal tight.

Place the folded wontons in the lightly greased cooking basket. Cook at 360 degrees F for 10 minutes. Work in batches and **Serve:** warm. Bon appétit!

Broccoli Bruschetta with Romano Cheese

(**Ready in about** 20 minutes | **Servings:** 3)

Ingredients

6 slices of panini bread
1 teaspoon garlic puree
6 tablespoons passata di pomodoro (tomato passata)
1 cup small broccoli florets

3 tablespoons extra-virgin olive oil
1/2 cup Romano cheese, grated

Directions

Place the slices of panini bread on a flat surface.

In a small mixing bowl, combine together the garlic puree and extra-virgin olive oil. Brush one side of each bread slice with the garlic/oil mixture.

Place in the Air Fryer grill pan. Add the tomato passata, broccoli, and cheese. Cook in the preheated Air Fryer at 370 degrees F for 10 minutes. Bon appétit!

Polenta Bites with Wild Mushroom Ragout

(**Ready in about** 50 minutes | **Servings:** 3)

Ingredients

2 cups water
2 tablespoons butter, melted 1 tablespoon olive oil
1/2 red onion, chopped
1/2 cup polenta
Sea salt and freshly ground black pepper, to taste
1 teaspoon cayenne pepper

1 teaspoon salt
6 ounces wild mushrooms, sliced

1/2 teaspoon fresh garlic, minced
1/2 cup dry white wine

Directions

Bring 2 cups of water and 1 teaspoon salt to a boil in a saucepan over medium-high heat. Slowly and gradually, stir in the polenta, whisking constantly.

Reduce the heat to medium-low and continue to cook for 5 to 6 minutes more. Stir in the butter and mix to combine. Pour the prepared polenta into a parchment-lined baking pan, cover and let stand for 15 to 20 minutes or until set.

In the meantime, preheat your Air Fryer to 360 degrees F. Heat the olive oil until sizzling. Then, add the mushrooms, onion, and garlic to the baking pan.

Cook for 5 minutes, stirring occasionally. Season with salt, black pepper, cayenne pepper, and wine; cook an additional 5 minutes and re**Serve:**.

Cut the polenta into 18 squares. Transfer to the lightly greased cooking basket. Cook in the preheated Air Fryer at 395 degrees F for about 8 minutes.

Top with the wild mushroom ragout and bake an additional 3 minutes. **Serve:** warm.

Cornmeal Crusted Okra

(**Ready in about** 30 minutes | **Servings:** 2)

Ingredients

3/4 cup cornmeal
1/2 teaspoon cumin seeds
Sea salt and ground black pepper, to taste
1 teaspoon cayenne pepper

1/4 cup parmesan cheese, grated
1 teaspoon garlic powder
2 teaspoons sesame oil
1/2 pound of okra, cut into small chunks

Directions

In a mixing bowl, thoroughly combine the cornmeal, parmesan, salt, black pepper, cayenne pepper, garlic powder, and cumin seeds. Stir well to combine.

Roll the okra pods over the cornmeal mixture, pressing to adhere. Drizzle with sesame oil.

Cook in the preheated Air Fryer at 370 digress F for 20 minutes, shaking the basket periodically to ensure even cooking. Bon appétit!

Tex Mex Pasta Bake

(**Ready in about** 40 minutes | **Servings:** 4)

Ingredients

3/4 pound pasta noodles
1 tablespoon olive oil
3/4 pound ground beef
1 bell pepper, seeded and sliced
1 ½ cups enchilada sauce
Sea salt and cracked black pepper, to taste
1/2 tbsp Mexican oregano
2 tbs fresh coriander, chopped

1 medium-sized onion, chopped
1 teaspoon fresh garlic, minced
1 jalapeno, seeded and minced
1 cup Mexican cheese blend, shredded
1/2 cup nacho chips
1/3 cup tomato paste

Directions

Boil the pasta noodles for 3 minutes less than mentioned on the package; drain, rinse and place in the lightly greased casserole dish.

In a saucepan, heat the olive oil until sizzling. Add the ground beef and cook for 2 to 3 minutes or until slightly brown. Now, add the onion, garlic, and peppers and continue to cook until tender and fragrant or about 2 minutes. Season with salt and black pepper.

Add the enchilada sauce to the casserole dish. Add the beef mixture and 1/2 cup of the Mexican cheese blend. Gently stir to combine. Add the tomato paste, Mexican oregano, nacho chips, and the remaining 1/2 cup of cheese blend. Cover with foil.

Bake in the preheated Air Fryer at 350 degrees F for 20 minutes; remove the foil and bake for a further 10 to 12 minutes. **Serve:** garnished with fresh coriander and enjoy!

Tyrolean Kaiserschmarrn (Austrian Pancakes)

(**Ready in about** 30 minutes | **Servings:** 4)

Ingredients

1/2 cup flour A pinch of salt
1 shot of rum
1/2 cup icing sugar
1/2 cup whole milk

A pinch of sugar
3 eggs
4 tablespoons raisins
1/2 cup stewed plums

Directions

In a mixing bowl, combine the flour, salt, sugar, and milk until the batter is semi-solid. Fold in the eggs, then add the rum and whisk to combine thoroughly. Allow it to stand for 20 minutes. Coat the baking pan of the Air Fryer with cooking spray. Fill the bowl with the batter.

Using a measuring cup, pour the liquid into the pan. Sprinkle the raisins on top. Cook for 4 to 5 minutes, or until golden brown, at 230°F. Repeat with the rest of the batter.

Cut the pancake into pieces, sprinkle with icing sugar, and **Serve:** alongside the stewed plums. Good appetite!

Rice Stuffed Peppers

Prep time: 10 minutes **Cooking time:** 15 minutes
Serve: 4

Ingredients

4 bell peppers, cut the tops & remove seeds
1 tbsp Italian seasoning
2 cups cooked rice
15 oz can tomato, diced
1 small onion, diced
Pepper

1 tsp garlic powder
2 cups Colby jack cheese,
8 oz tomato sauce
1 lb. ground beef
1 tbsp canola oil
Salt

Directions

Heat oil in a pan over medium-high heat. Add onion and sauté until softened. Add meat and cook until meat is no longer pink. Add garlic powder, Italian seasoning, rice, tomato sauce, tomatoes, pepper, and salt and stir until well combined.

Stuff rice mixture into the peppers and cook at 360 F for 10 minutes. Top with cheese and cook for 2 minutes more. **Serve:** and enjoy.

Apple Oats

Prep time: 10 minutes **Cooking time:** 15 minutes
Serve: 1

Ingredients

½ cup gluten-free oats
1 tbsp Greek yogurt
½ tsp cream of tartar
2 tbsp date spread
¼ cup apple, chopped

½ cup unsweetened
almond milk
½ tsp baking powder
1 tbsp protein powder

Directions

In a mixing bowl, mix together oats, baking powder, and protein powder. Add yogurt, milk, date spread, and cream of tartar and mix until well combined.

Add apple and fold well. Pour oat mixture into the greased air fryer baking dish. Place baking dish into the air fryer basket and cook at 330 F for 15 minutes. **Serve:** and enjoy.

Peanut Butter Oatmeal

Prep time: 10 minutes **Cooking time:** 15 minutes
Serve: 1

Ingredients

½ cup rolled oats
½ tsp baking powder
1/3 cup unsweetened
almond milk
1 tsp maple syrup

¼ tsp vanilla
½ tbsp peanut butter
½ banana
1/8 tsp salt

Directions

Preheat the air fryer to 350 F. Add oats into the food processor and process until get flour like consistency. Add remaining Ingredients and process until well combined. Pour batter into the greased ramekin. **Serve:** and enjoy.

Oats Granola

Prep time: 10 minutes **Cooking time:** 30 minutes
Serve: 8

Ingredients

3 cups old-fashioned oats
3 tbsp brown sugar
½ cup maple syrup
1 tsp vanilla

1 tsp cinnamon
3 tbsp coconut oil, melted
½ tsp salt

Directions

In a mixing bowl, mix together oats, vanilla, cinnamon, brown sugar, oil, maple syrup, and salt until well combined.

Spread oats mixture into the parchment-lined air fryer basket and cook at 250 F for 30 minutes. Stir after every 10 minutes. **Serve:** and enjoy.

Berry Oatmeal

Prep time: 10 minutes **Cooking time:** 8 minutes **Serve:** 4

Ingredients

2 eggs
5 tbsp unsweetened
almond milk
1 tbsp vanilla
2 tbsp mixed berries

7 oz banana
2 tbsp honey
2 tbsp Greek yogurt
4.5 oz quick oats

Directions

In a mixing bowl, add banana and mash using the fork.
Add oats, vanilla, honey, yogurt, milk, and eggs and mix until well combined. Add berries and fold well.

Spoon mixture into the four greased ramekins. Place ramekins into the air fryer basket and cook at 400 F for 8 minutes. **Serve:** and enjoy.

Chocolate Oats

Prep time: 10 minutes **Cooking time:** 15 minutes
Serve: 2

Ingredients

1 egg
½ tsp cinnamon
1 tsp vanilla
½ tsp baking powder
½ cup rolled oats

1 tbsp cocoa powder
¼ cup unsweetened
almond milk
1 tbsp maple syrup
½ banana Pinch of salt

Directions

Add oats and remaining Ingredients into the blender and blend until smooth. Pour blended oat mixture into the greased ramekins.

Place ramekins into the air fryer basket and cook at 330 F for 13-15 minutes. **Serve:** and enjoy.

Curried Chickpeas

Prep time: 10 minutes **Cooking time:** 18 minutes
Serve: 4

Ingredients

30 oz can chickpeas,
drained & rinsed
½ tbsp parsley, chopped
Salt

½ tsp chili powder
2 tbsp curry powder
2 tbsp canola oil

Directions

Add chickpeas and remaining Ingredients into the mixing bowl and toss until well coated. Spread chickpeas into the air fryer basket and cook at 375 F for 15-18 minutes. Stir after every 5 minutes. **Serve:** and enjoy.

Chocolate Chip Oats

Prep time: 10 minutes **Cooking time:** 18 minutes
Serve: 2

Ingredients

1 egg	1 cup rolled oats
¼ cup chocolate chips	½ tsp vanilla
½ tsp baking powder	1 ripe banana
½ cup unsweetened	1 tbsp maple syrup
almond milk Pinch of salt	

Directions

Preheat the air fryer to 350 F. Add oats, egg, vanilla, baking powder, maple syrup, banana, milk, and salt into the blender and blend until smooth.

Add chocolate chips and mix well. Pour oat mixture into the two greased ramekins. Place ramekins into the air fryer basket and cook for 18-20 minutes. **Serve:** and enjoy.

Ranch Chickpeas

Prep time: 10 minutes **Cooking time:** 17 minutes
Serve: 8

Ingredients

15 oz can chickpeas, drained & rinsed	2 tsp onion powder
	1 tbsp olive oil
2 tsp garlic powder	Salt
4 tsp dried dill Pepper	1 tbsp fresh lemon juice

Directions

Add chickpeas into the air fryer basket and cook at 400 F for 12 minutes. Transfer chickpeas into the mixing bowl. Add lemon juice, onion powder, garlic powder, dill, oil, pepper, and salt and toss until well coated.

Return chickpeas into the air fryer basket and cook at 350 F for 5 minutes more. **Serve:** and enjoy.

Better Spanish Rice

Prep time: 15 minutes **Cooking time:** 20 minutes
Serve: 1

Ingredients

1 tablespoon vegetable oil	½ onion, chopped
1 ¼ cups uncooked instant rice	1 (14.5 ounces) can diced tomatoes
½ cup chopped fresh cilantro	1 cup chicken broth

Directions

In a pan over medium-high heat, heat the oil and sauté and toss the chopped onion until browned, approximately 8 minutes.

Coconut Oats

Prep time: 10 minutes **Cooking time:** 18 minutes
Serve: 2

Ingredients

1 ripe banana	3 tbsp chocolate chips
2 tbsp unsweetened shredded coconut	½ tsp vanilla
	Pinch of salt
½ tsp baking powder	½ cup unsweetened almond milk
1 tbsp maple syrup	1 cup rolled oats

Directions

Preheat the air fryer to 350 F. Add banana, vanilla, baking powder, maple syrup, milk, oats, and salt into the blender and blend until smooth.

Add shredded coconut and chocolate chips and mix well.
Pour oat mixture into the two greased ramekins. Place ramekins into the air fryer basket and cook for 18-20 minutes. **Serve:** and enjoy.

Mango Ginger Rice

Prep time: 15 minutes **Cooking time:** 25 minutes
Serve: 1

Ingredients

2 tbs canola oil	¼ cup chopped dried mango
fresh cilantro (optional)	
2 teaspoons minced fresh ginger root	2 cups water
	1 cup uncooked jasmine rice
½ teaspoon salt	¼ cup chopped green onions
2 tablespoons chopped	

Directions

In a saucepan over medium-low heat, heat the oil. Cook for 2 to 3 minutes, or until the mango and ginger are aromatic. Cook, often stirring, until the rice is transparent, about 5 minutes. Bring the water and salt to a boil. Reduce heat to low and cover; simmer for 20 minutes or water absorbed.

Place the heated rice on a serving dish and garnish it with green onions and cilantro.

Carrot Rice

Prep time: 20 minutes **Cooking time:** 20 minutes
Serve: 1

Ingredients

1 cup basmati rice	¼ cup roasted peanuts
2 cups water	1 tablespoon margarine
1 onion, sliced	1tbs minced ginger root
¾ cup grated carrots	cayenne pepper to taste
salt to taste	
chopped fresh cilantro	

Directions

In a medium saucepan, combine rice and water. Bring the water to a boil over high heat. Reduce the heat to low, cover with a lid, and steam for 20 minutes, or until the vegetables are soft.

While the rice cooks, mix the peanuts in a blender and put them aside.

In a pan over medium heat, melt the margarine. Cook and stir for 10 minutes, or until the onion has softened and turned golden brown. Stir in the ginger, carrots, and salt & pepper to taste. Reduce the heat to low and cover for 5 minutes to steam. Add the cayenne pepper and peanuts and mix well. Add it to the skillet and gently toss to blend with the other Ingredients when the rice is done. Garnish with cilantro, if desired.

Persian Rice with Potato Tahdig

Prep time: 15 minutes **Cooking time:** 25 minutes
Serve: 1

Ingredients

2 cups basmati rice	2 tablespoons cooking oil
1 potato, sliced into 1/4-inch rounds	1 teaspoon salt

Directions

Rice should be rinsed and drained twice. A big pot of water should be brought to a boil. Cook for 6 minutes after adding the rice and salt. Drain through a colander. Rinse and re-drain the rice.

Place the potato slices in a single layer on top of the oil in the bottom of the saucepan. Pour prepared rice over potato slices, cover, and simmer for 20 to 30 minutes, or until soft rice and potatoes.

Carefully invert onto a serving platter to make the sliced potatoes on top of the rice.

Easy Cilantro-Lime Rice

Prep time: 15 minutes **Cooking time:** 20 minutes
Serve: 1

Ingredients

1 tablespoon olive oil	2 cloves garlic, minced
1 ½ cups chicken broth	2 tbs fresh lime juice
1 cup basmati rice	1 lime, zested
1 teaspoon salt	½ cup chopped cilantro
¼ cup whole-kernel corn	2 tbs green onions, chopped

Directions

In a saucepan over medium heat, heat the olive oil. Cook and stir rice and garlic in heated oil for 2 minutes or fragrant. Stir in the chicken broth, lime juice, and salt; bring to a boil, lower to medium-low heat, cover with a lid, and cook for 15 minutes, or until the rice is soft and the liquid has been absorbed. Cilantro, corn, green onions, and lime zest until well combined.

Jasmine Rice

Prep time: 20 minutes **Cooking time:** 25 minutes
Serve: 1

Ingredients

2 tablespoons olive oil	2 tbsp chopped onion
¼ cup green peas	1 ½ cups dry jasmine rice
salt to taste	3 cups water
1 bay leaf	

Directions

Warm the oil in a large saucepan over medium-low heat. Sauté the onion for 3 to 5 minutes. Next, incorporate the green peas, bay leaf, and jasmine rice. To coat the rice, give it a good stir.

Pour in 3 cups of water and season with salt in a pot. Increase the heat to medium and bring the rice to a rapid boil. Reduce the heat to low and let the rice gently simmer, uncovered until all of the liquid has been absorbed. Remove the rice from the heat and cover it with a lid. Allow for a 40-minute resting period.

Black Rice

Prep time: 15 minutes **Cooking time:** 18 minutes
Serve: 1

Ingredients

2 tablespoons butter	¼ cup diced onion
¼ cup slivered almonds	1 ¾ cups water
1 cube chicken bouillon	1 cup black rice

Directions

In a saucepan over medium heat, melt the butter. Cook and stir for 5 to 10 minutes, or until the black rice, onion, and almonds are gently toasted. Bring the water and bouillon cube to a boil. Reduce the heat to low, cover, and simmer for 25 to 30 minutes, or until the rice is cooked and the liquid has been absorbed.

Yellow Rice with Vegetables

Prep time: 10 minutes **Cooking time:** 18 minutes
Serve: 1

Ingredients

1 teaspoon vegetable oil	½ cup chopped broccoli florets
1 small onion, chopped	
¼ cup diced red bell pepper 1 clove garlic, minced	3 cups vegetable broth
	1 carrot, diced
1 ½ cups rice	
1 dash adobo seasoning with pepper (such as Goya®)	1 (1.41 ounces) package sazon seasoning with coriander and achiote (such as Goya®)

Directions

In a saucepan over medium heat, heat the oil. Cook and stir onion, carrot, broccoli, red bell pepper, and garlic in heated oil for 5 minutes, or until garlic just begins to brown.

Pour the vegetable broth into the saucepan, whisk in the rice, season spice, and adobo seasoning. Bring the liquid to a boil, then lower to low

heat and simmer for 25 minutes, or until the liquid is absorbed and the rice is soft. To **Serve:**, fluff the rice with a fork.

Dirty Rice

Prep time: 15 minutes **Cooking time:** 22 minutes
Serve: 1

Ingredients

1 tablespoon vegetable oil	6 ounces boneless pork shoulder, diced
1 yellow onion, diced	
½ cup diced celery	½ cup diced green bell pepper
1 tablespoon paprika	
2 teaspoons ground cumin	2 tbsp ground black pepper
½ teaspoon cayenne pepper	½ teaspoon garlic powder
¼ teaspoon dried oregano	¼ teaspoon dried thyme
1 andouille sausage, diced, or to taste	2 cups long-grain rice
4 cups chicken broth	8 ounces chicken livers, minced
2 teaspoons kosher salt, or to taste	1 bay leaf
¼ cup chopped Italian parsley	1 dash Worcestershire sauce
	¼ cup sliced green onions

Directions

In a high-sided pan over medium-high heat, heat the oil. 5 to 7 minutes, cook and stir meat until thoroughly browned and fat is released. Cook until the onion, celery, and bell pepper are transparent, about 5 minutes. In a mixing bowl, combine paprika, cumin, black pepper, cayenne pepper, garlic powder, oregano, and thyme.

Cook, stirring regularly, for 5 minutes, or until veggies continue to soften. Reduce the heat to medium and stir in the andouille sausage. Cook and stir for 2 to 3 minutes to release some flavor. Stir in the chicken livers and rice until thoroughly coated. Season with salt, add stock and bring

to a boil over medium-high heat. Combine the bay leaf and Worcestershire sauce in a mixing bowl. Reduce the heat to medium- low and cover securely. Cook, without stirring, for approximately 25

minutes, or until most of the liquid has been absorbed and the rice is starting to become soft. Mix in the green onions and parsley. Cook for another 10 minutes over
low to medium-low heat until the rice is tender. Before serving, taste for seasoning and discard the bay leaf.

Basmati Rice

Prep time: 15 minutes **Cooking time:** 25 minutes
Serve: 1

Ingredients

1 ¾ cups water	1 cup basmati rice
¼ cup frozen green peas	1 teaspoon cumin seeds

Directions

Bring water to a boil in a saucepan. Stir in the rice.
Reduce the heat to low, cover, and leave to simmer for
20 minutes.
When the rice is done, add the peas and cumin. Allow
to stand for 5 minutes, covered.

Almond Wild Rice

Prep time: 18 minutes **Cooking time:** 20 minutes
Serve: 1

Ingredients

cooking spray	2 ½ cups chicken broth
1 ½ cups brown and wild rice mix	1 cup slivered almonds
2 tablespoons dried parsley	3 tablespoons butter
¼ teaspoon salt	1 cup sweetened dried cranberries
	¼ teaspoon ground black pepper

Directions

Preheat the oven carefully to 375°F (190 degrees C).
Coat an 8-inch square baking dish with nonstick
cooking spray.
In a saucepan, bring chicken broth to a boil.

Place the rice mixture in the prepared baking dish.
Pour the boiling chicken stock over the rice with care.
Wrap the dish with aluminum foil. Bake it in a
preheated oven for 1 hour or until the rice is soft.

In a pan over medium heat, melt the butter. Cook and
stir almonds in heated butter for 3 to 5 minutes, or
until they brown. Continue to simmer and stir until
the almonds are lightly toasted, about 3 to 5 minutes
more.

In a large mixing basin, combine the baked rice,
almond mixture, cranberries, salt, and pepper; toss to
combine.

Thai Fried Rice

Prep time: 20 minutes **Cooking time:** 20 minutes
Serve: 1

Ingredients

6 slices bacon, sliced crosswise into 1/2-inch pieces	1 onion, finely chopped
	1 large tomato, cubed
	2 cloves garlic, minced
½ cup chopped fresh pineapple	5 cups cooked jasmine rice, cooled
2 tablespoons light soy sauce 1 tablespoon white sugar	¼ teaspoon freshly ground white pepper
½ cucumber, sliced	3 eggs, beaten
¼ cup chopped fresh cilantro	2 green onions, chopped
	4 green Thai chili peppers
1 lime, cut into wedges	2 tablespoons ketchup

Directions

Cook the bacon in a large pan or wok over medium
heat until it is browned and crisp, about 5 minutes.
Drain, saving the bacon fat in a separate basin. Return
2 tablespoons of the fat to the skillet.

Increase the heat to medium-high and sauté the garlic for
30 seconds, or until fragrant. Cook often turns until the
onion is softened, 2 to 3 minutes. Stir in the tomato and
pineapple and cook for 2 minutes, or until heated through.
1 cup bacon grease 1 tablespoon bacon grease 1
tablespoon bacon grease 1 tablespoon bacon grease 1 Stir
in the rice, breaking it up with a spatula so that it is fully
covered with the bacon oil. Cook for approximately 3
minutes. Ketchup, soy sauce, sugar, and white pepper to
taste. Place the rice mixture on one side of the skillet or
wok and pour the beaten eggs on the other. Stir-fry for 2 to
3 minutes, or until the eggs are almost set. Combine eggs
and rice mixture. Fold in the bacon pieces. Cucumber,
green onions, cilantro, lemon wedges, and chili peppers

Sweet Coconut Rice

Prep time: 15 minutes **Cooking time:** 20 minutes
Serve: 1

Ingredients

1 ½ cups long-grain white rice	1 ¼ cups water
	1 tbsp shredded coconut
1 teaspoon white sugar	1 (14 ounces) can of coconut milk

Directions

In a saucepan, bed by the rice. Turn off the heat and
leave the pot on the fire for another 5 to 10 minutes to
allow the rice to simmer until sticky. Garnish with
shredded coconut if desired.

Rice Patties

Prep time: 15 minutes **Cooking time:** 18 minutes
Serve: 1

Ingredients

1 cup cooked rice
1 teaspoon minced garlic
½ small onion, chopped
1 egg, beaten
¼ teaspoon salt

¼ cup shredded Cheddar cheese
¼ teaspoon ground black pepper, or more to taste
¼ tbs chopped fresh parsley

1 tablespoon vegetable oil, or more to taste

Directions

In a mixing bowl, combine rice, onion, Cheddar cheese, egg, garlic, salt, red pepper flakes, black pepper, parsley, and onion powder by hand.

Refrigerate for at least 30 minutes, covered with plastic wrap. Make four tiny patties out of the rice mixture.
In a large skillet over medium-high heat, heat the vegetable oil. Fry patties in heated oil for 5 minutes per side or lightly browned

Brown Rice Pudding

Prep time: 15 minutes **Cooking time:** 25 minutes
Serve: 1

Ingredients

1 ½ cups heavy cream
½ cup short-grain brown rice
½ cup raisins (Optional)
½ teaspoon ground cinnamon
2 teaspoons vanilla extract

1 ¼ cups water
¼ teaspoon salt
3 egg yolks
¼ cup white sugar
1 tablespoon butter, softened

Directions

In a saucepan, bring the heavy cream, water, brown rice, and salt to a boil; decrease the heat to low, cover, and simmer for 80 minutes, or until the liquid is entirely absorbed. Fold the raisins into the mixture and simmer for another 10 minutes, or until the raisins are plump.
In a mixing dish, combine the egg yolks, sugar, and cinnamon; gently pour into the saucepan with the rice

Cherry Wild Rice

Prep time: 15 minutes **Cooking time:** 20 minutes
Serve: 1

Ingredients

2 ½ cups water, divided
¼ cup brown rice,
¼ cup sliced almonds
⅓ cup fresh orange juice
1 cup pitted and sliced cherries

½ cup wild rice
½ cup brown sugar
½ cup sliced celery
2 tablespoons red wine vinegar
1 teaspoon grated orange zest

Directions

In a saucepan, bring 2 cups of water and wild rice to a boil. Reduce the heat to medium-low, cover, and cook for 30 to 45 minutes, or until the rice is soft. Drain excess liquid, fluff rice with a fork, and cook for another 5 minutes, uncovered.

In a saucepan, bring 1/2 cup water and brown rice to a boil. Reduce the heat to medium-low, cover, and simmer for 45 minutes, or until the rice is cooked and the liquid has been absorbed.

In a large nonstick pan, combine cherries, brown sugar, and almonds; cook and stir over medium heat until brown sugar melts and coats cherries and almonds, about 6 minutes. Combine the brown rice, wild rice, celery, orange juice, red wine vinegar, and orange zest in a mixing bowl. Cook, stirring regularly, until well heated, approximately 5 minutes.

The Perfect Egyptian Rice with Vermicelli

Prep time: 20 minutes **Cooking time:** 25 minutes
Serve: 1

Ingredients

1 ½ tablespoon olive oil
1 cup Egyptian rice (short-grain rice)
salt to taste

¼ cup 1/2-inch-long vermicelli
1 ¾ cups water

Directions

In a saucepan over medium heat, heat the oil. Cook, stirring regularly until the vermicelli is golden brown, 3 to 5 minutes. Turn off the heat. Pour in the rice and salt, stirring until evenly covered with oil.

Turn down the heat to low. Cook the rice mixture, stirring regularly, for 3 to 5 minutes, or until the rice turns pasty white. In a saucepan, bring water to a boil.

Incorporate water into the rice mixture. Cook, covered, for 10 to 15 minutes, or until most of the water has been absorbed. Turn off the heat and set it aside for 5 minutes to allow the remaining water to soak. With a fork, fluff the rice.

Baked "Fried" Rice

Prep time: 15 minutes **Cooking time:** 20 minutes
Serve: 1

Ingredients

2 cups long-grain white
rice 2 tablespoons canola
oil
½ cup sliced green onions
3 cloves garlic, crushed
½ cup diced carrots
1 pinch salt to taste
(Optional)
2 teaspoons chili paste

1 tablespoon sesame oil,
or to taste
½ cup diced red bell
peppers
½ cup green peas
3 tablespoons soy sauce
1 cup diced ham
3 cups chicken broth

Directions

Preheat the oven carefully to 400 degrees Fahrenheit
(200 degrees C). In a large baking dish, place the rice.
Drizzle canola and sesame oils over rice and toss to
cover fully. Combine the garlic, green onions, bell
peppers, carrots, peas, and ham in a mixing bowl.
Season with salt and pepper. Stir until everything is
completely blended.

Combine the chicken broth, soy sauce, and chili paste
in a saucepan over high heat. Bring to a boil, stirring
constantly. Pour over the rice and give it a quick swirl.
Wrap the top securely in heavy-duty aluminum foil.
Bake for 32 minutes in a preheated oven. Remove
from the oven and set aside for 10 minutes. Remove
the lid and fluff the rice with a fork. Seasoning should
be tasted and adjusted.

Raise the oven temperature to 475°F (245 degrees C).
Return to the oven for 10 minutes or until the rice is
toasted and crusted.

Mushroom Rice

Prep time: 15 minutes **Cooking time:** 22 minutes
Serve: 1

Ingredients

2 teaspoons butter
1 clove garlic, minced
1 green onion, finely
chopped
½ teaspoon chopped
fresh parsley
salt and pepper to taste

6 mushrooms, coarsely
chopped
1 cup uncooked white rice
2 cups chicken broth

Directions

In a saucepan over medium heat, melt the butter.
Cook the mushrooms, garlic, and green onion until
the liquid has evaporated and the mushrooms are
tender. Combine the chicken broth and rice in a
mixing bowl. Season with parsley, salt, and pepper to
taste. Reduce the heat to low, cover, and leave to
simmer for 20 minutes.

Island-Style Fried Rice

Prep time: 18 minutes **Cooking time:** 20 minutes
Serve: 1

Ingredients

1 ½ cups uncooked
jasmine rice
1 (12 ounces) can fully
cook luncheon meat (such
as SPAM®), cubed

2 tablespoons canola
oil
½ cup chopped green
onion 3 tablespoons oyster
sauce

2 teaspoons canola oil
3 cups water
½ cup sliced Chinese
sweet pork sausage (lap
Cheong)
3 eggs, beaten
1 (8 ounces) can pineapple
chunks, drained
½ teaspoon garlic powder

Directions

In a saucepan over high heat, bring the rice and water
to a boil. Reduce the heat to medium-low, cover, and
cook for 20 to 25 minutes, or until the rice is soft and
the liquid has been absorbed. Allow the rice to cool
fully.

Brown the luncheon meat and sausage in a pan with 2
tablespoons of oil over medium heat. Set aside the
beaten eggs and pour them into the heated skillet. Set
aside the scrambled eggs.

In a large nonstick pan over normal heat, heat 2
tablespoons of oil and toss in the rice. Toss the rice in
the hot oil for approximately 2 minutes, or until
cooked through and beginning to brown. Toss the rice
for 1 minute longer to enhance the garlic flavor, then
add the luncheon meat, sausage, scrambled eggs,
pineapple, and oyster sauce. Cook and stir for 2 to 3
minutes, or until the oyster sauce covers the rice and
other Ingredients. Stir in the green onions and **Serve:**.

Cindy's Yellow Rice

Prep time: 15 minutes **Cooking time:** 25 minutes
Serve: 1

Ingredients

2 cups water
¼ cup dried minced onion
2 tablespoons olive oil

1 teaspoon ground black
pepper

1 cup white rice
1 teaspoon ground
turmeric 1 teaspoon garlic
powder

1 teaspoon salt

Directions

In a saucepan, bring water to a boil. Combine the rice,
onion, olive oil, turmeric, garlic powder, black pepper,
and salt in a mixing bowl. Cover the pot, decrease the
heat to low, and simmer for 20 minutes, or until the
water is absorbed and the rice is tender. With a fork,
fluff the rice.

Sarah's Rice Pilaf

Prep time: 10 minutes **Cooking time:** 18 minutes
Serve: 1

Ingredients

2 tablespoons butter
½ cup diced onion
½ cup uncooked white
rice 2 cups chicken broth

½ cup orzo pasta
2 cloves garlic, minced

Directions

In a covered skillet over medium-low heat, melt the butter. Orzo pasta should be cooked and stirred until golden brown. Sauté until the onion becomes transparent, add the garlic, and cook for 1 minute. Combine the rice and chicken broth in a mixing bowl.

Turn the heat up to high and bring it to a boil. Reduce the heat to medium-low, cover, and cook for 20 to 25 minutes, or until the rice is soft and the liquid has been absorbed. Remove from the heat and set aside for 5 minutes before fluffing with a fork.

Vegan Korean Kimchi Fried Rice

Prep time: 15 minutes **Cooking time:** 25 minutes
Serve: 1

Ingredients

1 tablespoon vegetable oil
1 tablespoon minced garlic
½ cup finely chopped kimchi
1 tablespoon rice wine vinegar
2 tablespoons reduced-sodium soy sauce
½ tablespoon sesame oil
salt to taste

¼ cup diced red onion
1 ½ teaspoon minced ginger (optional)
1 cup day-old cooked white rice
2 tablespoons white sugar
2 tablespoons kimchi brine
ground black pepper to taste

Directions

In a large nonstick skillet over medium heat, heat the oil. Mix in the red onion, garlic, and ginger. Cook, stirring periodically, for 3 minutes, or until the onion softens.

Turn the heat up to high and add the kimchi and vinegar. Cooked rice, soy sauce, sugar, soy sauce, kimchi brine, and sesame oil should all be combined. Cook and stir for 5 minutes, or until heated through; scrape the bottom of the skillet to prevent sticking. Season with salt and pepper to taste.

Garlic Rice

Prep time: 20 minutes **Cooking time:** 20 minutes
Serve: 1

Ingredients

2 tablespoons vegetable oil
2 tsp ground pork
4 cups cooked white rice

1 ½ tablespoons chopped garlic
1 ½ teaspoon garlic salt
ground black pepper to taste

Directions

In a large skillet over medium-high heat, heat the oil. Add the garlic and ground pork after the oil is heated. Cook, constantly stirring until the garlic is golden brown. This is the hue you want for optimum taste; the flavor will be bitter if it burns.

Season with garlic, salt, and pepper and stir in the white rice. Cook and stir for 3 minutes, or until well cooked and well combined. **Serve:** immediately and enjoy.

Cauliflower Rice (Biryani-Style)

Prep time: 15 minutes **Cooking time:** 22 minutes
Serve: 1

Ingredients

1 head cauliflower, broken into florets
1 clove garlic, minced,
½ tbs ground coriander
½ teaspoon ground turmeric
salt and ground black pepper to taste
1 lime, cut into wedges

3 tablespoons butter
1 pinch cayenne pepper
½ teaspoon cumin
½ teaspoon garam masala
¼ teaspoon minced fresh ginger, or to taste
¼ cup chopped fresh cilantro, or to taste

Directions

In a blender or food processor, break cauliflower florets into little pieces the size of rice. Melt the butter in a pan over medium-high heat and add the cauliflower
rice, garlic, cumin, coriander, garam masala, turmeric, ginger, cayenne pepper, salt, and black pepper. Cook, stirring periodically, for approximately 10 minutes, or until cauliflower is softened. Remove the skillet from the heat and stir in the lime wedges and cilantro.

Quinoa Fried Rice

Prep time: 20 minutes **Cooking time:** 25 minutes
Serve: 1

Ingredients

1 ½ cups water
1 ½ tablespoons teriyaki sauce
1 tablespoon olive oil, divided
3 scallions, chopped, divided 3 cloves garlic, minced
½ cup frozen peas

2 ½ tablespoons soy sauce
¾ teaspoon sesame oil
1 cup quinoa salt to taste
¼ onion, chopped
2 carrots, peeled chopped
½ teaspoon minced fresh ginger

2 eggs, beaten

Directions

Bring the quinoa and water to a boil, season with salt. Reduce the heat to medium-low, cover, and cook for 15 to 20 minutes, or until the quinoa is tender and the water is absorbed. Turn off the heat and put aside for 5 minutes before fluffing the quinoa with a fork. Refrigerate for at least 8 hours and up to overnight.

In a mixing bowl, combine soy sauce, teriyaki sauce, and sesame oil until equally combined. Heat 1 1/2 tsp oil and sauté carrots and onion in a large pan over high heat for 2 minutes. Sauté the remaining 2 scallions, garlic, and ginger for 2 minutes, or until aromatic. Cook until heated through, approximately 2 minutes, with the remaining 1 1/2 tablespoons oil and quinoa.

Cook and swirl the sauce into the quinoa mixture for 2 minutes or evenly covered. In the center of the quinoa mixture, make a well. Pour the eggs into the well; heat and stir for 2 to 3 minutes, or until the eggs are scrambled and cooked through. Cook for 2 to 3 minutes, or until peas are cooked through. Stir in the remaining scallions.

Cinnamon Rice

Prep time: 15 minutes **Cooking time:** 18 minutes
Serve: 1

Ingredients

1 cup uncooked rice
2 cups water
2 teaspoons margarine
1 teaspoon sugar

2 tablespoons nonfat milk
5 tablespoons raisins
½ teaspoon ground cinnamon

Directions

In a saucepan over medium-high heat, bring rice, water, milk, raisins, and margarine to a boil, stirring periodically. Reduce the heat to low, cover, and simmer for 15 minutes, or until the liquid has been absorbed and the rice is soft. To **Serve:**, combine cinnamon and sugar and sprinkle over rice.

One-Pot Rice and Beef Pilaf

Prep time: 15 minutes **Cooking time:** 20 minutes
Serve: 1

Ingredients

½ cup olive oil

2 pounds bone-in beef pot roast, boned and cubed
1 onion, peeled, halved, and thinly sliced
2 fresh red chili peppers hot water to cover

2 cups uncooked white rice
4 carrots, peeled and cut into matchsticks
2 teaspoons ground cumin salt to taste
1 head garlic, unpeeled (optional)

Directions

Place the rice in a bowl and cover with warm water to soak while the meat cooks. Heat the olive oil in a saucepan over medium-high heat and sauté the bones for 5 minutes, or until gently browned.

Place the bones on a platter. Cook until the onion is tender and translucent, about 5 minutes, in the same saucepan. Brown the meat on both sides, 5 to 10 minutes. Return the bones to the pan and add the carrots. Garnish with cumin. Stir in the entire chili peppers and garlic, then season with salt. Fill the container halfway with boiling water. Bring to a boil, then lower to low heat and continue to cook for 35 to 40 minutes, or until the flavors are fully integrated.

With kitchen tongs, remove the bones and add the rice. Pour in 2 cups hot water and level out the rice to sit flat on top, but do not stir. Cook, covered, over low heat for 20 to 25 minutes, or until tender rice. Before serving, mix everything.

Classic Fried Rice

Prep time: 18 minutes **Cooking time:** 20 minutes
Serve: 1

Ingredients

6 strips bacon, cut into 1/2-inch pieces
1 egg, beaten
1 tablespoon minced garlic

8 green onions and tops, sliced
4 cups cold, cooked rice
3 tablespoons Kikkoman Soy Sauce

Directions

In a large pan over medium heat, cook bacon until crisp. Transfer the bacon to the side of the pan; add the egg and scramble it. Move the egg to the skillet, add the green onions, cook for approximately a minute. Next, stir in the rice, followed by the garlic and soy sauce. Toss until the mixture is properly combined and thoroughly cooked.

Morel Mushroom and Wild Rice Risotto

Prep time: 10 minutes **Cooking time:** 18 minutes
Serve: 1

Ingredients

6 cups chicken broth
¼ cup heavy cream
2 stalks celery, diced
1 onion, diced
2 tablespoons unsalted butter
½ pound fresh morel mushrooms
salt and ground black pepper to taste

1 teaspoon dried thyme
2 carrots, diced
2 tablespoons olive oil
3 cups water
1 cup wild rice
1 cup brown rice
½ cup dry white wine
2 cloves garlic, minced

Directions

In a large stockpot, combine chicken broth and water. Bring to a boil over medium-high heat; lower to low heat and keep warm.

Heat 1 tablespoon butter and 1 tablespoon olive oil over medium heat until the butter melts in a large Dutch oven. Cook, stirring regularly, until the brown rice is toasted, about 5 minutes. Stir in the wild rice, carrots, celery, onion, and garlic, as well as half of the morel mushrooms. Cook, stirring regularly, for 3 to 5 minutes, or until onions are transparent. Pour in the white wine and heat for 2 to 3 minutes, or until it has evaporated.

1/2 of the chicken broth mixture should be mixed into the rice; toss to incorporate. Cook, covered, over medium heat for 30 minutes, stirring every 5 minutes, until thickened. Pour in the rest of the chicken broth mixture, morel mushrooms, and thyme. Cook, covered, over medium heat for 30 to 40 minutes, stirring every 5 minutes, until wild rice is soft.

Combine the remaining 1 tablespoon butter and heavy cream in a mixing bowl. Cook for 1 minute more, or until the butter has melted. Season with salt and pepper to taste. **Serve:** with Pecorino Romano cheese on top.

Parmesan Asparagus Rice

Prep time: 15 minutes **Cooking time:** 25 minutes
Serve: 1

Ingredients

1 cup UNCLE BEN'S®
Basmati Rice - cooks in 10 minutes
3 tablespoons butter, divided
1 pinch salt and ground black pepper

1 small, sweet onion, diced
1 clove garlic, minced
2 cups vegetable stock
2 tablespoons freshly grated Parmesan cheese
1 cup chopped fresh asparagus

Directions

In a 3-quart saucepan over medium heat, melt 2 tablespoons of butter. Cook and stir onion for 1 minute or until softened and translucent. Cook for another minute after adding the garlic. Combine the rice, asparagus, and stock in a mixing bowl. Reduce the heat to medium-low and cover.

Stir the rice occasionally to keep it from sticking to the bottom of the pan. Cook for another 10 minutes, or until
the rice is soft.

Remove from the heat and whisk in the Parmesan cheese and remaining butter. **Serve:** right away.

Easy Oven Brown Rice

Prep time: 20 minutes **Cooking time:** 20 minutes
Serve: 1

Ingredients

1 ½ cups brown rice
2 tablespoons butter

1 teaspoon salt
3 cups boiling water

Directions

Preheat the oven carefully to 400°F (200 degrees C). Combine the rice, salt, and butter in a casserole dish with a lid. Pour boiling water over the rice and toss to combine.

Cover and bake in a preheated oven for 1 hour, or until liquid is absorbed and rice is soft. Remove from the oven, fluff with a fork, and **Serve:** immediately.

Yellow Rice with Meat

Prep time: 15 minutes **Cooking time:** 25 minutes
Serve: 1

Ingredients

1 tablespoon olive oil
2 pork chops
1 onion, diced
2 green bell peppers
4 sprigs of fresh thyme
2 teaspoons cloves
1 (10 ounces) package
yellow rice
1 lemon, cut into wedges
chili sauce

2 boneless, skinless
chicken thighs
2 cloves garlic, finely
chopped
3 bay leaves
1 sprig of fresh rosemary
1 cup peas
1 fresh jalapeno pepper
diced

Directions

In a skillet over medium heat, heat the olive oil. Cook until the pork chops and chicken thighs are browned on both sides, the chicken juices run clear, and the pork chops are done. Set aside after removing from skillet.

Cook until the bell peppers are cooked in the pan, then put aside. Mix in the onion and garlic. Combine rosemary, thyme, cloves, and bay leaves in a mixing bowl. Add rice to the pan, along with the amount of water specified on the rice bag. Cook for another 10 minutes.

Combine the pork chops, chicken, rice, peppers, and peas in a pan. Cook for another 10 minutes, or until the rice is soft. Remove the rosemary, thyme, and bay leaves. To **Serve:**, pour lemon juice over the meats and rice, then top with chopped jalapeño and chili sauce.

Perfect White Rice

Prep time: 15 minutes **Cooking time:** 20 minutes
Serve: 1

Ingredients

2 teaspoons unsalted
butter
2 cups water
½ teaspoon salt

1 cup uncooked long-grain
white rice

Directions

In a medium saucepan over medium heat, melt the butter. Stir in the rice to coat it. Cook for 1 to 2 minutes, or until the rice grains become opaque; do not brown. Pour in the water and salt.

Bring to a boil, then lower to low heat. Allow boiling for 15 minutes, covered. Do not remove the cover. Remove from the heat and set aside for 5 minutes, covered. Before serving, fluff with a fork.

Jeera Rice

Prep time: 20 minutes **Cooking time:** 25 minutes
Serve: 1

Ingredients

1 cup basmati rice
4 whole cloves
4 whole black peppercorns
1 ½ cups water salt to
taste

2 teaspoons vegetable oil
1 teaspoon cumin seeds
1 bay leaf
2 cardamom pods

Directions

Rinse rice three to four times before placing it in a bowl; cover with water and soak for at least 30 minutes.
Cook and swirl cumin in a pan over medium heat until it begins to pop, 2 to 4 minutes. Cook and stir for 1 1/2 minutes, or until the cloves, peppercorns, cardamom pods, and bay leaf are aromatic.

Drain the rice and combine with spice mixture; add 1 1/2 cups water and salt to taste. Cook for 5 minutes, covered, over high heat. Reduce the heat to medium and cook for another 10 minutes. Reduce the heat to low and continue to cook for 15 minutes. Remove skillet from heat and set aside for 15 minutes with the lid on.

Remove the lid and fluff the rice with a fork. Remove the bay leaf, cardamom pods, cloves, and peppercorns from the mixture.

South Indian-Style Lemon Rice

Prep time: 15 minutes **Cooking time:** 20 minutes
Serve: 1

Ingredients

4 cups water

¼ cup raw peanuts
6 tablespoons vegetable oil
½ teaspoon mustard
seeds
¼ cup lemon juice
1 ½ teaspoons salt

2 cups uncooked white
rice
½ teaspoon ground
turmeric
4 green chili peppers,
chopped
15 fresh curry leaves
(Optional)

Directions

Bring water and rice to a boil in a saucepan. Reduce to medium-low heat, cover, and simmer for 20 to 25 minutes, or until the rice is mushy and the water has been absorbed.

In a large skillet over medium heat, heat the oil. Cook and stir the peanuts, turmeric, and mustard seeds for 2 to 3 minutes, or until the peanuts are browned.

Combine the green chili peppers, lemon juice, curry leaves, and salt in a mixing bowl. Fold the cooked rice into the lemon juice mixture.

Cajun Wild Rice

Prep time: 15 minutes **Cooking time:** 18 minutes
Serve: 1

Ingredients

1 cup uncooked wild rice	1 (14 ounces) can of
1 tablespoon minced garlic	chicken broth
¼ cup water	½ pound andouille
mushroom soup	sausage
½ cup diced sweet onion	1 cup chopped fresh
1 (10.75 ounces) can	mushrooms
condense cream of	
mushroom soup	

Directions

Combine the wild rice, chicken broth, water, sausage, onion, mushrooms, and garlic in a saucepan. Bring to a boil, lower to low heat, cover, and leave to cook for 25 to 30 minutes, or until the rice is tender.

Next, take the pan off the heat and whisk in the cream of mushroom soup. It's just that simple!

Delicate Jasmine Rice

Prep time: 18 minutes **Cooking time:** 20 minutes
Serve: 1

Ingredients

3 cups water	1 jasmine herbal tea bag
1 ½ cups uncooked brown	2 tablespoons chopped
rice	fresh cilantro
1 tablespoon butter	1 cube vegetable bouillon

Directions

In a large saucepan, bring 3 cups of water and the tea bag to a boil. Take the teabag out of the boiling water. Return the flavored water to a boil after stirring the rice and bouillon cube. Reduce heat carefully to low and cover the pan.

Allow rice to steam for 45 minutes or until the water has been absorbed and the rice is soft. Remove from the heat and set aside for 5 minutes. With a fork, fluff the cooked rice and whisk in the butter. Garnish the rice with chopped cilantro.

Linnie's Spanish Rice

Prep time: 15 minutes **Cooking time:** 22 minutes
Serve: 1

Ingredients

1 cup uncooked white rice	1 teaspoon minced garlic
1 (16 ounces) jar salsa	2 cups water

Directions

In a large pot, combine the rice and garlic. Pour the rice mixture with the water and salsa.

Bring the water to a full boil before lowering the heat to a simmer. Cook, occasionally stirring, for 20 minutes, or until the rice is tender. When the rice is done, fluff it with a fork.

Kheer (Rice Pudding)

Prep time: 10 minutes **Cooking time:** 18 minutes
Serve: 1

Ingredients

2 cups coconut milk	3 tablespoons white sugar
½ cup Basmati rice	¼ cup raisins
½ teaspoon ground	½ teaspoon rose water
cardamom	(Optional)
¼ cup sliced almonds,	¼ cup chopped pistachio
toasted	nuts
2 cups milk	

Directions

In a large saucepan, bring the coconut milk, milk, and sugar to a boil. Cook, occasionally stirring, until the stew thickens, and the rice is cooked for about 20 minutes. Cook for a few minutes more after adding the raisins, cardamom, and rose water. Garnish with almonds and pistachios before ladling into serving dishes

Whole Grain Pancakes

Prep time: 20 minutes **Cooking time:** 25 minutes
Serve: 1

Ingredients

1 cup whole wheat flour	½ cup rolled oats
¼ cup cornmeal	3 tablespoons flaxseed
1 teaspoon baking powder	meal
½ teaspoon baking soda	2 cups buttermilk
1 egg, beaten	cooking spray
3 tablespoons brown sugar	

Directions

Combine the whole wheat flour, oats, cornmeal, flaxseed meal, brown sugar, baking powder, and baking soda in a large mixing basin. Pour in the buttermilk and the egg. Only stir until smooth. Melt butter in a large pan or skillet over medium heat. Coat with nonstick cooking spray. Drop batter onto the griddle in large spoonsful and heat

Chicken and Multi-Grain Stir Fry

Prep time: 20 minutes **Cooking time:** 20 minutes
Serve: 1

Ingredients

1 bag Minute® Multi-Grain Medley, uncooked
½ teaspoon sesame oil
2 cloves garlic, chopped
½ cup snap peas
½ cup broccoli florets
½ cup red bell pepper, sliced
2 cups cooked chicken, shredded

2 large eggs, lightly beaten
1 cup chicken broth
2 tablespoons olive oil, divided
½ cup red onion, thinly sliced
½ teaspoon Chinese five-spice powder (Optional)

Directions

Make Multi-Grain Medley according to package directions
but use broth instead of water. Whisk together the eggs and sesame oil in a small bowl.

12 tbsp olive oil, heated in a large pan at medium-low heat Soft scrambled eggs in a hurry. Remove from skillet and set aside to stay heated. Heat the remaining olive oil in a medium saucepan over medium heat. Sauté for 3 minutes with the garlic, onions, peas, broccoli, bell peppers, and five-spice powder.

Cook for 2 minutes more, or until the chicken, Multi-Grain Medley, and eggs are crisp-tender.

Spent Grain Wheat Bread

Prep time: 15 minutes **Cooking time:** 25 minutes
Serve: 1

Ingredients

1 ¼ cups water
3 tablespoons butter, softened
1 ½ tbsp powdered milk
½ cup rye flour

1 ½ cups bread flour
1 teaspoon active dry yeast

3 tablespoons honey
¼ cup spent grain
1 teaspoon white sugar
1 teaspoon salt
1 ½ cups whole wheat flour
¼ cup vital wheat gluten

Directions

Place the Ingredients in the bread machine's pan in the sequence indicated by the manufacturer. Choose the complete wheat cycle and hit the Start button. Reduce the water by 1 tablespoon if using the delay timer.

Cranberry Pecan Multi-Grain Stuffing

Prep time: 15 minutes **Cooking time:** 25 minutes
Serve: 1

Ingredients

1 tablespoon olive oil
¼ cup chopped celery
½ cup dried cranberries
1 cup chicken broth
½ cup chopped pecans, toasted

½ cup chopped onion
¼ tbs poultry seasoning
1 bag Minute® Multi-Grain Medley, uncooked
1 pinch salt and ground black pepper

Directions

In a medium saucepan, heat the oil over medium heat. Cook for 2 minutes after adding the onion and celery. Combine the chicken seasoning, cranberries, and broth in a mixing bowl. Bring to a boil, then add the Multi-Grain Medley. Cover, decrease the heat to low and cook for 5 minutes. Remove from the heat and set aside for 5 minutes. Season with salt and pepper, if preferred, and stir in the pecans.

Whole Grain Pancakes with Fresh Fruit

Prep time: 15 minutes **Cooking time:** 20 minutes
Serve: 1

Ingredients

1 cup whole wheat flour
1 tablespoon Reddi-wip®
2 tablespoons firmly packed brown sugar
½ teaspoon salt
½ cup Egg Beaters® Original
½ teaspoon vanilla extract
¼ cup honey
No-Stick Cooking Spray
½ cup fresh blueberries
Canola Oil

¼ cup quick cooking rolled oats
1 ½ teaspoons baking powder
¾ cup fat-free milk
¼ cup plain nonfat yogurt
1 tbsp Pure Wesson® PAM® Organic Canola Oil
2 medium bananas, peeled and sliced
Fat-Free Dairy Whipped Topping

Directions

In a large mixing basin, combine the flour, oats, sugar, baking powder, and salt; set aside. Next, combine the milk, Egg Beaters, yogurt, oil, and vanilla extract in a small mixing bowl. Add to the flour mixture and whisk just until combined. (Avoid overmixing.) The batter should still be a little lumpy.)

Coat the skillet with frying spray. Heat over medium heat until hot, or preheat an electric skillet to 400°F. For each pancake, pour roughly 1/4 cup batter onto a heated griddle. Cook for 2 to 3 minutes, or until bubbles appear on the surface and the bottom is golden brown. Cook until golden brown on the other side. Rep with the remaining batter. Drizzle 1 tablespoon honey over each serving and top with fresh fruit. **Serve:** right away.

Rustic Grain Cereal

Prep time: 15 minutes **Cooking time:** 22 minutes
Serve: 1

Ingredients

½ cup water	⅓ cup wheat berries
1 cup steel-cut oats	⅓ cup chopped pecans
⅓ cup slivered almonds	1 cup chopped dried
3 cups boiling water	apples
⅓ cup white sugar, or to	1 ½ tablespoon ground
taste	cinnamon
1 teaspoon butter	1 teaspoon salt

Directions

In a small saucepan, combine 1/2 cup water and the wheat berries; bring to a boil. Cover saucepan, remove from heat and leave aside for 10 minutes to allow wheat berries to soak.

Melt butter in a 2-quart saucepan over low heat; cook and stir oats, pecans, and almonds in melted butter for 5 minutes, or until brown and aromatic. Pour boiling water into the nut mixture, add the wheat berries and dried apples. Cook, covered, over low heat for 25 minutes, or until wheat berries are soft; mix in sugar, cinnamon, and salt.

Grain and Nut Whole Wheat Pancakes

Prep time: 15 minutes **Cooking time:** 18 minutes
Serve: 1

Ingredients

1 ½ cups old-fashioned	1 ½ cups whole wheat
oatmeal	flour 2 teaspoons baking
	soda
1 teaspoon baking powder	½ teaspoon salt
1 ½ cups buttermilk	¼ cup vegetable oil
1 cup milk	1 egg
⅓ cup sugar	3 tbs chopped walnuts

Directions

In a blender or food processor, grind the oats until fine. Combine ground oats, whole wheat flour, baking soda, baking powder, and salt in a large mixing basin. In a separate dish, whisk together the buttermilk, milk, oil, egg, and sugar with an electric mixer until smooth. Then, combine the wet and dry components with a few quick strokes. If using nuts, toss them in at the end.

Easter Grain Pie

Prep time: 15 minutes **Cooking time:** 20 minutes
Serve: 1

Ingredients

5 cups water	½ cup whole wheat berries
1 cup white sugar	1 (8 ounces) package
6 eggs	mixed candied fruit
1 ½ pound ricotta cheese	½ teaspoon ground
1 teaspoon vanilla extract	cinnamon
2 teaspoons grated orange	1 tbs grated lemon zest
zest	2 tbs confectioners' sugar
1 teaspoon salt	2 pastries for 9-inch
1 tablespoon shortening	lattice-top pies

Directions

In a big saucepan, bring water to a boil. Allow wheat to boiling for 40 minutes. While the wheat is cooking, beat the eggs in a large mixing basin while gradually adding 1 cup sugar.

Combine the fruit, ricotta, vanilla essence, cinnamon, lemon rind, and orange rind in a mixing bowl. When the wheat is done, strain it in a strainer and rinse it with warm water. Combine 3/4 cup cooked wheat, shortening, and salt in a small bowl. Stir until the shortening is melted, then fold in the wheat mixture and the remaining cooked wheat berries.

Preheat the oven carefully to 375°F (190 degrees C). Fill two 9-inch pie tins halfway with pastry. Cut the leftover pastry into strips for the pies' tops. Half of the filling should be placed in each pan. To make lattice tops, cover with pastry strips. Crimp the edges.

Bake for 45 minutes, or until the crust is golden brown, in a preheated oven. Allow each pie to cool at room temperature before sprinkling with 1 tablespoon sugar. Allow chilling overnight before serving. Any leftovers should be refrigerated.

Whole Grain Carrot Peach Muffins

Prep time: 10 minutes **Cooking time:** 18 minutes
Serve: 1

Ingredients

2 tablespoons butter, slightly softened
1 tablespoon dark brown sugar
½ cup all-purpose flour
1 tbsp ground cinnamon
½ cup oat flour
½ teaspoon baking soda
½ cup white sugar
2 large eggs
1 cup grated carrots
¼ cup rolled oats
1 tbsp all-purpose flour
¼ teaspoon ground cinnamon
½ cup white whole-wheat flour
1 ½ tbsp baking powder
½ cup canola oil
1 teaspoon vanilla extract
1 ½ cups diced peaches

Directions

Preheat the oven carefully to 350°F (175 degrees C). Prepare a muffin tin by lining it with paper liners. Combine the butter, rolled oats, dark brown sugar, 1 tablespoon all- purpose flour, and 1/4 teaspoon cinnamon in a mixing dish. Mix with a fork or your fingertips until the mixture is crumbly.

In a large mixing bowl, combine 1/2 cup all-purpose flour, white whole-wheat flour, oat flour, baking powder, 1 teaspoon cinnamon, and baking soda.

Combine the oil, sugar, eggs, and vanilla essence in a separate dish. Pour into the flour mixture and fold until barely mixed. Next, gently fold in the peaches and carrots.
Fill prepared muffin tins about 2/3 full of batter. Garnish with oat topping.

Bake for 15 minutes, or until a toothpick inserted into the center comes out clean. Cool for 5 to 10 minutes in the pan before transferring muffins to a wire rack to cool fully.

Zucchini Banana Multi-Grain Bread

Prep time: 18 minutes **Cooking time:** 20 minutes
Serve: 1

Ingredients

1 bag Minute® Multi-Grain Medley, uncooked
1 teaspoon vanilla extract
½ cup sugar
3 tablespoons vegetable oil, ¼ cup milk
½ cup walnuts, chopped
3 large eggs, lightly beaten
1 serving Nonstick cooking spray
1 ripe banana, mashed
1 medium zucchini, grated
2 cups baking mix

Directions

Preheat the oven carefully to 400°F. Follow the package directions to make the Multi-Grain Medley. Using nonstick cooking spray, coat a loaf pan.

In a large mixing basin, combine the eggs, sugar, and banana. Stir I the rice, oil, milk, vanilla, zucchini (approximately 1 1/2 cups shredded), and walnuts. Stir in the baking mix until all of the Ingredients are mixed. Pour the mixture into the prepared pan.

45 minutes in the oven, or until a toothpick inserted into the middle comes out clean. Allow to cool for 10 minutes before removing from pan and cooling on a rack.

Special Events

Flavorful Chicken Skewers

Prep time: 10 minutes **Cooking time:** 20 minutes
Serve: 4

Ingredients

1 1/2 lbs. chicken breast, cut into 1-inch cubes	For marinade
2 tbsp dried oregano	1/2 cup low-fat yogurt
2 tbsp fresh rosemary, chopped	1 tbsp red wine vinegar
1/2 cup lemon juice	1 cup olive oil
1/4 tsp cayenne Pepper	4 garlic cloves
	Salt
	1/4 cup fresh mint leaves

Directions

Add all marinade Ingredients into the blender and blend until smooth. Pour marinade into a mixing bowl.
Add chicken and coat well, cover and place in the refrigerator for 1 hour.

Thread marinated chicken onto the soaked wooden skewers. Place chicken skewers into the air fryer basket and cook at 400 F for 15-20 minutes. **Serve:** and enjoy.

Turkey Meatballs

Prep time: 10 minutes **Cooking time:** 18 minutes
Serve: 6

Ingredients

1 lb. ground turkey	1 tbsp dried onion flakes
1 tbsp garlic, minced	2 eggs, lightly beaten
1 tsp cumin	1/3 cup almond flour
2 cups zucchini, grated	1 tbsp basil, chopped
1 tsp dried oregano	Pepper
Salt	

Directions

Preheat the air fryer to 400 F. Add turkey and remaining Ingredients into the mixing bowl and mix until well combined.

Make small balls from the turkey mixture and place into the air fryer basket and cook for 15-18 minutes. Turn halfway through. **Serve:** and enjoy.

Tandoori Chicken Drumsticks

Prep time: 10 minutes **Cooking time:** 15 minutes
Serve: 4

Ingredients

4 chicken drumsticks	For marinade
1/2 tsp garam masala	1 tsp chili powder
1/2 tsp turmeric	1 tbsp fresh lime juice
1 tbsp ginger garlic paste	1 tsp salt
1/4 cup yogurt	1 tsp ground cumin

Directions

Preheat the air fryer to 360 F. In a mixing bowl, add marinade Ingredients and mix until well combined.

Add chicken in marinade and mix until well coated. Cover and place in the refrigerator for overnight. Place marinated chicken drumsticks into the air fryer basket and cook for 15 minutes. Turn halfway through. **Serve:** and enjoy.

Chicken Burger Patties

Prep time: 10 minutes **Cooking time:** 18 minutes
Serve: 4

Ingredients

1 lb. ground chicken	2 oz mozzarella cheese, shredded
3 oz almond flour	
1 tbsp oregano Pepper	Salt

Directions

Preheat the air fryer to 360 F. Add chicken and remaining Ingredients into the mixin bowl and mix until well combined. Make four patties from the chicken mixture.
Place chicken patties into the air fryer basket and cook for 18 minutes. Turn halfway through. **Serve:** and enjoy.

Flavorful Stew Meat

Prep time: 10 minutes **Cooking time:** 25 minutes
Serve: 4

Ingredients

1 lb. beef stew meat, cut into strips	1/2 tsp onion powder
1 tbsp garlic powder	1/2 fresh lime juice
1/2 tbsp ground cumin	1 tbsp olive oil
Salt	Pepper

Directions

Preheat the air fryer to 380 F. Add stew meat and remaining Ingredients into the mixing bowl and mix well.
Add stew meat into the air fryer basket and cook for 25 minutes. Stir halfway through **Serve:** and enjoy.

Cheesy Lamb Patties

Prep time: 10 minutes **Cooking time:** 8 minutes **Serve:** 4

Ingredients

1 lb. ground lamb	1/4 cup mint leaves, minced 1/4 cup fresh parsley, chopped
1 tsp dried oregano	
1/2 tsp kosher salt	
1 cup goat cheese, crumbled 1 tbsp garlic, minced	8 basil leaves, minced
1/4 tsp pepper	1 tsp chili powder

Directions

Preheat the air fryer to 400 F. Add ground lamb and remaining Ingredients into the mixing bowl and mix until well combined. Make four equal shape patties from the lamb mixture. Place patties into the air fryer basket and cook for 8 minutes. Turn halfway through. **Serve:** and enjoy.

Chipotle Rib-eye Steak

Prep time: 10 minutes **Cooking time:** 10 minutes
Serve: 3

Ingredients

1 lb. rib-eye steak	1/2 tsp coffee powder
1/8 tsp cocoa powder	1/4 tsp onion powder
1/8 tsp coriander powder	1/4 tsp garlic powder
1/4 tsp chipotle powder	Pepper
1/4 tsp paprika	1/4 tsp chili powder
Salt	

Directions

Preheat the air fryer to 390 F. In a small bowl, mix together all Ingredients except steak. Rub spice mixture all over the steak and allow to sit steak for 30 minutes.
Place steak into the air fryer basket and cook for 10 minutes. Turn halfway through. **Serve:** and enjoy.

Yogurt Beef Kebabs

Prep time: 10 minutes **Cooking time:** 15 minutes
Serve: 8

Ingredients

1 1/2 lbs. beef, cut into 1-inch pieces	1/4 cup Greek yogurt
1 onion, cut into chunks	1 tsp garlic, minced
pepper	Salt
	2 bell pepper, cut into chunks

Directions

Preheat the air fryer to 350 F. Add meat and remaining Ingredients into the mixing bowl and mix well. Cover and place in refrigerator for 30 minutes. Thread marinated beef pieces, bell pepper, and onion pieces onto the skewers.
Place meat skewers into the air fryer basket and cook for 15 minutes. Turn halfway through. **Serve:** and enjoy.

Amazing Buttermilk Air Fried Chicken

Prep time: 15 minutes **Cooking time:** 25 minutes
Serve: 1

Ingredients

1 cup buttermilk	½ teaspoon hot sauce
⅓ cup tapioca flour	½ teaspoon garlic salt
⅛ teaspoon ground black pepper	½ cup all-purpose flour
	2 teaspoons salt
1 ½ teaspoons brown sugar	½ teaspoon paprika
	1 egg
1 teaspoon garlic powder	
½ teaspoon onion powder	¼ teaspoon oregano
¼ teaspoon black pepper	1-pound skinless, boneless chicken thighs

Directions

Add buttermilk and spicy sauce; stir to blend. Shake together tapioca flour, garlic salt, and 1/8 teaspoon black pepper in a resealable plastic bag. In a small dish, beat the egg. In a gallon-sized resealable bag, add flour, salt, brown sugar, garlic powder, paprika, onion powder, oregano, and 1/4 teaspoon black pepper.

Dip the chicken thighs in the following order buttermilk mixture, tapioca mixture, egg mixture, and flour mixture, brushing off the excess after each dipping. Preheat an air fryer carefully to 380°F (190 degrees C). Then, using parchment paper, line the air fryer basket. Fry the coated chicken thighs in batches for 10 minutes in the air fryer basket.

Asian Pork Chops

Prep time: 10 minutes **Cooking time:** 12 minutes
Serve: 2

Ingredients

2 pork chops, boneless	1 tbsp sesame oil
3 tbsp lemongrass, chopped	1 tbsp garlic, chopped
1 tsp soy sauce	1 tbsp fish sauce
1 tbsp shallot, chopped	1 tsp liquid stevia

Directions

Preheat the air fryer to 400 F. Add pork chops and remaining Ingredients into the mixing bowl and mix well. Cover and place in refrigerator for 2 hours.

Place marinated pork chops into the air fryer basket and cook for 12 minutes. Turn halfway through. **Serve:** and enjoy.

Air-Fried Sweet and Sour Chicken Wings

Prep time: 20 minutes **Cooking time:** 20 minutes
Serve: 1

Ingredients

2 pounds party chicken wings	1 tablespoon extra-virgin olive oil
½ teaspoon salt	¾ cup white sugar
⅔ cup distilled white vinegar	⅓ cup water
2 tablespoons reduced-sodium soy sauce	1 tablespoon ketchup
	2 tablespoons cornstarch

Directions

Preheat the air fryer carefully to 380°F (190 degrees C).
Place the wings in a large mixing basin. Drizzle the oil over the top, then sprinkle with the salt and mix until evenly blended. Place half of the wings, skin side down, in the air fryer basket.

10 minutes in the air fryer. Cook for 10 minutes longer after flipping the wings with tongs. Raise the temperature to 400°F (200 degrees C). Cook until the wings are crispy on the other side, about 5 minutes more. Rep with the remaining wings.

Meanwhile, add sugar, vinegar, water, soy sauce, cornstarch, and ketchup in a saucepan over medium-high heat. For 3 to 5 minutes, whisk until sauce has thickened. Turn off the heat and set it aside to cool somewhat.
Place the wings in a large mixing basin. Pour the sauce over the top, mix to coat, and **Serve:** right away.

Cheese Balls

Prep time: 10 minutes **Cooking time:** 12 minutes
Serve: 8

Ingredients

2 eggs	1/2 cup almond flour
1/4 cup parmesan cheese, shredded	1/2 cup cheddar cheese, shredded Pepper
1/2 tsp baking powder Salt	1/4 cup mozzarella cheese, shredded

Directions

Preheat the air fryer to 400 F. In a mixing bowl, whisk eggs. Add almond flour, parmesan cheese, mozzarella cheese, baking powder, cheddar cheese, pepper, and salt and mix until well combined. Make 8 equal shapes of balls from the cheese mixture and place into the air fryer basket and cook for 12 minutes. **Serve:** and enjoy.

Crumbed Chicken Tenderloins

Prep time: 15 minutes **Cooking time:** 25 minutes
Serve: 1

Ingredients

1 egg	½ cup dry breadcrumbs
2 tablespoons vegetable oil	8 chicken tenderloins

Directions

Preheat an air fryer carefully to 350°F (175 degrees C). In a small bowl, whisk the egg. Combine breadcrumbs and oil in a separate dish until the mixture is loose and crumbly. Dip each chicken tenderloin into the egg, then shake off any excess.

Dip the chicken into the crumb mixture, coating it evenly and completely. Place the chicken tenderloins in the air fryer basket. Cook until the center is no longer pink, approximately 12 minutes. In the middle, an instant-read thermometer should read at least 162 degrees F. (74 degrees C).

Air-Fried Peruvian Chicken Drumsticks with Green Crema

Prep time: 15 minutes **Cooking time:** 20 minutes **Serve:** 1

Ingredients

olive oil for brushing
2 cloves garlic, grated
1 teaspoon ground cumin
1 tablespoon honey
½ teaspoon dried oregano
6 (4 ounces) chicken drumsticks
1 cup baby spinach leaves, stems removed
¼ cup cilantro leaves
½ jalapeno pepper, seeded

1 tablespoon olive oil
1 teaspoon salt
½ teaspoon smoked paprika
¼ teaspoon ground black pepper
1 clove garlic, smashed
¾ cup sour cream
2 tbsp fresh lime juice
¼ tbsp ground black pepper
¼ teaspoon salt

Directions

Brush olive oil into an air fryer basket. In a large mixing bowl, combine garlic, honey, 1 tablespoon olive oil, salt, cumin, paprika, oregano, and pepper. Toss in the drumsticks to coat. Arrange the drumsticks in the prepared basket vertically, resting against the basket wall and one another.

Cook in the air fryer at 400 degrees F (200 degrees C) for 15 to 20 minutes, or until an instant-read thermometer placed into the thickest section of the drumstick registers 175 degrees F (80 degrees C). To ensure consistent cooking, rearrange the drumsticks using kitchen tongs halfway through.

Meanwhile, mix spinach, sour cream, cilantro, lime juice, garlic, jalapeño pepper, salt, and pepper; process until crème is smooth. Drizzle some cream sauce over the drumsticks and **Serve:** the rest of the crema.

Grandma Egan's Chicken Stock

Prep time: 18 minutes **Cooking time:** 20 minutes **Serve:** 1

Ingredients

1 (8 pounds) chicken

3 stalks celery, chopped
1 onion, quartered

Directions

In a large stockpot, combine the chicken, celery, and onion. Fill the container halfway with water. Bring the water to a boil.

Remove any extra fat. Reduce the heat to a simmer and cook for 2 to 3 hours. Take out the chicken and veggies. Using a cheesecloth, strain the soup.

Dry-Rub Air-Fried Chicken Wings

Prep time: 20 minutes **Cooking time:** 25 minutes **Serve:** 1

Ingredients

1 tbs dark brown sugar
1 tablespoon sweet paprika
½ tbs ground black pepper
1 tbs poultry seasoning

½ tablespoon kosher salt
1 teaspoon garlic powder
1 teaspoon onion powder

½ tbs mustard powder
8 chicken wings, or more as needed

Directions

Preheat the air fryer carefully to 350°F (175 degrees C).
In a large mixing bowl, combine brown sugar, paprika, salt, garlic powder, onion powder, poultry seasoning, mustard powder, and pepper. Toss in the chicken wings and work the spices into them with your hands until they are well covered.

Arrange the wings in the preheated air fryer basket, standing up on their ends and resting against each other and the basket wall. Cook for 35 minutes, or until the wings are soft on the inside and golden brown and crisp on the exterior. Place the wings on a dish and **Serve:** immediately.

Mustard Fried Chicken

Prep time: 15 minutes **Cooking time:** 20 minutes **Serve:** 1

Ingredients

5 pounds chicken wings, separated at joints, tips discarded
2 tablespoons garlic powder
2 tablespoons onion powder
1-quart oil for frying, or as needed

2 tablespoons ground black pepper
1 tablespoon seasoned salt
3 tablespoons prepared yellow mustard

3 cups all-purpose flour

Directions

Season both sides of the chicken wings with seasoned salt, garlic powder, onion powder, pepper, and MSG. I prefer to spread everything out on a large plastic bag for simpler cleanup. Apply a little coating of mustard on each slice. You may use a basting brush or your fingers to apply the sauce. Fill a plastic bag halfway with flour, add the chicken, and shake to coat.
Heat the oil in a deep-fryer or heavy skillet to 350°F (175 degrees C). Cook the chicken for 6 minutes on each side, or until the juices run clear after the oil is heated. Cool for 5 minutes on paper towels before serving.

Garlic and Parmesan Chicken Wings

Prep time: 15 minutes **Cooking time:** 22 minutes
Serve: 1

Ingredients

cooking spray
⅓ cup balsamic vinegar
1 teaspoon dried thyme
1 teaspoon dried oregano
1 pinch salt
1 bay leaf
1 tablespoon freshly ground black pepper
2 tbs red pepper flakes
1 cup finely grated cheese, divided

3 quarts cold water
¼ cup salt
1 teaspoon dried rosemary
8 cloves garlic, minced
3 tablespoons olive oil, or as needed
4 pounds chicken wings, separated at joints, tips discarded
2 tbsp fine breadcrumbs

Directions

Preheat the oven to 450°F (230 degrees C). Line a baking sheet with foil and spray with cooking spray. Bring water, vinegar, 1/4 cup salt, bay leaf, thyme, oregano, and rosemary to a boil in a large stockpot. Return to a boil and cook the chicken wings for 15 minutes. Transfer the chicken wings to a cooling rack and set aside for 15 minutes to dry.

In a mortar and pestle, mash garlic with a pinch of salt until smooth. Combine the mashed garlic, olive oil, black pepper, and red pepper flakes in a large mixing bowl. Toss in the chicken wings and breadcrumbs to coat. Add 1/2 cup Parmigiano-Reggiano cheese on top. Sprinkle with the remaining 1/2 cup Parmigiano-Reggiano cheese and place on the prepared baking sheet. Cook in a preheated oven for 20 to 25 minutes or until browned.

Beer Can Chicken Texas Style

Prep time: 15 minutes **Cooking time:** 18 minutes
Serve: 1

Ingredients

1 (3 pounds) whole fryer chicken
2 limes, quartered
¼ teaspoon ground allspice
1 tbsp ground black pepper
¾ (12 ounces) can beer
4 cups water
6 tablespoons Worcestershire sauce
1 red onion, chopped

2 lemons, quartered
1 cup vinegar
½ teaspoon garlic salt
salt and ground black pepper to taste

1 (12 fluid ounces) can or bottle beer
1 red bell pepper, chopped
3 tablespoons minced garlic
1 tablespoon salt
6 tablespoons minced garlic, divided

Directions

Rinse and pat dry the chicken with paper towels. Squeeze the quarters of lemon and lime over the chicken. In a mixing bowl, combine garlic salt, allspice, salt, and black pepper to taste, massage the spices over the chicken skin, insert squeezed lemon and lime quarters into the chicken cavity. Fill the cavity with 3 teaspoons of minced garlic. Wrap the chicken in plastic wrap and place it in the refrigerator for 6 to 8 hours.

Preheat the grill to medium-low heat; a grill thermometer should read 275°F (135°C) with the lid closed.
Place the remaining 3 tablespoons garlic into the partially filled can of beer and place the chicken upright atop the beer can, careful not to spill any lemon and lime quarters or garlic.

In a saucepan over medium heat, combine water, 1 12-ounces can of beer, vinegar, and Worcestershire sauce; toss in red onion, red bell pepper, 3 tablespoons minced garlic, salt, and black pepper. Bring the mopping sauce to a boil, then reduce to low heat and leave to simmer for 10 minutes. Set aside the sauce.

Cook until the skin is browned, and the flesh is no longer pink inside, about 2 hours, over a hot grill with the chicken standing erect with the beer can. Inserting an instant-read meat thermometer into the thickest breast section should yield a temperature of at least 160 degrees F. (70 degrees C). As the chicken cooks, use a brush to sprinkle mopping sauce on it every 30 minutes. Discard any remaining sauce.

Gluten-Free Almond Flour Chicken Nuggets

Prep time: 10 minutes **Cooking time:** 18 minutes
Serve: 1

Ingredients

1 ¼ pounds ground chicken 2 teaspoons salt, divided	2 teaspoons ground black pepper, divided
½ teaspoon dry mustard	½ teaspoon paprika
½ tbs dried oregano	2 cups King Arthur Almond Flour
2 tablespoons olive oil	
¼ cup cornstarch	¼ cup water

Directions

Preheat the oven to 375 degrees Fahrenheit. Set aside an oven-safe wire rack on top of a baking sheet. Combine the chicken, 1 teaspoon salt and pepper, and the other spices

in a large mixing basin. Set aside after thoroughly mixing.
Whisk the almond flour and the remaining salt and pepper in a separate basin. Set aside this dish as well. Combine the cornstarch and cold water in a third bowl to make a slurry.

Take roughly 2 teaspoons of chicken and form it into a tiny disk with damp palms. Coat in almond flour first, then dip in the cornstarch slurry, coat again in almond flour, and place on a wire rack to cool (which is on top of your baking sheet).

This technique should be repeated until no chicken remains. In a nonstick skillet, heat the 2 tablespoons olive oil. When the pan is heated, add half of the chicken nuggets. Cook for 1 minute or until the bottoms start to brown. Cook for another minute on the other side to brown. Return the nuggets to the wire rack.
Continue frying until all of the nuggets are golden. Bake for 10 minutes with the full baking sheet (with the wire rack on top) on the middle rack of the oven.

Remove the nuggets from the oven and place them on a cooling rack to cool. Toss with your favorite dipping sauce and **Serve:**. Enjoy!

Smoked Chicken Drumsticks

Prep time: 15 minutes **Cooking time:** 25 minutes
Serve: 1

Ingredients

12 chicken drumsticks	¼ cup vegetable oil
⅓ cup BBQ rub	

Directions

Remove the drumsticks from the package and set them on a rack over a drip tray or baking sheet. Refrigerate for 8 hours to overnight to air dry. Preheat an electric smoker to 275°F (135 degrees C). Follow the manufacturer's Directions for adding wood chips. Brush the drumsticks with a little vegetable oil. Put the drumsticks in a resealable plastic bag with the rub and shake to coat. To coat evenly, toss everything together.

Air-Fried Popcorn Chicken Gizzards

Prep time: 18 minutes **Cooking time:** 20 minutes
Serve: 1

Ingredients

1 pound chicken gizzards	⅓ cup all-purpose flour
1 ½ teaspoon seasoned salt (such as LAWRY'S®)	½ teaspoon ground black pepper
½ teaspoon garlic powder	½ teaspoon paprika
1 pinch cayenne pepper (Optional)	cooking spray
	1 large egg, beaten

Directions

A big pot of water should be brought to a boil. Add the gizzards, cut into bite-sized pieces, to the boiling water. 30 minutes at a boil Drain. Combine the flour, seasoned salt, pepper, garlic powder, paprika, and cayenne in a flat plastic container. Put the lid on and shake until everything is mixed.

Combine the seasoned flour with the gizzards. Replace the cover and shake until evenly coated. In a separate dish, beat the egg. Each gizzard piece should be dipped in the beaten egg and then into the seasoned flour. Snap the cover back on and give it one more shake. Allow resting for 5 minutes while the air fryer warms up.

Preheat the air fryer carefully to 400°F (200 degrees C).Spray the tops of the gizzards with cooking spray and place them in the basket. For 4 minutes in the oven, Shake the basket, and re-spray any chalky areas with cooking spray. Cook for another 4 minutes.

Crispy Honey Sriracha Chicken Wings

Prep time: 15 minutes **Cooking time:** 20 minutes
Serve: 1

Ingredients

2 tablespoons baking powder	1 teaspoon freshly ground black pepper
1 tablespoon kosher salt	1 tsp smoked paprika
2 ½ pounds chicken wing sections	⅓ cup honey
⅓ cup sriracha sauce	¼ teaspoon sesame oil
	1 tbsp seasoned rice vinegar

Directions

Preheat the oven to 425°F (220 degrees C). Then line a baking sheet with aluminum foil and set an oven-safe wire rack on top. Combine the baking powder, salt, black pepper, and paprika in a small mixing bowl. In a large mixing basin, combine the chicken wings. Toss the wings in 1/2 of the baking powder mixture to coat. Toss the wings with the remaining baking powder mixture to coat. Place the wings on the rack of the baking sheet that has been prepared.
Bake for 20 minutes in a preheated oven. Bake the wings for another 20 minutes. Bake for another 15 minutes, or until the wings are golden and crispy. Place the wings in a large mixing basin. Combine honey, sriracha sauce, rice vinegar, and sesame oil in a mixing bowl until smooth. Drizzle glaze over wings and toss to coat evenly. Place the wings on a serving plate and garnish with sesame seeds.

Air Fryer Gluten-Free Fried Chicken

Prep time: 10 minutes **Cooking time:** 18 minutes
Serve: 1

Ingredients

1 ¼ cups gluten-free flour	salt and freshly ground black pepper to taste
6 large eggs	¼ cup vegetable oil
1 ¼ cups Gluten-free crackers	2 pounds boneless, skinless chicken breast

Directions

In a small dish, whisk together the eggs and season with salt and pepper. In a separate bowl, properly combine the flour and cracker crumbs.

Dredge the chicken pieces in flour, then in eggs, and then in cracker crumbs. Next, place the pieces on an air fryer rack, ensuring they don't touch. Finally, brush the tops of the birds with oil.

Air-fried chicken for 10 minutes at 375°F (190°C) until cooked through and crisp.

Restaurant-Style Extra Crispy Chicken

Prep time: 15 minutes **Cooking time:** 25 minutes
Serve: 1

Ingredients

4 cups water	1 tablespoon salt
½ teaspoon monosodium glutamate	4 cups oil for deep frying
1 (4 pounds) whole chicken	1 egg, beaten
	2 ½ teaspoons salt
1 cup milk	2 cups all-purpose flour
¾ tbsp monosodium glutamate	¾ tbsp ground black pepper

Directions

Mix the water, salt, and monosodium glutamate in a big glass dish or basin. Cover and refrigerate for 20 minutes, flipping a couple of times to marinate the chicken.

Combine the egg and milk in a shallow dish or bowl. Separately, combine the flour, salt, pepper, and monosodium glutamate in a shallow dish or basin. Drain the chicken after removing it from the marinade (discarding the excess marinade). Preheat the oil in a deep fryer to 350°F (175 degrees C).

Dip chicken pieces one at a time into the flour mixture, then the egg/milk mixture, and finally the flour mixture, ensuring sure each piece is fully coated. Place the coated pieces on a dish or baking sheet.

Place the chicken, one piece at a time, into the heated oil. Fry half of the chicken parts (4 pieces) for 12 to 15 minutes, or until golden brown, then repeat with the remaining pieces. (Note Stir the chicken halfway through the frying time to ensure that each piece cooks evenly.) Before serving, drain the fried chicken for 5 minutes on paper towels or a wire cooling rack.

Airline Chicken Breast

Prep time: 20 minutes **Cooking time:** 20 minutes
Serve: 1

Ingredients

1 whole chicken
ground black pepper to
taste 2 pinches herb de
Provence
3 tablespoons butter,
divided
1 sprig of fresh rosemary
½ cup chicken stock

kosher salt to taste
¼ teaspoon cayenne
pepper 1 tablespoon olive
oil
2 sprigs of fresh thyme
1 drizzle olive oil

Directions

By cutting through the junction where the wing joins
the drumette, take 1/2 of each chicken wing. Cut the
flesh between the thighs and the breasts. To separate
the breasts, make a shallow cut along the breastbone
and two deep cuts on either side.

Using the knife's point, cut each breast from the
carcass, keeping the blade pushed against the bone.
Then, remove the breast with the wing connected by
cutting through the
cartilage.

Tenders should be removed and trimmed as needed.
Season with olive oil, salt, pepper, herbs de Provence,
and cayenne pepper to taste.

To separate the skin from the flesh, carefully push
your finger beneath the skin of each breast, exactly
adjacent to the wing bone. Next, 1 tender should be
slid beneath the skin, centered, and smoothed over the
skin. Then, season the breasts with salt.

In a pan over medium-high heat, heat 1 tablespoon
olive oil. Place the chicken breasts, skin side down, in
a baking dish. Cook for 6 to 7 minutes, or until the
bottom is browned. Reduce heat to medium and cook
until the interior is no longer pink, 7 to 10 minutes
more. 1 tablespoon butter, rosemary, and thyme are all
good additions. Baste the chicken with butter. Take
the chicken out of the skillet.

Pour in the stock and turn up the heat to high. Boil
for about 2 minutes or until the required thickness is
reached. Remove from heat and whisk in the
remaining butter. Divide each chicken breast into
thirds and cover with the pan sauce.

Crispy Flautas

Prep time: 15 minutes **Cooking time:** 25 minutes
Serve: 1

Ingredients

1 teaspoon vegetable
oil
½ onion, finely diced
1 (1 ounce) package taco
seasoning mix
¾ cup water

½ cup shredded Cheddar
cheese
2 cups vegetable oil for
frying

½ green bell pepper,
chopped
1-pound skinless, boneless
chicken breast
1 (10 ounces) package
corn tortillas (such as
Ortega®)
24 toothpicks
1 cup salsa

Directions

In a pan over medium heat, heat 1 teaspoon vegetable
oil. Stir in the bell pepper and onion; simmer and stir
for 5 minutes, or until the onion has softened and
turned translucent. Raise the heat to medium-high and
add the chicken breast. Cook and stir for 10 minutes,
or until the chicken breast is no longer pink in the
middle. Using two forks, shred the chicken. Combine
the taco seasoning and water in a mixing bowl.
Simmer for 10 minutes, stirring regularly, until the
liquid has evaporated. Remove from the pan and set
aside the Cheddar cheese.

Brush a thin coating of salsa onto each corn tortilla.
Along the bottom border of the tortilla, place roughly
2 teaspoons of the chicken mixture. Roll the tortilla
tightly into a cylinder, then attach the ends with one or
two toothpicks. Rep with the remaining tortillas.

Heat 2 cups vegetable oil to 375 degrees F. (190
degrees C) in a large pan. Fry the flautas, no more than
four at a time, in the hot oil until golden and crisp,
about 4 minutes. Drain the flautas on a dish lined with
paper towels. Remove toothpicks and top flautas with
remaining salsa.

Crispy Baked Moroccan Chicken Wings with Yogurt Dip

Prep time: 15 minutes **Cooking time:** 20 minutes
Serve: 1

Ingredients

2 ½ pounds chicken wings	1 ½ tablespoon vegetable oil
1 teaspoon ground cumin	¼ teaspoon ground cinnamon
1 teaspoon paprika	
¼ teaspoon ground ginger	¼ teaspoon cayenne pepper
¼ tbsp ground turmeric	½ teaspoon salt
¼ teaspoon pepper	Reynolds Wrap® Non-Stick Aluminum Foil
1 cup plain Greek yogurt	
2 tablespoons fresh lemon juice	1 tablespoon chopped fresh cilantro
1 ½ tablespoon honey	½ teaspoon salt
¼ teaspoon pepper	1 tbsp chopped fresh mint

Directions

Preheat the oven to 400 degrees Fahrenheit. Reynolds Wrap® Nonstick Foil should be used to line a baking pan. Toss the chicken wings in a large mixing basin with the vegetable oil until they are fully covered.

Combine the paprika, cumin, cinnamon, ginger, cayenne pepper, turmeric, salt, and pepper in a small mixing bowl. Toss the wings in the spice mixture until thoroughly covered. Arrange the wings on the baking sheet in a single layer, spreading them apart, so they don't touch.
Bake the wings for 40 to 45 minutes, or until cooked through, before transferring them to a serving tray.

Combine the yogurt, lemon juice, mint, cilantro, honey, salt, and pepper in a small mixing dish. Season the dip with extra salt and pepper to taste. With the yogurt dip, **Serve:** the wings.

Air Fryer Rotisserie Chicken

Prep time: 15 minutes **Cooking time:** 20 minutes
Serve: 1

Ingredients

1 tablespoon sea salt	2 teaspoons ground paprika
1 teaspoon ground thyme	1 teaspoon ground white pepper
1 teaspoon onion powder	
½ tbs. ground black pepper	½ teaspoon cayenne pepper
½ teaspoon garlic powder	1 (4 pound) whole fryer chicken, giblets removed
3 tablespoons vegetable oil	

Directions

According to the manufacturer's instructions, preheat an air fryer carefully to 350°F (175°C).
In a small bowl, combine salt, paprika, onion powder, thyme, white pepper, black pepper, cayenne pepper, and garlic powder.

Rub half of the oil and half of the spice mixture over the chicken. Cook for 30 minutes in a preheated air fryer. Remove the chicken from the frying with care. Turn the chicken over. Brush the opposite side with oil and sprinkle with the remaining spice mixture.

Return to the air fryer and cook for another 30 minutes, or until the meat is no longer pink at the bone and the juices flow clear. An instant-read thermometer implanted near the bone into the thickest section of the thigh should register 165 degrees F. (74 degrees C).

Remove from the fryer, cover with a double layer of aluminum foil, and set aside 10 minutes before slicing.

Chicken Fajita Egg Rolls

Prep time: 10 minutes **Cooking time:** 18 minutes
Serve: 1

Ingredients

vegetable oil for frying
2 tablespoons olive oil
1 red onion, minced
1 green bell pepper, chopped
½ cup finely chopped mushrooms (Optional)
16 egg roll wrappers, or more as needed
2 tablespoons milk
1 red bell pepper, chopped
2 eggs
1 jalapeno pepper, seeded and minced (Optional)
2 pounds skinless, boneless chicken breasts cayenne pepper
2 (8 ounces) packages of shredded pepper Jack cheese

Directions

Heat the oil in a deep fryer or big saucepan to 350°F (175 degrees C). To prepare egg wash, combine eggs and milk in a mixing bowl.

In a sauté pan over medium heat, heat the olive oil. Cook and stir the onion, peppers, mushrooms, and cayenne for 5 minutes, or until slightly softened. Cook until the chicken is no longer pink, about 5 minutes. 1 to 2 minutes, mix in the pepper Jack cheese until fully incorporated and beginning to melt.

Fill each egg roll wrapper with an equal amount of the filling mixture. Fold in the side corners and wrap up, using egg wash to seal the edges.

Cook the egg rolls in the heated oil for 3 to 5 minutes, or until they float to the top and turn golden brown. To minimize overpopulation, work in bunches. Then, lay flat on paper towels to drain, standing on end to drain any excess oil.

Zesty Broiled Chicken Thighs

Prep time: 15 minutes **Cooking time:** 18 minutes
Serve: 1

Ingredients

1 large onion, chopped
¼ cup orange juice
2 tablespoons avocado oil
2 teaspoons ground cumin
2 teaspoons Mexican oregano
½ teaspoon smoked paprika
3 pounds boneless, skinless chicken thighs
¼ cup lime juice
8 cloves garlic, peeled
2 teaspoons ground coriander
1 teaspoon chipotle chili powder
1 pinch salt and ground black pepper

Directions

In a blender or food processor, combine onion, lime juice, orange juice, garlic, avocado oil, coriander, cumin, Mexican oregano, chipotle chili powder, and smoky paprika. Pulse several times to combine, then puree for 1 minute, or until no visible chunks remain.

Place the chicken thighs in a 1-gallon resealable bag and pour the marinade. Squeeze the majority of the air out and seal. Squeeze the contents of the bag gently until the chicken pieces are coated. Marinate for 30 minutes to 3 hours in the refrigerator.

Preheat the oven's broiler and position an oven rack approximately 4 inches from the heat source. On a broiler pan, place the marinated chicken thighs. Broil the chicken thighs for 8 minutes or until they begin to brown.

Broil for another 7 minutes, or until gently browned the second side. An instant-read thermometer put into the thickest section of the chicken thigh should register at least 165°F (74 degrees C). Transfer the chicken to a serving plate.

Baked Panko-Crusted Chicken Tenders

Prep time: 20 minutes **Cooking time:** 25 minutes
Serve: 1

Ingredients

½ cup plain fat-free Greek yogurt
1 tbsp balsamic vinegar
¼ teaspoon dried basil
⅛ teaspoon black pepper
¼ teaspoon garlic powder
¼ teaspoon salt
1 pound chicken tenders
1 cup Italian-seasoned panko (Japanese breadcrumbs)

¼ cup jarred roasted red peppers - drained, patted dry, and chopped
⅛ teaspoon salt
⅛ teaspoon garlic powder
¼ teaspoon onion powder
¼ teaspoon freshly ground black pepper
1 large egg, lightly beaten

Directions

Preheat the oven to 400 degrees Fahrenheit (200 degrees C). Preheat the oven to 350°F. Line a baking sheet with parchment paper.

In a tiny food processor, combine Greek yogurt, red peppers, balsamic vinegar, basil, salt, pepper, and 1/8 teaspoon garlic powder. Blend until smooth, then chill the dipping sauce until ready to use.

Combine 1/4 teaspoon garlic powder, onion powder, salt, and pepper in a small bowl. Toss the chicken tenders in the seasoning mixture to coat evenly. Place aside.
In a skillet over medium-high heat, toast panko crumbs
until golden brown, 4 to 5 minutes. Put the panko in a shallow dish. Separately, crack one egg into a shallow dish. Dip chicken tenders into the egg, allowing excess to drop out, and then cover with panko. Place the tenders on the baking sheet that has been prepared.

Bake it until the chicken is no longer pink in the center and the juices run clear, 12 to 15 minutes total, flipping halfway through. In the middle, an instant-read thermometer should read at least 160 degrees F. (74 degrees C). **Serve:** it with the dipping sauce on the side.

Paper-Wrapped Chicken

Prep time: 15 minutes **Cooking time:** 22 minutes
Serve: 1

Ingredients

½ cup teriyaki sauce,
2 cloves garlic, minced
1-pound skinless, boneless chicken breast halves - cut into bite-size pieces
oil for deep frying

¼ teaspoon crushed red pepper flakes
30 4x4-inch squares aluminum foil, or as needed
1 (1 inch) piece fresh ginger, grated

Directions

Combine the teriyaki sauce, garlic, ginger, and red pepper flakes; whisk in the chicken pieces until fully covered.
Refrigerate the chicken for 3 to 4 hours or overnight in a covered bowl.

Remove a piece of marinated chicken and lay it in the center of an aluminum square. Fold the square in a triangular shape over the chicken piece; fold up the open corners of the triangle several times and press tightly together to seal the chicken inside the foil. Rep with the rest of the chicken pieces. Remove the used marinade.

Heat the oil in a deep fryer or big saucepan to 350°F (175 degrees C). Add the wrapped foil packets to the heated oil and fry for 2 to 4 minutes, or until the chicken is tender and cooked through. Allow the packets to drain on paper towels and cool slightly. Tear apart the packages along the sealed edges to **Serve:**.

Air-Fried Chicken Calzone

Prep time: 15 minutes **Cooking time:** 18 minutes
Serve: 1

Ingredients

1 teaspoon olive oil,
¼ cup finely chopped red
onion
⅓ cup shredded cooked
chicken breast
6 ounces prepared pizza
dough

⅓ cup low-sodium
marinara sauce
3 cups baby spinach leaves
⅓ cup shredded
mozzarella cheese
cooking spray

Directions

In a nonstick skillet, heat the oil over medium-high heat.
Cook occasionally turns until the onion is soft,
approximately 2 minutes. Cover and simmer until the
spinach is wilted, about 1 1/2 minutes. Remove from the
heat and mix in the marinara and chicken. According to the
manufacturer's instructions, preheat an air fryer carefully to
325°F (165°C).

Cut the dough into four equal pieces. Roll each piece
into a 6-inch circle on a lightly floured work surface.
1/4 of the spinach mixture should be spread over the
bottom half of each dough round. Top with a quarter
of the mozzarella cheese on each. Fold the dough over
the filling to make half-moons, then crimp the edges
to secure. Coat well

Chicken and Waffle Sandwich

Prep time: 20 minutes **Cooking time:** 20 minutes
Serve: 1

Ingredients

2 cups all-purpose flour
1 teaspoon salt
¼ teaspoon granulated
garlic
1 ½ cups warm milk
Cookig spray
⅓ cup shredded Cheddar
cheese
2 large eggs
1 pinch salt

4 teaspoons baking
powder
¼ teaspoon Italian
seasoning
⅓ cup salted butter,
melted
1 (24 ounces) package
frozen breaded chicken
breast fillets (such as
Kirkwood®)

Directions

In a large mixing bowl, combine the salt, garlic, flour,
baking powder, and seasoning; set aside. Combine the
eggs, milk, and melted butter in a separate dish. Pour
the milk mixture into the flour mixture and stir until
combined. Mix in the Cheddar cheese.

Preheat an air fryer carefully for 5 minutes at 400
degrees F (200 degrees C).
7 minutes in the air fryer. Cook for another 6 minutes
after turning the chicken pieces.

Meanwhile, preheat the oven to 200°F (95 degrees C).
Preheat a waffle maker according to the
manufacturer's Directions

Coat the waffle maker with nonstick cooking spray.
Pour 3 tablespoons batter onto the waffle maker.
Cook for 5 minutes, or until the waffle is golden
brown and the iron stops steaming. Place on a baking
sheet lined with parchment paper and keep heat in the
oven. Rep with the remaining batter.

Once all waffles are done, assemble the waffle and
chicken sandwiches.

Hot Bean and Bacon Dip with Air Fryer Tortilla Chips

Prep time: 15 minutes **Cooking time:** 25 minutes
Serve: 1

Ingredients

avocado oil cooking spray
½ cup chopped onion
2 cloves garlic, minced
1 (29 ounces) can pinto beans, undrained
1 teaspoon chili powder
1 cup shredded sharp Cheddar cheese
1 cup shredded pepper Jack cheese
½ pound bacon
1 (4 ounces) can chop green chiles
½ cup chicken broth
12 (6 inches) corn tortillas
2 tsp cream cheese
salt and ground black pepper to taste

Directions

Preheat the oven to 350 degrees Fahrenheit (175 degrees C). Spray an 8x8-inch baking dish lightly with cooking spray.

Cook the bacon in a large pan over medium-high heat, stirring periodically, for approximately 10 minutes, or until uniformly browned. On paper towels, drain the bacon slices. Once cool, crumble.

In the same skillet, cook the onion until transparent, about 4 to 5 minutes. Cook for 2 minutes more after adding the green chilies and garlic. Bring the pinto beans to a boil. Combine the chicken broth and chili powder in a mixing bowl. Reduce to low heat and mash the beans. Allow boiling for 5 to 6 minutes, or until slightly thickened. Next, stir in the cream cheese until it is melted. Simmer for 5 to 6 minutes, or until slightly thickened. Finally, stir in the bacon until completely mixed. Season with salt and pepper to taste.

Layer 1/2 of the bean mixture, 1/2 cup pepper Jack, and 1/2 cup Cheddar cheese in the prepared baking dish. Layers should be repeated.

Bake for 15 minutes, covered, in a preheated oven. Uncover and bake for 5 to 7 minutes more, or until the cheese is melted or lightly browned.

Meanwhile, prepare an air fryer to 350°F (175°C) according to the manufacturer's recommendations. Each tortilla should be cut into fourths. Avocado oil should be sprayed on both sides of each tortilla. Place in a single layer in the air fryer basket. 4 to 6 minutes in the air fryer. Cook for another 2 to 3 minutes, or until crisp. Because they can burn fast, always keep an eye on your basket. **Serve:** with a hot-dip and a sprinkle of salt.

Air Fryer Stuffed Chicken Thighs

Prep time: 20 minutes **Cooking time:** 25 minutes
Serve: 1

Ingredients

6 ounces Swiss cheese
1 tablespoon salon seasoning
salt and freshly ground black pepper
6 medium boneless skinless chicken thighs
nonstick cooking spray
1 cup panko breadcrumbs
½ cup flour, divided
2 large eggs
6 slices turkey lunch meat

Directions

Preheat an air fryer carefully to 400°F (200 degrees C). Swiss cheese should be cut into six 2 x 1/2 x 1/2-inch pieces.

Set up a breading station by putting breadcrumbs, 2 teaspoon sounder spice, 1 tablespoon flour in one shallow dish, remaining flour and sounder seasoning in another shallow dish, and eggs in a third shallow dish. Whip the eggs until they are golden and foamy. Season the eggs with salt and pepper to taste.

Place one piece of Swiss cheese on top of each piece of turkey meat. Wrap luncheon meat in a layer of Swiss cheese.

Open the chicken thighs and insert the turkey cheese bundle in the center. Wrap the chicken thigh around the bundle. Place the chicken bundles in the air fryer, seam side down. Nonstick spray should be sprayed on the chicken bundles.

Reduce the temperature of the air fryer to 380 degrees F (193 degrees C) and air-fried the chicken for 15 minutes. Turn the bundles over, coat with nonstick spray, and reduce the temperature of the air fryer to 370 degrees F. (187 degrees C). Cook until the chicken is cooked through, about 8 minutes more in the air fryer. **Serve:** right away.

Air-Fried Breaded Chicken Thighs

Prep time: 15 minutes **Cooking time:** 20 minutes
Serve: 1

Ingredients

4 medium bone-in, skin-on chicken thighs	¼ cup all-purpose flour
¼ cup plain breadcrumbs	1 cup buttermilk
1 teaspoon garlic powder	2 tablespoons grated Parmesan cheese
½ teaspoon ground paprika	1 teaspoon salt
½ teaspoon onion powder	½ teaspoon black pepper
	nonstick cooking spray

Directions

Combine the chicken thighs and buttermilk in a nonreactive container with a cover or a resealable plastic bag. Marinate for at least 1 hour or overnight in the refrigerator.

Take the chicken out of the refrigerator. Pour out the buttermilk and let the chicken aside to rest while preparing the breading mixture.

In a wide, shallow dish or pie plate, whisk or mix the flour, breadcrumbs, Parmesan cheese, paprika, garlic powder, salt, onion powder, and black pepper until equally blended.

Preheat the air fryer carefully from 375°F to 380°F (190 to 195 degrees C). Lightly coat the air fryer basket with nonstick spray.

Once the air fryer is heated, dip the chicken thighs, one at a time, into the breading mixture, making sure the breading adheres to both sides as much as possible. Then, place gently in the air fryer basket. Repeat until all thighs have been breaded and placed in the basket. They should not be stacked on top of one other.

Set the timer for 25 minutes in the air fryer. When the timer goes off, use an instant-read thermometer to check the temperature. The inside temperature should be 180 degrees Fahrenheit (82 degrees C).

If they aren't quite done but the breading is turning black, simply seal the basket and set them aside to rest or turn the air fryer back on for a few minutes and check again. **Serve:** right away.

Crispy Chicken Salad with Yummy Honey Mustard Dressing

Prep time: 15 minutes **Cooking time:** 22 minutes
Serve: 1

Ingredients

2 tablespoons olive oil	1 ½ cups panko breadcrumbs
¼ teaspoon garlic powder cooking spray	2 tablespoons chopped fresh parsley
½ cup all-purpose flour	¼ teaspoon salt
¼ teaspoon ground black pepper	2 tablespoons water
1 ½ pound skinless, boneless chicken breast halves	2 large eggs
¾ cup mayonnaise	2 large carrots, peeled and sliced diagonally
8 cups mixed spring salad greens	1 cup sliced radishes
4 teaspoons Dijon mustard	3 tablespoons prepared yellow mustard
	3 tablespoons honey
	1 tablespoon lemon juice

Directions

In an extra-large skillet, heat the oil over medium heat. Mix in the panko and garlic powder. Cook, constantly stirring, for 2 to 3 minutes, or until toasted. Allow cooling in a shallow dish for 2 to 3 minutes. Mix in the parsley.
Preheat the air fryer carefully to 400°F and coat the air fryer basket with cooking spray (200 degrees C).

Meanwhile, combine the flour, salt, and pepper in a separate shallow dish. Finally, whisk together the eggs and water in a third shallow dish.

Cut chicken breasts into 1x3-inch strips lengthwise. To coat, dip the chicken strips in the flour mixture, then egg mixture, and finally the panko mixture.

Add the chicken to the prepared air fryer in batches. Cook, rotating once, for 5 to 7 minutes, or until an instant-read thermometer inserted into the thickest sections registers 165°F (74°C). Transfer to a platter, cover with foil and keep warm.

In a large mixing basin, combine salad leaves, carrots, and radishes. In a small mixing bowl, combine the mayonnaise, yellow mustard, honey, Dijon mustard, and lemon juice for the dressing. Salad should be divided among plates, topped with chicken, and drizzled with dressing.

Alphabetical Index

SNACKS & APPETIZERS

Made in the USA
Monee, IL
24 June 2022